HISTORY OF BEHAVIOR MODIFICATION
Experimental Foundations of Contemporary Research

D0945173

One of a series of historical monographs sponsored by the Committee on Brain Sciences, Division of Medical Sciences, Assembly of Life Sciences, National Research Council.

The preparation of this publication was supported by the National Institute of Mental Health, of the Alcohol, Drug Abuse, and Mental Health Administration, under Contract No. N01-MH-1-0094 (ER).

HISTORY OF
BEHAVIOR
MODIFICATION #6
Experimental Foundations
of Contemporary Research

by

[Alan E. Kazdin, Ph.D.
Professor of Psychology
The Pennsylvania State University

University Park Press
Baltimore

UNIVERSITY PARK PRESS
International Publishers in Science and Medicine
233 East Redwood Street
Baltimore, Maryland 21202

Copyright © 1978 by University Park Press
Typeset by American Graphic Arts Corporation
Manufactured in the United States of America by
the Maple Press Company.

Library of Congress Cataloging in Publication Data:
Kazdin, Alan E.
History of behavior modification.

Bibliography: p.
Includes index.
1. Behavior modification—History.   2. Psychology, Experimental—History.   3. Psychology,
Physiological—History.   I. Title.

BF637.B4K42   153.8′5   77-25180
ISBN 0-8391-1205-X

Contents

COMMITTEE ON BRAIN SCIENCES

SUBCOMMITTEE ON BEHAVIOR MODIFICATION

Howard F. Hunt, Ph.D., *Chairman,* Professor of Psychology in Psychiatry, New York Hospital-Cornell Medical Center, White Plains, New York

Sidney W. Bijou, Ph.D., College of Education, Department of Special Education, The University of Arizona, Tucson, Arizona

John Paul Brady, M.D., Professor of Psychiatry, University of Pennsylvania Medical School, Philadelphia, Pennsylvania

Sigmund Diamond, Ph.D., Professor of Sociology and History, Department of Sociology, Columbia University, New York, New York

Jarl E. Dyrud, M.D., Professor of Psychiatry, University of Chicago, Chicago, Illinois

Cyril M. Franks, Ph.D., Psychological Clinic, Graduate School of Applied and Professional Psychology, Rutgers University, New Brunswick, New Jersey

Richard T. Louttit, Ph.D., Professor of Psychology, University of Massachusetts, Amherst, Massachusetts

Joseph Zubin, Ph.D., Biometrics Research Unit, New York State Psychiatric Institute, Columbia University, New York, New York

The project that is the subject of this report was approved by the Governing Board of the National Research Council, whose members are drawn from the Councils of the National Academy of Sciences, the National Academy of Engineering, and the Institute of Medicine. The members of the Committee responsible for the report were chosen for their special competencies and with regard for appropriate balance.

This report has been reviewed by a group other than those involved in its preparation according to procedures approved by a Report Review Committee consisting of members of the National Academy of Sciences, the National Academy of Engineering, and the Institute of Medicine.

Foreword

In 1969, the Committee on Brain Sciences of the National Research Council/ National Academy of Sciences commissioned a series of reviews inquiring into the history of selected scientific achievements that had brought major social benefits to contemporary life. The Committee began the project by considering discoveries that have had great practical value in the treatment of nervous and mental disorders. The history of these achievements, the Committee believed, not only could indicate something of the complex sequence of discoveries and events leading up to the achievements but could also shed light on conditions that would favor still further scientific progress and new social benefits.

The present volume, the third in the series,[1] explores the contributions of basic laboratory research in psychology and physiology to the development of behavior modification. The Subcommittee on Behavior Modification was fortunate indeed in securing Dr. Alan E. Kazdin as the author of this review. He is an outstanding authority on this topic, the unfolding of his own professional career has been contemporaneous with the most exciting developments in the field, and he writes clearly and with a critical scholarship. Although the Subcommittee suggested the scope and general range of coverage, credit for the quality of the report must belong to him. We are indebted to him for the fine work he has done.

Howard F. Hunt, Ph.D.
Chairman, Subcommittee on
Behavior Modification

---

[1] *Chlorpromazine in Psychiatry: A Study of Therapeutic Innovation* by Dr. Judith P. Swazey was published in 1974 by MIT Press, Cambridge, Mass., and *Science and Epilepsy: Neuroscience Gains in Epilepsy Research,* by Drs. James L. O'Leary and Sidney Goldring, Raven Press, New York, followed in 1976.

Preface

The field of behavior modification has emerged as a departure from many traditional views and approaches in psychiatry, clinical psychology, and other mental-health related fields. It has grown to encompass heterogeneous treatment, rehabilitation, and educational practices. Although the field includes several specific behavior-change techniques, its unifying characteristic is an experimental and empirical approach toward developing those techniques. Behavior modification can be defined as the application of basic research and theory from experimental psychology to influence behavior for purposes of resolving personal and social problems and enhancing human functioning.

The purpose of this book is to review the evolution of findings and approaches underlying contemporary applications in the field of behavior modification. Several reasons exist for such a history. First, the field illustrates how basic scientific research can lead to the resolution of clinical and social problems. Behavior-change techniques and innovative applications can be traced to specific experimental findings and theoretical insights. However, beyond the specific techniques, the influence of experimentation in general can be felt in the behavioral approach toward treatment. Behavior modification, unlike many other forms of psychological treatment, has drawn extensively upon experimental findings and methods of psychology; thus, the field is an applied endeavor that stresses an empirical, analytical stance in designing and evaluating treatment techniques.

There are other reasons for singling out behavior modification as a contemporary subject for historical study. The movement represents a revolution in the field of mental health: in less than 20 years, it has brought about a major reconceptualization of psychological problems and their treatment. With this reconceptualization has followed application of behavior-change techniques to many areas that previously were outside the domain of the mental-health professions. Behavior modification not only has helped alleviate clinical disorders that have been the prominent and traditional focus of psychiatry and clinical psychology but also has been extended to ameliorate diverse and unexpected aspects of rehabilitation, education, and social and community problems. Moreover, the breadth of application has been accelerated by deprofessionalization of many therapeutic methods. Several behavior modification techniques can be administered by parents, teachers, or peers; in some cases it is the clients themselves who are instrumental in altering their own behaviors. In the mental-health fields, no other approach or set of techniques has achieved such widespread applicability.

Another reason for tracing the evolution of behavior modification pertains to general social concerns about the abridgment of individual freedom. Advances in the field have been a target of much criticism because of the putative power of behavioral techniques and their potentially coercive use to alter the conduct of individuals or even of society at large. Media dramatizations of behavior control have aggravated the belief in behavior modification as a tool of oppression by portraying fictional cases in which behavior change has been used in service of cruel or despotic ends. Even within the field, writers occasionally have imagined speculative accounts of cultures redesigned in such a way that behavioral techniques would control nearly all facets of human life.

Despite the great attention that such dramatizations and speculations receive, they bear little, if any, resemblance to contemporary behavior modification. The fears of personal abuse and societal control derive from a failure to recognize the purposes, foci, and indeed, the technological limitations of behavior modification. As highlighted in this volume, behavior modification is devoted explicitly to increasing rather than decreasing human freedom. Helping a person to achieve greater individuality and responsibility is a goal accomplished by the voluntary employment of specific behavior-change techniques to overcome deficits and to develop positive social behaviors to enhance day-to-day functioning. Understanding the historical development and contemporary applications of the field may help dispel the basis for many of the concerns about extensions of behavior modification to clinical and social problems.

The field is multifaceted, encompassing a variety of philosophical stances, assumptions about the nature of behavior and its causes and alteration, theoretical approaches, experimental findings, and therapeutic techniques. To be sure, the separate areas included under the rubric of behavior modification have many points of convergence, and this history addresses the field's growth and evolution by tracing these points. Although attention is paid to the separate traditions within the field and behavior modification in its entirety is addressed, the laboratory and applied work in operant conditioning receive the greatest emphasis. Through his research on operant conditioning, B. F. Skinner has exerted tremendous influence. Treatment programs based on principles of operant conditioning have been extended to almost every type of treatment, education, and health-care facility from preschools to nursing homes, as well as to client populations ranging from psychiatric patients to the mentally retarded. Within behavior modification, no single conceptual and experimental approach has generated the breadth of applications that operant conditioning has.

Another reason for highlighting operant conditioning is that it represents a relatively clear progression from experimentation to application. Skinner and his colleagues' animal experiments provided basic findings that were extrapolated directly to hypotheses about human behavior, initially in laboratories and eventually in clinical settings. The history of this translation of operant conditioning from laboratory to applied settings has yet to be traced. Applied operant conditioning merged with largely independent research efforts that became behavior modification. This volume surveys the mutual and idiosyncratic historical antecedents of separate traditions within behavior modification.

Writing a history on such a recently evolved area as behavior modification has unique obstacles and rewards. Because the author is directly influenced by and is engaged in behavior modification research, it is very easy, if not inevitable, to distort aspects of the field in light of ongoing developments that in time will take on different value. Thus, it is difficult to place with any certainty much of contemporary research into a larger context of clinical research. However, there are compensations in writing a history that can be compiled almost as it unfolds. Prominent individuals who played pivotal roles in experimental and applied research can testify about important influences and events, recall anecdotes, resolve ambiguities, and, in general, richly supplement the archival records to which many histories are confined.

Many people instrumental in bringing this project to completion need to be acknowledged within a space not at all commensurate with the extent of their contributions or my gratitude. Howard F. Hunt (Chairman), Sidney W. Bijou, John Paul Brady, Sigmund Diamond, Jarl Dyrud, Cyril M. Franks, Richard T. Louttit, and Joseph Zubin, of the Subcommittee on Behavior Modification of the Committee on Brain Sciences, all contributed helpful support and suggestions in planning the monograph and evaluating the initial product. Bernice Grafstein, Jerome Kagan, and Mark Rosenzweig of the parent committee also reviewed the manuscript.

I also profited greatly from the generous assistance of numerous colleagues, many of whom explained in interviews and in correspondence the evolution of their own work or emerging trends of which they were a part. In addition to furnishing historical material, several individuals were kind enough to review portions of the monograph. I am grateful to Teodoro Ayllon, Donald M. Baer, Beatrice Barrett, Wesley C. Becker, Peter Dews, Hans J. Eysenck, Charles B. Ferster, Jacob Gewirtz, Thomas F. Gilbert, Israel Goldiamond, John Hall, R. J. Herrnstein, Fred Keller, Leonard Krasner, Arnold A. Lazarus, Frederick Lemere, O. Ivar Lovaas, Richard Malott, Jack Michael, Gerald R. Patterson, Ellen Reese, Leo J. Reyna, Henry C. Rickard, Todd R. Risley, Andrew Salter, Kurt Salzinger, Nathan Schoenfeld, B. F. Skinner, Arthur Staats, Stephanie B. Stolz, Charles Taffel, Montrose M. Wolf, and Joseph Wolpe.

The staff of the Assembly of Life Sciences of the National Research Council were very helpful in coordinating the project. Henry S. Parker, Acting Executive Secretary of the Division of Medical Sciences, facilitated completion of the project. Avis Berman, Editor, brought to bear truly remarkable skills to mold the manuscript into its final form.

Most of the manuscript was written while I was a Fellow at the Center for Advanced Study in the Behavioral Sciences, Stanford, California. The Center provided idyllic conditions for writing. In addition, several scholars in the field of behavior modification were in residence at the Center, including W. Stewart Agras, Nathan H. Azrin, Walter Mischel, Jack Rachman, and G. Terence Wilson. Conversations with these colleagues enhanced my understanding of important developments and insights into the current status of the field. In addition, discussions with others at the Center, including Gardner Lindzey (Director), Alexander George, David Krantz, Lauren Resnick, and Elliot S. Valenstein, were invaluable.

Finally, I am grateful for the time and resources made possible by support from the Foundations Fund for Research in Psychiatry, the National Institute of Mental Health, the Spencer Foundation, and The Pennsylvania State University Central Fund for Research.

Alan E. Kazdin, Ph.D.

1
Introduction

Throughout civilization, theories of human nature have been posed to explain behavior. The types of theories and factors to which they attribute individual differences in personality and behavior have virtually exhausted the available possibilities. Body fluids, body build, genetic and environmental influences, family interaction, biological and psychological instincts, needs, or traits, and a host of other factors have been proffered to account for the ways individuals behave. Explanations of human nature are not simply an academic subject. The theory to which one adheres in explaining behavior is important for practical matters because it dictates whether personality and behavior can be changed and, if so, in what way.

The practical concern about the ability to change behavior may be more pervasive than the speculations about human behavior. This concern encompasses different levels of human interaction, ranging from very few individuals (e.g., parents changing the behavior of their children) to large groups (e.g., international relations). Social organization, even in its most primitive form, requires unified behavior of groups. Hence, managing and directing individuals to perform in certain ways is essential. In any society, the development of customs, laws, and moral codes implicitly or explicitly codifies normative ways of behaving and the consequences for behavior deviating from these norms. In general, government, law, religion, education, and similar social institutions dictate ways of behaving.

Psychology has developed as the scientific study of behavior and has explicitly addressed many of the questions pertaining to behavior change. Recently, an area has developed within psychology that has applied psychological principles, findings, and methods to psychological treatment and therapy. This area, behavior modification or behavior therapy, consists of the application of experimental findings from psychological research for the purpose of altering behavior.[1] The applications are directed toward eliminating debilitating behavior and enhancing human functioning. Behavior modification, as used in its technical sense, refers to a methodological approach for developing, implementing, and evaluating behavior-change techniques derived from psychological research.

Although the problems of defining behavior modification are addressed later, it is important to specify the domain of the field very carefully. When used in the *nontechnical* sense, the term "behavior modification" can refer to any method or means of influencing an individual so that his/her behavior is modified. Several methods, including physical coercion, psychosurgery, "brainwashing," psychotherapy, encounter groups, and other procedures, might be called "behavior modification" because they do, or at least attempt to, modify behavior. Yet, they are not behavior-modification techniques as that term is defined in psychology.

Behavior modification encompasses a particular content area, therapeutic focus, and methodological approach to treatment. The content area is based on theories and findings from psychology, often from the psychology of learning. The techniques involved often include ways of modifying features of the environment or social situation. The therapeutic focus is the direct alteration of overt behavior rather than the inferred psychological forces that traditionally have been assumed to underlie it. The therapeutic focus is directed toward fostering socially appropriate behavior and eliminating inappropriate behavior. Finally, the methodological approach refers to a stance that emphasizes the empirical evaluation of treatment.

As a term, "behavior modification" leaves a great deal to be desired because of the confusion of its technical and nontechnical uses. Because many procedures in everyday experience (persuasion, advertising) as well as less commonly used odious practices (torture) might modify behavior, the term has been used to embrace any or all technique for its alteration. This overuse has had deleterious conse-

---

[1] The terms "behavior modification" and "behavior therapy" will be used interchangeably throughout the text. Occasionally, authors have distinguished behavior modification from behavior therapy according to the theoretical ties upon which treatment techniques are based (e.g., Keehn and Webster, 1969; Krasner, 1971a), according to the countries in which behavioral techniques and approaches have developed (e.g., Yates, 1970a), or based upon whether the techniques are applied to individuals or to social systems such as institutions (e.g., Franzini and Tilker, 1972). Because none of these distinctions have been widely adopted, the field ordinarily has used "behavior modification" and "behavior therapy" interchangeably.

quences for the field as a whole. As will be discussed, some of the objections levied against behavior modification have applied to procedures that are not really a part of this research and application.

This book traces the history of behavior modification through the converging trends and lines of research that have led to its emergence. Within the field, behavior modification is not a unified area of research and clinical application. It encompasses diverse behavior-change techniques, conceptual and theoretical positions, and methodological approaches for evaluating treatment. There are several subareas of behavior modification, many of which can be traced along historical lines of their own and somewhat independent historical developments.

One area within behavior modification that has stimulated much work is founded upon laboratory research in operant conditioning, a particular type of learning developed by B. F. Skinner and based upon the use of rewards and punishing events to modify behavior. In this volume, particular emphasis is placed on applications relying on operant conditioning because of the extensive contributions of the research to applied work and the widespread use of operant techniques in clinical, educational, and rehabilitation settings.

OVERVIEW OF THE BOOK

Within clinical psychology and psychiatry, behavior modification represents a departure from traditional models of abnormal behavior and its treatment. Traditionally, abnormal behavior has been considered within the domain of medicine. Indeed, the terminology of deviant behavior and its amelioration reflect a strong medical orientation, as exemplified in such terms as "mental illness," "psychopathology," "psychiatric hospital." Behavior modification differs from this stance in its formulation of deviant behavior in terms of a psychological rather than a disease-based model. To convey the shift in paradigms that this formulation represents in the mental-health related fields, the traditional approach toward disturbed behavior and its assessment and treatment is described. This description provides the contemporary context in clinical psychology and psychiatry against which the overall development of behavior modification can best be understood. Traditional approaches to abnormal behavior and its treatment are discussed in Chapter 2.

The traditional views in clinical psychology and psychiatry do not convey the specific historical events to which behavior modification can be traced. Of central importance to contemporary behavior modification was the introduction of behaviorism into psychology in the early 1900s. John B. Watson, who crystallized and proposed behaviorism, emphasized rigorous methodological requirements for scientific research in psychology. Watson rejected the subjective areas of inquiry and methods of study that characterized the psychology of his day. He insisted upon objectivity and the concentration on overt events in studying behavior rather than the prevalent subjectivism associated with private experience (thoughts, images).

Inseparable from Watson's work and behaviorism in general was research in the psychology of learning. The foundations of behavior modification rely heavily upon learning theory and research. Much of this work derived from physiology experiments in Russia and animal learning in the United States; in many ways, learning theory was the foundation upon which behaviorism was built. The psychology of learning has been important in providing conceptual bases for behavior in general and for many of the therapeutic techniques developed to change behavior. The growth of behaviorism and the psychology of learning are traced in Chapter 3.

One aspect of the psychology of learning is operant conditioning. Operant research, which grew directly out of the behaviorist tradition, focuses primarily upon behaviors that are influenced by their consequences. Whereas the influence of consequences (i.e., reinforcing and punishing events) on behavior had been known for some time, Skinner brought its importance into sharp focus in the late 1930s. Operant conditioning developed within experimental psychology and included its own substantive questions and research methodology. Both the substantive findings and methodology of operant conditioning have had considerable impact on contemporary behavior modification. The evolution of operant conditioning and its approach toward behavior are described in Chapter 4.

Obviously the history of behavior modification cannot be traced along a single line. In the late 1950s and early 1960s, several parallel developments in different areas of the world eventually converged into a unified movement. In the United States, laboratory research in and conceptual extensions of learning increased, with resulting implications for the treatment of clinical disorders. Demonstrations in learning research showed that the methodology of experimental psychology as well as specific substantive findings were useful in studying or influencing abnormal behavior. Indeed, psychotherapy increasingly came to be viewed in terms of learning theory. In South Africa, research and theory from the psychology of learning were relied upon to generate techniques to eliminate anxiety. The techniques developed in the context of providing psychological treatment with an empirical basis. In England, dissatisfaction with traditional clinical methods served as the background for creating new models and treatments of abnormal behavior. The psychology of learning was proposed as the basis for conceptualizing and treating psychological disorders. This emergence of behavior modification is presented in Chapter 5.

Several methodological features were common among different views of behavior therapy research and applications of learning theory. Generally, the separate developments in different countries included a focus on changing overt behavior, conceptualizing abnormal behavior and its treatment from the standpoint of learning, and empirically deriving and examining treatment methods. Although these features characterize behavior modification in general, specific areas and approaches within behavior modification require qualification and amplification of these characteristics. Contemporary behavior modification and its characteristics and specific techniques are presented in Chapter 6.

One area of behavior modification represents an extension of operant conditioning to problems of clinical, educational, and social importance. Operant-conditioning research, primarily based on animal investigations, increasingly examined the application of its methodology and findings to human behavior. Eventually the methods and general model of operant conditioning were shown to provide important insights into the study of human behavior, in particular, the behavior of various clinical populations such as psychiatric patients and retarded children. Finally, operant techniques were extended to clinical populations for therapeutic and rehabilitative purposes. The applied extension of experimental research on operant conditioning quickly developed a subject matter and methodology of its own, for use in treatment, rehabilitation, education, and other areas. This applied extension is called "applied behavior analysis." The emergence of applied behavior analysis and its evolution from laboratory research are traced in Chapter 7. The characteristics and accomplishments of contemporary applied behavior analysis are reviewed in Chapter 8.

Throughout the history of behavior modification, overt behavior has been emphasized. Until recently, the influence of such events as thoughts, fantasies, and private verbalizations has been minimized. Several techniques have been created that are collectively referred to as "cognitive behavior modification," in which private events are focused upon directly as a means of changing overt behavior. These techniques are based upon the assumption that an individual's thought patterns and perceptions of the world account for problematic behaviors. Cognitive therapies focus upon altering these thought processes so that overt behavior is changed. Related to the development of cognitive therapies is the creation of behavior-change techniques that individuals can apply to themselves. These "self-control" techniques are necessary for changing private events (e.g., obsessive thoughts) not open to public scrutiny. Only the individual can detect the occurrence of these events and can be in a position to do something about them. Yet self-control techniques also have been used to alter a variety of overt behaviors and currently constitute a major area of research. The development of cognitive behavior modification and self-control is discussed in Chapter 9.

The success of behavior modification has caused increased concern about ethical and legal issues in treatment, which appears to reflect a general social awareness of protecting individual rights rather than a response to a particular form of treatment. Yet, the term "behavior modification" itself suggests that someone's behavior is going to be changed, perhaps against the volition of the individual who is the focus of the technique. Ethical discussions of behavior modification have questioned the desirability of technological advances in behavioral control and who should control behavior, and for what ends. Recently, the courts have increased their involvement in judging aspects of treatment to ensure the protection of individual rights. Many of the decisions have had direct implications for conducting behavior modification. Ethical and legal issues of behavior modification and issues pertaining to the protection of client rights are reviewed in Chapter 10.

Behavior modification has matured considerably in its relatively brief period of formal existence. Contemporary behavior modification consists of diverse theoretical positions about the development of behavior and the nature of motivation, research methods, and intervention techniques. Because of the heterogeneity of the field, relatively few characteristics of behavior modification can be enumerated that adequately encompass its variety. The positive characteristics that apply universally across techniques pertain primarily to methodological rather than to substantive or conceptual issues. In expanding its conceptual and technological scope, behavior modification also has enlarged upon aspects of clinical psychology. Extensions include applications of behavior-change techniques beyond the traditional confines of treatment to social problems, reliance upon non-professionals for direct delivery of treatment, and expansion of the criteria for evaluating psychological treatment in general. New extensions of behavior modification are discussed in Chapter 11.

2

Traditional Approaches to Conceptualization, Diagnosis, Assessment, and Treatment of Deviant Behavior

Until behavior modification emerged as a competitive theoretical basis for research and applied uses, a particular model or general view of abnormal behavior and its treatment dominated the mental-health profession.[1] This perspective has been generally referred to as a "medical" or "disease" model of abnormal behavior. The disease model was widely adopted to explain maladaptive or deviant behavior studied in psychology and psychiatry as an extrapolation of a successful approach used in medicine to explain physical disorders. In medicine, the belief that physical symptoms are traceable to underlying physical pathology has contributed to successful identification and control of physical disease. In particular, discoveries in pathology have supported the validity of the model for medical diagnosis and treatment. The success of the general approach stimulated the extension to psychological problems.

---

[1] The development of behavior modification might be viewed generally from the standpoint of a social movement reflected by diverse aspects of cultural growth beyond the mental health professions. However, the emergence of behavior modification in a social, cultural, and perhaps political context is outside the scope of this monograph.

When extended to abnormal behavior, the disease model implies that maladaptive behaviors are symptoms resulting from underlying processes analogous to "disease." The underlying processes could include biological factors. When biological factors are shown to cause disordered behavior, the disease model has been accepted as an appropriate extension of the model to behavior. In contrast, when the disease model has been extended to account for behavior with no known organic basis, debate has ensued over the suitability of the extrapolation. The model in this latter sense might be better characterized as an *intrapsychic-disease* model of abnormal behavior because disordered psychological processes are posited to account for maladaptive behaviors or psychological symptoms.

Traditional conceptualizations of abnormal behavior have emphasized an intrapsychic-disease model. This model and its implications are what behavior modifiers generally have referred to as the "medical model."[2] Proponents of behavior modification have objected to the medical orientation of this model, as reflected in formulations of abnormal behavior in such terms as "symptomatology," and "pathology." In addition, they have been opposed to positing intrapsychic processes that are presumed to account for deviant behavior.

Conceptualization and treatment of abnormal behavior have resided largely within the realm of medicine, specifically, psychiatry. Adhering to the medical approach toward abnormal behavior has had far-reaching consequences, because, once an orientation is selected, it dictates the terminology used to describe behavior, the type of procedures and facilities employed for modifying it, the type of research questions asked, and the training given to professionals who change behavior. The pervasiveness of the medical orientation in psychiatry and clinical psychology is evidenced by the fact that one cannot describe the topics of the field without implicitly embracing the

---

[2] In actuality, no single model exists in medicine that adequately characterizes its approach toward physical disorders. Thus, to speak of a single disease model begins with an oversimplified characterization of medicine and the approach that might have been extended to abnormal behavior. To illustrate the complexity of the disease orientation, at least three types of models can be distinguished based upon the type of physical disorder that is treated, including infection (e.g., as in bacterial diseases), systemic dysfunction (e.g., as in malfunction of an organ or regulatory system), and noninfectious trauma (e.g., as in externally induced injury) (Buss, 1966). Each of these disease models has different characteristics and would have different implications when extrapolated to nonmedical areas.

basic approach reflected in terms such as "mental illness and health," "treatment," and "therapy."

The development of behavior modification can be viewed as a reaction to the traditional conceptualization of abnormal behavior and its treatment. Thomas Kuhn, the noted historian of science, has suggested how reactions or revolutions arise in science (Kuhn, 1962). Initially, the field experiences growing dissatisfaction and skepticism with the adequacy of the existing model or paradigm that has guided research. Traditional methods of study or approaches to the subject matter may reveal large problems or inadequacies that fail to be resolved within the existing paradigm. The growing dissatisfaction sets the stage for the emergence of a new paradigm that clashes with the traditional approach. The new paradigm addresses the subject matter differently, with new definitions and relationships, and seems to resolve many problems that appeared to be unresolvable within the previous paradigm.

Within the field of mental health, behavior modification has been viewed as a new paradigm (Kanfer and Phillips, 1970; Krasner, 1971a). The stage for this paradigm was set by increasing disappointment with and criticism of diverse aspects of the traditional view of mental illness and its treatment. With the emergence of the behavior modification came a reconceptualization of deviant behavior and how it should be changed. As is characteristic with the presentation of a new approach, a great deal of research was stimulated in areas that seemed recalcitrant to inquiry within the previously dominant paradigm. In particular, behavior modification encouraged new suggestions for changing behavior.

This chapter discusses the paradigm or model against which behavior modification reacted. The extension of the medical approach to abnormal behavior and its implications in diagnosing, assessing, and treating abnormality are outlined.[3] The general characteristics of contemporary clinical practice based upon the disease model are described. The source of dissatisfaction with clinical practice and research derived from the traditional approach need to be pointed out because they are *direct* sources of confrontation of the traditional intrapsychic and contemporary behavioral paradigms.

---

[3] The development of the disease model, its implications, and sources of criticism and dissatisfaction with it can only be highlighted here. Various histories of psychiatry and clinical psychology are recommended to the interested reader (Alexander and Selesnick, 1968; Deutsch, 1946; Kraepelin, 1962; Lewis, 1941; Zilboorg and Henry, 1941).

EXTENSION OF THE
DISEASE MODEL TO ABNORMAL BEHAVIOR

The development of treatment methods in psychiatry and clinical psychology has been closely tied to conceptualizations or models of abnormal and normal behavior. Factors assumed to account for abnormal behavior have shaped the different treatments for individuals whose behaviors were deviant. Theories of behavior have varied so much throughout human history that treatment has been the province of different specialists and disciplines. In ancient times, prevailing explanations of behavior were based upon demonology. Individuals who acted abnormally were believed to be possessed by evil spirits. Spiritual notions were invoked to explain many aspects of life that were not understood, including deviant behavior. When deviant behavior was interpreted as a sign of evil spirits, treatment was based primarily upon exorcism. Diverse techniques, including prayer, flogging, and primitive psychosurgery, were designed to release or drive away evil spirits. Treatment and patient care were thus in the domain of priests, who were assumed to have the power to influence spirits.

Eventually, demonology was replaced with biological or medical conceptualizations of mental disorders. Hippocrates rejected intervention of spirits and demons and suggested biological causes related to brain functions and body fluids to explain abnormal behavior, and many other Greeks and Romans attributed abnormal behavior to biological causes. Once biological factors were assumed to underlie abnormal behavior, treatment changed. It generally became more humane than it had been when demons were thought to cause aberrant behavior. Treatment included providing patients with pleasant surroundings, exercise, special diets, cultural events, and massages. The notion that abnormal behavior had physiological roots brought treatment within the realm of physicians rather than priests and deviant behavior within the domain of medicine.

During the middle ages, demonology again became the dominant explanation for maladaptive behavior, and priests regained control over treatment. Physical punishment and torture often were used to drive away evil spirits. Increasingly, individual patients were blamed for their abnormal behavior in that it was taken as proof of having sinned.

By the sixteenth century, emphasis on biological causes of disordered behavior began to regain ascendancy over demonology

(Zilboorg and Henry, 1941). Once again, the resurgence of a biological and more scientific approach to deviant behavior led to humane rather than punitive treatment and to major reorganization of institutions for treatment purposes. By the eighteenth century, scientific inquiry and approaches toward abnormal behavior reached a zenith. Not only did advances in the biological sciences and general medicine accelerate, but specific findings also linked organic pathology to many physical disorders. The early successes in understanding physical maladies suggested that organic pathology might well account for disordered behavior as well. Accordingly, brain pathology was assumed to account for mental illness, and a disease model of behavior was constructed systematically. As with physiological disorders, mental disorders were viewed as reflecting an underlying pathological cause. Of course, for many mental disorders, a clear organic basis did exist (i.e., those disorders currently referred to as "organic"). Yet the disease model was extended to deviant behavior for which no organic basis was evident.

Establishing the organic basis of select manifestations of abnormal behavior markedly advanced extrapolations of the illness paradigm of mental disorders in general. The most prominent and influential catalyst was the discovery of the cause of general paresis, a neurological disorder that, in its late stages, may include several psychological symptoms such as intellectual impairment, grandiose ideation, and distorted perceptions. A remarkable series of breakthroughs led to Hideyo Noguchi's (1876–1928) demonstration in 1913 that the syphilitic spirochete (*Treponema pallidum*) was the cause of general paresis. Moreover, effective treatments were found along with discovery of the cause. The discovery and treatment of syphilis were especially dramatic because they provided the first case in which medical science conquered what was considered to be a mental illness, i.e., general paresis (Zilboorg and Henry, 1941). This contribution, along with discoveries pertaining to other disorders with much lower prevalence, provided a major impetus for the identification of psychological disorders with organic pathology.

Despite the success of an organic model for mental illness, there was a trend toward other lines of inquiry. For a major portion of the mental diseases, no evidence existed of organic pathology. In the late nineteenth century, the disease model was modified by many who looked for psychological rather than biological factors that might cause abnormal behavior, supported by reports of effective psychological techniques used to treat abnormal behavior. Elaborate procedures believed to be based upon suggestion (such as mesmerism, hypnosis, couéism) were developed as dramatically effective treatment strategies in Europe, especially in France, for treating a wide array of disorders. Select demonstrations in hospital settings established that symptoms of mental disorders (e.g., hysterical paralysis) could be induced or eliminated entirely through suggestion. The development of such methods to treat disorders, particularly neuroses, accelerated the search for psychological rather than organic factors in determinants of mental illness. However, no comprehensive theory was available to account for how psychological factors could cause mental illness or how psychological treatments might alleviate symptomatic behaviors. This lack was remedied by Sigmund Freud (1856–1939).

Freud and Psychoanalysis

In discussing the history and conceptualization of mental illness and its relationship to behavior modification (however indirect), it is important to focus on Freud for at least two reasons. As is obvious, Freud's influence on contemporary conceptualizations and treatment of abnormal behavior has been monumental. Moreover, behavior modification can be viewed as a reaction to many of the basic tenets of Freudian theory and therapy, particularly intrapsychic conflicts as determinants of behavior.

Background   Freud was trained in physiology and had a special interest in neuroanatomy. For financial reasons, he turned to medicine which he practiced in Vienna. His interest and training led him to specialize in "nervous" disorders, for which he consistently embraced an organic view. Freud thought that abnormal behaviors and psychological symptoms were based upon neurological and other physiological problems.

Freud began to study psychiatry and observed the work of Jean Charcot (1825–1893) and Hippolyte Bernheim (1837–1919) in France. They had successful therapy practices and had advanced influential theoretical formulations about the causes of mental disturbances. Their treatment was based upon hypnosis, which provided not only a method of treatment, but also a way to investigate the possible psychological concomitants or causes of mental disorders. When Freud returned to Vienna, he incorporated hypnosis into his own practice.

In Vienna, Freud collaborated with Josef Breuer (1842–1925), a neurophysiologist and clinician. Breuer also used hypnosis and reported its utility in helping patients recall early experiences. Hypnosis helped patients recall early traumas that appeared to be related to their disorders. Recollection or catharsis of the original traumatic event led to therapeutic change. On the basis of their therapeutic applications, Breuer and Freud attributed the development of neurotic disorders to unconscious processes. This hypothesis constituted a major advance toward the development of a psychological view of mental disorders because it provided a clear instance in which the cause of a disorder had been revealed while attempting to treat it. Thus, etiology, treatment, and cure were shown to be within the realm of psychological rather than organic factors (Zilboorg and Henry, 1941).

Since both Breuer and Freud had been trained in neurophysiology, it is not surprising that their theories retained an organic slant despite their advocacy of unconscious forces as causes of psychological disorders. Initially, the effects of cathartic treatment were explained in neurophysiological terms by referring to the conversion of energy and organic forces. Freud and Breuer parted when Freud embraced the view that sexual impulses underlie psychological problems and increasingly began to rely on his own theory of psychopathology. In addition, Freud abandoned hypnosis as a form of treatment because of its short-lived effects. He developed other methods (such as free association and dream analysis) to illuminate early memories and experiences that were thought to underlie a patient's problems.

Freud's clinical practice led to the development of his own theory of personality and system of therapy—psychoanalysis. On the basis of clinical observations, he postulated psychological processes that could account for behavior. These explanations were constantly being revised in light of material revealed in treatment. Psychoanalysis became a theory of personality, a treatment technique, and a method of investigation that sought to determine the psychic bases of behavior.

General Characteristics of Psychoanalysis Psychoanalysis as a theory of personality is a complex network of psychological mechanisms, structures, impulses, and developmental stages that explain behavior. Although the specific features of the theory are beyond the scope of the present chapter, some general characteristics warrant mention.[4] Freud conjectured that personality development can be traced to the expression of biological or sexual energy (libido) and to the sources of gratification toward which that energy is directed. He believed that psychological processes unfold in early childhood when instinctual gratification is a function of different sources of stimulation. Freud explained psychological development as passing through a series of psychosexual stages. The stages were determined primarily by the focus of expression of libidinal energy on various parts of the body (i.e., oral, anal, genital areas) as well as by psychic mechanisms he assumed to be operative during those stages.

Freud's initial interest was in accounting for neurotic behavior of "symptoms." He regarded neurotic symptoms as substitute gratifications for unconscious impulses that had been denied expression. The goal of therapy was to uncover these repressions and unconscious processes. He found that sexual themes, usually related to early childhood, were uniformly implicated in the patient's problems. Initially, he believed that sexual experiences in childhood played a role in later adult psychopathology. Later, he revised this view and referred to the patient's *fantasies* of such experiences as an influence on psychopathology. He developed a theory of childhood psychosexual development that provided a hypothetical account of specific developmental stages and critical events that explained personality and behavior. Freud interpreted neurotic disorders as a return to early levels of psychosexual development. The goal of treatment was to provide insight into the client's psychosexual evolution and to understand the developmental bases of symptomatic behavior. The therapeutic focus was on unraveling unconscious processes as expressed in dreams, free associations, and interpretations of overt behavior.

Along with the psychosexual stages of development, Freud posed an intricately related series of concepts, including various structures of personality (id, ego, superego), mechanisms to ward off or express

---

[4] Psychoanalytic theory has evolved considerably, beginning with Freud's first disciples and still continuing with contemporary theorists. Many of the basic tenets of Freudian psychoanalysis have been altered. For example, Freud stressed instinctual conflicts, psychic impulses, and unconscious processes as determinants of behavior, whereas neo-Freudians and ego psychologists who have revised the theory have emphasized social influences and conscious processes (e.g., Erikson, 1963; Hartmann, 1964). These later developments, although important in their own right, are tangential to the emergence of behavior modification. Behavior modification reacted to both the specific substance and methods of orthodox psychoanalysis and the basic intrapsychic model upon which its revisions have been based. Hence, this discussion provides an overview of Freudian psychoanalysis and features characteristic of the intrapsychic model.

otherwise threatening impulses (e.g., repression, sublimation, reaction formation), and processes to explain ordinary as well as abnormal behavior (e.g., primary and secondary processes). Many of these specific features of psychoanalysis came to be continually altered by Freud and revised extensively by the neo-Freudians, who adhered to the general psychoanalytic model but varied its content and emphasis.

It cannot be overemphasized that psychoanalysis was based on an organic approach to psychopathology, as Freud's original training as a physiologist predisposed him to explain psychological phenomena from the standpoint of physiology and neurology. Psychoanalytic theory also reflects the more general influence of the organic approach that was popular in his day. For example, the physiologist Ernst Brücke (1819–1892), with whom Freud had studied, emphasized that the physiology of organisms could be understood from dynamic physical processes such as the influences of forces and energy relationships. Similarly, the English neurologist, John Hughlings Jackson (1835–1911), whose work was familiar to Freud, emphasized the hierarchical organization of physical and psychological functions. He theorized that a breakdown of one level led to a regression and expression of another (lower) level. The nervous system was dynamic—energy was stored and expended by it—which provided the basis for psychological and physical functioning. Many features of psychoanalytic theory were grounded in accepted premises about the function of the organism and thus represented a plausible extension of basic tenets of biological and physical sciences to psychic phenomena. Freud's theory stressed the *dynamic* properties of psychological energy and the transformation of energy into various manifestations (behaviors and symptoms). The principle of conservation of energy, which had been formulated in early nineteenth-century physics, exerted influence and reflected the thought about both physical and psychological energy systems. Psychoanalytic theory fit into this general mode. Indeed, the psychological processes to which Freud referred often are called "psychodynamic processes."

Several concepts within psychoanalytic theory reflected the concern with psychological energy and its transformations. An important example is the notion that symptoms of psychopathology reflect expressions of psychic (libidinal) impulses. Alleviation of the symptom depended upon eliminating or rechanneling the energy source that was manifested in the symptom. Merely altering the symptom was considered undesirable unless the presumed psychic basis for its appearance was corrected. The treatment of a specific symptom without treating its underlying psychic cause would merely lead to substitute problem behaviors that would be reexpressions of the psychic energy, a phenomenon termed "symptom substitution."[5] The general model of Freudian psychoanalysis is an intrapsychic-disease model in that disordered underlying psychic processes (e.g., repression, conflict, thwarted impulses) are considered to cause a symptom (overt problematic behavior). As in many forms of illness, treatment of the symptom without alleviation of the underlying disorder would not be expected to effect cure.

As suggested earlier, important gains were made during the nineteenth century in identifying specific factors that accounted for various physical disorders. By analogy, the model was extended to "mental illness," which in some instances successfully revealed specific physical pathology to which psychological symptoms (i.e., deviant behavior) could be traced. Yet with many forms of psychological disturbance, the underlying disorder was assumed to be psychological and the general disease model was preserved. Freud's contribution was to provide an elaborate conceptual framework for determining what these abnormal psychological factors were. Psychoanalytic theory advanced a particular view of the processes that might account for abnormal behavior and suggested treatment that would alleviate them.

Along with his substantive contribution to personality theory and psychotherapy, the general approach advocated by Freud represented a major advance. Psychoanalytic theory assumed a determinism whereby every behavior, thought, and idea, however minor, were caused by underlying psychological mechanisms. By emphasizing the necessity of processes that often were assumed to be random (e.g., dreams, humor, slips of the tongue), he clearly moved psychological processes within the realm of scientific inquiry. Another contribution was the scope with which Freud endowed psychoanalysis. He applied the concepts of psychoanalysis to account for general psychological functioning rather than merely abnormal actions. Freud attempted to

---

[5] Symptom substitution is discussed later because it is a fundamental issue in the development of behavior modification. It is important to reemphasize here that variations of a disease model and orthodox psychoanalytic theory do not necessarily predict the appearance of substitute symptoms after problem behaviors are treated. For example, Freud himself (1936) explicitly noted that psychological symptoms may at some point become free from the psychic energy from which they were derived. Thus, elimination of the "symptom" would not necessarily result in reexpression of the energy.

show that psychological processes could account for all behavior; indeed, he extended his theory beyond individual behavior and speculated about social processes, cultural development, anthropology, and history.

Dissatisfaction with the Psychoanalytic Model

Psychoanalysis and the model of behavior that it embraced has dominated thought about the nature of psychological disorders and their treatment. Within the last 25 years, dissatisfaction with psychoanalysis and the intrapsychic-disease model has increased. A major source of dissatisfaction with psychoanalysis has been its status as a scientific theory. An essential ingredient of a scientific theory is that it should yield readily testable hypotheses. The hypotheses must be falsifiable so that they can be rejected in light of empirical tests. Psychoanalytic theory has been formulated in such a way that a large part of its basic assumptions and statements about personality are not tested easily. Many writers have criticized psychoanalytic theory on the basis of its immunity to falsification (Bailey, 1956; Ellis, 1949; Eysenck, 1960c; La Piere, 1948; Oberndorf, 1953; Rachman, 1963; Salter, 1952; Sears, 1943; Shaffer, 1936).

Different features of psychoanalysis contribute to its inadequacy as a scientific theory. In general, the relationship between psychodynamic processes and behavior is not clear. The presence or absence of a certain behavior in and of its own right is not necessarily evidence for particular psychological processes. An individual's behavior may be related to psychological processes only very remotely through a complex chain of symbolic derivations. Two sources of ambiguity illustrate the difficulty in deriving predictions from psychoanalytic theory. First, a given behavior may be a sign of different (and opposite) psychological processes. For example, a habit such as cigarette smoking can be traced to childhood sources of gratification. Yet smoking could illustrate either excessive or insufficient gratification (oral stimulation) early in life. The behavior does not necessarily argue for one of these interpretations. Similarly, neurotic symptoms might develop as a substitute satisfaction of a sexual impulse or as a measure to avoid such a satisfaction. Indeed, compromises between these two choices may be the impetus for neurotic symptoms (Freud, 1949).

The above examples suggest that a given behavior can result from different and incompatible psychological processes. Conversely, a given psychological process can be evidenced by different manifestations of behavior. For example, repression of psychic impulses can lead to symptomatic behavior. However, repression also can lead to creative expression of the psychic impulses if the individual can express them through a socially acceptable behavior (sublimation).

As a rule, psychoanalytic interpretations of given processes, symbolic expression, or overt behavior can vary drastically to achieve opposite conclusions about behavior. Because contradictory inferences can be derived from the same information about the individual, falsifiable hypotheses are difficult to generate.

Psychoanalytic theory has shielded itself from criticism as a scientific theory in other ways. Initially, Freud noted that psychoanalysis was intended to be primarily retrospective, designed to describe the past basis for contemporary behaviors (Freud, 1933). Prediction was not the goal of psychoanalytic propositions, and thus they were free from empirical test. By stressing *ex post facto* formulations, the theory was considered to be immune from scientific refutation.

Freudian theory protected itself from criticism in other ways. Presumably, if empirical evidence is difficult to bring to bear to psychoanalytic theory, its theoretical propositions might be criticized on logical grounds. Yet Freud argued that criticism of psychoanalytic theory *per se* only serves as support for the theory. He observed that criticism of psychoanalytic theory was based primarily upon the reaction of critics to the place it accorded sexuality. The rejection of the pansexuality of psychoanalysis was itself based upon neurotic processes that had been fully explained by the theory (Freud, 1950). In addition, Freud noted that individuals who themselves had not experienced analysis or had not studied others through psychoanalysis were not in a position to judge independently the theory's validity (Freud, 1949). Essentially, psychoanalytic theory might only be criticized by individuals who in some way were already trained in analysis. Such individuals, of course, were those most likely to be active proponents of the theory.

Although the bulk of psychoanalytic theory is not readily amenable to scientific verification, many researchers have derived particular propositions to test aspects of the theory. In general, the evidence has not supported many of the assumptions and speculations about behavior and its antecedents. This conclusion was reached in an influential report completed in 1943 by Robert S. Sears, who evaluated 166 articles dealing with attempts to verify empirically select Freudian propositions about personality. Sears concluded that the evidence at that time did not offer support for the theory. Indeed,

Sears noted that "perhaps a dozen other theories would provide as good or better explanations" of the findings (1943, p. 134).

Many statements in psychoanalytic theory link early childhood experiences and development with later behavior. Several investigators have indicated that many specific connections between early experiences and adult behavior have not been supported (Caldwell, 1964; Hovey, 1959; Jastrow, 1932; Orlansky, 1949; Sewell, 1952). Specific developmental events regarded as important determinants of subsequent behavior—for example, breast feeding and toilet training— have not been shown to relate consistently to particular characteristics of adults (e.g., Livson and Peskin, 1967; Orlansky, 1949; Sewell, 1952).

Attempts have been made to assess the universality of many of the claims about personality and psychological development. Freud viewed unfolding of psychological processes as biologically deter- mined in the sense that specific developmental obstacles and events were universal rather than culturally based. For example, Freud viewed progression through stages of psychosexual development and specific psychic events such as the Oedipus complex as basic aspects of psychological growth. Many writers have suggested that insofar as the processes Freud described were present at all, they were restricted to Western Europeans and Americans of his era (Benedict, 1946; Malinowski, 1937; Mead, 1928, 1935). Indeed, Freudian theory has been criticized for ignoring cultural and sociological variables that would limit its applicability.

A major source of dissatisfaction with psychoanalytic proposi- tions pertains to its assumptions about symptom formation and elimi- nation. The theory assumes that maladaptive behaviors are symptoms of underlying disorders. The notion of a psychological "symptom" embraces a particular theoretical position that dictates not only the individual's problem but also the appropriate focus of treatment. If a patient's problems are viewed as symptoms of underlying disorders, treatment must focus upon these disorders. The psychological "disease" rather than the problem behavior must be treated.

Within psychodynamic theory, symptom formation was seen as a welling up of psychic energy that sought expression. The system of psychic energy within psychodynamic theory can be imagined as a closed hydraulic model. If one channel of energy expression is shut off, another may appear. To extend the metaphor, altering a sympto- matic behavior might lead to reexpression of the original psychic energy in another form. Specifically, psychodynamic theory has sug- gested that if the treatment focuses upon symptoms without the underlying disorder, substitute symptoms might develop. The notion of symptom substitution in psychodynamic theory has been a subject of major controversy in its own right (e.g., Eysenck, 1959; Mowrer, 1950; Yates, 1958b).

Several reasons have been given for dissatisfaction with symptom substitution. Initially, as with other psychodynamic concepts, it is not easy to ascertain if substitute symptoms appear after treatment. The nature of the substitute symptoms that might arise, the circumstances under which they arise, and the length of time one must wait for their appearance are not specified by psychodynamic theory. And, as noted, the very notion of "symptom" substitution presupposes an intra-psychic-disease model of abnormal behavior as well as specific notions about the function of psychic energy and its expression. Perhaps most important, many therapists have reported that treatment of behavior regarded as "symptomatic" (such as enuresis or fear) does not necessarily result in the appearance of other maladaptive behaviors (e.g., M. C. Jones, 1924b; Mowrer and Mowrer, 1938; Yates, 1958b). The absence of maladaptive behaviors following treatment of the presenting problem calls into question the model upon which symptom substitution was based.

PSYCHIATRIC DIAGNOSIS

Application of the disease model to abnormal behavior has led to attempts to devise a method of identifying specific or distinct disease entities or disorders that can be treated. The identification of specific disorders has been undertaken through classification of mental illness and psychiatric diagnosis.

Throughout the history of psychiatry, investigators have endeavored to differentiate types of disorders and describe their unique characteristics. Successful delineation of specific disorders would contribute to discovering the cause of the disorders, providing treatment, and predicting the outcome. The search for disease entities had proved to be valuable in the area of medicine, particularly by the nineteenth century, when advances made in diagnosis were beginning to be accompanied by many gains in treatment and understanding of etiology.

Although many previous attempts to distinguish personality types and psychological disorders can be cited, the basis for modern psychiatric diagnosis is credited to the German psychiatrist Emil

Kraepelin (1856–1926). Kraepelin developed a diagnostic system that exerted a major influence on psychiatry. He first advanced his classifications in a brief publication outlining disorders (1883), and his work culminated in a massive textbook on psychiatry that provided specific details of a large number of disease entities (published posthumously in 1927).

Like many other psychiatrists of his time, Kraepelin adhered to an organic view of mental illness that emphasized brain pathology and that was compatible with contemporary discoveries revealing that organic pathology was the basis of select mental disorders. He extended this general organic approach to mental disorders through his identification of specific "disease" entities. He isolated various entities by systematically collecting thousands of case studies on hospitalized psychiatric patients. He described the history of each patient, the onset of the illness, and the outcome of the disorder. From this extensive clinical material, he elaborated various types of mental illness. His system was based upon the assumption that specific mental disease entities existed and that each of them had a predetermined or fixed course. Disorders were classified on the basis of their presumed outcome, i.e., whether or not the diseases remitted or were curable. In addition, the classification of disorders was made on the basis of presumed etiologies (e.g., endogenous versus exogenous). His system distinguished various psychogenic or functional disorders, with no known biological basis, from organic disorders, based upon identified brain pathology and toxic states. It is important to note that specific features of Kraepelin's system as well as his basic approach toward mental illness have been largely retained.

Kraepelin's work brought mental disease (deviant behavior) clearly into the realm of medicine. Mental disease was now recognized as being very much like physical disease, with its own specific etiology and particular course. Other individuals before Kraepelin, as well as several of his contemporaries, adhered to the notion that mental disorders represented distinct physical diseases. However, Kraepelin provided a system based upon extensive clinical data, in which disorders were classified according to specific entities with a specific prognosis (Zilboorg and Henry, 1941).

Contemporary diagnosis is based upon a system that attempts to classify patients in terms of specific nosological categories. The system is described in the *Diagnostic and Statistical Manual of the Mental Disorders* published and periodically revised by the American

Psychiatric Association (1952, 1968, in preparation). Three major categories are delineated: organic syndromes, psychogenic disorders, and mental retardation. Several subcategories and types of disorders are listed under each of the main classifications. The different disorders included in the diagnostic system are identified by their actual or proposed etiology, patterns of symptomatic behavior, deviance from social norms, and other dimensions. The system is mainly descriptive and identifies or names disorders rather than extends information about them. More important than the specific content of the contempoary diagnostic system is its clear medical orientation. With most disorders, psychological and behavioral problems are viewed as evidence of underlying psychological disturbance ("mental illness").

Dissatisfaction with Psychiatric Diagnosis

Psychiatric diagnosis has been the center of extensive research, and a comprehensive review is beyond the scope of this volume. Two general criticisms have emerged. One source has focused upon specific characteristics of the system and its utility. The other has examined psychiatric diagnosis *per se* and the assumptions entailed by labeling people as mentally ill based upon their behavior.

Several specific characteristics of the diagnostic system have been criticized. The first pertains to the reliability of diagnosis, which includes the extent to which a given diagnosis is made consistently by different diagnosticians at a given time as well as the extent to which an initial diagnosis is consistent with a later one. In general, research has shown that agreement among different diagnosticians who observe the same patient is often relatively low. Although the precise percentages of agreement across studies differ, even broad categories of diagnosis still lead to large discrepancies between observers. The more specific the diagnosis, the lower the agreement between the two diagnosticians (e.g., Ash, 1949; Hunt, Wittson, and Hunt, 1953; Schmidt and Fonda, 1956). These results across several studies have raised questions about the utility of the system, because diagnosticians do not agree on the labels they assign to patients. After reviewing the literature on reliability of psychiatric diagnosis, Joseph Zubin (1967) concluded that ". . . the degree of overall agreement between different observers with regard to specific diagnoses is too low for individual diagnosis. The overall agreement on general categories of diagnosis, although somewhat higher, still leaves much to be desired" (p. 383).

In addition to lack of agreement among observers for a given patient, the consistency of a patient's diagnosis over time also has been a source of dissatisfaction. Although findings differ across diagnostic categories, it has been generally shown that patients receiving a given diagnosis at a certain time are not likely to receive the same diagnosis later (Masserman and Carmichael, 1938).

The validity as well as reliability of psychiatric diagnosis has been doubted. Validity refers to the question of how well diagnosis achieves its purposes. The question is inherently difficult to address because of the multiple purposes (e.g., deciding treatment, predicting prognosis) for which diagnosis is used. One means of assessing validity is to determine if the patient's symptomatic characteristics can be revealed through different means of assessing behavior. Some studies have compared results from psychometric assessment with clinical application of diagnostic labels (see Mischel, 1968). Little correspondence was found between assessment of diagnosis (e.g., through psychological tests) and clinical diagnosis (e.g., through interviews). Another means of evaluating the validity of diagnosis is the extent to which it predicts outcome of the disorder. Generally, some association has been established between specific diagnoses and predictions of outcome (e.g., Zubin, Sutton, Salzinger, Salzinger, Burdock, and Peretz, 1961).

Diagnostic validity also has been studied by examining the extent to which knowledge of one or a few symptoms predicts other characteristics of a given diagnostic group. Research has demonstrated enough overlap among diagnostic groups to illustrate that knowledge of a specific symptom does not in itself predict a specific syndrome (group or patterns of symptoms) (Freudenberg and Robertson, 1956; Phillips and Rabinovitch, 1958). In general, there is sufficient homogeneity of symptoms across many diagnostic categories and heterogeneity of symptoms within a given category to raise serious questions about the basis of many diagnostic categories (e.g., Katz, Cole, and Lowery, 1964).

Along with concerns about reliability and validity of psychiatric diagnosis, reservations have been expressed about the utility of diagnosis. For medical diagnosis of physical ailments, classifying specific disorders has been productive for discovering etiology, treatment, and prognosis. The utility of psychiatric diagnosis along these dimensions has been less marked. Psychiatric diagnosis has been important in aiding the study of patients with similar diagnoses or symptoms. Etiological hypotheses and specific forms of treatment have resulted from such research. However, the direct implications of diagnosis for patient care have been minimal. To many investigators, diagnosis merely provides a label; it does not supply clear implications about what will happen in the course of the disorder or treatment.

Many of the above objections focus upon specific inadequacies of the existing classification. Broader criticisms of the classification of abnormal behavior as disease also have emerged, particularly in the late 1950s and 1960s. Criticisms came from several quarters, including psychiatry, clinical psychology, and sociology. The basic assumption of psychiatric diagnosis as it derives from a disease model initially was questioned. For example, Thomas Szasz, a psychiatrist, has been particularly vocal in rejecting the disease model. Szasz suggests that so-called psychogenic mental illnesses are really problems in living that individuals experience as a result of stress. He has claimed that a "myth of mental illness" is fostered by treating deviant behavior within the realm of a disease model (Szasz, 1961). Deviant behavior, according to Szasz, reflects a departure in someone's behavior from ethical, legal, and social norms and does not reflect an organic malfunctioning. That deviant behavior and psychological dysfunction arise from the social context rather than a disease process has been argued by several other writers (e.g., Ellis, 1967; Ferster, 1965; Laing, 1967; Mowrer, 1960c; Scheff, 1966; Ullmann and Krasner, 1969). In addition, psychiatric diagnosis and the disease model upon which it is based are very misleading, because they imply that individuals have discrete and distinct handicaps that can be treated in a manner analogous to physical disorders (Ellis, 1967).

Many authors have objected to the diagnostic process as well as the fundamental disease model presupposed by psychiatric diagnosis. Objections to labeling individuals as "mentally ill" and providing a specific diagnosis have been raised because the diagnosed individual may be subjected to social discrimination and criticism, may enter a career of deviant behavior as a result of the manner in which he/she views him/herself or is viewed by other people, and may be removed from many social, vocational, and educational opportunities that provide constructive influences in his/her life (Ellis, 1967; Sarbin, 1967; Scheff, 1966).

Thus, virtually all facets of psychiatric diagnosis have been questioned, from inadequacies of the system currently used to diagnosis *per se* based on the disease model. Many writers believe it is inappropriate to view abnormal behavior defined and identified in the social context from the standpoint of disease. Thus, even if diagnosis did not suffer from such fundamental problems as reliability and validity, much of the contemporary dissatisfaction would not dissipate.

CLINICAL ASSESSMENT

Early in clinical psychology, assessment devices were developed to appraise intellectual abilities and educational achievement. In France in the 1890s, Alfred Binet (1857–1911) attempted to distinguish "bright" from "dull" children by having them perform diverse tasks related to sensorimotor skills, memory, imagination, perception, and comprehension. Binet was successful in differentiating children according to their academic performance. His results were a major impetus for devising psychological tests for personality and psychopathology.

In the United States, the advent of World War II made it necessary for the military to begin extensive psychological assessment of enlisted personnel and victims of war-related injuries, and research on personality and psychopathology was stimulated by this imperative. Psychologists entered the military in large numbers and became involved in screening recruits with psychological impairment who might not be suited for the military. Tests were also required to select individuals with particular skills for the military. Furthermore, psychologists became involved in treating individuals who had become psychologically disturbed by participating in the war. Thus, psychologists became more clearly engaged in clinical practice.

Concomitant with the practical needs of the military, theoretical developments contributed to the refinement of psychological measurement. Psychoanalytic theory in particular provided a conceptual framework for explaining behavior based upon underlying psychological processes. These processes could not be discerned from overt behavior because individuals disguised or only symbolically expressed them. Thus, a large effort developed to evaluate underlying personality.

Psychoanalytic theory accelerated the search for and the use of available assessment procedures that might reveal unconscious processes. Much of the influence of psychoanalysis was indirect. For example, psychoanalysis stimulated the formulation of theories of personality that generated their own methods of personality assessment.

In addition, psychoanalysis helped unify independently devised methods of personality assessment that developed without allegiance to a particular theoretical framework.

Psychoanalysis and the intrapsychic-disease model encouraged work in personality assessment. The aim of personality assessment is to uncover the individual's psychological impulses, traits, and attributes that underlie behavior. In clinical uses of assessment, such as testing psychiatric patients, the purpose is to elaborate the personality traits or dynamics that might help explain motives and conflicts that account for behavior. A battery of inventories and tests to measure attributes and processes related to psychopathology are administered.[6]

Of the available methods, it is important to single out *projective techniques* because they are products of the prevailing concept of the disease model in clinical psychology. Projective techniques are a collection of many different methods for assessing psychological functioning. They did not develop out of a unified theory such as psychoanalysis. However, the tests were greatly influenced by the psychodynamic theory of personality. As psychodynamic theory began to dominate clinical psychology, investigators sought techniques that would allow the study of personality and unconscious motives. The Rorschach test, which had already been available as a method of personality study, was one method incorporated into psychodynamic assessment (cf. Reisman, 1966). Many other projective techniques have developed from particular theories or with the express purpose of assessing psychodynamic processes (cf. Klopfer and Taulbee, 1976).

Projective techniques are characterized by presenting the subject with an ambiguous task. The task is ambiguous so as to minimize cues that will dictate the response given by the subject. Presumably the individuals will project their own meanings and interpretations onto the situation. If external stimuli do not contribute markedly to the form of the client's response, internal psychological processes are assumed to account for the responses provided. With the administration of many tests, the purpose of revealing underlying psychological processes is disguised further and the person is told to respond freely.

A quintessential example of the projective techniques is the Rorschach test, consisting of bilaterally symmetrical ink blots that are

---

[6] For a comprehensive list of available tests and critical reviews, the *Mental Measurement Yearbook*, published every few years, should be consulted (e.g., Buros, 1972).

shown to the subject (Rorschach, 1942). The subject describes what he/she sees and responds to general questions from the examiner. The Thematic Apperception Test (Murray, 1943) presents ambiguous pictures of events that are considered to represent important themes in personality development (e.g., need for achievement, handling of aggression and sexuality, relations with family members). Because the pictures are ambiguous, individuals can interpret what is going on very differently. Responses to both the Rorschach test and the Thematic Apperception Test are analyzed as reflections of the respondent's personality.

Dissatisfaction with Projective Techniques

Diagnostic testing and the use of projective techniques reached a peak in the 1940s and 1950s. The reliability and validity of projective assessment techniques began to be criticized in the 1950s and continues today (Davenport, 1952; Garfield, 1974; Mischel, 1968; Zubin, 1954). Studies of reliability have shown that examiners often do not agree about the personality processes reflected in a particular response to a projective test or across several tests (e.g., Datel and Gengerelli, 1955; Howard, 1962; Little and Shneidman, 1959). Different interpretations are reached from identical test procedures. In addition, validity studies have shown that different measures of the same psychological process, attribute, or trait rarely show a positive relationship that would suggest the utility of the construct assumed to account for the responses (e.g., Goldberg and Werts, 1966; Holland and Nichols, 1964). Thus, with many measures, it is unclear precisely what is being measured and what inferences can be drawn on the basis of test performance.

Moreover, psychological assessment often has little or no applied influence in the treatment or disposition of patients. For example, in psychiatric hospitals, psychologists often spend many hours administering a battery of psychological measures, including projective techniques and inventories of specific traits and states. The final scoring and interpretation of these tests are similarly time-consuming. Once completed, the psychological report frequently has little effect upon the diagnosis given to the patient in the hospital or upon the treatment administered (Peterson, 1968). Surveys have revealed that most therapists do not believe that psychological assessment of the client's personality is relevant for treatment (Meehl, 1960). Thus, the practical importance and the utility of assessing a patient's personality have been questioned (Mischel, 1968; Peterson, 1968).

Complex psychological assessment procedures predict no better how an individual will behave than measures that are more easily obtained, such as self-report from the individual or standing on demographic or subject variables such as socioeconomic class (e.g., Eschenbach and Borgatta, 1955; Mischel, 1965; Peterson, 1965). Indeed, predictions about behavior based upon psychological assessment often are below the level of accuracy that can be achieved by taking into account base rates for the behavior (Meehl and Rosen, 1955).

A major criticism of projective techniques is their heavy reliance upon clinical judgment. The psychologist's interpretations are the basis for predicting an individual's behavior or for describing features of the subject not directly revealed in test performance. Reliance upon the therapist's interpretations has been influenced by psychodynamic theory, in which the overt responses of the client are taken solely as signs of underlying personality. Interpretations are derived from taking into account diverse responses, perhaps from different tests, as well as from subtleties of a person's behavior during test administration. The clinician combines all of the information available to provide a statement or prediction about the patient.

Clinical interpretation and judgment have been demonstrated to be grossly inadequate in predicting behavior; clinical judgment often is no better than applying stereotypic predictions about behavior based upon such general information as age or sex (Mischel, 1968). Indeed, the extent to which the clinician deviates from general stereotypic statements and takes into account nuances of client test performance is related to decreases in accuracy of the predictions or characterizations of the client (Soskin, 1959; Taft, 1955). Frequently individuals who are neither professional clinicians nor trained in test interpretation and interview or therapy skills make judgments of interpretations about clients that are as accurate as those of trained clinicians (Crow, 1957; Goldberg, 1959; Horowitz, 1962; Sarbin, Taft, and Bailey, 1960).

In addition, clinical judgment tends to be strongly oriented toward interpreting behavior in terms of psychopathology. Clinicians are likely to interpret projective test performance in terms of disordered psychological processes and psychiatric impairment. Even the test responses of "normal," well-adjusted subjects are interpreted as impaired and characteristic of diagnosed psychiatric patients (Little and Shneidman, 1959).

Dissatisfaction with clinical judgment as a way of predicting behavior has led to suggestions for more reliable and valid methods. One alternative is derived from actuarial methods of combining data to predict behavior (Meehl, 1954), which refers to making decisions based upon how the data (usually, test performance) are shown empirically to relate to subsequent behavior. Once the relationship is demonstrated, test performance can be interpreted automatically without recourse to judgment. Actuarial methods of combining data have proved to lead to more accurate predictions than does clinical judgment (Gough, 1962; Meehl, 1954, 1955). The superiority of actuarial over intuitive methods of prediction precipitated several discussions over the future of clinical judgment itself (Holt, 1958; Meehl, 1956, 1957; Sawyer, 1966).

TREATING ABNORMAL BEHAVIOR

Two general categories of treatment have been derived from the intrapsychic-disease model in contemporary clinical practice: psychotherapy and institutionalization. Although many forms of therapy and institutional treatment are available, the context out of which behavior modification developed can be illustrated by a general discussion of traditional psychoanalysis or psychoanalytically oriented psychotherapy and by custodial ward care. Psychotherapy and institutionalization have characterized the bulk of outpatient and inpatient treatment, respectively.

Psychotherapy

The advent of psychoanalysis had a great impact on the practice of psychotherapy. Before psychoanalysis, psychotherapy primarily consisted of methods explicitly based upon prescriptive advice or suggestion (e.g., hypnosis and mesmerism). Psychoanalysis, however, placed treatment within a complex theoretical framework that at once accounted for the development of psychopathology and provided recommendations for treatment.

In the early 1900s, psychoanalytically oriented therapy dominated treatment in psychiatry and clinical psychology. Although relatively few individuals were trained in psychoanalysis or had undergone analysis themselves, the bulk of the practitioners drew upon Freudian theory to conceptualize client behavior and treatment. The language of psychoanalysis became the jargon of therapy. Also, the basic approach toward treatment tended to be widely incorporated by practitioners.

The goal of psychoanalytic treatment is to provide the patient with insight into the unconscious processes that motivate his/her behavior. Several techniques are used to reveal unconscious psychodynamic processes, including dream interpretation and free association. Therapeutic change is a complex process that results from resolving early childhood conflicts, overcoming sources of resistance in therapy, and uncovering repressed material expressing itself in symptom formation or currently influencing psychodynamic functioning. The task of therapy is to alter the psychological processes to which causes of behavior are attributed.

The focus upon underlying psychological processes rather than the symptomatic behaviors or problems themselves is embraced by many other verbal psychotherapeutic techniques. Many therapeutic techniques are based on differing assumptions about which particular psychological processes account for behavior, yet they fall within the general intrapsychic approach to treatment. A major example of treatment that has been extremely influential is nondirective or client-centered psychotherapy. The technique was proposed by Carl Rogers, a clinical psychologist, who developed a phenomenological self-theory of personality (Rogers, 1942, 1951). The theory of personality and therapeutic practice advocated by Rogers can be readily distinguished from psychoanalysis. Rogers' therapy focuses upon events in the individual's contemporary life rather than historical sources of conflict, eschews interpretations about psychodynamic processes, and rejects most Freudian notions about personality development. A person's self-concept and perception of the environment account for symptomatic behavior. The task of treatment is to help the client accept him/herself and assimilate those portions of reality that are rejected, denied, or distorted. Treatment is directed toward altering self-perceptions rather than focusing upon problematic behavior (Rogers, 1951).

Most psychotherapy practiced in the 1950s and 1960s was based upon psychoanalytic or nondirective therapy. Nondirective therapy was a strong competitor of psychoanalytically oriented psychotherapy in terms of popularity among psychologists because it evolved from psychology rather than medicine. Within psychology, a number of other therapeutic techniques were usually based upon elaborate theories of personality. In addition, Freudian psychoanalysis branched out into divergences, including new approaches pioneered by individuals who left orthodox psychoanalysis to apply their own related theories, notably Carl Jung and Alfred Adler.

Despite the variations, most psychotherapies adhere to an intrapsychic-disease model. As behavior modification evolved, diverse forms of psychotherapy based upon the intrapsychic model were grouped together and referred to as "insight" or "evocative" therapy (e.g., London, 1964; Ullmann and Krasner, 1965). The distinctions among insight therapies became less important than their adherence to basic features of the intrapsychic-disease model. Objections were directed at psychodynamic therapy in particular because of its prominence in clinical work and its vulnerability to criticism.

Dissatisfaction with Psychotherapy

A major impetus for behavior modification stemmed from a dissatis- ✓ faction with traditional psychotherapy, particularly psychoanalysis and psychoanalytically oriented therapy. The most significant and challenging criticism of traditional therapy was an evaluation of its efficacy. Until the 1950s, psychotherapy was not subjected to major critical evaluation. Most professionals believed in the efficacy of therapy because of their own case experiences and testimonials of patients and colleagues. Although several investigators had questioned the efficacy of psychotherapy (e.g., Denker, 1946; Landis, 1937; Salter, 1952; Wilder, 1945; Zubin, 1953), the most influential critical evaluation of psychotherapy appeared in Hans J. Eysenck's article, "The Effects of Psychotherapy," published in 1952. Eysenck investigated whether rigorous evidence existed for the proposition that psychotherapy was effective.

Eysenck examined several outcome studies that primarily evaluated treatment of neurotic patients. To assess the effects of psychotherapy, he attempted to derive an estimate of improvements in patients that occurred in the absence of therapy. Using data from available studies, he concluded that approximately 67% of neurotic patients recover within two years, even in the absence of formal psychotherapy. Having established an approximate baseline against which treatment could be evaluated, Eysenck found that review of the literature on therapy outcome showed a cure rate of approximately the same magnitude as remission without treatment (termed "spontaneous remission"). He concluded that the published psychotherapy research failed to demonstrate that therapy was effective over and above spontaneous remission.

The 1952 article was revised in 1960 and in 1965, and similar conclusions were reached. The main conclusions were:

1. When untreated neurotic control groups are compared with experimental groups of neurotic patients treated by means of psychotherapy, both groups recover to approximately the same extent.

2. When soldiers who have suffered a neurotic breakdown and have not received psychotherapy are compared with soldiers who have received psychotherapy, the chances of the two groups returning to duty are approximately equal.

3. When neurotic soldiers are separated from the service, their chances of recovery are not affected by their receiving or not receiving psychotherapy.

4. Civilian neurotics who are treated by psychotherapy recover or improve to approximately the same extent as similar neurotics receiving no psychotherapy.

5. Children suffering from emotional disorders and treated by psychotherapy recover or improve to approximately the same extent as similar children not receiving psychotherapy.

6. Neurotic patients treated by means of psychotherapeutic procedures based on learning theory improve significantly more quickly than do patients treated by means of psychoanalytic or eclectic psychotherapy, or not treated by psychotherapy at all.

7. Neurotic patients treated by psychoanalytic psychotherapy do not improve more quickly than patients treated by means of eclectic psychotherapy and may improve less quickly when account is taken of the large proportion of patients breaking off treatment.

8. With the single exception of the psychotherapeutic methods based on learning theory, results of published research with military and civilian neurotics, and with both adults and children, suggest that the therapeutic effects of psychotherapy are small or nonexistent and do not in any demonstrable way add to the nonspecific effects of routine medical treatment, or to such events as occur in the patients' everyday experience. (From Eysenck, 1960b, pp. 719–720.)

In the original version, Eysenck's main conclusion was that psychoanalysis and psychoanalytically oriented therapy had not demonstrated their efficacy. Essentially, the effects of psychotherapy, according to Eysenck, were unproved. In the revised article, the conclusion was altered slightly. In light of subsequent research that continued to show a similar pattern of results, he suggested that a stronger negative conclusion might be warranted. The conclusion, not stated directly, was that belief in the effectiveness of psychotherapy was no longer tenable.

The only conclusion warranted from the analysis Eysenck made of the literature was that therapy had not proved its efficacy, assuming for a moment that no controversy surfaced about the interpretation of the individual studies. Yet the reanalysis and critical evaluation were taken by many writers as *proof* that psychotherapy did not work (Luborsky and Spence, 1971). Certainly the latter conclusion was implied strongly by Eysenck and no doubt crystallized opinion and dissatisfaction about the effects of therapy in the field.

On the more constructive side, the revised versions of Eysenck's article brought out important points that had been overshadowed by the overall thesis. Eysenck emphasized the need for carefully controlled therapy research that not only took into account spontaneous remission but also controlled for nonspecific treatment effects. He noted that showing that therapy is superior to no treatment was not sufficient to demonstrate that any particular technique or ingredient of therapy was effective. Nonspecific treatment effects such as attending treatment and meeting with a therapist would still have to be ruled out to argue for specific benefits of treatment.

Eysenck also pointed to the positive effects of therapies based upon "learning theories." By the time the final revision of the article was published (1965), a few outcome studies had become available (e.g., Lang and Lazovik, 1963; Lazarus, 1961; Lovibond, 1963a, 1963b) as well as case reports of the efficacy of select behavior therapy techniques (e.g., Wolpe, 1958). Eysenck concluded that techniques derived from learning theory appeared to be effective and to produce results beyond those that would be incurred by nonspecific treatment.

Eysenck's conclusions about the effects of psychotherapy, or rather the lack of demonstrated effects, exerted profound impact on the field. Numerous articles were written to reply to his claims and to his interpretation of research on the outcome of therapy (see Eysenck, 1966). Eysenck was criticized for not presenting select studies that argued for the efficacy of psychotherapy, for how he decided whether or not patients improved after completing treatment, for adhering to stringent criteria when evaluating psychoanalytically oriented therapy yet abandoning these standards when evaluating therapies based upon learning, and so on (Duhrssen and Jorswieck, 1962; Luborsky, 1954; Rosenzweig, 1954; Strupp, 1963). The historical importance of Eysenck's thesis was that it challenged psychotherapy to demonstrate its efficacy and to acknowledge the limited information available.

The failure of traditional psychotherapies to prove their efficacy was taken up by many others (e.g., Cross, 1964; Oberndorf, 1953; Meehl, 1955). For example, Eugene E. Levitt reviewed (1957, 1963,

1971) the research on psychotherapy with children and reached a conclusion similar to that of Eysenck. After studying 35 years of reports on child psychotherapy that covered thousands of patients, Levitt concluded that about 67% of the patients improved to a noticeable extent at the end of treatment. However, this improvement rate was similar to the "spontaneous remission" rate based upon the outcome of those children who were offered formal treatment at a clinic but who failed to take advantage of the opportunity.

Evaluations of the effects of psychotherapy certainly led to dissatisfaction with conventional methods of treatment. They also clearly pointed to the complexity of therapy and of assessing its effects. Initially, the notion of spontaneous remission brought into sharp focus by Eysenck made evaluation of treatment difficult. The concept of spontaneous remission itself was not clear. The improvement that individuals make without formal treatment is not "spontaneous" in the sense that it occurs randomly or without a clear cause. It is likely that individuals who do not receive formal treatment often seek other means to resolve their personal problems, and thus therapeutic effects are obtained in some other way. For example, research has demonstrated that most people who want help for their personal problems seek professionals not primarily trained in psychiatry or psychology such as physicians and clergymen (Frank, 1961; Gurin, Veroff, and Feld, 1960). Thus, the process leading to change was not illuminated by the notion of spontaneous remission.

More central to the evaluation of treatment, the percentage of individuals who did not receive formal treatment in therapy studies but who did improve was not clear. Although Eysenck (1952b) suggested that about 67% of neurotics who did not receive treatment improved anyway, this figure was questioned. The rate of remission appears to be a complex function of several variables, including diagnosis of the patient, age, and measurement devices used (cf. Bergin, 1971; Kiesler, 1971; Subotnik, 1972). Overall, spontaneous remission and its assessment are complex phenomena in their own right that will obscure simple evaluations of therapy outcome.

A second complexity of therapy evaluation pertains to the different effects that therapy has on different people. The evaluations of therapy outcome by Eysenck, Levitt, and others stressed the mean improvements across patients who received treatment. On the average, patients who received treatment were considered to improve no more than those who did not receive treatment. However, comparing average improvement rates across groups hides the effects of treatment on individuals in the groups. Allen Bergin (1966, 1967) pointed out that therapy and no-treatment control groups have similar overall effects yet nonetheless produce marked differences in individual patients. He noted that patients who participated in treatment increased in their variability of responding on outcome measures, whereas those who had not received treatment did not. The increase in variability suggested that some patients improved with treatment while others became worse. Bergin labeled such adverse consequences a "deterioration effect" and presented data in support of its generality across studies. Demonstration of a deterioration effect indicated that although some people became worse with treatment, others became better. Thus, the question for therapy outcome was not whether or not therapy was effective, but rather for *whom* therapy was effective. In general, ensuing research concerned with therapy shifted somewhat to examine the effects of specific techniques upon particular individuals.

Another factor that increased the difficulty of therapy evaluation was the nonspecific effects of treatment. In the 1950s and 1960s, authors became increasingly concerned about the possibility that general ingredients of treatment, such as attending therapy and talking with a professional therapist might have accounted for change rather than a specific treatment (Bailey, 1956; Eysenck, 1965; Rosenthal and Frank, 1956).[7]

Jerome Frank argued this position in his influential book, *Persuasion and Healing* (1961). He suggested that four features common to all psychotherapies and other methods of healing account for change:

1. The existence of a specific relationship between the patient and the help-giver. The relationship arouses the patient's faith in the confidence of the therapist and his desire to help.
2. Treatment is conducted in a locale designated by society as a place of healing. Hence, the patient's expectancies for help are aroused.
3. A rationale is provided that presents a patient's problem in an optimistic light. The rationale explains the cause of the problem as well as specific goals and processes of the therapy.
4. A task or procedure is presented that requires the therapist's and patient's participation. These tasks serve as a medium through which a therapist can exert his/her influence.

---

[7] Certainly the belief that nonspecific effects of treatment accounted for therapeutic change was not new in the 1950s and 1960s. Early in the history of psychotherapy, many authors had noted that faith, belief in the therapist, and suggestion accounted for change (e.g., Brown, 1929; Charcot, 1893; Dejerine and Gauckler, 1911).

Overall, these treatment ingredients may provide hope for the patient and new opportunities for changing cognitions, attitudes, and behaviors, may enhance a patient's hope of relief, may provide success experiences, and may generally restore the patient's morale (Frank, 1961). Frank's analysis of the processes that account for change suggests that specific forms of therapy achieve their effects through common ingredients, rather than through their theoretical rationale or unique practices (Parloff and Rubinstein, 1962). Thus, Frank questioned the effectiveness of psychotherapy as a specific entity, yet somewhat differently than did Eysenck.

Many other problems make the evaluation of therapy complex. For example, selection of homogeneous patient populations was itself an obstacle to conducting research. Patient selection often depends upon psychiatric diagnosis which, because of its own problems, presents difficulties. Similarly, assessment of therapeutic change presented multiple problems. Many measures of therapeutic change were a topic of study in their own right and subject to diverse problems such as uncertain reliability and validity. Also, deciding the primary mode of assessment and evaluating therapy was problematic. Different types of measures (e.g., self-report, therapist ratings, overt behavior) led to different evaluations of treatment outcome.

In general, the criticism of therapy outcome and recognition of the complexity of treatment elevated the interest in establishing requirements for experimental evaluation. In the 1950s and 1960s several authors recommended how to conduct psychotherapy research (Edwards and Cronbach, 1952; Eysenck, 1960b; Frank, 1959; Hunt, 1952; Kiesler, 1966, Meehl, 1955; Rogers and Dymond, 1954; Sargent, 1960; Scriven, 1959; Thorne, 1952; Watson, 1952a, 1952b; Watson, Mensh, and Gildea, 1951; Zubin, 1953). Major evaluations were made of psychotherapy to clarify its empirical status and to outline the problems and requirements of research.[8]

Evaluation of psychotherapy research in the late 1950s and early 1960s revealed an increasing trend toward asking more specific questions about therapy rather than global questions about overall efficacy. Much of the research turned to process questions, theory testing, and, in general, "basic" therapy research (Parloff and

---

[8] In the late 1950s, a major conference was initiated on research in psychotherapy under the sponsorship of the Division of Clinical Psychology of the American Psychological Association. The purposes of the conference were to provide objective evaluations of psychotherapy, to examine the present status of the research, and to stimulate further research. Conferences were held in 1958, 1961, and 1966, and each resulted in separate proceedings entitled *Research in Psychotherapy* (Rubinstein and Parloff, 1962; Shlien, 1968; Strupp and Luborsky, 1962).

Rubinstein, 1962; Strupp and Luborsky, 1962). Yet, the evaluation of psychotherapy did not merely alter the focus of research within traditional therapy: it led to some dissatisfaction with traditional treatment. This dissatisfaction alone made the possibility of new treatments such as behavior therapy more acceptable. In addition, the complexities of traditional therapy research revealed that evaluating treatment and change in a patient's condition required refined research and methodological advances. Behavior modification emerged out of this context of doubt pertaining to both substantive and methodological issues in psychotherapy.

Institutional Treatment

Early in the development of psychological treatment, institutionalization rather than psychotherapy was the fate accorded those whose behavior was severely abnormal. Throughout the middle ages, religious sanctuaries and prisons provided care for deviant individuals. Hospitals gradually assumed the function of housing patients, although treatment and rehabilitation were rarely goals. For instance, in sixteenth-century England, St. Mary of Bethlehem was converted from a monastery into a mental hospital. Patients lived under harsh conditions, which included confinement, inadequate provision of basic amenities, and public display for ridicule. By the 1700s and 1800s, asylums were being used throughout the world to house the mentally ill. Typically, patients were confined to small quarters, placed on exhibition to entertain the public, and treated as cruelly as prisoners. "Treatments" often consisted of plunging individuals into cold water, shackling, solitary confinement, head shaving, bleeding, and similar abusive procedures. Basic amenities such as food, warmth, and sleeping quarters were poor or minimal.

Phillippe Pinel (1745–1826) effected humanitarian reforms in asylums in France when he departed from the traditional attitude toward mental patients by treating them kindly. He removed the chains of inmates at La Bicêtre Hospital. Cruel and restrictive conditions were replaced with pleasant living quarters, opportunities to exercise, and attention from the staff. The humane treatment was dramatically successful in enhancing the demeanor and tractability of the patients. Pinel and his successor, Jean Esquirol (1772–1840), extended the humanitarian approach to several other French hospitals with similarly successful results.

In England, William Tuke (1732–1822) independently established a hospital based upon procedures similar to those inaugurated by

Pinel. He began a treatment facility in a country house where patients worked and rested. Somewhat later, Benjamin Rush (1745–1813) also established humane treatment of the mentally ill in America, although some residual primitive and punitive practices remained. The pioneering work of Pinel and Tuke helped accelerate the improved care of mental patients and equate treatment of mental illness with that of physical illness.

The movement toward humanitarian treatment was associated with the widespread application of moral treatment (Bockoven, 1963).[9] Moral treatment derived from the work of Pinel and Tuke and was based upon the premise that the mentally ill were normal in many ways and would benefit from desirable living conditions. Stresses of living and psychological problems were viewed as responsible for mental illness, and treatment was directed toward helping individuals with their difficulties. Moral treatment was characterized by extending compassion to the patients. It was designed to appeal to the moral sense of patients by setting examples of appropriate behavior and by providing a relationship between the physician and the patient. The social influences of treatment and the physical setting were accorded an important curative role (Bockoven, 1963). Patients were expected to improve in their behaviors and assume responsibility for their actions. They were housed in small numbers so that the staff and superintendent could maintain a close relationship with the patients, know their individual problems, and interact both therapeutically and socially. The size of the hospital and the relationship fostered by the staff attempted to make treatment home-like rather than institutional. Moral treatment reached its peak in the early nineteenth century. Its effectiveness was appreciable when compared to prior and subsequent institutional treatment. Discharge rates from the hospital were relatively high, often ranging from 70–90% (Bockoven, 1963; Tourney, 1967).

Despite the success of moral treatment, it declined in the latter half of the nineteenth century. The illness view of deviant behavior was gaining adherents. The notion that disordered behavior was an illness fostered the assumption that patients could not meet minimal

---

[9] The term "moral" denoted that problems of psychiatric patients were based upon stresses of a psychological or emotional nature. Also, "moral" conveyed that disturbed individuals would be treated according to their moral rights. Moral treatment was designed to help patients discuss their difficulties and to provide them with comfortable living conditions and purposeful activities to reduce psychological stress (Bockoven, 1957, 1963).

expectations of reasoning, performance of routine behavior, or decision-making normally possible among healthy individuals. Kraepelin's influence helped to synthesize thought along these lines, although he was not alone in believing that disordered behavior reflected illness. His system of diagnosis encouraged the idea that prognoses of psychiatric disorders were fixed and predetermined despite attempts at intervention. That is, the mentally ill needed only to be housed and the illness would run its natural course. Thus, interventions were eventually discouraged, because acceptance of behavioral disorders as illness made social interventions such as moral treatment less plausible than organic ones.

The decline of moral treatment also resulted from the development of large hospitals to handle increased numbers of patients. Dorothea Dix (1802–1887), a proponent of humane conditions for mental patients, helped extend the scale of hospitalization of patients in the United States. Dix sought to eradicate the harsh and deplorable treatment for patients in almshouses, jails, and asylums and successfully lobbied for legislative reform that provided institutional care for large numbers of patients. The success of her efforts increased the size of hospitals so that the relatively intensive care provided in moral treatment was no longer available. The large number of patients in need of hospitalization also stemmed from massive immigration. Increased numbers of foreign-born patients lessened the desire of many administrators and the feasibility of most hospitals to provide intensive treatment (Zilboorg and Henry, 1941).

Institutional care in the late 1800s and early 1900s became characterized by large hospitals, overcrowding, a small ratio of staff to patients, and a continual decline of effectiveness in discharging patients (Bockoven, 1963; Ullmann, 1967). Patients rarely participated actively in treatment and assumed little responsibility for their own behavior. Passivity and custodial care dominated. Instead of treatment or rehabilitation as a primary focus, care had shifted to managing patients to have them adhere conveniently to hospital routines.

Contemporary institutional treatment for psychiatric patients consists largely of custodial care in large hospital settings. In addition to psychotherapy, many somatic treatments are used as part of care, including chemotherapy, electroconvulsive shock, insulin treatment, and psychosurgery. Most prominent is chemotherapy, which has been widely adopted since its development in the 1950s. Patients with diverse symptoms can be maintained with drugs that reduce specific bizarre or disruptive symptoms such as anxiety, aggression, hallucinations, delusions, and depression.

In addition to somatic treatments, psychosocial programs have been created. Milieu therapy is one example of a psychosocial treatment for institutionalized patients (Jones, Baker, Freeman, Merry, Pomryn, Sandler, and Tuxford, 1953; Paul, 1969a). With milieu therapy, all events in the institution are viewed as relevant for patient treatment. The purpose of the institution is to provide a therapeutic community in which the patient has the opportunity to interact with staff in a normal fashion. Patients are given responsibility for their own behavior and take an active part in making decisions about hospital life, their own treatment, and discharge. Staff attempt to break down the usual boundaries between patients and themselves and treat the patients as fellow humans. In many ways, the characteristics of milieu therapy parallel those of moral treatment.

Contemporary treatment has stressed facilities that integrate patients into the community. For example, halfway houses are patient residences located in the community. Patients may have outside jobs and utilize community resources while they live in a sheltered environment. Treatment has been extended to the community in other ways. For example, local mental health centers provide services to individuals in need of treatment and attempt to avoid hospitalizing individuals away from their usual living situation.

Dissatisfaction with Institutional Treatment

The need to confine individuals in institutions has been questioned. The usual rationale for institutionalizing psychiatric patients is that they either are a danger to themselves or to others, or are incapable of functioning in the community. However, it has been shown that these conditions are rarely met by individuals who are considered for hospitalization and are finally confined (Cooper and Early, 1961; Scheff, 1966).

The process of institutionalization begins with screening and labeling the individual as mentally ill. Several investigators have objected to the labeling processes that precede hospitalization and that continue once the individual is hospitalized. The belief that an individual is mentally ill, when held by others or by the individual him/ herself, leads to certain kinds of performances or attributions of performance that support the label (cf. Farina, Gliha, Boudreau, Allen, and

Sherman, 1971; Farina and Ring, 1965). Thus, labeling the deviant individual as mentally ill may help crystallize deviant behavior that would otherwise only be temporary (Scheff, 1966).

The initial process of labeling individuals as mentally ill merely *begins* a series of events that has deleterious effects on the individual patient's behavior. Once hospitalized, the individual suffers numerous other consequences of general "institutionalization." Newly hospitalized patients often become worse in their behavior in a relatively short time along several dimensions, such as increased symptomatology, apathy, and withdrawal from activities (cf. Goffman, 1961; Gruenberg, 1967; Mahrer and Mason, 1965; Paul, 1969a; Sommer and Osmond, 1961; Ullmann, 1967). Indeed, the longer a patient remains in the hospital, the more his behavior deteriorates, and the less likely are his/her chances for release (Honigfeld and Gillis, 1967; Wanklin, Fleming, Buck, and Hobbs, 1956).

Hospital treatment *per se* also has its critics. Generally, the lack of specific therapeutic treatments used with patients in a large psychiatric setting has been looked upon with disfavor. Patients may be given drugs to control bizarre or disorderly behaviors. It is common for patients to receive group psychotherapy for a brief period of time, regardless of their diagnosis.

Release from the hospital and success in staying in the community has been shown to be somewhat independent of the treatment provided in the hospital or the psychological status of the patient. The individual's release from the hospital may depend upon such factors as obtaining a job, having relatives who will take care of the patient, and so on (Paul, 1969a). Thus, social contingencies rather than success in treatment play a major role in discharge and readmission. This reality has led investigators to question whether hospitalization is relevant or necessary for most individuals who behave abnormally. Because successful placement of individuals in the community partially depends on the patients being supported after release, i.e., in the form of employment, close social relationships, and type of living arrangements to which the patients return, developing resources in the community would seem to be more important than institutional care (Fairweather, Sanders, Maynard, and Cressler, 1969; Miller, 1965, 1967). Along related lines, hospital treatment exacerbates rather than ameliorates bizarre behavior (Freeman and Simmons, 1963; Miller, 1965, 1967). Even if bizarre behavior were reduced in the hospital, it might have little bearing once the patient returns to the community.

The overall outcome of patient hospitalization is disappointing. Conventional care successfully discharges relatively high proportions of patients within the first few years of hospitalization, yet individuals who remain longer have a very low probability of being discharged (Paul, 1969a; Ullmann, 1967). Of the individuals who are discharged, a high percentage are readmitted (e.g., Dinitz, Lefton, Angrist, and Pasamanick, 1961). Indeed, for many patients, the cycle of hospital discharge and rehospitalization is a frequently completed one.

The discharge and readmission data suggest 1) that patients do not change while in the hospital, 2) that they do change but the changes are short-lived, or 3) that the changes made in the hospital are not relevant to community adjustment. Several authors believe that hospital treatment is no more effective for treating many disorders than is no treatment (e.g., Hastings, 1958; Perrow, 1965) or noninstitutional care (Langsley, Machotka, and Flomenhaft, 1971). Spending time in a hospital may even interfere with subsequent community adjustment (Mendel, 1966, 1968). Among the many criticisms of hospital care has been the charge that hospital life bears little resemblance to the social environment of the community to which the patient must return.

Custodial treatment aside, a number of specific procedures utilized in psychiatric hospitals have been criticized. Many treatments in the hospital include biological or somatotherapies such as psychosurgery, insulin, pentylenetetrazol (Metrazol), and electroconvulsive shock. A critical evaluation across several studies suggested that somatotherapies are superior to ordinary custodial treatment immediately after treatment with schizophrenic patients (Staudt and Zubin, 1957). Yet typically after two or three years of follow-up, these treatments are no more effective than general hospital care in improving patient behavior.[10] Thus, at least some of the specific treatment practices in institutional care appear to produce only short-lived alterations of the patient's psychiatric status.

Other treatments within the hospital also have been criticized. For example, treatments directed at developing specific skills in patients (e.g., vocational abilities) have failed to produce lasting effects. Efforts to provide vocational rehabilitation combined with supportive psychotherapy for hospitalized patients does not seem to

---

[10] It is of interest to note that, at follow-up on a number of studies, patients who received a specific form of somatotherapy during their hospitalization showed a lower incidence of death up to five years after treatment than did patients who received nonspecific hospital treatment (Staudt and Zubin, 1957).

improve the posthospital adjustment of patients in the community or their subsequent readmission rates (Criswell, 1967; Neff and Koltuv, 1967).

However, changes have been made in hospital treatment to move away from custodial care. Although they are too extensive to detail here, they include many efforts at restructuring activities and providing responsibilities for inpatients. Some treatments are enmeshed directly into the community as, for example, in special transitional living situations, community mental health treatments, and self-help groups (see Greenblatt and Levinson, 1965).

SUMMARY AND CONCLUSIONS

The conceptualization and the treatment of abnormal behavior, as derived from an intrapsychic-disease model, have been traced across interrelated areas of research and practice in psychiatry and clinical psychology. Specific sources of dissatisfaction with the model and its most prominent variation, orthodox psychoanalysis, also have been highlighted. Criticisms were examined more generally by looking at the broader context in which a paradigm shift from an intrapsychic-disease to a behavioral model of deviant behavior was made.

Much of the basis of that shift is summarized in the notion of *mental illness*. Within the traditional model, deviant behavior is viewed as a disease. It has been demonstrated that the notion of psychological disease and all that it entails is not particularly productive in generating effective treatment for most psychiatric disorders. Indeed, many treatments within the intrapsychic-disease model have been accused of being deleterious.

The dissatisfactions with a disease-oriented view of deviant behavior were multiple. Even at the most basic level, the model presents problems. For example, no objective criteria can be used to define "mental illness." The field has been continually plagued by difficulties in obtaining objective or operational definitions of mental illness and health (Scott, 1958; Ullmann, 1967; Zubin, 1953).

Many aspects of disordered behavior point to the importance of the social environment rather than an intrapsychic-disease process that unfolded in the individual. Identification and diagnosis of mental illness seem to depend upon social and cultural factors (Jackson, 1964). Particular behaviors that appear to be "symptoms" do not solely define disease unless individuals evincing these behaviors disrupt others in the social environment. Many believe that behavior identified as mental illness is not disturbed so much as disturbing (e.g., Ferster, 1965).

The importance of the individual in a social context is further evidenced in the extent to which patients who have been treated (e.g., through institutional care) successfully function in the community. Social factors, such as having a job, living with other individuals, undertaking responsibilities for others, and similar criteria, determine the success of staying in the community to a greater extent than does psychiatric status (degree of "pathology") at discharge. Overall, the evidence increasingly has pointed to the importance of social variables in identifying and treating individuals with deviant behavior and raises questions about conceptualizing behavior as diseased or healthy. The concept of behavior as diseased or healthy would have been challenged less if a medical approach to abnormal behavior had generated potent treatment techniques. The lack of clearly effective treatments further supports arguments that deviant behavior may be more profitably conceived from some other perspective.

Because the traditional view of abnormal behavior was derived explicitly from medicine, it made virtually no contact with psychology in conceptualizing behavior. For example, Freud's own training was in physiology and neurology, and many concepts from these fields characterized the psychological mechanisms and processes of his theory of personality and behavior. When Freud was formulating his interpretations in the late 1800s and early 1900s, relatively little was known in psychology that could provide sophisticated theoretical accounts of behavior and its acquisition, alteration, and elimination. The psychology of learning, which generated theories of behavior, eventually provided an alternative to the psychoanalytic model. However, research and theory in learning evolved in the early 1900s, which was after Freud had set forth most of his ideas. By the time that the psychology of learning did evolve to the point that it might provide a tentative theory of behavior, Freudian theory had achieved prominence and widespread acceptance. Abnormal behavior and its treatment had been established in the domain of psychiatry long before the appearance of psychoanalysis. However, when psychic forces, as espoused by Freud, were advanced as an account of abnormal behavior, psychology had no real alternative that could be offered to challenge psychoanalysis.

As the science of behavior grew, experimental findings from psychology remained without impact upon psychoanalytic theory. Research findings about behavior and its development were not incorporated into psychoanalysis. Eventually, enough theory and research in psychology had accumulated to construct another account of deviant behavior and its alteration. In an important sense, the behavioral model of deviance that developed out of psychological research helped to provide an identity to psychology independent of medicine. The study and alteration of behavior rather than the treatment of disease allowed psychology to address problems from a unique perspective (London, 1972). A psychological theory of behavior provided a substantive alternative to a disease model and psychoanalysis on subjects such as the development of deviant behavior, theory of behavior change, and recommendations for therapeutic practice.

The science of behavior offered a new methodological advance, too. Psychoanalytic theory and therapy evolved from clinical work and observations of therapy cases. Freud "tested" his views in therapy and revised them according to progress in treatment or personality dynamics revealed in his patients. Despite Freud's reputation for careful observation, the type of observations and methods of study were outside of the realm of science. His procedures were not based upon objective observations and were not replicated. Most important, the theory and practice developed free from attempts at experimental evaluation. Support for theoretical claims were based upon interpretation, intuition, and judgment of the therapist: *ergo*, neither the method of support nor its results were a part of a replicable process. Many statements supportive of the theory relied upon intuitive rather than objective criteria (Reik, 1937). Overall, verification in psychoanalysis departed from the scientific method.

The paradigm shift from an intrapsychic-disease model to a behavioral model in part represents a recognition of the inadequacies of psychoanalysis as a scientific theory. Treatment techniques developed from extrapolations of laboratory research and have been described in such a way as to permit empirical verification. Thus, the paradigm shift provided by behavior modification entailed both substantive and methodological diversion from the traditional approach.

The traditional intrapsychic-disease model and the dissatisfaction it generated provide the context from which behavior modification developed. As Kuhn (1962) has noted, no model or theory in science is ever rejected on the basis of criticism of its inadequacies alone. What is required is a clearly superior theory or at least an alternative that permits research to progress in areas that previously were not well handled. Behavior modification provided such an alternative in many areas of clinical research. The major dissatisfaction with the traditional disease model, or at least that most vociferously expressed, was directed at changing behavior, i.e., therapy. It was in this area in particular that behavior modification contributed to major advances in research.

3
Foundations of Behavior Modification

The scientific foundations of behavior modification are relatively new. The nineteenth century saw the beginnings of conceptual and methodological advances in the sciences, characterized by objective research methods and experimentation. Progress in the biological sciences dramatically shaped psychology. This influence stemmed in part from the common interests of biological sciences and psychology, which included investigation of the functioning of organisms in relation to the environment. The mutual interest was associated with Darwin's theory of evolution, which stressed, among other things, the adaptability of organisms to their environment. Adaptability included physiological adaptation as well as behavioral adjustments to external stimuli, and it encompassed the study of numerous species.

Although the foci and levels of analysis in biological sciences and psychology were different, specific areas did overlap. For example, physiologists and zoologists entered into discussions and research of major interest to psychologists, such as sensation, perception, and cognition, as well as the development of overt patterns of behavior in lower organisms and humans. The mechanistic and materialistic approach of nineteenth-century biological sciences, coupled with the success of objective methods in developing a knowledge base, served as an impetus for objectivism in psychology.

Objectivism in psychology crystallized in the movement referred to as "behaviorism," which was primarily a methodological revolt to establish the scientific basis of psychology. Behavior modification relies upon empirical methods and owes allegiance to behaviorism and its methodological stance.

[Behavior modification is concerned with how organisms adapt in relation to the environment. Its focus is upon how behaviors develop, are maintained, and can be altered, or, more simply, how behaviors are learned. The psychology of learning as an area of interest can be traced to the philosophy of associationism, which was first recorded in Aristotle's explanation of how ideas become connected. Yet the scientific study of learning, the basis of most work in behavior modification, is a relatively recent development and one strongly associated with research conducted in the methodological tradition of behaviorism.

Chapter 3 reviews the experimental foundations of behavior modification, emphasizing the evolution of methodological advances in psychology and the psychology of learning. The discussion ranges from research on conditioning in Russia and research on comparative psychology in England, Europe, and America to the rise of behaviorism and the psychology of learning in America.

CONDITIONING AND REFLEXOLOGY IN RUSSIA

An important antecedent to behaviorism and behavior modification is the work of three prominent Russian physiologists: Ivan M. Sechenov, Ivan P. Pavlov, and Vladimir M. Bechterev. These investigators were deeply committed to objective methods of research and advanced the course of experimentation in neurophysiology. Through empirical investigation of the nervous system, they eventually pursued topics that overlapped with the subject matter of psychology. At the time, psychology concentrated upon subjective explanations of behavior rather than upon objective scientific methods. The major methodological contribution of Russian physiologists was their strict mechanistic interpretations of subjective processes as well as overt behavior. They insisted on the application of objective methods of physiology to problems of psychology.

Ivan M. Sechenov (1829–1905)

Sechenov received medical training in Russia and studied in Germany, Austria, and France with many eminent anatomists and physiologists, including Johannes Müller (1801–1858), Karl Ludwig (1816–1895), Claude Bernard (1813–1878), and Emil DuBois-Reymond (1818–1896). Objective experimentation and the materialistic and mechanistic scientific climate of Europe had not yet reached Russia. Russian physiology had been primarily theoretical until Sechenov returned to Russia to take a faculty position at the Medico-Surgical Academy of St. Petersburg (later renamed the Military Medical Academy) in 1860. Sechenov introduced experimental methods into Russian physiology, an achievement that helped to establish him as the "father of Russian physiology."

Sechenov had studied psychology as a student and retained his interest in psychological research. However, he regarded psychology as an inexact science because it relied upon subjective accounts of psychological events rather than upon objective experimentation. On the basis of his work in neurophysiology, he advocated applying the methods of physiology to the study of psychological problems.

Sechenov's interest in combining neurophysiology and psychology derived from his work on reflexes. He had demonstrated the inhibitory influence of the brain on spinal reflexes, which led him to speculate on the reflexive nature of psychological phenomena and behavior of humans. Such an extrapolation was tenuous, which he realized. However, applying findings from the study of nervous systems of lower animals to humans was consistent with Darwin's monumentally influential theory of evolution introduced in *On The Origin of Species by Means of Natural Selection* (1859). Sechenov advanced his formulations in a treatise entitled, "An Attempt Physiologically to Explain the Origin of Psychical Phenomena," which was published serially in 1863 under the revised title "Reflexes of the Brain."[1,2] In 1866, the revised text was published under the latter title in book form.

In this book, Sechenov declared that all behavior, whether referred to as involuntary or voluntary, was entirely reflexive. Although many reflexes emanated from the brain rather than the spinal cord and thus were relatively complex, they were reflexes nonetheless. Given particular environmental stimulation, the resulting behavior would occur inevitably. In explaining reflexes, Sechenov noted that behavior in a given instance might not be initiated by external stimuli. Behaviors could be initiated by thoughts, images, or memory traces of particular events that initiated previous behavior.

---

[1] "Psychical" as used in this title referred to phenomena now embraced by the word "psychological" (Koshtoyants, 1965).

[2] The original manuscript was censored. Sechenov changed the title to "An Attempt to Establish the Physiological Basis of Psychical Processes," which was no less offensive. With another change in title to "Reflexes of the Brain," and the deletion of a few paragraphs, the manuscript was deemed suitable for publishing (Koshtoyants, 1965).

However, all psychical or internal events themselves were the result of external stimuli and reflexive in nature. Thus, he stated, ". . . the initial cause of human action lies outside of man" (Sechenov, 1965, p. 106).

Sechenov asserted that the complex reflexes comprising human behavior are acquired through learning. For Sechenov, learning consisted of the association of stimuli (e.g., visual, aural, tactile) with muscular movements. Repetition of muscle movements in the presence of particular external or internal stimuli made the acts habitual and involuntary.

Sechenov noted that the reflexive nature of human behavior often may be disguised. Not all behavior initially involves the performance of discrete acts—its inhibition may be a reflex response to some external stimulation. One may learn to block responses to a particular sort of environmental stimulation as in the case of fear. Similarly, according to Sechenov, thought is a reflex response in which overt action is inhibited. Sechenov's speculations about inhibitions of reflexes were not without some basis. His own research demonstrated the inhibition of spinal reflexes in the frog through chemical stimulation of the brain. However, the nature of the processes involved in inhibition in the animal or human brain were not known.

The reflexive nature of behavior may also be disguised by self-consciousness, awareness, and other psychical processes. Sechenov effectively questioned the commonly accepted notion that volition, self-consciousness, and choice were the only causal agents of behavior.

> The man of high moral principles . . . acts as he does solely because he is guided by the high principles acquired by him in the course of his life. Prompted by these principles he cannot act otherwise: his activity is the inevitable result of these principles. . . . *given the same internal and external conditions the activity of man will be similar.* Choice of one of the many possible ends of the same psychical reflex is absolutely impossible; its apparent possibility is merely a delusion of self-consciousness (Sechenov, 1965, p. 105).

Sechenov's analysis of psychical phenomena and behavior was radical. At once he eliminated the distinction between voluntary and involuntary behavior and between mental and physical processes. As a whole, his book showed that psychical phenomena could be explained by concrete entities such as reflexes and were subject to scientific scrutiny. In its advocacy of the deterministic nature and scientific scrutiny of behavior, Sechenov's treatise was highly controversial, and it was initially banned because its materialistic and mechanistic views ran counter to prevailing idealistic thought in Russia. Indeed, court action was initiated against Sechenov for undermining public morals (Boring, 1950). Eventually the book became widely read and was a source of intellectual debate.

In 1870, Sechenov published an expansion of *Reflexes of the Brain* entitled, "Who Must Investigate the Problem of Psychology and How?" This paper was more explicit in outlining the methodological changes that he felt were essential for studying psychical phenomena. The investigation of psychical processes had been restricted largely to subjective accounts, which Sechenov believed to be unscientific. His answers to the two questions posed by the title of his paper were the physiologist and the study of reflexes, respectively. Sechenov felt that the only appropriate domain of psychology was the study of reflexes, and the only suitable methods were those employed by the physiologist.

Sechenov's recognition of the importance of reflexes in behavior made him a pioneer in conditioning and reflexology. His main contribution to conditioning and reflexology has been heuristic, because his propositions on the role of reflexes in accounting for behavior were hypothetical. The neurological mechanisms upon which his analysis depended, as he readily admitted, remained to be demonstrated.

Sechenov's contribution to psychology was twofold. First, he attempted to free psychology from unsubstantiated and metaphysical concepts and to place it clearly in the realm of science. He advocated the methods of physiology for investigating psychical phenomena because they allowed an empirically based and objective analysis. Second, he emphasized the role of reflexes and learning in explaining behavior. Thus, the significance of the environment in explaining psychological processes and overt behavior was endorsed. Indeed, Sechenov believed that all psychical life was stimulated and maintained by environmental factors. From the standpoint of subsequent work in behavior modification, Sechenov's search for external causes of behavior was extremely innovative.

Ivan P. Pavlov (1849–1936)

Pavlov was influenced greatly by *Reflexes of the Brain,* because it suggested a scientific resolution of the relationship between physical and psychical acts (Pavlov, 1927). Like Sechenov, Pavlov was deeply committed to the scientific approach and the study of the central nervous system. He applied methods derived from physiology to examine Sechenov's hypotheses about neurological functioning.

Pavlov was on the faculty of the Military Medical Academy of St. Petersberg. He studied digestion, specifically, reflexes of the alimentary canal. Conducted almost exclusively with dogs as experimental subjects, his work revealed that glandular secretions were evoked by substances placed directly into the digestive system. Pavlov's careful observations of salivary and gastric secretions were facilitated by surgical techniques that made it possible for him to obtain secretions directly from the glands. The techniques required the establishment of permanent fistulas in the glands or major organs of digestion (e.g., salivary glands, stomach, intestines, pancreas). The secretions passed through the fistula outside the body, and then they were collected. They could be measured in drops, thereby permitting careful quantification of digestive functions. Implantation of the fistula required delicate surgery that would not interfere with the animal's subsequent recovery and functioning.[3]

Pavlov's research led naturally to the study of conditioned reflexes. As part of his studies on digestion, he demonstrated that greater amounts of gastric secretions followed if the animal saw the food placed into its stomach than when the food was concealed. Pavlov realized that the perception of food contributed to gastric secretions (Pavlov, 1902). Moreover, he noted that gastric secretions regularly occurred in the absence of any physical stimulation in the digestive system. Secretions occurred in response to stimuli such as the sight of the experimenter or of a particular substance that had not yet been ingested. These latter secretions could not be inherited reflexes because the stimuli to which the animal responded were associated with unique features and the routine of the laboratory. Pavlov referred to the reactions as "psychical secretions" because they were not evoked through direct physical stimulation. He attributed the secretions to expectancies of the dog based upon its experiences of the laboratory. Initially, Pavlov did not investigate the "psychical secre-

---

[3] Although Pavlov did improve gastrointestinal surgical techniques considerably in his study of digestion, he did not devise the technique of implanting fistulas. Fistulas already had been used in Russia, France, and Germany. Yet in techniques heretofore employed to assess secretions of the stomach, gastric fluid could not be separated from food, an obstacle to analyzing pure secretions. Pavlov devised a technique of isolating a portion of the stomach so that gastric secretions could pass uncontaminated through a fistula (Cuny, 1965). The surgery required was extremely difficult and reached a successful conclusion only after several animals had been sacrificed.

tions"—he tried to minimize them so they would not interfere with observing digestive processes in response to physical stimulation.

In Pavlov's laboratory during 1901–1902, Ivan F. Tolochinov (1859–1920) completed the first systematic investigation of "psychical secretions" to determine if they could be studied from a purely physiological point of view. Before these efforts, Pavlov and his colleagues sought to explain "psychical secretions" in subjective psychological terms from the standpoint of the animal. However, Pavlov's insistence upon an objective explanation increased as the futility of the subjective approach became apparent and the lawfulness of the "psychical secretions" was demonstrated. The objective stance was reflected in the change in terminology from "psychical secretions" to "conditioned reflexes" (Pavlov, 1902).

> At first, in our psychical experiments with the salivary glands (for the time being we shall use the term "psychical"), we conscientiously endeavoured to explain our results by imagining the subjective state of the animal. But nothing came of this except sterile controversy and individual views that could not be reconciled. And so we could do nothing but conduct the research on a purely objective basis; our first and especially important task was completely to abandon the very natural tendency to transfer our own subjective state to the mechanism of the reaction of the animal undergoing the experiment and to concentrate instead on studying the correlation between the external phenomena and the reaction of the organism, i.e., the activity of the salivary glands (Pavlov, 1955, p. 155).

From 1902 until his death in 1936, Pavlov conducted programmatic research on the characteristics of conditioned reflexes. He already had turned to investigation of conditioned reflexes by the time he received the Nobel Prize in 1904 for his work in digestion. Upon receipt of the prize, he did not greatly elaborate the specific research for which it was rewarded. In his address, entitled "The Future Sure Steps Along the Path of a New Investigation," he gave only a résumé of the work on digestion. Greater attention was given to the conditioned reflex and its utility in studying functions of the cerebral cortex. Here Pavlov was covering largely unexplored ground, because most of his work on conditioned reflexes was still in the future.

Pavlov's research on conditioning focused upon the salivary reflex of dogs. This reflex was selected because the salivary gland was a relatively simple organ that did not involve muscle function (which might augment the complexity of the reaction). The conditioned reflex was established by repeatedly pairing a stimulus that elicited a reflex reaction (an *unconditioned stimulus*) with a neutral stimulus that did not (a *conditioned stimulus*). Pairing the conditioned stimulus with the unconditioned stimulus was called *reinforcement*. Repeated reinforcement was required to establish a conditioned reflex.[4]

As a typical example of conditioning from Pavlov's laboratory, food (the unconditioned stimulus) would be paired with a tone (the neutral or conditioned stimulus). Initially, the salivary reflex (the *unconditioned response*) would be elicited only in the presence of food. Yet by repeatedly pairing food with the tone, the tone alone would elicit salivation (a *conditioned response*). Pavlov demonstrated that diverse stimuli (olfactory, auditory, visual, and tactual) acquired the power to elicit the salivary reflex. The specific apparatus that Pavlov employed to investigate conditioned reflexes in dogs is illustrated in Figure 3.1.

The importance of Pavlov's work on "psychical secretions" did not lie in discovering their presence. Learned reflex reactions were recognized well in advance of his investigations (Bechterev, 1933; Franks, 1969b; Hilgard and Bower, 1966). For example, in 1763, the physiologist Robert Whytt (1714–1766) noted that the sight or the idea of food caused secretion of saliva. In Russia, conditioning of the salivary reflex had been demonstrated as early as 1833 (cf. Bechterev, 1933). In the mid-nineteenth century, Claude Bernard described salivary conditioning of the horse (Rosenzweig, 1959). During the same period in Germany, two investigators reported that simply showing food to a dog was sufficient to evoke gastric secretions and stated further that in humans the sight or mere thought of food could provoke salivary secretions (Bidder and Schmidt, 1852).

Pavlov's unique contribution was in objectively investigating conditioned reflexes from the standpoint of a physiologist, as originally recommended by Sechenov. He investigated several processes associated with the development and elimination of the conditioned

---

[4] It is generally agreed that "conditional" rather than "conditioned" reflex would be closer to the meaning of the Russian term employed by Pavlov. The reflexes performed in response to previously neutral stimuli were conditional in that their development and maintenance depended upon special circumstances (Pavlov, 1928, Lecture II). Use of the word "conditioned" has been attributed to translating the German *bedingte Reflex*, where *bedingte* means "conditional." However, the word form is more readily translated into English as "conditioned" (Hilgard and Bower, 1966; Konorski, 1948). Although some translations have adhered to the original intent by using the word "conditional," "conditioned" is widely accepted. (A journal published in English devoted to Pavlovian research has retained the original terminology and is called *Conditional Reflex*.) For an additional discussion of the reasons "conditioned" rather than "conditional" reflex has enjoyed wide usage, see Franks (1969b, 1970) and Gantt (1966).

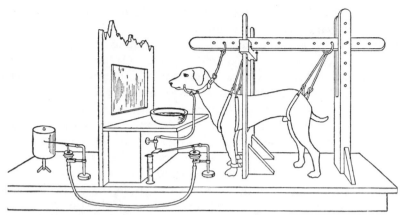

Figure 3.1. The apparatus used by Pavlov to study conditioned reflexes. (From Yerkes and Morgulis, 1909.)

reflex. Some of the more well known processes include extinction, generalization, and differentiation. Extinction is the repeated presentation of the conditioned stimulus by itself once it acquires the capacity to elicit a conditioned reflex. After repeated presentations in the absence of reinforcement, the conditioned stimulus gradually loses its capacity to elicit a response. Generalization and differentiation are complementary processes. A conditioned reflex evoked by the stimulus to which it was conditioned also can be elicited by similar stimuli even if it has not been associated with these latter stimuli (generalization). Conversely, through training, the conditioned reflex can be evoked in the presence of a particular stimulus but not in the presence of similar stimuli (differentiation). Pavlov thoroughly investigated other features of conditioning, including the temporal relationships of reinforcement required to establish a conditioned reflex and techniques to inhibit a conditioned reflex once the response was established (Hilgard and Bower, 1966; Kimble, 1961). He conducted meticulous programmatic analyses of the conditioned reflex and established clear, lawful relationships.

Pavlov viewed conditioning as a means of elaborating nervous activity of the brain. He speculated about cortical processes that would account for the lawful relationships he established for the acquisition and extinction of conditioned reflexes. His theorizing about cortical processes was inferential and included assumptions about the physiology of the cortex that were based on behavioral observations. (Pavlov's major assumptions about cerebral functioning are discussed later.)

Pavlov was also interested in how higher nervous processes pertained to language and human learning. He wished to account for unique features of human learning and formulated a "second signal system" to account for the effect of language on behavior. He believed that animals and humans have a repertoire of inborn adaptive reactions (reflexes) to the environment. These innate reactions eventually are elicited by the presence of various conditioned stimuli. Pavlov referred to the stimuli in the environment to which reflex responses became associated as the "first signal system," because the stimuli to which reflexes were directly conditioned served as "signals for reality." It is this first signal system to which Pavlov devoted his research. He hypothesized that in humans, learning progresses beyond the conditioning of each reflex response to a particular stimulus in the environment. Speech, Pavlov proposed, is associated with stimuli of the first signal system and can evoke responses in its own right. Thus, to Pavlov, language served as a "second signal system" that accounted for the acquisition of complex behavior (Pavlov, 1955). Pavlov's interest in language (the second signal system) and its connections to behavior are noteworthy because of contemporary techniques in behavior modification that stress similar relationships.

Vladimir M. Bechterev (1857–1927)

Bechterev obtained his medical degree two years after Pavlov and also was on the faculty of the Military Medical Academy of St. Petersberg for part of his career. Several similarities may be observed between the training and research of Pavlov and Bechterev. Both were influenced by Sechenov, trained under German physiologists, and created their own research programs through application of methods from physiology to study complex functioning of the brain. Like Sechenov and Pavlov, Bechterev renounced the subjective and mentalistic notions that had constituted topics of psychology. In their place, he advocated the scientific study of organisms and how the environment affected them.

Bechterev was a physiologist, neurologist, and psychiatrist, and held a faculty position in mental and nervous disease at the Medical Academy. His own professional career was characterized by investigations of the anatomy and physiology of the brain and spinal cord, the treatment and observation of nervous and mental disease, and numerous publications in experimental, developmental, and social psychology. For the purposes of this volume, it is important to note his work on conditioning. Although Bechterev employed an experimental paradigm somewhat different from that of Pavlov, the similarity in their work is marked.

In the 1880s Bechterev began work with reflexes. He mainly used dogs as subjects to discover cortical localization of reflex behavior. Initially he investigated respiratory reflexes in response to shock. However, most of his work examined reflexive behavior of the striated muscles (i.e., motor responses) rather than of the glands or smooth muscles of the digestive system focused upon by Pavlov. During 1906–1907, Bechterev encountered the responses that Pavlov had first called "psychical secretions" and, later, "conditioned reflexes" (1902), and he, too, began to examine their characteristics (Flugel and West, 1964). Bechterev labeled the learned responses "associative reflexes," and observed them by applying shock to the animal's paw to evoke muscle flexion.

To demonstrate the associative reflex, shock was paired with some neutral stimulus (e.g., sound) in a manner employed by Pavlov (Babkin, 1949). Bechterev's study of associative reflexes also was extended to humans: shock was applied to the palm of the hand, fingertips, or foot as the reflex response and various visual, auditory, and tactile stimuli were supplied as neutral stimuli. Bechterev noted several advantages of his method over Pavlov's in studying learned reflexes. Bechterev's method did not require surgery to implant fistulas or the use of a harness to restrict the animal, and it avoided the problem of deprivation and satiation as a possible influence in salivary conditioning (Bechterev, 1933). Unquestionably, his method was more practical for studying conditioning in diverse species, a feature that contributed to its early acceptance in America.

Bechterev felt that complex habits involved a series of motor reflexes: indeed, thought itself might be related to specific motor impulses depending upon the inner activities of the speech musculature. He was convinced that problems of psychology could be analyzed by an examination of reflexes, and proposed this in his monograph, *Objective Psychology* (1913), published serially from 1907 to 1912. Later editions in book form substituted the words *psycho-reflexology* and finally simply *reflexology,* a term for which he is credited. Bechterev viewed reflexology as a separate discipline distinct from the physiological study of reflexes. In his own words,

> the new science, which we call reflexology, has for its aim the study of personality by means of objective observation and experiment, and the registration of all its external manifestations and their external causes, present or past, which arise from the social environment and even from

the framework of inherited character. In other words, the aim of reflexology is the strictly objective study, in their entirety, of the correlations of the human being with the environment through the mediation of man's facial expressions, his gestures, the content and form of his speech, his behaviour, and, in general, everything by which he manifests himself in the environment (Bechterev, 1933, p. 81).

He believed that reflexology would replace psychology, which traditionally dealt with subjective topics inaccessible to experiment and scientific inquiry. Psychology had consisted primarily of the study of consciousness. Internal processes were studied by having individuals report on their subjective experiences. Reflexology did not focus upon subjective experience, but "... explication and investigation of response patterns in general, and, in particular, of association reflexes. . . ." (Bechterev, 1933, p. 171). Bechterev extended the revolt against subjective concepts in psychology more than Pavlov by explicitly stating that external behavior was the only suitable area for scientific inquiry. Extending Sechenov's theory, Bechterev explained how reflexes and the combination of reflexes were responsible for behavior, a point later seized upon by American behaviorists. The influence of reflexology in Russia was at least as great—numerous professional organizations passed resolutions that medical and pedagogical institutions should provide a course on reflexology as part of their training (Bechterev, 1933).

Along with similar research interests and techniques, a longstanding rivalry developed between Pavlov and Bechterev pertaining to specific points about conditioning. The rivalry began when Pavlov and his colleagues were unable to replicate a study by a student in Bechterev's laboratory who had established the role of a particular cortical center in the salivary reflex (Babkin, 1949). The ultimate resolution of the issue favored Pavlov's findings. The friction grew to encompass general criticism of the applicability of each other's methods. In the long run, however, their differences were less outstanding than their similarity, that is, their total rejection of subjectivism in examining psychological phenomena.

Bechterev's interest in associative reflexes and their applicability to psychological problems was wider than that of Pavlov. Pavlov's interest in psychiatric disorders developed late in his career and grew out of his work on experimental neurosis. In contrast, Bechterev's involvement in psychiatric disorders and treatment began during his training and continued throughout his career. In 1907, he founded the Psychoneurological Institute, with departments for mental cases, alcoholics, epileptics, and neurosurgery patients. The institute served both training and research functions. Concurrent with the establishment of this institute, he founded several others for abnormal psychological behavior, developmental psychology, childhood deficiencies, antisocial disorders, speaking and hearing disorders of children, and retarded children. Thus, his interest in applied research was coextensive with his work in anatomy and physiology of the central nervous system and in reflexology (Gerver, 1933).

Summary

The evolution of conditioning in Russia was a relatively clear progression. Sechenov proposed hypotheses about the nervous system and learning and vigorously advocated the use of objective methods of physiology to study the issues of psychology. Pavlov and Bechterev extended Sechenov's work in somewhat different ways despite the marked similarities of much of their work. Pavlov examined conditioning in detail and established several lawful relationships. Throughout his research, he emphasized the importance of conditioning as a way of investigating processes of the nervous system. Bechterev's interest in conditioning was more than merely methodological. He extended conditioning to diverse problems of psychology to the point of attempting to replace psychology with a scientific discipline called "reflexology." Bechterev also applied the tenets of reflexology to explain psychiatric disorders and treatment.

COMPARATIVE PSYCHOLOGY

The rise of objectivism in physiology and reflexology in Russia was not without parallel elsewhere. Increasingly, research in England, Europe, and America extended scientific and objective methods, particularly in the area of comparative or animal psychology. Research on animal behavior was stimulated by Darwin, who theorized that continuity existed between human and animal species in both mental and physical functioning. This proposition was particularly explicit in *The Descent of Man* (1871) and *The Expression of the Emotions in Man and Animals* (1872). One outcome of Darwin's books was to establish firmly the importance of animal research. By assuming the continuity of species, animal research would come to have great meaning in understanding human behavior.

Initially, much of the animal work focused upon discovering the "animal mind," that is, an evolutionary antecedent to the human mind. In England, this approach was taken by George J. Romanes (1848–1894), a contemporary of Darwin who made observational studies of various species. Romanes observed the behavior of birds, fish, domestic animals, and monkeys to examine the evolution of mental capacities. He reported his findings in *Animal Intelligence* (1883), considered to be the first text devoted to comparative psychology. The book was based on anecdotal rather than experimental methods and, therefore, lacked the rigor that would characterize subsequent research in comparative psychology. The subjective method was accompanied by anthropomorphic accounts of animal behavior. Thus, complex traits and mental processes characteristic of human behavior were ascribed to animals.

C. Lloyd Morgan (1852–1936) opposed anthropomorphic descriptions of animal behavior. Indeed, he is famous for appealing to the law of parsimony (in comparative psychology, referred to as Lloyd Morgan's canon), which states that behavior must not be interpreted in terms of higher mental processes if it can be interpreted in terms of lower evolutionary processes. Thus, processes assumed to underlie human behavior should not be used to account for animal behavior if more parsimonious interpretations are available. In addition, Morgan advanced research in comparative psychology by improving upon anecdotal methods. He conducted a number of experiments by introducing various events in the animal's natural environment and observing the resulting behavior. Although the experiments did not achieve the rigor of laboratory investigations, they were marked advances in the scientific study of animal behavior.

In Germany, investigators increasingly focused upon animal behavior and mechanistic interpretations of it. Jacques Loeb (1859–1924), a German zoologist and physiologist, came to America in 1891 to continue his work on animal behavior. He developed the concept of tropism or forced movement to explain animal behavior. In the tropistic view, an animal's response is a direct function of environmental stimulation. Behaviors of lower organisms are thought of as reactions to stimuli and do not depend upon consciousness. To account for the adaptation of animal behavior, Loeb (1899) introduced the concept of "associative memory," which meant that, through learning, a previously performed response became attached to new stimuli. Associative memory resembled the idea of conditioning explored by Pavlov and Bechterev. A mechanistic and objective approach to animal behavior developed in Germany and was maintained after Loeb had come to America. For example, Beer, Bethe, and Uexküll (1899) wrote about the objective study of psychological problems and disparaged anthropomorphic accounts of the behavior of lower organisms.

Work in experimental animal psychology was expanding in America at the end of the nineteenth century independent of Loeb's contributions. Edward L. Thorndike (1874–1949), who received his doctorate in 1898, had begun laboratory studies on learning at Columbia. Thorndike conducted careful laboratory experiments with diverse species, including chicks, cats, dogs, fish, and monkeys. Similarly, Robert Yerkes (1876–1956), began a research program in 1900 in comparative psychology at Harvard that investigated even more animals than Thorndike had. Yerkes was an important figure not only for his careful investigations of animal behavior but because he also introduced Pavlov's method of studying the conditioned salivary reflex to American psychologists. In 1909 he and a Russian student who translated Pavlov's work published an article entitled, "The Method of Pawlow [sic] in Animal Psychology."

The experimental method of investigation in animal work was well established by 1900. In 1898, apparatus such as the "maze" by W. S. Small (1859–1920) and the "puzzle box" by Thorndike had been introduced, which permitted directed laboratory research rather than naturalistic observation. By 1911, the *Journal of Animal Behavior* appeared; it eventually became the *Journal of Comparative Psychology*. The importance of this early research in animal behavior lay in its firm commitment to experimentation and the elimination of subjective and anthropomorphic concepts.

JOHN B. WATSON AND BEHAVIORISM

Foundations of Behaviorism

Conditioning in Russia and comparative psychology in England, Europe, and America represent independent advances in methodology and applications of the scientific approach to the subject matter of psychology. In America, John B. Watson (1878–1958) was responsible for crystallizing an existing trend toward objectivism.

American psychology at the time of Watson's graduate training was characterized by functionalism. Watson worked with James R. Angell (1869–1949) and studied under John Dewey (1859–1952), two prominent functionalists at the University of Chicago where he received his doctorate in 1903. Functionalist psychology was concerned with analyzing the operations of consciousness. Functionalism developed in reaction to structuralism, a school of psychology devoted to describing the elements or components of thought rather than the operation of thought processes. Both structuralism and functionalism employed introspection as their method of investigation. Introspection involved carefully "observing" one's own conscious mental creations such as thoughts and images. The behavioristic revolt led by Watson was against the subject matter as well as the method of investigation.

Watson became interested in animal psychology as a graduate student. In addition to his training in psychology, he studied biology and physiology with Loeb, who had formulated a mechanistic interpretation of animal behavior. Watson started an animal laboratory at the University of Chicago, where he remained until 1908, when he went to the Johns Hopkins University. He continued his animal work there, and his research increasingly convinced him that animal psychology was an objective science that could function independently of mentalistic underpinnings. He believed that investigations of human psychology could profit from the objectivity achieved in animal studies. Objectivity in psychology in general, Watson believed, would be improved if all references to consciousness were eliminated and reliance upon introspection were abandoned.

Generally, Watson is credited with catalyzing a movement toward objectivism that was already well in progress. Several texts had appeared that minimized or rejected the study of consciousness in psychology, including *Physiological Psychology* (1905) and *An Introduction to Social Psychology* (1909) by William McDougall, *The Essentials of Psychology* (1911) by Walter Pillsbury, and *The Fundamental Laws of Human Behavior* (1911) by Max Meyer. In these and other books, psychology was defined as the science of behavior or conduct rather than of private experience.

Watson himself was directly influenced by the emergence of objectivism in psychology. As early as 1904, he had heard an address by James McKeen Cattell (1860–1944), who endorsed objective experimentation independently of introspection. At Johns Hopkins, Watson became increasingly behavioristic in his outlook, a position which is traceable in his personal letters and professional presentations (Burnham, 1968) and was strengthened by the direct influence of his colleagues. Herbert S. Jennings (1868–1947), a zoologist at Johns

Hopkins with whom Watson studied, had written a text on the *Behavior of the Lower Organisms* (1906). The book advocated the objective study of animal behavior and focused upon observations rather than alleged mental states. Another colleague, Knight Dunlap (1875–1949), had publicly denounced introspection in 1912 in an article called "The Case Against Introspection" and encouraged Watson's behavioristic philosophy (Dunlap, 1932; Herrnstein, 1969).

Watson announced his behavioristic position in an address delivered at Yale in 1908, and elaborated upon it in 1912–1913 in a series of lectures he delivered at Columbia at the invitation of Cattell. The first published statement of his position appeared in 1913 in the highly influential article, "Psychology as the Behaviorist Views It." The paper clearly defined what Watson considered the appropriate domain of psychology, and it rejected the focus and methodology of structuralism and functionalism. The following passage has become a classic statement:

> Psychology as the behaviorist views it is a purely objective experimental branch of natural science. Its theoretical goal is the prediction and control of behavior. Introspection forms no essential part of its methods, nor is the scientific value of its data dependent upon the readiness with which they lend themselves to interpretation in terms of consciousness. The behaviorist, in his efforts to get a unitary scheme of animal response, recognizes the dividing line between man and brute. The behavior of man, with all of its refinement and complexity, forms only a part of the behaviorist's total scheme of investigation (Watson, 1913, p. 158).

In 1914, Watson completed a book, *Behavior: An Introduction to Comparative Psychology,* in which he described experimental work in animal psychology and discussed the legitimacy of this area of inquiry as an objective science. In 1919, his second book, *Psychology, From the Standpoint of a Behaviorist,* appeared and applied the methods and principles of animal psychology to human behavior. In this work, Watson reported his research on the development of reactions in infants. In subsequent books and articles, he continued to expound the tenets of behaviorism and to extend the application of conditioning to diverse human behaviors.

Watson's position was based on two methodological points. First, psychology should no longer consider consciousness as its domain of study. The study of consciousness led to irresolvable discussions about the nature of "mental" events such as sensations, images, and thoughts. Watson asserted that the proper domain of psychology was the study of overt behavior. Specifically, psychology should study various environmental stimuli (S) and the responses (R) they evoke. This emphasis eventually was termed S-R psychology. Second, introspection as the method of psychological "observation" should be abandoned, because it did not allow the objective study of behavior. In place of introspection, the psychologist was to assess behavior in much the same way that animal experimenters had successfully done. Watson suggested that the conditioned reflex method elaborated by Pavlov and Bechterev could replace introspection and establish psychology as an objective science.

Watson's views were consistent with, but did not necessarily follow from, adherence to the objective orientation he advocated. It was important for Watson to address himself to diverse classical topics in psychology—including the role of instincts and behavior, emotions, and thought processes—to demonstrate that behaviorism could encompass any subject matter previously investigated through introspection.

The role accorded thought or consciousness in Watson's system of behavior was particularly interesting because thought processes were considered inaccessible to objective experimentation. Therefore, his solution was to reduce thinking to observable sensorimotor behavior. He explained that thinking consisted of "implicit" speech movements, i.e., subvocal talking, a notion that may have been derived from Sechenov (1965) and Bechterev (1913). Some of Watson's investigations did reveal slight movements of the vocal musculature during thought, but such movements are not always correlated with reports of thinking.

Watson regarded emotions as somatic reactions made in response to external stimuli rather than conscious processes or perceptions. They could be understood in terms of specific responses, including visual responses, changes in breathing and pulse, and other physiological manifestations. Watson investigated stimuli that produced emotional responses in human infants and identified what he considered to be the three fundamental unlearned emotions, namely, fear, rage, and love. He believed that all other emotions evolved from these basic emotions through conditioning.

Watson's view of instincts changed radically over the course of his career. Although he initially accepted instincts as important in explaining human behavior, he finally denied their influence. Behaviors that seem instinctive, he argued, actually result from conditioning. He concluded that inheritance contributed little to behavior.

His confidence in the influence of learning and environment is revealed in this now well known declaration:[5]

> Give me a dozen healthy infants, well-formed, and my own specified world to bring them up in and I'll guarantee to take any one at random and train him to become any type of specialist I might select—doctor, lawyer, artist, merchant—chief and, yes, even beggar-man and thief, regardless of his talents, penchants, tendencies, abilities, vocations, and race of his ancestors. I am going beyond my facts and I admit it, but so have the advocates of the contrary and they have been doing it for many thousands of years. Please note that when this experiment is made I am to be allowed to specify the way the children are to be brought up and the type of world they have to live in (Watson, 1924, p. 104).

Watson's dramatic challenge cannot convey the extent of his intensive investigations and elaborate extrapolations of conditioning to account for behavior. He set forth his position enthusiastically, both in academic and popular publications. Behaviorism, as espoused by Watson, began as a methodological stance against current schools of psychology. His insistence upon an objective approach to psychological topics, the rejection of introspection, and the study of consciousness are the formal foundations of behaviorism. (However, the methods of behaviorism already had been widely adopted before Watson's manifesto (Herrnstein, 1969).)

The Influence of Conditioning and Reflexology on Behaviorism

The methodological tenets espoused by Watson were quite similar to those advanced by Sechenov, Pavlov, and Bechterev, particularly the replacement of speculative and introspective inquiry into subjective states with the objective study of overt behavior. However, Watson

---

[5] Although not as extreme an environmentalist as Watson, Sechenov held a similar position. In pointing out the limitations of his book *Reflexes of the Brain*, Sechenov noted that he failed to discuss individual differences of the nervous mechanisms as a function of heredity. However, he stressed the negligible influence of heredity in explaining behavior:

> In the present investigation nothing is said about the individual peculiarities of the nervous mechanisms in the newborn child. These peculiarities undoubtedly exist (ancestral and inherited from the nearest kindred), and they must, of course, influence man's entire subsequent development. However, it is absolutely impossible to detect these peculiarities, because in the overwhelming majority of cases 999/1000 of the psychical content of man is determined by education in the broadest sense, and only 1/1000 depends on individuality. By this I do not mean to say that a fool can be made intelligent; this would be the same as trying to develop hearing in a person born without the auditory nerve. What I have in mind is that a clever Negro, Lapp or Bashkir brought up in European society and in a European manner will differ very little intellectually from educated Europeans (Sechenov, 1965, p. 107).

did not restrict the study of behavior to physiological responses, because the differences between a physiology and psychology lay in the behaviors that were observed. The objective study of psychology would include not only specific physiological responses such as reflexes and firing of nerve cells but molar behaviors as well. However, Watson believed that psychology should *focus* on larger units of behavior involving the entire organism (Watson, 1919), although he was interested in behaviors ranging from molecular responses, such as discrete muscle movements, to molar responses, such as verbal statements.

The crystallization of Watson's position, set forth in the 1913 manifesto, occurred somewhat independently of the Russian work on conditioning. However, the influence of both Bechterev and Pavlov became increasingly heightened in Watson's publications. In Watson's 1915 presidential address to the American Psychological Association, "The Place of the Conditioned Reflex in Psychology," he outlined the methodology of conditioning, with particular emphasis on the work of Bechterev (Babkin, 1949). Watson also described his collaboration with Karl S. Lashley (1890–1958), a student at Johns Hopkins who later became a prominent physiological psychologist. Their work on conditioning, conducted in 1914, was stimulated by the French translation of Bechterev's book, *Objective Psychology*, which had become available in 1913. Watson and Lashley applied Bechterev's method of conditioning motor reflexes to diverse animals.

Bechterev's work helped Watson recognize the importance and the implications of conditioning. In his early writings (Watson, 1913, 1914, 1916), conditioning was regarded as only an investigative tool with which to replace introspection. Eventually, conditioning became more than a method of study—a concept central to explaining mechanisms of complex behavior (Watson, 1924). Watson assumed that units of behavior were integrated series of reflexes. The assumption had tremendous heuristic value, because it signaled that complex behavior could be investigated by examining simple reflexes and their combinations.

It is interesting to note that conditioned reflexes were being studied in America at the time Pavlov's research on "psychical secretions" had begun. In 1902 at the University of Pennsylvania, Edwin B. Twitmyer (1873–1943) completed his doctoral dissertation on the knee jerk, a reflex elicited by physical stimulation of the tendons near the patella. With an automatically controlled tap of a hammer, Twitmyer paired stimulation of the tendons with a bell, a procedure that led him to the accidental discovery of the conditioned reflex.

> During the adjustment of the apparatus for an earlier group of experiments with one subject (Subject A) a decided kick of both legs was observed to follow a tap of the signal bell occurring without the usual blow of the hammers on the tendons. It was at first believed that the subject had merely voluntarily kicked out the legs, but upon being questioned, he stated that although quite conscious of the movement as it was taking place, it had not been caused by a volitional effort, and further, that the subjective feeling accompanying the movement was similar to the feeling of the movement following the blow on the tendons with the exception that he was quite conscious that the tendons had not been struck. Two alternatives presented themselves. Either (1) the subject was in error in his introspective observation and had voluntarily moved his legs, or (2) the true knee jerk (or a movement resembling it in appearance) had been produced by a stimulus other than the usual one (Twitmyer, 1902, pp. 24–25).

He examined the reactions further to assess the reliability of the reflex evoked without physical stimulation. After having been paired repeatedly with physical stimulation, the bell alone was sufficient to elicit the knee jerk in several subjects. Twitmyer did not extend his work on the conditioned reflex beyond these demonstrations, although he noted that ". . . the phenomenon occurs with sufficient frequency and regularity to demand an inquiry as to its nature" (p. 29).

Publication of his dissertation did not attract attention. Behaviorists who subsequently relied heavily upon conditioning did not give particular credit to Twitmyer. Rather, they turned to Bechterev, whose conditioning of motor reflexes was very similar. However, conditioning merely had been demonstrated in America. In Russia, it had been thoroughly exploited. By the time accounts of the Russian experiments were available through translations, Pavlov and Bechterev had clearly established several processes of conditioning, the utility of conditioning as an experimental method, and the applicability of conditioning to study and explain diverse psychological processes.

Watson drew upon the work of Bechterev and Pavlov. Bechterev influenced Watson's early work on conditioning, although Pavlov's methods and terminology ultimately were adopted (Babkin, 1949). Along with the greater accessibility of Bechterev's work through French and German translations, he expressed a broader theory of behavior than did Pavlov and addressed a variety of psychological topics objectively. In addition, the experimental arrangements of Pavlov seemed restrictive and inapplicable to investigating the conditioned reflex in humans and animals other than dogs. The apparatus (e.g., a restrictive harness) and assessment techniques (measuring saliva from a fistula) seemed impractical for more mobile organisms (Lashley, 1916). Recognizing the importance of Bechterev's work, Watson and Lashley began experiments on conditioning. To expand their knowledge, Watson made arrangements for Lashley to work in Bechterev's laboratory. Unfortunately this plan was interrupted by World War I.

Some of Pavlov's work was available in English before the translations of Bechterev's writings. As early as 1906, he published an article in *Science* entitled "The Scientific Investigation of the Psychical Faculties or Processes of Higher Animals," and in 1909 the Yerkes and Morgulis paper on Pavlov's method appeared. This second article was one of several papers in comparative psychology that comprised a single issue of the journal, with Watson as guest editor. The article did not generate an immediate response although it described the application of Pavlov's method to the study of sensation and perception, which was of interest to psychologists. Pavlov's extensive research did not appear in English until his two major books, *Conditioned Reflexes* (1927) and *Lectures on Conditioned Reflexes* (1928) were made available.

A major factor that may have contributed to the greater influence of Pavlov over Bechterev on Watson was not only Pavlov's recognition as a Nobel Laureate, but the nature of his research. Pavlov's work was systematic and reflected a concern for careful laboratory control and minute details of experimentation. He made great progress in his elaboration of the conditioned reflex by investigating a number of processes in a programmatic fashion.

Although Bechterev had conducted extensive research, he could not match Pavlov's reputation, at least in Russia, for methodological rigor (Babkin, 1949). Also, Bechterev's main interest was not in studying conditioning, but in extrapolating from his research to forge a general theory of behavior. Bechterev extended reflexology to a variety of psychological problems, including some that Watson rejected outright as subjective. However, Bechterev's influence on Watsonian behaviorism was evident. For example, the notion espoused by Watson that thought is subvocal conditioned-reflex behavior appears to come directly from Bechterev. Yet Bechterev's concern with phenomena that psychologists had referred to in subjective terms made his own position appear more subjective than that of Pavlov (Watson, 1919). Bechterev attempted to interpret various mental concepts (e.g., ego, thought, dreams) in terms of reflexology. Lashley noted that Pavlov's work was preferred over Bechterev's because the latter recognized subjective states (Babkin, 1949). Because Pavlov was more explicit in rejecting internal processes, his terminology was ultimately adopted.

THE PSYCHOLOGY OF LEARNING IN AMERICA

The research on conditioning in Russia and America stressed the adaptability and modifiability of behavior. Pavlov had clarified the manner by which stimuli came to acquire the capacity to evoke responses. Watson and Bechterev attempted to formulate broad theories of behavior based upon the notion of conditioning. Watson's own work on conditioning, his rejection of instincts, and his emphasis upon environmental influences on behavior helped establish learning as a central topic.

Watson regarded all learning as analogs of Pavlovian conditioning. Individuals learn to respond to new situations by having reflexes elicited in the presence of neutral stimuli that eventually acquire the capacity to elicit the behavior. Yet, all behavior is not simply a matter of learning to respond to different situations or stimuli. New responses are learned that do not appear to be simple reflex behaviors. Watson explained the acquisition of new responses as a sequence or combination of simple reflex responses. For example, according to Watson, a behavior such as walking is a sequence of many responses, including putting the weight on one foot, swinging the other foot forward, bringing it down, putting the weight forward on the other foot, and so on. The sequence was a function of each response providing muscle sensations that served as a stimulus for the next response. The sequence of behaviors was assumed to be a series of conditioned reflexes (Watson, 1924). Watson explained complex habits and responses such as emotional reactions, acquisition of knowledge, verbal behavior, and ultimately all learning as combinations of conditioned reflexes.

In America, several theories of learning were proposed to explain the acquisition of responses. They differed in the assumptions made about learning processes, the degree of theoretical sophistication, and the amount of research generated in support of particular interpretations. Generally, these premises adhered to the basic methodological tenets of behaviorism: focus upon stimuli and responses, reliance upon objective evidence, and rejection of consciousness. However, several important theorists, notably Thorndike, Hull, Tolman, Guthrie, Mowrer, and Skinner, carved out individual positions within the larger realm of behaviorism. These theorists have contributed to the evolution of specific behavior modification techniques. In addition, controversies about the nature of learning have their roots in the application of techniques based upon their theories. Because each man's theory of learning cannot be presented in detail, the basic assumptions about how behaviors are learned are provided and the role of reward and punishment is described.[6]

Edward L. Thorndike and Connectionism

In addition to introducing laboratory methods of research to animal psychology, Thorndike distinguished himself in education and psychological measurement. Although he is not usually identified as a behaviorist, his animal research was well within the behaviorist tradition. Like Watson, Thorndike employed objective methods and dismissed mental events and consciousness as a topic of psychology. Before receiving his doctorate in 1898, Thorndike worked at Columbia with Cattell, another early behaviorist (Burnham, 1968).

Thorndike's research on learning was distinct from that of the Russian physiologists. Pavlov and Bechterev had focused upon reflexive behavior and determined how various stimuli acquired the capacity to elicit reflexive responses. Learning was thought to result from a change in the stimuli that elicited a particular reflex response. The reflex responses elicited were already in the repertoire of the organisms and merely were evoked in the presence of diverse stimuli. Conditioning actually involved changes in the responses, as the conditioned response was not identical with the unconditioned response. However, that difference was not immediately regarded as important in early research on conditioning.

Thorndike's research centered on the acquisition of responses not initially in the repertoire of the organism under specific, unvarying stimulus conditions. He completed experiments with different species to discover how responses came to vary. His dissertation at Columbia in 1898 was expanded into a book, *Animal Intelligence: Experimental Studies of the Associative Processes in Animals* (1911). The research reported included his experiments with cats in puzzle boxes, studies

---

[6] Detailed explanations and analyses of learning theories can be found in Deese and Hulse (1967), Gagne (1970), and Hilgard and Bower (1966).

which have since become classic in the psychology of learning. The puzzle box was employed to see how animals learned to escape from a confined situation to procure food. The puzzle box allowed the experimenter to make various behaviors such as turning a button, pulling a string or loop, pushing a lever, or moving a latch necessary to escape. Because the responses were instrumental in leading to escape, Thorndike coined the term *instrumental behaviors*. A typical puzzle box he used is illustrated in Figure 3.2.

Thorndike would place a hungry cat in a box with a small piece of food lying outside the box. The animal immediately attempted to escape by exploring diverse solutions in a trial-and-error fashion. Eventually the animal removed the barrier and was allowed to consume the food. The cat was placed in the box again to examine behavior leading to escape. Repeated trials revealed that the random movements and errors that preceded escape decreased substantially over time. After several trials, the cat immediately performed the required response to escape as soon as a new trial began. Thorndike kept records of performance by plotting the amount of time required to escape over successive trials. Figure 3.3 is a typical learning curve showing that as training continues, less time is required for solution.

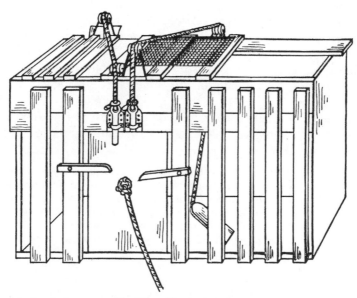

Figure 3.2. Puzzle box created by Thorndike for learning experiments with cats. (From Garrett, 1951; reprinted by permission.)

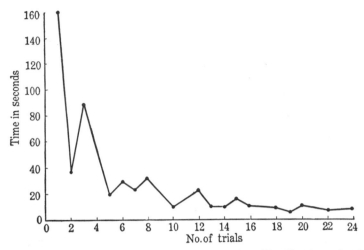

Figure 3.3. Learning curve for a cat as recorded by Thorndike. The time taken by the cat to escape in successive trials is represented by the ordinate; the successive trials are represented by the abscissa. (From Garrett, 1951; reprinted by permission.)

The general characteristic of the learning curve was shown in other animals as well. The differences among animals pertained to the variability of responding across trials, i.e., consistency of performance, and the speed with which the errors decreased over time.

Thorndike referred to trial-and-error learning as a "stamping in" of correct responses and a "stamping out" of incorrect ones. He explained learning in terms of *connecting* responses to various stimulus conditions. Indeed, he explicitly stated that "learning is connecting" (Thorndike, 1931, p. 122). That connections become strengthened or weakened by the consequences of behaviors is the foundation of Thorndike's two basic laws of learning: the law of effect and the law of exercise.

> The Law of Effect is that: *Of several responses made to the same situation, those which are accompanied or closely followed by satisfaction to the animal will, other things being equal, be more firmly connected with the situation, so that, when it recurs, they will be more likely to recur; those which are accompanied or closely followed by discomfort to the animal will, other things being equal, have their connections with that situation weakened, so that, when it recurs, they will be less likely to occur. The greater the satisfaction or discomfort, the greater the strengthening or weakening of the bond.*
> The Law of Exercise is that: *Any response to a situation will, other things being equal, be more strongly connected with the situation in proportion to*

the number of times it has been connected with that situation and to the average vigor and duration of the connections (Thorndike, 1911, p. 244).

The law of effect explained how the successful response was acquired. In the case of animals in the puzzle box, Thorndike observed that several responses were made until the successful one was achieved. The successful response resulted in food or "satisfying consequences" and, therefore, was learned. Unsuccessful responses were associated with "annoying consequences" and were eliminated. Thorndike specified the consequences that determined whether the response was to be "stamped in" or "stamped out."

> By a satisfying state of affairs is meant one which the animal does nothing to avoid, often doing such things as attain and preserve it. By a discomforting or annoying state of affairs is meant one which the animal commonly avoids and abandons (Thorndike, 1911, p. 245).

In addition to the consequences of behavior, aspects about the performance of the response itself were important for learning. As suggested by the law of exercise, the more frequently, the more recently, and the more vigorously a response is exercised or performed, the more effectively it is learned.

Thorndike later revised his laws of learning based upon his own research, much of which was reported in *The Fundamentals of Learning* (1932) and *An Experimental Study of Rewards* (1933). He had qualified his major law (the law of effect). He found that, whereas rewards tended to strengthen behavior, as originally posed, punishment did not weaken it. His belief in the ineffectiveness of punishment resulted from laboratory research in which he used small monetary fines and admonition with the word "wrong." Thus, only one-half of the original law of effect was retained. The law of exercise was completely retracted. Repetition was no longer considered essential for learning, but only facilitative of performance. Frequent performance of a response was important only insofar as it allowed the law of effect to operate.

Thorndike, Pavlov, and Behaviorism

Both Thorndike and Pavlov were working independently on learning at the end of the nineteenth century. Pavlov later acknowledged the importance of Thorndike's *Animal Intelligence* (Pavlov, 1928). Later, the similarity between their work in describing stimulus-response learning was clearly recognized. Indeed, as will be discussed, the distinction between associating new stimuli with a particular response (Pavlov) and between associating particular stimulus with new responses (Thorndike) is not easily maintained in many learning situations. One of Thorndike's secondary laws (the law of associative shift) stated that when two stimuli are presented and one elicits a response, the other acquires the capacity to elicit the same response. This, of course, is close to Pavlov's conditioning model (Murphy and Kovach, 1972).

Interesting methodological similarities were immediately apparent in the work of Pavlov and Thorndike. Both investigators conducted experiments with individual subjects over time to examine the process of learning in depth. Second, both insisted upon careful quantification of events to establish clear relationships between stimuli and response conditions.

One difference in their work may have resulted from the different disciplines with which they were associated. As a physiologist, Pavlov insisted upon eliminating references to consciousness or subjective states of the organism. Thorndike's work, however, developed within the traditions of animal psychology and functionalism, in which frequent references to consciousness were made. His experiments, like those of Pavlov, were objective and did not require the discussion of subjective or conscious states of the organism. Given particular stimulus conditions, the resulting behavior could be observed objectively. However, Thorndike introduced notions that were indicative of subjective states. For example, instead of talking about certain events or consequences affecting behavior, Thorndike described outcomes in terms of "satisfying" or "annoying" consequences. Thus, because the law of effect included subjective states and allusions to consciousness of the organism, Watson rejected Thorndike's formulation as not completely behavioristic (Watson, 1919).

Although Thorndike was not accepted as a behaviorist by Watson, he used the methods of behaviorism. Thorndike's experimental contributions to learning were substantial. By stressing the importance of the consequences that would alter behavior, he initiated a productive line of research in the psychology of learning. This work, which will be traced later, served as the basis for many contemporary behavior modification techniques.

Edwin R. Guthrie and Contiguous Conditioning

Guthrie (1886–1959) was the behaviorist whose stance on learning remained the closest to Watson's (Hill, 1963). Guthrie posited a major principle of learning in his book *The Psychology of Learning* (1935): "A combination of stimuli which has accompanied a movement will on its recurrence tend to be followed by that movement" (p. 26). In other words, a response performed in a given situation is likely to be repeated in that same situation. According to Guthrie, the pairing of a stimulus and a response is all that is required for learning.

Guthrie's association of stimuli and responses is deceptively simple. The "stimuli" did not merely mean environmental cues nor did "movements" simply refer to molar behavioral acts. Stimuli included environmental events that brought about specific movements of the organism. These activities (such as particular muscle movements) were considered as small components of larger behavioral acts and the responses that actually became conditioned.[7] Yet, the movements, in turn, produce proprioceptive stimuli that serve as conditioned stimuli for further movements. Any learned act involves both environmental and internal stimuli. The pairing of stimuli with specific acts is all that is required for learning.

Because the pairing of a stimulus and a response was all that was needed for learning, Guthrie maintained that successful consequences or rewards did not strengthen the learned connection. He considered rewards to be important in an ancillary fashion in that they can change the stimuli or situation so that no new response can be associated with the previous stimulus. A reward removes the organism from the stimulus to which the response was conditioned. The response is conditioned to the situation if it is the last thing done in that situation. The consequence of a behavior, by altering the stimuli, ensures that unlearning will not take place. Unlearning would result from associating a new or incompatible response with the previous stimulus.

Based upon his contiguity interpretation of learning, Guthrie (1935) described these techniques for breaking habits or unlearning undesirable behaviors. Applying the techniques meant finding the cues that initiate the undesirable action and practicing another response to them. The first technique requires gradual introduction of stimuli to prevent the evocation of the undesirable response. The stimulus is

---

[7] Pavlov used the term "conditioned reflex" to refer to automatic and involuntary acts elicited by various stimuli. American psychologists extended the notion of conditioning to a variety of behaviors that had no clear unconditioned stimuli and were not reflexes in the Pavlovian sense. To account for contiguity or association learning in general, which encompassed conditioned reflexes, the term "conditioned response" was introduced (Smith and Guthrie, 1921).

gradually increased in strength so that the response to be eliminated never occurs. By not performing the undesirable response in the presence of mild doses of the stimulus and by gradually increasing its prominence, the stimulus can be presented at full strength without eliciting the response. For example, to overcome fear of cats, an individual can acquire a kitten. Because the kitten is so small and helpless, the fear is not evoked. The kitten's growth is so gradual that habits of caring for it and petting it continue even when it reaches maturity. These nonfearing responses become conditioned to the animal and fear will no longer be evoked.

A second technique for breaking habits is the repeated presentation of the stimulus at full strength to evoke the undesirable response again and again. The response should be evoked until fatigue, exhaustion, or adaptation results and the response no longer occurs. According to Guthrie, the last response to the situation (not responding) becomes conditioned to the stimulus. For example, many individuals overcome stage fright by repeatedly making public appearances. If individuals continue to appear publicly after the excitation and anxiety of stage fright has subsided, the sight of an audience no longer evokes fright. The stimulus that caused fright is still present in subsequent public appearances but fright has been replaced with other responses.

The final method of breaking a habit is pairing the stimulus that produces the undesirable response with a stronger stimulus that produces an incompatible one. The original stimulus associated with the undesirable response becomes attached to this new response. For example, a student may be unable to study in a library because of distracting noise. If he reads an engrossing book, he will quickly adapt to the noise. If the book includes enough material of interest to the student, it will provide a stronger stimulus than the noise and, hence, produce responses that are incompatible with being distracted. By repeatedly reading in the library, the distractability of the noise will be diminished and reading will be established as a firm response.

It is interesting to note that in writing about altering behavior, Guthrie did not refer to reward or punishment as Thorndike had done in his original law of effect. It has been demonstrated that consequences that follow behavior do strengthen the connection between stimuli and responses, thus refuting Guthrie's major tenet (Hilgard and Bower, 1966). However, his emphasis on contiguity has remained important in learning and in behavior modification. His techniques for changing undesirable behavior have been incorporated directly into behavior modification, although the interpretation of these techniques transcends Guthrie's straightforward application of contiguity.

Edward C. Tolman and Purposive Behaviorism

Tolman (1896–1961) adhered to the major methodological tenets of behaviorism, although he differed from Watson in at least two respects. First, Tolman was interested in studying behavior solely at the molar rather than at the molecular level, i.e., in terms of stimulus-response connections. Tolman's insistence on studying the behavior of the entire organism rather than specific individual acts can be appreciated more fully when the second major distinction between Watson and Tolman is considered.

The second difference is in the notion of *purposive* behavior, a major concept articulated by Tolman. Tolman maintained that all behavior was goal-directed or purposive. An organism learns a means to an end. For example, in the puzzle-box situation constructed by Thorndike, cats learned how to escape a puzzle box to achieve a particular end—food. According to Tolman, molecular movements made by an animal were less descriptive of behavior than the goal toward which the movements led.

The notion of purposive behavior seemed to violate a fundamental tenet of behaviorism in its assumption that the animal is conscious of a particular goal or has a particular end in mind. Indeed, Watsonian behaviorists criticized Tolman for attributing purpose to behavior (Schultz, 1975). Yet Tolman attempted to eliminate consciousness from the notion of purpose by focusing upon the response itself. If conscious awareness of a goal did exist, he affirmed that it was unavailable to scientific scrutiny. Thus, his interest was in the responses that resulted in definite ends.

When Tolman made reference to concepts that seemed to reflect consciousness, he was interpreting behavior. However, his approach to the phenomenon under study remained behavioristic because the data he reported were objective. Yet Tolman relied heavily upon *intervening variables,* that is, constructs for inferring processes that intervene between the stimulus and the response. The intervening variables were posited to account for the relationship between some environmental manipulation and behavior.

Tolman's theory of learning differed from other theorists discussed so far. Unlike the proponents of stimulus and response theories, who maintained that specific behaviors were learned under specific conditions, Tolman argued that organisms did not learn specific responses. Rather, they learned *meanings* and developed *cognitions* about various stimuli vis-à-vis a goal. Tolman's purposive behavior has been characterized as a theory of "what leads to what" (Hilgard and Bower, 1966, p. 203). Repeated experience with a sequence of events leading to a goal results in an expectancy for that goal. If an organism's expectancy is confirmed by goal attainment, the likelihood of the behavior is increased. Thus, reward is important only insofar as it provides confirming experiences or reveals what environmental stimuli lead to what consequences (Tolman, 1952). Because Tolman claimed that learning was based upon acquiring knowledge or cognitions about related stimulus conditions, his position is often called a stimulus-stimulus rather than a stimulus-response learning theory.

Although Tolman's work has not been drawn upon directly in behavior modification, the field's recent focus on cognitive processes in explaining the development and amelioration of adaptive behavior is one that bears close resemblance to Tolman's ideas. Specifically, cognitive behavior modification makes assumptions about the nature of learning and posits intervening variables that go beyond simplistic stimulus-response accounts of learning (see Chapter 9).

Clark L. Hull and a Hypothetico-Deductive Theory

Clark Hull (1884–1952) was familiar with and apparently impressed by the writings of Pavlov and Thorndike, both of whom provided accounts of learning in special situations. One of Hull's major contributions was his synthesis of Pavlov's work on reflexes and Thorndike's work on trial-and-error learning. From 1915 to his death in 1952, Hull worked on a hypothetic-deductive theory of behavior. The theory included definitions, postulates, corollaries, and theorems for predicting behavior.

Behaviorism had begun to move away from a straightforward stimulus-response (S-R) account of behavior emphasized by Watson. Experimental psychologists such as Robert S. Woodworth (1869–1962) had suggested a stimulus-organism-response (S-O-R) formula to be used to replace the S-R account of behavior (Woodworth, 1938). The organism stands for the intervening conditions of the stimulus and the response. The stimulus and the organism, according to the S-O-R position, affected the final response. What goes on in the organism is a matter of inference. Like Tolman, Hull used intervening variables to account for the relationship between stimuli and responses. Posing intervening variables to explain a variety of specific stimulus-response relationships allowed for deductions of new phenomena and empirically testable predictions. Hull's system attempted a careful association of intervening variables with environmental events. Predictions deduced from the postulates could be examined empirically to determine the plausibility of the postulates and the utility of the intervening variables upon which they relied. The postulates could be revised in light of the experimental findings.

The intervening variables were organized into a multistage predictive scheme. The first stage consisted of the independent variables (stimuli) and the last stage consisted of dependent variables (responses). The next stages included constructs varying in their relationship to the independent variables. Some intervening variables (e.g., drive) posed by Hull were affected directly by manipulating environmental events (e.g., hours of food deprivation). Yet other intervening elements were used to encompass several first-stage intervening variables and were not themselves directly related to any single independent variable. For example, one intervening variable, termed a reaction potential ($_sE_R$) consisted of the probability of performing a particular response. The $_sE_R$ was a complex function of several other intervening variables which themselves could be affected by manipulating independent variables.

Two important intervening variables for Hull were habit strength ($_sH_R$) and drive (D). Habit strength referred to the strength of a connection between a stimulus and response learned through reinforced practice. Drive was an activated state of the organism which, when reduced, served as reinforcement. Hull concluded that a drive such as hunger or thirst produces a characteristic stimulus (i.e., a drive stimulus) emanating from some internal need. Any response that occurs immediately before the reduction of the drive stimulus tends to be learned as a response to any stimuli that were present. Although habit and drive were important in predicting performance in a given situation, several other intervening variables, such as magnitude of the reward, the amount of effort required for response, and other factors, affected the equation for predicting performance.

In his synthesis of the work of Thorndike and Pavlov, Hull posed reinforcement as the one principle central to learning (Hull, 1937). For Hull, reinforcement meant drive reduction. He accepted Thorndike's revised law of effect, which stated that rewarding consequences tend to strengthen a stimulus-response connection. To this, Hull added a notion of drive. To explain habit formation as discussed by Thorndike, Hull claimed that any response made prior to terminating a drive would become connected to that drive. When the drive recurs, the response will be set off more promptly and more vigorously. Thus, drive reduction was posed to explain strengthening or "stamping in" of a connection between a response and its consequences.

To explain Pavlov's theory of conditioned responses, Hull suggested that drive reduction could strengthen the connection between stimuli present when the drive had been reduced. Thus, if a response were followed by drive reduction, any stimulus associated with drive reduction would eventuate in a response without the drive reduction itself. The conditioned response made by the organism would be an anticipatory response. Pavlov had emphasized the importance of the onset of the event (e.g., shock) as the unconditioned stimulus resulting in a response. However, Hull (1943) assumed that the critical element was drive reduction.

To reiterate, Hull accounted for habit formation as discussed by Thorndike by a relationship between a response and drive reduction that served as a reward or reinforcement. In conditioning as described by Pavlov, the connection was formed between the unconditioned response and some stimulus other than the one whose reduction provided a reinforcing state (Mowrer, 1960a). Thus, as Hull proposed in his major book *Principles of Behavior* (1943), the differences between trial-and-error learning and conditioning did not involve "the action of fundamentally different principles or laws but only differences in the conditions under which the principle operates . . . (p. 78)." The commonality of learning was in the reinforcing state or drive reduction.

Hull's original work in learning was influential because it permitted concrete predictions about behavior. He never completed the specific theory of learning, but the revisions were published in his *Essentials of Behavior* (1951) and *A Behavior System* (1952, published posthumously). The theory was constantly evolving; it was based upon predictions, alteration of postulates in light of empirical data, and subsequent predictions. Although the substance and generality of Hull's theory have been criticized, its heuristic value has been great (Hilgard and Bower, 1966; Koch, 1954). In addition, behavior modification has drawn upon aspects of Hull's theory to generate and to explain behavior change techniques.

O. Hobart Mowrer and Two-Factor Theory

Mowrer, a colleague of Hull's at Yale, also attempted to integrate the work of Pavlov and Thorndike in his two-factor theory of learning (Mowrer, 1947, 1960a). The importance of Mowrer's position derives from its integration of Pavlov's and Thorndike's theories and from its attention to development of emotional reactions (e.g., fear, anxiety), a concern relevant to clinical psychology and psychiatry.

Mowrer was interested in the nature of reinforcement, especially the drive-reduction view posited by Hull. For Hull, all learning depended upon reinforcement (drive reduction or drive-stimulus reduction); reinforcing events reduced drives such as hunger or thirst or removed some aversive state such as pain. Mowrer pointed out that drive reduction did not adequately account for all learning, particularly the learning of emotional reactions. Nor could punishment be explained fully by Hull's conception of reinforcement. For example, in acquiring fear in response to an aversive situation such as burning oneself on the stove, what is the reinforcing event for learning to avoid the stove? Drive reduction could not easily explain avoidance learning under conditions of punishment. Thus, avoidance behavior and punishment became central concerns of Mowrer because these concepts were not completely addressed by previous interpretations of learning.

Thorndike's original law of effect stated that responses followed by rewards were "stamped in" and those followed by punishing consequences were "stamped out." Mowrer observed that the delivery of punishing consequences can be associated with the development of specific behavior. Punishment not only stamped out responses but could stamp them in as well. For example, a child punished for playing with valuable china learned how to behave in a particular way, namely, to avoid certain situations. Thorndike's law of effect was inadequate in accounting for avoidance learning because new behaviors were included through punishment. Pavlovian conditioning was no more helpful in explaining avoidance learning. In conditioning, pairing an unconditioned stimulus such as shock with a conditioned stimulus such as a buzzer could lead to avoidance behavior. However, this pairing by itself was not as effective for fostering or maintaining avoidance behavior as allowing the organism success in preventing the aversive event in subsequent trials. Learning to avoid aversive events appeared to contribute to the development of avoidance behavior, which was not addressed by Pavlov.

Mowrer was not the first to reveal the shortcomings of Thorndike, Pavlov, and Hull in accounting for avoidance learning. In the 1920s, Russian studies had showed that conditioning alone was not sufficient to account for avoidance learning (Razran, 1956). However, Mowrer appears to have been responsible for clarifying the problem raised by avoidance learning.

In 1947, Mowrer formulated a two-factor theory of reinforcement that encompassed the different types of learning investigated by Thorndike and Pavlov. Mowrer posed that there were two kinds of learning—sign learning and solution learning. Sign learning involved the conditioning of involuntary responses of organs and glands, including various emotional reactions. An unconditioned aversive stimulus, such as shock, elicited an emotional response. A conditioned stimulus associated with the unconditioned stimulus becomes a sign that an aversive event will follow and itself become aversive and elicit a response. Solution learning, the problem-solving responses acquired in drive reduction, is demonstrated in the performance of behavior to reduce drives. Voluntary responses of the skeletal muscles are part of the solution learning.

The distinction between responses that were learned on the basis of conditioning and on the basis of law of effect was not new when Mowrer published "On the Dual Nature of Learning: A Reinterpretation of 'Conditioning' and 'Problem Solving'" in 1947. (See Woodworth, 1918; and, later, Konorski and Miller, 1937; Schlosberg, 1937; and Skinner, 1935, who brought the distinction into particularly sharp focus.) Mowrer's contribution was to describe the way in which these two types of learning were united.

After several experiments, he emphasized the importance of the intervening variable of fear in avoidance learning (Mowrer, 1939; Mowrer and Lamoreaux, 1946). For Mowrer, avoidance learning was a two-stage process in which fear became conditioned to some stimulus through sign learning. The fear produced stimuli, which then acted as a drive. Thus, fear is a secondary drive acquired as a result of conditioning. Furthermore, any instrumental behavior that reduces drive is learned through the process of solution learning. That is, fear is reduced by escaping from the conditioned stimulus that arouses it. By explaining the acquisition of fear through Pavlovian conditioning (sign learning) and the elimination of fear through Thorndikian learning (solution learning), Mowrer could account for avoidance behavior.

The best evidence to indicate that drives could be acquired and could motivate subsequent learning came from Neal Miller, a

colleague of Hull and Mowrer at Yale's Institute of Human Relations. Miller (1948) completed laboratory investigations showing that
fear could be acquired as a drive and subsequently could motivate
performance. He conditioned rats to fear an experimental chamber
through shock. Once the fear was acquired, as evidenced by agitation,
urination, and defecation when exposed to the chamber, various
responses such as turning a wheel to raise a door or pressing a lever
could be acquired to escape from a situation. The fear conditioned to
a particular situation was labeled an acquired or secondary drive
because the animal was not initially or innately fearful before conditioning. Once anxiety was established, escape to a situation not
associated with the fear could reinforce new responses. Thus, Miller's
work clearly established Mowrer's thesis that fear had motivating
properties that could in fact reinforce new learning (see Miller, 1951).

Mowrer revised his two-factor theory in *Learning Theory and
Behavior* (1960a). The revision encompassed the acquisition of fear
and avoidance reactions to reduce fear under sign learning. Fear reactions (signs of anxiety or danger) were developed by an animal
associating certain responses with environmental stimuli. Escape or
avoidance responses instrumental in removing such reactions became
signs of fear reduction or "hope." In this way Mowrer explained the
dual features of learning as sign learning, that is, as association with
particular consequences.

Mowrer's ideas were important to learning theory and its applications to clinical psychology and psychiatry. His contribution to learning was in combining conditioning and trial-and-error learning to
account for avoidance behavior. His focus upon emotional reactions
had immediate implications for psychopathology: Mowrer was suggesting that maladaptive avoidance behavior in humans might be conceptualized and, by implication, treated according to learning theory.
Specific behavior change techniques have been formulated on the
assumption that fears are acquired and maintained according to
Mowrer's original two-factor theory (despite Mowrer's revision of it).

SUMMARY AND CONCLUSIONS

Research in conditioning, reflexology, and comparative psychology
stimulated the objective study of behavior in psychology. The
methodological advances made in these areas were applied to the field
in general. Behaviorism, epitomized by the work of John B. Watson,
is credited with making explicit the methodological changes required

in psychology and insisting upon the study of overt behavior rather than private experience.

Learning became a central topic of psychological study. The Russian experiments with conditioning provided a method and a means for explaining human and animal learning. Initially the conditioning of reflex behavior was thought to account for all learning, at least in America. But soon the inadequacy of conditioning or of any single principle in explaining learning became clear. Thorndike had demonstrated learning of behaviors that could not be fit readily into the conditioning framework of Pavlov. Several other theorists, notably Guthrie, Tolman, Hull, and Mowrer, attempted to construct accounts of learning and posited different mechanisms and principles; their research has contributed to contemporary work in behavior modification.

However, the experimental foundations of behavior modification have not been delineated completely in this chapter in that the experiments of B. F. Skinner have been omitted. Skinner, who focused upon learning in a fashion similar to Thorndike, has had more impact than any other single learning theorist on behavior modification. Because of his intellectual influence—comparable to that of Watson in the early part of the century—Skinner's research and conceptualization of behavior are treated separately (see Chapter 4).

4
Operant Conditioning and the Experimental Analysis of Behavior

Skinner's approach to the study of learning has been crucial to diverse developments and applications in behavior modification. Like Hull and Mowrer before him, Skinner attempted to clarify the relationship between the learning paradigms of Pavlov and Thorndike. In each paradigm, a connection was made between a stimulus and a response. In Pavlov's paradigm, a connection was made between a new stimulus and a reflex response; in Thorndike's paradigm, a connection was made between a given stimulus and a new response. Skinner (1935, 1937, 1938) sought to clarify these models by distinguishing two types of responses and two types of conditioning. The two classes of responses were *respondents* and *operants*. Respondents are those responses that are *elicited*. Reflex responses—including salivation in response to food, a knee jerk in response to a patellar tap, and pupillary constriction in response to bright light—are examples of elicited responses. Operants refer to those responses that are not elicited by stimuli. These responses are *emitted* or performed "spontaneously." No eliciting stimulus may be detected when an operant response occurs. Respondent and operant behaviors are measured differently. The strength of a respondent usually is measured by its magnitude. In contrast, an operant usually is measured by its frequency of occurrence.

Skinner (1937) distinguished these two types of conditioning according to class of responses involved. *Type S conditioning* is the conditioning of respondent behavior. Respondent conditioning was called Type S because the reinforcement is correlated with the stimulus. That is, a conditioned stimulus is paired with an unconditioned stimulus and eventually can elicit the response. Type S conditioning refers to Pavlovian or classical conditioning. The laws of Type S conditioning are:

> The Law of Conditioning of Type S: *The approximately simultaneous presentation of two stimuli, one of which (the "reinforcing" stimulus) belongs to a reflex existing at the moment at some strength, may produce an increase in the strength of a third reflex composed of the response of the reinforcing reflex and the other stimulus.*
> The Law of Extinction of Type S: *If the reflex strengthened through conditioning of Type S is elicited without presentation of the reinforcing stimulus, its strength decreases* (Skinner, 1938, pp. 18–19).

Type R conditioning is the conditioning of operant behavior. Operant conditioning is termed Type R because the reinforcement is correlated with the response. For example, a response such as pressing a lever or escaping from a puzzle box is followed with food. Reinforcement is correlated with or contingent upon the response. Type R conditioning refers to conditioning in the manner described by Thorndike in his law of effect. The laws of Type R conditioning are:

> The Law of Conditioning of Type R: *If the occurrence of an operant is followed by presentation of a reinforcing stimulus, the strength is increased.*
> The Law of Extinction of Type R: *If the occurrence of an operant already strengthened through conditioning is not followed by the reinforcing stimulus, the strength is decreased* (Skinner, 1938, pp. 18–19).

Skinner's classification of learning into categories largely based upon Pavlovian versus Thorndikian paradigms was similar to the classifications of several others (Konorski and Miller, 1937; Miller and Konorski, 1928; Razran, 1939; Schlosberg, 1937; Thorndike, 1911). However, he sharpened the distinction and pointed to areas in which the two types of conditioning appeared indistinguishable.[1] In 1935, Skinner announced his twofold classification of conditioning, plus a pseudotype of conditioning. The pseudotype of conditioning referred to those instances in which operant responses were stimulus-correlated. For example, operant behavior can be induced in the presence of a particular stimulus. By developing a response in the

---

[1] Skinner (1935) originally saw the distinction between these learning paradigms in terms of Type I and Type II learning, which referred to conditioning in which reinforcement was correlated with the response or with the stimulus, respectively. Since Miller and Konorski (1928; Konorski and Miller, 1937) had made a similar distinction but used Type I and II conditioning in a somewhat different way, Skinner (1937) altered the terminology to avoid confusion and elaborated the differences in learning paradigms in terms of Type R and Type S conditioning.

presence of one stimulus but not in its absence, presentation of the first stimulus alone results in the response. Thus, operant behavior may become correlated with a stimulus. The response performed in the presence of a stimulus is referred to as a *discriminated operant*. It appears to be elicited in the fashion of Type S conditioning. However, the stimulus does not elicit the response in the way that reflexes are elicited. Rather, the stimulus previously associated with operant reinforcement sets the occasion for the response. The stimulus serves as a cue that reinforcing consequences are likely to follow and increases the likelihood that the response occurs.

Skinner emphasized that Type S and Type R conditioning could not always be distinguished; indeed, the two frequently occurred simultaneously. For example, when an animal approaches and consumes food, both types of conditioning probably are operative (Skinner, 1935). Conditioned stimuli associated with the approach toward food signals that food will be presented. Salivation then is elicited. Yet, eating the food reinforces emitted responses that lead to procuring food.

Similarly, it is difficult to separate respondents from operants in many practical situations. Behaviors that may begin as respondents may become operants eventually, thereby making the distinction difficult to maintain. For example, respondent behaviors such as a child's crying in response to an injury may be maintained by consequences that follow behavior. Thus, the behavior (crying) has both respondent and operant components that may be difficult to separate at any given time.

The significance of Skinner's distinction of the types of conditioning was manifold. In many early investigations of respondent conditioning, the sources of ambiguity surrounding the types of conditioning were not really recognized. Indeed, respondent and operant conditioning was investigated simultaneously in situations in which conceptual and empirical distinctions might have been made. For example, in some investigations, a conditioned stimulus (e.g., a buzzer) was presented to an animal followed by an unconditioned stimulus (food). This sequence closely follows the procedures of respondent conditioning. However, the unconditioned stimulus would not be delivered unless a particular response (e.g., head moving) occurred. That is, food was response-contingent. The response followed by the unconditioned stimulus would increase in strength (cf. Grindley, 1932; Konorski and Miller, 1937), which closely follows the procedures of operant conditioning.

Bechterev's early research in 1886-1887 exemplifies some of the earliest operant conditioning, although of course, it was not formulated in terms of reward training. Bechterev taught dogs to make specific movements such as giving the front paw or dancing on the hind paws. The dogs learned to make the movements upon demand by the experimenter providing contingent rewards (e.g., sugar) for performance of the response (Bechterev, 1933). Much of Bechterev's research on motor conditioning clearly falls within the realm of contemporary operant conditioning.

Pavlov's followers also utilized the general paradigm in which response-contingent events were delivered.[2] A series of experiments was conducted in which children obtained food and other rewards by pressing a bulb when specific neutral stimuli appeared (Ivanov-Smolensky, 1927). Similarly, in 1928, Miller and Konorski trained dogs to lift a paw by making food contingent upon leg flexion. Initially, the experimenter moved the dog's leg and rewarded the movement. Eventually, the dog learned to flex at a signal that preceded leg flexion.

Although several instances of conditioning based upon delivering response consequences had been reported, the implications of classifying different types of responses and conditioning had not been recognized clearly. Skinner elaborated these implications. Along with distinguishing the types of conditioning and sources of ambiguity between them, the significance of Skinner's early work stems from his shifting of emphasis in learning from respondent to operant behavior. Before Skinner, great stress was laid on respondent conditioning in explaining behavior. Stimulus-response psychology had adhered to the assumption that behavior could be accounted for by an eliciting stimulus (Skinner, 1938). Even if an eliciting stimulus could not be identified, it was assumed to be present. For example, Watson (1919) had defined the goal of psychology as ". . . *ascertaining of such data and laws that, given the stimulus, psychology can predict what the response will be; or, on the other hand, given the response, it can specify the nature of the stimulus*" (p. 10).

---

[2] Pavlov inadvertently noted what later would be considered to be a clear example of operant conditioning. While experimenting with a feeding method and conditioning reflex behavior, he observed that the dog could obtain food by shaking the defective apparatus (a tube through which food passed). The animal quickly learned to shake the tube repeatedly and the response occurred continuously (Pavlov, 1932). Although Pavlov described this performance in terms of stimulus substitution, the description strongly suggests that performance was a function of response-contingent food.

Skinner maintained that elicited behavior could not account for most of the responses that organisms normally perform. Thus he gave prominence to operant behavior and operant conditioning.

> Operant behavior with its unique relation to the environment presents a separate important field of investigation. The facts of respondent behavior which have been regarded as fundamental data in a science of behavior (Sherrington, Pavlov, and others) are, as we have seen, not to be extrapolated usefully to behavior as a whole nor do they constitute any very large body of information that is of value in the study of operant behavior (Skinner, 1938, p. 438).

Another contribution of Skinner was his programmatic investigation of operant behavior. From his research, he elucidated several principles of operant conditioning and discovered empirical relationships among diverse variables of the contingencies of reinforcement and behavior. Before the substantive and methodological features of his work are discussed below, Skinner's personal and intellectual development is described.

DEVELOPMENT OF OPERANT CONDITIONING

Skinner's Background and Influences on Him

As an undergraduate, Skinner had been exposed to the writings of Loeb and Pavlov. However, his interest in psychology and behaviorism did not blossom until after his undergraduate years (Skinner, 1970), when he read a series of articles by Bertrand Russell criticizing Watson's book, *Behaviorism*. These articles prompted him to learn more about Watson before beginning his graduate work at Harvard University.

At Harvard, research was more structuralist than behaviorist. Skinner's behaviorist leanings were influenced by Fred S. Keller and Charles K. Trueblood, two fellow graduate students. Keller was a behaviorist and very familiar with the language, methods, and interpretations of behaviorism. Trueblood was involved in experimental animal research. Visiting professors at Harvard, including Tolman and Walter S. Hunter, conducted experimental animal research and offered an "academic taste of behaviorism" (Keller, 1970, p. 31).

While at Harvard, Skinner read books by Ernst Mach, Henri Poincaré, and Percy Bridgman; these writings helped solidify his general positivistic approach. He met Hudson Hoagland and W. J.

Crozier (1892–1955), both of whom were in the department of general physiology at Harvard. Hoagland introduced Skinner to the writings of Rudolf Magnus and Charles Sherrington. Crozier was a direct influence on his approach toward research (see below).

At Harvard, Skinner began animal research and became interested in the concept of the reflex, evidently a result of his immersion in the works of Pavlov, Watson, Loeb, Magnus, and Sherrington.[3] He sought to study the reflex from a purely behavioral standpoint without the physiological concomitants discussed by investigators before him. His initial work focused on changes in rate of eating and drive and reflex strength, which fulfilled his thesis requirements for a doctorate at Harvard, granted in 1931.

After Skinner received his degree, Crozier supported him for two years on a fellowship. He studied the central nervous system at Harvard Medical School and continued to conduct his own animal research with laboratory space provided by Crozier. He received three years additional support from Harvard as a Junior Fellow and worked on his animal research full-time. In 1936, Skinner was hired by the University of Minnesota. In 1945, he went to Indiana University as department chairman, and then he returned to Harvard in 1948, where he has taught ever since.

Crozier's influence on Skinner seems particularly noteworthy. Crozier, who had been a student of Loeb, extended the research of his mentor by studying the responses of diverse animals to various stimuli such as light. General and specific features of Crozier's approach to research bear similarity to Skinner's position. Initially, and perhaps most importantly, Crozier advocated study of the organism as a whole. This focus derived directly from Loeb, who had published a book entitled *The Organism as a Whole* (1916). Skinner also studied the behavior of the organism as a whole and its relationship with the environment. He was interested in behavior in its own right rather than the processes of the nervous system to which it might be related.

Another similarity between Crozier and Skinner was their general attitude toward theory. Crozier tended to eschew theory in favor of a

---

[3] It is of interest to note that Leonard Troland (1889–1932) of Harvard investigated the reflex. He theorized about the influence of environmental stimuli on behavior, described in his book, *The Fundamentals of Human Motivation* (1928). In this book, he discussed influences on behavior that resembled Skinner's later distinction between positive and aversive events. Presumably Skinner and Troland were aware of each other's work—Troland was on the committee that approved Skinner's doctoral thesis. Despite the similarities between their work, Troland appears to have exerted no influence on Skinner (Herrnstein, 1972). Skinner's approach to the study of reflexes had its roots in the work of physiologists.

strong base of empirically established relationships. He viewed the primary task of research as describing relationships between independent and dependent variables after which interpretation of behavior was possible (Crozier and Hoagland, 1934). Skinner, too, has emphasized the priority of establishing empirical relationships rather than generating theory.

Features of Crozier's research methodology also were apparent in Skinner's subsequent work. Crozier advocated single-organism research. Experimental control could be demonstrated by obtaining measures of the individual organism as a number of values or parametric variations of the experimental condition were invoked. He believed that the variability of an organism's response at any time was a function of external conditions and changes in that organism. He viewed variation as lawful rather than random. The task of research was to determine the factors of which such variation was a function. Crozier advocated looking at experimental effects over time in light of intrasubject variability in behavior rather than merely comparing means across conditions or characterizing the variability statistically. Skinner's research has amplified the importance of studying the individual organism, its variations in behavior, and the conditions of which the variation is a function.[4]

Evolution of Skinner's Research: An Overview

Skinner's research goal was to discover lawful behavioral processes of the organism as a whole (Skinner, 1956). He focused upon animal behavior and was interested in describing lawful relations without theorizing about abstract physiological processes to account for them. In this regard, his approach resembled that of Crozier, who investigated behavior and avoided conjecture about the nervous system. Pavlov's research also influenced Skinner, but he was interested in the behavior Pavlov studied rather than his speculations about neurological processes.

Skinner used the white rat as an experimental subject. His first research pertained to the animal's response to novel stimuli; later, he studied postural reflexes. As part of his experiments, he often designed equipment that allowed him to observe select responses that could

---

[4] In comparing the methodological features of Crozier and Skinner, it is important not to exaggerate the overlap. Crozier's own approach included features not apparent in Skinner's work. For example, Crozier relied heavily upon mathematical models and derived predictions deductively. Skinner's initial research was formulated in mathematical terms occasionally, e.g., his research in which eating was studied as a power function in time (cf. Herrnstein, 1972). However, mathematical models *per se* have not been advocated by Skinner.

easily be recorded. Skinner (1956) has traced the evolution of his research and the changes in equipment that partially guided and led him to the research topics of operant conditioning.

An apparatus used early in his research was a tunnel in which a rat was placed. To study the animal's adaptation to novel stimuli, a click sounded when the rat emerged from the tunnel. The rat would re-enter the tunnel at the sound. After repeated exposures, it would retreat less and less. Skinner manually recorded the advances and retreats of the rat by moving a pen back and forth across a moving paper tape. In subsequent experiments, the apparatus took over this manual function so that these data could be gathered automatically. The automatic recording of data greatly facilitated later experimentation in operant conditioning.

One early piece of equipment was a runway attached to a kymograph that would record vibrations caused by running. To improve running over repeated trials, Skinner provided a back alley to allow rats to return to the beginning of the runway after a single trial. Food (wet mash) was given to the animals after they left the runway and ran down the alley. However, animals hesitated after traversing the runway obtaining the food before returning to the start of the runway. Skinner timed and plotted these pauses that appeared to show orderly changes. He modified the equipment to make the delivery of food automatic after completion of traveling the runway. The movement of the rat down the runway tilted it on its fulcrum. The tilt was recorded on a slow-moving kymograph and advanced the food dispenser (magazine) so that the animal received food. The kymograph was modified to produce a curve to record the movement caused by running. The curve of cumulative responses readily revealed changes in response rate.

Eventually the runway was eliminated, and Skinner observed the rat simply reaching for food by removing the cover of a tray (Skinner, 1930). Movements of the cover were recorded automatically with the cumulative curve used with the previous apparatus. The curve showed that the rate of eating declined over time. To further investigate rate of responding to obtain food, he modified the apparatus, which now included a horizontal bar or lever that could be pressed by the rat (Skinner, 1932). Depressing the lever closed a switch that operated the food magazine. The response was recorded automatically on a cumulative record of lever-pressing. Once the food magazine jammed and the apparatus broke down, and the cessation of food delivery resulted in extinction curves. Skinner repaired the equipment, but eventually he deliberately disconnected the apparatus to study extinction.

The evolution of experimental apparatus culminated in the construction of a soundproof box with a lever, a food magazine, and a cumulative recorder. The apparatus has come to be known as a "Skinner box." An early version is shown in Figure 4.1. The lever-pressing responses are recorded automatically on a graph of the total number of responses plotted over time. The records are made by a slow kymograph and vertically moving pin. Each response moves the pin an equal distance and produces a step-like line. The slope of the response record reflects the rate of response. The steeper the slope, the higher the rate of responding. These slopes are illustrated in Figure 4.2.

In the classic operant conditioning experiment, the animal is first trained to operate the food magazine. Magazine training begins by placing a rat in a cage into which food pellets are discharged from the magazine for a specific period of time. The magazine produces a sound when food is delivered. The rat learns to discriminate between the presence of the tray alone and the tray plus the sound of the food magazine operating. Eventually, the rat comes to the magazine only when it hears the sound. After magazine training, the conditioning experiment can begin. Operant conditioning in the usual experimental

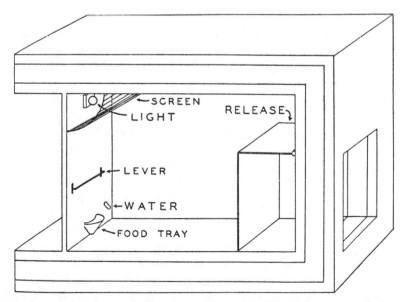

Figure 4.1. A typical experimental box constructed by Skinner. One side has been cut away to show the part occupied by the animal. The space behind the panel at the left contains the rest of the lever, the food magazine, and other pieces of apparatus. (From Skinner, 1938; reprinted by permission from Prentice-Hall, Inc.)

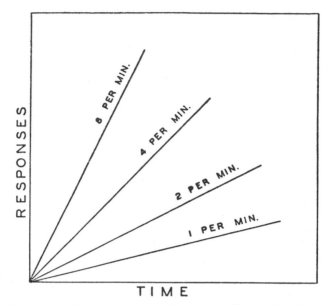

Figure 4.2. Lever-pressing responses plotted over time. The number of responses per minute represented by each slope is indicated. The actual records are step-like. (From Skinner, 1938; reprinted by permission from Prentice-Hall, Inc.)

situation refers to the increase in responding that results from providing some event (usually food) contingent upon responding (usually lever- or key-pressing). Using this basic procedure, Skinner investigated various phenomena, including delayed reinforcement, extinction, spontaneous recovery, reconditioning, schedules of reinforcement, discrimination training, response differentiation, deprivation, the effect of drugs on conditioning and extinction, and others. Skinner's early research in operant conditioning was synthesized in his book *The Behavior of Organisms: An Experimental Analysis* (1938).

In the 1930s and 1940s, Skinner used the methods of operant conditioning to study such topics as inherited maze behavior, the effects of drugs and food deprivation on acquisition and extinction, and reaction time. At the University of Minnesota, he and several colleagues attempted to apply operant methods to devise a guidance system for air-to-ground missiles. The system was based upon the performance of pigeons that had been trained to respond to patterns of visual stimuli in the missile to keep it on target. Training the pigeons required developing responses to diverse stimulus patterns, sustaining performance under intermittent reinforcement, and devising a complex apparatus to simulate conditions of combat.

After Skinner came to Harvard in 1948, he established a pigeon laboratory and conducted extensive research on operant conditioning. From 1951 to 1955, Charles B. Ferster, who received his doctorate at Columbia University, was an assistant in Skinner's laboratory. Ferster and Skinner collaborated on an elaborate series of studies which culminated in *Schedules of Reinforcement* (1957). During this time, Skinner also set up a laboratory at the Metropolitan State Hospital in Waltham, Massachusetts to study operant behavior of psychotic patients. This research initiated important applications of operant conditioning with heterogeneous treatment populations and is discussed in Chapter 5.

OPERANT CONDITIONING AND THE EXPERIMENTAL ANALYSIS OF BEHAVIOR

To understand subsequent developments in behavior modification, it is important to distinguish separate aspects of Skinner's research. First, he elaborated basic principles of operant conditioning and variables that contribute to operant performance. An extremely diverse set of behavior modification techniques has been derived from these basic principles. Second, he adhered to a particular conceptual and methodological approach toward behavior and its investigation. Although this approach was related directly to the substantive questions Skinner addressed, it transcends the content of operant conditioning. The substantive principles that Skinner has described are referred to collectively as the principles of operant conditioning. The conceptual and methodological approach of operant research is called the experimental analysis of behavior.

Basic Principles of Operant Conditioning

The principles of operant conditioning describe the relationship between behavior and the environmental events that influence it.[5] Most of the principles describe the effects of consequences that follow behavior. The basic principles of operant conditioning include reinforcement, punishment, extinction, and stimulus control.

Reinforcement   The principle of reinforcement refers to an increase in the frequency of a response that is immediately followed by certain consequences. Any consequence increasing the frequency of behavior is called a *reinforcer*. Positive and negative reinforcers

---

[5] Numerous books are available that describe operant conditioning principles and concepts in detail (e.g., Catania, 1968; Ferster, Culbertson, and Boren, 1975; Holland and Skinner, 1961; Keller, 1954; Reynolds, 1968; Skinner, 1953a; Williams, 1973).

constitute the two kinds of events that can increase the frequency of a response. Positive reinforcers are events presented after a response that increase its frequency. Negative reinforcers refer to events that are removed after a response and increase the frequency of the response that preceded their removal. Events that serve as positive or negative reinforcers are defined solely by the effects they exert on behavior.

There are two variations of the reinforcement principle. *Positive reinforcement* is an increase in the frequency of a response that is followed by a positive reinforcer. *Negative reinforcement* refers to an increase in the frequency of a response that is followed by removal of an aversive event. A common laboratory example of positive reinforcement is delivery of food to an animal contingent upon pressing a bar. An example of negative reinforcement is the termination of shock contingent upon bar-pressing. In these examples, bar-pressing increases as a function either of food delivery or cessation of shock.

Punishment   Punishment refers to the presentation or withdrawal of an event contingent upon a response that decreases the probability of the response. As with reinforcement, the principle specifies not only a procedure but also the effect of that procedure on behavior. The two variations of punishment correspond to the variations of reinforcement. The variations are the presentation of an aversive event or removal of a positive event, either of which will decrease the behavior they follow.[6] A laboratory example of the first variation of punishment is the presentation of shock when an animal presses the bar, which will bring about a suppression of bar-pressing. The second variation is illustrated by withdrawal of the food magazine after a response.

Extinction   Extinction means discontinuing delivery of a reinforcer after a response. Extinction differs from punishment, although both operations result in reduced frequency of the response. With punishment, an aversive event follows a response or a positive event is taken away. With extinction, no consequence actually follows a response, i.e., an event is not delivered or taken away. Instead, an event that was administered previously for the response is no longer provided. A laboratory example of extinction is termination of the delivery of food for bar-pressing. Once food no longer follows bar-pressing, extinction eventually leads to its reduction and elimination.

---

[6] The removal of a positive event that results in a decreased response also is referred to as time-out from reinforcement if the positive event is withdrawn for a specific period of time (cf. Ferster, 1957).

Stimulus Control   Operant behavior is influenced by antecedent events as well as consequences. The control of antecedent stimuli results from associating different consequences for a particular response across different stimuli. A response may be followed with a reinforcing or punishing consequence in the presence of one stimulus (referred to as S^D or S^+) but not in the presence of another (referred to as a S^Δ or S^-). For example, when a response is reinforced in one situation but not in another situation, behavior comes under the control of the different situations. The situation previously associated with reinforcement of the response will increase the probability that the response is performed when compared to the situation previously associated with no reinforcement. When an organism responds differentially to different stimuli, it has made a *discrimination* and behavior is considered to be under *stimulus control*. For example, in the laboratory, the concept of stimulus control is illustrated by reinforcing bar-pressing when a red light above the bar is on but not when a green light is on. After differentially reinforcing behavior on the basis of the different stimulus conditions, turning on the red (S^D) or green (S^Δ) light will lead to bar-pressing or cessation of bar-pressing, respectively. The stimulus conditions exert control over behavior because of the different contingencies with which each stimulus is associated.

Other Concepts and Variables   The basic principles of operant conditioning and their operations and effects on behavior are summarized in Table 4.1. The basic principles are presented in a general form. Thus, distinctions among the kinds of operations for a given principle are omitted. For example, different types of operations are subsumed under reinforcement. Negative reinforcement alone encompasses several procedures for escape and avoidance training. Although Table 4.1 lists the basic operations accurately, it implies that specific operations invariably result in certain effects on behavior. The influence of antecedent and consequent events on behavior is determined by multiple factors. Hence, the interrelationships of the environment and behavior are complex and reflect a dynamic rather than static interaction. (The complexities of the relationships of operant consequences and behavior are highlighted later in this chapter.)

Another crucial determinant of operant behavior is the schedule of reinforcement (see Morse and Kelleher, 1970; Skinner, 1938; Zeiler, 1977). Reinforcement schedules are the rules used for providing reinforcing stimuli. They specify the conditions that must be met

Table 4.1. Summary of basic principles of operant conditioning

Principle	Characteristic procedure or operation	Effect on behavior
Reinforcement	Presentation or removal of an event after a response	Increases the frequency of the response
Punishment	Presentation or removal of an event after a response	Decreases the frequency of the response
Extinction	Ceasing presentation of a reinforcing event after a response	Decreases the frequency of the previously reinforced response
Stimulus control and discrimination training	Reinforcing the response in the presence of one stimulus (S^D) but not in the presence of another (S^Δ)	Increases the frequency of the response in the presence of the S^D and decreases the frequency of the response in the presence of the S^Δ

for a reinforcer to be delivered. Extensive research has demonstrated that the development, maintenance, rate, and pattern of responding are shaped by the manner in which reinforcing consequences are scheduled. Among the many types of schedules, the most widely studied are those based upon the administration of consequences according to the number of responses performed and the temporal pattern of responding (Ferster and Skinner, 1957). Schedules may vary according to whether consequences are provided for a predetermined number of responses or time period or are presented at random and independent of responding. The diverse schedules reveal systematic and orderly effects within individual subjects and are highly replicable across subjects (Morse, 1966; Zeiler, 1977).

Several secondary concepts, experimental conditions, and variations of the contingencies influence behavior. Concepts important in the operant analysis of behavior include primary and conditioned reinforcement, shaping, chaining, generalization, and the Premack principle. Such experimental conditions as the magnitude, immediacy, and quality of the consequences that follow behavior and the contingencies that operate on other behaviors affect reinforcement and punishment. Finally, variations in the type of reinforcing and punishing stimuli, procedures for enhancing response acquisition and maintenance, and characteristics of the desired response classes dictate the effects of different operations on behavior.

The Experimental Analysis of Behavior

Skinner adhered to a particular approach in conceptualizing the subject matter of psychology and in conducting research. He was adamant about the importance of establishing empirical relations between environmental events and behavior. Research was to describe these relationships and not generate theory and models of behavior. Skinner is known for his opposition to theory construction. Theory, in the sense that he has used the word, refers to ". . . any explanation of observed fact which appeals to events taking place somewhere else, at some other level of observation described in different terms, and measured, if at all, in different dimensions" (Skinner, 1950, p. 193). Skinner has acknowledged that empirical statements are never wholly free of theory. Certain basic assumptions and predictive statements make most proposals theoretical in some sense, and he did not object to that aspect of theory. However, he rejected theories expressing empirical findings in terms not confirmed by the same methods of observation used to obtain them.

Skinner's rejection of theory was directed primarily at theories that relied on intervening variables and hypothetical constructs in the organism. He reacted against theorists who posited an S-O-R interpretation of learning in which O referred to aspects of the organism rather than well-grounded stimulus and response components (Keehn, 1972).[7] He has been opposed particularly to statements made about the central nervous system in explaining behavior, which he relabeled the conceptual nervous system (Skinner, 1938). He objected to explanations of behavior made in terms of physiological functioning. He noted: ". . . no fact of the nervous system has yet ever told anyone anything new about behavior, and from the point of view of a descriptive science this is the only criterion to be taken into account" (Skinner, 1938, p. 425). Skinner's argument was not aimed at ruling out relationships between findings at one level (e.g., physiology) and findings at another (e.g., behavior). However, he did feel that such explanations were separate. Moreover, even to begin explanations across levels requires a complete description of behavior at its own level. Skinner advocated a science of behavior in which description and explanation are on the direct level of behavioral observation. Explanations of behavior do not have to appeal to natural sciences such as physiology or to abstract theoretical notions within psychology. Laws of behavior are valid in their own right.

Skinner's rejection of theory was an outgrowth of his view of scientific progress. He viewed theory as something constructed to compensate for inadequate data or imperfect control over the subject matter. That is, theory develops from a lack of understanding of the basic phenomena of interest. The methodology advocated by Skinner directly reveals behavior and the variables of which it is a function. Experimental control is achieved through a functional analysis, i.e., an analysis of behavior in terms of cause and effect relationships in which the causes themselves are manipulated directly. When control can be demonstrated unambiguously and the relevant variables identified, theories of behavior, he maintains, have little value (Skinner, 1956).

---

[7] Skinner originally adopted a concept in his own formulation of behavior that had the status of an intervening variable. The concept was "reflex reserve," meaning a reservoir of responses that were ready to be emitted during extinction (Skinner, 1938, p. 26). He subsequently rejected the concept because it did not contribute any useful explanation (Skinner, 1950). The phenomenon that the concept was used to explain is now called resistance to extinction. This latter term is descriptive of the extent to which responses do or do not decline when the previously administered reinforcer is no longer provided.

Skinner is acknowledged for his rigorous insistence on a science of behavior. He emphasized "pure behavior" and provided a method of study that could be applied widely. Of course, behavior was a topic in its own right with no need to appeal to other levels of analysis, and it had been studied by investigators stressing objectivity and precision such as Pavlov, Bechterev, Watson, and Thorndike. However, they had relied on physiological analysis or abstractions that went beyond the data. Skinner's approach toward the subject matter of psychology at the descriptive level of behavior is bound up inextricably with the methods he employed to study operant responding, the use of frequency or response rate as the experimental datum, and the focus on the individual organism.

Operant Responding   The notion of operant responding has obvious substantive implications. Operants refer to classes of behavior rather than to isolated responses (see Schick, 1971). A response class is defined by those behaviors that meet the requirements for reinforcement in a given situation. Responses that share the property required to obtain the reinforcer are part of the operant. Thus, there are no inherent limitations set by preexisting responses of the organism on what an operant will be. The notion of an operant as a class of responses defined largely by the contingency widens the range of behaviors that can be studied as compared to predefined response units such as reflexes. Operant behavior refers to performance that influences or operates on the environment and which constitutes the majority of human behaviors. Thus, principles explaining the development, maintenance, and elimination of operants are likely to have wide generality.

Operant behavior has been investigated in experimental situations that permitted free responding. Free-operant responding means that the response can occur repeatedly without discrete trials or interruptions. Free-operant responding allows the rate of responding to assume a wide range of values within a given period. Thus the direct influence of experimental manipulations can be readily determined by differences in response rate.

Lever- or bar-pressing is the response most commonly used in operant conditioning research, one that has been used in testing various animal species and human populations. Lever-pressing can be performed by many species despite differences in anatomy and response repertoires. The utility of the operant method can be seen by comparing laboratory responses of three different animals under a

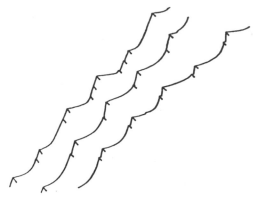

Figure 4.3. Cumulative records of a pigeon, rat, and monkey for a given schedule of reinforcement. (From Skinner, 1972, p. 119; reprinted by permission from Prentice-Hall, Inc.)

complex reinforcement schedule. Figure 4.3 shows that pigeons, rats, and monkeys respond similarly to a given schedule of reinforcement. These similarities in responding suggest that certain basic behavioral processes are common among organisms. The generalization possible with operant responding and its sensitivity to assorted experimental manipulations has led to its adoption in other areas of research.

Frequency or Rate of Responding   The recording of frequency or rate of responding (frequency as a function of time) as the experimental datum provides distinct advantages:

1. Frequency of responses is an *extremely orderly datum*. The curves which represent its relations to many types of independent variables are encouragingly simple and smooth.

2. The results are *easily reproduced*. It is seldom necessary to resort to groups of subjects at this stage. The method permits a direct view of behavioral processes which have hitherto been only inferred. We often have as little use for statistical control as in the simple observation of objects in the world about us. If the essential features of a given curve are not readily duplicated in a later experiment—in either the same or another organism—we take this, not as a cue to resort to averages, but as a warning that some relevant condition has still to be discovered and controlled. In other words, the uniformity of our results encourages us to turn, not to sampling procedures, but to more rigorous experimental control.

3. As a result of (2), the concepts and laws which emerge from this sort of study have an *immediate reference* to the behavior of the individual which is lacking in concepts or laws which are the products of statistical operations. When we extend an experimental analysis to human affairs in general, it is a great advantage to have a conceptual system which refers to the single individual, preferably without com-

parison with a group. A more direct application to the prediction and control of the individual is thus achieved. The study of frequency of response appears to lead directly to such a system.

4. Frequency of response provides a *continuous* account of many basic processes. We can follow a curve of extinction, for example, for many hours, and the condition of the response at every moment is apparent in our records. This is in marked contrast to methods and techniques which merely sample a learning process from time to time, where the continuity of the process must be inferred. The samples are often so widely spaced that the kinds of details we see in these records are missed.

5. We must not forget the considerable advantage of a datum which lends itself to *automatic experimentation*. Many processes in behavior cover long periods of time. The records we obtain from an individual organism may cover hundreds of hours and report millions of responses. We characteristically use experimental periods of eight, ten, or even fifteen hours. Personal observation of such material is unthinkable.

6. Perhaps most important of all, frequency of response is a valuable datum just because it provides *a substantial basis for the concept of probability of action*—a concept toward which a science of behavior seems to have been groping for many decades (Skinner, 1953b, p. 77).

In addition, the use of frequency has some intuitive appeal because it dovetails with beliefs about the learning process. As learning increases so does rate of responding; as unlearned (extinction or forgetting) takes place, the rate declines.

The utility of frequency was augmented by plotting responses over time as a cumulative record. Graphing responses as a cumulative record allows interpretation of the overall rate and characteristics of performance, as the effect of experimental manipulations can be seen immediately upon behavior. Use of a cumulative record also allows a large amount of data to be collected and interpreted relatively easily through visual inspection. Because behavior change can be observed directly, statistical analyses of the data are not necessary. The effects of the experimental manipulation need not be "teased out" to reveal the behavioral process. Skinner drew an analogy between the use of rate of behavior and the cumulative record to the use of a microphone or telescope in other sciences. The tool makes the phenomenon under study directly visible (Skinner, 1956).

The study of frequency of behavior provided a major methodological advance for psychology in general, and behaviorism in particular. As Skinner noted, if the goal of a science of behavior is to predict and possibly control behavior, then the dependent variable must address the probability of a response. The task of a science of behavior is to explain the conditions that dictate response probability. Rate of responding, although not a direct measure of probability, comes close enough to make predictions about behaviors.

Study of the Individual Organism   A major feature of the experimental analysis of behavior is the focus on the individual subject rather than on the performance of a large group, as is common in traditional psychological experimentation. The purpose of the experimental analysis of behavior is to reveal behavioral processes of the individual. Data based upon group performance reveal changes made in the "average" organism and may not represent the performance of any individual subject whose data were used to achieve the average (Skinner, 1950). The experimental analysis of behavior governs the performance of the individual by controlling sources of variability and demonstrating over time the variables of which behavior is a function. The goal is to produce orderliness in the behavior of the single subject, which will allow development of a "science of the individual" (Skinner, 1956).[8]

The study of the individual requires experimental designs that differ from those used in between-group research. Experimental design is not used in the experimental analysis of behavior in quite the same way as in traditional experiments. Customarily, the designs are based on preplanned arrangements of the experimental situation. In the experimental analysis of behavior, the design is not completely preplanned or conducted in an unvarying fashion to meet *a priori* requirements. Rather, the design is improvised and changed as a function of the data (Skinner, 1969). Because the effect of a variable upon behavior is immediately evident, the experimental contingency can be altered as soon as such effects become apparent.

The experimental designs used for single-subject research are called intrasubject-replication designs (Sidman, 1960). The effect of a given variable is usually replicated over time for one or a few subjects. The effect of a manipulation is evaluated against premanipulation or baseline performance rates. The point is to demonstrate experimental control of the individual subject so that performance will be predictable over time (e.g., across sessions). The extent to which behavior

---

[8] Characteristically, Skinner has studied the individual organism, observing a single subject or a few subjects intensively. However, for a brief period at the University of Minnesota (in collaboration with W. T. Heron), he did conduct large between-group investigations in which mean performance and average learning curves were studied rather than the individual organism.

changes as a function of a given variable is determined by comparing the individual subject's performances across different conditions replicated over time. After the effect of a given variable is demonstrated, the performance levels under conditions without the manipulation usually can be recovered by withdrawing or altering the manipulation. Before evaluating the influence of a given variable, a stable baseline performance is required. The variable then is manipulated. If behavior changes, the premanipulation condition may be reinstated to recover operant performance levels.

Examples of the type of design and experimental demonstration are shown in Figures 4.4 and 4.5. They record demonstrations of shock on performance in two monkeys. In these demonstrations, lever-pressing was established and maintained for food reinforcement under a particular schedule (variable interval reinforcement). The manipulation consisted of presenting unavoidable shock that was preceded by a clicking stimulus for a five-minute period. As shown in Figure 4.4, performance rate is stable before shock is applied. Delivery of the shock terminated lever-pressing (horizontal line). Once the shock ceased, the monkeys returned to the previous stable rate of performance. The results suggested that the manipulation was responsible for the pause in responding. The demonstration is more convincing in Figure 4.5, which shows that the clicking and shock were presented nine different times. Shock was associated consistently with the termination of responding whereas baseline conditions were not. These data provide a simple demonstration that the stimulus presentation suppressed performance.

Automation of the Experimental Situation   An important characteristic of operant research has been its reliance upon automated electrical apparatus. Use of such equipment has had distinct advantages. First, responses such as lever- or bar-pressing are recorded automatically during an experiment. For a response to activate the equipment, a certain unvarying criterion is met (e.g., pressure). The response is detected and recorded reliably because human judgment need not decide if a response has occurred. The unvarying standard eliminates one source of variability in assessment.

Second, presentation of antecedent stimuli and response consequences can be programmed automatically. The ability to program equipment allows for complex variations in arranging the environment that otherwise would not be feasible if an experimenter were required to carry out the procedures constantly. Also, the reliability of administering a contingency is maximized with automation.

Third, a cumulative record of behavior is plotted automatically, which means that response records can be interpreted during the experiment. The effects of a given manipulation are immediately obvious and do not have to be subjected to complex statistical analyses in order to evaluate them. In addition, the immediacy of the results allows the experimenter to alter experimental conditions on the spot to determine the variables of which behavior is a function. In general, the use of automated equipment allows completion of complex experiments over extended periods. Once the equipment is

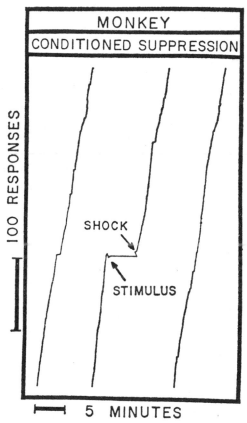

Figure 4.4. A cumulative record of a monkey's lever-pressing behavior. The ongoing baseline behavior is clearly disrupted by a stimulus that precedes unavoidable shock. After the shock, the animal returns to its normal performance. (From *Tactics of Scientific Research: Evaluating Experimental Data in Psychology,* by Murray Sidman, p. 89. Copyright 1960 by Basic Books, Inc., Publishers, New York.)

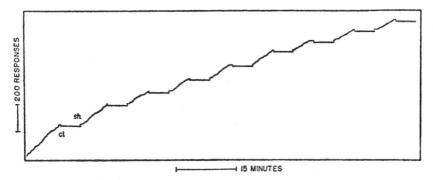

Figure 4.5. Nine intrasubject replications, within a single session, of the behavioral change illustrated in Figure 4.4. (From *Tactics of Scientific Research: Evaluating Experimental Data in Psychology,* by Murray Sidman, p. 90. Copyright 1960 by Basic Books, Inc., Publishers, New York.)

programmed, the experiments can be completed without the direct supervision of the experimenter.

Overview of Laboratory Research in Operant Conditioning

Characteristically, research in operant conditioning uses rats, pigeons, or monkeys. The behavior of individual animals is observed for extended periods of time, often including daily sessions over several days. The experiment is programmed automatically so that the apparatus handles both the assessment of response rate and the implementation of the experimental manipulations. The data for individual organisms, who are exposed to each manipulation, usually are entered in detail on cumulative records. This general method has been used in diverse areas of investigation, such as schedules of reinforcement, stimulus control, conditioned reinforcement, punishment, avoidance, concurrent operants, superstitious behavior, and behavioral pharmacology. The investigative focus of each of these areas is highlighted below.

Schedules of reinforcement refers to the ways in which discriminative or reinforcing stimuli are presented in relation to responses. Research has explored such questions as the influences of diverse schedules on acquisition and extinction, reinforcement for specific response characteristics such as interresponse times or high or low rates of behavior, and variations in frequency and magnitude of reinforcement on schedule effects.

Stimulus control is the extent to which antecedent stimuli determine the probability of a response taking place. Research has examined the conditions required to establish stimulus control, factors that control generalization across stimuli, and differences in performances as a function of learning to discriminate with and without errors in responding.

Conditioned reinforcement is concerned with transforming nonreinforcing events into reinforcers through conditioning. Research has focused on such topics as the conditions necessary to establish the reinforcing value of neutral stimuli, how responses are maintained by stimuli previously associated with reinforcing events, how sequences or chains of behaviors are maintained under different reinforcement schedules, and the consequent and discriminative functions of conditioned stimuli.

Punishment means the administration of consequences contingent upon a response that reduces the frequency of that response. Punishment research has focused on factors that contribute to response suppression and recovery, effects of different aversive consequences on behavior, withdrawal of positive events, reinforcement variables that contribute to punishment, and the side effects of punishment.

Avoidance behavior refers to postponing or preventing the delivery of aversive events. Research has centered upon variables affecting acquisition and extinction of avoidance responses, signaled versus unsignaled aversive events, temporal discriminations important in avoidance, and stimulus control and generalization in avoidance learning.

Concurrent operants is the term for simultaneous conditioning of two or more responses, each of which may be controlled by different contingencies. The influence of different reinforcement schedules, punishment, and conditioned reinforcement, and the differences in behaviors as a function of exposure to a given manipulation in isolation or as part of concurrent operant conditioning have been investigated.

Superstitious behaviors are those changes that result from repeated presentation of a reinforcer soon after, yet independent of behavior. The noncontingent delivery of consequences increases the rate of actions performed at the time the reinforcer was delivered. Aspects of superstitious behavior that have been studied include the temporal relations between response consequences and behavior, extinction of superstitious behavior, stimulus control, and the dominant responses of species that may contribute to a particular response topography.

Behavioral pharmacology assesses the effects of drugs on behavior. Research has evaluated the effects of different classes of drugs, the relationship between dose and response, the temporal course of a drug's effects, side effects of drugs, and the influence of drugs on such basic operant processes as reinforcement, punishment, stimulus control, and schedules of reinforcement.

The above list cites subjects that have been paid detailed attention in the literature (Catania, 1968; Honig, 1966; Honig and Staddon, 1977). Along with these topics, operant methods have been used extensively elsewhere: the study of sensory processes, in which operant responding is used to detect the sensory capacities and threshold levels of different animals; sensory reinforcement, in which special reinforcers involving sensory stimuli (such as visual or auditory stimulation), as well as the conditions under which such events become reinforcing are studied; the study of brain functions, in which anatomical, neurological, physiological, and pharmacological variables that contribute to brain stimulation are examined; space-flight research, in which the stresses of space launch, reentry, and living in space for extended periods are evaluated through operant responding; and physiological research, in which somatic correlates of behavioral processes such as changes in respiratory, cardiovascular, neurophysiological, and endocrine functions are studied.

Not all areas of laboratory operant research have relied upon animal subjects. Operant methods have been extended to study normal infants, children, adolescents and adults, as well as diverse psychiatric populations. For example, workers in programmed instruction have tested variables with humans; they have experimented with specific methods of programming materials that are to be learned, the manner in which individuals emit their responses, factors that control learning, including immediacy and magnitude of reinforcement, and the use of prompts. The extension of operant conditioning research to human behavior is the subject of Chapter 7.

Complexities of Operant Conditioning

Descriptions of the basic principles and areas of research in operant conditioning do not convey the complexity of the relationships of antecedent and consequent events to behavior change. Often operant behavior is discussed as being a function of different kinds of consequences labeled "reinforcers" or "punishers." However, particular consequences are not invariably one or the other. The focus on *events* in the environment that can alter behavior draws attention away from the complex and dynamic characteristics of behavior and behavior change.

The effect of a particular consequence on behavior often depends on several factors. Events such as food are not invariably positive reinforcers and their power is bound up with such diverse entities as the level of deprivation and the particular food used. Electric shock, usually considered to suppress behavior, can be made to increase or decrease behavior depending on the manner in which it is scheduled. Often identical consequences can have opposite effects on behavior, their result depending on schedule variations. For example, scheduling will determine if intracranial brain stimulation of a given intensity and location is to be a positively reinforcing or punishing event. Similarly, physical activity, visual and auditory stimuli, and injection of drugs can serve as positive reinforcers or punishing stimuli (Kish, 1966; Morse and Kelleher, 1977; Premack, 1971). Changes in magnitude, intensity, or duration of a given event also can determine whether it is a positive reinforcer or a punishing event. For example, responses that produce intracranial stimulation usually will increase in frequency as intensity or duration of stimulation is increased over a specific range of values, gradually decrease as these variables are increased, and eventually cease (Morse and Kelleher, 1977).

The experimental history of the organism also contributes to the effect of a given contingency. The delivery of an event such as shock may or may not suppress the behavior it follows if the subject has been exposed to shock previously in the context of punishment or avoidance schedules. Presentation of shock independent of responding can increase the responding of animals previously conditioned on avoidance schedules (Morse and Kelleher, 1977). The influence of history is illustrated further by the effects of variations in the magnitude of reinforcement, which are in part controlled by the magnitude of reinforcement previously delivered for the response.

Identifying specific conditions upon which the effect of a given contingency depends still does not convey the complexity of predicting behavior change. Complex interactions among variables also determine the direction and extent of behavior change. The type of events delivered, the manner in which they are scheduled, stimulus intensity, concurrent contingencies, and other factors contribute to behavior change. For example, the suppressive effects of an aversive stimulus of a given intensity depend upon the schedule of reinforcement maintaining the response to be suppressed, the level of deprivation of the positive reinforcer, and the concurrent contingencies for other responses (Azrin and Holz, 1966; Morse and Kelleher, 1977). An aversive event may suppress a response maintained under one schedule of reinforcement but not a response maintained on another schedule, or may suppress a response under low levels of deprivation but not under high levels, or when concurrent contingencies provide the reinforcer for other responses but not when response alternatives are absent.

Just as factors related to the delivery of consequences determine the effect of the contingency, so do characteristics of the response itself. Although the principles of operant conditioning are formulated generally, difficulties may emerge when they are applied across behaviors. Some behaviors are much more readily alterable than others (Dunham, 1977; Hinde, 1973). For example, presentation of a positively reinforcing event can much more readily alter a response involving a discrete activity than a response involving little or no activity. It is difficult to use a reinforcer to decrease the level of responding or to develop a response such as "standing still" (Blough, 1958; Morse and Kelleher, 1977).

Rate of responding also determines the effect of a contingency. A response with a relatively low frequency can be more readily increased than one with a higher frequency. Indeed, the ability of a given event to serve as a reinforcer may depend in part on the rate of responding. At low rates, some events have been shown not to affect performance, whereas at higher rates some events may be incentives (Goldberg, 1973). In other cases, making an event already demonstrated as a "positive reinforcer" contingent upon a response that is performed relatively frequently decreases rather than increases behavior (Skinner and Morse, 1958). Rate of responding also determines the effect of specific condition of reinforcement. For example, changing the magnitude of reinforcement sometimes readily alters behavior when the rate of responding is low, but not when it is relatively high (Morse, 1966).

More general complexities of operant conditioning than contingencies based upon response rate have been found when investigating the contingencies of reinforcement, particularly the extensions of conditioning principles. Breland and Breland (1961, 1966) have extended operant conditioning beyond the usual range of laboratory animals and have encountered response patterns that seem to violate the contingencies of reinforcement. Specifically, when conditioning some responses in an animal, stereotyped response patterns often evolve that are not explained readily by the operant consequences programmed in the situation. Animals occasionally develop response patterns that compete with the receipt of reinforcement. The response to be conditioned may be learned and performed adequately but eventually breaks down as competing behaviors surface and interfere with the learned response. For example, a pig was trained to deposit wooden coins in a container to obtain food. Although the response was learned, the animal increasingly engaged in competing behaviors such as dropping, throwing, and rooting the coins. These behaviors postponed the delivery of food. Increasing food deprivation did not alter these behaviors. Indeed, the competing behaviors continued to gain in strength. Breland and Breland (1961) noted similar examples with different species in which the conditioned response was lost gradually, although operant consequences continued to be delivered. Because the behaviors interfering with the learned response resemble responses exhibited by animals in the natural habitat and are connected with consummatory behavior, these authors labeled the phenomenon "instinctive drift." They suggested that instinctive drift represents response patterns not readily explained by operant conditioning principles.

Only a fraction of the complexities of operant conditioning and the effects of reinforcement contingencies have been mentioned, and many other examples are available. Operant responses such as keypecking in birds can be generated through Pavlovian conditioning (Brown and Jenkins, 1968; Schwartz and Gamzu, 1977). The response is instilled merely by pairing a conditioned stimulus (e.g., a lighted disc) and an unconditioned stimulus (e.g., food). No operant consequences need to be provided to attain the response (see Moore, 1973). As another example, altering behavior by contingent delivery of a particular reinforcer may increase the frequency of other behaviors that are not directly reinforced. Specifically, food reinforcement for bar-pressing can markedly increase the frequency of drinking and running (Falk, 1961, 1972; Keehn, 1972). Animals can be trained to avoid an intense aversive event and receive in its place a milder aversive event for making the avoidance response. However, the original avoidance response is maintained, even when the milder event increases in intensity, and eventually equals or surpasses the intensity of the original stimulus (Keehn, 1972; Sandler and Quagliano, 1964). Finally, avoidance learning with several species has shown that high levels of response proficiency often decline over time despite the apparent lack of change in experimental conditions (Keehn, 1972).

The above discussion illustrates rather than exhausts the intricacies of operant conditioning (see Dunham, 1977; Hinde and Stevenson-Hinde, 1973; Morse and Kelleher, 1977). Its purpose is to convey that a simplistic formulation of behavior based solely on the basic principles of operant conditioning is inadequate. The complexities themselves are not explored completely and remain unresolved; much of their significance lies in their recalcitrance to explanation through existing principles of behavior.

Overview of Professional Developments

The professional development of operant conditioning has expanded markedly over the past 30 years, evident in the establishment of organizational structures and associations that provided investigators interested in operant conditioning with the means to affiliate and discuss their research. One of the earliest organizational activities emerged in the 1940s when relatively few investigators were working in operant research. A small group, composed of faculty and students from Columbia and Indiana Universities interested in operant conditioning and the experimental analysis of behavior, started to hold informal meetings on these subjects. The first meeting was held at Indiana University in 1946. Eventually the conferences were conducted in conjunction with the annual meetings of the American Psychological Association. During the late 1940s and 1950s, the group put out a newsletter that described activities of the conference and reported ongoing operant research. As operant research became more popular, other organizational structures and publications replaced the conference and the newsletter.

Another milestone in the professional development of operant conditioning was the institution of specific college curricula. Many investigatiors must have introduced operant principles into their courses, but Fred S. Keller and William N. Schoenfeld developed a psychology curriculum based upon reinforcement theory. The curriculum began in 1946 with the offering of a course in introductory psychology at Columbia College (Keller and Schoenfeld, 1949), in which topics of psychology were contemplated from a Skinnerian standpoint. A few years later, Keller and Schoenfeld (1950) completed their influential book, *Principles of Psychology*, which was designed as a text for this course. The introductory course combined lectures and seminars with direct laboratory animal research to teach basic principles of behavior. The course was extremely successful and, indeed, enrollments exceeded department facilities (Keller and Schoenfeld, 1949). The success of the introductory course led to a revision of the whole psychology undergraduate curriculum, for which reinforcement theory was used as a unifying conceptual approach. Most courses in the department were taught in terms of operant principles. A graduate program in operant conditioning also was instituted to continue the general approach at an advanced level.

The impact of the curriculum at Columbia was great—it provided a training program almost completely based upon operant conditioning and reinterpreted traditional topics in light of its principles (Keller and Schoenfeld, 1950). Although the program was criticized as a "cult" (Wendt, 1949), both the program and the criticism it engendered helped to demarcate a distinct movement and particular school of thought (Krantz, 1971).

Laboratory research in operant conditioning grew rapidly in the 1950s. Yet there continued to be no satisfactory publication outlet for operant research. This void was related primarily to the methodological characteristics of operant research, which relies upon small sample sizes, intrasubject analysis of experimental variables, absence of statistical evaluation, use of cumulative records, and other features described earlier. These characteristics deviate from traditional experimental research and journals were not constituted to handle such differences. In 1958, operant investigators formed the Society for the Experimental Analysis of Behavior (SEAB). Its sole purpose was to provide a corporate organization to publish a journal devoted to operant research. The *Journal of the Experimental Analysis of Behavior* (*JEAB*) began publication in 1958 under the editorship of Charles B. Ferster.

The problem in finding an appropriate outlet for publicizing operant research extended to the presentation of experimental findings at professional meetings. At American Psychological Association annual conventions, the number of hours for presenting papers is allocated according to the divisions that comprise the organization. In the late 1950s and early 1960s, many investigators in the area of operant conditioning belonged to the Division of Experimental Psychology (Division 3). However, this division represented many interests, only one of which was operant conditioning. When presentations for the annual convention were assigned, the number of operant conditioning papers scheduled would be relatively small because of the heterogeneity of interests that had to be included in those hours allocated to the Division of Experimental Psychology. Investigators in operant conditioning decided to form their own division, called the Division of the Experimental Analysis of Behavior (Division 25). Once a separate division existed, individuals interested in operant conditioning could be given more time for presenting papers at the annual convention. The division, established in 1964, also publishes a newsletter. More recent professional advances in operant conditioning have pertained to applied rather than laboratory research. This growth is discussed in Chapter 7, in which the history of applied operant work is traced.

SUMMARY AND CONCLUSIONS

Skinner's contributions to the psychology of learning and to behaviorism were both substantive and methodological. At the substantive level, he developed and elaborated operant conditioning. His initial contribution was the clarification of differences between respondent and operant conditioning. He was neither the only one to recognize the differences between the paradigms investigated by Pavlov and Thorndike nor the only one to show the importance of response consequences in developing behavior. However, he shifted the emphasis in learning from respondent to operant conditioning to account for behavior. His own programmatic research elaborated the principles of operant conditioning and revealed the importance of diverse aspects of reinforcement under carefully controlled laboratory conditions. Skinner also extended operant conditioning principles to social behavior; the impact and implications of his extrapolations for behavior modification are discussed in Chapters 7 and 8.

At the methodological level, Skinner advanced a particular approach for studying behavior, termed the "experimental analysis of behavior." The investigator generally seeks to establish relationships between behavior and environmental stimuli in order to develop a science of behavior without appealing to constructs outside of the descriptive level of behavior. The methodology includes the study of free-operant behavior, i.e., responses such as lever- and key-pressing that can be repeated without interruption and take on a wide range of values. The response rates of individual organisms are studied over extended periods while the experimental variable is manipulated. The effect of the experimental variable is seen immediately on a cumulative record that shows changes in free-operant response rates.

Laboratory research on operant conditioning with animals proliferated in the 1950s. Areas investigated included schedules of reinforcement, stimulus control, conditioned reinforcement, punishment, avoidance, concurrent operants, superstitious behavior, and behavioral pharmacology. The expansion of operant conditioning research is attested to by the institution of curricula based on operant principles and the publication of the *Journal of the Experimental Analysis of Behavior,* a periodical devoted entirely to operant conditioning research. In the early 1950s, operant techniques were systematically extended to humans in laboratory investigations. These extensions began as exploratory attempts to apply the methodology of operant conditioning to humans, but by the late 1950s and early 1960s, both operant techniques and the methodology of the experimental analysis of behavior had been adopted for clinical and educational purposes.

5

The Emergence of Behavior Modification

The emergence of behavior modification reflects the transition from experimental work on learning to clinical applications of laboratory findings. As increasing information became available about the acquisition of behavior, it was applied to explain adaptive and maladaptive behavior. Thus, learning theorists frequently used clinically related topics to frame their notions about learning—Mowrer, for instance, discussed the etiology of maladaptive behaviors, and Guthrie wrote about methods of behavior change.

The transition from laboratory research to clinical applications of learning was gradual, although experimental findings and concepts were applied to clinical topics even in the early work on conditioning. For example, Pavlov, Bechterev, and Watson were concerned with maladaptive behavior as it related to conditioning principles. Advances in basic conditioning research provided a new way of looking at abnormal behavior, personality change, and the therapy process. The actual use of conditioning techniques in clinical practice began with a few isolated applications and then expanded in scope. The conceptual, methodological, and clinical extensions of learning all converged in behavior modification.

Chapter 5 traces the emergence of behavior modification through research on experimental neuroses, applications of conditioning to human behavior, the extension of learning concepts to explain personality and psychotherapy processes, and verbal conditioning and psychotherapy. In addition, the history of behavior modification in South Africa, England, and the United States is outlined.

EXPERIMENTAL NEUROSES

Experimental neuroses are laboratory-produced emotional responses considered to resemble neurotic behavior commonly found in humans.[1] Investigation of experimentally-induced neuroses is germane to the history of behavior modification for at least two reasons. First, the discovery of experimental neuroses pointed to the role of learning in the acquisition of emotional responses. Before the establishment of laboratory-induced neurotic reactions, the evolution of neurotic behavior had been largely a matter of conjecture. Experimental neuroses suggested a clear basis for pathological behavior. Second, the production of experimentally-induced neuroses in animals and eventually humans suggested procedures to ameliorate these reactions. If neurotic reactions were acquired through learning, they also might be eliminated through unlearning. Thus, research on experimental neuroses led directly to the concern with and study of therapeutic techniques.

Investigations in Pavlov's Laboratory

The discovery of experimental neuroses emerged from the two experiments conducted independently by Mariya Nikolayevna Yerofeyeva (1867–1925) and Nataliya Rudolfovna Shenger-Krestovnikova (1875–1947), working in Pavlov's laboratory in 1912 and 1913. The first instance was found while establishing a conditioned salivary reflex to electric shock in a dog. In the experiment, shock served as a neutral or conditioned stimulus (i.e., prior to conditioning it did not elicit the salivary reflex) and was paired with food. Although the shock was usually accompanied by its own defensive reflex response, eventually the dog was not aroused by the shock and gave the conditioned salivary reflex. As trials continued, the strength of a shock was increased markedly, and the dog continued to make the conditioned salivary

---

[1] The term "experimental neuroses" has been criticized because it implies that the experimentally induced reactions are the same as clinical neuroses (Russell, 1950). The term has been retained because of its historical significance that began with Pavlov. "Experimental neuroses" has been used to denote deviant or aberrant behavior that includes an extremely broad spectrum of responses (depending in part upon the species), such as general irritability, regressive behavior (characteristic of an earlier period in animal development), avoidance, head-tossing, tics, withdrawal, aggression, and disturbances in physiological activities such as pulse, heart, and respiration rates (Russell, 1950). There is some resemblance between select symptoms of experimentally induced neurotic behaviors of animals and human neuroses. However, serious questions have been raised as to whether experimental neurosis bears any more than a superficial relation to human neurosis (see Hunt, 1964).

reflex. However, changes were also made in the location of electrical stimulation on the skin. When several new places on the skin were stimulated, the animal became greatly agitated. Also, all conditioned responses previously made to weak shocks, whether or not they were applied to the original location used during acquisition, did not elicit a conditioned reflex. Apparently, altering the location of electrical stimulation resulted in a breakdown of the connection between the conditioned stimulus and the response and was associated with a general disruption in behavior.

A second instance of a breakdown of the conditioned response was obtained in a study on the discriminability of increasingly similar stimuli. In this experiment, the dog was exposed to two stimuli, a circle and an elipse, which were individually projected onto a screen. The projection of a circle was always followed by the presentation of food, whereas an elipse was not. Thus, the conditioned salivation response was performed in the presence of a circle but not in the presence of the elipse. The axes of the elipse were altered progressively so that the elipse increasingly resembled a circle. The animal continued to respond to the circle but not to the elipse even when the elipse became almost circular. However, after a few weeks of experimentation with a difficult discrimination, the animal no longer improved and became worse in performing the conditioned response. Furthermore, the animal's general behavior changed abruptly. The dog, although usually quiescent, now struggled, became agitated, barked violently, and attacked the apparatus. In addition, all the simple differentiations that had been acquired previously were lost. Retraining to discriminate between the gross differentiations of the circle and elipse was resumed. When retraining reached the point of the final discrimination, the dog again became very agitated and lost all the discriminations that had been relearned. This disturbance of the conditioned reflex and the resulting emotional responses were termed an "experimentally induced neurosis" (Pavlov, 1927).

Pavlov hypothesized that excitation and inhibition, two fundamental processes of the cerebral cortex, were implicated in experimentally induced neuroses. Pavlov noted that three methods from his laboratory could be used to create experimental neuroses, and each could be explained in light of these two neurological processes. The method involved overstimulation of either the inhibitory or excitatory processes or alternating stimulation of each. For example, a conflict between excitation and inhibition was established by providing stimuli that led to incompatible responses such as salivating and not salivating. The animal's inability to switch from excitatory to inhibitory responses either within a very brief period or across stimuli that appeared similar led to a breakdown (Pavlov, 1927). The breakdown in behavior was assumed to result from the inability of the cortical cells to change from one process to another in rapid succession. In the case of a conflict between the two processes, one process finally dominated. The dominant process was reflected in different behaviors, for example, extreme agitation (if excitation dominated) or withdrawal (if inhibition dominated). The breakdown of inhibitory and excitatory processes was temporary. After a period of rest or drug treatment, the animal's behavior returned to normal. However, repeated stimulation of inhibitory and excitatory processes, according to Pavlov, could result in chronic functional damage to the cortex (Pavlov, 1927).

Excitation and inhibition were not sufficient to account for the breakdown in behavior. Dogs exposed to identical laboratory conditions did not show neurotic reactions invariably. Moreover, similar stimuli tested in different animals led to different manifestations of emotional responses. Some animals became inhibited and others became excited as a function of the same procedure. The different reactions led Pavlov (1934) to develop a typology of nervous systems based upon the extent of the animal's excitation or inhibition before conditioning.

Beginning in 1921, Pavlov and his colleagues extensively studied the production of experimental neuroses to understand the cortical processes thought to underlie the development of different reactions. Thus, as with the conditioned reflex, experimental neuroses were viewed primarily as a method to investigate higher nervous processes. Yet Pavlov did recognize the potential connection in his work to the psychopathology of humans. He became familiar with neurotic and psychotic disorders in humans by visiting various clinics. He continued research that produced states in dogs he believed to be analogous to neurotic and psychotic disorders. On the basis of his experiments, he theorized about the causes of specific psychiatric symptoms, including apathy, negativism, stereotyped movements, fear of specific situations, and catalepsy (Pavlov, 1928). Although most of Pavlov's work on experimental neuroses was concerned with etiology, he did treat the animals. Treatment consisted either of prolonged rest from experimentation for several months or drugs such as bromides or calcium salts, which led to recovery within one or two weeks (Pavlov, 1927).

Extensions of Experimental Neuroses

Pavlov's work on experimental neuroses occurred late in his career after the importance of conditioning had been recognized. Research on conditioning and experimental neuroses was made available with the translation of his two books in the late 1920s. Several experimenters elaborated upon his work by investigating the conditions under which experimental neuroses could be produced and by extending the range of animals studied and the types of cures used to ameliorate the reactions.

In America, two investigators, who had conferred with Pavlov previously, established their own laboratories. At Cornell University, Howard S. Liddell (1895–1962) began a laboratory in 1926. Liddell visited Pavlov's laboratory and was interested in conditioning as a method to study the effect of thyroidectomy on learning and intelligence in dogs and sheep (Liddell, 1956). In the course of his research, he inadvertently produced experimental neuroses in sheep. This accident led to the systematic examination of stress-inducing aspects of conditioning that resulted in neurotic behavior. Peter S. Kupalov (1888–1964), who had worked with Pavlov, visited the United States in 1929 and guided Liddell's progress. Liddell and his colleagues studied experimental neuroses with such species as sheep, goats, pigs, rabbits, and dogs (Anderson and Liddell, 1935; Anderson and Parmenter, 1941; Liddell, 1938; Liddell and Bayne, 1926).

In 1931, W. Horsely Gantt, who had worked with Pavlov for six years, came to the Phipps Clinic of the Johns Hopkins University Hospital, where he began a conditioning laboratory.[2] Gantt systematically studied experimental neuroses for over a decade. One of his subjects, a dog named Nick, was studied for more than 13 years and remained "neurotic" through all that time (Gantt, 1944). Liddell, Gantt, and Kupalov, who had met in Russia, continued to confer in the United States on their research.

Liddell and Gantt found numerous new ways to produce experimental neuroses and extended the list of symptoms across various species. Liddell, and to a greater extent Gantt, adhered closely to a Pavlovian interpretation of experimental neuroses. Eventually, however, they introduced concepts such as frustration, conflict (of

---

[2] In May 1955, an anniversary of the Pavlovian Clinic at Johns Hopkins, Gantt initiated a society for the advancement of objective psychiatry based upon Pavlov's work.

drives), fear-meaning of the stimuli presented to the animal, and apprehension to account for neuroses (e.g., Gantt, 1942; Liddell, 1956). Other investigators began to question Pavlov's concepts of excitation and inhibition in light of research on cortical functioning and learning (cf. Denny-Brown, 1932; Hilgard and Marquis, 1940; Lashley, 1933; Tolman, 1932).

A major reinterpretation of experimental neuroses and extension of experimental research to human psychopathology and treatment were made by Jules H. Masserman, a psychiatrist at the University of Chicago. Masserman conducted research on experimental neuroses in cats and a few dogs. He established experimental neuroses by allowing the animal to open a food box in an experimental cage after hearing an auditory signal. At the moment of taking food, an aversive stimulus (shock or air blast) was delivered. According to Masserman, pairing the aversive agent with food-taking produced a motivational conflict (fear versus hunger). One or two repetitions of the procedure produced experimental neuroses including symptoms such as restlessness, crouching, hiding, escaping, and disturbed physiological responses. Animals would not approach the food unless some procedure was involved to overcome their symptoms.

Masserman's work on experimental neuroses were published in a book, *Behavior and Neuroses: An Experimental Psychoanalytic Approach to Psychobiologic Principles* (1943). Masserman's book stands out for its integration of conditioning and experimental neuroses with psychopathology and psychoanalytic theory, its evaluation of specific treatment techniques in animals to overcome their neurotic reactions, and its attempt to provide an experimental basis for psychoanalytic therapy.

Masserman integrated experimental research with psychoanalytic theory. He applied dynamic concepts such as symbolic expression and motivational conflicts to the experimental investigation of behavior. In his book, he applied findings on experimental neuroses to a wide array of psychopathological behaviors and psychological mechanisms, including compulsions, obsessions, fixations, regression, intractable behavior, negativism, masochism, and sexual aberrations. Thus, Masserman combined his research with a theory of psychopathology in general, and with psychoanalytic theory in particular.

Another important feature of Masserman's work was his investigation of procedures for treating neurotic behaviors. He evaluated several methods designed to increase an animal's approach toward food and to overcome its neurotic symptoms. One method was to let the animal rest after the neurotic reactions had been established. Rest periods ranging from two weeks to five months had little effect on the cats. When they were reintroduced into the cage where the reaction had been established, their symptoms returned.

A second method, referred to as "reducing one of the conflictional drives," consisted of manually or forcibly feeding the cat before placing it in the cage. The animal would not be hungry in the experimental cage and did not experience the conflict between hunger and fear of the aversive event associated with food. This method was ineffective in eliminating the neurotic reaction: as the cat's hunger increased, the aberrant behaviors returned.

A third method, termed the "transference technic," consisted of the experimenter handling, stroking, and petting the cat as it was coaxed to approach the food box and eat. The experimenter's contact with the animal was stressed as important in inducing approach behavior. If the experimenter ceased contact, the cat withdrew from the food. Continued contact and reassurance led to a reduction of anxious behavior.

A fourth method, called "environmental manipulation," was to increase the hunger drive by food deprivation coupled with the sight and smell of food. This high drive was accompanied by actual physical manipulation. The starving cat was placed in the cage with a movable barrier that forced close proximity of the food, which together led to feeding in the cage and a reduction of the neurotic symptoms. Environmental manipulation was one of Masserman's more effective methods for reducing neurotic symptoms.

A fifth method, referred to as "social example," consisted of placing a neurotic cat in the experimental cage with a cat that responded normally to the feeding situation. The normal cage-mate fed and eventually the neurotic cat approached the food and ate. This method was one of the least reliable for overcoming neurotic reactions.

The final method, termed "working through," allowed the animal to control the situation to overcome fear on its own. Specifically, the cat was trained to control a switch that made food available. After the neurotic reaction was established, the animal was given the switch so that it could control food delivery from the feared food box. Eventually, the cat delivered food to itself, ate, and overcame neurotic behaviors. Of all the methods used, working through was the most effective in eliminating neurotic reactions.

Masserman extrapolated concepts from psychotherapeutic practices and clinical disorders to explain his therapeutic procedures, which he viewed as analogous to features of psychoanalytic therapy. For example, "working through," the most effective procedure in overcoming the animal's neurotic reaction, was considered comparable to the "working through" of psychoanalysis. In therapy, the patient resolves his/her own anxieties and motivational conflicts through symbolic representations of reality and transference relationships to his analyst. After symbolic adaptations to the environment, the patient can test out his/her own behavior in relation to the formerly neurotic objects and in actual interpersonal relationships. Although the similarities between the specific methods used to overcome aberrant behaviors in cats and psychotherapeutic practices in clinical cases can be questioned, Masserman's work is significant for attempting to provide an empirical basis for existing therapeutic techniques.

APPLICATIONS AND EXTENSIONS
OF CONDITIONING TO HUMAN BEHAVIOR

Early Investigations in Russia and the United States

Up to 1925, research on conditioning and experimental neuroses was based largely upon animal subjects, but some major exceptions can be cited. In Russia, Bechterev had experimented with human subjects; in the United States, Watson and Lashley, influenced by Bechterev's writings, explored conditioning with humans beginning in 1915. As early as 1902, Twitmyer studied human conditioning without knowledge of the work of Pavlov and Bechterev. However, research from Pavlov's laboratory was responsible for stimulating widespread use of human subjects in conditioning in this country.

In 1907, Nikolay I. Krasnogorski (1882–1961), one of Pavlov's students, studied conditioning by using children (Krasnogorski, 1925). In his initial work, he investigated the conditioned reflexes of a 14-month-old infant. Krasnogorski used a sight of food as the conditioned stimulus, food as the unconditioned stimulus, and swallowing as the unconditioned and conditioned response. Because salivation induces swallowing, the frequency of swallowing was taken as an indication of salivary secretions. Eventually, he employed wide ranges of children—including "idiots," imbeciles, cretins, epileptics, as well as "normals"—and conditioned stimuli, including auditory, visual, and tactile stimuli. Like Pavlov, Krasnogorski investigated diverse processes in an attempt to understand neurological mechanisms.

During the course of his research, Krasnogorski discovered behavior similar to the experimentally induced neurotic reactions of dogs. He noted that when difficult discriminations were required, the children became irritable. Moreover, the reactions extended beyond the laboratory. For example, when one child was required to make a difficult discrimination in the laboratory, he began to attack other children on the ward, cried frequently, and wanted to leave the hospital (Krasnogorski, 1925). Consistent with Pavlov, Krasnogorski used rest from the experimental situation and bromides to treat the neurotic reactions.

Some of Krasnogorski's work on conditioning was published in German in 1909 and 1913. These writings came to the attention of William H. Burnham (1855–1941) at Clark University, who incorporated these ideas into his lectures for a course on mental hygiene in education. About 1914 Florence Mateer (1887–1961), one of Burnham's students, became interested in conditioning of children, and decided to replicate and extend Krasnogorski's work for her dissertation research. Although Mateer emphasized the significance of Krasnogorski's work, she criticized his reports because they lacked sufficient detail for replicating his procedures. For example, Krasnogorski had failed to specify dimensions of conditioning such as the duration of the conditioned stimuli, number of conditioning trials, and how the children were induced to enter the conditioning situation (Mateer, 1918; Razran, 1933).

Mateer extended Krasnogorski's procedures by studying a large number of children up to the age of seven, including normal and mentally retarded children and several infants. Her conditioning procedure was similar to that of Krasnogorski in that she used food as the unconditioned stimulus and swallowing (automatically recorded) as the unconditioned response. Mateer placed a blindfold over the child's eyes as the conditioned stimulus. Seconds before presenting food, it was pulled down over the child's eyes.[3] Along with examining the acquisition of conditioned swallowing in response to placement of the blindfold, Mateer also studied forgetting, discrimination, and inhibition of the conditioned reflex. A notable feature of her research was her examination of demographic and diagnostic variables (e.g., age, sex, intelligence), which she correlated with conditioning per-

[3] In Krasnogorski's procedure, the child was blindfolded throughout conditioning. Mateer's pilot work indicated that children did not allow the blindfold to stay on. Thus, she used the blindfold itself as a conditioned stimulus and it was removed in between trials.

formance. Thus, her study provided both methodological refinements and substantive extensions of Krasnogorski's work. Her dissertation was published in 1918 as a book, *Child Behavior: A Critical and Experimental Study of Young Children by the Method of Conditioned Reflexes.*

As a result of her findings (which were important in their own right), Mateer strongly endorsed the use of the conditioned reflex to study children:

> It is easily applicable with very young children. It is independent of the acquisition of speech and hence enables one to study the development of mental processes without considering the language factor. . . . So far as an investigation of the factors influencing the learning process is concerned this method allows of such wide variation that time factors, effect of frequency and distribution of stimulations, of intensity and complexity of stimuli, of modes of presentation, quality of stimuli, of effect of affective toning, near and distance stimulation may all be studied while the child thinks he is playing a game (Mateer, 1918, pp. 194–195).

In promoting the use of the conditioned reflex method, Mateer advocated the work of Pavlov and Krasnogorski over that of Bechterev on both methodological and substantive grounds. She noted that Pavlov had been especially sensitive to the many details of the laboratory that needed to be controlled in conditioning studies. Extraneous events, if not controlled, would readily become conditioned stimuli. In addition, Mateer rejected Bechterev's method of shock as the unconditioned stimulus because of its potentially adverse effects on children. Mateer's work firmly established the relevance of conditioning to child behavior. As discussed below, her research directly influenced her teacher, William Burnham, who applied conditioning concepts to education and mental hygiene in children.

John B. Watson, Rosalie Rayner, and Mary Cover Jones: The Conditioning and Deconditioning of Emotions

One of the most influential applications of conditioning to human behavior was made by Watson, who studied the conditioned emotional reactions of human infants. Watson's research is noteworthy for at least two reasons. First, by conditioning emotional reactions, Watson showed that behavioral notions and objective methods could be applied to explore states of feeling and private experience. Second, observations of how emotional reactions evolved provided potential clues as to how fears might be created and, by implication, be treated.

Watson's interest in the conditioning of emotions derived largely from his own theory that innate emotional reactions were limited to fear, rage, and love, all of which were evoked by a narrow range of stimuli at birth. In adults, a broad range of stimuli elicited emotional responses, which suggested to Watson that innate emotional reactions are conditioned to a variety of environmental stimuli. Watson began research to demonstrate whether neutral stimuli could elicit fear reactions through conditioning.

In 1920, Watson and Rosalie Rayner (1898–1935), a graduate student at Johns Hopkins (and eventually the wife of Watson), reported an experiment to condition fear in an 11-month-old infant, named Albert, who had been reared in a hospital environment. As part of tests provided to several children, Albert was exposed to assorted stimuli, including small animals such as a white rat, a rabbit, a dog, and a monkey. He showed no fear of any of these animals. Among the stimuli that did elicit a reaction was a loud noise produced by striking a hammer on a steel bar. The boy was startled in response to the noise and cried, trembled, and showed changes in breathing.

Watson and Rayner wished to determine if the startle reaction could be conditioned to previously neutral stimuli. A white rat that had not elicited fear served as a conditioned stimulus and was paired with the loud noise (the unconditioned stimulus). The rat was presented to Albert followed by a loud noise. Initially, Albert fell over or withdrew and sometimes whimpered and cried. After a total of seven pairings of the noise with the rat over a one-week period, the joint presentation of the rat and noise was associated with crying. Subsequently, the rat was presented alone. As soon as the rat was presented, the child fell over, cried, and began to crawl away. Thus, a conditioned fear response had been established.[4]

Following conditioning, Watson and Rayner tested Albert's responses to various stimuli that previously had not elicited fear to determine whether the conditioned reaction transferred to other objects. When he was presented with stimuli that resembled the white rat, including a rabbit, dog, fur coat, cotton, wool, the experimenter's hair, and a Santa Claus mask, the fear reaction was elicited. In

---

[4] Watson and Rayner conceived of their demonstration as an application of classical conditioning. However, the actual technique deviated from this paradigm. In a strict classical conditioning paradigm, the presentation of the unconditioned stimulus is not necessarily preceded by performance of a particular response. That is, the stimulus is not contingent upon a response. However, Watson and Rayner did not adhere to this requirement. The presentation of the unconditioned stimulus (loud noise) followed after Albert began to reach or when he touched the rat. Thus, the unconditioned stimulus was response-contingent. This paradigm more closely follows a punishment procedure as commonly practiced in operant model with components of classical conditioning.

contrast, no fear was elicited in the presence of inanimate objects such as blocks. Five days later, Albert was reexamined and continued to show the conditioned fear reaction.

The experiment had indicated that fear could be conditioned, that conditioned reactions generalized beyond the original conditioned stimulus, and that the reaction was maintained up to at least a week. For reasons unrelated to the experiment, Albert left the hospital so that persistence, and more importantly, elimination of the fear could not be studied. Nevertheless, Watson and Rayner noted several procedures that they might have used had time been available.

Three years after the case of Albert had been reported, Mary Cover Jones, under the advice of Watson, studied the effects of the therapeutic techniques suggested by Watson and Rayner (M. C. Jones, 1924a). Jones tested the reactions of institutionalized children between the ages of three months and seven years to being left alone, being in a dark room, being with other children who showed fear, being exposed to various animals (snakes, rabbits, frogs, white rats), hearing a loud noise, and so on. After selecting individuals with fear reactions, seven methods, originally suggested by Watson and Rayner, were used alone or in combination to eliminate these reactions.

The first method was "disuse," which attempted to eliminate fear by not exposing the child to the feared stimuli for several weeks or months. This method was not successful in decreasing fear. The second method, "verbal appeal," consisted of talking to a child to overcome his negative reactions to the stimulus by associating verbally pleasant experiences with the feared stimulus. For example, a child who feared rabbits would hear brief stories about rabbits (Peter Rabbit) and discuss make-believe stories of "real" rabbits. This method was also unsuccessful in decreasing fear of the actual stimulus when it was presented again. Jones described the effect of the verbal treatment method with one girl as follows: "She had learned to speak freely of rabbits, but this altered verbalization apparently was not accompanied by any change in her responses to the rabbit itself" (Jones, 1924a, p. 385).

The third method, "negative adaptation," consisted of repeatedly presenting the feared object so that the subject adapted to it. The method was based upon the common notion that "familiarity breeds indifference." However, repeated presentations of the stimulus did not consistently reduce fear. The fourth method, "repression," associated punishment from peers (social ridicule, teasing) with the fear. Punishment was not programmed specifically, but evolved at the stimulus was presented to the fearful child in a group of fearless children. Adverse social consequences were expected to suppress or contain the child's fear, but the method was unsuccessful.

The fifth method, "distraction," involved substituting another activity for the fear response. The child's attention was diverted from the feared object by conversation or by toys. Although the distraction did soothe the frightened child temporarily, this method did not appear to produce permanent change.

The sixth method, "direct conditioning," associated the feared object with a different stimulus capable of arousing a positive (pleasant) reaction. Hunger, according to Jones, appeared to be the most effective motive in conditioning a positive reaction. The procedure consisted of placing the hungry child in a high chair and feeding him. The object of fear then was brought into the room, which would trigger in a fear reaction. The stimulus was removed gradually until it was far enough away not to interfere with eating. While the child ate, the stimulus was slowly brought closer to the child, and eventually close enough to be touched. Jones commented upon the difficulty inherent in the procedure:

> Two response systems are being dealt with: food leading to a positive reaction, and fear-object leading to a negative reaction. The desired conditioning should result in transforming the fear-object into a source of positive response (substitute stimulus). But a careless manipulator could readily produce the reverse result, attaching a fear reaction to the sight of food (Jones, 1924a, p. 389).

The seventh method, "social imitation," was based on placing the individual who feared a particular object with other individuals who did not. The fearless children approached and played with the stimulus. The fearful individual imitated his peers and overcame his fear. Jones reported several cases in which the fear was eliminated and induced on the basis of social imitation.

As an overall evaluation, Jones noted that only two methods, direct conditioning and social imitation produced "unqualified success." The results of the two most effective methods were demonstrated in the second paper, which has become a classic in the area of behavior modification (Jones, 1924b). This report described the case of a 34-month-old boy named Peter. Tests of Peter in the laboratory revealed he was afraid of diverse stimuli, including a white rat, rabbit, fur coat, cotton, and wool, but not inanimate objects like blocks and toys. Because the rabbit elicited greater fear than the rat, it was used as the feared object during treatment.

Initially, social imitation was used. Three children who were un-afraid of the rabbit came into the laboratory daily with Peter for a play period. The rabbit was placed in the cage. Throughout the play period, the rabbit was brought increasingly closer in progressive steps or "degrees of toleration." The laboratory notes reflected the progression of steps as follows:

1. Rabbit anywhere in the room in a cage causes fear reactions.
2. Rabbit 12 ft away in cage tolerated.
3. Rabbit 4 ft away in cage tolerated.
4. Rabbit 3 ft away in cage tolerated.
5. Rabbit close in cage tolerated.
6. Rabbit free in room tolerated.
7. Rabbit touched when experimenter holds it.
8. Rabbit touched when free in room.
9. Rabbit defied by spitting at it, throwing things at it, imitating it.
10. Rabbit allowed on tray of high chair.
11. Squats in defenseless position beside rabbit.
12. Helps experimenter to carry rabbit to its cage.
13. Holds rabbit on lap.
14. Stays alone in room with rabbit.
15. Allows rabbit in play-pen with him.
16. Fondles rabbit affectionately.
17. Lets rabbit nibble his fingers. (Jones, 1924b, pp. 310–311)

The procedure ceased for two months because Peter contracted scarlet fever. When he returned, his fear worsened, apparently because of an encounter with a large dog that startled him. Jones began a direct conditioning procedure to eliminate his fear. Peter was given food that he liked while in the presence of the rabbit. The rabbit was placed in a cage and brought as close to the child as possible without eliciting fear that would interfere with eating. As Jones noted, "Through the presence of the pleasant stimulus (food) whenever the rabbit was shown, the fear was eliminated gradually in favor of the positive response" (1924b, p. 313).

To hasten the deconditioning of fear, other children were included occasionally. The children were not afraid of the rabbit. At the end of the deconditioning procedure, Peter's fear was eliminated. Indeed, he reacted favorably to the rabbit and occasionally stated, "I liked the rabbit." In the last session, Peter's reactions to other stimuli that previously evoked fear were also assessed. He failed to show fear to these objects. New stimuli (a mouse and tangled mass of worms) to which Peter had not been exposed previously in the laboratory also were presented. Although he was distressed initially and moved away, by the end of the session he was undisturbed and actually interested in these stimuli. This report suggested the direct effects of deconditioning fear and the generalizability of these effects across stimuli.

The work of Watson, Rayner, and Jones is monumental in light of subsequent developments in behavior modification. The initial experiment by Watson and Rayner suggested that learning could account for fear reactions in humans. Although the demonstration did not establish that fears normally are acquired through classical conditioning, it showed that conditioning is a useful model from which fear development might be viewed. Conditioning provided a parsimonious account of the acquisition of fear, and the results directly challenged psychodynamic formations of emotional reactions. Watson and Rayner dryly fabricated a typical psychoanalytic interpretation acquired fear that might be advanced if Albert's conditioning history were unknown.

> The Freudians 20 years from now, unless their hypotheses change, when they come to analyze Albert's fear of a seal skin coat—assuming that he comes to analysis at that age—will probably tease from him the recital of a dream which upon their analysis will show that Albert at 3 years of age attempted to play with the pubic hair of the mother and was scolded violently for it. (We are by no means denying that this might in some other case condition it.) If the analyst has sufficiently prepared Albert to accept such a dream when found as an explanation of his avoiding tendencies, and if the analyst has the authority and personality to put it over, Albert may be fully convinced that the dream was a true revealer of the factors which brought about the fear (Watson and Rayner, 1920, p. 14).

Interestingly, attempts to replicate the conditioning of fears with young children did not corroborate the original experiment consistently. With some exceptions (e.g., H. E. Jones, 1931), children have not developed conditioned fears with procedures similar to those used by Watson and Rayner (Bregman, 1934; English, 1929). The inconsistent effects obtained in this research did not limit the influence of Watson and Rayner's demonstration in interpreting fears and their acquisition.

M. C. Jones' elimination of fear with diverse methods challenged existing beliefs about the need to treat underlying psychodynamic states rather than overt behavior. Jones demonstrated that fears could be deconditioned directly. The impact of her work on treatment has been great. As discussed later, some of the specific methods she employed continue to be used in contemporary behavior modification. Overall, the work of Watson, Rayner, and Jones has greatly influenced the development of behavior modification. By producing and eliminating fears, they encouraged the extension of conditioning concepts to explain normal and abnormal behavior and to generate direct methods of behavior change.[5]

William H. Burnham and Mental Hygiene

Burnham, who was at the department of pedagogy at Clark University, was interested in conditioning as it related to child development and mental hygiene.[6] In 1917, he published an article entitled, "Mental Hygiene and the Conditioned Reflex," in which he reviewed the accumulating research on conditioning as reflected in the writings of Pavlov, Watson, Twitmyer, Krasnogorski, and his own student, Florence Mateer. Burnham credited the conditioned reflex method of study as "... an epoch-making contribution to genetic pedagogy and school hygiene" (p. 462). He viewed conditioning as a means of understanding child behavior. According to Burnham, mental hygiene could be viewed as the development of appropriate conditioned reflexes required for physical and mental health.

In 1924, he published a lengthy book entitled *The Normal Mind: An Introduction to Mental Hygiene and the Hygiene of School Education*, which greatly elaborated the role of conditioning in child adjustment. The book focused on the acquisition of appropriate and productive behaviors and the prevention and elimination of adjustment problems, particularly those exhibited by children in educational settings. Burnham viewed behavior from a conditioning framework:

> ... in every act of our daily lives conditioned reflexes are involved. Every habit is made up of conditioned reflexes. Every attitude and interest, too, probably involved conditioned reflexes. Thus learning consists in the formation of associations, conditioned reflexes, and systems of conditioned reflexes. Education is a systematic attempt to develop conditioned reflexes that signify normal adjustment to one's environment and efficient activity (Burnham, 1924, pp. 144–145).

Conditioning research explained how behavior evolved and provided recommendations for altering it. For example, to treat fear, Burnham extrapolated from Pavlov and Krasnogorski's work on inhibiting conditioned responses. He advocated thwarting inhibitions, i.e., interfering with the conditioned fear response.

---

[5] Recently, M. C. Jones (1975) has published an interesting personal account of her seminal work on fear and the place of early behaviorism in the growth of behavior therapy.

[6] The department of pedagogy was equivalent to educational psychology and mental hygiene.

Burnham was critical of psychoanalytic notions and believed psychoanalytic interpretations to be ". . . merely a form of psychological astrology . . ." (1924, p. 628). He regarded Freudian concepts as unparsimonious when compared to formulations of behavior based on learning. Burnham criticized psychoanalytic treatment. Any therapeutic effects derived from psychoanalysis, he maintained, probably resulted from suggestion and placebo effects.

Perhaps the most striking feature of *The Normal Mind* is its anticipation of numerous techniques that were implemented formally years later in behavior modification.[7] Burnham placed greatest emphasis on techniques that now would be included as applications of operant conditioning, and made recommendations for education that resemble many current practices. He stressed the importance of designing the school environment so as to initiate student performance and ensure success (i.e., positive consequences). He noted, "The function of the teacher is to provide opportunity for a suitable task and the conditions that make success for the individual possible" (p. 228). He also believed that ". . . the maxim for the teacher should be to make the work so easy at first that the child will believe he can do it and success will be assured." (p. 470). Burnham criticized the use of aversive events in the classroom because of their potentially deleterious effects on children: frequent experiences of failure, coupled with punishment and blame by the teacher, could contribute to a student's negative attitudes or misbehavior. Favorable consequences (success) were accorded a major role in developing adaptive behavior in general.

> For those who have to deal with social failures, with the people who are down and on the verge of being out, the problem is much like that of the teacher and physician; it is the problem of giving each case something to

---

[7] Burnham's discussion of learning was based upon Pavlovian conditioning. He applied the conditioning paradigm to a variety of situations and behaviors. Ironically, most of the applications, recommendations, and examples—such as his emphases on the consequences of behavior, stimulus control, and shaping—are much closer to law-of-effect learning, which was not reviewed in his book. Thorndike was cited by Burnham but only for his work in educational psychology rather than for the learning laws he formulated. The failure to refer to Thorndike and law-of-effect learning is not a criticism of Burnham's applications of learning concepts. As noted in Chapter 4, the distinction between the different learning paradigms was not actively discussed until the late 1930s. Of the several authors who made the distinction, it was not until Skinner's (1938) work that differences were drawn sharply. The distinction reached a larger audience when Hilgard and Marquis (1940) contrasted classical conditioning (Pavlovian paradigm) and instrumental conditioning (Thorndikian paradigm) in their book, *Conditioning and Learning*.

> do that is worth while, and of placing each individual in a situation where success is likely to occur; and, when we recall the essential psychology of success, we find that this is possible in many forms of work, and that the psychological success in doing ordinary work properly, in itself is a stimulus to further work, and often the most important condition of mental health (Burnham, 1924, pp. 479–480).

Along with Burnham's explicit endorsement of the use of positive consequences in a classroom, his book included several other procedures that have been since employed as behavior modification techniques. For example, in his discussion of the elimination of fear, he advocated bringing the individual in contact with the fear stimulus and associating the stimulus with a "rival stimulus" that did not evoke a fearful response, thus inhibiting fear. Burnham's recommendations were influenced by Watson and Rayner's (1920) suggestions for eliminating fear. However, Burnham suggested that anything that was able to concentrate attention or thought would inhibit fear. The procedure of employing fear-inhibiting responses—including thought and imagery—antedate the use of systematic desensitization in behavior modification. Burnham also recommended "direct action" to eliminate fear by having the individual enter situations in which he is afraid. By exposing himself to the situation, the individual will habituate himself to the fear, which should weaken its power. Throughout the book, Burnham refers to procedures that closely resemble current behavior modification techniques, including stimulus control, modeling, contingency contracting, cognitive rehearsal, self-instruction, and self-control. These procedures are implicit in the recommendations for handling adjustment problems in education and child rearing.

The scope encompassed in *The Normal Mind* was another exemplary feature. Although Burnham discussed mental hygiene in the context of education and child rearing, he envisioned the principles of conditioning to be widely applicable.

> The writer believes that the application of the simple knowledge we already have of the conditions of mental health would improve human health everywhere—that it would be helpful to the schools, would prevent many neuroses, and favor the mental health and increase the efficiency of all normal children, and afford a social training vitally important for the health of the state. . . . Thus the application of the principles of mental hygiene in all forms of education, whether in the home, the school, on the playground, or in industry, is essential for efficiency, happiness, and normal development (Burnham, 1924, pp. xi, 684).

Current applications of principles of behavior change to diverse social problems are consistent with Burnham's statement.

Burnham's work is significant for applying conditioning concepts to mental hygiene and education and for anticipating a wide range of behavioral techniques. In *The Wholesome Personality: A Contribution to Mental Hygiene*, published in 1932 and an update of the 1924 book, Burnham accorded conditioning a relatively minor role, although he continued to stress techniques for altering behaviors that were described in *The Normal Mind*.

O. Hobart Mowrer and Willie M. Mowrer: Treatment of Enuresis

A major advance in the application of conditioning was reported by O. Hobart Mowrer and Willie M. Mowrer, who developed a treatment for enuresis. In 1935, Mowrer and Mowrer began to experiment with 30 enuretic children, ages 3 to 13, at the New Haven Children's Center. The formulation of enuresis and method of treatment were based upon Pavlovian conditioning.

The Mowrers viewed enuresis as a failure to respond to cues (bladder distension) that preceded urination. Full bladder distension, which did not awaken the child, eventually resulted in the reflex response of urination. The Mowrers believed that the child could be trained to anticipate full bladder distension by awakening in time. Waking is associated with contraction of the bladder sphincter which inhibits urinating.

The Mowrers attempted to establish bladder distension as the conditioned stimulus for sphincter control and inhibition of urination. A loud noise served as the unconditioned stimulus and awakening (accompanied by sphincter contraction) as the unconditioned response. To condition awakening and sphincter contraction to bladder distension, the children were awakened at the immediate onset of urinating. The Mowrers reasoned that with repeated trials, awakening and sphincter contraction eventually should occur in time to precede urination. Thus, before urinatng, bladder distension alone should result in sphincter contraction and inhibit urination.

The Mowrers devised an electric pad for placement in the child's bed. The pad was connected to a bell that provided the noise to awaken the child. The pad consisted of cotton fabric that encased an incomplete electrical circuit. The circuit was connected to the bell that rang at the onset of urination. The electrical circuit was completed by the urine thereby sounding the bell. The bell-and-pad apparatus was extremely effective and successfully eliminated enuresis in all 30 participants.

The Mowrers' contribution does not derive from discovering or inventing the technique to eliminate enuresis, because similar apparatus already had been devised. As early as 1830, J. Nye, a pediatrician, suggested placing a circuit apparatus in bed that would be completed by the urine. The completed circuit would result in a shock delivered to the individual to wake him up. Nye did not have the opportunity to test his procedure (Glicklich, 1951).

A bell-and-pad apparatus was used by M. Pfaundler (1905), a German pediatrician. The apparatus was used in a hospital to signal nurses when a child urinated. A bell, which sounded at the onset of urination, appeared to have therapeutic consequences and inhibited urination. Following this accidental discovery of an effective treatment, the method was applied directly for therapeutic purposes in France. Two published reports indicated that the method rapidly effected bladder control (Genouville, 1908; Roux, 1910). Despite the success of the method, it was not used widely, perhaps because of some of the cumbersome and inefficient features of the apparatus (Mowrer and Mowrer, 1938). Independently of the previous discoveries, a similar apparatus was devised in Russia and it was reported in the *Baltimore Sun* (1936, May 4). Indeed, the brief report suggested that the device already was in use in a Russian hospital, indicating a wider application than the Mowrers had achieved in the United States. At about the same time that the Mowrers had explored the conditioning method, two other investigators independently developed the procedure in the United States (Morgan and Witmer, 1939).

The contribution of the Mowrers extended beyond designing a more efficient apparatus and introducing the procedure in the United States. Their conceptualization and treatment of enuresis from a learning orientation and their discussion of related issues figured prominently in behavior modification. The Mowrers viewed enuresis as inadequate habit training rather than as an expression of psychodynamic processes, a theory that had been commonly held. They did not rule out the possible role of psychodynamic factors in the same cases. However, they pointed out the difficulty in determining what these factors might be and how they might be altered. Thus, their approach was directed toward the behavior itself rather than any underlying psychological processes. The Mowrers conceptualized treatment from the point of Pavlovian conditioning.[8] Previous treatments of enuresis in Germany and France did not rely explicitly on learning principles. (In the United States, the heuristic value of looking to the psychology of learning for ameliorating child problems was already clearly evident in the work of Watson and Rayner, M. C. Jones, and Burnham.)

The Mowrers also criticized psychoanalytic concepts and psychodynamic treatment and endorsed a learning approach as a legitimate conceptual alternative. Part of the clinical *Zeitgeist* was the advocacy of conditioning concepts as an alternative for psychoanalytic concepts in explaining etiology and treatment of maladaptive behavior. Such espousals are to be found in the writings of Pavlov and Bechterev as well as in the work of the Mowrers' contemporaries, including Watson and Rayner and Burnham.

The Mowrers addressed the issue of symptom substitution, which

---

[8] Although the Mowrers conceived their treatment in terms of Pavlovian conditioning, there is some question about the exact paradigm(s) used. In classical conditioning, events occur in the following sequence: conditioned stimulus, unconditioned stimulus, and unconditioned response. The sequence of events in the Mowrer's procedure was more complex. Ostensibly, the only elements involved were conditioned stimulus (bladder distension), followed by an unconditioned stimulus (noise), which resulted in an unconditioned response (waking and sphincter control). Yet there were other inevitable components to the series. Although bladder distension is a neutral stimulus when paired with waking, it is an unconditioned stimulus for urinating. The loud noise used in the procedure served as an unconditioned stimulus and followed urinating. Therefore, the sequence of events might be viewed legitimately as follows: unconditioned stimulus (bladder distension), unconditioned response (urination), and another unconditioned stimulus (loud noise). That is, an unconditioned stimulus (noise) followed urination. Insofar as the loud noise followed urinating, it was response-contingent. In classical conditioning, the presentation of an unconditioned stimulus is not response-contingent. If episodes of urinating are suppressed when followed by an event, this consequence qualifies as a punishment paradigm, i.e., operant conditioning.

Another discrepancy pertains to the conditioned response. If the unconditioned response is awakening and sphincter contraction, the conditioned response should be a close approximation. Bladder distension alone should come to elicit awakening and inhibit urination. Yet the goal of treatment is to have the individual sleep through the night without urinating and not wake up at all. Thus, the development of a conditioned response is unclear.

Finally, the long-term effects of treatment do not conform to a classical conditioning paradigm. Based upon classical conditioning, one might expect that without repeated reinforcement (i.e., pairing the conditioned stimulus of bladder distension with the unconditioned stimulus of loud noise), the relationship between the conditioned stimulus and conditioned response should extinguish. However, the learned response typically does not relapse. Evidently, operant and classical conditioning are both at work in the bell-and-pad procedure. (For an elaboration of conceptual problems associated with the bell-and-pad treatment method, see Lovibond (1964).)

figured prominently in discussions of psychoanalytic treatment. As a result of their treatment, they stated categorically, "In no case has there been any evidence of 'symptom substitution'" (Mowrer and Mowrer, 1938, p. 451). Some cases relapsed within a few weeks or months after treatment, but these were children who returned to an ". . . intolerable home situation where emotional stresses are too great and newly acquired habits give way to old ones" (p. 452).

The Mowrers criticized not only the notion of symptom substitution but also the "disease model" in general. They objected to the uncritical acceptance of the "careless medical analogies" (p. 454) that were used in child training and education. For example, referring to problem behaviors as "symptoms," in their opinion, was an overextension of the medical analogy. Indeed, such usage reflected the value-laden nature of diagnosing behavior as "symptoms": ". . . whether a given item of child behavior is or is not a 'symptom'. . . seems to be whether somebody who is important in the life of the child objects to it" (p. 454). The Mowrers' ideas on the nature of deviant or symptomatic behavior were taken up by later theorists of behavior modification.

The treatment devised by the Mowrers was of great importance, too. Consistent changes were obtained in a large number of subjects, and therapy never took more than two months. Follow-up of the children revealed that bladder control had been maintained up to two-and-one-half years after treatment. Further, the technique could be used by parents under the supervision of professionals without altering the child's environment. Indeed, some of the most dramatic successes had been effected in the home. Thus the technique did not require isolating children in an institutional setting or seeing the child in an outpatient treatment. Overall, the treatment technique seemed to have a conceptual advantage in that it was based upon learning and, by implication, well grounded in objective science and practical advantages in that it was effective, quick, and durable.

Additional Applications of Conditioning for Clinical Purposes

When conditioning began to be studied in Russia in the 1900s, its concepts were extended to psychiatric populations. By the 1920s and 1930s, conditioning methods had been applied in several countries to explain or to treat a number of psychopathological disorders. The first systematic applications of conditioning or reflexology were conceptual extensions by Pavlov and Bechterev to explain various disorders (e.g., Pavlov, 1932, 1934, 1941; Bechterev, 1912). The extension of conditioning to explain psychopathology spread to Europe (e.g., Kostyleff, 1927; Marinesco and Kreindler, 1935; Meignant, 1935; Morhardt, 1930) and to the United States (e.g., Bagby, 1928; Kubie, 1934; Levin, 1934).

Bechterev used conditioning to treat hysterial deafness (1912) and sexual perversion (1923). Conditioning was particularly well suited to investigate hysterical disorders, because verbal reports could be avoided entirely to determine responsiveness to external stimulation. Bechterev's work on hysteria stimulated similar work by others in Russia (Myasishchev, 1929), Europe (Marinesco, Sager and Kreindler, 1931), and the United States (Cohen, Hilgard, and Wendt, 1933); Sears and Cohen, 1933). Conditioning sometimes was successful in treating hysteria. For example, establishing a conditioned response to a part of the body in which the hysteria was manifest (e.g., in the case of hysterical anesthesia) resulted in a disappearance of the disorder (cf. Sears and Cohen, 1933).

Conditioning methods were applied to addictive behavior. In Russia, Kantorovich (1929) used conditioning to treat alcoholics. Alcohol was used as the conditioned stimulus and shock as the unconditioned stimulus to establish an aversive reaction to alcohol. Kantorovich's work, which is discussed again in Chapter 6, stimulated many other investigators in Russia, Germany, France, Belgium, and the United States in the mid-1930s to apply conditioning to treat alcoholism. Conditioning methods also were tried with drug addicts. In the United States, Rubenstein (1931) eliminated morphine addiction by establishing a conditioned drug reaction by pairing a neutral stimulus (e.g., sound of a tuning fork or a massage) with morphine injections. Gradually, saline solution was substituted for morphine and paired with the conditioned stimulus. Eventually, patients no longer were addicted to morphine.

Classical conditioning was instituted for clinical purposes other than treatment. Acquisition and extinction of conditioned responses were used to diagnose disorders and provide correlates of various disorders such as brain damage, psychoses, mental retardation, deafness, alcoholism, and physical and psychogenic pain (Aldrich, 1928; Alexander, 1962; Dix and Hallpike, 1961; Franks and Franks, 1962; Gantt, 1938, 1942; Gantt and Muncie, 1942; Reese, Doss, and Gantt, 1953; Vogel, 1961; Wells and Wolff, 1960). In addition, conditioning was used to evaluate clinical interventions such as psychotherapy, electroconvulsive shock, and various drugs (Alexander, 1961; Brown, 1957).

The increased applications of classical conditioning and other concepts of learning stemmed from advances in learning theory and research. Research in learning addressed topics of direct clinical relevance such as frustration, conflict, and avoidance. Learning concepts became extended to provide a general theory of behavior that also encompassed abnormal conduct.

Extensions of Learning Concepts to Personality and Psychotherapy

Increased applications of conditioning to treat clinically relevant behaviors were associated with attempts to extend learning to provide a general theory of behavior. Of course, initial attempts to extend conditioning to explain behavior were made by Pavlov, and to a much greater extent, by Bechterev and Watson, and Watson, Rayner, Jones, Burnham, and the Mowrers proved the value of such extrapolations.

From the 1930s through the 1950s, explanations of normal and abnormal behavior and psychotherapy based upon learning increased markedly (Cameron and Magaret, 1951; French, 1933; Kubie, 1934; Magaret, 1950; Masserman, 1943; Mowrer, 1950; Shaffer, 1947; Shaw, 1948; Shoben, 1949). Most of them focused upon particular aspects of psychopathology or therapy. One of the most comprehensive attempts to integrate learning concepts with personality theory was made by John Dollard and Neal E. Miller.

Dollard, a sociologist, and Miller, an experimental psychologist, were affiliated with the Institute of Human Relations at Yale University. The Institute was established in 1933 to foster closer integration and collaboration among the behavioral sciences and the work of Dollard and Miller reflected these goals. They brought diverse aspects of social sciences together in their writings. A major influence at the Institute was Clark Hull, who, in his own writings, had attempted to formulate a general theory of behavior. Dollard and Miller adopted the Hullian concepts of drive, reinforcement, primary stimulus generalization, and habit formation. However, they did not employ his formal theoretical approach.

In 1950, Dollard and Miller published *Personality and Psychotherapy: An Analysis in Terms of Learning, Thinking and Culture*, which provided a comprehensive theory of behavior and united learning, psychopathology, and psychotherapy. They tried to integrate three traditions: Freud and psychoanalysis, experimental psychology as represented in the works of Pavlov, Thorndike, and Hull, and modern social sciences, as represented in the influence of culture on behavior.

The underlying assumption of *Personality and Psychotherapy* was that psychopathology and psychotherapy obey the laws of learning. Thus, symptom development and elimination could be explained by the same principles. Although Dollard and Miller drew heavily from Hull's theory (1943), more recent advances in learning research also were included, such as O. H. Mowrer's work on acquired drives and Miller's own research on acquired drives and the analysis of conflict. The findings from learning research were applied to psychoanalytic theory and therapy, that is, psychoanalytic concepts were translated into learning terms. For example, the pleasure principle, transference, and neurotic conflict were rephrased and explained in terms of reinforcement, stimulus generalization, and acquired drives, respectively. The goal of the book was to accomplish more than reexplanation or interpretation of a specific theory or therapy. Dollard and Miller intended their interpretation to explain the development of normal and abnormal behavior in general and to explain therapy independently of a specific theoretical approach. Freudian therapy was used as a mechanism to accomplish this end.

Dollard and Miller's interpretations encompassed more than the psychology of learning. Their approach recognized the importance of the social and cultural climate in which the individual matured:

> No psychologist would venture to predict the behavior of a rat without knowing on what arm of a T-maze the feed or the shock is placed. It is no easier to predict the behavior of a human being without knowing the conditions of his "maze," i.e., the structure of his social environment. Culture, as conceived by social scientists, is a statement of the design of the human maze, of the type of reward involved, and of what responses are to be rewarded. It is in this sense a recipe for learning. This contention is easily accepted when widely variant societies are compared. But even within the same society, the mazes which are run by two individuals may seem the same but actually be quite different. . . . No personality analysis of two . . . people can be accurate which does not take into account these cultural differences, that is, differences in the types of responses which have been rewarded . . . (Miller and Dollard, 1941, pp. 5–6).

Such a broad approach to behavior—extending beyond the psychology of learning to cultural influences—has been advocated in behavior modification (Krasner and Ullmann, 1973).

Another extension of learning to personality and psychotherapy was made by Julian B. Rotter. He attempted to translate and relate basic knowledge of experimental psychology to clinical situations in general, as elaborated in his book, *Social Learning and Clinical Psychology* (1954). Rotter drew upon several sources, including Hull, Tolman, Thorndike, and Kurt Lewin. Based upon evidence in learning, he devised a series of postulates to explain and predict behavior in a fashion similar to Hull. Rotter viewed behavior as an interaction of the individual with his environment. To understand behavior, Rotter believed that one must know an individual's expectancy for reinforcement and the perceived value of the reinforcing event.

Rotter's emphasis on expectancies of reinforcement and reinforcement value extended to psychotherapy. Therapy was seen as a learning process in which an individual's perceptions and expectancies needed to be altered. To be cured, a client needs insight into his problems, but he must learn new ways of behaving as well, so that he can achieve his goals through other means. The therapist's role is to influence the behavior of the client directly by providing reinforcement.

Despite the behavioral features he advocated, Rotter's theory was based largely upon conventional psychotherapeutic practice. The focus of therapy was on insight, expectancies, and perceptions rather than overt behavior for its own sake. In addition, his regimen depended upon mechanisms of change customarily employed in conventional therapy, including the therapeutic relationship, acceptance, reassurance, and interpretation. What Rotter added was the need to change behavior and the view of the therapist as a reinforcing agent who could effect behavior change.

The precise impact of the work of Dollard and Miller and Rotter and several other authors who applied learning concepts to behavior and psychotherapy is difficult to evaluate. The efforts to translate therapeutic processes into learning can be distinguished from contemporary behavior modification. A major difference between the translation of concepts of psychotherapy into learning and behavior modification is that the former begins with existing treatment (e.g., psychoanalytic therapy) and incorporates learning after the fact. Behavior modification, however, begins with concepts of learning and develops a program for behavior change before the fact (Ullmann and Krasner, 1965). The efforts to translate psychodynamic theory and therapeutic processes did not generate new therapeutic techniques. Learning concepts were offered as parsimonious interpretations of behavior change. For example, Shoben (1949) discussed diverse forms of psychotherapy, each of which claimed to be effective but for different reasons. Despite the dissimilarities in the therapies, common ingredients based upon learning might account for the effects of treatment.

In the late 1940s, concern about the bifurcation of clinical and experimental psychology increased. The translation efforts helped achieve a rapprochement between these areas. Learning was seen as a possible bridge between experimental science and clinical practice. In the words of Shoben (1949),

> ... there is one slender lead that might be profitably followed in the attempt to provide a basis for the conceptualization and investigation of psychotherapy as a problem in general psychology. This is the widespread recognition that psychotherapy is essentially a learning process and should be subject to study as such (Shoben, 1949, p. 367).

Thus, a general theory of behavior based upon the psychology of learning might be developed through experimentation and applied clinically.

VERBAL CONDITIONING AND PSYCHOTHERAPY

The extension of learning concepts to psychotherapy provided a fresh way to view traditional practices. However, merely explaining therapy in terms of the psychology of learning did not by itself generate research on processes of therapy or suggest new therapeutic techniques. In some ways, reinterpreting traditional psychotherapy in terms of learning may have interfered with changing therapy practice. By couching therapy practices in the terminology of learning, conventional treatment received a new theoretical justification (Salzinger, 1959).

Research on operant conditioning of verbal behavior began in the early 1950s. In verbal conditioning, verbal behavior of a speaker was altered by following specific responses with contingent events such as comments by the experimenter. Unlike conceptual extensions of learning concepts, research in verbal conditioning influenced both the method of investigation and the techniques of developing specific behaviors in therapy. The advent of verbal conditioning was particularly significant for behavior modification because it provided a direct tie between operant methods investigated in the laboratory and individual psychotherapy.

The impetus for studying verbal behavior in its own right derives from Skinner, who began to apply operant principles to verbal behavior in the early 1940s. He considered verbal behavior to be like any other emitted behavior and thus subject to the same principles. Of particular interest in verbal behavior, according to Skinner, was the behavior of the listener, who reinforced the verbalizations of the speaker. Specifically, he noted that the listener provided generalized conditioned reinforcers (e.g., attentiveness, approval) that maintained speech. Skinner's ideas were disseminated through unpublished mimeographs, courses, and lectures and finally in a book, *Verbal Behavior* (1957).[9] His ideas were widely available in summary form before the book appeared. For example, in their influential book, *Principles of Psychology,* Keller and Schoenfeld (1950) drew upon Skinner's William James Lectures on verbal behavior delivered at Harvard in 1948. Also, Skinner provided a brief outline of the application of operant conditioning to explain verbal behavior in *Science and Human Behavior* (1953a).

Interest in verbal conditioning stimulated much original experimental research. Its main purpose was to demonstrate the extent to which verbal behaviors could be manipulated as a function of consequences provided by the social environment, i.e., the listener. As it is usually conducted, verbal conditioning involves identifying a response class to be reinforced (e.g., statements of a particular type of word, such as plural nouns) and having the experimenter note instances of the target class of responses by giving some overt sign, usually either a verbal comment such as "mmm-hmm," "good," "fine," or nonverbal cues such as a nod or smile.

Initial research in conditioning verbal behavior was conducted by Joel Greenspoon (1951) for his doctorate at Indiana University. The purpose of his study was to create an experimental situation with humans that would parallel an operant conditioning model with animals. College students were instructed to say words individually rather

---

[9] Skinner's book provided an interpretation of the acquisition and use of language based on operant conditioning. An operant theory of linguistics has been criticized primarily because it attributes the causes of language to environmental events such as reinforcing and discriminative stimuli. Other dimensions, such as the internal structure of the individual and the manner in which incoming information is processed, are neglected (e.g., Chomsky, 1959). In general, the contribution of the organism has been viewed as essential in understanding language.

The linguistic theory embraced by *Verbal Behavior* is somewhat tangential to the direct line of research underlying behavior modification traced in this monograph. Skinner's views of behavior stimulated research in verbal conditioning, as discussed below. The investigation and application of operant conditioning in the context of verbal conditioning can be embraced without subscribing to an operant theory of ordinary verbal behavior. Critics of an operant analysis of language have recognized the utility of verbal conditioning as a research area in its own right (see Chomsky, 1959, p. 32fn).

than in sentences or phrases. For part of the session, the experimenter followed certain words (plural nouns) with contingent reactions such as saying "mmm-hmm," "huh-uh," or presenting visual (light) or auditory (tone) feedback. For the second part of the session, these stimuli were no longer delivered. Greenspoon found that contingent events increased plural nouns, except for "huh-uh," which was intended to suppress behavior. Thus, verbal behavior in a dyadic situation could be manipulated by the experimenter's contingent delivery of reinforcement.

Other methods were used to study verbal conditioning than the conditioning of plural nouns. A frequently used paradigm was a sentence-construction task, in which subjects selected one of six pronouns to form a sentence with verb stems printed on cards (Taffel, 1955). Selection of a particular pronoun (e.g., "I") is followed with contingent events. A less commonly used paradigm for verbal conditioning was, in the course of normal conversation, the noting of specific types of responses such as opinion statements by delivering contingent stimuli (Verplanck, 1955).

In the 1950s and 1960s, verbal conditioning received a great deal of attention. Several variables were investigated, including the effect of preconditioning experiences of the subject (e.g., allowing the subject to interact with the experimenter before conditioning), experimenter characteristics (e.g., attractiveness, sex), subject characteristics (e.g., suggestibility, aggressiveness), schedules of reinforcement, and subject awareness of the contingency (cf. Bandura, 1969; Greenspoon, 1962; Krasner, 1958, 1965b; Salzinger, 1959).

Verbal conditioning studies were extended quickly to areas of clinical work. One of the earliest was worked out by Charles Taffel (1955) in his dissertation research at Indiana University. Taffel showed that pronoun selection by psychotic patients was altered as a function of the experimenter saying "good." Several other studies extended verbal conditioning to neurotic, psychotic, mentally retarded, and geriatric patients (cf. Greenspoon, 1962).

Verbal conditioning was also applied to the psychological testing situation, particularly projective testing (Fahmy, 1953). Investigators demonstrated that clients' responses to projective tests could be controlled by consequences delivered by the examiner. For example, as a patient talked about an inkblot test, the examiner could alter specific classes of verbal responses to the test stimuli by saying "good," "all right," or by nodding, smiling, or leaning forward.

An important extension of verbal conditioning to clinical situations was the investigation of verbal behavior in interview and therapy situations. Another graduate student at Indiana University, R. S. Ball (1952), was the first to investigate the conditioning of verbal responses in a situation analogous to a clinical interview. Subjects were instructed to make up a brief story that included references to a man, woman, and an animal. Across several sessions, references to animals were increased by following them with verbal stimulus of "mmm-hmm" delivered by the examiner.

Devising a story or responding to general questions are common in assessments of verbal conditioning. A general and somewhat ambiguous task like storytelling provides a situation that more closely resembles actual therapy or interview sessions than specific responses to grammatical classes. Thus, conditioning in interviews increasingly focused upon responses assumed to resemble the therapeutic process. Affect statements, emotional words, statements about one's mother, or early family and other memories, "neurotic" or "hallucinatory" verbalizations, confiding statements, and self-acceptance and self-reference statements were conditioned in college students or psychiatric populations (Krasner, 1962).[10]

The clinical relevance of verbal conditioning was further suggested in studies of clinical populations demonstrating that changes in verbal behavior affected changes in symptomatically relevant behaviors. For example, some studies showed that conditioning emotional words with psychotic patients was associated with changes in the recognition of threatening material, anxiety, and adequacy in interpersonal relationships (cf. Krasner, 1962, 1965b). Also, reinforcement of self-acceptance or positive self-reference statements during interviews or experimental sessions sometimes altered self-descriptions and performance on psychological inventories (cf. Kanfer and Phillips, 1970).

Initially, verbal conditioning resembled psychotherapy insofar as they both represented dyadic interaction in which the prime medium of exchange is verbal. From the patient's standpoint, too, the role of language has been regarded as crucial. Maladaptive behavior may

---

[10] An advantage of procedures in which subjects state words individually (e.g., plural nouns) or tell a story is that they comprise a free-operant task. Responding is almost unrestricted and the rate of behavior can assume a wide range of values. In contrast, Taffel's task, in which subjects selected pronouns from a limited number of opportunities, restricted the response options. Taffel's task also has been criticized because the responses reinforced were limited and bore little similarity to operants usually reinforced. Operant responses usually refer to a response class with several members, not a single response (cf. Greenspoon, 1962).

consist, in part, of an inability to control one's own behavior through linguistic symbols (Shaffer, 1947; Shaw, 1946). The verbal component of therapy must be taken into account because words recreate the events that lead to the disorder. Through verbalizations, the repressed material is lifted (Shoben, 1949). Thus, a major task in treatment is getting the patient to talk (Shaffer and Lazarus, 1952).

From the therapist's standpoint, verbal conditioning also bears similarity to psychotherapy. In conventional therapy, the therapist provides cues, including brief comments such as "mmm-hmm" or "fine" or repetition and interpretation of material stated by the client. These responses were demonstrated to serve as reinforcers for specific client responses. The role of verbal conditioning in psychotherapy was emphasized by Krasner (1955), who asserted that a common factor in all psychotherapy was the presence of another person (the therapist) listening, paying attention, and showing interest, i.e., providing generalized conditioned reinforcers. By stressing the responses of the therapist, verbal conditioning studies drew attention to the directive nature of the therapeutic process and the control of the therapist. Krasner (1962) stressed the counselor's power by referring to the therapist as a "social reinforcement machine" (p. 61). This statement did not mean that the therapist was dehumanized and performed mechanically, but that he was programmed through training to exert control over client behavior by delivering generalized conditioned reinforcers contingently.

The notion that psychotherapy could be viewed through the lens of verbal conditioning was bolstered in a study by Charles Truax (1966). Truax examined the role of reinforcement in controlling client behavior by analyzing tape recordings of a therapy case handled by Carl Rogers. The analysis revealed that Rogers provided comments reflecting empathy and warmth, contingent upon specific responses of the client. This finding was dramatic, of course, because Rogerian therapy ordinarily is labeled as nondirective—the therapist is thought not to control client behavior. Truax was able to imply that therapy techniques depended upon conditioning to influence the client regardless of whether conditioning principles were acknowledged in the theoretical underpinnings of the techniques.

Psychotherapy seen from the point of view of verbal conditioning provided a rapprochement between general experimental and clinical psychology. The substantive findings of experimental work—specifically, operant conditioning—appeared to be germane to psychotherapy. The rapprochement was consistent with the work of

Dollard and Miller and others who attempted to apply learning to therapy. Yet the implications of verbal conditioning transcended psychotherapy—they suggested that certain principles and laws of behavior could apply to most social interaction (Rotter, 1960). Thus, a general theory of behavior beyond a specific therapeutic context was advanced.

A second and related aspect was that verbal conditioning provided a methodology by which various processes could be studied empirically in situations analogous to therapy. The response studied in verbal conditioning experiments were defined clearly, were recorded reliably, and were sensitive to a wide range of manipulations that were usually consequences provided by the therapist. The consequences were measurable and could be controlled readily to investigate laboratory variables such as schedules of reinforcement and types of reinforcers. In addition, the methodology permitted evaluation of factors not derived specifically from operant conditioning such as status, prestige, and experience of the therapist, atmosphere of therapy, and the expectations and personal characteristics of the subject.

Verbal conditioning research inevitably called into question some traditional assumptions of diagnosis and personality theory. Many of the responses used as the basis of diagnosis were shown to be under the control of the interviewer or experimenter's responses. Although such a finding does not mean that such responses usually *are* controlled in this way during diagnostic interviews, the modifiability of such responses suggests that they may mirror the experimenter's behavior rather than or as well as the nonverbal client behavior they supposedly reflect. The patient's report about his/her behavior or emotional states may be a function of immediate contingencies of therapy. Thus, verbal conditioning research pointed out that "personality," at least as revealed through verbal behavior, was partially a function of environmental stimuli rather than internal processes (Krasner, 1963).

The verbal conditioning research, of course, was not without limitations. Initially, the extrapolation of laboratory findings to verbal behavior was not entirely straightforward. A number of complex influences interacted to determine whether conditioning was achieved at all (Heller and Marlatt, 1969). Several studies failed to find conditioning effects (Krasner, 1958). Perhaps, more importantly, several investigators stressed that verbal conditioning and psychotherapy were dissimilar in important respects (cf. Heller and Marlatt, 1969; Kanfer, 1968; Luborsky and Strupp, 1962). In therapy, focal responses, the structure of the situation (e.g., task provided to the client), expectancies of the client, and extent of behavior change were considered to differ from verbal conditioning.

After several years of verbal conditioning research in interview and quasi-therapeutic situations, verbal conditioning was tried as a direct treatment. These applications were made in cases in which verbal behavior was of direct therapeutic interest. For example, irrational talk in psychotic patients was decreased (Ayllon and Michael, 1959; Rickard, Dignam, and Horner, 1960) and speech was reinstated in mute psychotic patients (Isaacs, Thomas, and Goldiamond, 1960; Sherman, 1965). In general, these latter applications transcended the verbal conditioning analogs that resulted from Skinner's analysis of verbal behavior. Although verbal conditioning research represented an application of operant techniques to change behavior, it should be distinguished from direct application of operant techniques to alleviate deviant or symptomatic behavior. Verbal conditioning studies developed primarily as a means to examine if verbal behavior could be altered within an operant paradigm and as a laboratory counterpart of individual psychotherapy. These investigations usually did not have a direct therapeutic focus that could be demonstrated through the responses commonly altered (e.g., use of pronouns, sentence construction) and subjects studied (e.g., college students). In contrast, the application of operant techniques for clinical purposes concentrated upon disordered behavior and clients with a diagnosed psychiatric impairment. The application of operant techniques to clinical problems was concurrent with advances in verbal conditioning. (Chapter 7 traces the progress of applied operant work.)

DEVELOPMENT OF BEHAVIOR MODIFICATION

The application of learning principles to related behavior problems, as demonstrated by Watson, Rayner, M. C. Jones, and the Mowrers, provided a preview of behavior modification. These investigators saw beyond the immediate goals of applying learning principles to alter behavior: they viewed their work as a way to demonstrate the utility of a new approach to psychopathology. Accordingly, the earlier behaviorists' work remained a valuable theoretical base for later investigators of behavior modification. Although no precise beginnings of behavior modification in its own right can be pinpointed with any ease, its incipient emergence as a formal movement is evident in South Africa, England, and, to a lesser extent, the United States.

South Africa: Wolpe and Reciprocal Inhibition

The growth of behavior therapy in South Africa derives primarily from the work of Joseph Wolpe in Johannesburg in the 1940s and 1950s. Wolpe completed research for his medical degree at the University of Witwatersrand in the late 1940s and remained on the faculty until 1959. He introduced systematic desensitization, one of the most widely employed and researched behavior therapy techniques for the treatment of neurotic disorders. Other individuals who played important roles in developing behavior therapy in South Africa were James G. Taylor and Leo J. Reyna, who influenced Wolpe's orientation and research, and Stanley J. Rachman and Arnold A. Lazarus, who worked directly with Wolpe after desensitization proper had been developed.

Wolpe was trained in traditional psychodynamic therapy, but he became dissatisfied with results of psychoanalytically oriented treatment and sought ways to alleviate emotional problems. He studied research in the psychology of learning, particularly the work of Pavlov and Hull, and became acquainted with Masserman's research on experimental neuroses. Taylor, an experimental psychologist in South Africa and avid follower of Hull, was responsible for introducing Wolpe to Hull's work. Taylor was interested in formulating a behavioral theory of perception using the hypothetico-deductive approach and select concepts of Hullian learning theory (Taylor, 1962). Although the subject was out of the mainstream of his own work, he was interested in applying learning principles to treat psychological disorders (e.g., Taylor, 1963).

Wolpe's study of learning also was facilitated by the arrival of Reyna, an American psychologist who went to Johannesburg, where he remained until 1949. Reyna received his Ph.D. in 1947 at the University of Iowa with Kenneth Spence, whose research extended Hullian theory. Reyna's interest and area of specialization was unlearning and inhibition (Reyna, 1947). Wolpe frequently consulted with Reyna, particularly about Hullian theory. He attended Reyna's seminars on the topic and Reyna served as a reader for Wolpe's dissertation for his M.D. degree.

Wolpe began research on the production and elimination of experimental neuroses in cats. He produced neurotic reactions in cats either by presenting shock alone or in conjunction with approach toward food, as Masserman (1943) had done. The animals showed a variety of symptoms, including a resistance to being placed in the experimental cage in which the neuroses had been established, signs of anxiety when placed in the cage, and a refusal to eat (meat pellets) in the cage even after one to three days of starvation.

As had been observed by Pavlov and others, the neurotic reaction transferred beyond the situation (experimental cage) in which the reaction had been established. Wolpe noted that the severity of the cats' neurotic reactions appeared to be a function of the similarity of their surroundings to the situation in which the neuroses had been developed. Specifically, the more similar the room in which the cats were placed to the room in which fear had been established, the more severe the symptoms. Wolpe relied upon Hull's notion of primary stimulus generalization to explain the transfer of neurotic reactions and speculated about the neurophysiological mechanisms to account for generalization (Wolpe, 1950a, 1950b, 1952a, 1952b, 1952d). He hypothesized that generalization was explained by common afferent neurons that the stimuli (e.g., experimental and nonexperimental rooms) shared as a function of their similarity.

The association of shock with approach toward food helped to produce the neurotic symptoms. Wolpe saw that the neurotic symptoms were linked to the inhibition of feeding, a finding also evident in Masserman's research (Masserman, 1943). This suggested that under different circumstances, feeding also might inhibit anxiety. In other words, the two reactions might be "reciprocally inhibiting" (Wolpe, 1952a).

Wolpe attempted to have animals eat in the presence of the cage in which the neurotic symptoms were established by inducing the animal with the human hand or by forcing the animal with a movable barrier to approach food. Like Masserman, he found that neurotic reactions diminished once eating had been established. However, not all the animals that Wolpe treated with induced feeding were cured. Therefore, he next attempted to induce feeding in rooms that resembled the original room in which the fear had been established. He reasoned that if the anxiety responses were relatively mild, eating would be more likely to occur. Also, if the animal ate and the anxiety diminished, lack of anxiety would generalize to the originally fear-provoking stimulus.

Wolpe (1952a) devised a procedure whereby animals ate in one of three rooms that resembled the original room in which neuroses were established. To determine the cage in which to place the animal, he began by attempting to feed the animal in the original experimental room. If the animal did not eat in this room, it was placed in the room that most resembled the original room. If the animal did not feed here either, it was placed in the next room that resembled the original room even less. The sequence was continued across all four rooms until the animal ate. Once the animal ate in a given room, it was given several opportunities to eat until all signs of anxiety decreased in that room. After anxiety diminished, the animal was placed in the next room in the series that *more* closely resembled the original experimental room. Feeding the animal in a given room until anxiety diminished and progressing to the room more similar to the original experimental room were continued until the animal ate in the setting in which neuroses were induced. In each room, food pellets were placed on the floor. When the animal progressed to the original experimental room, pellets first were placed on the floor around the room, then moved increasingly closer to the experimental cage, and finally put in the cage itself. When the animal ate in the cage, anxiety was considered eliminated (Wolpe, 1952a).

Wolpe accounted for the cure of experimental neuroses as follows:

> . . . in every instance feeding was made possible in the presence of stimuli conditioned to anxiety responses which, under other circumstances, inhibited feeding. When stimuli to incompatible responses are present simultaneously, the occurrence of the response that is dominant in the circumstances involves the reciprocal inhibition of the other. As the number of feedings increased, the anxiety responses gradually became weaker, so that to stimuli to which there was initially a response of the anxiety pattern there was finally a feeding response with inhibition of anxiety (Wolpe, 1958, p. 67).

Feeding was regarded as a response incompatible with fear. Eating in the presence of anxiety-provoking stimuli overcame anxiety. Wolpe formulated a general principle of reciprocal inhibition that stated the basis for the cure:

> *If a response antagonistic to anxiety can be made to occur in the presence of anxiety-evoking stimuli so that it is accompanied by a complete or partial suppression of the anxiety responses, the bond between these stimuli and the anxiety responses will be weakened (Wolpe, 1958, p. 71).*

To eliminate fear in cats, reciprocal inhibition involved exposing the animals to a graded series of situations that were progressively more anxiety-provoking and then pairing each situation with a response that appeared to inhibit anxiety.[11]

Wolpe extended the principle of reciprocal inhibition to treat neurotic reactions in humans. But first he had to devise methods for exposing individuals to a hierarchy of anxiety-provoking situations and creating eventual inhibitory responses. Because he felt that eating was incompatible with anxiety, he assumed that responses of the parasympathetic (craniosacral) portion of the autonomic nervous system were likely to be antagonistic to anxiety, a response primarily of the sympathetic (thoracolumbar) portion. In working on a method to inhibit anxiety that could be used readily in therapy with humans, Wolpe happened to read a book by Edmund Jacobson, a physiologist at the University of Chicago.

In his *Progressive Relaxation: A Physiological and Clinical Investigation of Muscular States and Their Significance in Psychological and Medical Practice* (1938), Jacobson said relaxation could reduce the tension produced by many disabilities. He had successfully used relaxation to treat an extremely wide range of disorders, including general anxiety, phobias, hypertension, colitis, stuttering, insomnia, tics, and depression (Jacobson, 1938). Treatment consisted of intensive and prolonged training in muscular relaxation. Wolpe seized upon Jacobson's method because it had obvious "anxiety-countering effects" (Wolpe, 1958, p. 136). However, Jacobson's method usually required between 100 and 200 training sessions. Wolpe adapted the procedure so it could be employed in only a few sessions (usually less than seven). Relaxation, often induced by hypnosis in Wolpe's original procedure, was used as an anxiety-inhibiting response, just as feeding had been used with neurotic cats (Wolpe, 1954).

The hierarchy of situations used with cats was extended to humans in two ways. Wolpe first exposed his clients *in vivo* to situations that were anxiety-provoking in a graded fashion. However, because *in vivo* confrontation with objects of fear was cumbersome, he began to explore the use of imagery. Clients imagined a graded series of anxiety-provoking situations. For example, a client who experiences severe anxiety about physical illness or becoming ill might rank the following items in descending order of anxiety-arousing value:

---

[11] The term "reciprocal inhibition" was introduced by Charles S. Sherrington (1906), who meant the inhibition of one spinal reflex by another. Wolpe extended the concept well beyond its original definition.

1. Feeling of being about to lose consciousness
2. Feeling of falling backwards
3. Marked dizziness
4. Feeling of lightness in the head
5. Moderate dizziness
6. Smell of ether
7. Receiving an injection
8. Racing heart (anxiety increasing with rapidity of heartbeat)
9. Weak knees
10. Seeing syringe poised for an injection
11. Sight of bandages (Wolpe and Lazarus, 1966, p. 70)

The items are imagined in ascending order when the client is deeply relaxed. As relaxation is maintained in the presence of items that elicit relatively low anxiety, the client proceeds up the hierarchy until the final item is imagined with no anxiety.

Wolpe also used assertive and sexual responses to inhibit anxiety. The use of assertive responses had been advocated by Andrew Salter (1949), whose therapy technique was based upon Pavlovian concepts. Salter claimed successful treatment of several disorders by having individuals behave assertively in everyday interpersonal situations.[12] Wolpe was impressed with Salter's results although he rejected the theoretical basis of the technique. Wolpe used assertive responses for inhibiting anxiety in interpersonal situations but interpreted the technique according to the principle of reciprocal inhibition. Sexual responses, i.e., those behaviors leading up to and including intercourse, were reserved for situations in which anxiety inhibited sexual performance. Wolpe instructed his clients to perform only those responses associated with sexual arousal rather than with anxiety. As the client progressed, increasingly intimate contact served to eliminate anxiety. Eventually, sexual arousal dominated and intercourse was successful.

Relaxation, assertive behavior, and sexual responses constitute the major responses used in reciprocal inhibition treatment (Wolpe, 1954).[13] Assertive and sexual responses generally are used in actual

---

[12] Salter's work is reviewed later in the discussion of the emergence of behavior modification in the United States.

[13] Wolpe noted no *a priori* reason to assume that inhibition of anxiety could be accomplished only by responses that were "physiologically opposite" (Wolpe, 1958, p. 73) to anxiety. He cited previous research (e.g., Mowrer and Viek, 1948) showing that developing motor responses helped an animal to overcome anxiety. Wolpe sometimes used respiratory responses to inhibit fear, although he did not believe these exercises to be physiologically antagonistic to anxiety. However, the main responses most frequently employed by Wolpe (relaxation, assertiveness and sexual behaviors) were conceived as being incompatible with anxiety.

situations in which behavior is problematic, such as interpersonal and sexual encounters, whereas relaxation is usually used in the therapy session. Other responses that have been used to inhibit anxiety include conditioned avoidance responses, respiratory responses (inhaling carbon dioxide), anxiety relief, and motor responses. By far the most frequently used reciprocal inhibition technique is the pairing of muscular relaxation with hierarchically arranged anxiety-provoking situations presented in imagination. This latter procedure is called systematic desensitization.

The refinement of systematic desensitization and other related techniques is traced in Wolpe's book, *Psychotherapy by Reciprocal Inhibition*, published in 1958. The work details the theoretical and empirical underpinnings of reciprocal inhibition therapy, cases demonstrating the use of relaxation, assertive, sexual, and other treatments of neurotic disorders, as well as an overall evaluation of the success of patients treated by Wolpe up to the time of publication. He claimed that psychotherapy by reciprocal inhibition cured about 90% of 210 patients.[14]

Wolpe's work is striking from several standpoints. The major contribution was the devising of specific therapy techniques based upon the principle of reciprocal inhibition. On the basis of more than 200 cases, the techniques were claimed to be effective in alleviating a wide range of neurotic disorders, particularly when compared to traditional psychotherapeutic treatment. Case comparisons, of course, do not provide rigorous evidence of a therapy's success. However, Wolpe compared results of his clinical cases with those reported from several treatment centers using traditional therapy, and asserted the superiority of his cure rate (Wolpe, 1952c, 1958). In addition to its promising success rate, reciprocal inhibition treatment required relatively few sessions. Thus, treatment appeared to be efficient as well as effective for neurotic disorders.

Aside from the appeal of Wolpe's techniques, broader aspects of his approach and development of treatment may be of greater significance. First, Wolpe conceptualized the growth and treatment of

---

[14] The improvement rates reported by Wolpe (1958) have not gone unchallenged. Stevenson (1964) noted that Wolpe excluded from his improvement figures clients he considered not to have received a thorough exposure to reciprocal inhibition therapy. Stevenson estimated that inclusion of all patients who entered the treatment evaluation process would reduce the success rate from 90% to 65%. Also, Stevenson raised the possibility that Wolpe applied criteria for improvement differently from others evaluating their psychotherapy results. Thus, the relative efficacy of reciprocal inhibition therapy and traditional psychotherapy could not be determined with any certainty.

neuroses through learning theory. He relied heavily upon the theories and research of Pavlov, Hull, Mowrer, Miller, Masserman, and others. Learning concepts were supplemented with hypotheses about neurophysiological substrates of behavior. Thus, systematic desensitization grew out of a "respectable" research—that is, "hard" science—and scientific base encompassing both the psychology of learning and physiology. The scientific respectability of the treatment may have been an attractive feature of his approach, particularly because criticism of traditional psychoanalytic treatment and its unscientific tenets had increased in the early 1950s (e.g., Eysenck, 1952b; Salter, 1952).

Second, Wolpe extrapolated from his cures of experimental neurosis in animals to invent treatment techniques for clinical patients. Masserman (1943) also had devised treatment procedures to eliminate neurotic reactions in cats, and Wolpe's work followed Masserman's procedures very closely. However, Masserman applied psychoanalytic concepts to explain the laboratory techniques that eliminated neurotic reactions in animals. He reinterpreted his laboratory-based techniques in terms of concepts and procedures used in psychoanalysis (e.g., transference, working through). Wolpe's unique contribution was in employing laboratory procedures, generating a principle to explain these procedures, and deriving "new" therapy techniques based upon that principle. Thus he established a direct tie between laboratory-animal research and new clinical treatment.

Finally, Wolpe made specific and testable claims about his conceptualization of therapy. He asserted that for reciprocal inhibition treatment to be effective, certain conditions had to be met. By asserting that specific features of therapy were essential, he stimulated a plethora of research (see Chapter 6).

The combination of the above factors contributed to the innovative quality of Wolpe's approach. The combination of ingredients appears to be especially important because particular elements were already available in the literature. Several other investigators had suggested techniques that very closely resembled or were identical to desensitization (e.g., Herzberg, 1945; Jones, 1924a, 1924b; Salter, 1949) and some had relied upon learning theorists to account for their findings. Wolpe was familiar with the literature of the psychology of learning and the generation and elimination of neuroses, and he was able to integrate theoretical positions and laboratory findings from both areas to provide an account of the etiology and treatment of clinical neuroses.

Wolpe developed his techniques while in South Africa. In 1956, he left South Africa for one year to become a Fellow at the Center for Advanced Study of the Behavioral Sciences in Stanford, California. It was during this year that he completed *Psychotherapy by Reciprocal Inhibition.* In traveling to and from the United States and South Africa, Wolpe gave colloquia on reciprocal inhibition therapy at various universities in the United States. He also visited Eysenck in London, who was instrumental in promoting behavior therapy in England. In 1962, Wolpe left South Africa to join the faculty at the University of Virginia School of Medicine. In 1965, he went to work at Temple University Medical School, where he is a professor of psychiatry.

Two other individuals worked with Wolpe before he left South Africa. Stanley J. Rachman and Arnold A. Lazarus, both undergraduate and graduate students at the University of Witwatersrand, later collaborated with Wolpe. In 1955–1956, Rachman completed his degree; he remained on the faculty at the University and informally received training from Wolpe (cf. Rachman, 1959; Wolpe and Rachman, 1960). When Wolpe left for his sabbatical in California, Rachman took over treatment of some of his patients. To work with Eysenck, Rachman moved to England in 1959, and he introduced Wolpe's technique of desensitization there. Since 1960, Rachman has had a major influence on the course of behavior modification in England.

Arnold A. Lazarus also became interested in Wolpe's technique and collaborated with Rachman on using desensitization with clinical cases (Lazarus and Rachman, 1957). In 1960, Lazarus completed his doctoral degree in psychology under the supervision of Wolpe. Lazarus' dissertation research extended the practice of desensitization to groups of individuals (Lazarus, 1961). After completion of his degree, Lazarus continued his therapy work. Based on his extensive practice, Lazarus reported the results of treatment of his own 408 cases with a relatively high rate (78%) of improvement (Lazarus, 1963). In 1963, Lazarus came to Stanford University for one year, where he trained others in desensitization. After two more years in South Africa, he returned to California in 1966 to found an institute for behavior therapy.

Lazarus' contributions include the introduction of the term "behaviour therapy" in South Africa. He used the term in 1958 to refer to an objective, laboratory-derived therapy that contrasted with traditional techniques (Lazarus, 1958). He also extended systematic desensitization to phobic children (Lazarus, 1959) and to groups (Lazarus, 1961). Finally, he experimented with pleasant imagery rather than relaxation as an anxiety-inhibiting response (Lazarus and Abramovitz, 1962).

England: The Maudsley Group

The growth of behavior modification in England began independently of Wolpe's work in South Africa. Two individuals who have exerted the greatest influence are Hans J. Eysenck and, less directly, M. B. Shapiro at the Institute of Psychiatry of the University of London, which is associated with the Maudsley Hospital.

Eysenck completed his Ph.D. in psychology at the University of London in 1940. Before obtaining a job, he met Alexander Herzberg, a German psychoanalyst who fled to London during World War II. Although Herzberg adhered rather closely to orthodox psychoanalysis, he had invented a direct form of treatment that deviated from standard analytic practice. In 1941, Herzberg proposed a short-term treatment of "graduated tasks" and presented several cases attesting to its efficacy. The technique required patients to perform a graduated series of tasks to overcome their symptoms. For example, a patient who was fearful of walking out on the street was given a series of progressively more demanding tasks, such as walking briefly near a park, on a quiet street, and eventually alone at more difficult locations. Herzberg elaborated the graduated-task procedure in a book entitled *Active Psychotherapy* (1945). The book recorded numerous cases with diverse problems—including fear, headaches, insomnia, depression, homosexuality, impotence, masochism, and exhibitionism—that were successfully treated in a relatively brief period of time.

Herzberg held informal group meetings in London on psychiatry. Eysenck attended these meetings and became interested in the graduated-task method independent of its ties to psychoanalytic therapy. The technique appeared to focus directly upon problem behavior. Eysenck questioned whether the effects of the technique depended upon the psychodynamic processes to which Herzberg referred. Herzberg and Eysenck debated if the graduated-tasks method were an adjunct to psychotherapy or an effective method in its own right (Eysenck, 1966). Several years later, the graduated-tasks method was shown to be effective in its own right (see below).

A few years after completing his degree, Eysenck took a position as a research psychologist at Mill Hill Hospital in London. After the end of World War II, he and others at the hospital transferred to the Maudsley, a psychiatric teaching hospital in London that had been closed down during the war. He accepted a position as head of the department of psychology at the Institute of Psychiatry at Maudsley. As he expanded the department, Eysenck altered the usual role of the clinical psychologist. He advanced the notion that a psychologist should serve primarily as a researcher and rely upon findings from general psychology for clinical practice (Eysenck, 1949, 1950, 1952a; Paynes, 1953). This position derived from his scientific and experimental training as well as his dissatisfaction with traditional psychiatric practices.

Eysenck was trained as an experimental psychologist and was critical of the scientific status of psychiatry and clinical psychology. His criticism, in part, resulted from some of his own research that had demonstrated the unreliability of psychiatric diagnosis and his evaluation of traditional psychotherapy. He evaluated the efficacy of psychoanalysis and psychoanalytically oriented treatment by reviewing the psychotherapy literature. In 1952, the review was published as a paper entitled, "The Effects of Psychotherapy: An Evaluation."[15] He found no firm evidence that psychotherapy was more effective than spontaneous remission (improvement without specific treatment.) The review was extremely influential and controversial because it challenged the efficacy of traditional therapy. It precipitated an increased concern with experimentation in psychotherapy in general and with the limitations or possible limitations of traditional treatment.

Another of Eysenck's interests lay in the psychology of learning. Much of his research focused upon a dimensional approach to personality and drew upon learning theorists, particularly Hull and Spence. He made direct use of Hull's ideas to explain causes of anxiety in *The Dynamics of Anxiety and Hysteria: An Experimental Application of Modern Learning Theory to Psychiatry* (1957). The book is notable for its concise review of some therapeutic applications of learning theory to psychiatric disorders, including early work of Wolpe, and cases at Maudsley conducted by H. Gwynne Jones, Victor Meyer, and Aubrey Yates.

In 1959, Eysenck published the first paper that introduced the term "behavior therapy" in England. The paper, "Learning Theory

---

[15] A revision of this paper was published later in book form in which eminent psychiatrists, psychologists, and psychoanalysts served as discussants (Eysenck, 1966).

and Behaviour Therapy," criticized psychoanalytic theory and the disease model. An important feature of this article was Eysenck's comparison of Freudian psychotherapy and behavior therapy, set forth in Table 5.1.

In 1960, Eysenck edited a book entitled *Behaviour Therapy and the Neuroses: Readings in Modern Methods of Treatment Derived from Learning Theory*. It presented many classic works in the field and various treatment applications, including desensitization, negative practice, aversion therapy, and other techniques. This book was the first general text in any country that had brought together diverse treatment methods under the rubric of behavior therapy.[16] In 1963, Eysenck initiated *Behaviour Research and Therapy,* the first journal devoted to behavior therapy.

Under Eysenck's direction, the department of psychology as a whole was firmly committed to the role of the psychologist as a scientist-researcher. This approach was supported and fostered by M. B. Shapiro, who came to the Institute of Psychiatry after World War II. Eysenck was head of the research section of the psychology department, and Shapiro was head of its clinical-teaching section.

Shapiro rejected the routine administration of psychological tests as the primary task of clinical psychologists. His dissatisfactions with the traditional role of clinical psychologists were multiple. They included the apparent irrelevance of test performance to important diagnostic questions given that diagnosis had no treatment or etiological implications, the invalidity of many tests, and the futility of routinely testing all patients (Yates, 1970b). He felt that the unique role of the psychologist should be to approach the patient from a scientific perspective. From knowledge of general psychology, the psychologist should formulate hypotheses about the possible etiology of behavior and treatment. According to Shapiro, the role of the psychologist was to determine: ". . . whether general and experimental psychology have anything to offer in the way of explanation of the patient's disorders, and whether this explanation offers leads for further investigation, treatment, and disposal of the patient" (1957, p. 100).

Although both Eysenck and Shapiro believed that the clinical psychologist should be a researcher, their approaches differed. As head of the psychology department, Eysenck conducted research related to basic theoretical questions about psychopathology by using

---

[16] Other books that appeared before Eysenck's treatise included descriptions of specific techniques (e.g., Salter, 1949; Wolpe, 1958). They were not general texts on behavior modification.

Table 5.1. Comparison between Freudian psychotherapy and behavior therapy[a]

Freudian psychotherapy	Behavior therapy
1. Based on inconsistent theory never properly formulated in postulate form.	Based on consistent, properly formulated theory leading to testable deductions.
2. Derived from clinical observations made without necessary control observations or experiments.	Derived from experimental studies specifically designed to test basic theory and deductions made therefrom.
3. Considers symptoms the visible upshot of unconscious causes ('complexes').	Considers symptoms as unadaptive conditioned responses.
4. Regards symptoms as evidence of *repression*.	Regards symptoms as evidence of faulty learning.
5. Believes that symptomatology is determined by defense mechanisms.	Believes that symptomatology is determined by individual differences in conditionability and autonomic lability, as well as accidental environmental circumstances.
6. All treatment of neurotic disorders must be *historically* based.	All treatment of neurotic disorders is concerned with habits existing at *present*; their historical development is largely irrelevant.
7. Cures are achieved by handling the underlying (unconscious) dynamics, not by treating the symptom itself.	Cures are achieved by treating the symptom itself, i.e., by extinguishing unadaptive conditioned responses and establishing desirable conditioned responses.
8. Interpretation of symptoms, dreams, acts, etc., is an important element of treatment.	Interpretation, even if not completely subjective and erroneous, is irrelevant.
9. Symptomatic treatment leads to the elaboration of new symptoms.	Symptomatic treatment leads to permanent recovery provided autonomic as well as skeletal surplus conditioned responses are extinguished.
10. Transference relations are essential for cures of neurotic disorders.	Personal relations are not essential for cures of neurotic disorder, although they may be useful in certain circumstances.

[a] From Eysenck, 1959, p. 67; reprinted by permission.

large groups of subjects. As head of the clinical-teaching section, Shapiro conducted research pertinent to the clinical study and treatment of the individual.

Two aspects of Shapiro's approach are especially noteworthy. He advocated the use of individualized measurements of a patient's behavior. Instead of using a standardized battery of tests for all patients, specific measures could focus on the patient's particular problem (Shapiro, 1951, 1961a). He criticized traditional research for its emphases on patient performance, batteries of tests, experimental tasks such as puzzles and games that were not of immediate clinical relevance. He recommended direct measurement of clinically relevant behavior (i.e., the patient's symptoms) so that any behavior change effected with treatment would be of clinical and research import (Shapiro, 1961a). He favored the intensive study of the single case—the individual patient could be utilized in clinical research (Shapiro, 1961b, 1966; Shapiro and Ravenette, 1959). He believed that the demands of a given patient could not await the findings from group studies. The individual patient could be subjected to research to test different hypotheses about explanations of the disorder and procedures to ameliorate it. If experimental control could be demonstrated in a single case, he believed that the same control could be expected with other patients as well (Shapiro, 1961b).

Shapiro's role in the development of behavior modification is a subtle one, because his primary commitment has been oriented toward the individual patient rather than behavior modification techniques (Shapiro, 1951, 1952, 1957). However, Shapiro helped foster the use of conditioning in the clinical-research section by meeting with other psychologists to discuss Pavlov, Hull, Osgood, and others, and by designing behavioral interventions. He worked with H. G. Jones, Meyer, and Yates in applying behavioral techniques to various clinical cases at Maudsley Hospital during the 1950s.

Applications of learning principles in the clinical-teaching section involved diverse methods. H. G. Jones (1956) made one of the earliest applications when he treated an adult female patient who complained of frequent urination (about one instance every half hour) and anxiety in public situations. To decrease the frequency of urination, Jones used a procedure whereby saline solution was placed directly into the patient's bladder.[17] Bladder-pressure readings were displayed in front of

---

[17] The procedure was based upon experiments of Bykov (1953). Warm water was introduced into the bladder and bladder pressure changes were displayed to the subject. Bykov conceptualized his research as Pavlovian conditioning.

the patient on a manometer. The patient's urge to urinate was associated with low levels of fluid in the bladder. As the trials progressed, more fluid was introduced; however, the pressure readings were altered so as not to reflect these changes. As the patient tolerated more fluid, veridical readings were provided. After only a few sessions in a period of one week, bladder control was gained and frequent urinating ceased.

To treat the patient's anxiety, Jones associated responses that did not trigger stress with the presence of stimuli that approximated the anxiety-provoking stimuli (i.e., other people). The patient was instructed to engage in a progressive series of behaviors that did not provoke anxiety. Because the patient once had been a dancer, she performed dance-related tasks such as dancing before an imaginary audience, performing in front of the experimenter, and performing in an amateur show. In two weeks, the patient no longer reported anxiety in public situations and treatment was terminated.[18]

Meyer (1957) treated fear of going outdoors and fear of enclosed and crowded places in two adult patients. He assumed that nonanxious responses could be performed in mild approximations of the anxiety-provoking stimulus, i.e., across a series of graduated tasks as used by Herzberg. Eventually, as being unafraid began to increase across diverse situations, the original feared situation would not be associated with anxiety. Patients were exposed to a series of stimuli similar to the anxiety-provoking situation. For example, the patient who feared going outside was provided with a series of tasks in which she went out on the enclosed roof of the hospital, to a main garden of the hospital, outside the hospital grounds, along main and back streets, on bus rides, and other tasks. The daily frequency of the excursions was increased along with the anxiety-provoking nature of the tasks. Throughout treatment, the experimenter initially accompanied the patient into the situation before she performed the task alone. Within five weeks, the patient made excursions alone without difficulty and treatment was terminated.

Yates (1958a) treated an adult female who had multiple tics (a complex stomach-contraction tic, and nasal, coughing, and eyeblink tics). Yates employed a technique known as negative practice (Dunlap, 1932), which involves repeating the behavior one wishes to eliminate. Yates provided a rationale for the technique based upon

---

[18] The procedure was conceived in terms of Guthrie's method of breaking habits, i.e., by associating a given response with approximations of the anxiety-provoking stimuli. The procedure was similar to Wolpe's use of imagery.

Hullian theory and tested various predictions about the effect of manipulating variables of practice.[19] The patient voluntarily performed the tics during several sessions. Treatment reduced three of the four tics, but none were eliminated.

These early applications of learning principles at Maudsley led to investigation of several techniques, including the graduated-task method, biofeedback, aversion relief, and negative practice.[20] The techniques were based on the ideas of Hull, Guthrie, and Mowrer. Wolpe's research exerted relatively minimal influence on this early work. Although his work was cited, it was used only as support for techniques already in use at Maudsley. For example, the technique of presenting graduated tasks was not conceptualized as desensitization or reciprocal inhibition *per se*. Instead, the graduated-task procedure closely resembled what is now termed *in vivo* desensitization, in which patients perform a graded series of responses in actual situation rather than in imagination.

In the 1960s, application of behavior therapy techniques increased at the Institute with the appearance of Stanley J. Rachman, Michael Gelder, and Isaac M. Marks. After his training with Wolpe, Rachman came to Maudsley to work with Eysenck (on a project unrelated to behavior therapy); in 1961, he joined the faculty in the department of psychology. Rachman introduced Wolpe's method of systematic desensitization based on imagery, although *in vivo* desensitization already had been piloted by H. G. Jones and V. Meyer.

In the early 1960s, Gelder, who was a psychiatrist at the Institute, became interested in Meyer's clinical work with phobias. He worked on a few cases with Meyer and believed that the graduated-task technique or desensitization was sufficiently promising to warrant further consideration. After studying learning theory and research on his own, he began a research program on desensitization. In 1960, Marks came to the clinical-teaching section for training in psychiatry. He worked with Shapiro (e.g., Shapiro, Marks, and Fox, 1963) and eventually collaborated with Gelder. Gelder and Marks completed a series of studies on desensitization (e.g., Cooper, Gelder, and Marks, 1965; Gelder and Marks, 1966; Marks and Gelder, 1965).

---

[19] According to Hullian theory, massed practice of a response builds up inhibition (i.e., reactive inhibition or I_R). When I_R reaches a critical level, the individual is forced to rest or not perform the response. The habit of not performing the response is acquired because it is reinforced through drive reduction. The learned inhibition (i.e., conditioned inhibition or $_sI_R$) replaces performance of the response.

[20] Many additional cases by investigators at Maudsley are unpublished, but some are reviewed by H. G. Jones (1960).

Rachman, Marks, and Gelder have been responsible for many investigations of behavior therapy techniques, including desensitization, flooding, modeling, and aversion therapy. The Institute of Psychiatry at Maudsley Hospital remains the nucleus of behavior therapy in England as well as the editorial center for *Behaviour Research and Therapy*.

The United States: Negative Practice, Aversion Therapy, Conditioned Reflex Therapy, and Operant Conditioning

The emergence of behavior modification in the United States is not as readily demarcated as it is in South Africa and England. Before behavior modification became a specific domain of study in the United States, select behavioral techniques were used or advocated, as reflected in the seminal work of Watson, Rayner, M. C. Jones, the Mowrers, Burnham, and others. Early uses of behavioral techniques showed an increased application of learning principles to clinical problems, but they were not unified as part of a single approach or movement labeled "behavior modification." Many of these applications did not differ from current behavior modification practices, although they tend to be accorded embryonic status in contemporary behavior modification. Because the work of Watson and his followers, the Mowrers, Burnham, Mateer, and others was summarized earlier, this section will turn to the contributions of other American psychologists, psychiatrists, and clinicians.

Applications of conditioning to therapeutic purposes expanded along independent lines in the United States. The most notable clinical applications were made by Knight Dunlap, who devised a therapeutic technique called "negative practice," Walter L. Voegtlin and Frederick Lemere, who developed aversion therapy to treat alcoholics, and Andrew Salter, who created conditioned reflex therapy to treat diverse disorders. Concomitant with these advances, operant conditioning methods were extended to human behavior. The extensions, reflected primarily in the laboratory work of Ogden R. Lindsley and Sidney W. Bijou, became the bases for subsequent refinements in applying operant techniques for clinical purposes. (Chapter 7 elaborates the application of operant techniques for clinical purposes.)

Knight Dunlap and Negative Practice An experimental psychologist at the Johns Hopkins University and a colleague of John B. Watson, Dunlap was interested in the formation and elimination of habits, particularly the role of response repetition in learning. He believed that repetition *per se* did not necessarily increase response strength. Repetition was important only insofar as it allowed other factors to operate. Dunlap posed that repetition operated on behavior in one of three ways: increased a response (referred to as the alpha hypothesis), had no influence on the response (beta hypothesis), or decreased the response (gamma hypothesis).

His own interest focused upon the role of repetition in eliminating undesirable habits. He published two articles (1928, 1930) and a book (1932), *Habits, Their Making and Unmaking,* which described this interest and its therapeutic applications. The procedure, known as *negative practice,* involves the voluntary performance of some behavior that an individual wishes to eliminate. If an individual repeats a behavior, the expectation of improvement and the satisfaction of eliminating the response will break the habit. Thus, by voluntarily engaging in the behavior, the habit is eradicable. After the undesirable habit is eliminated, positive practice of the desired behavior develops the new habit.

Although the term "negative practice" suggests the importance of repetition of the behavior, repeated practice alone was not sufficient for behavior change. The effectiveness of the repetition depended upon the individual's "thoughts, desires, and ideals" (Dunlap, 1932, p. 202). The individual must practice the response with the mental set that the response will be eliminated. The desire to stop the habit, according to Dunlap, was the fundamental curative agent. Based upon actual case histories, he claimed that negative practice was effective in eliminating stuttering, nail-biting, daydreaming, tics, thumbsucking, masturbation, and homosexuality. To eliminate these behaviors, the individual either repeatedly performed the unwanted behavior or a close approximation of it. Although Dunlap claimed that negative practice could treat all sorts of habits successfully, he did not offer a complete rationale for its efficacy.

> The "explanation" of the efficacy of the method of negative practice is not a matter of great moment. The facts can probably be speciously fitted into any theory of learning, however useless such a theory may otherwise be. Unfortunately, any "explanations" of learning at present are assumptions in the realm of the unknown, and should be sedulously avoided (Dunlap, 1932, p. 314).

The significance of Dunlap's work in behavior modification derives not only from his technique of negative practice but also from his general approach toward psychological treatment. His view of treatment is one to which most contemporary practitioners of behavior modification would subscribe:

> The salvation of the neurotic lies in the application to him of the results of scientific psychology. Of these results, the principles of learning are by

far the most important, but the application must be based in a broad psychological understanding of the patient's situation and processes (Dunlap, 1932, p. 193).

Although learning is accorded the most prominent place in behavior modification, many writers have argued for a broader approach in understanding behavior (e.g., Krasner and Ullmann, 1973; Lazarus, 1971a; Ullmann and Krasner, 1969).

Dunlap's work anticipated the course of behavior modification in the United States because he suggested and applied a learning-based therapy technique and advocated a scientific approach toward therapy. His work on negative practice was pursued by various authors, most notably Yates (1958a) in England. Yates applied the procedure clinically and added a theoretical base derived from Hullian learning theory. Other investigators have applied negative practice to such problems as speech difficulties, and phobic and obsessive disorders (e.g., Case, 1960; Fishman, 1937; Lehner, 1954; Malleson, 1959).[21]

Walter L. Voegtlin, Frederick Lemere, and Aversion Therapy for Alcoholics   In 1935, aversion therapy was proposed as a way to help alcoholics. Treatment commenced at Shadel Sanatorium, a facility in Seattle, Washington, devoted to treating voluntarily admitted alcoholics. The program was directed by Voegtlin, a gastroenterologist who developed nausea-inducing agents (emetine and emetine derivatives) for use in the cure. Treatment entailed pairing nausea with alcohol according to the tenets of classical conditioning. In 1937, two years after the procedure was tested, Lemere, a psychiatrist, came to Shadel. Voegtlin and Lemere collaborated for several years on the treatment of alcoholics.

The use of aversion conditioning developed over a lengthy period at the institution, during which several procedures were tried, including group therapy and follow-through rehabilitation (Shadel, 1944). Of all the available techniques for treating alcoholics, conditioning appeared to be the most promising (Voegtlin and Lemere, 1942). The earliest reports of aversion therapy as an effective treatment came from Russia. In Russia, Kantorovich (1929) had used electric shock as the unconditioned stimulus and alcohol as the conditioned stimulus to bring about an aversive reaction. Other Russian investigators

---

[21] Negative practice is no longer popular because it is unreliable. Negative practice has alleviated problem behaviors in some cases, but it has exacerbated them or has had minimal effects in others (e.g, Case, 1960; Feldman and Werry, 1966; Fishman, 1937; Rutherford, 1940; Walton, 1961; Yates, 1958a). Moreover, numerous other techniques to eliminate undesirable habits are available.

established conditioned aversion by using apomorphine as the unconditioned stimulus (Markovnikov, 1934; Sluchevski and Friken, 1933).
As a result of the early work in Russia, investigators in France, England, Germany, Belgium, and America began to use techniques to
develop an aversion toward alcohol.

The treatment used at Shadel Sanatorium, known as "conditioned reflex treatment," (Voegtlin, Lemere, and Broz, 1940) paired
the sight, smell, and taste of alcohol with nausea- and emesis-inducing
agents that were taken orally or injected. The goal of treatment was to
develop an aversion reaction. Treatment was brief (lasting from four
to seven sessions over an average of 10 days, with individual sessions
of 30 minutes to one hour). At the end of several months, patients
routinely received booster sessions to correct or decrease the likelihood of relapses.

The most compelling feature of the work of Voegtlin and Lemere
was the thorough follow-up evaluation of treatment. Follow-up ranged
from 1 to 13 years and encompassed over 4,000 patients. The success rates, using abstinence as the criterion, were impressive. Sixty
percent of the patients remained abstinent for 1–2 years, 38% for 5–10
years, and 23% for 10–13 years after treatment (Lemere and Voegtlin,
1950). The possibility of sustained abstinence was enhanced by conducting booster sessions one year after treatment (Voegtlin, Lemere,
Broz, and O'Hollaren, 1942). In addition to durability of treatment,
variables that influenced treatment efficacy were evaluated. Among
them were effects of administering different drugs (apomorphine and
emetine), the role of personal and demographic variables, and the
results of booster sessions on abstinence rates. The story of the Shadel
program was well documented in the 1940s and 1950s (Lemere and
Voegtlin, 1940, 1950; Lemere, Voegtlin, Broz, and O'Hollaren, 1942a,
1942b; Voegtlin, 1940; Voegtlin, Lemere, Broz, and O'Hollaren,
1942). Publication of treatment results led several other investigators
in the United States to use the conditioned reflex treatment with alcoholics, although on a much smaller scale than employed in Seattle
(e.g., Edlin, Johnson, Hletko, and Heilbrunn, 1945; Kant, 1944;
Thimann, 1949a, 1949b).

The work at Shadel stands out among other applications of conditioning in the United States available in the 1930s and 1940s. The
aversive conditioning techniques then used continue to be used in
behavior modification. Thus, the applications at Shadel are not
precursors to behavioral techniques or merely demonstrational
projects but behavior modification practiced on a large scale before
behavior modification became a formal movement. Moreover, the

research of Voegtlin and Lemere remains one of the most thorough records of aversion therapy in the literature.

Andrew Salter and Conditioned Reflex Therapy   Andrew Salter received his undergraduate degree at New York University in 1937. A few years later, he began private practice in New York City, where he developed therapy based upon theory and research in the psychology of learning. During his undergraduate years, Salter had become interested in hypnosis as a therapeutic method. Clark Hull's book, *Hypnosis and Suggestibility: An Experimental Approach* (1933), provided a behavioristic interpretation of hypnosis that greatly influenced Salter. The primary mechanism of hypnosis, according to Hull, was the experimenter's or hypnotist's speech, which served as conditioned stimuli to evoke reactions from the client.

Salter explored the use of hypnosis in private clinical practice and developed techniques of autohypnosis, which he posed as self-control techniques (Salter, 1941). He applied autohypnosis to problems such as stuttering, nail-biting, insomnia, smoking, and overeating. In 1944, Salter published *What is Hypnosis; Studies in Auto and Hetero Conditioning*, in which he expanded Hull's interpretation of hypnosis to include conditioning. In this book, he referred directly to Pavlov and Bechterev's discussion of what Pavlov had termed the "second signal system." Salter also emphasized that words spoken by oneself or by someone else could become conditioned stimuli (cf. Hudgins, 1933). He reasserted Hull's idea that words serve as conditioned stimuli in hypnosis and evoke previously conditioned reactions on the part of the client.

Viewing hypnosis as conditioning in the manner suggested by Hull led Salter to a more general concern with conditioning and therapeutic change. He published another book, *Conditioned Reflex Therapy; The Direct Approach to the Reconstruction of Personality* (1949), based on conditioning as the major instrument of therapeutic change with hypnosis relegated to a comparatively minor role. This work described a general theory of maladaptive behavior and specific therapeutic procedures called "conditioned reflex therapy."[22] The writings of Pavlov and Bechterev were the primary sources for the treatment. Specifically, the notions of excitation, inhibition, and disin-

---

[22] The term "conditioned reflex therapy" used by Salter was developed independently of the term "conditioned reflex treatment" used by Voegtlin and Lemere. Both procedures were conceived of as descending from Pavlov's and Bechterev's work. Salter set forth a general therapeutic strategy based upon a Pavlovian theoretical base; Voegtlin and Lemere meant aversion therapy based upon the method of establishing conditioned responses.

hibition—neurological processes originally suggested by Sechenov and discussed by Pavlov and Bechterev—were appropriated to explain maladaptive behavior.

Salter believed that maladjustment primarily consists of excessive inhibition. The basis of adjustment is a balance between excitation and inhibition: "[m]ental health is a matter of balance between inhibition and excitation, although in therapy we emphasize the excitatory side of the picture" (p. 199). According to Salter, social development frequently inculcates so much inhibition that individuals are not free to express themselves. The goal of therapy is to liberate inhibitions and nurture an excitatory personality. As he noted, to "disinhibit the inhibitory" (p. 187) is the guiding principle of conditioned reflex therapy:

> Our goal is to disinhibit the inhibitory, and this we attain by what may be termed *verbal chemistry*. Words, spoken by the therapist, travel along appropriate nerve tracts in the person under treatment, and produce chemical modifications in his nervous system. These changes are associated with behavior changes, which in turn precipitate more biochemical modifications and more behavior changes.
>
> Maladjustment is a learning process, and so is psychotherapy. Maladjustment is malconditioning, and psychotherapy is reconditioning. The individual's problems are a result of his social experiences, and by changing his techniques of social relations, we change his personality. Experience is not only the best teacher, it is the only teacher. We are not especially concerned with giving the individual stratified knowledge of his past—called "probing." What concerns us is giving him reflex knowledge for his future—called "habits" (Salter, 1949, p. 316).

To encourage one's excitatory side, individuals must practice expressing their emotions in everyday life. General rules of conduct or techniques to improve emotional expression include: *feeling talk* (deliberate utterance of spontaneously felt emotions); *contradiction and attack* (expression of disagreement); *use of the word "I"*; *agreement with praise*; and *improvisation* (engaging in acts spontaneously) (Salter, 1949).

Engaging in excitatory behaviors during social interaction constituted a general strategy recommended by Salter for all psychological problems. However, he employed several adjunctive procedures to induce, liberate, or eliminate various feelings depending upon the specific behaviors being modified. For example, individuals who occasionally experienced anxiety learned to relax to reduce tension in stressful settings. Individuals were trained to relax by the therapist and then to make themselves relax in problematic situations. Similarly, imagery connected with positive experiences or events was evoked to help overcome particular problems. For example, calmness would be induced with pleasant imagery to overcome anxiety or insomnia or to foster desired behavior, such as appropriate sexual functioning.

The importance of Salter's work to behavior modification lies in its roots in conditioning and learning theory and its emphatic focus on therapy. His initial theory of maladaptive behavior and therapy leaned upon concepts and research in conditioning. His position owed the most to Pavlov and, to a lesser extent, Bechterev, but he also synthesized the research of Gantt, Masserman, Mowrer, N. R. F. Maier, Hull, and Guthrie. Salter viewed maladaptive behavior and formulated treatment in terms of learning—a clear departure from traditional psychotherapy. His notions of conditioning were bolstered by his references to a successful therapy approach based upon learning as espoused by Watson and Rayner, Voegtlin and Lemere, and Dunlap. The innovative feature of Salter's approach was not simply to use conditioning principles to explain existing therapy techniques, as Dollard and Miller had done, but to devise specific treatments and apply them clinically.

A second striking feature of Salter's work was its therapeutic focus. Treatment focused upon the behavior itself rather than underlying psychodynamics, thoughts, and traits. Therapeutic change was effected by having the individual *behave* differently:

> People tell me what they think, but this does not concern me very much. I want to know what they *did*, because it is what they do that gets them into trouble, and what they *will do* that gets them out of it. To change the way a person feels and thinks about himself, we must change the way he acts toward others; and by constantly treating inhibition, we will be constantly getting at the roots of his problem (Salter, 1949, p. 100).

Behavior in the problematic situation was what counted—Salter did not believe that improvement was made in the therapist's office. Thus, clients were instructed how to perform in everyday situations in a way that would lead to therapeutic change. Salter's clients completed therapeutic tasks *in vivo*, still an integral strategy of a number of contemporary behavioral techniques.

Salter made sure that patients concentrated on the here and now rather than past conflicts. The assumption that maladaptive behavior was caused by inappropriate conditioning was useful as a rationale for the techniques employed, but conditioned reflex therapy did not dwell on history. As Salter (1949) noted, "Finding and exploring the situations that have caused the psychological difficulty does nothing to facilitate the cure" (p. 38). For practical purposes, "how the individual 'gets that way' is of little therapeutic importance" (p. 143).

Conditioned reflex therapy was also useful in that it could be applied to diverse behaviors. Previous applications of conditioning had remained within a relatively narrow focus: M. C. Jones treated specific fears, the Mowrers dealt with enuresis, Dunlap tried to break maladaptive habits, and Voegtlin and Lemere devoted themselves to reducing alcohol abuse. Through Salter, conditioned reflex therapy was now applied to various neurotic disorders, sexual deviance and dysfunction, insomnia, and more. Testimony could be offered to its wide generality.

Salter used several therapeutic procedures based upon conditioning that eventually became more systematically studied. Cases reported in *Conditioned Reflex Therapy* include applications of techniques closely resembling systematic desensitization, self-control, behavioral rehearsal, and covert conditioning based upon imagery. Although the specific Pavlovian notions of inhibition and excitation that were posed as the theoretical base of conditioned reflex therapy have been refuted, fuller versions of techniques initiated by Salter are still being employed by contemporary practitioners of behavior modification.

Extensions of Operant Conditioning to Human Behavior The systematic application of operant conditioning to human behavior provided a major impetus for work in behavior modification. In the 1950s, operant conditioning became increasingly investigated in animal-laboratory research. The first major extensions of operant principles to complex human behavior were conceptual rather than empirical. Keller and Schoenfeld (1950) described the pervasiveness of operant principles as follows:

> The principle of operant conditioning may be seen everywhere in the multifarious activities of human beings from birth until death. Alone, or in combination with the Pavlovian principle, it is involved in all the strengthenings of behavior with which we shall be concerned in this book. It is present in our most delicate discriminations and our subtlest skills; in our earliest crude habits and the highest refinements of creative thought. It accounts, in large part, for our abnormal "fixations" as well as our normal "adjustments"; for our parades of power and our shows of weakness; for cooperation no less than competition. It may be seen in our friendly relations with, and our withdrawals from, our fellows; in our expressions of bigotry and toleration; in our virtures as well as our vices (Keller and Schoenfeld, 1950, pp. 64–65).

Skinner also was quite explicit about the generalizability of operant principles and their relevance to complex human behavior. Perhaps the most ambitious extension was in *Walden Two* (1948), in which he described a utopian society based upon operant principles. Operant principles also were shown to be functioning in all types of behavior and social institutions in his *Science and Human Behavior* (1953a), which explained the role of reinforcement contingencies in government and law, religion, psychotherapy, economics, and education.

The methodology of operant conditioning, as well as its potential to explain social behavior, began to receive greater attention from the larger field of psychology. The procedures required for conducting laboratory operant research, along with the advantages of the experimental analysis of behavior as a general scientific approach were touted in widely read professional publications (Ferster, 1953; Skinner, 1953b). Investigators suggested that operant methods might be useful in studying specific content areas such as child development (Keller, 1950). The enthusiasm for a general science of human behavior based upon operant methodology was expressed by Keller and Schoenfeld (1950):

> All behavior, as we can now discern it, is composed of variations on a few basic themes. For the first time in mankind's saga, these themes are open to all who wish to see them in the steady light of science, rather than by the rare illuminations of intuitive minds. We are on the frontier of an enormous power; the power to manipulate our own behavior scientifically, deliberately, rationally (Keller and Schoenfeld, 1950, p. 401).

Specific topics related to clinical psychology and psychiatry also were addressed in the conceptual extensions of operant principles and methods. Skinner discussed the etiology and treatment of psychiatric disorders from a behaviorist standpoint. Many of his comments anticipated the formal development of behavior modification and the application of operant techniques to clinical problems. He challenged the traditional intrapsychic view of abnormal behavior and its focus on treating mental events. According to him, the traditional interpretations of behavior have:

> encouraged the belief that psychotherapy consists of removing certain inner causes of mental illness, as the surgeon removes an inflamed appendix of cancerous growth or as indigestible food is purged from the body. We have seen enough of inner causes to understand why this doctrine has given psychotherapy an impossible assignment. It is not an inner cause of behavior but the behavior itself which—in the medical analogy

of catharsis—must be "got out of the system." . . . We have to ask why the response was emitted in the first place, why it was punished, and what current variables are active. The answers should account for the neurotic behavior. Where, in the Freudian scheme, behavior is merely the symptom of a neurosis, in the present formulation it is the direct object of inquiry (Skinner, 1953a, pp. 373, 376).

He anticipated criticism that might be made against a behavioral approach, namely, that direct treatment of behavior would not resolve the underlying psychological problem:

In emphasizing "neurotic" behavior itself rather than any inner condition said to explain it, it may be argued that we are committing the unforgivable sin of "treating the symptom rather than the cause." This expression is often applied to attempts to remove objectionable features of behavior without attention to causal factors—for example, "curing" stammering by a course of vocal exercises, faulty posture by the application of shoulder braces, or thumb-sucking by coating the thumb with a bitter substance. Such therapy appears to disregard the underlying disorder of which these characteristics of behavior are symptoms. But in arguing that behavior is the subject matter of therapy rather than the symptom of a subject matter, we are not making the same mistake. By accounting for a given example of disadvantageous behavior in terms of a personal history and by altering or supplementing that history as a form of therapy, we are considering the very variables to which the traditional theorist must ultimately turn for an explanation of his supposed inner causes (Skinner, 1953a, p. 379).

Skinner described the effects of psychotherapy in terms of operant principles. He noted that therapeutic change probably resulted from specific reinforcement contingencies managed by the therapist. The therapist reinforces various behaviors, primarily through approval, in the process of effecting change. Extinction also plays an important role in therapy. Behaviors of the client that have been punished previously are emitted in the presence of the therapist. Eventually, escape or avoidance of emotional stimuli once associated with punishment are extinguished because the therapist is not an agent of punishment. Along with direct manipulation of the contingencies, the therapist helps the patient restructure his own environment to alter stimuli that adversely affect behavior.

Skinner's extension of operant principles to human behavior, particularly to clinically relevant behaviors, suggested the utility of a behavioral approach as an alternative to the intrapsychic model. The application of operant methods to achieve clinical changes followed several years after his pronouncements. In the early and mid 1950s, operant research was extended to human behavior. The research on verbal conditioning has already been noted, and other investigations were soon initiated. The goals of these studies were more general than observations of particular facets of verbal behavior. The laboratory extensions examined the utility of the operant paradigm by looking at diverse behavioral processes studied in animal experiments. Particularly noteworthy were the extensions of operant methods by Skinner and Ogden R. Lindsley to psychotic patients and by Sidney W. Bijou to child behavior. Operant work with an applied or clinical rather than laboratory purpose that grew out of this research is discussed in Chapter 7.

In 1953, Skinner and Lindsley, a graduate student at Harvard, began research contracted by the Office of Naval Research to determine the applicability of operant conditioning to the experimental analysis of the behavior of psychotic patients. The research, directed by Lindsley, was conducted at the Metropolitan State Hospital, Waltham, Massachusetts. The purpose of the research was

> to attempt to modify and make clinically relevant the methods of free-operant conditioning in order to produce medically useful, objective laboratory measures of the psychoses (Lindsley, 1960, p. 66).

The behaviors of chronic and acute psychotic adults and children as well as "normal" individuals were studied in a laboratory situation at the hospital. Patients were observed as they performed a plunger-pulling task. They were left alone in a small (6 × 6 ft), indestructible room for an hour a day over several days. The room included an apparatus with a manipulandum (plunger or lever), a reinforcement magazine, and a stimulus panel. The patient's task was to pull the plunger repeatedly while seated in front of the apparatus. Plunger-pulling was a free-operant response so that the patient could respond at any time. The task allowed a large number of responses to be made each session. Small physical objects that served as reinforcers could be presented automatically through an aperture next to the plunger. In the early research, plunger-pulling was followed by such reinforcing objects as candy, cigarettes, or projected pictures (Skinner, Solomon, and Lindsley, 1953; Skinner, 1954a; Skinner, Solomon, Lindsley, and Richards, 1954). These events were scheduled intermittently and followed two simple reinforcement schedules. An important feature of the task was that performance was recorded automatically on a cumulative recorder in another room and that response consequences were delivered automatically when the schedule requirements had been met.

The initial reports indicated that response patterns of psychotic patients were orderly and resembled the response characteristics of lower organisms. In subsequent reports (Lindsley, 1956, 1960, 1963), the investigations were extended in the number of patients used, the length of time that patients were studied, the range of reinforcing events, and the characteristics of responding that were revealed. Some patients were studied in daily experimental sessions for nearly five years. Responses were varied—food, money, male and female nude pictures, music, tokens, the opportunity to give milk to kittens, and escape from loud noise or a dark room were all employed as incentives.

Several important characteristics of responding were found. First, many patients tended to have lower rates of responding than did normal adults and lower organisms under the schedules of reinforcement investigated. Second, performance was often interrupted by long pauses in responding, during which idiosyncratic psychotic symptoms (e.g., vocal hallucinatory behaviors) could be observed. (The patients could be watched unobtrusively through a periscope.) Third, marked rhythms in response rate were noted. Over time, patients sometimes alternated between consistently high or low rates of performance although the reinforcement contingencies remained the same.

The investigations revealed several distinct advantages of exploring the free-operant paradigm with hospitalized persons. First, the method provided a way to assess the behavior of psychotic patients. For many patients, psychometric methods of assessment are useless. The free-operant method yielded a readily quantifiable, objective measure of behavior that worked for extended periods. Second, although the task itself was not clinically relevant, it revealed response characteristics that were. Long pauses in responding were associated with the appearance of psychotic behaviors such as pacing, laughing, swearing, staring, and destroying objects, suggesting that objective measures of response rate aided in indirect assessments of psychotic symptoms. Third, operant principles were useful in ascertaining the effect of treatment interventions. Electroshock, insulin coma, chemotherapy, and psychotherapy were experienced by various patients during the course of the project, and their effects were reflected in rates of responding. Because patients were used as their own control, the relative efficacy of different treatments for a given individual could be evaluated over time. In summarizing his research and its methodological significance, Lindsley noted:

> For the first time we have brought a few facts of psychosis into the body of natural science. In so doing much of what we have brought in looks

just as the clinicians always said it did. But remember that we now have the advantage of measuring these things automatically in the laboratory. And also remember that we have left many things that clinicians say in the clinic (Lindsley, 1960, p. 78).

Free-operant methods are especially appropriate to the problems of psychotherapy, because both fields (1) emphasize behavioral modification and control, (2) deal with single individuals, (3) use frequency of response over a period of time as a datum, (4) concentrate on the consequences of behavior, and (5) are interested in the functional and dynamic relationships between individuals and their social and non-social environments (Lindsley, 1963, p. 48).

Although the studies originally had not been designed to *treat* psychotic patients, the findings had obvious implications for designing treatment. Increased response rates for a task were sometimes associated with diminished psychotic behavior (Lindsley, 1960). For patients whose symptomatic behavior involved motor responses, plunger-pulling constituted a competing response. Thus, increasing nonpsychotic responses reduced some psychotic behaviors. For some patients the lessening of symptoms during the sessions appeared to transfer outside the experimental environment (Lindsley, 1963). In addition to the specific relationship observed between plunger-pulling and symptomatic performance, the overall project suggested more generally that the behavior of psychotic patients could be altered as a function of environmental consequences. This implication was exploited subsequently to alter many behaviors of psychiatric patients.

An important historical feature of the work of Lindsley and Skinner is that they were the first users of the term "behavior therapy" (Skinner *et al.* 1953, 1954), meaning the direct focus on behavior and the use of operant conditioning. Although their use of "behavior therapy" antedated other coinages (e.g., Eysenck, 1959; Lazarus, 1958), it was restricted to unpublished research reports that were not widely circulated. Thus, the term became popularized through its widespread adoption in publications originating in England, and to a lesser extent in South Africa.

While Skinner and Lindsley were exploring operant methods with psychotic patients, Sidney W. Bijou was trying out operant conditioning on children. Bijou had trained with Kenneth Spence at the University of Iowa, where he received his doctorate in 1941. He was first interested in Hullian theory, experimental neuroses, and conflict, but shifted toward the experimental analysis of behavior during his appointment at Indiana University from 1946 to 1948. Skinner, chairman of the psychology department, and J. R. Kantor, a prolific commentator on the philosophy of science and behaviorism, were on the faculty at Indiana. Both men questioned the utility of unobservable constructs in explaining behavior and encouraged a behaviorist and natural science approach to psychology. Skinner's work advocated experimental analysis in accounting for behavior without the addition of complex abstractions and provided a methodology to determine lawful relationships between stimulus and response functions. In 1948, Bijou left Indiana to take a position at the University of Washington. The position included the directorship of the University's Institute of Child Development.

In the early 1950s, Bijou, after abortively investigating children through the study of doll play, began to apply the methodology of operant conditioning to study child behavior at the Institute. Skinner's *Science and Human Behavior* (1953a) was particularly influential. Bijou conducted a series of studies on children aged between two-and-one-half and five years. The primary purpose of the research was methodological.

> The aim is to devise a situation which will provide (a) a well-defined and readily recordable dependent measure of behavior change, and (b) a well-controlled situation allowing precise manipulation of independent variables. A methodology of this kind, once fully developed, should enable one to study problems and behavior processes in children by relating the direct effect of one variable upon another (Bijou, 1957a, p. 243).

In his preliminary research, Bijou evaluated different types of reinforcers (e.g., candy, balls, appearance of a toy dog, pleasant-sounding tones, trinkets) and responses (e.g., push buttons and lights, peg boards and lights, pump handles). One early task required children to drop a ball through a hole. After the ball returned, the child would perform the response again. This task was eventually abandoned in favor of a lever-pressing response. Unlike ball-dropping, which was interrupted by a delay, lever-pressing was a free-operant response. It could occur at a high rate without interruptions and was more sensitive to various contingency manipulations (Bijou, 1957a).

Bijou studied basic behavioral processes observed in animal research, including acquisition, extinction, discrimination, and differentiation (Bijou, 1957a). The effect of various manipulations on humans, such as continuous and intermittent reinforcement on extinction, echoed the results obtained with animals (Bijou, 1957b). The research was carried out along several lines, including the study of retarded and normal children and the effects of various reinforcement schedules on behavior (cf. Bijou and Oblinger, 1960; Bijou and Orlando, 1961; Orlando and Bijou, 1960).

Bijou's work is significant because he extended operant conditioning to children and looked for an experimental method that allowed investigation of diverse manipulations of contingencies. The method came out of exploring various laboratory tasks and reinforcing events. He conducted programmatic research that examined a variety of behavioral processes, facilitated by his establishment of carefully controlled laboratory conditions. To this end, a trailer was converted into a laboratory to make it portable (Bijou, 1958a). The procedures could readily be brought to the subjects. Although some studies preceding Bijou's work had demonstrated instrumental conditioning with children (e.g., Fattu, Auble, and Mech, 1955; Fattu, Mech, and Auble, 1955; Grosslight and Child, 1947; Ling, 1941), they were isolated attempts concerned with select hypotheses. In contrast, Bijou worked to extend operant methodology.

Bijou's broader concern was reflected in his conceptualization of mental retardation (Bijou, 1963, 1966) and developmental psychology in general (Bijou, 1959). In each of these fields, he recommended that emphasis be placed upon carefully establishing empirical laws of behavior for individual development. He suggested that a functional analysis be used rather than the study of hypothetical mental processes, physiological states, or segregated aspects of behavior (e.g., motor, social, and intellectual). The individual could be studied from the standpoint of stimulus and response functions, which had proved their worth in animal experiments. Stimulus events were those antecedent conditions, settings, and consequences associated with production of the response. The responses included respondent and operant behaviors and their combinations. Rather than merely constructing analogies between principles established through observations of animal and human behavior, Bijou suggested that animal research should be a base for direct studies of human behavior. His own research with normal and retarded children was a systematic fulfillment of this objective.

While Bijou was doing his laboratory research, other investigators were applying operant methods to developmental psychology. At the University of Chicago, Jacob L. Gewirtz began operant research with children. Gewirtz completed his graduate work at the University of Iowa in 1948, where he became interested in the formation of social behavior. After receiving his Ph.D., he joined the faculty at the University of Chicago. He was influenced by Skinner's writings and

began to incorporate operant methodology into the study of social
behavior. At the University of Chicago, he was influenced by Howard
F. Hunt, chairman of the department of psychology, who was engaged
in operant research with animals.

Gewirtz's early operant research was conducted with Donald M.
Baer, a graduate student at the University of Chicago (Gewirtz and
Baer, 1958a, 1958b; Gewirtz, Baer, and Roth, 1958). They studied the
effect of social deprivation (brief isolation) on responsiveness to social
approval. Gewirtz continued work on social learning, using the
operant model to explain general developmental processes, observational learning, deprivation, attachment, dependency, and other
behaviors.

Baer completed his undergraduate and graduate work at the
University of Chicago, learning operant concepts and methodology
from Hunt and Gewirtz. In 1956, he was hired by Bijou, under whose
direction he began his own laboratory research on social development.
At the University of Washington, Bijou and Baer collaborated in
extending learning principles to developmental psychology (Bijou and
Baer, 1961, 1965, 1967). They advanced a general theory that viewed
child behavior in relation to observable environmental events. In the
early 1960s, Bijou, Baer, and other investigators at the University of
Washington began to apply operant principles and methods to achieve
clinical change (see Chapter 7).

Overall, the initial extensions of operant conditioning to psychotic patients and to normal and retarded children were motivated by
a search for a methodology to study human behavior. Free-operant
responses were used, discriminative stimuli and response consequences
were presented automatically, and behavior was recorded automatically. The operant method that had proved so useful in studying
animal behavior in the laboratory was equally valuable in studying
human activity. And in turn, the laboratory research had predicted
that reponse consequences could readily affect human performance.
This general finding had obvious implications for treatment, which
were acted upon soon thereafter.

In summary, diverse applications of behavioral techniques to
therapies and the initial extensions of operant research with humans
represented somewhat independent efforts. The applications were
isolated from each other, in many cases, both geographically and con-
ceptually. Whereas the behavioral approach in South Africa and England developed in localized centers with a relatively clear focus of
treatment, efforts in the United States were diffuse, although all were

evidence of a general *Zeitgeist* of applying learning theory and research methodology to clinical topics. However, in the United States no distinct and unified behavior modification movement had emerged by even the late 1950s. The formal recognition of behavior modification in England in the late 1950s and early 1960s crystallized existing practices in the United States, which are discussed in Chapter 6.

The Spread of Behavior Modification Research Across Countries

Results of behavior modification research in South Africa, England, and the United States were quickly reported so that some areas of distinction were removed. Publications brought the news of numerous applications from different countries together under the rubric of behavior therapy (Eysenck, 1960a, 1964; Franks, 1964; Wolpe, Salter, and Reyna, 1964), and individuals moved across geographic boundaries to confer, write, and teach. Wolpe, for example, visited the United States in 1956 and introduced desensitization. By 1962, he had settled in the United States. In 1963, Lazarus worked in the United States for a year, and made the move permanent in 1966. Desensitization also was introduced relatively early in England. In the late 1950s, Wolpe visited London and met briefly with Eysenck, who already had read some of Wolpe's early papers on reciprocal inhibition. In addition, Rachman, who had worked with Wolpe, came to England in 1959. Thus, developments in South Africa were communicated to the United States and England.

The cross-fertilization between English and American investigators was less clear. The appearance of operant techniques in the United States quickly attracted attention in England and was explored to some extent in the early and mid 1960s. However, operant techniques appear to be used much less in England than the United States. One reason for the difference in popularity may be a function of the way in which training resources are distributed. In the United States, a few universities became major centers for laboratory and applied research on operant conditioning. The growth of operant research in academic centers provided opportunities for many students who contributed directly to the proliferation of operant techniques (see Chapter 7). Academic training centers in operant conditioning were unavailable in England—thus, no established resources for training operant researchers came into being.

Another reason for the more widespread adoption of operant techniques in the United States involves the treatment focus generally

preferred. In the United States, many laboratory and clinical extensions of operant conditioning incuded hospitalized psychotic patients.
Operant techniques appeared readily applicable for evaluating the
responsiveness of psychotic patients to their environment and useful in
managing ward behavior. In England, the population of institutionalized psychotic patients is proportionately smaller than in the
United States, and the major therapeutic emphasis in institutions such
as the Institute of Psychiatry at Maudsley is on neurotic disorders.
Behavioral treatments of anxiety-based disorders tend to rely upon
classical rather than operant conditioning.

The differences in behavior modification in England
diverge from the operant conditioning view popular with American
investigators. Behavioral treatments of neurotic disorders tend to rely
more heavily upon such intervening variables as anxiety, drive, and
drive reduction. Hence, such theorists as Mowrer and Miller—rather
than Skinner, who has eschewed intervening variables—have received
more attention in England. In general, the theoretical work of such
influential psychologists as Eysenck alone may make the atheoretical
approach of Skinner less attractive in England than in the United
States.

The differences in behavior modification research and therapy in
England and the United States should not obscure the many similarities. The conceptual roots, specific techniques, and many
approaches toward clinical problems all are shared. One interesting
similarity is the approach taken toward the individual client. In England, behavior modification included experimenting with the single
case through the work and influence of Shapiro (Yates, 1970a, 1970b).
In the United States, this approach characterized operant methods
that had been devised much earlier and were extended to treatment
populations. Of course, the bulk of the research in behavior modification in both England and the United States has been with groups
rather than the single case.

SUMMARY AND CONCLUSIONS

The transition from experimental research to clinical applications of
conditioning began with work on experimental neuroses. The development of experimentally induced neurotic reactions suggested conditioning as a basis for the etiology and, by implication, treatment of
human disorders. Indeed, research on the elimination of experimental

neuroses ultimately led to the discovery of such important therapeutic techniques as systematic desensitization.

As conditioning research was extended to humans, learning became increasingly important as a fundamental explanation of both normal and abnormal behavior. This role was bolstered by the dramatic demonstrations of creating and eliminating fear in children by Watson and Rayner, and M. C. Jones, all under the rubric of conditioning. Varied therapeutic applications followed from their work.

The progress of learning theory and research in the United States led to conceptual models of psychopathology, personality, and therapy that were combined with traditional conceptualizations. Dollard and Miller provided the most comprehensive attempt to integrate learning theory and psychodynamic concepts. However, the influence of learning in its own right emerged in relation to clinical issues as, for example, in the study of verbal conditioning. The early applications of conditioning to psychopathology, personality, and therapy were the roots of behavior modification, and important advances in the field were made in South Africa, England, and the United States.

6
Contemporary Behavior Modification

The growth of behavior modification in different countries encompassed diverse techniques. By the early 1960s, investigators were sharing ideas across national boundaries, and this communication led to their convergence into a major movement. Chapter 6 continues to trace the course of behavior modification as a unified movement and the expansion of professional activities. Characteristics of the behavioral approach are outlined and major behavior modification techniques are reviewed, including systematic desensitization, flooding and implosion, aversion therapy, covert conditioning, modeling, and biofeedback. Applied techniques extrapolated from operant principles are detailed in Chapter 7.

EVOLUTION AND EXPANSION OF BEHAVIOR THERAPY

Behavior therapy became a visible movement in the early 1960s. Early publications (Eysenck, 1960a, 1964), including the first behavior therapy journal, *Behaviour Research and Therapy* (1963), provided an identity for individuals working with distinct behavioral techniques, problems, and settings. During this time, considerable attention was devoted to criticizing the traditional intrapsychic approach toward psychopathology and to defending behavior modification as a legitimate alternative to the prevailing model.

Behavior therapy, like many other movements, began largely as an attack against the existing dominant position in psychiatry and clinical psychology, namely, the "disease model" conceptualization of abnormal behavior, and specifically, psychoanalytic theory (e.g., Eysenck, 1959; Rachman, 1963; Salter, 1949, 1952; Wolpe, 1961; Wolpe and Rachman, 1960).[1] And, as with many other ideologies, criticism of traditional explanations served to unify its proponents. Although many of the distinguishing features of behavior modification vis-à-vis psychodynamic therapy later became blurred, that first consensus on the inadequacies of traditional psychodynamic theory and treatment served an important function.

Perhaps as important as the attack of behavior modification against traditional conceptualizations of behavior was the defense of behavior modification against criticism of its own position. As behavior therapy developed, its own tenets and claims were challenged, including the scientific status of behavioral techniques, the ties to learning theory, and the efficacy of treatment. The criticism and ensuing controversy helped the field formulate the definition of behavior therapy, which has evolved since its inception.

In the mid and late 1960s an increasing number of defenses or criticisms of behavior therapy appeared in the literature. The most noticeable attack was made in 1965 by Louis Breger and James L. McGaugh in their article, "Critique and Reformulation of 'Learning-Theory' Approaches to Psychotherapy and Neuroses" in the *Psychological Bulletin.* The article prompted a series of rebuttals and rejoinders pertaining to the assumptions and validity of behavior therapy (Breger and McGaugh, 1966; Eysenck, 1970; Katahn and Koplin, 1968; Rachman and Eysenck, 1966; Wiest, 1967). The series of articles served at least two purposes: the criticism brought considerable attention to behavior therapy, and the articles provided a relatively clear confrontation of issues that had not been previously expressed in the literature.

Breger and McGaugh (1965) challenged the theoretical basis of behavior therapy and the empirical evidence in support of behavioral techniques. At the time, behavior modification was defined as a series of therapeutic techniques based upon learning theory. Behavioral techniques were considered to be applications of well established "laws of learning." Breger and McGaugh pointed out that the "laws of learning" remained to be established themselves, because fundamental issues such as the role of mediational events in behavior change, the nature of responses learned, and the limitations of a stimulus-response

---

[1] See Chapter 2 for a history of dissatisfactions with the "disease model" and the major criticisms leveled against it.

analysis had not yet been resolved. They argued that behavior therapy mistakenly assumed a monolithic learning theory to which it could appeal. If learning theory itself had not resolved major issues, then how could therapy rely on it as an established theoretical base?

A second issue raised by Breger and McGaugh was that the tie between behavior therapy techniques and the notions of learning was purely metaphorical. They asserted that many *terms* used in behavior therapy were derived from the psychology of learning. Although the terms added scientific respectability to the techniques, their actual relation to learning theory was tenuous. For example, in systematic desensitization, an anxiety-provoking scene imagined by the client is viewed by behavior therapists as a "stimulus." Yet, in experiments in the psychology of learning, the stimulus usually is an unambiguous event defined in objective terms rather than as a private event. While one may borrow the terminology of learning, Breger and McGaugh claimed, it is a mistake to assume similarity across learning theory and behavior therapy practice.

Breger and McGaugh also maintained that the evidence in support of behavior therapy was inadequate. When their article was published, much of the evidence was founded upon case material (Eysenck, 1960a, 1964; Grossberg, 1964; Lazarus and Rachman, 1957; Rachman, 1959). Indeed, Wolpe (1954, 1958) and Lazarus (1963) based their claims for the efficacy of desensitization largely upon an accumulation of cases rather than upon empirical evidence. Breger and McGaugh emphasized the possibility of biases in presenting the data, selecting cases, evaluating improvement, and the absence of carefully controlled studies.

Rachman and Eysenck (1966) addressed the criticisms of Breger and McGaugh by pointing out that behavior therapy relied upon empirical *findings* of learning rather than on a monolithic theory. Basic findings such as those obtained in classical and operant conditioning could be extrapolated to develop behavior therapies. Rachman and Eysenck stressed the heuristic value of relying on the best available theories, even if the ones in question were not complete or unified. Although terms and findings from learning might not account for a given technique, they were useful in generating techniques (Eysenck and Beech, 1971; Rachman and Eysenck, 1966).

Rachman and Eysenck also reviewed the evidence in support of behavior therapy. Several publications appeared between the time Breger and McGaugh originally submitted their article for publication and when Rachman and Eysenck wrote the reply. To Rachman and

Eysenck, the evidence in support of behavior therapy appeared even more convincing than before. In a rejoinder, Breger and McGaugh (1966) reiterated that virtually all the evidence provided in support of behavioral techniques was based upon case material and that bias in reporting, selecting subjects, and producing therapeutic change still could not be ruled out. Breger and McGaugh's debate with Rachman and Eysenck revealed that the data in favor of behavior modification were not uniformly convincing.

In the late 1960s, polemics against traditional treatment and criticism and defenses of behavior therapy appeared to decrease. Considerably more attention was paid to research that could demonstrate the efficacy of diverse techniques. Comprehensive behavior modification texts appeared that reviewed the experimental evidence bearing on various techniques (e.g., Bandura, 1969; Franks, 1969a; Kanfer and Phillips, 1970; Rachman and Teasdale, 1969; Ullmann and Krasner, 1969; Yates, 1970a). Thus, a fundamental criticism—that behavior therapy had not demonstrated effective treatment outside of case material and a few select studies—was no longer compelling. With the proliferation of research and accompanying professional activities, behavior modification had arrived as a well established school of thought. Solidification of the movement no longer depended heavily upon confrontation of behavior therapy and the "disease model," but upon developing a body of empirically based therapy techniques.

Attempted Synthesis of Behavior Therapy and Psychotherapy

Because behavior therapy was a rejection of the psychodynamic model of abnormal behavior and treatment, an early goal of behavior therapists was to formulate a treatment that radically differed from traditional psychotherapeutic theory and practice. As various behavior therapy techniques were demonstrated to be effective in managing certain clinical problems, attempts were made to integrate behavior therapy and psychotherapy. Of course, such attempts at integration were not new: they commenced soon after basic tenets of conditioning became well known (French, 1933; Humphrey, 1933; Kubie, 1934). The translation effort of Dollard and Miller (1950) and the research and theoretical issues raised by Masserman (1943) also combined learning theory and traditional psychotherapy. However, with the formal acceptance of behavior therapy, several authors raised the possibility and advisability of integrating behavior therapy and psychotherapy in clinical practice (Birk, 1970; Feather and Rhoads, 1972a, 1972b; Kraft, 1969; Porter, 1968).

Integration evolved as a major concern because of the realization that similarities did exist between behavior therapy and traditional practices. When behavior therapy was defined originally, differences between it and traditional therapy were somewhat exaggerated. The positions had been polarized and oversimplified to point out the divergence of behavioral treatment (Hunt, 1975). However, once behavior therapy was established, similarities rather than differences vis-à-vis traditional treatment became clearer.

Behavior therapy originally was distinguished from psychotherapy along a number of dimensions including the reliance upon "consistent theory" and scientific research and the focus on overt behavior rather than underlying causes (Eysenck, 1959). A few years later, some of the alleged dissimilarities came to be questioned. For example, behavior therapists claimed that their demonstrations in support of treatment efficacy were more scientific than demonstrations of conventional therapy. Yet behavior therapy relied heavily upon case material which, of course, is scientifically unacceptable for establishing efficacy of a technique. In addition, pointing to the tenuous relation of behavior therapy to learning theory challenged the scientific status of behavior therapy. Indeed, some of the techniques included in behavior therapy did not rely upon learning principles at all (cf. Heller and Marlatt, 1969; Ullmann and Krasner, 1965).

Proponents of behavior modification claimed to focus on behaviors rather than underlying causes. However, for some behavioral problems, behavior therapists alluded to underlying causes that had to be ameliorated. For example, Eysenck (1959) noted that some motor behaviors (e.g., tics, compulsive acts) may be activated by their anxiety-reducing properties. To alter the motor behavior without changing the anxiety that led to its performance would not be a true cure. Although Eysenck cited motor behaviors maintained by anxiety as an exception to the rule that "symptomatic" behaviors could be treated directly, the example illustrates a concern with underlying causes similar to that in traditional therapy (Dyrud, 1971). In any case, many of the specific or unique characteristics of behavior therapy seemed less clearcut over time. Specific substantive issues supposedly distinguishing behavior therapy from psychotherapy began to look weak (Hunt, 1975). For example, behavior therapists noted that symptom substitution would be predicted from the psychodynamic position and the disease model in general but not from behavioral treatment (Ullmann and Krasner, 1965). Yet, psychodynamically as well as behaviorally oriented writers pointed out that symptom substitution was not predicted necessarily from the disease model or even from orthodox Freudian theory (cf. Weitzman, 1967). Also, behaviorally oriented writers noted that in many situations in which target behaviors are focused upon directly, new maladaptive behaviors might well occur at the termination of treatment (Cahoon, 1968b). Thus, the issue of symptom substitution, which had served as one locus for distinguishing behavior therapy from psychodynamic therapy, was not that clear.

Other similarities between behavior therapy and psychotherapeutic practices became increasingly evident. For example, in the late 1960s, the clinical work of Wolpe and Lazarus, who were both at the Eastern Pennsylvania Psychiatric Institute in Philadelphia, was observed. Behavior therapy (i.e., systematic desensitization) in practice revealed marked similarities to traditional individual psychotherapy (Klein, Dittmann, Parloff, and Gill, 1969). In desensitization such factors as the therapeutic relationship, suggestion, and the manipulation of client expectancies for improvement appeared to play a large role. Also, in the face of complex clinical cases, the efficacy and efficiency of desensitization appeared to decrease compared to earlier claims (cf. Lazarus, 1963; Wolpe, 1958). Finally, a major similarity to traditional therapy, focusing on themes related to the patient's complaint rather than the presenting behavioral problem itself, was the rule (Klein et al., 1969). Overall, many of the procedures employed in behavior therapy did not stem from learning theory *per se* (Heller and Marlatt, 1969).

The similarity between behavior therapy and traditional therapy was evident in the role assigned private events. Psychodynamic therapy had been distinguished from behavior therapy in that the former focused upon private or "mental" events such as thoughts, feelings, dreams, unconscious processes, and ideas, whereas the latter focused upon overt behavior. However, behavior therapy increasingly dealt with private events, including beliefs, thoughts, cognitions, and feelings. (The relationship of cognitive processes to behavior modification is explained in Chapter 9.)

One of the strongest bases for distinguishing behavior therapy from psychotherapy was treatment efficacy. Early in the literature, behavior therapy was proposed to be more effective than traditional psychotherapy (e.g., Eysenck, 1960b, 1965). For example, Wolpe (1958) presented case material arguing that 90% of the clients receiving behavior therapy based upon reciprocal inhibition were much improved or cured, whereas only 60% of clients from clinics with traditional psychotherapy met these criteria. Thus, behavior therapy techniques were viewed from the beginning as being much more effective than other methods, at least by proponents of behavior therapy.

Recently, the relative efficacy of behavior therapy and psychotherapy techniques has received considerable attention not only in reviews of the literature (Luborsky, Singer, and Luborsky, 1975) but also in comparative outcome studies with diverse behavior therapy and psychotherapy techniques and treatment populations (e.g., Argyle, Bryant, and Trower, 1974; Hall, Hall, DeBoer, and O'Kulitch, 1977; Hartlage, 1970; Obler, 1973; Sloane, Staples, Cristol, Yorkston, and Whipple, 1975). Some authors have suggested that the effects of behavior therapy and traditional psychotherapy for the treatment of neurotic disorders, for instance, are roughly the same (Luborsky et al., 1975; Sloane et al., 1975). Moreover, the multiplicity of techniques subsumed under the general term "behavior therapy" makes any global comparative statements of unclear value. The effects of specific behavioral techniques (e.g., systematic desensitization, flooding) can be compared with traditional techniques (e.g., psychoanalytically oriented therapy) for a given clinical problem. Kazdin and Wilson (1978) reviewed the comparative literature for the gamut of clinical problems studied and noted that conclusions reached about the relative efficacy of different techniques vary according to the therapeutic problems at issue. For most clinical problems, insufficient experimental evidence is available to make unequivocal statements for the superiority of one technique over another. Yet there are certain areas for which behavior therapy techniques have a decided advantage over traditional methods (see Kazdin and Wilson, 1978).

The attention that the comparison of behavior therapy and psychotherapy has been paid reflects skepticism about the alleged superiority of behavior therapy. Many authors have challenged the view that behavior therapy techniques are more effective than traditional avenues for a particular clinical problem. Reservations about the differential efficacy of behavior therapy and traditional psychotherapy techniques have further blurred the dissimilarities between them.

The distinction between behavior therapy and psychotherapy may have become even less clear with attempts to synthesize these methods of treatment. Suggestions have been made to combine aspects of behavior therapy and psychotherapy, especially in the area of individual (outpatient) treatment. An integration of behavior therapy and psychotherapy was suggested partially because of the assumed utility of combining diverse approaches to treat intractable patient populations. The combination of behavior therapy and psychotherapy had been reported as effective in various clinical cases (Feather and Rhoads, 1972b; Kraft, 1969).

Defenders of behavior modification have tended to reject the idea of integrating behavior therapy and traditional psychotherapy on theoretical, methodological, and empirical grounds (Krasner, 1960; Levis, 1970; Rachman, 1970). At the theoretical level, integration has been opposed because some of the fundamental notions of the psychodynamic model, such as symptom formation and psychosexual development, appear incompatible with formulations based upon learning theory. At the methodological level, the objection is that behavior therapy, unlike psychodynamic therapy, is firmly committed to a scientific and empirical approach. Psychodynamic notions have not lent themselves well to empirical verification (Levis, 1970). Finally, at the empirical level, integration of different methods is rejected because of the absence of evidence supporting the proposition that combined behavior therapy and psychotherapy is superior to behavior therapy alone. Indeed, the failure of psychotherapy in its own right to demonstrate behavior change convincingly demoted the value of an attempted integration (Eysenck, 1952b; Rachman, 1971).

Rather than a complete integration of behavior modification and psychodynamic theory, some authors have suggested that the behavioral approach may illuminate concepts that have been troublesome to define in psychoanalytic work (Hunt and Dyrud, 1968). Behavior modification may be useful in making it possible to test empirically influences addressed by psychodynamic concepts. At the clinical level, reformulation of dynamic concepts in behavioral terms might suggest variables important to consider and alter in behavioral treatment (Hunt, 1976). Conceivably, psychodynamic variables could be translated into behavioral terms and suggest foci that might otherwise be neglected. However, proponents of behavior modification are not likely to explicitly embrace concepts from a theoretical position and an overall model of human behavior that have served as sources of departure since the field's inception.

Expanding the Domain of Behavior Therapy

Although behavior therapy resisted integration with traditional techniques, it has become much broader than originally conceived. In the early descriptions of behavior therapy, the definition was tied closely to learning theory and research. For example, Eysenck (1964) defined behavior therapy as ". . . the attempt to alter human behavior and emotion in a beneficial manner according to the laws of modern learning theory" (p. 1). Similarly, Wolpe and Lazarus (1966) saw behavior therapy as ". . . the application of experimentally established principles of learning" (p. 1) to overcome persistent maladaptive habits.

The definition of behavior therapy has been broadened, and the role of learning theory has been reduced substantially to the point that the precise role of learning theory in actual practice of behavior therapy has been questioned. For example, Lazarus (1971b) commented:

> When a behavior therapist admonishes a patient to stand up for his rights, and when he assures him that masturbation is neither sinful nor harmful, or when he role-plays a significant personal event, where, we might ask, is his allegiance to Thorndike or to Hull? Can the work of Guthrie or Tolman, or perhaps even Pavlov, always contribute meaningfully to his decision whether an abortion is indicated, whether suicide is imminent, or if a divorce is justified (Lazarus, 1971b, p. 370)?

Most behavior therapists maintain that any empirically established findings might be useful for clinical practice. Although findings from learning research have been especially useful, many authors believe that behavior therapy should not be restricted to learning theory. Identifying behavior therapy with learning theory may retard the utilization of other important areas of knowledge from experimental psychology and the social sciences (Lazarus, 1967, 1971a; Ullmann and Krasner, 1975; Yates, 1970b). The current definition of behavior therapy has been extended to include the application of empirical results from psychology and the social sciences to effect behavior change (Franks and Brady, 1970; Krasner and Ullmann, 1973; Mahoney, Kazdin, and Lesswing, 1974).

Perry London (1972) has stressed the historical importance of relying upon learning theory in the development of behavior therapy. However, the relationship of the techniques employed to the theoretical base is questionable. As elaborated later in this chapter, the theoretical basis of many techniques such as systematic desensitization, covert conditioning, and aversion therapy is doubtful although their efficacy generally is accepted. London asserted that the technology of behavior therapy should be viewed independently of the theories with which it has been associated.

> In reality, behavior therapists never did have so much a theory as an "ideology". . . . What behavior therapists called theory actually served as bases for commitment or a rallying point for talking about disorder and treatment in a certain way and, more important, about acting on it within particular sets of limited operations, that is, technical limits (London, 1972, p. 916).

Recent innovations in behavior therapy have stressed a methodological and empirical rather than a theoretical approach to behavior therapy. That is, rather than limiting behavior therapy to techniques derived from learning, any technique that can be demonstrated to effect behavior change should be incorporated into treatment. As London has declared,

> theory has worn itself out in behavior modification and . . . technology, essentially of treatment, should now be a primary focus, perhaps, in the long range, even for serving scientific purposes. . . . the proper development . . . reaches to the systematic exploration of all kinds of therapeutic things without inhibition or concern as to whether they fit ostensible *principles* of learning, or reinforcement, or whatever, but with a singular focus on whether they fit the *facts* of human experience (London, 1972, p. 919).

Lazarus has been the greatest advocate of diverse therapy techniques regardless of their theoretical origin (Lazarus, 1966, 1967, 1971a). He has encouraged "technical eclecticism," (Lazarus, 1967) in which the therapist draws upon any technique that is shown to be effective. Adherence to a particular domain such as learning theory has had the disadvantage, in Lazarus' opinion, of limiting the range of procedures from which the therapist might draw. In *Behavior Therapy and Beyond,* Lazarus (1971a) outlined a wide range of procedures that he used in his own clinical practice as supplements to existing behavioral methods. Lazarus' own approach, referred to as "broad-spectrum behavior therapy" (Lazarus, 1966) includes such assorted methods as hypnosis, time regression or projection (individuals fantasize unresolved events of the past or anticipated future ones), thought-stopping (individuals learn to interrupt their obsessive thoughts in response to the therapist or to their own instructions), exaggeration of fearful events (individuals imagine untoward consequences of anticipated events), and exaggerated role-playing. Lazarus believes that the more extensive the range of techniques, the more effective the therapist is likely to be. Lazarus' approach to therapy epitomizes an increased openness to explore techniques that do not derive directly from learning. He has employed techniques that *appear* to be effective. However, most of the techniques advocated by Lazarus for sole or combined use have not yet been evaluated empirically.

AN OVERVIEW OF PROFESSIONAL DEVELOPMENTS

The expanded scope of behavior modification has been associated with a proliferation of professional activities, evidenced in the establishment of professional organizations and conferences and the publication of journals and texts in the field.

Formation of Interest Groups and Societies

Two major professional organizations for behavior therapy in the United States are the Association for Advancement of Behavior Therapy (AABT) and the Behavior Therapy and Research Society (BTRS). A third and more recently formed organization is the Midwestern Association of Behavior Analysis (MABA), which tends to be restricted regionally but has gained increasing national prominence. Each organization serves a somewhat different purpose.

In 1966, AABT was formed as a multidisciplinary interest group. AABT is a national organization, although it affiliates with local groups at the state, regional, or city level throughout the United States as well as with foreign groups. Full membership in AABT has required membership in the American Psychological Association or the American Psychiatric Association. However, these criteria can be waived for individuals with experience in behavior therapy research or practice.

Originally the organization served two major functions, including circulating a newsletter and holding an annual convention. The newsletter, edited by C. M. Franks, reported meetings, symposia, notes, and therapeutic practices pertaining to behavior therapy. The newsletter also provided a forum for discussing controversial or theoretical issues and brought together information on behavior therapy from diverse sources. In 1970, the newsletter was superseded by a journal, *Behavior Therapy*, which serves as the official journal of AABT. The journal includes scholarly research. Recently a newsletter has been reestablished to report news and notes. The Association also holds an annual convention. Early conventions were conducted concurrently with the American Psychological Association's annual meeting, but beginning in 1972, conventions were scheduled independently.

The organization originally was called the Association for Advancement of Behavioral Therapies. However, an appeal was made in the newsletter by G. Terence Wilson and W. I. M. Evans (1967) to use the term "behavior therapy" rather than "behavioral therapies." Use of the singular form emphasized the general behavioral approach toward clinical intervention and a common theoretical and experimental base that encompassed heterogeneous techniques. "Therapies" was considered to imply a series of somewhat unrelated techniques. In 1969, the name of the organization was changed to the Association for Advancement of Behavior Therapy.

In 1970, the Behavior Therapy and Research Society was formed to promote basic research pertaining to behavior therapy, to foster exchanges of information, and to compile a roster of behavior therapists. The intent of the organization, in contrast to AABT, has been to develop a professional group of behavior therapists rather than merely an interest group. Membership is determined by having made a "significant contribution to behavior therapy or related fields" (*Journal of Behavior Therapy and Experimental Psychiatry*, 1970, p. 245), as determined by an executive committee. Emphasis on the professional qualifications was stimulated in part by attempts to establish a directory of behavior therapists without evaluating their qualifications (cf. Moss, 1972). The *Journal of Behavior Therapy and Experimental Psychiatry*, established in 1970, serves as the Society's official publication. Annual meetings are held in conjunction with the American Psychiatric Association. They are usually small and consist of a panel discussion by behavior therapists.

In 1974, the Midwestern Association of Behavior Analysis was formed. The organization developed, in part, because several midwestern universities have been major centers for experimental and applied operant research. (The centrality of the midwest to operant research is reflected in the administration of the operant journals, the *Journal of the Experimental Analysis of Behavior* and the *Journal of Applied Behavior Analysis*, by Indiana University and the University of Kansas, respectively.) The regional psychological meetings in the midwest (sponsored by the Midwestern Psychological Association) did not provide an outlet commensurate with the level of concentration in the area of operant research. MABA organized to fill that gap. The MABA convention runs concurrently with or immediately before the regional psychological association meeting. The convention is devoted entirely to experimental or applied behavior analysis.

In addition to these major organizations in the United States, foreign behavior therapy organizations have been established, including the European Association of Behavior Therapy (1971). Separate organizations also have been founded in England, France, Germany, The Netherlands, Sweden, Israel, Japan, Mexico, and South America. Several of these groups have become affiliated with AABT, although they maintain their own independent professional activities.[2]

Conferences and Annual Meetings

A major sign of professional growth is the calling of conferences and annual meetings. The first behavior modification conference appears to have been conducted at the University of Virginia in 1962. The conference, instigated by Wolpe, Salter, and Reyna, focused upon the "conditioning therapies." The conference proceedings were published subsequently in book form under the same title (Wolpe, Salter, and Reyna, 1964).

By the late 1960s, the number of conferences and conventions had grown. As noted, AABT began sponsoring an annual convention in 1968, and several smaller regional conferences followed soon after within the United States. Major conferences with their date of inception include:

1. Southern California Conference on Behavior Modification (1969)
2. Conference on Behavior Analysis in Education (1969, Kansas)
3. Brockton Symposium on Behavior Modification (1971, Massachusetts)
4. National Behavior Modification Conference (1971, Colorado)
5. National Conference on Behavior Research and Technology in Higher Education (1973, Georgia)
6. Temple University Conference on Behavior Therapy and Behavior Modification (1974, Pennsylvania)
7. Drake Conference on Professional Issues in Behavior Analysis (1974, Iowa)
8. Convention of Midwestern Association of Behavior Analysis (1975, Illinois)

Some annual conferences in behavior modification outside of the

---

[2] The sources for ascertaining the foreign behavior therapy organizations were the *AABT Newsletter* and the News and Notes section of *Behavior Therapy*.

United States are:

1. Banff International Conference (1969, Alberta, Canada)
2. Annual International Symposium on Behavior Modification (1970, Mexico)
3. Conference on Behavior Modification (1970, New Brunswick, Canada)
4. European Conference on Behavior Modification (1971)
5. Latin American Congress on Behavior Analysis (1973)
6. Mexican Congress on Behavior Analysis (1974)

Training workshops, local conferences, and symposia on specific issues also are conducted frequently.

Publications in Behavior Modification

The ascendancy of behavior modification has been reflected in the growing number of publications in the field (Hoon and Lindsley, 1974). The increasing number of articles on behavior therapy in journals of psychiatry, clinical psychology, education, special education, counseling, speech, law enforcement, and other areas in the last decade has been documented (Brady, 1973; Kazdin, 1975c). In addition to publications in existing journals, new journals have been set up, and books and annual series have increased.

Journals   The heightened interest in behavior therapy is mirrored in the creation of several major behavior therapy journals.[3] Each of the journals has a different focus, as expressed in their editorial statements. In 1963, *Behaviour Research and Therapy* (Pergamon Press) began in England under the editorship of Eysenck and the assistant editorship of Rachman. The journal was designed to give direction to the behavior therapy movement. The journal publishes research and treatment investigations that apply "modern learning theory" to abnormal behavior. The title of the first behavior therapy journal was

---

[3] "Major behavior therapy journal" is used here to distinguish professional journals widely circulated by national organizations and/or publishers from those local publications whose circulation is relatively narrow. Concomitant with the proliferation of major journals in the late 1960's and 1970's, a large number of less prominent journals, newsletters, and magazines appeared. The journals include: *School Applications of Learning Theory* (1968), *Behavior Modification Monographs* (1970), and *Behavioral Engineering* (1973). The newsletters and magazines include: *Personalized System of Instruction* (1971), *Research Application of Techniques in Education* (1972), *The Boulder Behaviorist* (1973), *The Behavioral Voice* (1973), *Behavior Influence Newsletter* (1974), *Forum for Behavior Technology* (1975), and *Results Magazine* (1975).

significant in that the words "research" and "therapy" were included, stressing the importance of an empirical and scientific approach toward therapy. To accent the scientific outlook of the journal, Eysenck invoked Watson, who emphasized objectivity and experimentation as the best means of predicting and controlling behavior (Eysenck, 1963).

In 1968, the *Journal of Applied Behavior Analysis* (*JABA*) was founded. Published by the Society for the Experimental Analysis of Behavior, it is devoted to ". . . experimental research involving applications of the analysis of behavior to problems of social importance" (*Journal of Applied Behavior Analysis,* p. i). As applied operant research grew, particularly in the early and mid 1960s, it was clear that no appropriate publication outlet existed. Applied articles submitted to the *Journal of the Experimental Analysis of Behavior* (*JEAB*) were rejected because of the policy of that journal to publish primarily animal laboratory investigations in which responses were recorded automatically. In contrast, research in applied settings used human subjects and human observers to record behavior. *JEAB* published some articles with an applied focus using human observers (e.g., Ayllon and Azrin, 1964; Ayllon and Michael, 1959), but these were exceptions. To remedy this lack, the Society for the Experimental Analysis of Behavior sponsored an applied journal that would be devoted to operant work in applied settings.

JABA publishes applications of operant techniques. The methodology of experimental analysis of behavior is employed in relation to behaviors of clinical, social, and educational relevance. (The general domain of applied behavior analysis is described in the next chapter.) The editors of *JABA* have included Montrose M. Wolf, Donald M. Baer, Todd R. Risley, W. Stewart Agras, and K. Daniel O'Leary, plus a large number of associate editors.

In 1970, two additional behavior therapy journals were started in the United States. As mentioned, *Behavior Therapy* (Academic Press) was a publication of AABT. The editor was Cyril M. Franks and the associate editor, John Paul Brady. The first issue asked, "What is behavior therapy?" to help define the contents appropriate to the journal (Franks and Brady, 1970). The journal considered behavior therapy to be more related to how clinical data are approached rather than to particular therapeutic techniques employed. Rather than depending upon learning theory or a learning model, behavior therapy was defined as multidimensional. It was to include biogenic, developmental, and learned aspects of behavior.

In 1970, the *Journal of Behavior Therapy and Experimental Psychiatry* (Pergamon Press) began in the United States. (It is published in England but is edited in the United States.) Joseph Wolpe serves as editor and Leo J. Reyna is associate editor. The scope of the journal was somewhat broader than the other behavior therapy journals (Wolpe and Reyna, 1970). Although the journal was devoted to the applications of experimental psychology, it encompassed physiological and pharmacological research insofar as they related to etiology or treatment of conditions modifiable through learning. This journal also has devoted much space to training by providing information for the psychiatrist and clinical psychologist. To this end, didactic material such as transcripts of interviews, detailed description of methods, and cases, is included.

Several other journals have come into being within the last few years. In 1977, *Behavior Modification,* edited by Michel Hersen, was initiated to provide an outlet for diverse applications. The content overlaps with other behavioral journals in terms of specific techniques investigated. Also in 1977, *Cognitive Research and Therapy,* edited by Michael Mahoney, was begun primarily as an outlet for research on cognitive-therapy techniques. Recent foreign journals include the *Revista Mexicana de Análisis de la Conducta* (*Mexican Journal of Behavior Analysis*) (1975), devoted to applied operant investigations for Mexican and Latin American psychologists, and the *European Journal of Behavioral Analysis and Modification* (1975), which publishes behavior therapy articles based on diverse techniques.

Books   Texts began to be published on behavior modification in the late 1950s and early 1960s. The first books to use the term "behavior therapy" in their titles were *Behaviour Therapy and the Neuroses* (1960a) and *Experiments in Behaviour Therapy* (1964), both edited by Eysenck. In the United States, two important books on techniques of behavior therapy were *Conditioned Reflex Therapy: The Direct Approach to the Reconstruction of Personality* (1949) by Salter and *Psychotherapy by Reciprocal Inhibition* (1958) by Wolpe. Two other important books, not considered behavior modification books *per se,* were *Principles of Psychology* (1950) by Keller and Schoenfeld and Skinner's *Science and Human Behavior* (1953a). These books are significant in that they set both a general theory of human behavior and, particularly in the case of Skinner's book, applied operant principles to virtually all facets of human conduct, including psychopathology, psychotherapy, and education. The books by Salter, Wolpe, Keller and Schoenfeld, and Skinner are landmarks in the history of behavior modification although they are not general behavior modification texts. They advocated specific techniques or a general approach toward behavior encompassed by behavior modification.

In the mid 1960s, several important books on behavior modification appeared in the United States, including *The Conditioning Therapies: The Challenge in Psychotherapy* (1964) edited by Wolpe, Salter, and Reyna, *Conditioning Techniques in Clinical Practice and Research* (1964) edited by Franks, *Human Learning: Studies Extending Conditioning Principles to Complex Behavior* (1964) edited by Staats, *The Causes and Cures of Neuroses* (1965) by Eysenck and Rachman, *Research in Behavior Modification* (1965) edited by Krasner and Ullmann, *Case Studies in Behavior Modification* (1965) edited by Ullmann and Krasner, and *Behavior Therapy Techniques: A Guide to the Treatment of Neuroses* (1966) by Wolpe and Lazarus. Ullmann and Krasner's *Case Studies* appears to have been particularly influential. It has a lengthy introduction that provides a historical overview of behavior modification and outlines the general behavioral approach. A wide range of techniques and clinical problems are covered in the text.

By the late 1960s and early 1970s, comprehensive texts appeared that have now become standards in the field, including *Principles of Behavior Modification* (1969) by Bandura, *Behavior Therapy: Appraisal and Status* (1969a) edited by Franks, *Behavior Therapy* (1970a) by Yates, and *Learning Foundations of Behavior Therapy* (1970) by Kanfer and Phillips. Since 1970, books on the subject have increased markedly. They include comprehensive tests, handbooks, and pamphlets focusing upon particular techniques, treatment settings, or populations.

Along with individual texts, a number of annual series have been published. In 1969, the annual convention proceedings of AABT, entitled *Advances in Behavior Therapy* (Academic Press), were published with the editorship changing annually. (After four volumes and decreasing sales, the series was discontinued.) In 1972, an annual text on psychotherapy, counseling, and behavior modification (Aldine Press) was initiated under the editorship of Gerald R. Patterson, I. M. Marks, Joseph D. Matarazzo, Roger A. Myers, Gary E. Schwartz, and Hans H. Strupp. The series brings together previously published articles. Beginning in 1973, Franks and Wilson began the *Annual Review of Behavior Therapy* (Bruner/Mazel), a compendium of selected published articles. In 1975, Michel Hersen, Richard Eisler, and Peter M. Miller began an annual series entitled *Progress in Behavior*

Modification (Academic Press), which brings together original contributions in select areas of behavior modification.

THE BEHAVIORAL APPROACH

General Characteristics

Behavior modification can be characterized by several assumptions about the evolution and alteration of behavior, adherence to particular methodological concerns, and an approach toward diagnosis, assessment, and treatment. Many positions within behavior modification differ according to the theoretical ties (e.g., Hull versus Skinner), the behaviors emphasized (e.g., overt versus private events), the techniques applied (e.g., systematic desensitization versus contingency contracting), and methods of experimental evaluation (e.g., between-group versus intrasubject-replication methodology). Despite the variations, several common denominators of the behavioral approach are weighty enough that together they constitute a definition of the behavioral viewpoint.

The Behavioral Model of Abnormal Behavior A major assumption of the behavioral approach is the continuity of behavior, or the notion that behaviors considered to be normal and abnormal are not qualitatively different but on a continuum. By assuming the similarity between abnormal and normal behavior, the adherent of behavior modification believes that the principles of learning apply to all behaviors. Behaviors are learned, maintained, and modified by the same principles independent of whether the actions are referred to as "normal" or "abnormal," "healthy" or "sick." Practitioners of behavior modification do not deny that maladaptive behaviors exist and that individuals perform socially deviant behavior patterns. However, maladaptive behavior can be unlearned and replaced by adaptive behavior.

Reliance Upon Experimental Findings of Psychology Behavior modification attempts to apply well-established findings or to generate techniques derived from a particular theory to clinical practice. Most behavior modification techniques are indebted to the psychology of learning either to generate the techniques themselves or to provide an explanation of techniques that have developed somewhat independently of learning. This tradition of dependence upon learning has been well established: Pavlov, Bechterev, Watson, Masserman, and others directly applied the findings from conditioning to explain, develop, and ameliorate maladaptive behavior. The work of M. C.

Jones, Burnham, the Mowrers, Salter, and Wolpe constitute applications of concepts from learning theory and experimental research to clinical problems.

The definition of behavior modification has expanded over the years to include reliance upon theories and empirical findings of psychology in general. A definition of behavior modification that reflects increased breadth has been provided by Yates (1970a):

> Behavior therapy is the attempt to utilize systematically that body of empirical and theoretical knowledge which has resulted from the application of the experimental method in psychology and its closely related disciplines (physiology and neurophysiology) in order to explain the genesis and maintenance of abnormal patterns of behavior; and to apply that knowledge to the treatment or prevention of those abnormalities by means of controlled experimental studies of the single case, both descriptive and remedial (Yates, 1970a, p. 18).

Direct Focus on Behavior   Direct focus refers to an attempt to alleviate the maladaptive behavior for which the client seeks treatment. This emphasis is somewhat distinct from traditional therapies (such as psychoanalysis), which view behavior as *signs* of some psychodynamic process. The behavior therapist is interested in changing the behavior directly, usually without reference to hypothesized psychic states that allegedly underlie it.

Positions within behavior modification differ in the extent to which the focus on behavior should exclude references to internal states of the individual. Wolpe, for instance, posits intervening variables such as anxiety that are assumed to mediate avoidance behavior. The anxiety constitutes an internal state. Anxiety as employed in behavior modification is used as an intervening variable and is tied closely to more objective measures such as self-report, overt behavior, and physiological measures.

Behavior therapists sometimes refer to covert behaviors or private events such as thoughts, images, feelings, and other individual states that are not open to public scrutiny. Sometimes private events constitute the target problem, as in the case of self-criticism and obsessive thoughts, and thus may be examined directly. To some practitioners of behavior modification, private events (e.g., thoughts about other people) mediate problematic behavior and are the center of treatment. Many therapists eschew mediational states such as anxiety, covert behaviors, and cognitions. Professionals who rely upon operant techniques usually concentrate on overt behavior and the environment rather than mediational states or internal events.

Methodology   Behavior modification is characterized by assessment of behavior and experimental evaluation of treatment. The field has developed within a tradition of experimentation and evaluation, and investigators typically submit their techniques to experimental scrutiny by assessing the behavior to be changed and by testing the intervention. Different experimental research methods are used. Although most techniques are evaluated by between-group designs, those techniques developed from operant conditioning are usually evaluated by intrasubject-replication designs using only one or a few subjects. More than any other treatment, behavior therapy has been distinguished by a concern for combining scientific rigor with clinical practice in the evaluation of therapy (see Kazdin and Wilson, 1978).

Behavioral Diagnosis, Assessment, and Treatment

Diagnosis   Behavioral diagnosis focuses upon specific behaviors and the conditions under which they are performed. Unlike traditional diagnosis, behavioral diagnosis is not aimed at assigning individuals to diagnostic categories. Rather, the purpose is to make explicit recommendations for treatment. The target behaviors that need to be changed and the environmental events that might be useful in effecting change are weighed heavily.

One of the most explicit descriptions of behavioral diagnosis was provided by Kanfer and Saslow (1965, 1969). Their system is designed to improve decision-making about specific therapeutic interventions. The system consists of seven steps:

1. *Initial analysis of the problem situation,* in which the behaviors that brought the client to treatment are carefully specified;
2. *Clarification of the problem situation,* in which environmental factors (e.g., stimulus conditions under which the behavior is performed and consequences that may maintain the behavior) are specified;
3. *Motivational analysis,* in which positively reinforcing and aversive stimuli are identified;
4. *Developmental analysis,* in which biological, sociological, and behavioral changes of possible relevance to treatment are identified;
5. *Analysis of self-control,* in which the situations and behaviors the individual can control are identified;
6. *Analysis of social situations,* in which the relationship of individuals in the person's environment and their reinforcing or aversive qualities are specified;

7. *Analysis of the social-cultural-physical environment,* in which the normative standards of behavior and the client's limitations and opportunities for support are evaluated.

This listing clarifies the behaviors focused on and reveals environmental resources that can be used for treatment. The system is not intended as a substitute for assigning patients to traditional diagnostic categories when such labeling is useful for administrative or research purposes (Kanfer and Saslow, 1969). The method is designed solely to facilitate decisions about specific courses of treatment.

Another behavioral classification system has been posed as an alternative to psychiatric diagnosis (Cautela and Upper, 1973). This alternative, called the Behavioral Coding System, provides general descriptive categories of maladaptive behaviors such as fears, addictions, sexual disorders, thinking disorders, antisocial behavior, self-injurious behavior, and inappropriate habits of daily living. Within each category, several, specific behavioral variations are enumerated to add greater flexibility and specificity. For example, in the category of fears, specific types of fear are listed (e.g., being alone, heights, enclosed places, open places, crowds, water, darkness, germs or infection, animals, means of travel). In the category of thinking disorders, specific thoughts (covert comments to oneself) that lead to unsuitable affect or inappropriate overt behavior are listed (e.g., recurring thoughts accompanied by anxiety or fear, or by anger, or thoughts about harming oneself, being unjustly treated, exaggerated false beliefs). The Behavioral Coding System is for cataloging problems in terms of particular, directly observable behaviors and minimizing inferences made in diagnosis. Although the system serves as an index of specific behaviors, it makes no particular reference to the kinds of treatments that should be used.

In practice, no concrete system of behavioral diagnosis tends to be followed. Therapists frequently discuss general classes of behavioral problems such as behavioral deficits, excesses, inappropriate stimulus control, and aversive response repertoires (cf. Bandura, 1968; Bijou and Peterson, 1971; Bijou and Redd, 1975; Ferster, 1965; Gardner, 1971; Goldiamond and Dyrud, 1968; Kanfer and Saslow, 1969; Krasner and Ullmann, 1973; Stuart, 1970). However, these categories are extremely general and not a formal basis for classification or diagnosis.

Behavioral diagnosis first pinpoints what the person is doing or not doing that has brought him/her to treatment (Ullmann and Krasner, 1969). Once this specific target behavior has been identified, the next concern is the conditions under which the behavior occurs or fails to occur. Depending upon the particular target behavior, an analysis of the events that precede or follow the activity may also be of interest. Once the target behavior and the conditions under which it is or is not performed are known, the treatment strategy is selected. Thus, diagnosis consists of determining problematic behavior, isolating environmental events that control behavior, and selecting techniques to change behavior.

A major purpose of behavioral diagnosis is to reformulate the client's problem in behavioral terms. The reformulation is not merely a translation exercise. Rather, the purpose is to help apply laboratory-based concepts and procedures for altering, establishing, and maintaining behaviors (Goldiamond and Dyrud, 1968). The laboratory concepts help suggest variables that may be important to look for in the clinical situation. Once identified, the variables may be manipulable and behavior change can be examined. The reformulation of problems in behavioral terms also helps to identify response units so that behavior and behavior change can be viewed more analytically than is normally possible with global descriptions of clinical problems. Pinpointing the target response aids in observation and evaluation of behavior-change techniques once the techniques are applied. Essentially, the description of clinical problems in behavioral terms suggests substantive findings that may be useful to extrapolate to treatment and provides a methodology for the analysis of behavior change.

Assessment   As with diagnosis, behavioral assessment focuses upon the problematic behavior. Direct observation is the primary means of behavioral assessment. However, the methods of observation will vary according to specific target problems and therapeutic practices (Ciminero, Calhoun, and Adams, 1977; Hersen and Bellack, 1976). In many cases, behavior is observed in the actual situation in which it is a problem. This method would be especially likely for interventions relying upon operant conditioning in which treatment is conducted in the "natural environment" such as the home, school, or various community settings (e.g., Kazdin, 1975a; Tharp and Wetzel, 1969). A specific behavior will be observed under those conditions in which it needs to be changed.

Direct behavioral observation often is based upon performance in contrived situations (Nay, 1977). Clients are provided with a series of tasks in a clinical-laboratory setting that explore behavior directly related to their extralaboratory problem. For example, clients who are deficient in interpersonal skills may engage in role-playing tasks in which their social interactions can be seen firsthand. Similarly, phobic clients may complete a series of tasks through which they approach the feared object. Performance in the contrived situation is carefully quantified.

Behavioral assessment can center upon private events such as thoughts, feelings, and hallucinations. In these cases, assessment is direct only in the sense that the target response is at issue rather than some other event assumed to underlie that response. In the case of covert events, of course, assessment relies upon an individual's own reports or their overt behavioral correlates.

Self-report measures frequently are employed in behavior modification, particularly in individual behavior therapy (Cautela and Upper, 1976; Tasto, 1977). Written accounts by the client are used to sample select aspects of the target behavior. The employment of self-report measures in behavior modification often differs from traditional uses. Conventionally, performance on self-report measures is thought to illuminate signs of personality characteristics assumed to underlie behavior. In behavior modification, the self-report responses are considered as an important sample of behavior in its own right rather than a sign of some hidden trait.[4] Thus, self-report is a behavior of direct interest. For example, an individual's report of anxiety needs to be altered, along with maladaptive avoidance and physiological arousal that may be correlated with the report. Also, self-report measures sometimes are incorporated into direct behavioral assessment. For example, individuals may report their feelings as part of a test that directly assesses their overt avoidance behavior.

Physiological methods of assessment are used frequently in the treatment of anxiety, physiological disorders, and sexual deviance and dysfunction (Kallman and Feuerstein, 1977). Galvanic skin responses (GSR), blood pressure, and heart rate can register arousal in the presence of anxiety-provoking stimuli. Blood volume is commomly used, as in penile plethysmography, as a measure of arousal in response to sexual stimuli.

---

[4] There are clear exceptions to the use of self-report measures in behavior modification described here. In some studies, self-report measures are used as if specific traits (i.e., underlying psychological characteristics) *were* being examined. For example, in the treatment of assertive behavior, several measures of "assertiveness" are used to reflect change (cf. Hersen, Eisler, and Miller, 1973). It is unclear if investigators view the measure as samples of important behavior, signs of a general trait, or both.

Assessments of an individual's environment frequently accompany appraisals of his/her behavior. Antecedent and consequent events that may influence behavior or could be employed to influence behavior are noted. For example, instructions, praise, and other responses of individuals who interact with a client are observed directly.[5]

Treatment   In behavior modification, treatment is inextricably tied to diagnosis and assessment of behavior. Once the specific maladaptive behaviors are identified and measured, treatment centers on them. Generally, the direct focus on overt behavior distinguishes behavior therapy from traditional psychotherapy, which customarily concentrates on underlying psychic states to effect overt behavior change. The behavioral approach does not assume that problematic behavior is necessarily a symptom of some underlying intrapsychic cause that has to be treated independently of the problematic behavior itself. Eysenck (1959) reflected the prevailing orientation of behavior modifiers in treating neurotic disorders by flatly stating that "... there is no neurosis underlying the symptom, but merely the symptom itself. *Get rid of the symptom and you have eliminated the neurosis* (p. 65)."[6] Although the sentiment expressed in the above assertion continues to be supported, specific overt behaviors are not invariably the focus of treatment. Therapy may be working toward alleviating anxiety or shaping cognitive processes assumed to be responsible for particular overt acts. However, treatment concentrates on the identified problem and observable behavior is viewed as the confirmation of the wisdom of that approach.

The treatment strategy used to alter behavior varies according to the behaviors being studied. The diversity of techniques and their derivation from different models of behavior make it difficult to abstract specific commonalities of behavioral treatment. The major techniques of behavioral treatment and the behaviors for which they are used are reviewed below.

---

[5] For a detailed discussion of behavioral assessment, several sources may be consulted (Ciminero et al., 1977; Goldfried and Kent, 1972; Goldfried and Pomeranz, 1968; Goldfried and Sprafkin, 1974; Hersen and Bellack, 1976; Kanfer and Saslow, 1969; Mischel, 1968, 1971; Peterson, 1968).

[6] Some behavior modifiers have objected to the notion of a "symptom" in describing the behavioral approach. The word retains the medical analogy of a manifestation (e.g., symptom) of an underlying process (e.g., illness). Using "symptom" implies that there is an underlying problem (i.e., analogous to an illness) to which the maladaptive behavior is tied (Ullmann and Krasner, 1965).

REVIEW OF MAJOR BEHAVIOR THERAPY TECHNIQUES

This section reviews systematic desensitization, flooding and implosion, aversion therapy, covert conditioning, modeling, and biofeedback. For each technique, the historical foundations are outlined, as are variations of the technique in practice, the range of problems treated, and the current questions and unresolved issues. With few exceptions, procedures that constitute the major applications of operant techniques in treatment, rehabilitation, and educational settings are omitted. (They are detailed in Chapter 7.)

Systematic Desensitization

Systematic desensitization is one of the most widely employed and empirically researched techniques in behavior modification. The technique is used primarily for anxiety-based maladaptive behaviors or avoidance reactions. As usually practiced, desensitization includes three elements: relaxation training, a series of situations arranged hierarchically from least to most anxiety provoking, and pairing the hierarchy items, usually presented in imagination, with relaxation. In pairing relaxation with the hierarchy items, it is assumed that anxiety will be inhibited according to the principle of reciprocal inhibition.

Historical Foundations   As has been explained, Wolpe developed desensitization based on an overextension of the physiological notion of reciprocal inhibition. However, several therapeutic applications of procedures that closely resembled desensitization were available in the literature long before the technique was formally devised by Wolpe. Similar, and in some cases almost identical, procedures were reported in the writings of M. C. Jones, Jacobson, Herzberg, and Salter, all of whom have been acknowledged at some point by Wolpe.

Yet, many of the applications that resemble desensitization appear to have had no direct impact on the final development of the technique. For example, in France, in 1893, Edouard Brissaud (1852–1909) invented a procedure to relieve tics in which the patient was trained to perform exercises designed to teach him how to maintain immobility of the muscles. Gradually, the period of time the individual was required to remain motionless was increased. Some localized exercises were trained to replace the incorrect movement (tic) with normal movement. The use of exercises to control specific convulsions and chorea was reported much earlier (Blache, 1864; Jolly, 1892). In variations of Brissaud's technique, individuals sometimes merely performed behaviors incompatible with the response rather than not move their muscles (Meige and Feindel, 1907). In one version, deep breathing was the vehicle for eliminating tics. Continuous practice of the breathing exercises gradually weakened and eventually eliminated the tic (Pitres, 1888; Tissié, 1899). In any case, practicing inhibitory responses to eliminate tics had become relatively popular in France.

In the 1920s, a German psychologist, Johannes H. Schultz, developed a procedure referred to as "autogenic training" (cf. Schultz, 1932; Schultz and Luthe, 1959). The procedure was an outgrowth of investigations of autosuggestion and hypnosis. Inducing hypnotic states appeared to produce similar reactions, namely, feelings of heaviness and sensations of warmth. Schultz concluded that muscular relaxation (to account for "heaviness") and vasorelaxation (to account for "warmth") were basic to bringing about hypnotic states. He set forth a series of steps to induce relaxation, including self-suggestion of heaviness and warmth in the extremities, concentration on cardiac activity and respiration, and suggestion of abdominal warmth and cooling of the forehead. As a whole, these steps constitute autogenic training. Specific exercises, postures, and meditative themes are adjuncts to the basic procedure.

Autogenic training has been investigated extensively in Europe and has been the basis of successful treatments of a wide range of physiological and psychophysiological disorders of the respiratory, gastrointestinal, cardiovascular, and endocrine systems, as well as alcohol consumption, drug addiction, stuttering, writer's cramp, sleep disorders, and anxiety and phobic states. Certain applications of autogenic training closely resemble desensitization. For example, to deal with certain psychological or physical problems, individuals are trained to make self-suggestions to neutralize their feelings (e.g., by saying to themselves that something ordinarily disturbing to them does not really matter). Thus, individuals induce states incompatible with disturbing events, a process similar to desensitization.

In 1928, James Alexander published *Thought-Control in Everyday Life,* which gave instructions on how to control one's own thoughts. One technique, "direct switching," entailed thinking immediately of something that was the opposite of a disturbing thought that had come to mind. With each instance of switching, the unwanted thought should lose its power. Thus, Alexander suggested engaging in incompatible responses to eliminate an unpleasant idea.

English Bagby (1891-1955), a former student of Knight Dunlap, suggested various treatment procedures in his book *The Psychology of Personality: An Analysis of Common Emotional Disorders* (1928). Among the treatments he suggested was "substitution." Bagby broadened the method derived from M. C. Jones' experiments in which feeding was used as a substitute response in an anxiety-provoking situation. To eliminate maladaptive habits or thought patterns, regardless of whether or not they were based on anxiety, Bagby recommended that an individual perform a response incompatible with the habit to be eliminated.

In the 1940s, isolated therapeutic applications closely resembling desensitization were tried out in the United States. For example, films followed or accompanied by records of battle sounds were used to decondition war neuroses (Schwartz, 1945). The stimuli were presented in a hierarchical fashion beginning with animated cartoons and ending with intense combat (e.g., bombing, strafing). In another investigation, phobic patients engaged in various graded steps and performed responses that would distract them from anxiety (Terhune, 1949). For example, a patient would place him/herself in the feared situation and perform a relatively mild anxiety-provoking task (e.g., going for a walk with others for an agoraphobic). While walking, the patient would engage in other responses to compete with anxiety (e.g., draw a map of the area walked, eat in a restaurant). (These therapeutic applications resemble the graded-tasks procedure designed by Herzberg.)

These applications do not exhaust the procedures and therapeutic recommendations that resemble desensitization. However, they do indicate that in Europe and America the elimination of a problematic behavior was accomplished frequently by engaging in responses designed to compete with (or inhibit) the problematic response.

Current Practice Although desensitization usually consists of pairing relaxation with imagery of a progressive series of anxiety-provoking scenes, several variations of the basic procedure have evolved. Sometimes hypnosis or drugs (e.g., methohexitol sodium (Brevital)) are used to facilitate relaxation training and to inhibit anxiety during imagination of the hierarchy (Brady, 1972). Desensitization sometimes takes place *in vivo,* where the client has learned to relax in the presence of the anxiety-provoking stimuli. Graduated exposure to anxiety-provoking stimuli *in vivo* tends to be more effective than exposure to the stimuli in imagination. *In vivo* desensitization also has been used when responses other than relaxation inhibit fright. Assertive responses and sexual responses are expressed to overcome stress related to social interactions or to sexual situations. Other variations include automated desensitization (in which the presentation of a hierarchy of items and relaxation instructions are controlled by computer or tape recorder), group desensitization (in which several individuals are treated simultaneously, usually with a standardized hierarchy), and vicarious desensitization (during which individuals observe others being desensitized rather than undergo treatment themselves) (Paul and Bernstein, 1973; Rimm and Masters, 1974; Yates, 1970a).

Current Issues Desensitization has been extremely effective in alleviating a wide range of maladaptive behaviors, including fears and anxiety related to social situations, illness, injury, death, animals, and sexual encounters, "existential angst," nightmares, anorexia nervosa, obsessions and compulsions, depressions, epileptic seizures, and stuttering (Bandura, 1969; Paul, 1969b, 1969c; Paul and Bernstein, 1973; Rachman, 1967).

Because the efficacy of desensitization has been well established, a major issue is not the power of the technique but the mechanism(s) through which it operates. Wolpe originally argued that three ingredients were crucial to treatment: an anxiety-inhibiting response, a hierarchy of anxiety-provoking situations, and the pairing of the hierarchical items with relaxation. Yet it has shown repeatedly that none of these ingredients are crucial for effective treatment (see Jacobs and Wolpin, 1971; Kazdin and Wilcoxon, 1976; Marks, 1972; Wilkins, 1971). Thus, Wolpe's original interpretation of desensitization based upon Hullian learning theory, the notion of reciprocal inhibition, and speculations about neurological mechanisms of change upon which the "crucial" aspects of therapy were based have been largely dispelled. Reinterpreting desensitization through counterconditioning has become a popular alternative. This interpretation, very similar to Guthrie's (1935) notion about learning, poses that pairing anxiety-provoking cues with an alternative response is sufficient for relearning. However, a plethora of other interpretations are available—extinction, operant shaping, modeling, attribution, expectancy effects, and so on.

A related issue concerns the extent to which desensitization is an active therapy procedure or can be explained by nonspecific treatment or placebo effects. Desensitization research has served as a model of therapy research by including groups that control for spontaneous remission and nonspecific treatment effects (Paul, 1966). However, recent research has suggested that placebo control groups to which desensitized subjects have been compared are less credible and do not generate a client's expectancies for success to the extent that densensitization does (Borkovec, 1972; McReynolds and Tori, 1972; Nau, Caputo, and Borkovec, 1974). Moreover, when control groups do generate the expectancies for improvement equal to that of desensitized individuals, desensitization and the control conditions usually are not differentially effective (Kazdin and Wilcoxon, 1976). Thus, whether the effect of desensitization can unambiguously be attributed to active therapy ingredients or to nonspecific treatment effects is as yet undetermined.

Flooding and Implosive Therapy

Flooding, like desensitization, is a technique to treat avoidance responses (Marks, 1972, 1975). In systematic desensitization, anxiety-provoking stimuli are presented to the client in a hierarchical fashion in order to minimize the fear experienced during treatment. In contrast, flooding exposes the client to intense anxiety-provoking stimuli (either *in vivo* or in imagination) to heighten stress. The rationale of flooding is based upon the extinction of classically conditioned responses to anxiety-provoking cues, which are assumed to be conditioned stimuli that elicit avoidance responses. By repeatedly exposing clients to the conditioned stimuli at full strength, the stimuli lose their capacity to elicit fright. Thus, after prolonged exposure to anxiety-provoking cues, the cues no longer evoke anxiety.

Historical Foundations Flooding is derived from extensive laboratory work in experimental neuroses and avoidance learning. In the area of experimental neuroses, Masserman's (1943) work with cats is particularly seminal. Masserman demonstrated that experimentally induced neurotic reactions could be overcome by forcing the animals closer to the food box in the cage where shock previously had been administered. As the animal was brought closer to the food (by a movable barrier in the cage), its anxiety and attempts to escape initially increased. Eventually, the anxiety diminished and the animal ate from the food box. Masserman's work suggested that forced exposure to the anxiety-provoking stimuli could eliminate anxiety.

Similar findings were suggested by studies of avoidance learning. Laboratory work established that avoidance reactions under some circumstances were extremely resistant to extinction (Solomon and Wynne, 1953, 1954). In avoidance learning where the onset of an aversive event (shock) is preceded by a conditioned stimulus (tone or light), presentation of the conditioned stimulus alone without the shock eventually maintains avoidance behavior. Avoidance responses (such as jumping over a barrier of the cage to a "safe" area) do not extinguish because the animal never remains in the original situation after the conditioned stimuli are presented to encounter the new contingency (i.e., absence of shock). Experimental work revealed several procedures useful for extinguishing the avoidance response. For example, continuing the conditioned stimulus after the animal had made the avoidance response led to extinction of the avoidance behavior. Apparently, exposure to the conditioned stimulus for extended periods provided the opportunity for the animal to learn that shock was no longer associated with the conditioned stimuli (Katzev, 1967). Another procedure used to extinguish avoidance responses was repeated presentation of the conditioned stimulus without permitting the animal to escape (Baum, 1970). Extensive laboratory research strongly supported the effect of prolonged exposure to the conditioned stimulus without allowing the animal to make an avoidance response, and the technique has been extended to clinical cases.

Current Practice   The client imagines a particularly frightening scene or scenes for prolonged periods. The client may imagine anxiety-provoking scenes up to two or more hours, although 40 to 60 minutes per session is more common (Marks, 1972). Exposure time is related to therapy effectiveness, with longer durations of continuous scene presentation being associated with greater reduction in avoidance. Exposure time is usually determined by the client's behavior. Anxiety-provoking scenes are continued until the stress dissipates over time. Although most flooding is conducted in imagination, it has been used *in vivo*. As with desensitization, actual exposure to the anxiety-provoking stimuli tends to be more effective than exposure to the stimuli in imagination.

One major variation of flooding is *implosion* or *implosive therapy*, devised by Thomas Stampfl (Hogan, 1968; Stampfl, 1966, 1970; Stampfl and Levis, 1967). The unique feature of implosion is that it has attempted to combine behavior therapy and psychodynamic theory in a single technique. First the client experiences flooding by fantasizing scenes that arouse anxiety. In addition to imagining scenes directly related to avoidance responses, the client imagines scenes of psychodynamic import. Stampfl maintains that an individual's fear is a symbolic expression of repressed material. The repressed material is assumed to follow psychoanalytic themes, including conflicts related to sex and aggression and oral, anal, and genital needs. To maximize the anxiety elicited in treatment, clients imagine scenes devised by the therapist that directly reflect the conflicts thought to underlie the presenting problem. In practice, the therapist presents material so as to obtain the highest level of stress possible. To these ends, the scenes are often embellished upon in an unrealistic fashion to exaggerate the anxiety-provoking stimuli and the hypothesized repressed conflicts. Thus, implosion is sometimes distinguished from ordinary flooding not only by the use of psychodynamically relevant material but also by the exaggeration of the stimuli that are presented to the client.

Current Issues   Flooding has been effective in reducing a number of anxiety reactions, including fears of social situations, test-taking, blood and wounds, various animals such as spiders and snakes, agoraphobia, obsessions and compulsions, and "free-floating" anxiety (Marks, 1972, 1975). Some studies have suggested that implosion may be an effective variation of flooding although the efficacy of this procedure is not clearly established (Levis, 1974; Morganstern, 1973).

An unresolved issue in flooding is the mechanism through which the effects are achieved. Extinction generally is invoked to explain the process of change. As a result of nonreinforced exposure to the fear-provoking conditioned stimuli, the stimuli lose their capacity to elicit anxiety. Because the effect of flooding depends upon repeated and prolonged exposure to the fear-provoking stimuli—similar to the techniques used to eliminate avoidance in animals—extinction appears to provide a parsimonious interpretation. However, there are some dissimilarities between flooding in animal research and clinical applications.

With animals, flooding involves forcing physical contact with the feared stimulus, whereas in clinical applications the exposure is voluntary, i.e., the client can escape. Animals usually are exposed to the stimulus alone, whereas patients experience flooding in the presence of the therapist. In animal work, the presence of a naive animal during flooding facilitates elimination of avoidance. The therapist may operate in a similar capacity in therapy. Animal experiments usually have only one stimulus that is conditioned to evoke anxiety. In clinical cases, a variety of stimuli are responsible. In animal research, the fear-provoking stimulus has been conditioned to elicit fear. With humans, the process of fear acquisition is not clear and usually is not a simple matter of first-order conditioning. These factors merely suggest that the clinical application of flooding includes complexities that do not have to be considered in animal research. The influence of such complexities needs to be elucidated before the mechanism through which flooding operates is clear. In addition, expectancy and suggestion have been posited as mechanisms of change. As with desensitization, nonspecific treatment factors have not been ruled out as a possible explanation.

A final issue pertains to the advisability of using flooding. Systematic desensitization and flooding both have been successfully used in overcoming anxiety-based problems. However, the procedures differ in that desensitization attempts to minimize the patient's anxiety, whereas flooding tries to maximize it. Because both techniques appear to be effective and neither is clearly superior, the rationale for maximizing a client's fear during treatment has been questioned (Morganstern, 1973). At present, it is not clear whether desensitization and flooding are equally appropriate for the same anxiety-based problems or individuals with the same characteristics. Flooding may be required when desensitization has not been effective.

Aversion Therapy

Aversion therapy is a series of techniques in which aversive events are used to alter behavior. Both classical and operant conditioning paradigms are used. As a rule, classical conditioning is employed to alter the valence of a stimulus (e.g., alcohol) by pairing it with an unconditioned aversive event (e.g., shock). Operant procedures used include the presentation, termination, or avoidance of aversive events contingent upon behavior (e.g., shock delivery following consumption of alcohol). Typically, the procedure includes respondent and operant components.

Historical Foundations   The therapeutic use of aversive events to alter behavior has a long history. Anecdotal examples from Greek and Roman cultures illustrate early practices. According to Plutarch, Demosthenes had a shoulder tic and cured it by suspending a sharp sword above his shoulder. Whenever his shoulder raised during the tic, it was pricked by the sword, a procedure that quickly cured the tic. The Romans applied aversive measures to eliminate excessive alcohol consumption by placing an eel in a wine glass and making an individual drink it.

The experimental foundations of aversion therapy can be traced to Pavlov and Bechterev, who established aversive reactions in response to neutral stimuli. Bechterev's motor conditioning procedure, which involved pairing a neutral stimulus (tone) with shock closely resembles much contemporary work in aversion therapy. Another

Russian, Valentin A. Krylov (1892–1939), established an aversive reaction to a neutral stimulus by pairing the stimulus with injections of nausea-inducing morphine (Pavlov, 1927). Many current applications rely heavily upon electric shock and nausea-inducing agents as aversive stimuli.

In 1929, Nikolaï Kantorovich became the first investigator to employ aversion systematically (Razran, 1934). He developed an aversion in 20 alcoholics by pairing alcohol with shock to the hands. Eventually, an antagonistic reaction was established to the alcohol alone. Kantorovich claimed that the individuals were cured and did not recover the craving for alcohol over several months. After shock had been effectively used, other Russian investigators produced aversion toward alcohol by using apomorphine, an emetic drug (Markovnikov, 1934; Sluchevski and Friken, 1933). After Kantorovich's research, investigators in France, England, Germany, Belgium, and the United States applied conditioning to treat alcoholism in the 1930s and 1940s (cf. Voetglin and Lemere, 1942, and Chapter 5). Aversion also was extended to other behaviors than alcohol consumption. For example, one experimenter in the United States suppressed homosexual fixations by the use of electric shock (Max, 1935).

Current Practice   Contemporary aversion therapy takes several forms. In aversion therapy based upon classical conditioning, electrical or chemical stimuli typically serve as the unconditioned stimuli. Repugnant auditory and olfactory stimuli sometimes have been used. The conditioned stimuli have included alcohol, sexual stimuli (e.g., fetishistic objects, slides of individuals of the same sex for homosexual clients), food, cigarettes, and narcotic drugs.

In aversion therapy that incorporates operant conditioning, response-contingent consequences in the form of punishment, escape, and avoidance learning are used. For example, in punishment, performance of maladaptive behaviors (e.g., alcohol consumption) is followed by electric shock. In escape and avoidance learning, the aversive stimulus is terminated (escape) or averted (avoidance) by responding. For example, Feldman and MacCulloch (1965) used escape and avoidance to alter homosexual behavior of males. Shock was paired with the presentation of slides of nude males. Clients could terminate (escape) the shock by switching off the slide as soon as the shock was presented. Shock could be avoided altogether by quickly switching off the slide as soon as it was presented.

Another paradigm for aversion therapy is *aversion relief,* in which the termination of an aversive stimulus such as shock is associated with some neutral stimulus. The "relief" associated with shock termination is considered to establish the positive value of the neutral stimulus. For example, in the treatment of homosexual behavior through escape or avoidance, shock is terminated by removing a slide of a homosexual scene. The removal of the scene is associated with a heterosexual scene to enhance the positive valence of the heterosexual stimuli. Aversion relief can be viewed as a special case of escape training in which escape is associated with a particular stimulus. Symbolic or covert aversion has been employed whereby the clients imagine various attractive stimuli and aversive events. Classical conditioning, punishment, escape, avoidance, and aversion-relief have all served as the basis for imagery-based aversion techniques.

Current Issues   Aversion therapy has been effective in treating a wide range of disorders, including alcohol consumption, cigarette smoking, overeating, and sexual attraction toward socially censured stimuli (Barlow, 1972; Rachman and Teasdale, 1969; Rimm and Masters, 1974).

Aversion therapy has relatively close ties with learning theory and research, but the conceptual bases of many of its practices are not well understood (Rachman and Teasdale, 1969). Although some techniques appear to be relatively straightforward applications of experimental-laboratory paradigms, others are not. For example, some studies have reported success by using backward conditioning, in which the conditioned stimulus follows rather than precedes the unconditioned stimulus, but it is controversial whether backward conditioning should result in conditioning at all (cf. Eysenck, 1976; Kimble, 1961). Other deviations from laboratory findings in the application of aversion conditioning have included extended delays between the conditioned and unconditioned stimulus and the use of intermittent reinforcement, each of which should decrease or eliminate the formation of a conditioned response. However, aversion therapy that violates certain important laboratory conditions remains effective.

Rachman and Teasdale believe an important question in aversion therapy is why treatment has any effect at all:

> It could be said that the surprising thing about aversion therapy is *not* that its effects are uncertain, but rather that it works at all. One of the reasons for making this observation is the fact that patients know perfectly well that when they leave the clinic and approach the abnormal sexual object or indulge in the deviant sexual behaviour they will no longer receive electric shocks (Rachman and Teasdale, 1969, p. 65).

Therapy usually is conducted in a restricted clinical-laboratory or hospital setting, often in the presence of special experimental apparatus. The clients might be expected to discriminate between treatment and nontreatment settings because of the great differences in the stimulus conditions associated with their performance of the target response in the treatment setting. In addition, the resemblance of the particular stimuli used in treatment (e.g., slides of sexual stimuli) to the stimuli they actually represent should enhance the discriminability of treatment and nontreatment performance. Thus, any aversive reaction should be conditioned to the therapy or laboratory setting. However, when treatment is effective, the effects do not seem to be restricted to the treatment setting. The reasons why treatment effects generalize beyond the treatment setting are not readily understood.

The generality of treatment effects across settings is inconsistent with the highly selective effect that aversion therapy often has with respect to the target response class. The influence of therapy usually is very stimuli-specific. For example, in treatment of alcohol abuse, an aversion is often formed only in relation to the specific alcoholic beverage included in treatment (cf. MacCulloch, Feldman, Orford, and MacCulloch, 1966; Marks and Gelder, 1967; Quinn and Henbest, 1967).

Another controversy in aversion therapy is the relative utility of different aversive stimuli, especially chemical or electrical agents. Because of the ability to control aspects of the aversive event such as stimulus intensity, delay between conditioned and unconditioned stimuli or between the unconditioned response and the next presentation of the unconditioned stimulus, shock has been a preferred stimulus (Rachman and Teasdale, 1969). Yet the differential efficacy of various stimuli is not well established. Few comparative studies have evaluated different stimuli and their peculiar power to influence specific behaviors.

Covert Conditioning

A series of techniques termed "covert conditioning" has been developed by Joseph R. Cautela. Cautela (1972) assumes that imagined and actual events exert similar control over overt behavior.[7]

---

[7] Covert conditioning is based upon the client's imagining of various events. Although both systematic desensitization and flooding as usually practiced are based upon imagery, they are generally not classified as covert conditioning (cf. Cautela, 1972). This distinction derives, in part, from how the techniques were developed rather than from logical, conceptual, or practical differences. Covert conditioning techniques are adapted in the main from simple extrapolations of conditioning principles, usually operant conditioning, and refer to those methods devised by Cautela.

According to this assumption, overt behavior can be changed by imagining oneself performing a particular response and receiving various consequences. Cautela's formulations depend upon the strength of stimulus and response generalization—imaginary events and consequences must transfer to actual situations. Similarly, altered responses made by the client in imagination are assumed to generalize to overt behavior.

Historical Foundations   Imagery has been used extensively for therapeutic purposes, particularly in Europe (Singer, 1974). In psychoanalysis, imagery and fantasy have had at least an ancillary role in the therapeutic process. Both Freud and Jung used fantasy as a basis for assessing psychological processes. Variations of psychoanalytic practice have required patients to imagine psychodynamically significant scenes (e.g., pertaining to childhood) (cf. Clark, 1926; Kubie, 1943; Reyher, 1963). Other techniques, some of which are derived directly from analytic treatment, rely almost completely upon directed imagery and fantasy. In many of the procedures, clients imagine standard scenes that reflect such themes as interpersonal relationships, conflicts, and personal strivings. Or imagery can be somewhat less controlled and be allowed to unfold with little structuring by the therapist. The client is usually deeply relaxed and engages in imagery-construction for the entire therapy session. The curative effects of guided-imagery therapies are thought to result either from the imagery process itself or from the material revealed through the imagery (cf. Desoille, 1938, 1945; Fretigny and Virel, 1968; Leuner, 1969).

The use of imagery in behavior modification has developed independently of the European tradition (cf. Singer, 1974). The major impetus for the widespread adoption of imagery seems to be Wolpe's introduction of desensitization. Before Wolpe, uses of imagery in techniques resembling current behavioral practices were rare. For example, in the United States, Chappel and Stevenson (1936) used imagery to treat hospitalized patients with peptic ulcers. Patients were instructed to imagine positive life-experiences whenever they became anxious, a procedure that was shown to enhance recovery.

Salter (1949) may have been the first to employ imagery in behavior modification. He manipulated imagery to alter the client's mood and feelings in the therapy sessions as well as in his everyday experience to overcome maladaptive reactions such as anxiety. In therapy, Salter's use of imagery paralleled desensitization very closely.

Yet these applications appeared to exert little influence on contemporary behavior therapy. Wolpe's use of imagery as an alternative for *in vivo* desensitization was largely responsible for its adoption. His work stimulated further explorations of the therapeutic effects of imagery once individuals extended applications of desensitization. For example, Lazarus expanded the use of imagery in desensitizing children (Lazarus and Abramovitz, 1962). Instead of using relaxation as the anxiety-inhibiting response, which did not seem feasible with children, positive images were used. The images consisted of fantasized scenes of interest to the children. Lazarus reasoned that such "emotive imagery" could evoke positive feelings (e.g., self-assertion, pride, affection) that would inhibit anxiety.

Covert conditioning techniques were developed directly from desensitization. Desensitization is designed to eliminate maladaptive *avoidance* responses (e.g., phobias). Yet, no parallel technique had been advanced to eliminate maladaptive *approach* responses as seen in addictive behaviors or attraction toward socially censured sexual stimuli. Investigators began to explore the imagery of aversive events to develop avoidance reactions. An early application was provided by Gold and Neufeld (1965), who used aversive imagery (e.g., repulsive male images) to overcome an adolescent male's habit of soliciting men in public toilets. Similarly, Cautela (1966, 1967) reported a technique in which clients associated imagery of behavior they wished to eliminate or reduce with imagery of aversive events. The technique, called "covert sensitization," was illustrated with case material and supported with an investigation that treated alcoholics (Cautela, 1967). Several imagery-based techniques grew out of the development of covert sensitization and were applied across diverse target behaviors.

Current Practice These covert conditioning techniques each have distinct therapeutic foci, such as decreasing maladaptive approach (e.g., drug abuse) or avoidance (e.g., fears) and fostering appropriate responses in their place. In practice, each technique is conducted by having the client imagine various scenes described by the therapist. The scenes are built around behaviors the client wishes to alter and various response-contingent consequences.

Covert sensitization is used to develop avoidance responses and is applied to maladaptive approach behavior such as excessive drinking, overeating, smoking, and deviant sexual behaviors. (Cautela, 1966, 1967). The technique is based upon punishment, escape and avoidance, and aversion-relief paradigms. A client imagines him/herself engaging in the target behavior such as drinking in a bar followed by aversive consequences such as vomiting or being physically beaten. The aversive consequences usually are terminated once the individual ceases to perform the target behavior. Scenes are altered during the course of treatment. For example, for an alcoholic, initial scenes may include escaping from a bar followed by the introduction of positive imagery. Later scenes may include avoiding the bar entirely, to be followed by presentations of imagery of desirable consequences. The benefits the alcoholic imagines may be termination of vomiting or feelings of nausea.

Covert reinforcement is for encouraging approach behaviors and is applied to individuals with response deficits or avoidance behaviors (Cautela, 1970b). The technique is based upon operant reinforcement whereby behaviors are increased as a function of their consequences. In *covert positive reinforcement,* the individual imagines him/herself performing a particular behavior he/she wishes to acquire plus positive consequences that follow the behavior. Over the course of treatment, successive approximations of the final behavior are shaped (Ascher and Cautela, 1972; Cautela, 1971a, 1972).

Covert negative reinforcement is sometimes used with individuals who have a paucity of positively reinforcing consequences that can be imagined (Cautela, 1970a). In covert negative reinforcement, the individual imagines some aversive event or state. Once this activity is clearly imagined, the scene is terminated and the client is instructed to imagine the behavior he/she wishes to develop.

Two procedures used to eliminate behaviors are *covert punishment* and *covert extinction.* In covert punishment, the individual imagines some aversive consequence of a particular behavior (Cautela, 1976a). Although the procedure resembles covert sensitization, it does not include the escape, avoidance, and aversion relief components. Covert extinction is used to reduce maladaptive behaviors that ordinarily have positively reinforcing consequences (Cautela, 1971b). This procedure, based upon the principle of operant extinction, requires individuals to imagine the response they wish to eliminate followed by no positive consequences. Through repeated trials without reinforcement, it is assumed that the behavior will no longer be performed.

Covert modeling does not derive from the operant conditioning paradigm (Cautela, 1976b). It is used to build up or eliminate diverse responses. Clients imagine other individuals engaging in the behaviors they wish to emulate. Across several scenes, the imagined model engages in assorted behaviors associated with the target response.

Current Issues With the exception of covert sensitization, the covert conditioning techniques were formalized in the 1970s. Thus, the efficacy of these techniques has not been well established (cf. Mahoney, 1974). Nevertheless, the techniques have been applied to diverse behaviors, including overeating, smoking, homosexuality, phobias, social responses, and drug addiction (Cautela, 1972; Rimm and Masters, 1974).

A major debate in covert conditioning concerns the extent to which the techniques adhere to the principles and paradigms from which they were drawn (Kazdin, 1977c). Cautela has intentionally referred to the techniques in terms of learning principles such as reinforcement and punishment so that the conditions investigated in the laboratory can be extrapolated to therapeutic settings both for heuristic and clinical purposes (Cautela, 1970b). However, the extrapolation appears to be quite tenuous in many cases. For example, imagined positively and negatively reinforcing events differ from their overt counterparts. Positive reinforcement and aversive stimuli are selected in covert conditioning on the basis of the client's verbal report of desirable and undesirable events. To select reinforcing consequences, clients are required to complete self-report inventories by rating a large number of events that are rewarding. Technically, merely identifying an event as a reinforcer does not mean the event will be reinforcing. The reinforcing properties of an event can only be determined by examining changes in overt behavior that follow from its contingent application.

Some of the covert conditioning techniques themselves deviate drastically from the principles from which they were derived. For example, covert negative reinforcement does not employ the principle of negative reinforcement as typically conceived. As noted, negative reinforcement means an increased frequency of a response that is followed by termination of an aversive event. The response terminates some event. In the covert procedure, an aversive event is terminated and then the response is performed (Cautela, 1972). Response performance is not itself followed by any consequence. Thus, the procedure violates the principle from which it was derived. Indeed, in some of the covert negative reinforcement research (Ascher and Cautela, 1972), the paradigm seems to follow the punishment procedure, which would be expected to have the opposite effect of negative reinforcement. In any case, the deviation of covert techniques from the principles on which they are based brings into question the theoretical base and therapeutic mechanisms that account for behavior change (Kazdin, 1977c). Therefore, evaluation of the diverse covert conditioning techniques is still premature. Many cases and investigations for select problems have suggested the efficacy of the techniques. Yet, neither the reliability of outcome nor the specific mechanisms responsible for behavior change has been carefully determined.

Modeling Therapy

Modeling refers to learning by observing the performance of someone else. Through observation, clients can acquire desired responses without performing them themselves.

Historical Foundations   Modeling or imitative learning has been investigated in laboratory animals since the late 1800s. Simple motor, discrimination, and problem-solving tasks have been studied in cats, dogs, birds, chimps, and monkeys (cf. Hall, 1963; Riopelle, 1967; Simmel, Hoppe, and Milton, 1968). Extensions of modeling to human learning have been designed primarily to shed light on theoretical interpretations of imitative behavior and to understand mechanisms of personality and social development (e.g., Bandura and Walters, 1963; Miller and Dollard, 1941).

Historically, there are relatively few therapeutic applications of modeling. M. C. Jones (1924a, 1924b) used it to overcome fears of young children. She selected unafraid peers to interact with the object of fear while the fearful child observed, a technique that proved to be effective. Masserman (1943) used social imitation to treat experimental neuroses in cats. A cat who had learned to fear a section of the enclosure would be placed in the cage with an unfrightened cat who approached the food and fed. The fearful cat eventually emulated the other cat, fed, and showed a reduction of anxiety.

Current therapeutic applications of modeling are derived primarily from the work of Albert Bandura (Bandura, 1971a). His research was focused upon variables that contribute to observational learning, particularly with children in laboratory settings. In the late 1960s, he extended his work to therapeutic applications. Initial investigations demonstrated that children's fears could be altered through a live or filmed performance of a model. Since 1970, therapeutic applications of modeling have increased markedly (cf. Bandura, 1971a; Rachman, 1972, 1976).

Current Practice Several variations of modeling are used in treatment. In general, modeling consists of observing a live or filmed performance of the model. Recent research suggests that the model may be imagined rather than observed directly, as in covert modeling (Cautela, 1976; Kazdin, 1974a). A particularly effective variation of modeling is called *participant modeling* or *contact desensitization* (Ritter, 1968). In this version, the client observes a live model perform the response (e.g., the therapist) and then gradually performs the response him/herself. The therapist guides the client through various tasks that the therapist has modeled. The guidance continues until the client initiates all of the behaviors that have been demonstrated. In general, participant modeling results in greater behavior change than does modeling alone.

Current Issues Modeling has been used to treat a variety of behaviors such as fear of dogs, snakes, heights, and water, as well as test-taking, obsessions and compulsions, social withdrawal, unassertive behavior, dependent behaviors, and interview responses (Bandura, 1971a; Friedman 1972; Marlatt and Perry, 1975; Rachman, 1972, 1976). Adults, adolescents, and children in outpatient treatment as well as institutionalized psychiatric patients, delinquents, and retarded persons have undergone the treatment.

Modeling is a rather recent therapeutic technique. Thus, basic questions such as the extent to which treatment effects are maintained and carried over to situations not included in therapy, the range of problems that can be treated, and the relative effects of variations of modeling remain to be resolved. Laboratory research has suggested that several variables contribute to modeling effects, including similarity between the model and observer, competence, prestige, and status of the model, the number of models, characteristics of the observer, and consequences following emulated behavior (Bandura, 1971a; Flanders, 1968). These variables are beginning to be studied in the context of treatment (cf. Kazdin, 1976a).

A final issue involves the theoretical interpretation of modeling. Two major competing interpretations have been posed—a cognitive-mediational model (Bandura, 1969) and an operant model (Gewirtz, 1971). These positions and their variations diverge on the type of inferences made about the modeling process, the role accorded early training of the individual, and the events that control acquisition of imitative behavior. At present, any implications that these different interpretations might have in the therapeutic application of modeling have not been elaborated.

Biofeedback

Biofeedback consists of providing an individual with information about an aspect of his/her ongoing physiological processes (e.g., heart rate). The information is immediately displayed to the individual so that moment-to-moment changes can be monitored and response-contingent feedback can be provided for directional change (e.g., decrease in heart rate) (cf. Kamiya, Barber, DiCara, Miller, Shapiro, and Stoyva, 1971).

Historical Foundations   The conditioning of internal physiological responses has been studied by several contemporary investigators (see Franks, 1960; Razran, 1961, 1965), and the demonstrations of Pavlov and his colleagues are well known. One of the most systematic extensions of conditioning of internal functions was made by K. M. Bykov (1953, 1957). Bykov's work involved conditioning internal physiological responses by using direct stimulation to the internal organs as the conditioned or unconditioned stimulus, a procedure termed *interoceptive conditioning.* Diverse responses, such as glandular secretions, alteration of blood chemistry, uterine contractions, and vasoconstriction, could all be elicited by previous neutral stimuli.

In addition to the theoretical interest in the conditioning of physiological reactions, the clinical implications are enormous. Perhaps the most important is that maladaptive physiological reactions may become conditioned to events in everyday experience (cf. Bykov, 1953; H. G. Jones, 1960). For example, asthmatic responses have been shown to be controlled by specific environmental events, some of which have been paired directly with physiological irritants (cf. Dekker and Groen, 1956; Dekker, Pelser, and Groen, 1957). Therefore, classical conditioning has been accorded an important role in the acquisition of psychophysiological disorders. Despite the importance of classical conditioning, extrapolations from operant conditioning have been relied upon for clinical alterations of psychophysiological reactions.

The conditioning of physiological responses through operant methods was delayed in part because of early writings in the psychology of learning. The distinction between classical and operant conditioning led some authors (e.g., Konorski and Miller, 1937; Miller and Konorski, 1928) to suggest that glandular or muscle reactions could not be conditioned instrumentally. Although Skinner initially did not rule out the possibility of conditioning physiological responses instrumentally (Skinner, 1938), he eventually asserted that physiological functions could not be brought under control of operant reinforcement (Skinner, 1953a). The failure of separate experiments by Skinner and Mowrer contributed to the belief that autonomic functioning could not be conditioned, a belief perpetuated for many years in the literature (e.g., Keller and Schoenfeld, 1950; Kimble, 1961).

In the late 1950s, Neal Miller read a translation of Bykov's work that showed the wide range of internal responses that could be classically conditioned. Miller believed that a unity of all learning existed and began to look at the instrumental conditioning of internal functions (Jonas, 1973). In the late 1950s and early 1960s, he attempted to alter the frequency of stomach contractions, heart beat, and salivation in animals by following responses of a higher or lower rate with reinforcing consequences. To control for skeletal movements that might mediate changes in involuntary functions, he eventually used curare to immobilize all skeletal muscles. By the mid 1960s, he demonstrated that reinforcement (brain stimulation) effectively altered heart rate in curarized rats. Some animals received stimulation for an increase in rate, others for a decrease (cf. Miller, 1969). Thus, internal functioning appeared to be readily conditioned by operant consequences. More recently, Miller and others have reported a failure to replicate the results of experiments conditioning the heart rates of curarized animals (Brener, Eissenberg, and Middaugh, 1974; Miller, 1972; Miller and Dworkin, 1974; Roberts, Lacroix, and Wright, 1974). These findings have raised serious questions about conditioning effects and how the original results with curarized animals were obtained. However, replication difficulties have challenged rather than disproved the general belief, supported by research, that visceral conditioning does occur (Engel, 1972; Shapiro and Surwit, 1976).

In the late 1950s investigators in Russia, Canada, and the United States independently began studying instrumental conditioning of automatically mediated responses in humans. In Russia, digital vasodilation was successfully conditioned by making escape and avoidance from aversive events contingent upon dilation (Lisina, 1960; Razran, 1961). In Canada, attempts to condition galvanic skin responses (GSR) and heart rate were made by means of a response-contingent light (Mandler and Kahn, 1960; Mandler, Preven, and Kuhlman, 1962). In the United States, conditioning of GSR and heart rate through positive reinforcement and avoidance paradigms produced suggestive evidence that instrumental conditioning was effective (cf. Kimmell, 1967; 1974). In the early 1960s, an increasing number of investigators demonstrated the reliability of conditioning heart rate, GSR, and digital vasoconstriction. In these studies, visual or auditory feedback was provided to the subjects as part of avoidance, punishment, and positive reinforcement contingencies.

In the late 1960s, from a somewhat different research tradition than instrumental conditioning, Kamiya (1962, 1969) began to work on the alteration of electrocortical activity. His research stemmed from an interest in determining whether humans could discriminate higher nervous system activity and various subjective states if they received feedback for electroencephalogram (EEG) changes. The study of changing EEG waves became extremely popular, in part because of the association of wave patterns with altered states of consciousness, mood states, and feelings (Grossberg, 1972; Stoyva and Kamiya, 1968). Brain-wave biofeedback studies were viewed as an objective way to study consciousness (Brown, 1970; Green, Green, and Walters, 1970). Introspective reports of conscious experience could be believed more readily if the reports corresponded with specific physiological measures of brain activity (Stoyva and Kamiya, 1968). Thus, the conditioning of internal processes was viewed as a methodological advance to facilitate the study of consciousness.

The conditioning of glandular, visceral, and brain functions converged to constitute the area of biofeedback (Barber, DiCara, Kamiya, Miller, Shapiro, and Stoyva, 1975; Kamiya et al., 1971). Many demonstrations were made to show that individuals could be trained to control internal functions. Eventually, individuals selected for study were those who suffered physiological disorders that required intervention. The use of feedback and other consequences to alter disordered functioning thus became a therapeutic technique.

Current Practice   Biofeedback consists of attaching to the client an apparatus (e.g., polygraph or electroencephalograph) that automatically and continuously monitors the response of interest (e.g., GSR, heart rate, digital pulse volume, brain waves). Data on the monitored response are communicated to the client visually (e.g., display of a dial or meter) or auditorally (e.g., tone). Sometimes incentives such as money, verbal praise, slides, or other events are contingent upon achieving responses in the desired direction. Several training sessions are continued until change above baseline response rates are evident, or, in the case of clinical cases, until the extent of change is of therapeutic value (e.g., blood pressure is lowered beyond hypertensive levels).

Biofeedback requires sophisticated equipment that can sense and record various responses and can be programmed to provide consequences contingently. In addition to the target response, several responses typically are monitored to determine if they, too, are changing. Although biofeedback devices have been made available to the general public, they usually are used for EEG feedback. However, the clinical use of biofeedback generally has focused on cardiovascular responses, which require more elaborate and not generally available equipment.

Current Issues   Biofeedback has been used with such disorders as essential hypertension, cardiac arrhythmias, migraine headaches, Raynaud's disease, epileptic seizures, impotence, obsessive ruminations, and diarrhea (Barber et al., 1975; Blanchard and Young, 1974; Kamiya et al., 1971). Although the range of clinical disorders has been great, many of the reports have relied upon case material rather than upon experimental demonstrations (Blanchard and Young, 1974).

Various controversies remain to be resolved. A main issue is the extent to which changes in autonomic function are permanent. Studies have demonstrated that internal processes can be instrumentally conditioned, yet the effects may be somewhat exaggerated as compared to the available evidence (Miller, 1972). As noted, findings obtained in the early research have not been replicated consistently. For reasons that are not known, the effect of conditioning heart rate in animals has become progressively smaller over time. Whereas early studies produced rather marked effects, recent studies have obtained increasingly less significant effects under what appear to be similar laboratory conditions (cf. Miller, 1972; Miller and Dworkin, 1974).

From the standpoint of behavior therapy, several clinically relevant debates remain to be resolved. First, most biofeedback investigations have been conducted on volunteer college student populations with no major physiological disorders. While studies with such populations can demonstrate the effect of biofeedback of diverse body functions, they do not demonstrate whether or not actual physiological dysfunction can be altered. Second, the extent to which nonspecific treatment effects or client expectancies can account for the results have not been examined carefully. Third, although the effects of biofeedback are often statistically reliable, whether or not the changes produced are clinically important is less well established. Fourth, the effect of biofeedback compared to more easily implemented therapy techniques remains to be determined. Some studies have suggested, for example, that simple training in muscle relaxation may be as effective as biofeedback in controlling cardiac functioning (Blanchard and Epstein, 1977; Blanchard and Young, 1973).

Other Behavior Therapy Techniques

In addition to the techniques reviewed above, and operant and self-control techniques that are discussed later, several other procedures fall under behavior modification. Role-playing, behavioral rehearsal, thought-stopping, rational-emotive therapy, conditioning treatment of enuresis, negative practice, metronome-conditioned therapy, delayed auditory feedback, relaxation training, bibliotherapy, and induced anxiety are therapies that generally enjoy much less use than the techniques reviewed above. Behavior modification attempts to rely on techniques that are established empirically, independent of the theoretical derivations of the technique.

SUMMARY AND CONCLUSIONS

Behavior modification has evolved markedly in its brief history. Early developments emphasized the ties of behavior modification with learning theory and to a scientific approach in general, but contemporary practitioners place a substantially greater emphasis on a specific behavioral methodology. The movement seems to be devoted to developing behavior-change techniques with a well-established research base, somewhat independent of any narrow range of theoretical ties. Thus, behavior modification cannot be characterized by adherence to any one theory of behavior. Because of the diverse theoretical approaches and the unlimited range of admissible therapy techniques, the term "behavior modification" has become diffuse in meaning.

7
Emergence and Evolution of Applied Behavior Analysis

A major area within behavior modification is the application of techniques derived from operant conditioning and the experimental analysis of behavior. Operant conditioning is an outgrowth of learning research in the behaviorist tradition and it is based on a sophisticated laboratory methodology and technology. Within approximately two decades after its development in the 1930s, operant conditioning was extended systematically to human behavior in programmatic laboratory investigations. In these investigations, laboratory operant methods were applied to study the behavior of normal and clinical populations. These applications initially were designed to determine the utility of extending to humans operant principles and experimental methodology from laboratory investigations of animals.

Laboratory work with humans revealed characteristics of operant responding that were of clinical and applied relevance. Indeed, changes in behaviors of clinical interest occasionally were reported as side effects of laboratory investigations studying free-operant behavior. By the late 1950s and early 1960s, preliminary attempts were made to apply operant conditioning techniques directly to effect behavior changes in clinical populations. Many reports had shown that deviant and problematic behaviors could be altered by manipulating reinforcing and punishing consequences in the environment. Although these initial reports were primarily of demonstrational value, subsequent applications became explicitly therapeutic in their focus. By the mid 1960s, several applications had been reported, and as they proliferated, these extensions of operant conditioning and the experimental analysis of behavior were recognized formally as a new area of research: applied behavior analysis.

PRECURSORS OF APPLIED BEHAVIOR ANALYSIS

Several investigators of animal behavior were pioneers in the extension of operant conditioning to humans in experimental and applied contexts. From a historical standpoint, the evolution of applied work from laboratory research in operant conditioning is relatively direct. Since the basic principles of operant conditioning were elaborated by Skinner in the late 1930s, they have been increasingly extended to diverse aspects of human behavior.

Long before the principles of operant conditioning were investigated explicitly, various behavior-change techniques were used that bear similarity to contemporary operant techniques. The techniques, of course, were not conceived of as operant conditioning and, indeed, preceded the formal development of psychology itself. Nevertheless, they closely resemble contemporary applications and occasionally were attempted on a rather large scale.

Rewards resembling incentives based on operant conditioning have been used throughout civilization. Interpersonal interaction—as well as widespread institutional practices, such as religion, education, child rearing, military training, government and law, and business—has relied upon rewards and punishments to control behavior. For example, most cultures maintain armed forces to defend themselves. Throughout history, military training has relied heavily upon the contingent delivery of rewards for those behaviors valued in combat. The widespread use of incentives in military training resembles techniques based upon positive reinforcement.

Consider a sample of practices that illustrate the long-standing tradition of delivering rewards for military performance. During the first century A.D., Greek and Roman gladiators received special prizes ranging from wreaths and crowns to money and property for their victorious performances (Grant, 1967). Charioteers in Rome were freed from slavery and received financial rewards for repeated victories in their duels (Carcopino, 1940). Similarly, ancient Chinese soldiers received colored peacock feathers that could be worn as honorary symbols of their bravery during battle (Doolittle, 1865). Fifteenth-century Aztec soldiers received titles of distinction and the honor of having stone statues made of them for their triumphant military performance (Duran, 1964). American Indians of the Great

Plains tribes received attention and approval from their peers for skill in combat or hunting. Meritorious deeds earned the privilege of relating the experiences to others in public (Eggan, 1937). Of course, in contemporary military practice, all degrees of medals are awarded for deeds performed in the service of one's country.

Rewards frequently have been given by educators as incentives for learning. In twelfth-century Europe, prizes such as nuts, figs, and honey were used to reward individuals who were learning to recite religious lessons (Birnbaum, 1962). In the sixteenth century, fruit and cake were advocated as a means to help teach children Greek and Latin (Skinner, 1966). One particularly charming use of incentives for educational ends pertains to the perhaps apocryphal history of pretzels (Crossman, 1975). The invention of the pretzel has been traced to the seventh century A.D. A monk in southern Europe made pretzels from the remains of dough after baking bread. He shaped the remains into little biscuits to represent children's arms as they are folded in prayer. These biscuits were used to reward children who learned to recite prayers. The monk referred to these rewards as *petriola*, Latin for "little reward" and from which the word "pretzel" is derived.[1]

These examples of incentives in military training and education are only a fraction of the recorded instances of the use of rewards. The uses of punishment in criminology alone are too vast to begin to enumerate. From a historical standpoint, the importance of early applications of incentive systems lies in their similarities to contemporary behavior modification programs, a point even more apparent in practices illustrated below.

Joseph Lancaster and the Monitorial System

Reinforcement programs have been relatively common in the school classroom, where systems based upon points, merits, demerits, and similar tangible conditioned reinforcers are used to control behavior. An elaborate example of such a program was the educational system of Joseph Lancaster (1778–1838), which was implemented in countries throughout the world.

---

[1] Although a few sources have attributed the origin of "pretzel" to Latin words for "reward" (Shipley, 1945; *The World Book Encyclopedia*, 1975), other authorities trace it to the Latin *brachiatus* (having branches like arms), *brachium* (arm), or *bracellus* (a bracelet) (Klein, 1967; *The Oxford English Dictionary*, 1961; Partridge, 1966; *Webster's Third New International Dictionary*, 1967). "Pretzel" comes from the German *brezel* (also spelled *prezel*), which appears to be derived from the Latin words listed above.

In England in the early 1800s, Lancaster developed a system of teaching called the monitorial system (cf. Lancaster, 1805; Salmon, 1904). The system began when he initiated free education of the poor. This reform led to large enrollments (100–300 students in the early years and eventually over 1,000) in facilities that soon became overcrowded. Inadequate funds did not permit the hiring of assistants to handle the large number of students who were housed in one room, so Lancaster decided to use students in class as assistants or monitors (Kaestle, 1973).

Students who excelled in their work were appointed as monitors and were given responsibility for most of the functions traditionally reserved for teachers. The monitors were responsible for teaching the students, asking questions, grading answers, noting absences or misbehavior, preparing, distributing, and collecting supplies, and promoting students for improved academic performance. "Teaching monitors" responsible for presenting lessons had about 10 or 12 students in their groups. The groups differed in levels of ability, and the goal of the system was to advance an individual to higher levels of ability within his/her own group and eventually to other groups. The students were classified separately in reading, arithmetic, writing, and spelling and promoted to higher groups in these areas when competence was demonstrated.

Lancaster's system depended heavily upon positive reinforcement, particularly token reinforcement, both for the monitors and the students. The reinforcement system for the students was based upon competition. Students received rewards depending upon their correct responses in their group and their relative standing vis-à-vis their peers. The top individual in each group earned a rank of one and received a leather ticket of merit. Also, he wore a picture pasted on a small board and suspended on his chest to indicate his excellent performance. If his performance were surpassed by someone else in his group, he forfeited the honor of having the ticket and wearing the picture and the highest ranking number. However, he received another picture as a reward for having earned first place. Individuals were periodically examined by someone other than their monitor to determine if they could be promoted to a higher group. When a student knew the lesson and earned a promotion, he received a prize (e.g., a toy or picture). His monitor also received a prize of the same value.

Other reward systems were used besides the group ranking and ticket system. An "order of merit" was established for individuals who distinguished themselves by attending to their studies, helping others improve their work, or trying to check the misbehavior of others. Members of the order were distinguished by a silver medal suspended from their necks with a large plated chain. Another procedure was to reward a few outstanding children whose behavior appeared exemplary with engraved silver medals, pens, watches, and books (Lancaster, 1805).

Punishment was relatively infrequent in the system and was reserved for instances of idleness or disruptive behavior. For misbehavior, the offender would receive a ticket from his monitor. The offense was listed on the card. The card was turned into the head of the school, who admonished the offender. Repeated offenses were followed by such punishing consequences as having a wooden log tied to one's neck (making turning away from one's lesson difficult), placing one's legs in wooden shackles, having one hand tied behind one's back, or, on rare occasions, being placed in a sack or basket suspended from the ceiling.

Lancaster's system spread quickly in England and became popular in the British Empire, Europe, Africa, Russia, Asia, and South America, as well as in the United States and Canada (Kaestle, 1973). In the United States, the Lancasterian system was implemented shortly after it was created. The system was used in New York in the early 1800s and was adopted in New Jersey, Pennsylvania, Maryland, and Washington, D.C. (Ravitch, 1974; Salmon, 1904). Lancaster visited America to promote his system, established an institute, and published materials about his program.

The Excelsior School System

The use of reinforcement in the classroom seems to have become relatively popular in the United States in the late 1800s, somewhat independently of Lancaster's monitorial system of education. One program described in 1885 was called the "Excelsior School System" (Ulman and Klem, 1975). In this system, students earned merits in various denominations for appropriate behaviors, including punctuality, orderliness, and studiousness. Students could earn a token, referred to as an "excellent," for commendable performance or a different token, referred to as a "perfect," for perfect performance each day. Excellents and perfects were exchangeable for one or two merits, respectively. If a large number of merits were earned, the student could exchange them for a special certificate by the teacher attesting to his/her performance.

An interesting feature of the program was that parents were encouraged to ask the students how many merits they had earned and received feedback from the school. The Excelsior School System, which included tokens of different denominations, instructions, certificates, and slips to parents, was sold commercially. The program was reported to have been successful for almost 10 years, used by thousands of teachers in several states (Ulman and Klem, 1975).

Alexander Maconochie and the Mark System

A particularly interesting application of reinforcement was made by Alexander Maconochie (1787–1860), who established a program for managing and rehabilitating several hundred prisoners at Norfolk Island (Australia) (Maconochie, 1847, 1848). Maconochie was critical of inhumane methods of treating prisoners. He believed that prison should work to rehabilitate prisoners by developing conduct that would foster adjustment to society. He devised a system whereby prisoners could obtain release on the basis of their behavior rather than on the basis of merely serving the duration of their sentence.

Maconochie developed a "mark system" as the primary basis of rehabilitation. Sentences were converted into a fixed number of "marks" that individuals had to earn to obtain release. The number of marks needed by a prisoner was commensurate with the severity of the crime committed. Prisoners had to progress through a multistage system. Although some initial restraint and deprivation were included in the program, the main treatment consisted of inmates earning marks for work and for appropriate conduct. The marks could be exchanged for essential items, including food, shelter, and clothes. Disciplinary offenses were punished by fines and by withdrawal of privileges rather than by the cruel measures that had been commonly practiced (e.g., flogging and being bound in chains).

A given level of accumulated marks determined whether or not one earned release. The marks toward this final goal had to be accumulated over and above those marks spent on essential items or lost for offenses. After a prisoner had earned a large number of excess marks toward the terminal goal and, thus, had shown appropriate conduct for a protracted period, he joined other prisoners (in groups of five or six) and performed tasks as a member of a group. The group was organized so that individuals would become responsible for each other's conduct. To this end, offenses performed by one member of a group resulted in a fine for all group members. Correspondingly, marks were earned on a collective basis for the group.

Maconochie's system was beset with an extremely large number of obstacles (Barry, 1958). The prison in which he implemented his program housed particularly intractible inmates who had been sent for their multiple convictions. Extreme administrative and political opposition ensured that major conditions required in the program (e.g., guaranteeing release of prisoners contingent upon earning a predetermined number of marks) could not be enforced. Perhaps the most serious obstacle was that prison life during the time of Maconochie's work was based heavily upon brutal punishment and explicitly coercive treatment. Thus, his program was largely viewed as indulging the prisoners rather than providing the punishment and social revenge it was felt they deserved.

Despite these difficulties, there was some indication that his method was associated with superior outcome, as suggested by a recidivism rate claimed to be approximately 2% in five years (Maconochie, 1847). Other prisons throughout the British colonies showed a recidivism rate between 33–67%. Although the records do not permit an uncritical acceptance of these figures, evaluation of Maconochie's achievements by colleagues and contemporaries and by the verdict of history attest to the efficacy of his procedures (Barry, 1958; West, 1852).

From the standpoint of behavior modification, and more specifically, applied operant work, Maconochie's achievements are remarkable. His system entailed a reinforcement program in which behavior and rate of progress determined the consequences received. Prisoners were given clear guidelines of the required behaviors and predetermined rather than arbitrary consequences for specific offenses. Their treatment encouraged positive behaviors instead of merely punishing undesirable ones. It included approximations of social living through having to consider a group, which helped foster behaviors that would facilitate community adjustment after release.

Francois Leuret and the Treatment of Psychiatric Patients

Francois Leuret (1798–1851) was a French physician who spent most of his career at the Bicêtre Hospital in Paris. He treated hospitalized patients in a manner that appears consistent with contemporary behavior modification (Wolpe and Theriault, 1971). Leuret concentrated on changing the disordered conduct of his patients and sought means to alter it. For example, he treated patients with delusions by associating delusive verbalizations with aversive consequences. If a patient stated that he was Napoleon, he would receive an aversive event such as a cold shower, which was delivered repeatedly until the patient ceased making the offending statements. The patient could avoid the aversive event by denying the content of the delusive statements and by substituting rational statements in their place. Or he could engage in work in the hospital.

Leuret's technique of associating negative consequences with specific disordered behaviors does not appear to have been extended beyond his own practice. Indeed, his methods were considered as sadistic because they included ignoring the problems of the patient, administering unpleasant corporal consequences, and withholding food until the desired behavior was performed. These methods sharply contrasted with the more characteristic tendency of the time to treat patients kindly (Wolpe and Theriault, 1971).

Leuret's importance is not in his use of aversive events *per se,* because such procedures occupy a prominent place in the history of treating the mentally ill. Early in the history of psychiatry, treatment consisted of severe punishment, which was viewed as a means of exorcising the evil spirits assumed to be responsible for one's madness. In contrast, Leuret's approach was to provide contingent aversive events for specific deviant behaviors for the sole purpose of suppressing them. Contemporary operant techniques eschew punishment in cases in which positive reinforcers can be used to nurture socially adaptive behaviors.

The applications of incentive systems illustrated above describe only a few of such practices in the history of education, penology, and psychiatry. In some cases, such as the monitorial system of Lancaster, there are very close parallels to many contemporary practices (see Kazdin and Pulaski, 1977). Although many older practices provide clear precedents for current practices, they are outside the direct historical line leading to behavior modification. Contemporary behavioral applications can be traced directly to laboratory and clinical extensions of operant conditioning.

EMERGENCE OF APPLIED OPERANT RESEARCH

In the 1950s, several investigators extended operant conditioning research to humans. As this research evolved, the focus gradually shifted from basic research to clinical applications. At the extremes of the continuum, laboratory and clinical research can be delineated clearly. For example, the bulk of early human laboratory investigations focused on lever-pressing behavior in very much the same way as had the work with animals. Indeed, the experimental situation for human operant research was modeled after the laboratory. Purely clinical applications were evident when behaviors were selected for the purpose of effecting therapeutic change.

Before tracing the evolution of operant research from the laboratory to clinical work, its application in education warrants mention. That extension exerted tremendous impact on teaching and instruction by stimulating research on teaching machines and programmed instruction. Moreover, preliminary attempts were made to broaden educational applications to clinical problems.

From Laboratory Research to Educational Applications

The bulk of work on teaching machines and programmed instruction is outside the domain of behavior modification and, hence, is not detailed here. However, it should be noted that research in this area was a significant application of operant principles. In addition, extensions of the principles upon which programmed instruction is based were preliminary attempts to devise a technology that went beyond education.

Teaching machines are devices that present material to students and allow them to respond by completing an answer or providing missing information. Feedback and reinforcement are provided immediately for correct responses by allowing each student to progress as mastery of an individual item is achieved. The instructional material presented to the student by the teaching machine is referred to as the "program." The program presents substantive content and questions that require the student to respond. Typically, the program divides the subject matter into small and relatively simple units. The material presented may become increasingly complex within a program to develop a relatively sophisticated response repertoire of the material. Education based upon teaching machines and programmed instruction has several characteristics:

Provides immediate feedback for student performance;
Allows the individual student to proceed through the program at his/
    her own rate;
Tailors instruction to the level of the student;
Allows active participation by requiring the student to respond
    directly to the material as it is presented;
Divides the material into simple units that increase in complexity;
Specifies the final learning objectives in advance.

Many features of teaching machines and programmed instruction have their own historical precedents in education outside the realm of behavior modification (Dale, 1967; Lumsdaine and Glaser, 1960). However, it was operant conditioning that crystallized independent lines of research and directly stimulated research and applications of programmed instruction.

The earliest introduction of mechanical devices that resemble contemporary teaching machines was made in the 1920s by Sidney J. Pressey and his students at the Ohio State University (Pressey, 1926, 1927, 1950). Pressey's devices were designed for automatic testing (self-scoring), but they were soon shown to have instructional properties of even greater interest. To use these machines, students identified the correct answer among available solutions to a multiple choice question, and, following correct performance, progressed to subsequent questions. In the process, students learned the material that was presented. Thus, although the machines were designed for scoring purposes, they taught the subject matter. Pressey recognized the implications of his work and advocated widespread use of teaching machines. He envisioned an "industrial revolution in education" as a result of using these machines (Pressey, 1960).

Despite Pressey's enthusiasm, it was not until the 1950s that teaching machines became of major interest to educators. Skinner fueled this interest by his applications of operant conditioning to education (Skinner, 1953a) and his specific recommendations for changes in teaching methods (Skinner, 1954b). His 1954 paper, "The Science of Learning and the Art of Teaching," was particularly influential because it discussed how a technology of education was accessible through operant conditioning research. He described how learning research could serve as the basis for redesigning educational practices. According to Skinner, traditional practices relied primarily upon aversive rather than positive control, provided reinforcing events that were too infrequent and too delayed, and did not present academic material in a fashion that encouraged increasingly complex response repertoires. Because the pupil depended primarily upon the teacher for reinforcement, few children in the classroom could receive immediate incentives at any given time.

One change Skinner (1954b, 1958) recommended was the use of machines that presented academic material to the student individually and provided immediate reinforcement for responding. He suggested that teaching machines could gradually shape increasingly complex repertoires for whatever subject matter was involved. With Skinner's refinement, the student progressed through a series of questions (i.e., the program) based upon previously answered material. The program provided the stimulus materials, questions, and answers. The student responded to the questions by generating the answers, and immediate feedback was received for performance.

Within just a few years after he suggested the use of teaching machines and programmed instruction, Skinner, his students, and his colleagues were investigating the area actively by testing children, adolescents, and college students (Lumsdaine and Glaser, 1960).[2] Teaching machines and programmed instruction became an important area of research and application in education (Lange, 1967; Lumsdaine and Glaser, 1960, 1965).

The impact of teaching machines and programmed instruction was felt very quickly.[3] In the early 1960s, publishers began to produce an extensive amount of programmed material for classroom use (Hendershot, 1964). The availability of the material in published form meant that schools could easily adopt programmed instruction in text material without reorganizing the educational structure or retraining teachers (Lindvall and Bolvin, 1967). Hence, even in the early 1960s, a relatively high percentage of schools sampled in the United States were using programmed instructional materials (Hanson and Komoski, 1965). Programmed instruction also has greatly influenced training in industry and the military (Bryan and Nagay, 1965; Shoemaker and Holt, 1965): job training has been systematized through programmed materials, often in conjunction with machines for presenting the information. Independent of the specific setting in which programmed instruction has been extended, it has remained within the fold of education.

Programmed instruction flourished as a new area of research and application. In the 1960s the appearance of a special journal (*Journal of Programmed Instruction* in 1962) and major edited volumes (e.g., Lange, 1967; Lumsdaine and Glaser, 1960, 1965) provided a forum for

---

[2] Many individuals involved in early applications and research in programmed instruction later made seminal contributions to behavior modification. Among them were Nathan H. Azrin, Charles B. Ferster, James G. Holland, and Lloyd E. Homme.

[3] The use of teaching machines initially lagged behind the use of programmed instructional materials for a variety of reasons. For example, early teaching machines were no more efficient or effective in training students than was written programmed material provided without machines (e.g., Goldstein and Gotkin, 1962). Also, the material that could be presented was limited by the characteristics of the early machines. Contemporary applications have relied more heavily upon computer-assisted instruction in education, and this approach has been adopted widely.

assorted applications. The practical needs for training in industry and in the military accelerated the progress of research on programmed instruction in traditional classroom settings. Despite the popularity of programmed instruction and its close ties to psychological research and theory, it is not part of contemporary behavior modification. Programmed instruction has been investigated by individuals in operant conditioning and behavior modification research, and it is relied upon frequently when behavior modification is used in classroom settings. However, designing and evaluating programmed materials are distinct areas of education.[4]

Although most work on teaching machines and programmed instruction was done outside of the mainstream of contemporary behavior modification, advances in programmed instruction suggested applications of operant conditioning beyond traditional educational objectives. The generalizability of the principles of operant conditioning—upon which programmed instruction was based—was recognized within education. Some investigators have suggested that operant procedures could address the problems of human learning more generally than the confines of programmed instruction (Lindvall and Bolvin, 1967).

In the early 1960s, Thomas F. Gilbert extended the principles of operant conditioning beyond educational objectives. Gilbert was interested in self-instruction and operant conditioning. In the late 1950s, he attended Harvard for a year to do postdoctoral research with Skinner and the two worked together on programmed instruction. Eventually Gilbert became dissatisfied with the limited applicability of programmed instruction and devised a broader technology based upon operant conditioning. He called his technology "mathetics" and designated it as a new area of research (Gilbert, 1962c, 1962d).[5] In the *Journal of Mathetics,* which Gilbert founded in 1962, mathetics was described as

> the systematic application of reinforcement theory to the analysis and reconstruction of those complex behavior repertoires usually known as "subject-matter mastery," "knowledge," and "skill." Mathetics, like any technology, requires both an understanding of its principles and apprenticeship in conditions of the field to which it applies. . . . Its principles are few in number and are taken literally from the science of animal behavior (Gilbert, 1962c, p. 8).

---

[4] At least one area in behavior modification encompasses many specific aspects of programmed instruction. This area, the Personalized System of Instruction, is an interesting bridge between education and behavior modification and is mentioned later.

[5] "Mathetics" was taken from the Greek *mathein,* which means "to learn."

When applied to education, mathetics was to determine what needed to be learned and to arrange conditions ensuring that learning took place. The conditions were based on applying reinforcement principles to achieve particular educational objectives. Mathetics embraced the approach of the experimental analysis of behavior. Thus, the focus was on the behavior of the individual subject and the environmental conditions that altered behavior. The goal was to modify behavior rather than merely to predict how an individual would perform (Gilbert, 1962a).

Although Gilbert's description of mathetics stressed educational objectives, he envisioned the field as addressing a whole range of learning problems. Learning and education encompassed a variety of behaviors outside of traditional academic disciplines, including actions related to adjustment in general. This was especially true when the larger view was taken of education as a method to instill acceptable behaviors, which could include traditional learning tasks, personal habits, or child-rearing practices. In the two issues of the *Journal of Mathetics* published in 1962, some articles dealt with applications of operant techniques to solve clinical problems, such as overeating (Ferster, Nurnberger, and Levitt, 1962), stuttering (Goldiamond, 1962), and poor study habits (Fox, 1962).[6] The authors of these papers, which are detailed later, utilized principles of operant conditioning to analyze the nature of the problems and applied operant techniques to modify them. For example, Ferster and his co-workers analyzed eating habits of overweight individuals through an operant approach and recommended changes in those habits by restructuring environmental and self-imposed reinforcement contingencies. Some clients were reported as having profited from the investigators' suggestions.

These new publications suggested that mathetics embraced the application of operant conditioning to clinical problems. Hence, the field was a brief precursor of contemporary applied behavior analysis. However, the *Journal of Mathetics* ceased publication in 1962 after only two issues, in part because of the dissolution of the corporation that had supported it. Although Gilbert continued to refine his technology, which he introduced mostly in industry and education, general acceptance of applied operant conditioning as a basis for alleviating clinical problems was the result of other influences.

---

[6] Ljungberg Fox was a pseudonym used by Gilbert. Some of the articles in the journal were written by him and identified as such. The article on study habits, however, was published under a pseudonym so that too many papers would not seem to be presented by the same author—who was also the journal's founder and editor.

From Laboratory Research to Clinical Applications

The initial systematic extensions of basic operant conditioning to human behavior were primarily of methodological interest. Their purpose was to demonstrate the utility of the operant approach in investigating human performance and to determine if the findings of animal laboratory research could be extended to humans. The discussion highlights select studies of historical importance, major centers of operant research, and research programs that served as a basis for subsequent applications of operant techniques.

One of the first attempts to use operant conditioning with a human was made by Paul R. Fuller in 1948. Fuller, a graduate student at Indiana University, studied the behavior of an institutionalized, profoundly retarded 18-year-old whose behavior was that of a "vegetative idiot" (Fuller, 1949). After being deprived of food for 15 hours, the subject received warm sugared milk (injected into the mouth) as a positive reinforcer for moving his arm. The movements were initially recorded by hand by the experimenter and eventually by a polygraph. Movements increased during the contingent delivery of the reinforcer and decreased when the contingency was terminated.

Fuller's demonstration was a landmark because it showed operant responding in a human whose inability to learn anything had been assumed. Thus, achieving behavior change in a matter of a few sessions was especially dramatic. Fuller suggested that the transition of operant conditioning research from animal to human species might be made by studying relatively simple human behaviors. Despite the significance of Fuller's report, it did not mark the inception of a programmatic series of studies that could be converted directly into applied research. The initial programmatic extensions of operant conditioning to human behavior were begun in the early 1950s by Lindsley and Skinner, who studied the behavior of psychotics, and by Bijou, who studied the performance of normal and retarded children.

Lindsley and his colleagues made Harvard University and the surrounding areas one of the centers of human operant research. Studies were conducted either at the Metropolitan State Hospital in Waltham, Massachusetts or at various schools and institutions in Boston (e.g., the Harriet Tubman House, South Bay Union, and Walter E. Fernald State School). Nathan H. Azrin and Lindsley, both graduate students at Harvard working under the direction of Skinner, completed a laboratory study with 12-year-old children who were trained in pairs to engage in cooperative responses. An apparatus was designed so that reinforcing consequences (candy) were delivered only when both subjects simultaneously performed a response (placing a separate stylus in a hole). This initial demonstration with humans was a direct extension of a class demonstration at Harvard in which cooperative responses of pigeons were reinforced. Azrin and Lindsley (1956) demonstrated that cooperative behavior was a function of its consequences and developed as a single operant response, which mirrored the findings from animal research. The experiment pointed out that rudimentary interactive behaviors could be reinforced in a similar way as simple operant behaviors of one subject.

Another extension of operant techniques was reported in a collaborative study by Beatrice Barrett and Lindsley (1962). Barrett had worked at Indiana University School of Medicine, where she had met Ferster and was influenced by his interest in operant conditioning. In 1960, she went to Harvard Medical School on a postdoctoral fellowship to receive training in operant techniques and worked in Lindsley's laboratory. In her initial research, institutionalized retarded children and adults from the Fernald School were brought to the Metropolitan State Hospital where they executed the plunger-pulling response on an apparatus designed by Lindsley. The subjects (aged 7–20) received pennies or candies as reinforcers for responding over extended periods. As in Lindsley's original research with psychotic patients, Barrett found that specific response characteristics of retarded children distinguished them from normals, including stereotyped patterns of responding, highly variable responding for protracted periods, abnormally low response rates, abrupt loss of responding during and between sessions, and an occasional loss of responding during periods of symptomatic behaviors (Barrett and Lindsley, 1962).

Barrett's initial laboratory investigation extended the experimental analysis of behavior to retarded persons, although the focus was on basic rather than applied research. In a later investigation, she extended operant techniques and methodology to clinical behavior. At the Boston Veterans Administration Hospital, Barrett (1962) altered the multiple tics of a hospitalized patient. The patient experienced contractions of the neck, shoulders, chest, abdomen, and other parts of his body. These movements were recorded automatically as the individual sat in a chair connected to a relay. To decrease the frequency of tics, response-contingent events were delivered automatically, including an aversive noise or termination of ongoing music. Over extended sessions, these events reduced the rate of contraction, although tics were not eliminated. The report of this case demonstrated the potential clinical utility of operant techniques.

Through the efforts of Bijou and coworkers, the University of Washington became another important center for human operant research. In the late 1950s and 1960s, Bijou developed an extensive research program with normal and retarded children and examined many behavioral processes and characteristics of free-operant responding (e.g., Bijou, 1955, 1957a, 1957b, 1958a, 1958b, 1959, 1961; Bijou and Oblinger, 1960; Bijou and Orlando, 1961; Orlando and Bijou, 1960). A training center was established for operant research with children, and the University of Washington became the center for applying operant techniques for clinical purposes.

Baer, who also was at the University of Washington, began operant conditioning research with children under the influence and direct support of Bijou. Baer (1960, 1961) conducted laboratory investigations with preschool children and evaluated the effects of punishment, escape, and avoidance contingencies on bar-pressing responses. Aversive events presented to the subject consisted of an interruption of a positive ongoing stimulus (cartoons), which acted as a punishing stimulus and negative reinforcer. Baer (1962) extended his laboratory applications of operant techniques to a behavior of applied interest. Three 5-year-old children participated in an experiment in which thumbsucking was followed with the termination of ongoing cartoons. Thumbsucking was recorded by an observer looking through a one-way mirror and depressing a key that automatically recorded the rate of behavior. Alternating baseline periods with the withdrawal of cartoons contingent upon thumbsucking demonstrated the effect of the contingency.

Another center for operant research was the Indiana University School of Medicine. Ferster, who had collaborated closely with Skinner, continued his animal research after leaving Harvard. In 1957, he came to the department of psychiatry at the Indiana University School of Medicine where he extended operant research to study the behavior of autistic children. Ferster's work was especially notable because he began a programmatic series of investigations and influenced several individuals at Indiana and elsewhere who began to extend operant techniques to clinical problems. He collaborated with Marian K. DeMyer, who worked with autistic children at LaRue D. Carter Memorial Hospital (DeMyer and Ferster, 1962; Ferster and DeMyer, 1961, 1962). The investigations closely followed the laboratory operant approach pioneered in animal studies. As the children pressed keys, the apparatus automatically delivered consequences and recorded response rates. The experiments evaluated responses of varying complexity, beginning with simple key-pressing and discrimination tasks to complex match-to-sample tasks. Responses to various reinforcement schedules also were studied.

An important feature of the experiments was the reinforcement system used to sustain performance. Children usually worked alone in an experimental room. Coins were delivered for responding and served as generalized conditioned reinforcers. They could be exchanged for a variety of other prizes, including food, candy, toys, trinkets, viewing a pigeon that performed in a box for 30 seconds, access to a pinball machine, milk, and juice. Ferster and DeMyer found that autistic children were deficient in responding to some of the contingencies, for example, in their rate of behavior or responses to a complex reinforcement schedule compared to normal children. However, the basic patterns demonstrated with normal adults and children and animals also held for autistic children. The results of their experiments suggested that the response deficits found might be overcome by shaping increasingly complex response patterns and bringing behavior under control of antecedent and reinforcing stimuli. That is, additional training might widen the response repertoires of the children.

Joseph N. Hingtgen, Beverly J. Sanders, and DeMyer (1965) continued the line of research begun by Ferster and DeMyer with children with diagnosed schizophrenia as subjects. These investigators shaped cooperative responding on a lever-pressing task by rewarding the children with coins that would activate various devices. Cooperative responding was shaped on the task and was associated with an increase in physical and verbal contact with the partners. Subsequent research demonstrated that vocal responses and physical contact between subjects could be reinforced directly during experimental sessions (Hingtgen and Trost, 1966). Overall, research at the Indiana University School of Medicine suggested specific response deficits of autistic children and the possibility of building up complex repertoires and social behaviors through operant techniques.

John Paul Brady, who also worked at the Indiana University School of Medicine, was influenced by Ferster and his research with autistic children. Brady extended operant methods to psychiatric patients. In one study Brady, Nurnberger, and Tausig (1961) evaluated the relationship between operant performances of schizophrenic patients on a button-pressing task and their behavior on the ward. Individual patients were studied in daily sessions for weeks or months. Measures of a patient's responsiveness to a multiple schedule of reinforcement were shown to be correlated with the patient's adjustment outside of the experimental sessions, as measured by a behavioral rating scale. Because a clear relationship existed between symptomatic behavior and operant performance, Brady *et al.* (1961) suggested that the effects of different treatments could be evaluated through operant behavior. They noted the sensitivity of operant behavior to chemotherapy, as had Lindsley in his original research.

Brady also used operant methodology to study the hysterical blindness of an adult psychiatric patient (Brady and Lind, 1961). The purpose of the investigation was to demonstrate the advantages of operant methodology in studying behavior rather than to effect therapeutic cure. An attempt was made to determine the effect of manipulating visual cues on patient performance. The patient performed a button-pressing task that was designed so that the receipt of reinforcing consequences (buzzer, candy, praise) depended upon using visual cues in the situation. For example, illumination of the experimental room served as a cue to respond at the correct time. As the task progressed, correct responses became a function of making increasingly finer visual discriminations. The patient's vision was restored partially during treatment, as indicated by his own report and his identification of small print and other visual stimuli.

Follow-up of this patient was made after he was readmitted to the hospital, again claiming he could not see. Joseph Zimmerman and Hanus Grosz, at the Indiana University School of Medicine (Grosz and Zimmerman, 1965; Zimmerman and Grosz, 1966) conducted several experiments to replicate and extend the initial work of Brady and Lind. They too showed that the patient's operant responses on a laboratory task were influenced by available visual cues.

Southern Illinois University and Anna State Hospital also were sites of influential human operant conditioning research in the 1950s and 1960s. In 1955, Israel Goldiamond came to Southern Illinois. He had received his degree at the University of Chicago, where Howard F. Hunt had directed him to the operant conditioning literature. At Southern Illinois, Goldiamond continued his experimental work in perception. In addition, he taught courses with a clinical foundation, including an extension course for staff at Anna State, a nearby hospital. In the late 1950s, a project at Anna State grew out of Goldiamond's course in which operant techniques were applied to reinstate the verbal behavior of two hospitalized schizophrenics (Isaacs,

Thomas, and Goldiamond, 1960). Vocalizations were shaped in each patient in individual training sessions off the ward. For example, with one patient, gum was used to reinforce successive approximations of speech such as moving the lips, making spontaneous sounds, and eventually verbal responses prompted by the experimenter. Because the verbalizations were under the stimulus control of the experimenter, a nurse was brought into the sessions and eventually could evoke the verbalizations as well.

Goldiamond helped recruit Azrin to establish an animal laboratory at the hospital. Azrin, after completing his degree at Harvard, joined the Anna State staff in 1957, where he continued his own laboratory research and began to collaborate with Goldiamond, who began to study stuttering through an operant approach. In the early research, Flanagan, Goldiamond, and Azrin (1958, 1959) examined the possibility of stuttering and nonfluencies in normal speech being brought under operant control. For example, Flanagan et al. (1958) programmed specific consequences to follow stuttering of subjects as they read aloud. When the termination of an aversive noise was contingent upon stuttering, stuttering increased. In contrast, when the onset of noise was contingent upon stuttering, stuttering decreased. The control exerted by the contingencies designed to suppress stuttering is illustrated in Figure 7.1.

Goldiamond continued his work with stutterers and studied their behavior over protracted periods. Although he had experimented with noise and shock, he relied most heavily upon delayed auditory feedback of a subject's own voice as a consequence for stuttering (Goldiamond, 1965c). The early research was designed primarily to extend the operant methodology within the laboratory to study stuttering and nonfluencies. However, some of the changes in stuttering held outside of the training sessions, and Goldiamond was quick to follow up this advantage by initiating procedures to help control stuttering in and out of the training sessions. Stutterers were trained to analyze factors in their everyday situations that might be related to their stuttering. Also, stutterers were instructed to practice fluent speech outside of treatment and to engage in self-control exercises toward that end. (Those techniques for enhancing fluent speech were extended to other clinical problems and are addressed in Chapter 9.)

At Anna State, Azrin continued his research on animal and human operant behavior. Some of his investigations furthered the research begun by Lindsley. For example, using an apparatus similar to the plunger-pulling device engineered by Lindsley, the effects of

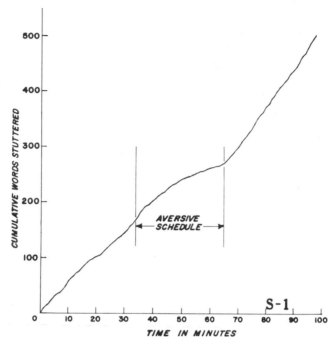

Figure 7.1. Cumulative record of words stuttered by one subject during the aversive period. (From "Operant Stuttering: The Control of Stuttering Behavior Through Response-Contingent Consequences," by B. Flanagan, I. Goldiamond, and N. H. Azrin, *Journal of the Experimental Analysis of Behavior,* 1958, 1:173-177. Copyright 1958 by the Society for the Experimental Analysis of Behavior, Inc.)

variations in reinforcement schedules and time-out from reinforcement were investigated (Holz, Azrin, and Ayllon, 1963; Hutchinson and Azrin, 1961). In the late 1950s and early 1960s, Azrin began to apply operant techniques to clinically diagnosed behaviors. These clinical extensions were seminal in the development of applied operant research, and will be discussed later.

Arizona State University became a center for operant research in the early 1960s. Arthur Staats promoted the application of learning theory and research to clinical and educational problems (e.g., Staats, 1964). As early as 1957, he suggested that learning principles could explain symptomatic behaviors of psychiatric patients. Specifically, he advanced the notion that bizarre speech patterns might be interpreted in terms of concepts such as verbal conditioning rather than psychodynamic causes (Staats, 1957).

Staats' interest in learning theory and application led to a programmatic series of studies, beginning in 1959, to investigate the reading behavior of children. He designed an apparatus to help teach children with learning disabilities to read. Stimulus presentation, response recording, and consequence delivery were partially automated, as the child worked individually in the laboratory (Staats, 1968a). Participants received marbles (which served as generalized conditioned reinforcers or tokens) for working at the apparatus and making correct responses. The marbles could be exchanged for such rewards as trinkets, prizes, toys, edibles, and pennies. The reinforcement system was shown to sustain a child's performance for prolonged periods at the task when other reinforcers—such as praise—could not. Staats and his colleagues studied normal, retarded, culturally deprived, and disturbed children as they performed responses designed to improve reading, writing, and arithmetic skills (Staats, Finley, Minke, and Wolf, 1962; Staats, Minke, and Butts, 1970; Staats, Minke, Finley, Wolf, and Brooks, 1964; Staats, Minke, Goodwin, and Landeen, 1967; Staats, Staats, Schulz, and Wolf, 1962). Their research allowed investigation of basic questions about different response consequences, schedule effects, and discrimination training, yet also revealed the applied value of training on such measures as vocabulary, achievement, and intelligence tests (Staats, 1968b; Staats and Butterfield, 1965).

Goldiamond moved to Arizona State in 1960 and continued his research on stuttering and application of self-control techniques, work that had direct applied value. In the same year, Jack L. Michael established an operant laboratory there. In subsequent years, several others with interest in applied or basic research in operant conditioning came to the department, including Frederick S. Keller, Lee Meyerson, J. Gilmour Sherman, Joel Greenspoon, and Arthur Bachrach.

The above research by no means exhausts laboratory extensions of operant conditioning to human performance that began in the last 25 years. Many investigations in developmental psychology evaluated the role of operant conditioning in shaping responses in children. For example, operant conditioning of infants was shown to influence such responses as smiling, speech sounds, neonatal sucking, and head-turning (Gelfand, 1969). Although research in child development might have supplied a laboratory foundation for application, the emphasis instead was on providing a theoretical and empirical basis for explaining social development. Investigations of the role of operant conditioning in child development contributed to the accumulating corpus of laboratory-based investigations. However, unlike the applications just reviewed, the investigations in child development provided somewhat less direct lines of influence on subsequent clinical application.

The bulk of human operant studies were oriented more toward basic research, although extensions along clinical dimensions were certainly apparent as well. Indeed, the continuum of human operant research assumed an increasingly applied focus. It began with pure laboratory research, in which free-operant responding was of interest in its own right. Research with a slightly more applied focus studied laboratory responses as a means of *evaluating* a clinical problem. Later investigations explicitly attempted to alter laboratory responses as a means of *changing* clinical problems.

The purpose of Lindsley's original laboratory research was to extend the methodology of operant conditioning to psychotic patients. Despite the absence of therapeutic goals, Lindsley found that the reinforcing of plunger-pulling responses tended to decrease symptomatic behaviors of some patients both in the laboratory and on the hospital ward (Lindsley, 1963).

More explicit excursions into the clinical domain were made by other investigators. For example, Ferster's laboratory research with autistic children was designed not only to attempt operant research with human sujects but to determine basic variables that might account for the deficits of autism (Ferster, 1961). Ferster provided a conceptual analysis of autistic behavior by explaining it in operant terms. He noted that problems of autistic children could be viewed in part as a lack of responsiveness to delayed conditioned reinforcers, to behavioral deficits such as inadequate speech repertoires, and to aversive social behaviors, as well as to the absence of certain forms of stimulus control. This interpretation provided a fresh basis for studying autistic behavior and, by implication, a way of treating deficits in responding to the contingencies that control behavior of normal children.

The clinical relevance of laboratory research was apparent in investigations that attempted to use operant conditioning methods to assess behavior of distinct treatment populations. Operant methods were considered an alternative to traditional psychometric methods. In the case of psychotic patients (Lindsley, 1956, 1960; Mednick and Lindsley, 1958), the mentally retarded (Barrett and Lindsley, 1962), and autistic children (Ferster and DeMyer, 1961, 1962), response characteristics peculiar to the population were posed as a means of diagnosis or behavioral assessment. More generally, Bijou suggested that operant methods had promise for the study of individual differences (Bijou, 1961; Bijou and Orlando, 1961). Because operant conditioning provides a detailed functional analysis of individual performance, the responsiveness of different individuals to a given set of manipulations can be compared easily.

Some of the laboratory research included distinct therapeutic goals that could be achieved by altering free-operant responding. An early study of this type was reported by Henry Peters and Richard Jenkins (1954), who used reinforcement to alter the behavior of schizophrenic patients at a hospital in Arkansas. Their purpose was to build up patients' problem-solving behaviors for specific tasks in the laboratory with the hope that successful behaviors would generalize to conduct on the ward. Food was delivered contingent upon successful performance on graded problem-solving tasks (e.g., tasks ranging from mazes to interpretation of proverbs). High-level motivation was maintained by increasing hunger with insulin injections. The problem-solving tasks improved performance of a variety of ward behaviors compared to a control group given the injections and noncontingent food.

Peters and Jenkins did not conceive of their research as an application of operant techniques. Yet the study was followed by similar applications by investigators with an operant orientation. For example, at a hospital in Michigan, Gerald F. King, Stewart G. Armitage, and John R. Tilton (1960) extended the Peters and Jenkins report by having schizophrenic patients respond to a multiple-operant, problem-solving apparatus that delivered candy and cigarettes for lever-pressing and complex motor behaviors. For 15 weeks, patients responded on the apparatus to increasingly complex tasks, including cooperative responding. Patients who performed the tasks showed greater clinical improvement on the ward than did control patients who received either verbal therapy, recreational therapy, or no treatment. The gains shown in the operant conditioning group were maintained up to six months.

An important bridge between laboratory and applied investigations of operant conditioning was verbal conditioning research. Several investigators in the early 1950s at Indiana University used positive reinforcement to increase verbal responses (notably, use of plural nouns and selection of specific pronouns in constructing sentences in simulated interview settings) (Ball, 1952; Fahmy, 1953; Greenspoon, 1951; Taffel, 1955).

Verbal conditioning research served as a transition between laboratory and clinical applications for several reasons. First, the extension of operant principles to human interaction departed dramatically from specific laboratory responses that had been customarily studied with animals and humans. Verbalizations could not be recorded automatically nor could response consequences be delivered automatically. Instead, human observers recorded verbal responses while an experimenter delivered reinforcing consequences (e.g., verbal approval in the form of "mmm-hmm"). Second, verbal conditioning with psychiatric patients concentrated on response classes believed to be related to psychopathology, such as affect statements, emotional words, statements about one's mother, early memories, "neurotic" or "hallucinatory" verbalizations, confiding statements, and self-reference and self-acceptance statements. As will be seen, verbal conditioning of psychiatric patients was one of the earliest applied focuses.

Early Extensions of Operant Techniques in Applied Settings

Applications of operant techniques generally increased in the early 1960s. One of its most influential extensions to clinical populations was initiated by Teodoro Ayllon, beginning in 1958. Ayllon was a graduate student at the University of Houston, and faculty members such as Jack Michael and Lee Meyerson were involved in operant conditioning research with children and the mentally retarded. During the summer of 1958, Ayllon took a summer job at Saskatchewan Hospital, where he devised a reinforcement system to alter behaviors of psychotic patients on the ward. After a brief stay at Houston, he returned to Canada to continue his work, some of which fulfilled the research requirements for his doctorate at the University of Houston. Ayllon completed his doctorate in 1959 and remained at the hospital, where he received a grant from 1959–1961 to continue his research.

Ayllon described his work in a series of articles. The first was a collaboration with Michael, his adviser at the University of Houston (Ayllon and Michael, 1959). This paper reported that 19 chronic psychotic or mentally defective patients had been exposed individually to operant conditioning. The nurses introduced the techniques on the ward and behaviors such as frequent visits to the nurses' station to interrupt their work, violent acts, psychotic talk, and hoarding all decreased. Behaviors such as self-feeding and socially interacting with the staff increased. Assorted techniques derived from operant principles were used, including positive reinforcement, negative reinforcement (escape and avoidance), extinction, punishment, reinforcement of incompatible behaviors, and satiation.

As an example, Ayllon and Michael (1959) used an extinction procedure to eliminate the frequency that a patient visited the nurses' office and interrupted their work. Nurses who had attended to a patient frequently and had bodily pushed her back to the ward were told not to pay attention to these visits anymore. Over an eight-week period, the average daily frequency of visits decreased. Another patient frequently attacked other patients and staff. To decrease these acts, staff reinforced the patient's remaining on the ward without committing violent acts. The episodes subsided during this intervention and increased when attention for nonviolent behavior was withdrawn during an extinction period.

Ayllon and Michael (1959) reported the effects of other operant interventions implemented by the nursing staff. Their report was the first to suggest the generality of operant methods across several patients and several behaviors within a hospital setting. Numerous reports from Saskatchewan Hospital completed between 1959 and 1961 followed (Ayllon, 1963, 1965; Ayllon and Haughton, 1962, 1964; Ayllon, Haughton, and Osmond, 1964; Haughton and Ayllon, 1965). In general, they provided dramatic experimental demonstrations that represented increasingly sophisticated applications of operant techniques.

Operant programs were successful with individual patients and with groups. For example, Ayllon and Haughton (1962) altered the behavior of 32 psychiatric patients to control their eating habits. The purpose of the program was to train patients to attend meals without being coaxed, reminded, escorted, or spoon- or tube-fed. To bring attending meals under the control of the availability of food rather than of the staff, nurses no longer provided social reinforcement (attention) for refusal to eat. Increasingly shorter intervals were allowed before the meal for patients to be admitted to the dining area. By limiting the time of entry to the meal, all patients eventually attended meals unassisted. Patients were trained to come within a relatively brief period (five minutes) after the meal was announced.

Work with individual patients demonstrated that careful control over behavior could be achieved with operant techniques, epitomized in one of the final reports that was completed at Saskatchewan (Ayllon and Haughton, 1964). Two experiments were reported. In the first experiment, the verbal behavior of a chronic schizophrenic was altered. The patient engaged in delusional statements and made frequent references to royalty (e.g., "I'm the Queen. How's King George, have you seen him?"). Before initiating techniques to alter behavior, the patient's verbal statements were recorded and categorized as psychotic or neutral. After this baseline period of observation, the staff provided attention and cigarettes whenever the patient made psychotic verbalizations. Neutral statements were ignored. Subsequently, staff were told to reinforce neutral statements and to ignore psychotic statements. The results, presented in Figure 7.2, indicated that the patient's verbal behavior was influenced by the manipulations of the nursing staff.

In the second experiment, Ayllon and Haughton (1964) reduced the frequent complaints of two patients. A depressed patient complained of sleeping difficulties and reported pains in her back, chest, head, and shoulders, although there was no evidence of organic dys-

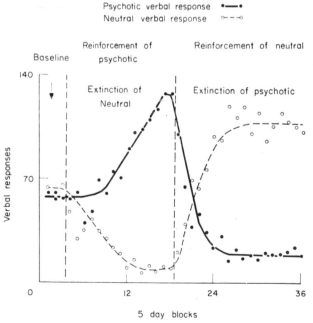

Figure 7.2. Verbal responses of a psychotic patient as a function of reinforcement and extinction procedures. (From Ayllon and Haughton, 1964; reprinted by permission.)

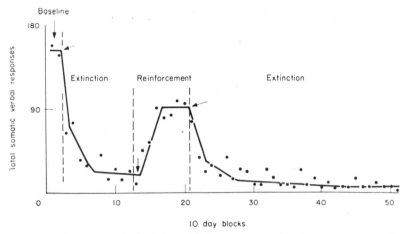

Figure 7.3. Frequency of complaints about somatic disorders during baseline, extinction, reinforcement, and extinction periods. (From Ayllon and Haughton, 1964; reprinted by permission.)

function. After baseline observations of somatic complaints, the staff ignored these statements rather than providing consolation, sympathy, and attention. Next, the staff attended to these statements again. In a final phase, staff attention was withdrawn. Throughout all phases, neutral statements were reinforced with attention. The data for one of the patients, shown in Figure 7.3, reveal the specific control that staff consequences exerted on verbal behavior. The patient's behavior consistently changed in response to the staff's reactions.

Although the studies by Ayllon and his colleagues were completed by 1961, many were not published until after Ayllon had already left Saskatchewan. In 1961, he joined Anna State Hospital in Illinois. At Anna State, he collaborated with Azrin, who had already conducted laboratory and clinically oriented research with patients, to evaluate the effect of operant techniques on the ward. For example, one of their early reports assessed the effect of providing reinforcing consequences (extra dessert) and instructions (statement of the contingency) to get psychiatric patients to use eating utensils (Ayllon and Azrin, 1964).

Ayllon and Azrin decided to experiment with operant techniques on an entire ward of psychiatric patients. In 1961, they began to design a total environment that would motivate a large number of patients. They constructed a comprehensive program by rearranging the hospital environment so that several reinforcers in the setting could be brought to bear to alter patient behavior. To incorporate a variety of reinforcing events, tokens (coins) served as a generalized conditioned reinforcer. The use of tokens permitted a way to monitor both the delivery of reinforcers by the staff and the progress of the patients as they earned tokens. The use of tokens in part was a continuation of earlier work at Saskatchewan. Ayllon and Haughton (1962) had demonstrated that psychiatric patients could learn to deposit a coin into a slot of a collection box to gain entry into the dining room and to make specific responses (button-pressing) to earn the coins.

At Anna State, tokens were earned for numerous behaviors, including performing various jobs on and off the ward as well as self-care activities. Select behaviors that could earn tokens for the patients on the ward and the events tokens could purchase are summarized in Tables 7.1 and 7.2. The program designed by Ayllon and Azrin, referred to as a token economy, was described in articles (e.g., Ayllon and Azrin, 1965, 1968a) as well as a book entitled, *The Token Economy: A Motivational System for Therapy and Rehabilitation* (Ayllon and Azrin, 1968b). Even before the appearance of these publications, the token economy created by Ayllon and Azrin had exerted immediate influence on other treatment, rehabilitation, and education programs. In the early stages of the program, several investigators visited the hospital or communicated with Ayllon and Azrin about their work. These contacts contributed to the establishment of several similar programs to help psychiatric patients, mentally retarded persons, delinquents, and other populations (Ayllon and Azrin, 1968b).

The token economy was a highly innovative and influential treatment strategy. It provided a way to implement an operant-reinforcement program on a large scale within one treatment setting. A general set of reinforcing events could be made available to patients; they could be purchased with tokens, a generalized conditioned reinforcer delivered to all individuals in the program. Idiosyncratic preferences for reinforcers could be exercised in exchanging the tokens for specific events. Many behaviors could be reinforced with tokens. Overall, the token economy provided a convenient way to reprogram entire institutional wards, classrooms, and rehabilitation settings (Kazdin, 1977d).

The work of Ayllon and Azrin at Anna State represents a landmark in the development of applied behavior analysis. The extensions of operant techniques with children in the late 1950s and early 1960s also were seminal in revealing the potential of the field. By far the

Table 7.1. Types and number of on-ward jobs

Type of jobs	No. of jobs	Duration	Tokens paid
Dietary assistant			
1. Kitchen chores	3	10 min	1
Patient assembles necessary supplies on table. Puts one pat of butter between two slices of bread for all patients. Squeezes juice from fruit left over from meals. Puts supplies away. Cleans table used.			
2. Pots and Pans	3	10 min	6
Patient runs water into sink, adds soap, washes and rinses all pans used for each meal. Stacks pans and leaves them to be put through automatic dishwasher.			
Waitress	6	10 min	2
1. Meals			
Empties trays left on tables and washes tables between each of four meal groups.			
2. Commissary	3	10 min	5
Cleans tables, washes cups and glasses used at commissary. Places cups and glasses in rack ready for automatic dishwasher.			
Sales clerk assistant			
1. Commissary	3	30 min	3
Assembles commissary items. Displays candy, cigarettes, tobacco, cosmetics, dresses, and other variety store items so that they can be seen by all. Prepares ice, glasses, and cups for hot and cold beverages. Asks patient what she wishes to buy. Collects the tokens from patient and tells the secretary the name of the patient and the amount spent. Puts commissary supplies away.			
Secretarial assistant			
1. Tooth-brushing	1	30 min	3
Assists with oral hygiene. Writes names of patients brushing teeth.			

Table 7.1. (Continued)

Type of jobs	No. of jobs	Duration	Tokens paid
2. Commissary Assists sales clerk assistant. Writes names of patients at commissary, records number of tokens patient spent. Totals all tokens spent.			
Ward cleaning assistant			
1. Halls and rooms Sweep and mop floors, dust furniture and walls in seven rooms and hall.	24	30 min	3
2. Special Cleans after incontinent patients.	1	30 min	4
Assistant janitor			
1. Supplies Places ward supplies in supply cabinets and drawers.	1	10 min	1
2. Trash Carries empty soft drink bottles to storage area, empties waste paper baskets throughout the ward and carries paper to container adjacent to building. Carries mops used during the day outside to dry.	3	5 min	2
Laundry assistant			
1. Hose Match and fold clean anklets and stockings.	1	15 min	1
2. Pick-up service Sorts dirty clothing and linens and puts items into bags marked for each item.	1	60 min	8
Grooming assistant			
1. Clothing care Patient sets up ironing board and iron. Irons clothing that belongs to patients other than self. Folds clothing neatly. Returns ironed clothing,	1	15 min	1

Table 7.1. (Continued)

Type of jobs	No. of jobs	Duration	Tokens paid
iron, and ironing board to nurses' station.			
2. Bath	2	45 min	4
Patient assists with baths, washing, shampooing, and drying. Cleans tub after each bath.			
Recreational assistant			
1. Walks	1	20 min	3
Assists ward staff when taking group of patients on walks. Walks in front of group.			
2. Exercise	1	20 min	3
Operates record player and leads patients in exercises.			
Special services			
1. Errands	1	20 min	6
Leaves the ward on official errands throughout the hospital grounds, delivering messages and picking up supplies and records pertaining to the ward.			
2. Tour guide	1	15 min	10
Gives visitors a 15-min tour of the ward explaining about the activities and token system. Answers visitors' questions about the ward.			
Self-care activities			
1. Grooming			1
Combs hair (three times daily); wears: dress, slip, panties, bra, stockings, and shoes.			
2. Bathing			1
Takes a bath at time designated for bath (once weekly).			
3. Tooth-brushing			1
Brushes teeth or gargles at the time designated for tooth brushing (once daily).			

Table 7.1. (Continued)

Type of jobs	No. of jobs	Duration	Tokens paid
4. Exercises			1
Participates in exercises conducted by the exercise assistant (twice daily).			
5. Bed-making			1
Makes own bed and cleans area around and under bed.			

From "The Measurement and Reinforcement of Behavior of Psychotics," by T. Ayllon and N. H. Azrin, *Journal of the Experimental Analysis of Behavior,* 1965, 8:357–383. Copyright 1965 by the Society for the Experimental Analysis of Behavior, Inc.

most influential application of operant techniques with children was work conducted in the early 1960s at the University of Washington. The University had become an important center for such work with Bijou as director of the Institute of Child Development, which consisted of a nursery school, a child development clinic, and on- and off-campus research laboratories. Bijou helped convert these facilities into applied operant research programs. In 1962, a number of projects with a clear applied and therapeutic focus were initiated; they established the University of Washington as a center for applied operant work.

An impetus for beginning an applied program with retarded children stemmed from Bijou's leave of absence during 1961–1962, when he studied at Harvard with Skinner. Bijou continued his laboratory research with retarded and normal children and studied complex behaviors and programmed instruction. In addition, he surveyed remedial education programs in the eastern United States. When he returned to the University of Washington, he believed that a treatment program based upon behavioral principles could be effective in shaping academic and social behaviors of retarded children. He helped initiate an experimental classroom at Rainier School, which already had a research laboratory coordinated by Jay Birnbrauer, a faculty member in psychology. An experimental classroom was set aside to improve academic behaviors of the retarded children.

The program began by giving students programmed instruction materials but no extrinsic reinforcement. Because academic performance was not accelerated by success on the materials, other rein-

Table 7.2. List of reinforcers available for tokens

		No. of tokens needed			No. of tokens needed
I.	Privacy	(daily)	IV.	Devotional opportunities	
	Selection of room 1	0			
	Selection of room 2	4		Extra religious services on ward	1
	Selection of room 3	8			
	Selection of room 4	15		Extra religious services off ward	10
	Selection of room 5	30			
	Personal chair	1	V.	Recreational opportunities	
	Choice of eating group	1			
	Screen (room divider)	1			
	Choice of bedspreads	1		Movie on ward	1
	Coat rack	1		Opportunity to listen to a live band	1
	Personal cabinet	2		Exclusive use of a radio	1
	Placebo	1–2		Television (choice of program)	3
II.	Leave from the ward				
	20-min walk on hospital grounds (with escort)	2	VI.	Commissary items	
	30-min grounds pass (3 tokens for each additional 30 min)	10		Consumable items such as candy, milk, cigarettes, coffee, and sandwich	1–5
	Trip to town (with escort)	100		Toilet articles such as Kleenex, toothpaste, comb, lipstick, and talcum powder	1–10
III.	Social interaction with staff				
	Private audience with chaplain, nurse (first 5 min)	free		Clothing and accessories such as gloves, headscarf, house slippers, handbag, and skirt	12–400
	Private audience with ward staff, ward physician (first 5 min) (for additional time—1 token per min)	free		Reading and writing materials such as stationery, pen, greeting card, newspaper, and magazine	2–5
	Private audience with ward psychologist	20		Miscellaneous items such as ashtray, throw rug, potted plant, picture holder, and stuffed animal	1–50
	Private audience with social worker	100			

From "The Measurement and Reinforcement of Behavior of Psychotics," by T. Ayllon and N.H. Azrin, *Journal of the Experimental Analysis of Behavior,* 1965, 8:357–383. Copyright 1965 by the Society for the Experimental Analysis of Behavior, Inc.

forcers were added—including candy, approval, and eventually tokens (stars and later checkmarks)—to reinforce completion of individually programmed academic assignments in vocabulary, arithmetic comprehension, and writing. Additional skills were learned, including instruction following, telling time, cooperative behavior, and classroom deportment.

The token system at Rainier was designed by Montrose M. Wolf. Wolf came to the University of Washington in 1962 after receiving his degree at Arizona State University. He had worked with Staats in the reading projects that had demonstrated the utility of token reinforcement in working with individual children. The token system at Rainier School was based on checkmarks that could be redeemed in the classroom for a variety of back-up rewards, including money, prizes, or edibles. In the 1960s, several investigations of the behavioral program at Rainier School confirmed the efficacy of this program in changing the behavior of retarded children (Bijou, Birnbrauer, Kidder, and Tague, 1966; Birnbrauer, Bijou, Wolf, and Kidder, 1965; Birnbrauer and Lawler, 1964).

As an example of the work at the school, Birnbrauer, Wolf, Kidder, and Tague (1965) provided an experimental evaluation of the reinforcement program with a class of 17 retarded students. Although approval for appropriate classroom behavior and time-out from reinforcement for inappropriate behavior were used throughout the study, the effect of token reinforcement superimposed upon these other procedures was evaluated carefully. The results showed that for most students the contingent delivery of tokens for correct academic performance decreased errors on the assignments compared to those phases in which no token reinforcement was provided.

At the same time that the experiments began at Rainier School, classroom applications of operant techniques were initiated at the laboratory preschool of the University of Washington. Wolf also influenced and directed the preschool programs, because the applications grew out of a seminar he conducted on operant techniques for the staff at the preschool. The interests and problems of the classroom teacher provided the impetus to create specific behavior-change programs. The preschool staff and assistants, including K. Eileen Allen, Florence R. Harris, Betty M. Hart, Margaret K. Johnston, Joan S. Buell, and others in collaboration with Wolf, generated several published reports. These reports dealt with behaviors such as increasing walking of a child who crawled excessively and decreasing crying in reaction to mildly distressful events (Harris, Johnston, Kelley, and

Wolf, 1964; Harris, Wolf, and Baer, 1964; Hart, Allen, Buell, Harris, and Wolf, 1964; Johnston, Kelley, Harris, and Wolf, 1966).

As an example of this series of studies, Allen, Hart, Buell, Harris, and Wolf (1964) increased the social interaction of a four-year-old retarded girl who isolated herself from other school children in a nursery school classroom. To foster social interaction in the classroom, the teacher ignored isolate play and delivered praise when peer play was initiated. During a later phase, the contingencies were altered so that the child received attention for isolate play and was ignored for peer interaction. As shown in Figure 7.4, peer interactions decreased when they were ignored and increased when they were reinforced. After the program was terminated (during the last month of school), a high rate of peer interaction was maintained.

The work at Rainier School and the laboratory preschool clearly established the utility of operant techniques in classroom settings with the retarded. At about the same time, additional work began with an

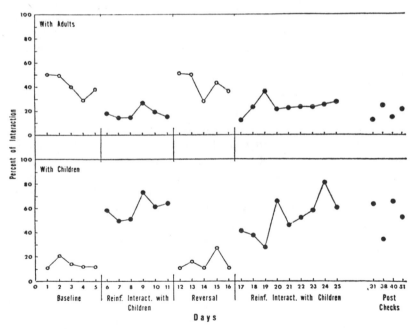

Figure 7.4. Percentages of time spent in social interaction by a four-year-old retarded girl during approximately two hours of each morning session, according to proffered and withdrawn reinforcement contingencies. (From Allen et al., 1964; reprinted by permission.)

autistic boy named Dicky, who was in a state psychiatric hospital for children. The hospital superintendent contacted Bijou about training the child to wear glasses. Wolf served as a consultant on the project and worked with Todd Risley, a graduate student at the University of Washington, and Hayden Mees, the psychologist at the hospital (Wolf, Risley, and Mees, 1964).

Among Dicky's many behavioral problems was his refusal to wear eyeglasses. Because of a history of eye difficulties and surgery, failure to wear the glasses was likely to result in partial loss of vision. Dicky also had continuous tantrums that included self-destructive behavior. The hospital staff and the boy's parents administered a program involving time-out from reinforcement (isolating him in his room or closing the door when he was already in his room), and tantrums and problems in going to bed decreased. Food and activities served as reinforcers and were used to shape wearing the glasses. Training proceeded gradually by reinforcing contact with the empty glass frames (e.g., picking them up, holding them) and eventually wearing the prescription lenses. Throwing the glasses, a problem that arose during training, was eliminated with time-out from reinforcement. Dicky was taught to increase his verbal responses and improve his eating habits. The case of Dicky provided a dramatic demonstration of the utility of operant techniques with several clinical problems and, hence, constituted an extremely influential report.

Although applications were attempted in other places in the country, the range of applications across settings, the number of projects reported, and the effects on child behavior were unsurpassed at the University of Washington. The work established the systematic basis for applying operant techniques in child treatment and education. The influence of applied operant research grew as the faculty and students eventually left the university and continued their work elsewhere. Individuals who were either faculty members or graduate students during the early and mid 1960s at the University of Washington are among the most prominent researchers in contemporary applied behavior analysis.

Additional Applications

Several investigators in the early 1960s altered the verbal behavior of psychiatric patients or children. As noted, Ayllon at Saskatchewan and Goldiamond and his colleagues (Isaacs et al., 1960) at Anna State Hospital modified the verbal behavior of psychiatric patients. At the University of Washington, James A. Sherman used reinforcement, shaping, and prompts to develop speech in mute psychotic patients (Sherman, 1963, 1965). Over a large number of sessions, increases were made in the number of words, sentences, and general vocabulary. In some cases, the changes transferred to a second experimenter who was brought into the training sessions but not to personnel on the ward who had not been associated with training.

At a hospital in Alabama, Henry C. Rickard, Patrick J. Dignam, and Robert F. Horner (1960) reinforced the rational statements of a chronic psychiatric patient with delusions. Social reinforcement from the experimenter (e.g., nods, smiles, expressions of interest) was delivered for rational speech. Over several sessions, rational speech was shown to increase as a function of contingent social consequences. The patient continued to respond to social reinforcement for rational speech in follow-up sessions conducted two years after the initial report (Rickard and Dinoff, 1962).

In a hospital in Georgia, R. V. Heckel, S. L. Wiggins, and H. C. Salzberg (1962) used a negative reinforcement technique to increase the frequency of verbalizations of a group of hospitalized psychiatric patients participating in group psychotherapy. The patients rarely talked in the group, so talking was reinforced. A loud noise, sounded from an audiometer placed in an air conditioning vent in the therapy room, served as an aversive event. To increase verbalizations in the group, the noise sounded during periods of silence and was terminated when a patient spoke. Speech increased during the experiment and periods of silence declined.

Although verbal behavior received the greatest attention in applications of operant techniques to psychiatric patients, some other responses compatible with the hospital setting also were studied. Gerald Mertens and Gerald Fuller (1963) used reinforcement to develop shaving in regressed male psychotic patients in a state hospital in Minnesota. The research was undertaken to apply operant techniques to a behavior of pragmatic value that would increase the patient's self-sufficiency. Patients received sweets, money, and praise for shaving correctly or engaging in responses that approximated shaving.

In the early 1960s, applications with children increased, and many dealt with modifying verbal behavior. For example, at Arizona State University, Kerr, Meyerson, and Michael (1965) shaped vocalizations in a nine-year-old mute, retarded, and physically handicapped girl. Using joggling while on the experimenter's lap and singing as positive reinforcers, vocalizations were developed. The authors noted that the gains made were especially important because the client might be called a "psychological terminal case" by virtue of her severe deficits and dysfunctions.

Kurt Salzinger and his colleagues at the New York State Psychiatric Institute used operant techniques to develop speech in hospitalized children (Salzinger, Feldman, Cowan, and Salzinger, 1965). In individual experimental sessions, a child received reinforcing consequences for vocalizations, which then were shaped into units of language gradually. Other problematic behaviors such as hyperactive responding were alleviated during training.

Clinical and applied work with children encompassed behaviors other than speech. For example, C. D. Williams (1959) at the University of Miami reported a case of a child who engaged in tantrums before going to sleep each night. They were eliminated by having the parents not attend to the outbursts after the child was placed in bed. Within a short time, all tantrums were eliminated, an effect that was maintained up to two years after the procedure had been terminated.

At the Indiana University School of Medicine, Zimmerman and Zimmerman (1962) altered the behavior of hospitalized children in a special classroom. Withdrawing attention for disruptive behaviors such as temper tantrums, use of baby talk, and bizarre spelling, and bestowing attention and praise for appropriate work markedly reduced classroom problems.

Several operant research programs for treating children were begun in the early and mid 1960s by individuals affiliated with the research at the University of Washington. For example, O. Ivar Lovaas began a program at the University of California at Los Angeles for autistic children. Lovaas had been a graduate student and then director of the child guidance clinic at the University of Washington. In 1961, he moved to UCLA and began an intensive program to improve the socialization of autistic children.[7] In 1964, Robert G. Wahler, also a former graduate and clinic director at the University of Washington, began a program at the University of Tennessee to alter behavior of children who were uncooperative at school and at home. Like Lovaas, Wahler had conducted a programmatic series of studies over several years.

In the late 1950s and early 1960s, Gerald R. Patterson at the University of Oregon conducted laboratory experiments on the responsiveness of children to social stimuli (Patterson, 1965c). In one

---

[7] Lovaas' program is discussed in Chapter 8.

early report, the hyperactive behaviors (e.g., being out of one's seat, hitting others, looking around instead of working) of one child were altered in a classroom setting (Patterson, 1965a). The child's attentive behavior was reinforced with a light as a signal and the advance of a counter from an apparatus on the child's desk. The signal and counter advance were backed with pennies or candies that were shared with his peers. The contingency was associated with a decline in hyperactive behaviors.

In another report, Patterson (1965b) used social reinforcement to help a seven-year-old overcome a school phobia. In doll-play sessions, the therapist praised the child for such behaviors as saying that the doll was not afraid in leaving his mother or for being brave when the doll incurred a minor injury. The child received candy and praise for increased independence (engaging in activities without the parents) both at home and at the clinic. The child successfully returned to school. After these early reports, Patterson continued to work with children with problem behaviors. In the late 1960s, he began an extensive research program to change behavior at home and at school (cf. Patterson, 1971).

In the mid 1960s, the University of Illinois started investigating operant techniques as they could be applied to children. In 1965, Bijou moved to the University of Illinois and helped to establish this focus on children. Wesley C. Becker, at the University of Illinois, was influenced by a project in which Bijou had been involved that trained parents to implement behavioral techniques for controlling their child's behavior in the home (Hawkins, Peterson, Schweid, and Bijou, 1966). Becker became more immersed in studying operant techniques with children in the home and, more extensively, in school settings. He was aided by several graduate students, including Charles Madsen, Donald Thomas, K. Daniel O'Leary, and others, who continued to attempt clinical and educational applications throughout the late 1960s. Becker and his colleagues completed a series of classroom studies showing the effects of praise, token reinforcement, and other teacher-implemented interventions in different classrooms. Other investigators at Illinois whose work and writings contributed to the recognition of that university as a behavior modification center in the mid and late 1960s were Leonard Ullmann (e.g., Ullmann and Krasner, 1965), Donald Peterson (e.g., Peterson, 1968), and Gordon Paul (e.g., Paul, 1966).

Another programmatic series of studies was initiated by Henry C. Rickard and his colleagues. Rickard, who received his degree from the University of Tennessee in 1959, was interested in verbal conditioning as a way of effecting change in therapy. Rickard initially employed verbal conditioning to alter the irrational verbalizations of a hospitalized psychotic patient (Rickard et al., 1960). Later he used it to treat stuttering in a child (Rickard and Mundy, 1965).

In 1963, Rickard and Michael Dinoff, both of whom were on the faculty of the University of Alabama, established a summer camp for emotionally disturbed boys. The camp, called Camp Ponderosa, provided a behaviorally oriented program in which boys received individual and group therapy to enhance adaptive behavior. Operant techniques were used on individual children at the camp to increase engaging in routine activities and complying with instructions, and to reduce fighting, stealing, and excessive crying. Other programs encouraged cleaning up, tooth-brushing, completing academic assignments, and developing problem-solving skills to resolve interpersonal conflict. The camp was in operation from 1963–1974. The significance of Camp Ponderosa lies in its application of operant techniques in a naturalistic setting before the formal development of applied behavior analysis.

Numerous other reports of operant techniques applied for therapeutic purposes began to appear in the literature. Many were collected with accounts of other applications of behavioral techniques and published in edited books (e.g., Staats, 1964; Ullmann and Krasner, 1965). Operant principles underlay programs for psychiatric patients, the mentally retarded, children in classroom settings, and outpatient treatment, and some of the results were made available in an edited volume (Krasner and Ullmann, 1965).

The Spread of Applied Operant Research

By the mid and late 1960s, operant techniques had been widely applied in diverse research centers, including Arizona State University, Florida State University, Indiana University, the University of Oregon, the University of Illinois, and the University of Washington. The spread of the applications, too extensive to trace, resulted from extensive movements of individuals to new employment where they continued and extended their research programs. Also, investigators who completed their doctoral research branched off into their own applied programs. In many cases, investigators were self-taught and explored the apparent promise of operant techniques for clinical ends on their own.[8]

---

[8] Goodall (1972) has traced the movements of many individuals active in applied operant research and has described the growth of research and training centers in behavior modification.

The role of the University of Washington in the proliferation and centralization of applied operant research has already been traced. However, the transplanting of many of its faculty and students to the University of Kansas—the center for applied operant research—has not. In 1965, Baer was recruited from the University of Washington by the department of human development of the University of Kansas. He was hired with the idea that he would help strengthen the department by bringing colleagues of similar interests with him. In 1965 and shortly thereafter, Wolf, Risley, Sherman, and other investigators previously affiliated with the University of Washington joined the University of Kansas. Over the years, others with interest in applied operant research have joined the department to make the University of Kansas the undisputed center for applied behavior analysis.[9] When applied behavior analysis became a formal area of research, investigators at the University of Kansas played a central role in defining its domain and suggesting its methodology (see Chapter 8).

SUMMARY AND CONCLUSIONS

In the 1950s, operant research was extended to investigate human behavior. Although its primary purpose was to be methodological, the value of clinical and applied implications of the research quickly manifested itself. For example, side effects of Lindsley's original laboratory research with psychotic patients included some positive changes in the patients. In the late 1950s and early 1960s, operant techniques were shown to be efficacious in treating maladaptive behaviors in several clinical populations.

Two programs of research in particular exerted a powerful influence on the evolution of applied behavior analysis. First, Ayllon began systematic applications of operant techniques in psychiatric wards to alter diverse behaviors. This work eventually led him to collaborate with Azrin, and together they devised the token economy as a way of redesigning whole treatment environments. Second, Bijou, Wolf, Baer, and several other investigators at the University of Washington began applied operant research that represented the most extensive efforts of the early 1960s and established the University of Washington as the nucleus of applied operant research.

Other programs of research were founded in the early 1960s, some of which derived directly from those that have been discussed in

---

[9] An analysis of publications in behavior modification journals that sampled articles over a four-year period revealed that the University of Kansas led all other institutions as a source of articles (Bornstein and Spitzform, 1974).

more detail. In addition, many disparate reports of operant techniques being applied to clinical ends began to be published. The extent of innovative and successful research begun in the mid and late 1960s contributed to the formal recognition of applied behavior analysis as a distinct area of research.

8

Contemporary Applied
Behavior Analysis

Employment of operant techniques to shape human behavior assumed an increasingly applied emphasis, one that grew to encompass more than an extension of the usual operant methods and techniques. Applied work had features of its own which distinguished it from basic research. Rather than restricting its subjects to laboratory animals and the complex apparatus necessary to record responses and deliver their consequences, the applied work relied heavily upon humans as observers and as agents for administering the contingencies. Operant techniques were investigated in such settings as the classroom and psychiatric ward, which meant that less control could be exerted over extraneous events and implementation of the contingency than in the laboratory. The responses performed in applied settings varied widely, as opposed to the key-, lever-, or button-pressing of the laboratory work. Such standardized responses in part allowed for sophisticated recording and programming equipment. In applied work, however, responses would vary with the individual's problem behavior or response deficit. The nature of the response scrutinized was of primary interest and not merely a means to reflect the effects of contingency manipulations. In applied operant work, different problems were to be encountered in assessing behavior *and* in programming consequences to follow behavior. The exigencies of applied problems did not allow for the precision of the laboratory. Laboratory and applied operant research had a similar experimental methodology and both sought causal relationships between interventions and behavior.

As applied research increased, it became evident that no distinct or large enough outlet existed for publishing the results. The methodology of applied research was based on the experimental analysis of behavior, which. was not popular within any particularly clinically oriented journal. The *Journal of the Experimental Analysis of Behavior* (*JEAB*) was devoted to operant research and published some of the early applied studies with humans. Yet the growing number of articles emanating from applied work could not all be absorbed by the journal. More importantly, *JEAB* chose to remain primarily a journal for basic animal research.

The Society for the Experimental Analysis of Behavior (SEAB), the corporation that published *JEAB*, recognized the need for a separate publication outlet for applied research, as did many of the researchers who published laboratory work in *JEAB* yet who also conducted applied work. Nathan Azrin, a member of SEAB, lobbied for a new journal for applied research. In 1968, SEAB established a second journal entitled the *Journal of Applied Behavior Analysis* (*JABA*) under the initial editorship of Montrose M. Wolf at the University of Kansas. The journal coined a label for the new area of research, "applied behavior analysis," and began to define the domain of this area explicitly.

CHARACTERISTICS OF APPLIED BEHAVIOR ANALYSIS

Definition

In 1968, an extremely influential paper, "Some Current Dimensions of Applied Behavior Analysis," by Donald M. Baer, Montrose M. Wolf, and Todd R. Risley, appeared in the first issue of *JABA*. This article was seen as a position paper that defined the realm of study for the journal. In addition, it explicitly distinguished applied from basic operant research in both methodology and substance. Part of the article's resonance was a function of the credentials of the authors, all extremely active researchers in applied work. All had been engaged in operant research at the University of Washington, and all had been recruited to the University of Kansas, where applied work had expanded. Wolf, Baer, and Risley, respectively, were the first three editors of *JABA*.

In their article, Baer, Wolf, and Risley (1968) defined applied behavior analysis according to substantive and methodological criteria. Substantive criteria pertain primarily to the focus of behavioral interventions. Applied behavior analysis concentrates on socially important behaviors, such as those related to mental illness, education, retardation, child rearing, and crime. Responses are selected for study because of their inseparability from everyday-life functions.

Relatedly, behavior is altered in social settings such as classrooms, institutions, the home, or other places where socially or clinically relevant behaviors need to be changed.

Another characteristic of applied behavior analysis pertains to the types of variables that are appropriate to study. Specifically, Baer et al. noted that applied research is constrained in that interventions that effect relatively large changes in behavior must be observed. Because the goal is to alter behavior of applied significance, the change made in behavior must make a difference in the functioning of the client.

To qualify as applied behavior analysis, the following methodological criteria had to be met:

> Analytic behavioral application is the process of applying sometimes tentative principles of behavior to the improvement of specific behaviors, and simultaneously evaluating whether or not any changes noted are indeed attributable to the process of application—and if so, to what parts of that process. In short, analytic behavioral application is a self-examining, self-evaluating, discovery-oriented research procedure for studying behavior (Baer, Wolf, and Risley, 1968, p. 91).

Although applied work should be experimental and analytical, the limitations that naturally arise as a function of treatment might constrain the type of experimental demonstrations possible. Applied behavior analysis thus must determine if those manipulated events are responsible for behavior change. Applied research usually cannot enjoy the same degree of control as basic laboratory research because social constraints of the setting and the demands of treatment might militate against repeated demonstrations that behavior can be increased and decreased as a function of the contingencies.

Evaluating Applied Interventions

The substantive and methodological characteristics of applied behavior analysis can be elaborated by examining the criteria for evaluating applied work. Risley (1970) noted that research in applied behavior analysis should be evaluated both by *experimental* and *therapeutic* criteria. The experimental criterion refers to determining the influence of some treatment intervention when compared to the absence of an intervention. This standard raises the question of what behavior would be like if the intervention had not been implemented and is characteristic of all psychological experimentation.

The experimental criterion is met by replicating intervention effects over time in one of several experimental designs. Usually data

are collected to determine the operant (or baseline) level of performance of the response before implementing a behavior-change technique. These data serve not only to characterize present performance,
but also to predict the level of behavior if no change had been made in
the contingencies. The intervention then is implemented to alter
behavior. The effect of the intervention is evaluated by comparing the
level of change attained with the projected level of baseline performance. If behavior diverges from this projected line, the intervention
may be withdrawn to ascertain whether the original level of behavior
shown during baseline was recovered or approached. The experimental
criterion is achieved by using particular experimental designs (outlined
below) that examine performance of an individual or group of individuals over time in much the same way that basic operant research
assesses performance of organisms in response to different contingency manipulations.

The therapeutic criterion is directed toward gauging the
importance or applied value of behavior change and the extent to
which the desired change has been achieved. Not only must the
behavior focused on be socially or clinically relevant, but the extent to
which the investigation is of applied value must be determined by the
level of behavior change achieved as compared to the level of change
needed by the client to function adequately in society (Risley, 1970).

Consistent but relatively small behavior changes may not meet
the therapeutic criterion even if the experimental requirements are
satisfied. For example, decreasing the self-destructive behavior (e.g.,
head-banging) of an autistic child from 100 to 50 instances per day
would not meet the therapeutic criterion. Although the change might
be reliable and shown to be a direct function of the intervention, the
extent of the change does not appreciably bring the child closer to
normative levels of functioning. In general, self-destructive behavior
needs to be eliminated to achieve a therapeutic criterion.

Whether or not a therapeutic criterion is met depends in part
upon the evaluations of individuals who commonly interact with the
client. For example, parents and teachers should determine if the
changes achieved in a child enhance his/her functioning. Baer et
al. (1968) emphasized the importance of the extent of behavior
change in evaluating the treatment intervention by noting, "If the
application of behavioral techniques does not produce large enough
effects for practical value, then application has failed" (p. 96). The
applied value of an intervention may be assessed in one of two ways.
The opinions of individuals in contact with the client may be solicited

after treatment to discover if the extent of change has made a difference in the client's functioning. Or, the degree to which the individual's conduct comes within the range of acceptable behaviors among the client's peers is assessed. The behaviors of the client and his/her normative group are compared to see if the client has moved within an empirically determined, acceptable level of performance.[1]

Methodology of Applied Behavior Analysis: An Overview

Applied behavior analysis and the experimental analysis of behavior share the same approach to data and experimentation. Both areas of operant research adhere to intrasubject-research designs for measuring the performance of the individual subject. Both observe behavior continuously for protracted periods and emphasize nonstatistical evaluation of the data. Methodological differences between applied and experimental behavior analysis pertain to how behaviors usually are observed and the manner in which behavior change is shown to result from application of the experimental variable (treatment intervention).

Several influential papers appeared in the late 1960s by individuals who played a major role in establishing applied operant research as a distinct entity. These publications described the methodology of applied behavior analysis and the differences between applied and basic research (Baer et al. 1968; Bijou, Peterson, and Ault, 1968; Bijou, Peterson, Harris, Allen, and Johnston, 1969). Laboratory and applied research approach the assessment of behavior differently. Most laboratory research uses frequency or rate (frequency over time) of response, a measure automatically recorded by an experimental apparatus. In applied operant work, frequency is used occasionally, especially when the response of interest is discrete and has a clear onset and termination (e.g., statement of a particular word). Yet many responses of applied interest are ongoing (e.g., studying, working, talking) and cannot be observed easily as self-contained events. Typically, then, other methods of observing behavior than frequency have to be employed.

One common method is *interval assessment*. With interval assessment, a client is observed daily for a given block of time (e.g., 30 minutes), which is divided into small temporal units (e.g., 20-second intervals). During each interval, an observer notes if the behavior of

---

[1] Procedures for evaluating the applied or therapeutic value of treatment in applied operant research have been detailed elsewhere (Kazdin, 1977a; Wolf, 1976).

interest has been exhibited. If the behavior occurs once or even several times in an interval, the interval is scored as one in which the behavior has taken place. At the end of the block of time, the percentage of intervals in which the behavior occurred can be used as the data. A variation of the interval method is called *time sampling*, which involves observing a client several times each day (e.g., once every hour). An observer merely records whether or not the behavior was occurring during the scheduled time of observation. The percentage of time that the behavior was performed out of all those times that observations were made constitutes the data for a given day. Another method of observation is *duration*, in which the amount of time spent performing the behavior in a fixed period is recorded. With duration, the cumulative time that a response occurs may be recorded each day. Frequency, interval, time-sampling, and duration together constitute the vast majority of observational methods used in applied behavior analysis. This preponderance, of course, differs from laboratory work, in which frequency or rate is observed almost exclusively.

Certainly a major difference between laboratory and applied assessment procedures is the reliability of the assessment instrument. In laboratory research, the response is recorded automatically. That a response has occurred is defined completely by the apparatus. Barring mechanical failure, there is no great concern that the apparatus is not recording reliably or is introducing systematic bias. In contrast, behavior in applied behavior analysis is almost always recorded by a human observer. Thus, a great possibilty exists that the observer may not be recording accurately and may introduce bias or inconsistencies in the scoring. In applied research, efforts are usually made to determine the extent to which observers agree in their scoring behavior. Independent observers are used to ascertain intraobserver agreement in applied projects.[2]

Applied behavior analysis is characterized by the use of specific intrasubject designs to evaluate the effect of interventions. The most commonly used experimental design is referred to as the reversal or *ABAB* design. In its simplest version, this design begins with the observation of behavior under baseline conditions in which no intervention is implemented (*A* phase). After the behavior shows a stable rate, the intervention is introduced to alter it (*B* phase). After a stable rate is achieved under these new conditions, the intervention is with-

---

[2] For an extended discussion of observational methods and interobserver agreement, see Bijou et al., 1968, 1969, and Johnson and Bolstad, 1973.

drawn. Thus, baseline conditions are reinstated (*A* phase). Finally, the intervention is reinstated (*B* phase). A causal relationship can be inferred between the intervention and behavior if behavior changes systematically each time the intervention is introduced or withdrawn.

Practical as well as ethical constraints sometimes militate against the use of the reversal design, because returning to baseline conditions is tantamount to making the client's behavior worse once some positive changes have been made. Usually, it is undesirable to remove treatment conditions until behavior is well established and more likely to be maintained. In some cases, the behavior might not return to baseline levels in the second *A* phase. In applied settings, behaviors that are developed during an intervention might come under the control of reinforcers available in the setting (e.g., peer attention) and may not revert to baseline levels when the intervention is withdrawn (Baer and Wolf, 1970).

Because of the obstacles provided by a return to baseline condition in the *ABAB* model, multiple-baseline designs are common. With these designs, no return to baseline conditions is required. For example, in the multiple-baseline design across behaviors, baseline data are collected for two or more behaviors of a given individual or group of individuals. After a stable rate of activity has been charted for each behavior, the intervention is implemented to change one of them. Baseline conditions remain in effect for the remaining behaviors and data continue to be collected for all behaviors. Once stable rates are achieved again, the intervention is extended to the second behavior. The first two behaviors are subjected to treatment while the remaining behaviors continue under baseline conditions. The intervention is extended across remaining behaviors sequentially at different times until all have been subjected to the intervention. A causal relationship between treatment and behavior is demonstrated if each behavior changes when and only when the intervention has been implemented for it.

There are other variations of the multiple-baseline design, in which multiple-baseline data are obtained for a single behavior across different individuals or situations. Other designs used in applied behavior analysis include the changing-criterion, simultaneous-treatment, and multiple-schedule designs.[3]

---

[3] For an extended discussion of experimental designs used in applied behavior analysis, several sources may be consulted (Hersen and Barlow, 1976; Kazdin, 1973b, 1978; Risley and Wolf, 1973; Wolf and Risley, 1971).

TECHNIQUES AND RESEARCH
IN APPLIED BEHAVIOR ANALYSIS

Applied behavior analysis is defined primarily by the nature of the behavior that is altered and the methodology used to evaluate behavior change. As long as the focus is on a behavior of applied relevance in nonlaboratory settings and the intervention meets the experimental and therapeutic criteria described above, the definition is met. Applied behavior analysis is not merely the application of techniques derived from operant conditioning, because operant techniques can be employed in such a way that the criteria for applied behavior analysis are not met. Conversely, many interventions derived from approaches other than operant conditioning might meet the applied and experimental characteristics outlined above. Of course, since applied behavior analysis grew out of operant conditioning and the experimental analysis of behavior, the most popular treatment techniques usually derive from operant principles.

Overview of Techniques

Operant techniques tend to be derived from the principles of reinforcement, punishment, and extinction, and their combination. Most applications use techniques based upon positive reinforcement. Positive reinforcement is appropriate to increase some target behavior, but it is also used when the primary goal is to decrease a response. A particular response (e.g., disrupting others in a classroom) can be decreased by reinforcing incompatible behaviors (e.g., working quietly on a task). Positive reinforcement techniques have been based upon the delivery of incentives such as food and other consumables, privileges and activities, feedback, praise, and tokens. These events delivered contingently on completion of the desired behavior have been used effectively across treatment populations and target behaviors.

Tokens, used as positive reinforcers in many programs, have been particularly effective in altering behavior. They can be earned for a variety of behaviors and can be exchanged for back-up events. Token economies afford a way to restructure the environment so that many incentives can be brought to bear to alter behavior. Several clinical populations have been treated with token economies (Kazdin, 1977d).

Various punishment techniques have been used in applied settings. Punishment frequently consists of withdrawing a positive event contingent upon behavior, as in time-out from reinforcement or response cost. With time-out, the client usually is briefly (e.g., a few minutes) removed from the situation (e.g., classroom, ward) in which the undesired behavior has occurred. Response cost consists of withdrawing some positive event, often a token, awarded for performance. Although both time-out and response cost involve the loss of some positive event, time-out is based upon removal of the reinforcers for a specific period of time. In contrast, there are no time constraints on response cost. Occasionally punishment techniques involve the presentation of aversive events such as reprimands or shock. Although shock tends not to be used, it has been very effective in eliminating such behavior as infliction of self-injury.

A recently created punishment technique is referred to as *over-correction and restitution* (Foxx and Azrin, 1972, 1973a). There are two components of this procedure: performing a response to correct the environmental consequences of the inappropriate behavior (e.g., cleaning up objects strewn upon the floor) and extensively rehearsing the correct form of the behavior (e.g., placing several objects in their rightful place). Research has shown that engaging in the latter component (sometimes called *positive practice*) often is sufficient to suppress unsuitable behavior. Requiring individuals to repeat appropriate responses contingent upon inappropriate behavior effectively develops the desired behavior.

Extinction techniques usually involve not paying attention to behaviors. In everyday situations, individuals inadvertently attend to and maintain the behaviors that they would like to eliminate. Withholding attention from undesirable behavior and attending to positive functioning has been an effective behavior-change technique.

So far, the discussion of techniques has implied that specific, narrowly defined interventions are selected for target behaviors. This impression is somewhat misleading, because in practice several procedures usually are combined to alter behavior. For example, to change behavior in an institutional setting, a patient usually will be exposed to reinforcement, punishment, and extinction techniques. Aides may deliver praise and tokens for adaptive behaviors in the setting as well as withdraw tokens for or not attend to bizarre behaviors. The intervention is multifaceted and may draw simultaneously from several principles and techniques. Programs may vary along with a number of other dimensions, including the procedures employed to initiate and encourage the response, the individual administering the contingencies, the role of peers in the contingencies, and so on. For example, in a reinforcement program, a wide range of prompts such as verbal, visual, and physical cues may be used to help initiate behavior, Also, shaping or chaining may be used to develop behaviors not originally in the client's repertoire.

The person administering the contingencies accounts for some of the differences in applications. Individuals who control reinforcing and punishing events in the environment—parents, teachers, spouses, etc.—usually administer the program. However, peers (e.g., other students in class) or the clients themselves may administer the program with little or no supervision.

The manner in which the program is conceived and constructed also may vary across interventions. Sometimes programs are superimposed upon the clients when they have had no input into the specific contingencies. On other occasions, the clients may help set up the conditions or negotiate the behaviors that are to be performed and the consequences earned for their performance. These negotiations often result in a written contract (a *contingency contract*) that is formally agreed to and signed by all participants in the program.

How the consequences are earned varies among programs. Usually the client earns or loses reinforcing consequences based upon his/her own performance. However, many programs are structured so that consequences earned by one individual are shared by others. Consequence sharing and group contingencies are effective in bringing to bear peer consequences for performance.

In general, the diversity of techniques afforded by the application of operant principles is too great to be sampled thoroughly here. Complex procedures for monitoring behavior, delivering and scheduling consequences, ensuring client progress in the program, and withdrawing the contingencies have been discussed extensively elsewhere.[4]

Overview of Research

Applied operant research is surveyed in this section by discussing the populations treated and the specific behaviors altered.

Psychiatric Patients   Hospitalized psychiatric patients have been exposed to operant techniques from the inception of applied behavior analysis (see Carlson, Hersen, and Eisler, 1972; Gripp and Magaro, 1974; Kazdin, 1977d; and Stahl and Leitenberg, 1976 for reviews). Token economies have been implemented in most applications with hospitalized patients. Typically, behaviors related to adjustment to the hospital routine are reinforced. These include self-care behaviors such

---

[4] For example, see Kazdin (1975a), Leitenberg (1976), Sulzer-Azaroff and Mayer (1977), and Ulrich, Stachnik, and Mabry (1966, 1970, 1974).

as grooming, making one's bed, and dressing and working at jobs on and off the ward. Self-care and work behaviors have been altered readily in the hospital. Moreover, making gains in adaptive behavior in the hospital frequently has been related to other improvements that might be more relevant to the patient's condition. Patients whose adaptive behaviors are increased in the hospital often show a reduction in bizarre behaviors ("symptoms"), improvements in mood, increases in communication and social skills, and more rapid discharge from the hospital (Kazdin, 1977d).

In many programs, symptomatic or therapeutically pertinent behaviors were made the direct focus of treatment. For example, programs have curbed delusional and irrational talk, somatic complaints, episodes of crying, aggressive outbursts, and social withdrawal. Several programs have increased the social skills of patients by reinforcing conversation and interaction with staff, peers on the ward, or visitors from the community. Reinforcement and punishment contingencies also have concentrated on such behaviors as overeating, pill-taking, making recommendations for treatment programs, decision-making, and participating in the administration of other patients' programs. However, most applications with hospitalized patients are targeted for routine ward behaviors.

Although most programs with psychiatric patients have been implemented in institutions, some have been conducted in half-way houses where patients receive reinforcing consequences for engaging in behaviors in the community such as seeking job interviews, attending social activities, or actually working on a job. Many local mental-health facilities have incorporated operant techniques in which patients participate in day treatment or outpatient treatment (Liberman, King, and DeRisi, 1976).

Follow-up data have been reported for some studies with psychiatric patients. The measures most consistently used to evaluate the long-term effects of treatment are discharge and readmission rates. Patients who participate in a reinforcement program in a hospital setting tend to show higher discharge and lower readmission rates than patients who receive custodial care (cf. Gripp and Magaro, 1974; Kazdin, 1977d). In many reports, the changes in discharge and readmission cannot be attributed unambiguously to the reinforcement program: they may reflect a change in hospital or ward philosophy regarding the criteria for release from and return to the hospital.

The Mentally Retarded Operant programs with the retarded encompass a variety of behaviors with clients of all levels of retardation (see Birnbrauer, 1976; Forehand and Baumeister, 1976; Gardner, 1971; Kazdin and Craighead, 1973; and Thompson and Grabowski, 1972 for reviews). The settings in which programs have been conducted include institutions, day-care facilities, sheltered workshops, and special classrooms.

In many programs, suppression of self-injurious responses, self-stimulation, aggressive outbursts, bizarre verbalizations, and inappropriate eating and social responses has been emphasized. However, the greatest attention has been devoted to developing self-care behaviors. These behaviors represent very basic skills, including feeding, toileting, dressing, bathing, wearing prosthetic devices, and exercising. Success has been achieved in treating several of them. For example, through a series of investigations, Nathan Azrin and Richard Foxx created a procedure to instill continence relatively quickly (Azrin and Foxx, 1974; Foxx and Azrin, 1973b). Several techniques are involved, including frequent and immediate reinforcement for dry pants and for urinating correctly, a large number of trials to practice the appropriate toileting responses, imitation and manual guidance to help initiate the behaviors, symbolic rehearsal of the desired behavior, and so on. The procedure has been effective in eliminating toileting accidents with institutionalized retarded as well as with "normal" children in a brief period of time (e.g., in less than a day). Follow-up suggest that the gains are maintained several months after treatment (Foxx and Azrin, 1973b).

Programs for the retarded have altered a wide range of other verbal behaviors and language skills. Receptive and productive language, imitative speech, use of vocabulary, responding to questions, correct articulation, and other skills have been acquired. In many programs, unsuitable speech or bizarre verbalizations are suppressed as part of the learning of appropriate verbal communication.

Work-related behaviors of individuals participating in sheltered workshop programs have been studied. Behaviors considered to be adaptive for ultimate community placement, including increased productivity, attendance, and punctuality, have been fostered by reinforcement. Social behaviors have been paid somewhat less attention than other behaviors of retarded individuals, although few applications have enhanced communicating with one's peers or playing cooperatively. Academic skills and achievement test performance have been investigated. Performance on achievement and readiness tests has been increased with remedial classroom programs or direct reinforcement of test-taking responses. (Academic responses are addressed below.)

Individuals in Classroom Settings   Operant techniques have been applied more in classrooms than any other setting (Kazdin, 1975b), and diverse populations have participated in the programs. Because these programs are similar in many ways, it is useful to treat them as a unit rather than as a separate category with each population. Reinforcement programs have been established in the classroom across varied populations (e.g., "normal," retarded, and delinquent children), across educational levels (e.g., preschool, high school, and college), and across settings (e.g., classes in public schools and psychiatric institutions, special education or adjustment classes) (see Drabman, 1976; Kazdin, 1977d; McLaughlin, 1975; O'Leary and Drabman, 1971; and O'Leary and O'Leary, 1976 for reviews).

Most programs are directed toward increasing attentive behavior and decreasing disruptive activities in elementary and preschool children. Students receive reinforcers, usually praise or tokens, for working on their tasks without disrupting others, for complying with teacher instructions, and, in general, for conforming to classroom rules. Programs have been extremely successful in improving classroom conduct.

The target of operant programs in the classroom has begun to shift (Kazdin, 1975b). Programs would uniformly emphasize deportment until recent investigations indicated that such improvements did not necessarily enhance academic performance. Thus, considerable attention has been given to direct alterations of academic performance through which students earn reinforcers for such behaviors as accuracy in reading, arithmetic, handwriting, spelling, and for completing homework, creative writing, and building vocabulary. Interestingly, the successful alteration of academic performance often leads to improvements in deportment. Classroom programs also have improved performance in responding to teacher requests, speaking correctly, participating in classroom activities, and socializing with other children.

Academic behaviors have been improved in operant programs conducted at colleges and universities. Operant techniques have been incorporated into college teaching in a method termed the Personalized System of Instruction, developed by Keller (1966, 1968; Ryan, 1974). Personalized instruction refers to a way of structuring a course so that specific contingencies are devised toward course completion. With personalized instruction, students progress through the material at their own pace, are allowed repeated opportunities to take exams until mastery is achieved, and receive immediate feedback after testing. Many techniques of operant conditioning—including shaping, immediate reinforcement, and reinforcing the rate of response—have been incorporated into the system. Students completing college work in a course structured according to personalized instruction tended to do better on exams on the course content both immediately after the course and after an interim follow-up period. As a rule, they find greater enjoyment in the course than those who receive the same curriculum in a traditionally managed class.

Some of the greatest gains in applied operant research have been demonstrated in work with preschool, elementary, and secondary students. Several investigations have shown that reinforcing academic performance improves scores on achievement tests. Occasionally, tested intelligence is assessed and shown to increase as well (cf. Kazdin, 1977d). Follow-up reports have indicated that gains are maintained in achievement or classroom deportment from six months to a year.

Children in Institutional Settings Most applications with children have been conducted in the classroom and have focused either on attentive or academic behavior. Severely disordered behavior often is treated in institutional settings. Children diagnosed as autistic[5] or hyperactive have been exposed to operant techniques in institutional settings (Lovaas and Bucher, 1974). Most investigators have worked on eliminating self-destructive and self-stimulatory behaviors, echolalia, and tantrums. With severe self-destructive behaviors, various punishment procedures have been effective, although electric shock has been the most potent and rapid. Autistic children have learned such positive behaviors as imitating others, responding to instructions, contacting and seeking out adults, language and speech, play, social interaction, and basic academic skills.

The work of O. Ivar Lovaas and his colleagues at the University of California at Los Angeles has been the most programmatic in designing and evaluating treatments for autistic children (Lovaas and Bucher, 1974). In Lovaas' program, children receive daily treatment for several hours during which various procedures are used and different behaviors are altered. The techniques include reinforcement

---

[5] A distinction often is made between autism and childhood schizophrenia. Behavior modifiers have not adhered to this distinction in designing treatment programs and frequently have used the terms interchangeably. Because the main focus is on the behaviors to be altered, no separation will be made here.

with such events as food and praise, extinction (including withdrawal of attention), and punishment and negative reinforcement (e.g., presenting and withdrawing of shock). Amelioration of specific problems such as self-destructive behavior, as well as the development of receptive and productive speech, have been well documented in Lovaas' program. Tested intelligence and social competence also have improved as a result of treatment.

Follow-up data for one to four years after treating autistic children have indicated that the extent to which gains were maintained depended upon the subsequent care the children received after leaving the program (Lovaas, Koegel, Simmons, and Long, 1973). Children returning to parents who had been trained to utilize behavior modification in the home retained their behavioral gains and, indeed, showed some improvements. In contrast, children placed in a state hospital lost most of what they had gained. Their psychotic acts such as echolalia and self-stimulation returned, whereas their appropriate verbal and social behaviors were lost. When some of the children in this latter group were returned to Lovaas for treatment, their adaptive behavior increased and psychotic behavior decreased. These gains, however, were lost again when the children were returned to institutional life.

Children diagnosed as hyperactive have been treated with operant techniques. The hyperactive behaviors that serve as a focus of treatment vary according to the setting in which behaviors are assessed. The problems usually include gross motor acts such as running around, being out of or constantly moving in one's seat, aggressing against others, failing to attend to a task, and so on. Reinforcement techniques have been used to encourage incompatible behaviors such as working on school assignments or sitting still. Because drugs are used so frequently to treat hyperactive children, reinforcement techniques have been compared with the major drugs used, including methylphenidate (Ritalin) and chlorpromazine (Thorazine). Evidence suggests that reinforcement techniques often are an efficacious substitute for drug treatment. In many comparative studies, reinforcement techniques have been superior to drugs decreasing hyperactive behaviors (Kazdin and Wilson, 1978).

Predelinquents and Delinquents   Many operant programs have been designed for juveniles who have committed antisocial behaviors (Braukmann and Fixsen, 1975; Braukmann, Fixsen, Phillips, and Wolf, 1975; Burchard and Harig, 1976; Davidson and Seidman, 1974; Stumphauzer, 1973). Most programs have been implemented in correctional facilities, although a major attempt has been made to alter behaviors of delinquents while they live in home-like living situations in a familial atmosphere or remain in the community.

Although programs sometimes attempt to eliminate specific anti-social behaviors, greater emphasis has been placed on reinforcing socially acceptable responses. Thus, programs have focused upon improving particular competences in academic and vocational skills as well as social interaction. The specific objectives and types of programs vary as a function of age of the individual and the setting to which he/she is assigned. A few programs have been designed as preventive measures for juveniles whose behavioral patterns (e.g., drop in grade levels, truancy, runaways from home, misbehavior in the community) suggest a high risk for later delinquent activities (Cohen, 1972; Filipczak and Cohen, 1972). Preventive programs enhance competencies in academic and social behaviors to increase the likelihood of pursuing socially compatible and nondelinquent behaviors (see Burchard and Harig, 1976).

Perhaps the most innovative and carefully evaluated program for juveniles has been conducted at Achievement Place, a home-style facility for adjudicated youths. The facility, located in Kansas, is supervised by Montrose M. Wolf and several of his colleagues, who have designed an elaborate contingency management program. A small number of youths live in the home that is managed by a husband and wife who have been carefully trained in applied behavior analysis. (Facilities are segregated by sex.) The delinquents participate in a token economy in which behaviors such as studying and completing school assignments, room cleaning, keeping up with the news, saving money, accepting criticism without aggressing, conversing appropriately with peers, and other behaviors are reinforced with tokens. Tokens can be exchanged for incentives such as watching television, staying up late, bicycling, snacks, and so on.

The purpose of the program at Achievement Place is to return the individual to his/her original living setting. To that end, the structured token-reinforcement program is gradually faded as the youths perform the target behaviors consistently and their parents are trained to manage the contingencies needed for maintaining behavior at home. Extensive research conducted at Achievement Place has established the efficacy of these diverse contingency manipulations for changes not only in specific behaviors but in general attitudes as well. The Achievement Place model has been adopted widely in many new home-style facilities.

Follow-up data on programs for delinquents have yielded diverse results, depending in part on the program. Follow-up data in a program referred to as CASE (Contingencies Applicable for Special Education) showed transient effects of treatment (Cohen and Filipczak, 1971; Filipczak and Cohen, 1972). The institutionalized boys received reinforcing consequences for engaging in academic tasks and select social behaviors. After release from the facility, inmates had lower recidivism rates and fewer warrants issued against them than other federal juvenile parolees. However, three years after release, the trends in the data suggested no long-term treatment effects. The initially positive results associated with the CASE program cannot be interpreted unambiguously because of the high percentage of attrition at follow-up, the dissimilarities between the juveniles at CASE and other institutional programs, and similar factors (Burchard and Harig, 1976).

Follow-up data from the Achievement Place program have been somewhat more favorable. A comparison was made between male delinquents who participated in the Achievement Place program with those either in an institutional boys' school or assigned to probation. Up to two years after treatment, graduates of Achievement Place had fewer run-ins with the police and courts, committed fewer delinquent acts that resulted in readjudication, and showed a markedly higher percentage of attendance at public school and slightly better grades than individuals who received institutional treatment or were placed on probation. These results were based upon nonrandomly assigned control groups and thus are only suggestive. Follow-up findings obtained at other facilities modeled after Achievement Place have been slightly less than favorable (Liberman and Ferris, 1974).

Adult Offenders   Programs for prisoners have been implemented to alter behaviors adaptive within the institution (Ayllon, Milan, Roberts, and McKee, in preparation; Kennedy, 1976; Milan and McKee, 1974). One of the more well-known programs, referred to as Special Treatment and Rehabilitation Training (START), conducted in Missouri by the Federal Bureau of Prisons (1972), was designed to foster adaptive behaviors in highly aggressive and resistive prisoners. The purpose of the program was to reinforce behaviors in otherwise intractible prisoners so they could return to their normal prison setting. Not engaging in aggressive behaviors, refraining from threats and fights, and similar behaviors led to privileges such as showering, exercising, and having access to personal items. The program was terminated because of pending litigation that challenged the involuntary assignment of prisoners to the program without due process, deprivation of privileges normally provided in prisons, aversive conditions used as part of treatment, and other aspects of contingencies.

Other prison programs have concentrated on developing specific positive behaviors rather than merely suppressing deviance. The greatest attention has been paid to improving academic behaviors. Prisoners receive reinforcing consequences such as money or special activities based upon their study habits and completion of academic tasks. Occasionally, inmates have received incentives for keeping informed of current events. Research in prisons has shown that scholastic behaviors are readily amenable to change. Programs also have been conducted in minimal security as well as hospital facilities. In the usual situation, prisoners receive reinforcing consequences for routine behaviors associated with prison or hospital life.

There are few data on the long-term effects of operant programs with adult offenders who are released. In one prison program that has been evaluated carefully, a comparison was made between inmates who participated in a reinforcement program (primarily to enhance academic behaviors) with those who received traditional prison treatment (primarily to provide vocational training) (Jenkins, Witherspoon, DeVine, deValera, Muller, Barton, and McKee, 1974). There were slight differences in arrest and recidivism rates immediately after release in favor of those who received the reinforcement program, although these differences were not statistically significant.

The military has reported follow-up data with a program for hospitalized "delinquent soldiers" who committed offenses in the military (Colman and Baker, 1969; Stayer and Jones, 1969). Soldiers participated in a token economy in a hospital where adaptive and self-care behaviors were reinforced. Follow-up assessment at three, six, and nine months after termination of the program revealed that 69.5% of the soldiers completed their tour of duty or were in good standing ("successes"), whereas 30.5% were discharged administratively, were AWOL, or were in a stockade ("failures"). A comparison group that did not undergo treatment showed only 28.3% successes and 71.7% failures by the same criteria.

Drug Addicts and Alcoholics   Most operant programs for drug addicts and alcoholics have been conducted in hospital settings (see Miller and Eisler, 1976 for a review). In these programs, special privileges or tokens backed by a variety of events are used to reinforce diverse adaptive behaviors on the ward, including self-care, participating in activities, and working. In some programs with alcoholics, patients have access to alcohol in the hospital setting and receive reinforcing consequences based upon drinking only small amounts (i.e., for social drinking). The purpose of such programs is to train individuals to engage in controlled levels of social drinking as an alternative to complete abstinence. Diverse reinforcement and punishment techniques have demonstrated control over drinking within the hospital.

There are few follow-up data for operant programs that deal with drug or alcohol abuse. One of the most carefully evaluated programs for drug addicts, conducted in Sweden, provided follow-up data up to one year after patients were released (Melin and Götestam, 1973). The percentage of drug-free patients was higher for those who participated in the program than for nonrandomly assigned, untreated control patients or for patients who had attended the hospital before the inception of the program.

Medical Patients Recently, medical applications of behavior modification, referred to as behavioral medicine (Birk, 1973; Blanchard, 1977), have proliferated. This area encompasses all behavioral techniques as applied to areas of medicine, health, and illness (Katz and Zlutnick, 1975; Knapp and Peterson, 1976; Price, 1974; Williams and Gentry, 1977). Perhaps the largest single component of behavioral medicine is the use of biofeedback to alter physiological responses related to such problems as cardiovascular disorders, headaches, seizures, tics, loss of muscle control, vaginismus, and incontinence (Blanchard and Epstein, 1977; Shapiro and Surwit, 1976). A few demonstrations have produced dramatic results. However, the lack of controlled investigations demonstrating the specific role of feedback restricts the conclusions that can be drawn at this time (Blanchard and Epstein, 1977; Blanchard and Young, 1974).[6]

Operant techniques have been used to treat a wide range of illness-related patient behaviors as part of diagnosed and undiagnosed conditions. One of the more well-studied examples is the reduction of pain-related behaviors performed by patients who complain and are medicated for chronic discomfort. Behaviors such as time out of one's bed, grimacing, moaning, verbal complaints, walking in a guarded or

---

[6] Biofeedback has been used to treat such disorders as hypertension, cardiac arrhythmias, and headaches. Although biofeedback utilizes operant principles, its scope extends beyond them, as discussed in Chapter 6. Biofeedback usually is viewed as an independent area of research rather than as a specialty of operant conditioning and applied behavior analysis (Shapiro and Surwit, 1976).

protective manner, reclining or sitting to ease pain, and relying upon medication have been altered by contingency management in the hospital or in the patient's everyday interactions with relatives. Behaviors accompanying chronic pain are altered by reinforcing activity and physical exercise, and by decreasing attention and delivery of medication based upon expression of pain (e.g., Fordyce, 1973; Fordyce, Fowler, Lehmann, DeLateur, Sand, and Trieschmann, 1973).

Other specific symptoms of hospitalized and nonhospitalized patients have been altered with operant techniques. Such disorders as epileptic seizures, asthmatic attacks, spasmodic torticollis, drooling, ruminations, constipation, and dermatitis have been ameliorated with behavioral techniques. In some cases, behavioral techniques are used to help maintain adherence to medical treatment regimens. For example, contingencies in the hospital or natural environment have been designed to ensure that patients take fluids, use prosthetic devices such as crutches, adhere to their medication schedule, and exercise (Gentry, 1977; Knapp and Peterson, 1976). In physical rehabilitation, operant techniques are useful in training patients to master prosthetic devices (Couch and Allen, 1973; Knapp and Peterson, 1976). Although the range of medical disorders and specific symptoms treated has been broad, to date most reports are uncontrolled case applications. Thus, conclusions cannot be drawn about the power of particular techniques to effect change.

Biofeedback and operant conditioning do not exhaust the range of techniques used in behavioral medicine. For example, inducements of calmness, including progressive relaxation, autogenic training, yoga, meditation, and hypnosis, have helped to control hypertension, headaches, and insomnia (e.g., Byassee, 1977; Jacob, Kraemer, and Agras, 1977; Knapp, Downs, and Alperson, 1976). Some of these aids (e.g., yoga) are not traditionally considered to be a part of behavior modification. However, behavioral medicine is developing as an area in its own right, and although it relies heavily upon the methodology of behavior modification, it is not necessarily restricted to a specific set of techniques.

Outpatient Applications   Operant programs have been popular for treating outpatients. Two categories can be distinguished, outpatient therapy and interventions in the natural environment. In outpatient therapy, individuals come for treatment in which the interventions are designed, described, and implemented. The therapist usually plays a major role in administering the contingencies that may control client behavior outside of treatment. Outpatient applications have been applied to such behaviors as overeating, cigarette smoking, dating, nail-biting, and excessive consumption of alcohol. Clients are instructed to engage in specific behaviors outside of treatment and meet regularly with a therapist. The therapist controls the delivery of reinforcing events such as a return of money previously deposited by the client contingent upon meeting specific response criteria. For example, to deal with an obese individual, the therapist may deliver or withdraw money based upon the client's change in weight or adherence to a particular diet or exercise regimen during the week. Treatment is carried out in the client's everyday environment insofar as the client engages in specific procedures agreed to in therapy. Yet, the major contingency may be controlled or monitored by the therapist.

Operant techniques have been applied much more extensively in the natural environment, where people ordinarily in contact with the client can administer the contingencies rather than the therapist. These individuals consult with a therapist, who helps design the program in conjunction with the clients. The therapist serves as an advisor to the agents who change behavior rather than as the active agent of change. For example, the therapist may help the client decide the reinforcing or punishing consequences that could be used to alter behavior and explain the manner in which the program needs to be conducted to effect change.

In the home, parents can be trained to administer reinforcement programs with their children (see Patterson, 1971; and Wahler, 1976 for reviews). For example, parents may systematically deliver praise, privileges, points, reprimands, or brief periods of time-out to encourage compliance with their requests, completion of chores, cooperative play with siblings, and similar behaviors. In some cases, programs are conducted simultaneously at home and at school and involve both the parents and teachers of the children being treated (e.g., Patterson, 1974; Patterson, Cobb, and Ray, 1973; Patterson and Reid, 1970; Wahler, 1969). A program in each setting appears to be necessary, because changes made in one setting usually do not transfer to the other.

Many programs with delinquent and predelinquent youths are conducted in the community rather than in treatment settings (e.g., Fo and O'Donnell, 1974; Tharp and Wetzel, 1969). In these programs, consultants vary program contingencies in the natural environment to promote behavior change. These individuals either directly administer the consequences for behavior or advise others more closely involved with the client. Treatment may be carried in diverse locations in the community (e.g., parks or the movies) where the appropriate behaviors need to be developed (see Ayllon and Skuban, 1973).

Interventions in the natural environment also have been implemented with adults. For example, at home, a spouse can monitor the contingencies to alter such behaviors as drinking alcoholic beverages or smoking. Occasionally, the interaction patterns of the spouses are modified as a way of resolving marital problems (Jacobson and Martin, 1976).

Other Populations and Applications   Operant techniques have been applied for clinical purposes to other populations, but only a few projects have been reported. Geriatric residents who live in hospitals or nursing homes have begun to be studied. For example, praise, attention from others, and tokens have been used to reinforce behaviors such as conversing with others, going for walks, writing letters, performing self-care tasks, and, in general, participating in activities (Nietzel, Winett, MacDonald, and Davidson, 1977).

Stutterers receiving outpatient treatment or institutionalized in a day-hospital program have decreased their stuttering through scheduled sessions in which they have been reinforced with praise or tokens or punished with noise or delayed auditory feedback. Reinforcement techniques have helped to develop language in adult aphasics whose speaking has been disrupted by cerebrovascular accidents. One of the newest extensions of applied behavior analysis has been to the environmental and social problems, in which behaviors related to pollution control, energy conservation, employment, and job performance have been altered (Kazdin, 1977b; Nietzel et al., 1977; Tuso and Geller, 1976). Such applications have expanded the realm of behavior modification beyond the confines of traditional psychiatric and educational interventions (see Chapter 11).

EVALUATING APPLIED BEHAVIOR
ANALYSIS: POTENTIAL PROBLEMS AND LIMITATIONS

Applied behavior analysis can be evaluated from different perspectives. From within its own research domain, several issues have implications for gauging the overall efficacy of the field and its impact on treatment, rehabilitation, and education. Three issues within applied behavior analysis are of especial importance; they involve the maintenance and transfer of changes made during treatment, the failure of some clients to respond to operant programs, and the training of individuals to implement behavioral programs. These issues point to the potential problems and limitations of contemporary applications. From the standpoint of the larger field of behavior modification, other potential limitations of applied behavior analysis have been cited. In particular, the model of human behavior embraced by operant conditioning—upon which applied behavior analysis heavily relies—has been criticized strongly.

Maintenance and Transfer of Behavior Changes

The overview of research in applied behavior analysis outlined some major accomplishments of operant techniques in changing behavior. Although the data for behavior change are vast, the evidence for long-term follow-up is sparse. Relatively few studies have examined the long-term effects of contingency manipulations in treatment settings or in the natural environment. Many authors have criticized the absence of follow-up in behavior modification in general (e.g., Cochrane and Sobol, 1976; Keeley, Shemberg, and Carbonell, 1976).

One reason for the relatively sparse follow-up evidence is that the field itself is relatively young: the bulk of the research has been produced since 1970. Some interesting follow-up data have been reported for the early applications of operant principles. For example, one of the first cases treated with operant techniques was an autistic child named Dicky who had several behavioral problems, such as refusing to wear glasses that would prevent impairment of vision, tantrums, self-destructive behaviors, and inappropriate social, verbal, and eating habits (see Chapter 7 and Wolf et al., 1964). The child had been a subject in several programs designed to develop diverse behaviors, including academic, verbal, and social functioning. A 10-year follow-up evaluation of Dicky revealed that he had maintained many of his gains (Nedelman and Sulzbacher, 1972). He was able to attend regular classes rather than special classes for the retarded, showed adequate reading ability, engaged in appropriate conversation, and was reported by his teacher to play with his peers. Although some autistic behaviors remained (e.g., rocking in his seat, hand clapping), his behavior had advanced considerably. The above report is especially interesting because it represents perhaps the longest follow-up of a systematic treatment with operant techniques. Additional follow-up reports have been made with psychiatric patients, individuals in classroom settings, autistic children, delinquents, and others.

The relative paucity of follow-up data in applied behavior analysis leads to the question of whether or not behavior changes are maintained after the intervention is terminated and after the individual leaves the setting in which the intervention was implemented. These issues refer to response maintenance and transfer of training, respectively, and currently are major areas of discussion and research in behavior modification (Kazdin, 1977d; Marholin, Siegel, and Phillips, 1976; Stokes and Baer, 1977; Wildman and Wildman, 1975). The relative absence of long-term follow-up data has not interfered with evaluating the extent to which responses are maintained or transferred to settings in which treatment has not occurred. Assessing behavior immediately after an operant program has been terminated or as soon as the client transfers to a new setting has revealed a relatively consistent pattern. As a rule, gains made during an operant program tend to be lost after the contingencies are withdrawn. Similarly, behavior changes in one setting usually do not transfer to another.

The failure of responses to be maintained after a contingency is withdrawn or to transfer across other settings is to be expected on the basis of the principles of operant conditioning. The overriding assumption of the operant approach is that *behavior is a function of its consequences.* Thus, if consequences for a given activity are discontinued in one setting or are never provided in another, behavior would be expected to adjust to these contingencies. Clients would be expected to discriminate in their performance across stimulus conditions (situations, settings) in which the consequences for performance differ. Behavior changes achieved through operant techniques are not always lost when the contingencies are withdrawn. However, cases in which the gains are retained without specific attempts to program maintenance appear to be exceptions.

The consistent finding that behavior tends to change only while the contingencies are in effect has fostered increased research on this phenomenon. Effective techniques for changing behavior seem to be somewhat different from those needed to maintain it and ensure its transfer across stimulus conditions. A variety of techniques have been studied to improve response maintenance and transfer of training.

The major techniques to program response maintenance and transfer of training include:[7]

1. Training individuals in the natural environment to expand or to continue a program conducted in a treatment setting.

---

[7] The techniques for ensuring that behaviors are maintained and transferred to everyday settings cannot be elaborated here. Several sources have described how these techniques are implemented and the evidence bearing upon their efficacy (Kazdin, 1975a, 1977d; Marholin et al., 1976; Stokes and Baer, 1977; Wildman and Wildman, 1975).

2. Substituting "naturally occurring" reinforcers (e.g., peer atten-tion) for behaviors initially enhanced through the use of extrinsic consequences.
3. Gradually fading the contingencies so that the client performs the desired behaviors for protracted periods without specific contingencies.
4. Developing the behavior in the presence of diverse stimuli (e.g., settings and experimenters) so that a broad range of stimuli con-trol the behavior and the client develops a generalized response pattern.
5. Scheduling intermittent reinforcement so that the behavior is maintained when consequences are delivered very infrequently or are eliminated entirely.
6. Increasing the delay between the consequences and behavior so that the client eventually receives no consequences while continu-ing to perform the behavior.
7. Building self-management techniques whereby the individual delivers his/her own consequences, provides self-instructions, or monitors his/her own behavior.

Although response maintenance and transfer have been paid increased attention in the literature in recent years, particular refine-ments of those techniques have not approached the advances in procedures for changing behavior. As it stands, many techniques usually are combined to maintain behavior change. Also, the evidence for the efficacy of many of the techniques is relatively sparse.

Failure of Some Clients to Respond to the Contingencies

Failure to respond to the contingencies means that changes in behavior have been absent or insufficient during the intervention over baseline rates. It is difficult to specify a percentage of clients who fail to respond because many programs have treated only a small number of participants. Thus, a few nonrespondents would inflate this percentage spuriously. Nevertheless, a large number of programs report that individuals do not respond to the contingencies (cf. Kazdin, 1973a).

Many explanations have been proposed to explain why some clients do not respond to a particular program. The failure to use suf-ficiently powerful reinforcers, the failure to reinforce successive approximations of behavior, and the failure of clients to comprehend the relationship between performance and response consequences have all been suggested as possible causes. Precise reasons for not responding to contingencies have not been well studied empirically. However, current evidence suggests that this deficiency is not a generalized response characteristic. Individuals who do not respond to a particular contingency frequently do improve when the contingency is altered (e.g., Ayllon, Garber, and Pisor, 1975; Mitchell and Stoffelmayr, 1973; Winkler, 1971). Thus, investigators have focused upon creating techniques to enhance performance when individuals do not respond to the contingencies at all or respond less well than desired in relation to the goals of the program. Several techniques can enhance performance in operant programs:

1. *Response priming* consists of initiating responses that otherwise might have a low frequency. To initiate the desired response, an individual is placed in a situation in which the response is more likely to be reinforced. Response priming relies upon the notion that responses near the end of a chain of responses are more likely to be performed than those at the beginning of a chain. The technique takes advantage of this relationship by placing the individual in stimulus conditions close to terminal reinforcement, which increases the likelihood of the response being performed.

2. *Reinforcer sampling* consists of providing the individual with a sample of the event that is designed to serve as a reinforcer. By providing a small sample (e.g., a portion of food or a few minutes of an activity), the individual is more likely to engage in behaviors that will earn the remaining portion of the activity.

3. *Reinforcer exposure* means exposing an individual to others who are engaging in the reinforcing event or activities. By seeing others engage in a reinforcing activity or partake of the reinforcing event, the subject is more likely to work for that event. As with reinforcer sampling, exposure tends to increase the value of the reinforcing event and the likelihood that the individual will engage in those behaviors that earn it.

4. *Varying the reinforcer* often is associated with increased performance for individuals who do not respond to the contingency as originally presented.

5. Using *individualized contingencies* can increase responsiveness to the program when a client has not responded to a general contingency that was designed for application to a larger population.

6. *Consequence sharing* is the dividing or sharing of reinforcers (e.g., tokens, a special activity) among one's peers. The event is earned only on the basis of the behavior of the individual, but the earn-

ings are shared by the peer group. Consequence sharing brings to bear peer encouragement and pressure to foster behavior change in the client.

In general, the initial failure of a client to respond to a program does not necessarily indicate more than unresponsiveness to a specific contingency. Altering the contingency in some way or increasing the likelihood of using the reinforcing consequences frequently improves performance. Nevertheless, the relative effectiveness of different types of contingencies, the factors that contribute to unresponsiveness of some clients, and the range of techniques useful in enhancing performance remain to be explored more fully.

Training Agents of Behavior Change

Training individuals in contact with clients to administer behavior-change techniques competently is crucial because the success of an intervention program is a function of how well the contingencies are implemented. The contingencies usually are not managed by the professional who designs them, but rather by someone else in close interaction with the client. These individuals include parents, teachers, spouses, aides, peers, or other acquaintances who control many of the reinforcing events that are brought to bear in an operant program.

Concern about the competence of individuals who serve as behavior-change agents is twofold. Often individuals in the natural environment can accidentally aggravate or contribute to the deviant behaviors they wish to alter (see Patterson and Reid, 1970). Subtle reinforcing contingencies can evolve inadvertently in which bizarre behavior patterns are attended to and gradually shaped to increasing levels of severity. Training individuals in contact with the client, or potential client, must include sensitizing them to the operation of operant principles in everyday interactions. Moreover, individuals who administer a behavior-change program frequently do not conduct the program with the consistency required to effect behavior change. Learning to modify behavior skillfully is a difficult task in its own right and beset with its own series of problems.

How to train people to conduct behavioral programs in institutions, classrooms, and the natural environment has been a topic of extensive research (see Berkowitz and Graziano, 1972; Patterson, 1976; and Yen and McIntire, 1976 for reviews). Typically, instructional techniques are employed whereby individuals who are to be trained are enrolled in didactic lectures, workshops, and extensive discussions of behavioral techniques and their implementation. With few exceptions, instructional techniques effect little or no behavior change in agents in the client's everyday experience (e.g., Katz, Johnson, and Gelfand, 1972; Pommer and Streedback, 1974; Quilitch, 1975).

Training conducted in the actual situation in which behavior is to be changed appears to be effective in altering actual behavior. In many programs, behavior-change agents receive feedback and social or token reinforcement (e.g., money, trading stamps) for their interactions with clients. Thus, the agents receive consequences for their own behaviors that are deemed appropriate to change a client's conduct. For example, psychiatric aides have received monetary incentives from a supervisor for contingently praising their patients or for interacting with them. Similarly, teachers have received points or trading stamps for attending to appropriate classroom behavior and for ignoring inappropriate behavior. Providing contingent consequences for staff and teacher behavior has led to marked behavior changes in their patients and students as well.

Occasionally, training is completed in simulated situations in which the staff or agents are exposed to models who perform the desired behaviors. Modeling sometimes is supplemented with role-playing, so that the individual can alternate in the roles of the client whose behavior is to be changed and of the agent who is changing it. Modeling and role-playing techniques, when used alone or in conjunction with incentives for performance, have been effective in improving the skills of behavior-change agents.

A problem in teaching individuals in contact with the client is that their behavior usually is not maintained once training is completed. Behavior will revert to baseline levels as soon as training and extrinsic consequences for performance are terminated (Kazdin, 1976b). The problem for nonprofessional agents of behavior change is that the existing system in which they may function may not actively support the desired behaviors. For example, teachers trained to conduct behavioral interventions in their classrooms often lose these skills. The rewards of being an effective teacher (e.g., seeing improvements in the students) apparently are too remote from the actual teaching behaviors to sustain performance. More immediate incentives are needed to maintain the teacher's conditioning, such as immediate consequences from supervisors or students. However, individuals who deliver consequences to the teachers need to receive reinforcing consequences themselves. Overall, it appears that in settings in which a hierarchy of individuals over the clients is found, accountability is required at all levels of staff; thus, contingent consequences need to be delivered for performance at each level. A change in only one level (e.g., the staff of an institution or the clients) may be transient unless the larger system within which these individuals behave is altered accordingly.

Conceptual Issues

Each of the considerations just discussed addresses specific areas for which the existing technology of applied behavior analysis needs to be refined. Within the larger field of behavior modification, more general issues are regarded by some authors as limitations of applied behavior analysis. They question the fundamental conceptual stance and assumptions about the nature of human behavior adopted by proponents of applied behavior analysis.

Applied behavior analysis relies heavily upon operant conditioning for its basic view of behavior, as evidenced by the emphasis on antecedent stimuli and consequences in altering behavior. This emphasis has been criticized, most notably by Bandura, whose theoretical position, referred to as social learning theory, contrasts with a strict environmentalism (Bandura, 1977). Bandura (1974) has challenged the operant conditioning model of human behavior because of its exclusive reliance upon environmental determinants. He has claimed that the strict environmentalism of operant conditioning perceives the individual as a passive agent merely subjected to the inevitable influences of his/her surroundings, an assumption that fails to recognize the existence of situations in which the individual can affect the environment. That is, influence is reciprocal. For example, social consequences (e.g., censure from others) that follow a person's actions may change those behaviors. However, the newly instilled behavior of the individual is likely to alter the environment in such a way as to produce different consequences (e.g., more positive reactions of others). Thus, although the consequences change the individual's behavior, the behavior in turn will alter subsequent consequences. Because of this constant give and take between the individual and environment, Bandura (1974) argues that emphasizing external determinants without recognizing the power of the individual to influence events is insufficient. One demonstration of a person's influence on his/her own behavior and surroundings is the ability to regulate behavior through processes termed self-control (see Chapter 9). Self-control refers to the different ways in which the individual can act to achieve particular self-selected ends. According to social learning theory, self-control dramatizes the influence that the individual rather than the environment exerts on behavior.

Another objection to the operant conditioning model of human behavior is its neglect of cognitive processes and their influence. By stressing environmental events, an individual's perceptions, expectancies, and thoughts about that environment are relegated to an ancillary or nugatory role. Cognitively oriented theorists have reiterated that the effect of external forces is heavily dependent on the individual's perceptions, thoughts, and reactions to them. Behavior therapy techniques designed to change cognitive processes, a relatively new aspect of behavior modification, have a strikingly different orientation from applied behavior analysis (see Chapter 9).

There is no doubt that fundamental differences do exist between operant conditioning and cognition-based learning models of human behavior in terms of self-control and cognitive processes in accounting for behavior. Some of the major conflicts, however, are a matter of emphasis even where there has been a tendency to draw sharp distinctions. For example, social learning theory gives due credit to external consequences and their influence on behavior. Similarly, operant conditioning does not merely maintain that individuals passively respond to environmental events. (Indeed, the very nature of reinforcement and punishment as dynamic processes would not allow such a simplistic analysis (Morse and Kelleher, 1977).) Proponents of operant conditioning have explicitly acknowledged the interaction between an individual and his/her external environment, thus illustrating the reciprocal relationship that Bandura has discussed. For example, Skinner (1971) has pointed out the phenomenon of counter-control, a reaction of individuals against others who exert coercive forms of control. This push and pull points to the interrelationship of behavior and the specific consequences it may generate. Other proponents of operant conditioning have recognized that when the environment affects an individual's behavior, the individual is likely to change in a fashion that will affect the environment (e.g., behavior of others) (Goldiamond and Dyrud, 1968).

Although the reciprocal interaction of the person and the environment has been noted by those employing applied behavior analysis, it is true that their interventions emphasize almost exclusively the manipulation of external events. The methodological heritage of the experimental analysis of behavior—to which applied behavior analysis adheres—dictates a focus on specific empirical operations and experimental manipulations and avoidance of intervening processes. Applied behavior analysis, with very few exceptions, has shown little interest in theoretical issues and in this way contrasts sharply with a social learning view of human behavior (Bandura, 1974, 1977).[8] Applied behavior analysis concentrates on producing behavior change in everyday settings, demonstrating those changes empirically, and determining the variables of which these changes are a function. The applied focus of the area has the greatest priority; accordingly, basic research and to a much greater extent theoretical issues play a minor role. If behavior change is shown to be of applied or clinical importance and these effects can be replicated, the task of applied behavior analysis is completed.

Debates about the role of the individual, cognitive influence on behavior, and reciprocal interaction have not been of great interest to investigators in applied behavior analysis because many of the issues have not proved themselves to be particularly helpful in designing treatment interventions. Actually, many of the variables and processes included in social learning theory—the use of instructions, vicarious reinforcement, modeling, and self-administration of reinforcing and punishing consequences—are fully embraced by applied behavior analysis. However, these notions are viewed from a conceptual standpoint, consistent with operant conditioning, that rejects the intervening variables so crucial to more cognitively oriented interpretations.

SUMMARY AND CONCLUSIONS

By the middle of the 1960s, operant techniques had come to be applied extensively for clinical purposes. The accumulation of clinical applications made it clear that applied research had a substantive focus and a methodological approach somewhat distinct from basic experimental research. Recognition of these differences led to the formal acknowledgment of applied behavior analysis as a separate research entity. This development is best marked by the appearance of the *Journal of Applied Behavior Analysis* in 1968. The journal not only provided a publication outlet for applied research but also defined the domain and characteristics of applied behavior analysis.

Applied behavior analysis is defined primarily by the social prominence of the behavior that is altered and by the methodology

---

[8] However, self-control and how it is to be interpreted has been paid considerable attention in that proponents of operant conditioning or social learning have debated the conceptualization and interpretation of self-control processes.

used to evaluate behavior change. Behaviors are selected because they figure in an individual's functioning rather than because they are conveniently measured laboratory responses. The methodology for evaluating the intervention includes both experimental and therapeutic criteria. To satisfy the experimental criterion, intrasubject-research designs are used to evaluate whether or not behavior change is a function of the intervention. To satisfy the therapeutic criterion, the applied value of behavior change is evaluated by assessing the impact of treatment on the individual's everyday functioning.

Contemporary applied behavior analysis consists of techniques mainly based upon reinforcement, punishment, and extinction. They have been applied to such populations as psychiatric patients, the mentally retarded, individuals in classroom settings, children in institutional settings, delinquents, adult offenders, drug addicts, alcoholics, and medical patients. Major research issues of concern to the overall evaluation of applied behavior analysis are the maintenance and transfer of behavior change, the failure of individuals to respond to reinforcement contingencies, and the behavior of administrators of contingencies. Preliminary research in each of these areas has suggested techniques to extend the effectiveness of operant techniques over time and across settings and clients.

9

Cognitive Behavior
Modification and
Self-Control

Contemporary applied behavior analysis represents one end of the spectrum of theoretical orientations within behavior modification. It evolved directly from operant conditioning, which has avoided mediating concepts and intervening variables in explaining behaviors and designing techniques to alter behavior. Both the substantive and methodological essentials of applied behavior analysis emphasize overt behavior and the environmental events that influence it. The methodological features of assessing and focusing on overt behavior characterize behavior modification in general and are not restricted to a specific area such as applied behavior analysis. However, major differences exist between conceptualizations of behavior and the techniques for altering it.

When compared with applied behavior analysis, cognition-based techniques (those which exploit cognitive processes to change overt behavior) are at the opposite end of the spectrum of behavior modification because internal, private, implicit, or covert events rather than the environment are manipulated to change behavior. (Yet, as is evidenced later in this chapter, select cognitively based techniques have been consistent with operant conceptualizations of behavior.) Most cognition-based techniques stress the individual's perception and interpretation of external events rather than the direct influence of the surroundings themselves.

The inclusion of cognition-based treatments represents a new direction in behavior modification that evolved out of dissatisfaction with stimulus-response explanations of behavior and in response to research that has demonstrated the role of thought processes in controlling behavior. Another reason for recognizing the importance of cognitive processes in behavior change is that many problems requiring therapeutic interventions are themselves based upon cognitions (e.g., obsessions, self-critical statements). Overt behaviors are not always the problem that serves as a basis for seeking treatments. Hence, focusing on thoughts, feelings, self-verbalizations, and other private events is required.

The influence of cognition on behavior has long been recognized throughout the field of psychology, and, naturally, the study of such processes has its own annals and antecedents. Because the history of cognitive processes and their role in behavior is beyond the scope of this volume, select antecedents within experimental and clinical psychology that illustrate the acceptance of cognitive techniques by behavior modifiers are highlighted.

Another recently acknowledged area within behavior modification is self-control. Self-control refers to procedures that clients can implement to modify their own behavior. The role of cognitive processes in behavior therapy and the development of self-control techniques can be seen as related, particularly when private events rather than overt behavior are the source of the client's problem. It is difficult to intervene therapeutically in such cases because the client is the only one who can detect the private event, by definition, and administer consequences for its control and alteration. The dilemma of modifying private events has helped stimulate research and treatment applications of self-control techniques.

EVOLUTION OF BEHAVIORISM AND
RELATIONSHIP TO COGNITIVE PROCESSES

The rise of therapeutic techniques based on cognition in behavior modification can be viewed as part of a much larger movement embraced by all of psychology. Indeed, the influence of cognitive processes in behavior modification has been quite delayed given the impact of these processes in other areas of psychology. The evolution of research and theory in cognitive psychology can be understood by examining developments in behaviorism. It is useful to examine the evolution of behaviorism, which can be traced through three overlapping stages (Koch, 1964), beginning with the formal inception of behaviorism and extending through contemporary research.

The initial stage can be marked by Watson's advocacy of radical changes in psychology, which strengthened the existing trend toward behaviorism. Watson of course exalted objectivism, emphasizing objective data rather than introspective reports of consciousness as the basis of a new psychology. Thus, he regarded consciousness and subjective states as inappropriate topics for scientific study. Mental events were thought to be explainable by stimulus-response laws and study of receptors, effectors, and nerve connections, i.e., physiological concomitants. Watsonian doctrine stressed learning as the central topic for psychology, especially stimulus-response learning as derived from Pavlov and Bechterev. The role of external influences on behavior was paramount; accordingly, behavior was assumed to be readily alterable through environmental manipulations. In general, many of the interrelated themes of early behaviorism were reactions to introspectionism and functionalism.

The second stage of behaviorism began to move beyond simple stimulus-response psychology and the descriptive level of analysis of learning. Several investigators, notably Hull, Tolman, and Mowrer, introduced concepts to mediate stimulus-response relationships. Intervening variables and complex theoretical structures were posed to explain how stimuli and responses were related. The account of learning began to stress variables within the organism (O) so that stimulus-response (S-R) psychology became S-O-R psychology. There were many reasons for this shift in emphasis. At the most general level, a simple stimulus-response analysis of behavior did not always account for complex learning phenomena in the laboratory (e.g., Goldstein, Krantz, and Rains, 1965).

Behaviorism still remained close to stimulus-response theory and, indeed, provided elaborate theoretical accounts with multiple levels of intervening variables to handle phenomena that might better have been handled by cognitive or perceptual theories. Much of the first 30 years of behaviorism in America was devoted to formulating laws of behavior based primarily upon animal research, which could help to illuminate the processes of human learning.

The third stage of behaviorist thought, as personified by such individuals as Robert C. Bolles, Gordon H. Bower, and Ulric Neisser, had interests in topics generally ignored by the other theorists of behaviorism, but not by other psychologists. For example, thinking, perception, complex motivational processes, and mediation in general would fall into this category. Many of the types of learning investigated in animals seemed inadequate for addressing the problems of human learning and thinking. Pavlov had recognized the differences between human and animal learning; both, he noted, shared conditioned reflex learning that resulted from direct exposure to unconditioned stimuli. This learning, which he had investigated extensively, was termed the *first signal system*. The difference in learning between humans and animals resulted from the property of language. As the unique human characteristic, speech, Pavlov believed, shaped learning by allowing humans to acquire responses without direct contact with unconditioned stimuli. He called this learning the *second signal system* (Pavlov, 1955). Pavlov's speculations about language anticipated subsequent concerns with the complex mental processes involved in human learning. As the inadequacy of simple stimulus-response theory became more and more evident, more experimenters became willing to embrace concepts that increasingly resembled those which classical behaviorism originally had rejected. However, the need to include mediating variables, private events, and conscious processes in the study of behavior had been evident from the inception of behaviorism and stimulus-response theory. Even Watson, who adhered to a particularly stringent stimulus-response version of learning and the complete rejection of private events, had to admit internal mechanisms to explain some behaviors. For example, he posited the notion of covert speech in his attempt to give an objective account of thinking.

The rejection of simple stimulus-response interpretations of learning became more explicit as time passed. For example, Guthrie, who began his work in the tradition of stimulus-response psychology, eventually arrived at the position that specification of stimuli alone was not sufficient to account for behavior. He believed that the learning process in humans required specification of the subject's perception of the stimuli and the meaning it conveyed (Guthrie, 1959).

The importance of cognition as a central theme in learning was first made explicit by Tolman. As noted in Chapter 3, Tolman emphasized that organisms developed cognitions about various stimuli and that the formation of these cognitions constituted learning. Rather than merely connecting stimuli and responses, as Watson had claimed, Tolman maintained that the organism learned strategies of responding and perceived general relationships in the environment. For example, he believed that to learn a maze, animals developed cognitive maps of the environmental stimuli. Tolman (1948) thought these cognitions and maps were responsible for behavior. He imagined the brain as

> ... far more like a map control room than it is like an old-fashioned telephone exchange. The stimuli, which are allowed in, are not connected by just simple one-to-one switches to the outgoing responses. Rather, the

incoming impulses are usually worked over and elaborated in the central control room into a tentative, cognitive like map of the environment. And it is this tentative map, including routes and paths and environmental relationships, which finally determines what responses, if any, the animal will finally release (Tolman, 1948, p. 192).

Other learning theorists in the behaviorist tradition have posed constructs and conceptualizations similar to those of Tolman to relate environment and overt behavior (e.g., Bugelski, 1956; Hull, 1943; Osgood, 1953).

Throughout the psychology of learning, debate has been continuous and spirited about what is learned, how learning takes place, and the role of mediating variables. The major positions taken may be reduced to cognitive versus stimulus-response theories of learning (Spence, 1950). The cognitive theorists believe that learning involves primarily the structuring of the cognitive field and perceiving relationships among environmental events (e.g., Koffka, 1935; Lewin, 1942; Tolman, 1934). Stimulus-response theorists have stressed stimulus-response connections, associations, and specific habits (e.g., Guthrie, 1935; Hull, 1943; Thorndike, 1932). Whereas cognitive theories tend to use mediating concepts, intervening variables, and private events (or central processing), stimulus-response theorists argue for the direct operation of environment on behavior (or peripheral processing).[1]

Within the behaviorist tradition, several attempts have been made to balance the different views by insisting upon the focus upon overt behavior and S-R functions while simultaneously recognizing mediating mechanisms. An interesting attempt to reconcile S-R psychology with cognition was made by George Miller, Eugene Galanter, and Karl Pribram. In their influential book, *Plans and the Structure of Behavior* (1960), they set forth a theory of "subjective behaviorism." The position was subjective (or rather cognitive) insofar as it recognized the influence of an individual's ideas and plans on behavior. Private events and processes that underlie overt behavior were acknowledged as important and legitimate areas of inquiry. The position was behavioristic because it stressed overt behavior and avoided the subjective methods characteristic of introspectionism.

Despite several different theories based upon cognition, there has been some reticence in behavior modification to embrace cognitive

---

[1] For detailed explanations of differences and similarities between specific cognitive and stimulus-response theories, see Kendler (1952) and Spence (1950).

variables as determinants of learning. A few influential writers sometimes are accorded partial responsibility for the relative neglect of cognitive factors. Of course, Watson's initial rejection of mental events as an area of scientific inquiry had considerable impact. Thorndike often is credited for having emphasized response consequences at the expense of cognitive events (Prentice, 1961), although this belief is probably a misrepresentation of his position (Farber, 1963). Thorndike noted that cognitive processes may well facilitate learning but are not essential for humans to learn (Thorndike, 1935). Similarly, Skinner has dismissed the role of cognitive events in accounting for learning, noting that a perception or private event is no more than a link in a causal chain leading to behavior (Skinner, 1953a).

In general, the discouragement in studying specific areas of inquiry that previously were regarded as unscientific has subsided. The expansion of interest to include cognitive variables in the scientific account of behavior is part of a much larger movement: cognitive factors have been recognized as important enough in explaining diverse phenomena in perception, language, memory, and thought processes to establish "cognitive psychology" as a formal area of study (Neisser, 1967; Weimer and Palermo, 1974).

Along with the reaction to narrow stimulus-response explanations of human behavior, another reason for the increasing interest in studying cognition may have been a function of dissatisfaction with methodological aspects of early behaviorism, particularly the search of general laws based upon animal research. For example, cognitive psychology, like humanistic psychology, rejects many notions of the supposed similarities in behavior and motivation between animals and people. Also, stimulus-response psychology by its nature implies that humans respond to the environment and certain laws of behavior in the same way as animals. Humanistic psychology emphasizes the uniqueness of the individual, conscious processes, and indeterminancy of behavior (free will, choice), which can be viewed as a reaction to movements such as behaviorism.[2]

---

[2] Humanism often is viewed as a reaction to tenets of both behaviorism and psychoanalysis, which share deterministic views and have stressed motivational processes outside of consciousness. Interestingly, the evolution of behaviorism and the increasing role accorded conscious components and determinants of behavior can be traced in an analogous fashion for psychoanalysis. The emergence of ego psychology within psychoanalysis represents the emphasis on ego functions (e.g., planning, problem-solving, conscious decision-making), which shifts the focus on unconscious, biological, instinctive sources of motivation (and primary processes) to cognitive influences (and secondary processes) (cf. Hartmann, 1964; Kris, 1952; Rapaport, 1951).

COGNITIVE PROCESSES IN HUMAN LEARNING RESEARCH[3]

Classical Conditioning

In human classical conditioning research, several investigators have noted that variables in the form of cognitions, perceptions, and interpretations of stimuli complicate the experimental results (Grings, 1965). In addition, specification of the nominal stimuli presented to the subject alone does not account for the results that are obtained. Subjects appear to design their own instructions that enhance or impede acquisition of conditioned responses. Also, subjects' expectancies about the occurrence of the unconditioned stimulus and its intensity relate directly to the performance of the conditioned response (cf. Branca, 1957; Chatterjee and Eriksen, 1962).

Ordinarily, subjects left to their own devices in laboratory conditioning experiments may construct idiosyncratic hypotheses and provide self-instructions that increase between-subject variability in learning (Gormezano, 1966). If information about the conditioning situation or specific instructions is provided by the investigator, the basic conditioning paradigm and its results are altered grossly (Bridger and Mandel, 1964; Cook and Harris, 1937; Razran, 1955; Spence, 1963). For example, extinction of a conditioned response can be immediate if the experimenter notifies the subject of the impending absence of subsequent pairings of conditioned and unconditioned stimuli (e.g., Grings and Lockhart, 1963; Notterman, Schoenfeld, and Bersh, 1952).

The influence of cognitive factors is considered to make a crucial difference between how humans and animals learn. For example, extinction of classically conditioned responses in the laboratory tends to occur much more rapidly among humans than animals (Spence, 1966). Indeed, without specific instructions, many individuals report making a discrimination in the shift from acquisition to extinction and may elect not to perform the conditioned response during extinction (cf. Spence, 1966; Spence, Rutledge, and Talbott, 1963).

Operant Conditioning

In operant conditioning research with humans, the role of cognition also has received attention, particularly in verbal conditioning. Aware-

---

[3] The influence of cognitive factors in human learning is a complex topic with an extensive literature. For details, the reader is referred to other sources (Mowrer, 1960b; Neisser, 1967; Weimer and Palermo, 1974).

ness of the reinforcement contingencies in learning and the possibility of learning taking place without awareness have been subjects of much study. Awareness usually is defined as the recognition of the relationship between behavior and its consequences. Various theories have been advanced to explain the relationship between learning and awareness. At one extreme are theorists who view awareness as necessary for learning and responsible for any behavior change that occurs in the conditioning situation. At the other are those who maintain that consequences act directly upon performance and that awareness is not mandatory for change (see Bandura, 1969, for a review). Reports indicate that learning is improved greatly when subjects can acknowledge or describe the contingency being managed. Indeed, depending upon how awareness is assessed, many experimenters have found that subjects who are aware of the contingencies demonstrate acquisition and extinction whereas those who are unaware do not (Dulany, 1962; Jacobson, 1969; Matarazzo, Saslow, and Pareis, 1960; Spielberger and DeNike, 1966).

Awareness also has been studied by providing instructions about the contingencies before the experiment rather than by measuring knowledge gained at the end of the study. As might be expected, instructions markedly influence responding to the contingencies. In many studies, the consequences for specific behaviors may have little or no effect until the subject is informed about the contingency. In addition, extensive research has shown that inaccurate instructions about the experimental situation may exert more control over behavior than the actual response-reinforcement relationship (Baron, Kaufman, and Stauber, 1969; Dulany, 1968). To many investigators of learning processes as well as proponents of behavior modification, the role of instructions in controlling behavior has constituted a powerful argument for the importance of cognitions in determining behavior.[4]

Awareness of the contingencies does not seem to be essential to all human operant learning. This phenomenon was demonstrated by the influential studies of Ralph F. Hefferline, who conditioned small muscle-movements in the thumb by providing reinforcing conse-

---

[4] To individuals who conceive of behavior in operant terms, instructions usually are accorded the status of discriminative stimuli that control behavior because of their association with reinforcing consequences. Thus the influence of instructions on behavior in an experiment does not violate an operant analysis. To proponents of operant conditioning, it only further demonstrates that antecedent stimuli and consequences control behavior. Mediating events in the form of intervening cognitive processes are avoided with this type of explanation.

quences (Hefferline, 1962; Hefferline and Bruno, 1971; Hefferline, Keenan, and Harford, 1959). He referred to the behavior as "covert" or "implicit" because the subject was unaware of it. Awareness of the contingency was regarded as unlikely because the response that was conditioned could not be detected by the subject.

Despite demonstrations of operant conditioning of subjects without their knowledge, the general view has been that consciousness is important in human operant learning. Some researchers have indicated that operant consequences in a verbal learning situation may be effective primarily because they communicate information to the subject about the contingencies rather than because they reflect the automatic and direct operation of reinforcement (Murray and Jacobson, 1971).

Observational or Vicarious Learning

Perhaps to a greater extent than classical and operant conditioning, observational or vicarious learning has emphasized the role of cognitive and symbolic processes. In observational learning, an individual can learn a response by merely watching someone else perform it. The observer need not perform the response in order to have learned it. Learning may be evinced long after the observational experience, for example, when appropriate environmental cues and incentive conditions evoke the response.

Although several interpretations of observational learning have been advanced, the one posed by Bandura (1969, 1977) has received the greatest attention. Bandura has attributed observational learning to several processes that influence the coding of modeling stimuli. This coding is based on verbal or imaginal representation of the modeled behavior (Bandura, 1970). An individual exposed to modeling stimuli can draw on the verbal or imaginal codes later and perform the response.

Explanation of observational learning does not necessarily require posing cognitive processes. To proponents of operant conditioning, for example, a history of reinforcement for imitative behavior and the discriminative stimuli under which such imitation occurs can explain modeling effects (Burgess, Burgess, and Esveldt, 1970; Gewirtz, 1971; Steinman, 1977). However, modeling has been widely discussed and investigated as a procedure based on cognition both in laboratory and applied research. Hence, in behavior modification, research on modeling has been regarded by many as a cognitive behavior-change technique.

This brief overview of specific areas of learning research merely begins to note the widespread attention that cognitive factors have been paid in different learning paradigms. Laboratory research has convincingly demonstrated the significance of cognition in the learning process. Because behavior modification techniques have drawn directly from findings in classical, operant, and vicarious conditioning, it is not surprising that extensions of learning phenomena to therapy also have incorporated cognitive factors.

COGNITIVE PROCESSES IN PERSONALITY
THEORY AND RESEARCH AND PSYCHOTHERAPY

Personality Theory and Research

Personality theories grouped under the rubric of phenomenological or self-theories are cognitive because they depend upon an individual's perceptions of the world as the primary impetus for behavior. Illustrative of this type of theory is Kelly's theory of personal constructs (Kelly, 1955), in which individuals categorize their experiences according to their own set of constructs and interpretations. Individuals generate constructs and hypotheses to anticipate and control events in their lives. These cognitions about the world account for one's behavior.

Personality theories based upon the psychology of learning also have relied upon cognitive notions in explaining behavior. For example, as reviewed in Chapter 5, Dollard and Miller (1950) formulated psychoanalytic theory and therapy in learning terms. Most of their interpretation was devoted to explaining processes such as mediated generalization and discrimination, verbal labels, and cue-producing responses. These cognitive processes were added to account for the complex mental processes that underlie human behavior. Rotter (1954) also posed a theory of personality based upon learning concepts. He stressed the power of the individual's expectancy of reinforcing consequences and his/her perception of events in the environment in shaping behavior. Expectancies and perceptions constitute important notions in cognitive psychology. Other notable personality theories emphasizing cognitive processes to account for behavior have been formulated by Allport, Lewin, Murray, Rogers, and others (cf. Hall and Lindzey, 1957; Mischel, 1971). Personality theory has had little direct impact on the development of behavior modification and, hence, is only mentioned peripherally.

Personality theories built on cognitive processes have stimulated research demonstrating the importance of cognitive determinants and correlates of behavior. For example, Rotter (1966), whose theory is based on a cognitive learning model, believes that an individual's perception of the relationship between his own behavior and its consequences may dictate behavior. He noted that some individuals tend to see themselves as the locus of control over their environment and attribute the events in their lives to their own behavior (referred to as internal control). In contrast, others see themselves as somewhat passive in that their lives are functions of luck, fate, chance, or the control of others (referred to as external control). Results of several experiments suggest that individuals who believe in different perceived loci of control also differ markedly in their responses to similar situations (e.g., exposure to painful stimuli) (Lefcourt, 1966; Phares, 1973). The theoretical importance of this locus of control is that it suggests the influence of perceptions about the world on actual behavior.[5]

Psychotherapy

The importance of cognitive processes in influencing behavior has been explored through various approaches in the context of traditional psychotherapy as well as in newer forms of interactive treatment experiences. In traditional therapy, techniques based upon phenomenological theories of personality attempt to change cognitions or perceptions of oneself or the world to modify behavior (e.g., Kelly, Rogers). The therapeutic goal is to alter an individual's reactions and interpretations of various events.

The specific therapeutic approaches that rely upon cognitive notions as the basis for therapeutic change are too numerous to review. Independent of specific psychotherapeutic techniques, several

---

[5] Actually, several areas within personality and psychological research have emphasized cognitive processes, including research on cognitive dissonance, attribution, person perception, and attitude change. These areas are important to mention in passing insofar as they illustrate the contemporary breadth of cognitive factors in psychological research. However, they have had little direct bearing on specific practices within behavior therapy. Attribution research has had a slight influence in stimulating work in behavior therapy. The laboratory work has confirmed that individuals can be made to assign their reactions to different environmental or self-generated cues and that these attributions control behavior (Davison, Tsujimoto, and Glaros, 1973; Schachter, 1964). However, extensions to therapy research have demonstrated that merely changing attributions is not very effective in altering the client's conduct. Thus, it is generally believed that alteration of attributions is not likely to be helpful in alleviating severe clinical problems (Bandura, 1977; Goldfried and Davison, 1976).

authors have suggested that psychotherapy, in general, works by altering cognitive or hypothetical mediating events of the client. For example, Shaffer (1947) emphasized the notion that therapeutic change results from the client's ability to learn to speak to him/herself in appropriate ways to control his/her own behavior. Thus, the client's internal verbalizations are credited with mediating behavior change. Similarly, Frank (1961) suggested that successful therapy entails altering the assumptions and perceptions that a person has about him/herself and his/her world. These assumptions will account for the maladaptive behaviors that led the client to seek therapy. The significance of these characterizations of psychotherapy is that they stress thinking, perception, and similar processes as a common denominator of therapeutic treatments.

The increased attention accorded cognitive processes is partially attested to by the emergence of many procedures similar to psychotherapy designed to expand awareness and to increase consciousness and human potential. In the late 1950s and early 1960s, encounter and marathon groups, sensitivity training, and other forms of human relations training have proliferated (see Gibb, 1971, for a review). Although there are many different procedures, each of which has multiple purposes, they share a similar general aim in increasing awareness of interpersonal processes. Implicit in the human relations training approach is the notion that cognitive and perceptual factors strongly influence individual behavior.[6]

The specific adoption of cognitive processes in clinical psychology as fundamental components of theoretical analysis of behavior or therapeutic practice has had little apparent impact on the development of cognitive techniques in behavior therapy. Indeed, from its inception, behavior therapy has tended to view "traditional" personality theory and therapy as a unified conceptual framework. Thus, various concepts and techniques that closely resemble contemporary features of behavior modification were rejected. It is important to

---

[6] Other related movements and interests have received wide notice and applications, notably, yoga, Zen, and meditation. Also, the popularity of biofeedback techniques to alter states of consciousness and the ingestion of psychotropic drugs might be considered as part of the rising tendency in Western society to seek consciousness-expanding experiences. However, the interest in cognitive influences expressed by practitioners of psychotherapy and behavior modification does not seem to derive from the consciousness-expanding experiences that have captured the popular imagination over the last decade. However, the concern with consciousness and its enhancement for handling the problems of everyday living seems to be apparent both in professional and lay circles.

mention the attention accorded cognitive factors in clinical psychology to establish a chronological relationship to concepts emerging in contemporary behavior modification. However, antecedents in clinical psychology do not appear to have exerted direct impact on theories or practices in behavior modification.

COGNITIVE PROCESSES IN BEHAVIOR MODIFICATION

The admission of cognitive processes to the field of behavior modification is not an entirely radical departure because private events and symbolic processes have been acknowledged for at least 20 years. Unlike classical behaviorism as espoused by Watson, behavior modification always has incorporated some private events in the form of images, self-statements, and thoughts. Although the focus and ultimate therapeutic goal of behavior modification consistently has been to alter overt behavior, this does not mean that private events cannot be used to effect such changes. For example, imagery has been employed in such techniques as conditioned reflex therapy (Salter, 1949), systematic desensitization (Wolpe, 1958), covert conditioning (Cautela, 1971a), and emotive imagery (Lazarus and Abramovitz, 1962).

Other applications also have exploited covert self-verbalizations. For example, Wolpe (1958) mentioned "thought-stopping," which is used to treat obsessions. The technique, devised by James G. Taylor in South Africa (Wolpe, 1958), entails the therapist shouting "Stop!" to interrupt the client's ruminations. Eventually, the client repeats "Stop!" to him/herself to control his/her own thoughts.[7] What should be noted is that self-statements and thoughts (i.e., the treatment technique and target focus) are private events and thus not clearly in the realm of "behavior," as that word is usually defined by the field.

Some investigators encouraged the explicit recognition and utilization of cognition-based strategies to change behavior. Breger and McGaugh's (1965) criticism of behavior therapy was written in part to show the inadequacy of stimulus-response learning theory in accounting for laboratory research and to illustrate the importance of cognitive variables in animal as well as human learning. For thera-

---

[7] Contemporary applications of thought-stopping can be traced to Taylor through the writings of Wolpe. However, earlier attempts to use related procedures have been recorded. As early as 1874, Lewis reported cases in which individuals with preoccupations of sexual indulgences were instructed to interrupt or stop their fantasies by engaging in competing thoughts (Lewis, 1874; Rosen and Orenstein, 1976).

peutic extrapolations, they suggested that it was more important to examine and alter "strategies" and "information" that guide an individual's behavior than to scrutinize discrete stimulus and response units minutely.

Select therapeutic applications also focused upon altering cognitive variables to change behavior. For example, in 1965, Peterson and London successfully toilet-trained a child by accompanying direct reinforcement with suggestions for, and information about, the behavior desired. These investigators advocated the study of cognitive-change strategies.

Although emphases upon cognitive and private events can be seen in many writings dealing with specific behavior modification techniques, there has been some resistance in endorsing behavior change techniques based upon cognitive theory. Some of this resistance may derive from the crucial role of cognitive and private events in orthodox psychoanalysis, which of course maintains that the unconscious dictates performance. The problems of verifying unconscious processes and tracing their influence have raised many of the methodological problems that behaviorists have tried to avoid. Because behavior modification has always been an endeavor antithetical to psychoanalytic theory and psychodynamics in general, its proponents may have overreacted in their eschewal of covert events. (Similarly, cognitive variables resemble the introspective concepts from which early behaviorists and their followers tried to free themselves.)

A major difficulty in considering covert events is methodological, because covert or private events such as images and thoughts can only be detected by the person who experiences them. This inability to assess covert processes represents an obstacle in behavior modification because the occurrence or absence of private events cannot be verified. Even if a covert event could be detected, it would still not be clear how to alter it. The principles of conditioning developed in the laboratory apply only to overt behaviors and do not suggest ways to influence thoughts, images, fantasies, and other private ideas.

Because an important issue in behavior therapy has been addressing difficulties in dealing with covert events, the problem has been paid some attention. Many practitioners of behavior modification maintain that cognitive, symbolic, and private events follow the same psychological laws as do overt behaviors. Skinner has long held this view, noting:

> We need not suppose that events which take place within the organism's skin have special properties for that reason. A private event may be dis-

tinguished by its limited accessibility but not, so far as we know, by any special structure or nature (Skinner, 1953a, p. 257).

Although private events might profitably be conceptualized as internalized responses, that approach did not suggest a way to affect covert events in service of behavior change. Having to detect internal responses by some external agent would result in private events largely being ignored.

A case for effective treatment of covert events through operant principles was set forth by Lloyd Homme (1965) in his article, "Control of Coverants: The Operants of the Mind." He extended the assumption that covert events might be viewed as responses and outlined techniques to change them. Homme called private events as "coverants" (a contraction of "covert" and "operant"), which included thoughts, images, reflections, fantasies, and similar notions commonly grouped together as mental or private events. He asserted that a technology of controlling coverants need not be impeded by the problems of detecting responses or of identifying reinforcers to follow their occurrence. The individual who experiences the coverant can detect it readily. Thus what remains is to identify the consequences that follow the event.

Homme suggested that coverants could be controlled by having the individual apply the consequences to himself, e.g., self-reinforcement. To define self-reinforcing events, he applied Premack's principle, which states that reinforcers are those events with a greater probability of occurring than the target response. Thus, to alter a covert event (or any overt behavior), an individual need only follow that behavior with some reinforcing consequence or high-probability behavior. The strength of a particular coverant might be increased by following it with some preferred activity. The significance of Homme's contribution was that it suggested a way to control private events and the ability of self-controlling operations to change behavior. His article synthesized control over cognitions and self-control operations and helped stimulate research in each of these areas. (Self-control is discussed below.)

COGNITIVE BEHAVIOR MODIFICATION:
OVERVIEW OF SELECT TECHNIQUES

The interest and movements toward the explicit consideration of private events in behavior therapy helped consolidate existing divisions within therapy that had developed somewhat independently. Several therapy techniques now included as part of behavior modification originally were not nurtured within behavior modification research. Rather, they were brought into the field as the interest in cognitive processes increased, and they have been classified as "cognitive behavior modification" or "cognitive therapy," meaning those specific techniques that consider private or internal events in their formulations (Beck, 1970, 1976; Meichenbaum, 1974).[8] They alter cognitions, usually in the form of thought patterns, to effect behavior change. Select techniques that have become subsumed under the rubric of behavior modification include rational-emotive therapy, self-instruction training, cognitive therapy, and problem-solving.

Rational-Emotive Therapy

Rational-emotive therapy, the creation of Albert Ellis, is based upon the notion that psychological disorders arise from faulty or irrational thought patterns. These patterns are evident in implicit verbalizations that arise from assumptions that an individual makes about the world and events that happen to him. Ellis was trained originally in psychodynamic theory and practice. During the course of his career, he became more concerned with cognitive factors in the client's present life than with his psychohistory and formulated rational-emotive theory as a result (Ellis, 1962).

Rational-emotive therapy and the process by which it effects change can best be understood by conceiving of behavior in terms of a chain of events, A-B-C-D-E (Ellis, 1971). A is an external event to which the individual is exposed, and B is a series of thoughts (implicit self-verbalizations) that the individual creates in response to A. C stands for the emotions and behaviors that result from B. D represents the therapist's attempts to alter what occurs at B. Finally, E stands for the altered emotions and behaviors that have resulted from D. The major purpose of the therapy is to examine the client's implicit self-verbalizations critically (at stage B) that account for his/her reactions to the environment (A). Therapy attempts to separate factual statements from the irrational conclusions derived from them.

---

[8] Cognitive behavior modification refers to techniques for altering thought processes to change behavior, a meaning that has been proposed only in the 1970s (Meichenbaum, 1974). The term "cognitive behavior modification" was used earlier by Staats in dealing with the cognitive deficit of reading ability in children with learning disabilities (Staats, Minke, Goodwin, and Landeen, 1967). Operant conditioning techniques were used to alter reading responses. Current usage denotes specific behavior-change techniques and an approach toward treatment rather than a particular response.

A commonly cited example that illustrates this distinction is the case of no longer being loved by a particular person. Because of the loss of love, an individual might believe or feel that he/she is worthless. However, because no longer being loved by a particular person does not lead rationally to the conclusion of worthlessness, rational-emotive therapy would focus on altering such illogical assumptions.

Ellis (1962) has identified many different irrational beliefs common to this culture that are the root of many problems he has seen in therapy. These include the belief that it is of the utmost necessity for an adult to be loved or approved by virtually every other important person in his/her life; that an adult must be totally competent, adequate, and efficient to be considered worthwhile; that life is miserable and disastrous when events are not turning out in the way one would like; and that human unhappiness depends upon external forces beyond the control of individuals. Therapy alters the client's beliefs or implicit self-statements, of the types excerpted above, along with other idiosyncratic interpretations of reality. The therapist may attack the irrational beliefs and demonstrate to the client that they need not be maintained.

In addition, the client is given "homework assignments" to practice appropriate self-verbalizations or interpretations of various situations. A client might write down situations that evoke negative emotions, the implicit thoughts that mediated these emotions, and various thoughts or self-statements that would affect these emotions. Also, the client is encouraged to confront feared objects or situations so that he/she can realize that the habitual thoughts are not accurate and can learn how to function better in those situations (e.g., looking for a job, seeking a date) (Ellis, 1970).

Although Ellis has promoted the efficacy and generality of rational-emotive therapy for more than 20 years (Ellis, 1957, 1962, 1971), it has only begun to receive attention in empirical research. This interest has stemmed from incorporating the technique into the realm of behavior modification, which has a strong analytical component. (Ellis supported his theory with evidence based on case studies.) Although research on rational-emotive therapy still is not extensive, the efficacy of the technique and specific component features considered important in behavior change have been confirmed. Several studies have suggested that rational-emotive therapy or procedures based on its tenets can alter anxiety associated with speech, examinations, and interpersonal encounters (e.g., DiLoreto, 1971; Montgomery, 1971; Trexler and Karst, 1972).

Self-Instruction Training

In this cognitive behavior modification technique, individuals are taught to make statements to themselves that will help change their behavior (Meichenbaum, 1973, 1975). Self-instruction overlaps somewhat with rational-emotive therapy but focuses less on belief systems and irrational assumptions and more on the ability of statements to direct or prompt one's own behavior and to guide performance.

This method for controlling psychological and physical disorders has some historical precedent (e.g., Coué, 1922; Johnson, 1946; Kelly, 1955; Korzybski, 1933; Shaffer, 1947). One of the greatest uses of self-verbalizations was made by Emile Coué (1857–1926), a psychotherapist who developed an extensive therapeutic practice in France based upon autosuggestion. First interested in hypnotism, Coué invented a technique of autosuggestion with which he treated individuals with such physical, psychophysiological, and psychological disorders as pain, paralysis, tumors, hernias, myopia, incontinence, insomnia, depression, and alcohol abuse (Coué, 1922, 1923). Treatment consisted of suggesting that the patient's condition would improve and prescribing a program of autosuggestion in which individuals repeatedly stated that they would improve (Coué, 1923). The role for autosuggestion was based on the assumption that believing something is a necessary and sufficient condition to bring about most changes in physical and psychological functioning. The most common phrase that individuals were instructed to declare was: "Day by day, in every way, I'm getting better and better" (Brooks, 1922, p. 27). Coué's writings indicate that he used autosuggestion to alleviate many disorders and a large number of patients sought out his/her clinic.

Research and theory of child development also have suggested the importance of self-verbalizations. Soviet psychologists in particular (see Luria, 1961 and Vygotsky, 1962) have stressed the influence of self-verbalizations in behavior, proposing that speech from others initially controls and directs a child's behavior. Only later will a child's own overt (and eventually covert) speech direct his own behavior.

Donald Meichenbaum has experimented with self-instructional training to alter various behaviors in laboratory and clinical settings. His initial interest in self-instruction training grew out of a study designed to train schizophrenic patients to engage in rational rather than irrational talk (Meichenbaum, 1969). In that project, Meichenbaum noted that patients occasionally instructed themselves aloud to engage in rational talk in the manner similar to the instructions that previously had been provided by the experimenter. These observations led to the direct study and manipulation of what individuals say to themselves as a form of treatment.

Self-instruction was first explored with impulsive children who tended to work rapidly and have high rates of error on specific tasks. Training consisted of having each child perform the task with the experimenter. As the experimenter performed several tasks, he stated various directives to guide performance. Essentially, the experimenter modeled thinking aloud and the verbalizations designed to control behavior (e.g., "work slowly," "be careful to do this," etc.). The verbalizations included questions about the nature of the task, plans of what to do next and how to go about the task, self-instructions, and self-praise when the task was performed correctly. Training consists of developing the self-instructional verbalization first aloud and then covertly in the client. At the end of training, the client can use the self-verbalizations to control behaviors beyond the tasks with which the skills were trained. In the case of the impulsive children, their training improved performance on several tasks reflecting intellectual and motor ability (Meichenbaum and Goodman, 1971).

Meichenbaum and his colleagues have completed numerous investigations demonstrating the effects of self-instruction training. Training individuals to speak covertly to themselves has been shown to be effective in reducing anxieties related to test-taking, harmless animals, and public speaking. Moreover, with psychiatric patients, self-instruction training has improved performance on tasks measuring competence in perception and abstraction as well as rational talk. Self-instruction training also has been applied to increase creativity (divergent thinking, originality, unusual uses of materials) and to reduce anxiety (see Meichenbaum, 1975, 1977 for reviews).

Meichenbaum's work appears to have exerted a major influence on the expansion of cognition-based therapies in general. His research has supported not only the efficacy of self-instruction training *per se* but is also consistent with other theorists, such as Ellis, who have argued the importance of self-verbalizations in behavior change. Meichenbaum's extensive program of research on self-instruction has helped to give cognitive therapies in general a more prominent place in contemporary behavior modification.

Cognitive Therapy

Although the words "cognitive therapy" might be used as a generic term synonymous with cognitive behavior modification, it has become associated with therapeutic methods espoused by Aaron Beck (1970, 1976). Cognitive therapy resembles the techniques of Ellis and Meichenbaum in that it concentrates on correcting self-verbalizations and thought patterns. Like Ellis, Beck was trained in psychodynamic therapy. From his observations of persons with affective disorders, especially depression, he came to view cognitive processes as the core of these maladies. A characteristic of many psychological problems is that they appear illogical and irrational when judged by someone other than the patient. Beck has suggested that from the standpoint of the patient's understanding and interpretation, many problems are quite logical. The logic may be rooted in assumptions and premises that are irrational in their own right, which led Beck to attempt to alter thought processes underlying specific problems and to formulate the notion of cognitive therapy (Beck, 1976).

To identify and change maladaptive cognitions, Beck has devised a sequence through which a patient must pass. First, the patient is trained to recognize idiosyncratic cognitions or "automatic thoughts" that reflect faulty or distorted appraisals of reality, and then to attend closely to them. Next, the client is trained to review the idiosyncratic cognitions objectively. He/she learns to realize that the offending thoughts bear no clear relation to reality; other interpretations may be available and just as logical. Following this step, the client is encouraged to correct cognitive distortions and deficiencies by reviewing fallacious thinking. Arbitrary inferences, overgeneralizations, magnification of the significance or meaning of events, and disregard of important events are analyzed for their consequences and questionable logic and corrected.

Cognitive therapy has been used with many populations, although relatively few controlled experiments have been conducted. Numerous studies suggest an effect of cognitive behavior modification therapies that supports Beck's approach and techniques. Outcome studies have shown the efficacy of cognitive therapy in treating depression (cf. Beck, 1976; Rush, Beck, Kovacs, and Hollon, 1977). At present, the specific mechanisms or components of treatment responsible for change have not been researched.

Problem-Solving

Independent of its therapeutic applications, problem-solving has been studied extensively in animal and human laboratory investigations dating back to Thorndike (cf. Riopelle, 1967). For example, effective problem-solving was described by John Dewey in his book, *How We Think* (1933). His strategy had five phases:

1. Recognizing the problem
2. Defining or specifying the difficulty
3. Suggesting possible solutions
4. Selecting an optimal solution from the suggestions
5. Executing the solution

Contemporary therapeutic applications of problem-solving closely resemble Dewey's prescription.

Thomas D'Zurilla and Marvin Goldfried (1971) suggested that training individuals in the general strategy of handling problems that normally confronted them would be appropriate for therapy. Problem-solving therapy is considered to be a cognitive behavior modification technique because it is directed toward building styles of reacting to various problems rather than focusing upon specific overt behaviors. The client is taught to think out how to solve particular problems. The therapist helps the client to compile a list of possible solutions and aids him/her in selecting the best solution among those choices for dealing with the difficulty at hand (D'Zurilla and Goldfried, 1971).

Treatment involves five steps for improving specific problem-solving skills, beginning with a general orientation that helps the client recognize problematic situations and his/her reactions to them and alerts him/her to which problems might be candidates for being solved. Second, translating the abstract or global statement of the problem into concrete features that can be dealt with specifically is required. Third, possible courses of actions are outlined, and the client is encouraged to generate all possible solutions that might be entertained. Fourth, the client must decide among the solutions by weighing the consequences of selecting a particular course of action. Finally, the client must execute the course of action that was decided upon and verify whether or not it was the best choice made. If the outcome is unsatisfactory, the client returns to an earlier stage in the sequence and entertains another solution.

The therapist helps the clients through each of the steps (Goldfried and Goldfried, 1975). Training begins by presenting the client with relatively simple problems. The therapist models the problem-solving method through each of the steps listed above. As training progresses, the problems increase in complexity and the therapist's role changes to that of a consultant by providing only occasional guidance in evaluating the real-life applications.

Experimental research has supported the importance of proceeding by specific steps when solving problems in laboratory contexts. Some applied research, as in industry for example, also has shown the importance of practicing the skills outlined above in reaching solutions to difficulties (e.g., Davis, 1973; Osborn, 1963). However, relatively few therapeutic applications of problem-solving have been reported in the literature (cf. Goldfried and Goldfried, 1975; Kifer, Lewis, Green, and Phillips, 1974; Mahoney, 1974).

Other Cognitive Behavior Modification Techniques

The domain of therapeutic techniques encompassed by cognitive behavior modification is not defined consistently; thus a definitive list of specific techniques is difficult to provide. However, treatments that might be counted are attribution therapy, acquisition of coping skills, thought-stopping, stress inoculation (engaging in self-suggestion and relaxation to handle stressful situations) and language behavior therapy (altering the connotations of words that elicit undesirable reactions) (Mahoney, 1974; Mahoney and Thoresen, 1974; Meichenbaum, 1974, 1975). Some investigators include any procedures that rely upon internal components, including imagery, thought patterns, and verbalizations (e.g., Mahoney, 1974; Meichenbaum, 1974). With such a broad definition, techniques such as systematic desensitization and covert conditioning can be admitted. Other investigators tend to restrict cognitive behavior modification to procedures that rely heavily upon thought processes (e.g., Beck, 1970).

SELF-CONTROL IN BEHAVIOR MODIFICATION

The major difficulty in treating problems involving covert or private events has been to detect such events and follow them with particular interventions. Homme's (1965) suggestion that clients themselves can detect disturbing covert events and might be able to alter them on their own has stimulated clinical applications.

The necessity of the client to control his/her own behavior transcends the alteration of covert events. Many overt behavior problems for which individuals seek treatment are maintained or fostered by everyday occurrences. If the behaviors are to be changed, events in the actual situations need to be scrutinized. For example, to stop overeating, it might be important to focus on day-to-day eating patterns. The need to concentrate on behavior in the natural environment has led to therapeutic innovations such as engaging friends and relatives to help operate programs or using self-control procedures (cf. Kanfer and Phillips, 1966). Because the client him/herself is in the best position to observe his/her own behavior, self-control techniques have received considerable attention.

The importance of self-control was recognized early in the evolution of behavior modification. Skinner (1953a) provided one of the first examples of self-control in the context of learning:

> . . . we must consider the possibility that the individual may control his own behavior. . . . When a man controls himself, chooses a course of action, thinks out the solution to a problem, or strives toward an increase in self-knowledge, he is *behaving*. He controls himself precisely as he would control the behavior of anyone else—through the manipulation of variables of which behavior is a function. His behavior in so doing is a proper object of analysis, and eventually it must be accounted for with variables lying outside the individual himself. (Skinner, 1953a, pp. 228–229).

He suggested that individuals frequently engage in one sort of response (*a controlled response*) that influences some other behavior they wish to alter (*a controlling response*). The controlling response manipulates variables of which the controlled response is a function. Based upon this formulation, he observed that individuals routinely practice several controlling behaviors as a form of self-control, including physical restraint and physical aid (e.g., holding a hand over one's mouth to offset laughing), changing the stimulus (e.g., moving away from someone who evokes specific kinds of feelings or behaviors), depriving and satiating oneself (e.g., deliberately eating or drinking to control subsequent performance), manipulating emotional conditions (e.g., "counting to ten" before reacting in anger), consuming drugs, alcohol, and other agents, providing contingent consequences, including positive reinforcers and punishers, and "doing something else" (e.g., performing behaviors that compete with or displace another response).

Contemporary definitions of self-control have adhered in varying degrees to aspects of Skinner's description. Many investigators maintain that self-control involves a change in the probability of performing responses that have both rewarding and aversive consequences (Kanfer and Phillips, 1970; Thoresen and Mahoney, 1974). An individual may respond in a way counter to obtaining some tempting and immediately reinforcing consequences. In other words, self-control is defined by performing a response that appears to act against the immediate contingencies.

Early behavioral applications of self-control were derived from operant conditioning formulations of behavior change. In 1962, Ferster, Nurnberger, and Levitt provided recommendations for self-control of overeating based on an operant conceptualization. They noted that the positively reinforcing aspects of eating immediately occur with the ingestion of food (e.g., taste). Excessive eating results in increased body fat, which is aversive to most individuals. A problem for the overeater is that the aversive consequences of eating are very delayed and thus exert relatively less impact on the eating response than do the immediately reinforcing consequences. Ferster et al. (1962) suggested that the individual who wishes to control overeating might be able to do something to bridge the time-span between the act of eating and the ultimate aversive consequences. Following Skinner's exposition, the subject might be able to perform a controlling response to limit overeating.

The recommendations advised that the therapist enumerate the aversive consequences of eating for a client and have him/her pair them (e.g., by verbal statement or imagery) with the thought or attempt to eat high-caloric foods. For example, situations could be described involving social rejection, difficulty in wearing certain clothes, and onset of specific physical disorders as a consequence of overindulging. Then the individual could invoke these unpleasant scenes at the point of eating fattening foods. Bringing the ultimately aversive consequences closer to the act of eating, it was reasoned, might help to reduce overeating.

In general, Ferster et al. (1962) provided a theoretical framework from which overeating might be viewed and specified practical recommendations that could be used in a self-control treatment program. The procedures attempted to bring eating under the control of a narrow range of stimuli (stimulus control), to lengthen the responses of eating during a given meal (extending chains of behavior), and to establish behaviors incompatible with eating (developing other prepotent responses). The report mentioned that the procedures had been used with a group of individuals with some success. However, specific results were not provided. Ferster, Nurnberger, and Levitt's report stimulated much new research in self-control and in the treatment of obesity.

In 1962, stimulus control also was suggested to improve the study habits of college students. Gilbert (pseudonym, Fox, 1962) reported how five students who had difficulty studying were helped by self-control. An operant analysis of study behavior served as the basis for the technique. Lack of studying was viewed as a problem in stimulus control in which specific times and places did not serve as a cue for working. It was brought under control by having individuals study for brief periods in specific settings at a designated time (e.g., library at 10:00 a.m.). Brief assignments initially were given, but these were gradually increased in length. Thus, shaping also was used to develop longer periods of studying. Results indicated an improvement in course grades for each of the five students, and suggested the promise of stimulus-control techniques that the individual client could apply on his/her own.

In the early 1960s Goldiamond began to use self-control as part of his work with stutterers in an attempt to have them control their speech disorder outside of the laboratory (Goldiamond, 1965c). He encouraged his clients to examine their everyday environment for influences which might exacerbate their stuttering and to modify their response to these influences as much as possible. Goldiamond eventually extended self-control training to individuals with other problems. In a major article published in 1965, Goldiamond (1965b) provided a rationale for self-control based upon operant conditioning and illustrated its application with specific cases. Self-control could be instilled by having individuals set up conditions for controlling their own behavior; they learned how to analyze the environment to determine for themselves the variables that should be altered. Goldiamond's cases were college students, some of whom had been referred to him by clinical psychologists. The clients studied the principles of operant conditioning before discussing the problem to be solved in treatment. After the clients were familiar with the basic concepts, Goldiamond instructed them how to implement a program. For example, to improve study habits, one subject learned to apply stimulus control to that behavior. The student was instructed to study at her desk and to perform no other behaviors there (e.g., letter writing, free reading). If distractions intruded during studying (e.g., daydreaming), she was instructed to leave her desk. The client reported increasing the duration of studying at her desk.

Goldiamond (1965b) also used self-control techniques to further interaction between spouses, improve handwriting, and increase academic performance. Each of these cases began with an analysis of the behaviors that needed to be changed, the stimulus conditions in which the behavior needed to be enacted, and consequences that could be provided to enhance performance. Usually the clients implemented the contingencies that were devised in consultation with the therapist. The procedures were based on self-control because the clients themselves manipulated their own environment to effect change.

Laboratory research on self-control that used children and adults began in the early 1960s. These investigations focused on how children can learn to control their own behavior, how patterns of self-evaluation and self-reward are transmitted across individuals, and how individuals can restrain from partaking of reinforcing events. One line of research, conducted by Walter Mischel and his colleagues, investigated variables that affect an individual's ability to delay consumption of reinforcers (e.g., Mischel and Gilligan, 1964; Mischel and Metzner, 1962; Mischel and Staub, 1965). Frederick H. Kanfer and co-workers explored the variables affecting the frequency of self-reward and the relation of self-reward to performance of specific experimental tasks (Kanfer, 1970). Bandura and his colleagues have examined the influence of observational learning on developing patterns of self-reward and self-evaluation and variables that affect acquisition of self-reward, including attributes and behaviors of the model, previous experiences of the observer, and other factors (e.g., Bandura, Grusec, and Menlove, 1966; Bandura and Kupers, 1964; Bandura and Whalen, 1966). These laboratory studies fall within the realm of child development and social learning theory in general rather than within the realm of clinical applications of self-control.

CONTEMPORARY APPLICATIONS
OF SELF-CONTROL TECHNIQUES[9]

Current Techniques

Self-control techniques constitute a major area of treatment within behavior modification. The major ones are stimulus control, self-observation, self-reinforcement and self-punishment, and alternate response training.[10]

Stimulus Control   Many behavioral excesses and deficits can be conceived as problems of stimulus control. Specific behaviors may or may not be performed in the presence of stimuli which, for most people, ordinarily control behavior. Three interrelated types of

---

[9] For a detailed review of self-control techniques and contemporary research issues, the reader may consult several sources (Goldfried and Merbaum, 1973; Mahoney and Thoresen, 1974; Thoresen and Mahoney, 1974).

[10] Self-instruction training and covert conditioning, described in this chapter and in Chapter 6, also are self-control procedures.

behavioral problems may result from maladaptive stimulus control. First, some behaviors are under control of stimuli that the client wishes to change (e.g., cigarette smoking). Second, some behaviors are not controlled by a narrow range of stimuli when such controls might be desirable (e.g., lack of studying, overeating). Third, some behaviors are under control of socially inappropriate stimuli (e.g., fetishism).

Typically, stimulus-control treatment proceeds by having the client identify the stimuli with which the behavior is (or should be) associated. As in the examples discussed earlier (Ferster et al., 1962; Fox, 1962; Goldiamond, 1965b), individuals are instructed to perform the designed behavior or approximations of that behavior only in the presence of a particular stimulus. Eventually, the behavior comes under control of the stimulus with which it has been systematically associated. Alternatively, when the goal is to eliminate control of the specific stimuli, the client is no longer under the control of stimuli that once increased the likelihood of the response. Stimulus control has been used alone or in combination with other procedures to alter such behaviors as insomnia, arousal to sadistic sexual fantasies, cigarette smoking, and overeating (Thoresen and Mahoney, 1974).

Self-Observation   Control over behavior can be enhanced by observing one's own conduct, although habitual actions frequently are outside of an individual's perception. Careful observation of behavior has been suggested to increase awareness of it and to indicate the extent to which that behavior deviates from some cultural or personal standard of performance (Kanfer, 1970). Self-observation may help individuals determine the extent to which their behavior is performed and to initiate action to alter undesired patterns. Whatever the mechanism of change, studies have shown that self-observation alters behavior in clinical and laboratory settings (Kazdin, 1974b).

As usually conducted, self-observation consists of having individuals collect data on some behavior they wish to change. For example, clients may observe the frequency with which they smoke cigarettes or that they experience self-defeating thoughts. Daily recording of the frequency of these behaviors has been shown to decrease or increase behavior, depending upon the desired direction of change. Self-observation has been shown to reduce such behaviors as tics, reported hallucinations, overeating, and cigarette smoking, and to increase such behaviors as paying attention in class, delivering approval to one's children, performing chores, working on an assignment, and participating in activities (Kazdin, 1974b). However, many studies have shown that this technique does not modify behavior. Moreover, if change is produced, it may be quite transient. In light of the variable results and transience of treatment effects, self-observation tends to not be used alone but rather to be supported by other self-control procedures.

Self-Reinforcement and Self-Punishment   Providing reinforcing or punishing consequences to oneself is a common self-control technique. The client is trained to administer consequences to him/herself rather than receiving them from an external agent. Self-reinforcement has received more attention than has self-punishment. The major requirement is that the individual be free to determine the responses that will be followed by the reinforcer and can reinforce him/herself at any time. To qualify as reinforcement, the behavior that is altered must increase in frequency.

Often self-reinforcement or punishment is preceded by an explanation of basic principles of operant conditioning. An external agent may implement the contingencies at first until the client can take over and work to change behavior or to maintain or accelerate the changes already achieved by the external agent. For the client to provide consequences contingently, he/she usually engages in self-observation.

As an illustration, the study behavior of elementary school students frequently has been improved with self-reinforcement contingencies. The program may begin with the teacher explaining the desired conduct and available reinforcers. Subsequently, the teacher may deliver reinforcers (e.g., tokens) for appropriate deportment and study habits. The children may observe their behavior along with the teacher. Eventually, the students administer points themselves at predetermined times or on cue from the teacher. Generally, self-administration of reinforcement improves attention and studying and reduces disruptive behavior in the classroom (Kazdin, 1975a).

Self-reinforcement and self-punishment have been used to treat outpatients and also have modified such behaviors as overeating, smoking, unsuitable social interactions and thoughts, drug abuse, and deviant sexual behavior (Jones, Nelson, and Kazdin, 1977; Mahoney and Thoresen, 1974). Many demonstrations of self-reinforcement and self-punishment are reports of case studies; therefore, the extent to which enduring changes can be made with clinical problems has not been established firmly.

Alternate Response Training   Learning to engage in responses that interfere with or replace another response to be moderated or eliminated is another self-control technique. The most frequent application of alternate response training is in the control of anxiety, with relaxation being the competing behavior. As usually implemented, a client relaxes deeply by contracting and relaxing different muscle groups (cf. Jacobson, 1938) or through self-suggestions of tranquility (cf. Schultz and Luthe, 1959). Once the client is trained to be calm, he/she applies this skill in any occurrence that evokes stress. Self-induced relaxation has been used to overcome anxieties elicited by the opposite sex, natural childbirth, interviews, public speaking, and other situations (e.g., D'Zurilla, 1969; Kondaš and Ščetnická, 1972; Zeisset, 1968).

Current Issues

Interpretation of Self-Control   There is some debate about the role of the individual in the self-control process and, indeed, the extent to which self-control is free from external determinants of behavior. The controversy primarily revolves around self-reinforcement and self-punishment operations. Investigators differ in the role accorded external forces in explaining self-control. Some investigators have asserted that self-reinforcement operations are relatively free from or at least appear to be free from environmental contingencies (Bandura, 1976; Thoresen and Mahoney, 1974). Others have maintained that external factors account both for engaging in self-reinforcement and for the effects this process has on behavior (Brigham, 1978; Catania, 1975; Goldiamond, 1976; Rachlin, 1974; Stuart, 1972). Aside from the conceptual debates, most results have not been documented in such a way as to allow ruling out the influence of external factors as the major component in self-reinforcement (Jones et al., 1977).

Role of External Factors in the Practice of Self-Control Although theoretical concepts of self-control vary in the role accorded external contingencies, it is generally agreed that environment is crucial in the execution of self-control in therapeutic applications. Evidence suggests that self-control contingencies depend upon surroundings to maintain their support. Thus, specific external consequences usually need to be programmed to follow the self-control responses so that adherence to the self-control regimen is maintained.

When individuals are taught to administer reinforcing consequences to themselves, they tend to reinforce their own behavior leniently or on a noncontingent basis (e.g., Felixbrod and O'Leary, 1973; McReynolds and Church, 1973; Santogrossi, O'Leary,

Romanczyk, and Kaufman, 1973). To avert the tendency to reward oneself noncontingently, some investigators have provided external reinforcement for adhering to the contingent delivery of consequences (e.g., Drabman, Spitalnik and O'Leary, 1973). It is unclear to what extent individuals can be trained to engage in self-control responses without the specific support of external contingencies.

Range of Applications of Self-Control Techniques   Another issue concerns the extent to which self-control techniques can be made available to various treatment populations. The method might be limited to those clients who have enough control to request treatment initially. Indeed, most self-control applications have been carried out with adults who seek treatment on an outpatient basis (Goldfried and Merbaum, 1973). Although self-control research and practice are in a relatively early stage of development, the results already have suggested that the techniques can be applied widely. Treatment groups have included adult and adolescent hospitalized psychiatric patients, children in elementary and junior high school classes, delinquents, and others. The range of problems treated includes addictive behaviors, various anxiety-based problems, poor academic performance, and bizarre conduct such as irrational verbalizations.

SUMMARY AND CONCLUSIONS

Behavior modification has begun to demonstrate an expanded interest in techniques that acknowledge cognitive processes. This attraction represents a departure from early endeavors in the field which, in the tradition of classical behaviorism, attempted to minimize the effect of private events and mediating processes. It also recognizes the growing dissatisfaction with nonmediating or simple stimulus-response formulations of human activity, supported by research confirming the importance of cognitive events on behavior. For example, the influence of cognition on overt behavior has been demonstrated in laboratory research in classical and operant conditioning and in vicarious learning. Cognitive processes also have been accorded an important role in research in personality and social psychology.

   The problems that arise in therapy often are based on thoughts, self-verbalizations, and other covert events. In these cases, private events are usually the primary focus of treatment. Because a number of investigators have attributed specific psychological disorders to maladaptive or illogical thoughts, perceptions, and interpretations of reality, cognitions and private events have been accorded etiological importance because they often underlie or aggravate specific overt behavioral problems (e.g., Beck, 1970, 1976; Ellis, 1957). Investigations of the role of self-instruction also have helped to attract interest in cognitive treatments. This research has demonstrated that giving oneself instructions can control behavior in laboratory and therapeutic contexts.

The term "cognitive behavior modification" encompasses treatments that attempt to change overt behavior by altering thoughts, interpretations, assumptions, and strategies of responding. The emergence of cognitive behavior modification stems from several autonomous lines of research and applications in therapy rather than a single historical progression or theoretical structure. Therapeutic approaches, derived somewhat independently, converged as their similarities were realized and as research began to support the basic assumptions of the influence of cognitive processes in ameliorating clinical problems. Some techniques labeled as cognitive behavior modification include rational-emotive therapy, self-instruction training, cognitive therapy, and problem-solving.

Another technique within behavior modification introduced because of the interest in cognitive processes is self-control. In cases in which the problem is a private event (e.g., obsession), only the individual client is in a position to monitor its occurrence. Impetus for self-control research stemmed partially from recommendations to conceive of private events as a behavior (covert behavior) and to follow such conduct with particular consequences as a therapeutic strategy. Because the client is the only one who can detect private events, he/she is the only one who can follow them with the most suitable consequences. Thus, the treatment of private events helped stimulate interest and research in self-control.

Interest in changing behavior in the client's natural environment also stimulated self-control research and applications. Most behaviors a person wishes to transform occur in everyday life and probably are best altered in his/her surroundings. Thus, others in contact with the client or the client him/herself can implement procedures to control behavior.

Self-control encompasses specific procedures that the client can employ to alter his/her own behavior. Major self-control techniques include stimulus control, self-observation, self-reinforcement and self-punishment, and alternate response training. These techniques have been implemented in the clinic and laboratory to foster or eliminate assorted behaviors.

10
Ethical and Legal Issues

The application of behavioral techniques offers promise in achieving various treatment, rehabilitation, and educational goals. However, as behavior principles are extended, people have become increasingly concerned about their misuse. Employing behavioral techniques to redesign institutional living of patients or inmates has stimulated considerable writings on client rights and mistreatment (Begelman, 1975; Davison and Stuart, 1975; Friedman, 1975; Goldiamond, 1974; Kassirer, 1974; Kittrie, 1971; Lucero, Vail, and Scherber, 1968; Mental Health Law Project, 1973; Stolz, 1976, in press; Wexler, 1973, 1975a, 1975b). Hypothetical extrapolations of behavioral principles to redesign society have led to even greater ethical concern because everyone's freedom seemingly is potentially jeopardized (London, 1969; Wheeler, 1973).

Before discussing salient ethical and legal issues, the domain of behavior modification needs to be clarified. Behavior modification or behavior therapy consists of a set of techniques and therapeutic procedures that have been derived from principles and experimental findings obtained in psychology. The techniques usually include interventions that are based upon rearranging social and environmental contingencies to alter client behavior. Thus, as a general statement, the domain of behavior modification is defined by the techniques that are employed and their basis in psychological research (Davison and Stuart, 1975; Martin, 1975; Stolz, Wienckowski, and Brown, 1975).

The defining characteristics of behavior modification have not always been recognized in ethical and legal criticisms of the field, partially because of a general confusion of terms. The term "behavior modification" has taken on a much broader meaning to individuals outside of the field and has been used to refer to the end product of an intervention (Davison and Stuart, 1975). Interventions of all sorts have as their end-goal the modification of behavior and, hence, have been grouped with behavioral techniques occasionally. For example, medical interventions such as psychosurgery have been included by individuals outside of the field as behavior modification techniques (Cooper, 1973; Subcommittee on Constitutional Rights, 1974), although these interventions are not classified by professionals as being a part of the narrowly and technically defined area of behavior modification. Chapter 10 addresses the ethical and legal issues as they pertain to this restricted definition of behavior modification.

The discussion of ethical issues encompasses behavioral control, the purposes for which behavior is controlled, the persons who exert control, and individual freedom. The section on legal issues reviews recent court decisions that have direct implications for implementing behavior modification programs. The issues addressed include infringements of rights associated with restricting the activity of individuals, use of aversive events, limitations of target behaviors that can be altered, rights of individuals to receive and to refuse treatment, and informed consent. Finally, means to ensure the protection of client rights are outlined.

ETHICAL ISSUES

The alteration of human conduct through psychological treatments has tremendous ethical implications. Behaviors, attitudes, thoughts, and feelings can be managed and, indeed, are regulated in order to effect therapeutic change; yet, decisions made in such contexts can precipitate outcomes far beyond the confines of clinical applications. The successes of behavior modification in treatment and rehabilitation have led to hypothetical extensions of behavioral principles to the behavior of whole segments of society at large. Some writers have viewed available behavior-change techniques as a preview or sample of a general technology of behavioral control easily appropriated for indiscriminate use (McConnell, 1970). Such an extrapolation from well-demonstrated, often limited methods in behavior modification to a broader technology of behavior change is purely a matter of conjecture. However, serious discussions of hypothetical extensions of behavioral principles (e.g., Skinner, 1948, 1953a, 1971) have incited fears that procedures used to change behavior of the populace, if available, could further despotic ends and control society (London, 1969; Wheeler, 1973). As presented in most ethical discussions, the frequently invoked "technology of behavior" refers merely to the extrapolation of principles to applications for which there is no empirical evidence. The techniques of controlling individuals cannot be made concrete because the so-called technology is hypothetical and extends beyond existing applications of behavior modification. Yet strong concern has been expressed by proponents of behavior modification, as well as its critics, who believe that continued research on behavior-change techniques will lead inevitably to a more general technology.

Behavioral Control

That advances in behavioral research will lead to control of the majority's behavior by a minority who know how to initiate mass conditioning entails several related issues, including the purposes for which behavior is controlled, the persons who will decide the ultimate purposes of this power, and the extent to which control over behavior interferes with individual freedom. The concerns subsumed under behavior control have become salient as references to a hypothetical technology of behavior have proliferated and have been widely disseminated. Popular books, most notably *Brave New World* and *A Clockwork Orange*, have presented vivid accounts of control and manipulation of behavior extending procedures well beyond their current level of efficacy and sophistication or have suggested practices that in some cases may even conflict with current knowledge (e.g., Burgess, 1963; Mitford, 1973). The concerns also have increased because of the number and types of behavioral control techniques that are available and the tendency to view all of these techniques as fundamentally similar and encompassed by the field of behavior modification. Some of the techniques represent extremely dramatic and irreversible changes in the individual (e.g., sterilization, psychosurgery) and are the subject of vehement protestations. It cannot be overemphasized that these techniques are not a part of behavior modification. They are not derived from psychological research nor do they depend upon reversible alterations of social and environmental conditions to change behavior. Rather, they represent medical and biological interventions that often produce irremediable changes in the individual. Although clear differences exist between medical and behavioral interventions, objections against severely intrusive interventions in one area tend to carry over to the other area in which they are less well founded.

Fears about molding behavior do not apply uniquely to behavior modification but extend to any procedures that influence behavior (London, 1969; Skinner, 1953a). Nevertheless, behavior modification has more frequently become a target of criticism than many other areas. Two reasons for this are that the field relies on such terms as "control," "conditioning," and "modification," and has drawn analogies to animal laboratory research, for which visions of manipulation and environmental control are great (Goldiamond, 1974). Indeed, a case could be made that it is not so much what behavior modifiers are doing that is objectionable as it is the way in which they refer to it (Woolfolk, Woolfolk, and Wilson, 1977).

In sciences other than psychology, technological developments make it necessary to deal with many of the same ethical issues of behavioral control. For example, research in biochemistry and pharmacology involves ethical decisions and questions about potential applications of drugs in chemical warfare and assassination attempts, or even actual occurrences of sustaining life "artificially" with drugs for protracted periods. Similarly, advances in electronics and neurophysiology and neurosurgery may foreshadow brain implantation techniques that could influence patterns of social interaction and conceivably control society (London, 1969). The advances in molecular biology that have led to the technology of recombinant DNA and its implications for genetic engineering are causing major reevaluations of the definition of human life and of the necessity of facing such issues as the possibility or desirability of human "perfectibility."

However, technology is hardly the lone culprit or a single agent of control. In general, technologies are subject to similar concerns about potential misuses that could result in human oppression. Social institutions such as government and law, business, education, religion, and the military explicitly attempt to alter behavior and all have specific techniques to achieve their ends (Skinner, 1953a). Behavioral control merely means influencing the behavior of others and is present in, if not the fabric of, ordinary social interactions with parents, teachers, employers, peers, spouses, siblings, and others. These agents provide or fail to provide consequences for behavior, which has some impact on one's own behavior. Thus, the behavior of every human in society is controlled in some way. The inevitability of control in everyday experience means that its existence is not the "fault" or harbinger of behavior modification or other advances in technology. As Skinner (1974) noted, "We cannot choose a way of life in which there is no control. We can only change the controlling conditions" (p. 190).

Purposes and Agents of Control

Behavioral technology, like any other technology, is ethically neutral: it has the potential for use and misuse. Thus, objections lie not with the techniques *per se*, but rather with the potential abuses. Critics have attacked the purposes for which behavior modification might be used and asked if such aims are consistent with the greater welfare of society. In one sense, behavior modification has no inherent goal. It consists of a series of principles and techniques and a methodological approach toward therapeutic change. It does not necessarily dictate how life *should* be led (Skinner, 1971).

Opponents of behavioral research and therapy frequently assume specific goals to be an inherent part of the technology. However, the scientifically validated principles that constitute behavior modification must be separated from applications that entail judgments about the ends toward which they should be directed. Behavior modification describes how to attain goals (e.g., develop certain behaviors) and not what the goals or purposes should be. A psychologist or psychiatrist might well be able to predict where preselected means or interim goals will lead and make recommendations to avert deleterious consequences, but initial selection of the goals is out of the professional's hands. However, the scientific study and practice of behavior change are not value-free (Gouldner, 1962; Krasner, 1965a; Rogers and Skinner, 1956; Szasz, 1960). Indeed, the values of the individual therapist influence the course of therapy and the beliefs of the client (London, 1964; Rosenthal, 1955). Although values enter in the process of behavior change, specialists in science and technology are not trained to dictate the social ends for which their specialties should be used.

In most applications of behavioral principles, the issue of purpose or goal is not raised because the psychologist or psychiatrist who uses the techniques is employed in a setting in which the goals have been determined in advance. Behavior modification programs in hospitals and institutions, schools, day-care treatment facilities, and prisons have many established goals already endorsed by society: for example, returning the individual to the community, accelerating academic performance, achieving self-help, communication, and social skills, and alleviating bizarre behaviors.[1]

In outpatient therapy, the client comes to treatment with a goal, namely, to attain some adaptive skill or to alleviate a problem that interferes with effective living. The primary job of the behavior

---

[1] One source of criticism that has come from within the field has been that the target behaviors of many treatment and educational settings may not be the most desirable ones to ameliorate (e.g., Davison, 1969; Kazdin, 1977d; Winett and Winkler, 1972). In many programs, the goals have been to change behaviors adaptive to the setting (e.g., performance of routine tasks of patients in a psychiatric hospital) rather than to focus directly upon community-relevant behaviors for effecting long-term therapeutic change.

modifier is to provide a means to obtain the goal insofar as it is consistent with the general social good. Freeing an individual from some behavior which impedes his/her functioning is consistent with the democratic value that, within limits, people should freely pursue their own objectives.

Another issue of behavioral control pertains to who would control society if a behavioral technology were available for societal design. It has been feared that one or a few individuals might be in charge of society and misuse behavioral techniques. Who should control society is not an issue especially related to behavior modification or advances in technology, because behavioral technology is compatible with any number of political philosophies. Indeed, the citizenry can be completely in charge of leadership and, essentially, exert ultimate control. A behavioral technology can help the citizenry achieve goals (e.g., alleviate social ills, improve education) with no actual change in who "controls" society. Society can determine the goals to be achieved and rely on technological advances to obtain them. There always exists the concern in society that despots will come to power, with their might fortified by mastery of the tools of behavioral control. Yet, tyrants—as well as more benign rulers or leaders—already have powerful control techniques (e.g., execution, imprisonment, manipulation of the press and other communications) at their disposal to achieve their goals.

Adversaries of behavior modification have charged that research advances will necessarily mean an abridgment of individual freedom. The deliberate control of human behavior may reduce an individual's ability to make choices. The extent to which an individual ever is free to behave counter to existing environmental forces has been discussed actively by philosophers, scientists, and theologians (e.g., Hospers, 1961; Novak, 1973; Platt, 1973; Rotenstreich, 1973; Skinner, 1953a). However, a source of agreement among those who posit or disclaim the existence of freedom is that it is exceedingly important for individuals to feel they are in fact free regardless of the actual situation (Kanfer and Phillips, 1970; Krasner and Ullmann, 1973; London, 1964).

The fear that behavioral techniques threaten to eliminate or reduce freedom and choice ignores much of the applied work in behavior modification. Applied work usually is conducted with individuals whose behaviors have been identified as problematic or ineffective in some way. The responses may represent deficits or behaviors that are not under the influence of socially accepted stimuli. Such clients ordinarily have a limited number of opportunities to obtain positive reinforcers in their life as a function of their deficient or "abnormal" behavior. Individuals who differ from those who function normally in society are confined by their behavioral deficits, in that their problems close off avenues of social participation.

Behavior modification aims to increase an individual's skills so that the number of response options are increased. By overcoming debilitating or imprisoning behaviors that restrict opportunities, the individual is freer to select from alternatives that were previously unavailable (Ball, 1968). As improved levels of performance are achieved, response opportunities increase. For individuals whose behavior is considered "normal," and even for those who are gifted in some way, behavior modification can increase performance or develop competencies beyond those already achieved. The increase in response opportunities and competencies expands the range of choices available (Goldiamond, 1965a). Thus, behavior modification, as typically applied, will increase rather than stifle individual freedom.

Despite the potential of behavior modification to increase an individual's freedom and choice, in actuality some individuals' rights have been abridged. For example, in cases in which persons are confined for treatment or are incarcerated, the abridgement of constitutional rights has been recognized. This issue, which is discussed below, points clearly to the need to define and protect rights of individuals who may be subjected to certain types of interventions and abuses. Once human rights are defined, behavioral interventions can be carried out within this framework.

There is little question that individual freedom can be abridged by a dictatorial ruler. It is unclear, however, to what extent behavioral techniques would enhance his powers. Governments already control such reinforcers as food, water, and money, and deliver aversive consequences such as imprisonment and immediate execution. The citizen has no counter-weapon for overcoming government control. In the structure of almost all governments are explicit means to handle individuals or groups whose purpose is to remove the government's control. The particular specter introduced by a behavioral technology is that a tyrannical leader will have even more means at his disposal to control the populace. While this may be true, the people still will have more means at their disposal to avert such domination.

Even if large-scale social control based on behavioral techniques were imminent, there would be sources of protection against oppression and they would be drawn directly from the techniques themselves. If the procedures provide would-be controllers with special powers, they also can be harnessed by individuals who are in danger of being controlled. The techniques can be applied toward self-selected ends that resist and run counter to the goals of the controllers. For example, members of resistance movements, political dissenters, and prisoners of war often engage in self-selected maneuvers against a coercive opposition. Self-control techniques, as described in Chapter 9, may be a partial deterrent against control by others (Platt, 1973; Skinner, 1971, 1973).

Awareness also is a partial defense against coercion and manipulation (Roe, 1959). Individuals who are unaware of those factors that control behavior are easily controlled by others. Although awareness alone cannot overcome oppression or counter overt manipulations (Bandura, 1974), consciousness of external forces of control can help individuals to resist their influence more effectively. Knowledge and awareness of the limits of controlling factors may be a condition for individual freedom (Ulrich, 1967).

LEGAL ISSUES

The increasing feasibility of behavior control made foreseeable by scientific advances has made the reexamination of many ethical issues necessary. As is often the case with such discussions, little in the way of resolution has transpired (Baer, 1970). However, several aspects of individual freedom have been the subjects of court rulings. Treatment programs in general have led to increased litigation, because their aim of controlling and modifying human behavior provides a potential conflict with individual rights guaranteed by the United States Constitution. When the state or its representatives in the form of responsible relatives or guardians intervenes and restricts an individual's choice of procedures (e.g., treatment, rehabilitation) designed to enhance his/her own or society's welfare, civil rights are being violated, a complex problem to resolve for individuals involuntarily confined in institutions. In other words, do institutionalized individuals have the right to accept or to refuse treatment? And to what extent can treatment curtail rights normally granted outside of institutional life?

In the United States, cases directly pertinent to behavior modification have been brought to trial only recently. Traditionally, the courts have assumed a "hands-off" policy, and institutions such as prisons and mental hospitals were free to determine at their discretion the type of treatment that would be used and the conditions under which treatment would be administered (Goodman, 1969; Martin, 1975; Wexler, 1973). This laissez-faire policy has been criticized because many therapeutic programs designed to help patients nevertheless have violated their constitutional rights (Ferleger, 1973). However, the courts have begun to intervene in questions of treatment. Despite the relative paucity of legal decisions and judicial pronouncements, the decisions already have far-reaching implications for behavior modification programs. The following discussion reviews major legal decisions in the United States as they pertain directly to the implementation of behavioral programs in institutional settings.

Contingent Consequences and Environmental Restraint

A common feature of institutional behavioral programs is the contingent delivery of reinforcing events to alter behavior. To increase the likelihood that clients will perform specific behaviors, a variety of reinforcers are made a part of the regimen. For example, in token economies for psychiatric patients, delinquents, and the mentally retarded, incentives may include such basic items as access to a room, bed, meals, clothes, or more commonly, improvements in each of these areas over very minimal facilities (i.e., a bed instead of a cot, a meal rather than a substitute food substance to maintain nutritive intake). Other events less essential to basic existence are made into rewards, such as engaging in recreational activities, walking on the institutional grounds, visiting home or a nearby community, having access to private space, and attending religious services. Patients may purchase these events with tokens earned for performing particular target behaviors. However, in most institutional settings that do not have behavior modification programs, these events are provided on a noncontingent basis, and the constitutionality of withholding positive events from patients has recently been addressed by the courts.

Wyatt v. *Stickney*, a landmark decision that set forth the conditions for client rights, arose from the reduction of employees in facilities for the mentally ill because of a paucity of funds in the state of Alabama. A complaint was made that adequate care was no longer provided in the facilities, and the case eventually extended to facilities for psychiatric patients and institutionalized retarded persons. Although the state argued that the adequacy of treatment was within the realm of judicial review, the court held that it could specify if care were adequate and what minimal conditions would be required for institutional treatment. Three major areas were decided to be substandard: conditions for humane psychological and physical environment, qualified and sufficient staff, and individualized treatment programs for each resident.

The ruling on conditions for humane psychological and physical environment affects what events may serve as reinforcers. The decision specified that patients had rights to a variety of events and activities, including a comfortable bed, a closet or locker for personal belongings, a chair, a bedside table, a nutritionally balanced meal, and the right to receive visitors, to wear one's own clothes, and to attend religious services. In addition, a patient is entitled to exercise several times weekly and to be outdoors regularly and frequently, to interact with the opposite sex, and to have a television set in the day room. For other populations, such as juvenile delinquents in residential facilities, the courts also have ruled that similar kinds of events and activities must be provided as part of the clients' basic rights (*Inmates of Boys' Training School* v. *Affleck; Morales* v. *Turman*).

These decisions mandating the basic amenities to which institutionalized populations are entitled have obvious implications for operant programs. In institutional programs, many amenities have been used as *privileges* (i.e., benefits enjoyed by a select group of individuals who earn them). The court rulings make these same amenities *rights* (i.e., conditions of life to which anyone has just claim). Items usually used for back-up events in token economies legally are not as readily available as they once were, at least on a contingent basis. The decisions do not completely rule out contingent administration of events to which patients are entitled by right. A patient may voluntarily yield his/her right by consent and have various events withheld as part of treatment. In addition, the rights of the individual may be waived in cases in which the state intervenes because the person is considered incompetent (Friedman, 1975). This sort of exception, which would allow use of specific events as reinforcers, needs to be decided on a case-by-case basis.

The numerous events that are now legally recognized as rights may present problems for operant programs. Indeed, some authors have noted difficulty in identifying reinforcers for select patients even before restrictions were placed upon withholding incentives (Ayllon and Azrin, 1965; Mitchell and Stoffelmayr, 1973). Many investigators have added highly attractive back-up events beyond those normally provided in the setting (e.g., Ayllon et al., in preparation; Milan, Wood, Williams, Rogers, Hampton, 1974). It is likely that the future use of reinforcement programs in institutionalized settings will have to be based on new reinforcing events over and above those basic rights to which the patients are entitled.

Court rulings affirming patients' rights to certain basic amenities are part of a broader guarantee that the environment to which an individual is committed will be the "least restrictive alternative" of confinement (Ennis and Friedman, 1973). The patient is entitled to the least restrictive conditions of confinement so that the interests of the public (confining someone of potential danger) and the individual (personal liberty) are balanced. The doctrine of the least restrictive alternative was first enumerated in *Lake* v. *Cameron.* In this case, an elderly woman unable to take care of herself was committed to a mental hospital, although she protested against institutionalization. A federal court of appeals decided that she was entitled to the least restrictive care available and that the state had to exhaust less restraining alternatives before deciding to select confinement. In general, the court ruled that deprivation of individual freedom should not exceed what is necessary for an individual's own protection. The doctrine of providing the least restrictive alternative has been extended to other cases, in which it was ruled that confinement of a patient to maximum security or even to full-time hospitalization is justified only when less constrained methods have proved ineffective (*Covington* v. *Harris*; *Lessard* v. *Schmidt*).

As a result of these decisions, institutions are now required to justify their choice of care given a patient. Because restrictions must be shown to be necessary, some conditions used in institutional behavior modification programs might conflict with the least restrictive alternative doctrine. Maintaining individuals on closed wards, confining them until certain behaviors are performed, limiting social interaction with other patients, or, indeed, in any way constraining their movement within the hospital might require justification. Also, the extent to which an individual's behavior is controlled by specific contingencies, the number of contingencies invoked, the duration of their implementation, alternatives provided for receiving back-up reinforcers outside of the specific contingencies, and similar issues all might have to be defended.

In many programs, deprivation of access to the hospital grounds or restrictive conditions within the ward serve as the basis for providing reinforcers. Initially, it is difficult, if not illogical, to argue against deprivation *per se* when discussing treatment of various institutionalized populations, because it is a fact of life. Most individuals who undergo behavior modification therapy are deprived in some significant way by virtue of their conduct (Lucero, Vail, and Scherber, 1968). Institutionalized clients are deprived of typical community living, friends, and freedom to choose where and how they would like to live. In educational settings, students with academic difficulties may have lost their access to employment, additional academic work, and economic opportunities as a direct function of their behavior. Delinquents fail to enjoy desirable features of social living because of their acts. Children and adults with debilitating albeit circumscribed problems also are deprived of moving about in life freely because of some thwarting behavior. One reason deprivation is a concept that usually provokes strong emotional reactions is that the social deficits and limited repertoires of the individuals exposed to treatment are not considered to be deprivations.

The social deprivation that individuals normally experience because of problem or deficient behaviors has to be weighed against any other restrictions that may be set as a function of treatment (Ball, 1968; Cahoon, 1968a). The issue of deprivation versus no deprivation would be relatively easy to decide. However, weighing the relative disadvantages of different types of deprivation and the duration of each type makes the issue more complex (Baer, 1970). For example, nonessential privileges versus social adequacy, short-term confinement for therapeutic purposes versus the remaining portion of one's life outside of the treatment facility, and the likelihood that a benign denial of amenities will alleviate a deprivation that has been the cause of much suffering are all possibilities to be contemplated (Kazdin, 1975a).

Deprivation can embrace both primary and secondary reinforcers. There is some agreement that primary reinforcers and other events essential to existence (e.g., food, water, shelter, physical activity, human contact) should not be restricted. In addition, as noted above, the courts have specified secondary reinforcers and nonessential events that should be provided, such as privacy and personal space. Therefore, the main question is what events can be withheld for purposes of rehabilitation. "Withholding" events is an appropriate term even when dealing with nonessential events or when luxuries such as extra recreation, extra furloughs from the facility, and extra food are introduced into a given treatment facility. If these events can be made available as part of a therapy, then one must question if they should be awarded on a noncontingent basis. In a sense, luxury items are already withheld from individuals participating in treatment.

Resolution of many aspects of deprivation, such as whether one deprivation or temporary abridgement of freedom justifies the goals of treatment, depends heavily upon ethical deliberation. Other questions, particularly those pertaining to decisions of treatment for a given client, need to be answered by empirical research. Perhaps the most important empirical question is whether depriving a client as a part of a treatment regimen is justifiable on the grounds of long-term treatment gains. The available evidence provides little information on the state of long-term gains resulting from any psychological techniques. Even with behavior modification techniques that have been successful in alleviating numerous problems, only sparse follow-up data are available (Kazdin and Wilson, 1978). Certain deprivations that are a part of behavior modification and other treatments—routine hospitalization, psychotherapy, incarceration—might be difficult to justify. The absence of clear evidence in support of the long-term effects of various treatments introduces obvious problems in carrying out the least restrictive alternative doctrine. The doctrine implies that *effective* treatments, differing in restrictiveness, do exist, and that the least restrictive treatment should be selected. However, evidence of posttreatment efficacy of even the most restrictive treatments is not especially convincing; indeed, no empirical research appears to have been conducted on selection of least restrictive and effective treatments.

Use of Aversive Techniques

Behavior modification tends to rely much more heavily on positive reinforcement than negative reinforcement and punishment. Aversive techniques, used as part of punishment and negative reinforcement contingencies, have become the subject of judicial review. Of course, punishing consequences have been used in psychiatry and penology long before the development of behavior modification. Physical restraint, confinement, beatings, mutilation, and similar penalties have been dispensed throughout history to discourage social deviance and occasionally such practices have been endorsed as treatment. For example, exorcism has been recommended to eliminate from one's body those evil spirits assumed to have been responsible for a mental disorder. In prisons, corporal punishment and unusually severe conditions of confinement have been common. Because of the pervasive use of aversive events and conditions, the courts have had a lengthy history of protecting individuals from cruel and unusual punishments and of determining what types of punishment can be used and their conditions of administration (Budd and Baer, 1976).

Many specific practices constitute punishment, as that term is commonly rather than technically used. For example, physically restraining, beating, and chaining individuals have often been means of disciplining institutionalized patients. Restraint has been used occasionally in behavior modification but only for very brief periods and typically as part of a larger program based upon positive reinforcement for adaptive behaviors. Other practices, such as corporal punishment or chaining individuals, are not part of behavior modification. The extensive use of corporal punishment in everyday life (e.g., in child rearing and education) may account for some of the stereotypic adverse public reaction to punishment when behavior modifiers include it as part of a therapeutic regime. In any case, legal rulings for punitive practices outside of the realm of behavior modification (primarily corporal punishment) are not reviewed here.

Judicial evaluations of punishments given in behavior modification programs have depended on the type of events employed and their conditions of administration. Obviously, the considerations that govern isolating an individual for a few minutes differ from those that govern the use of painful electric shock. For example, time-out from reinforcement consists of briefly removing an individual from sources of reinforcement. In time-out, the individual may be taken out of a situation and placed in seclusion, usually for only a few minutes. Courts have intervened in cases in which seclusion was a form of punishment. Specifically, extended periods of seclusion are not permissible and the client must have access to food, lighting, sanitation facilities, and so on (*Hancock* v. *Avery*). It has also been ruled that individuals have a right to be free from isolation (*Wyatt* v. *Stickney*).

Occasionally the courts have distinguished types of isolation and seclusion that may be used as punishment and have allowed for brief periods under close professional supervision for target behaviors such as those leading to physical harm or property destruction (*Morales* v. *Turman*; *Wyatt* v. *Stickney*). In other cases, this distinction has not been made and isolation for clients such as retarded persons has been ruled out (*New York State Association for Retarded Children* v. *Rockefeller*). Clear and consistent guidelines are not available for the use of time-out. Indeed, contradictory recommendations seem inevitable. For example, time-out as a brief period of isolation can be used; seclusion cannot be so employed. However, seclusion is sometimes defined by the courts as placing an individual in a locked room, which is what behavior modifiers occasionally mean by time-out.

Electric shock as a punishing stimulus is used infrequently. When applied, it is extremely effective for eliminating such behaviors as self-destruction (e.g., Lovaas and Simmons, 1969). The courts have delineated clear restrictions in the use of shock. For example, the *Wyatt* v. *Stickney* decision specified that for retarded clients, shock should only be called upon in extraordinary circumstances such as self-destructive behavior that was likely to inflict physical damage.

Moreover, shock could only be applied after other procedures had been attempted, after approval from a committee on human rights, and with informed consent from the client or a relative, and under direct order of the institution's superintendent. In general, the court ruled against shock for institutionalized residents without informed consent. It is understandable that shock should be restricted so carefully by the courts, because of its inherent risk and its potential for its being a cruel and unusual punishment as well as its history of misuse on many psychiatric patients.

Although behavior modifiers usually do not use drugs as punishers in applied settings, occasionally they have been delivered contingently to reduce obstreperous behavior. Certainly the most well-publicized program of this type was at a prison in Vacaville, California. Aggressive inmates were injected with succinycholine chloride (Anectine®), a preparation that inhibits respiration and simulates the experience of suffocation and drowning. The district court indicated that such punishment may have been unconstitutional because of a prisoner's claim that the drug was delivered involuntarily (*Mackey* v. *Procunier*).

In *Knecht* v. *Gillman*, administration of a drug inducing aversive states such as nausea with nonconsenting prisoners was ruled to be cruel and unusual punishment. The court mandated carefully monitored conditions under which drugs might be used—supervision by a physician, written consent of the client, and the opportunity to withdraw consent. In *Wyatt* v. *Stickney*, the court decided that drugs simply cannot be used as punishment.

The courts have not addressed some specific forms of punishment that are used in behavior modification. One procedure, overcorrection, consists of correcting the environmental effects of the inappropriate behavior and extensively rehearsing the correct forms of appropriate behavior (Foxx and Azrin, 1972, 1973a). For example, an individual who throws things might be punished by being made to pick up the things thrown (i.e., correcting the environmental effects) and to straighten up other areas beyond those disrupted by the original act (i.e., rehearsing correct behaviors). Another punishment is response-cost, which usually consists of withdrawing tokens contingent upon behavior.[2] Both overcorrection and response cost are common practices in behavior modification and probably constitute mild forms

---

[2] Ironically, the imposition of fines as practiced by the courts is a response-cost procedure.

of punishment in the eyes of the judiciary. Independent of the specific
procedures used. *' 　　　or element in the application of aversive
procedures s〔　　　　 〕btaining the consent of the client or a
guardian or r〔　　　　 〕resident is not able to give consent. The
issue of inform〔　　　 〕transcends the use of aversive techniques
and is addressed〔 〕

Selection of Targe〔　　 〕s

Most behaviors dea〔　　 〕n reinforcement programs have not raised
legal questions, no〔　　 〕ehaviors related to self-care, personal
hygiene, and particip〔　 〕n therapy groups. Some programs in psychiatric hospitals are b〔 〕d on work or job performance. Having
patients work for the institution without payment of the minimum
wage, termed "institutional peonage," is a widespread practice that is
not limited to behavior modification programs (Ennis and Friedman,
1973). It has been debated whether the client or institution reaps the
greater benefit from the work performed. Some authors have suggested that a patient's job can even be counter to therapeutic goals
because it may make retention of the patient essential to the institution and thus interfere with discharge (Bartlett, 1964; Mental Health
Law Project, 1973). In a large number of behavioral programs,
patients have engaged in work that maintains the effective operation
of the institution (e.g., Aitchison and Green, 1974; Arann and Horner,
1972; Ayllon and Azrin, 1965; Glickman, Plutchik, and Landau,
1973). Although work is seen as a way for patients to overcome
inactivity and institutionalization, concern has been expressed about
exploiting inmates. By making work part of a system of earning privileges, the possibility exists of coercing the patient to engage in work.

In an important decision on patient labor (*Jobson* v. *Henne*), the
court ruled that if the only purpose of patient work is saving money
and effort for the institution, and not therapeutic value, the individual's constitutional rights may be violated. (Involuntary servitude is
prohibited under the Thirteenth Amendment of the Constitution.) In
Jobson, it was decided that patients could be assigned some work if
the tasks were reasonably related to a therapeutic program.

The *Wyatt* v. *Stickney* decision was a more extreme ruling:
involuntary patient labor related to the operation or maintenance of
the hospital was not permitted even if the work had been deemed
therapeutic by the institution. Voluntary institutionalized work could
be performed by patients only if they were compensated with at least
the minimum wage. The court specified that incentives other than

wages (e.g., privileges or release from the hospital) could not be made contingent upon work performance. Thus, the use of work as a target behavior, at least as interpreted in many behavior modification programs, was ruled out because such labor violated patient's constitutional rights. Even if the patient volunteered for a job, performance of that task could not serve as a basis of obtaining privileges. However, the court did allow some exceptions to the rule against involuntary work. Patients could be assigned certain tasks viewed as therapeutic activities (e.g., vocational training) and jobs unrelated to hospital functioning (e.g., personal tasks such as making one's own bed). This distinction is consistent with the *Jobson* ruling, which stated that patients could be assigned normal housekeeping chores.

Right to Treatment

The client's right to treatment guarantees adequate care to individuals in institutional settings (cf. Birnbaum, 1960, 1969, 1972; Burris, 1969), even in instances of involuntary confinement. If an individual's freedom to receive therapy is denied through confinement, some intervention must be provided to return him/her to the community eventually. The right to treatment is also a part of due process of law. A patient should not be deprived indefinitely of his/her freedom in a "mental prison" if he/she is not receiving adequate care and treatment (Birnbaum, 1969).

In *Rouse v. Cameron*, a landmark case pertaining to the right to treatment, a patient was committed to a psychiatric hospital after determination that he was not guilty (of carrying a dangerous weapon) for reasons of insanity. He was hospitalized for longer than the term that would have resulted from criminal conviction. He attempted to obtain release, alleging that he received no psychiatric treatment. The outcome of the case was the ruling that a patient committed to a psychiatric hospital has a right to receive adequate treatment for the disorder that justified his commitment. Interestingly, the court ruled that the hospital need not show that the treatment will cure or improve the patient but only that it is a *bona fide* attempt to do so. A treatment must be provided that is adequate in light of present knowledge. The court cannot determine if care is optimal but only if it is reasonable when weighed against the patient's circumstances (cf. *Jones v. Robinson*; *Tribby v. Cameron*).

In another case, the court indicated that a patient was not receiving adequate psychiatric treatment, as defined by expert testimony (*Nason v. Superintendent of Bridgewater State Hospital*). The court ordered that suitable treatment be administered rather than custodial care and retained jurisdiction over the case to ensure that its mandate was followed. Similarly, the *Wyatt* v. *Stickney* ruling stipulated that involuntarily committed patients have a constitutional right to receive individual treatment that provides an opportunity to be cured or to improve one's psychiatric condition.

Other rulings have expanded upon the right to treatment, even asserting that patients cannot be confined without treatment if they present no danger to themselves or others (*Donaldson* v. *O'Connor*). Confinement without treatment is tantamount to unlawful imprisonment (*Renelli* v. *Department of Mental Hygiene*). The right to treatment has been extended to cases of sexual psychopaths, drug addicts, and juveniles (*Creek* v. *Stone*; *Millard* v. *Cameron*; *Morales* v. *Turman*; *People ex rel. Blunt* v. *Narcotic Addiction Control Commission*).

Guaranteeing a right to adequate treatment involves several problems. The definition of "adequate treatment," the methods by which that adequacy will be determined for a given patient, and the measures of therapeutic effects can all be disputed. Procedurally, the right may entail designing programs to improve the staff, individualizing treatment plans, systematically assessing program effects, and, in general, ensuring accountability on the part of the institution. Although the patient's right has been defined, many facilities might not be prepared to begin to evaluate the efficacy of treatment empirically.

Refusal of Treatment

Although the confined person has a right to treatment, it is possible that such care may abridge individual rights. Sometimes the individual's right may be temporarily curtailed. For example, in *Peek* v. *Ciccone,* a prisoner claimed that enforced administration of a tranquilizer was unlawful on the grounds that it was cruel and unusual punishment (in violation of the Eighth Amendment). Similarly, in *Haynes* v. *Harris*, an inmate protested that a medical treatment was being forced upon him. His complaint was directed primarily at the methods of prison discipline and supervision. In these cases, the courts ruled that since the purpose of commitment was treatment, all available treatments could be provided. In other cases, for example, in the treatment of drug addicts, the courts have ruled that compulsory practices do not violate constitutional rights (*In re Spadafora*). Indeed, the court has stated that individuals may have to sacrifice their liberty to benefit from treatment (*People ex rel. Stutz* v. *Conboy*).

Some inconsistencies can be noted in the debate on abridging individual rights with enforced treatment. For example, in *Winters* v. *Miller*, a psychiatric patient protested the chemotherapy she was forced to undergo because the use of drugs violated her religious convictions (as a Christian Scientist). The court noted that the interest of society was not clearly served by forcing unwanted medication and upheld her individual rights. Similarly, in *Knecht* v. *Gillman* and *Mackey* v. *Procunier*, the court has ruled against the use of drugs as part of aversion therapy (i.e., apomorphine, which induces vomiting, and succinycholine, which induces sensations of suffocating, drowning, and dying). The court also has denied authorization of electroshock with nonconsenting psychiatric patients (*New York City Health and Hospital Corporation* v. *Stein*). In general, the decision to override a patient's rights depends upon balancing the interest of the individual and society. Personal rights are most likely to be sacrificed when the state wishes to protect against some grave and immediate danger (cf. *Holmes* v. *Silver Cross Hospital of Joliet, Illinois*).

Individuals may refuse a treatment to which they are assigned, yet unwillingness does not necessarily absolve the treatment facility from responsibility for the client's welfare. For example, in one case, damages were awarded to a patient who allegedly refused treatment (*Whittree* v. *State*). The court implied that the hospital was obligated to provide treatment despite the patient's objections. Hence, the right to refuse treatment is complicated by an institution's responsibilities to attempt to improve the client and to protect itself against charges of negligence.

The assignment of individuals to treatment may conflict with due process. One of the more prominent cases pertaining to the remanding of individuals to treatment was raised in litigation against the Special Treatment and Rehabilitation Training (START) program, in which intractible prisoners were transferred to a special facility for a behavioral program (*Clonce* v. *Richardson*). Not all of the issues raised were considered because the program was terminated. However, the challenge from prisoners that transfer to the new facility violated the inmates' due process of law was addressed. Ruling in favor of the inmates, the court decided that the move to the START program involved a major change in their conditions of confinement, including a substantial loss of privileges such as denial of personal articles, the ability to receive and possess religious and legal materials, the opportunity to eat a satisfactory amount of food, and other conditions the inmates characterized as unbearable.

In general, the assignment of individuals to treatment is problematic for treatment facilities and complicated for courts to resolve. All of the issues already discussed in this section—including least restrictive environment, the individual's right to treatment, and right to refuse treatment—must be taken into account in this sort of litigation.

Informed Consent

Some of the difficulties inherent in the necessity to improve behavior by confining clients can be eliminated if the client provides his/her consent for receiving treatment. For example, the client can agree to waive rights of access to various aspects of hospital life (e.g., taking walks on the grounds) to have them serve as reinforcers for achieving some therapeutic goal. Essentially, the client can consent to the restrictions imposed by the intervention. Obtaining informed consent would seem to resolve many of the legalities of infringing on a client's rights, but it should be emphasized that ambiguities about informed consent and the precise role it can occupy in treatment of involuntarily confined populations are legion (Kassirer, 1974; Stolz, in press; Wexler, 1975a).

Consent involves three major elements: competence, knowledge, and volition (Friedman, 1975; Martin, 1975; Wexler, 1975a). Competence refers to the individual's ability to make a well-reasoned decision, to understand the nature of the choice presented, and to give consent meaningfully. It is questionable if certain individuals in behavior modification programs (some psychiatric patients, children, and retarded persons) are capable of providing truly informed consent. For these individuals, parents or guardians can give permission.

Even when client consent can be sought and obtained, it is unclear if such means are an adequate protection. This dilemma was illustrated in a study of informed consent, in which psychiatric patients who signed voluntary admissions forms to a psychiatric hospital were queried (Palmer and Wohl, 1972). Sixty percent of the patients questioned were unable to recall signing the admission form within 10 days after admission. Thirty-three percent of the patients did not recall or could not recall accurately the content of the form. Some of the patients even denied having signed it. Such results call into question either the competence of the patients or the procedures employed to secure consent.

The second element of consent is knowledge, which includes understanding the nature of treatment, the alternatives available, and the potential benefits and risks involved. It is difficult, if not impossible, to provide complete information to meet the requirements for a knowledgeable decision given that so little is known about many of the available treatments. An extremely important feature of consent is that the individual is aware that he/she does not have to give consent and that once given, consent can be revoked.

The third element of consent is volition—an individual must agree to be treated. Of course, agreement to participate must not be given under duress. Thus, giving a patient a "choice" between undergoing a particular treatment or suffering some sort of deprivation as a consequence is not an adequate or legal base for consent. It is difficult to ensure that individuals involuntarily confined to an institutional setting agree to participate in a program without some duress. In prisons and psychiatric hospitals, inmates may feel compelled to be in a program because of anticipated long-term gains from favorable evaluation by staff and administration whose opinions play an important role in release. For example, in one program in which mental patients consented to take a drug with unpleasant psychological and physiological side effects, several individuals claimed they participated because they felt pressure to do so from the doctor's request (Mattocks and Jew, undated).

Willing consent may be impossible because the institutional environment for an involuntarily confined patient may be inherently coercive, i.e., privileges and release may depend upon the individual's cooperation. Indeed, this was a conclusion reached in a landmark decision, *Kaimowitz* v. *Michigan Department of Mental Health*, in which the use of psychosurgery to control aggressive behavior of a psychiatric patient was examined. The court ruled that truly voluntary and informed consent was not possible, as the status of the patient militated against voluntary consent. Also, the nature of the experimental intervention (i.e., a dangerous and irreversible treatment) and lack of available information about its benefits and risks made "informed" consent impossible. Moreover, the treatment was regarded as unconstitutional independent of consent. The implication of the *Kaimowitz* decision is that involuntarily confined patients are not in a position to give voluntary consent because of the inherently coercive nature of institutional environments. Wexler (1975a, 1975b) has challenged the notion that involuntarily committed patients are necessarily forced by their status to comply with the institution. If the lure of release is regarded as inherently coercive, all therapy for involuntarily institutionalized persons would be coercive despite their expressed desire or consent.

The issue of consent involves a host of problems for treatment in general and for reinforcement practices in particular. Even if the client initially consents to a particular treatment, it appears that he/she may be allowed to withdraw consent at will (*Knecht* v. *Gillman*). For example, in a reinforcement program, a hospitalized patient may waive the right for meals, adequate sleeping quarters, and ground privileges and have them delivered contingently. Yet if the patient does not earn the events that he/she consented to waive as rights, he/she may withdraw consent and terminate the program, which may be easier than performing the behaviors that would earn the reinforcing events (Wexler, 1975b). From the standpoint of maintaining effective programs, obtaining consent does not guarantee that the contingencies could be managed adequately given that consent could be revoked. Because of the nature of the events that are absolute rather than contingent rights and the patient's ability to withdraw consent, therapies will have to rely heavily on highly attractive supplementary incentives.

REGULATION OF INTERVENTIONS
AND PROTECTION OF CLIENT RIGHTS

The guidelines issuing from the court decisions just described are the first statements of individual rights for persons being treated for problem behaviors, particularly for patients who are involuntarily committed and for prisoners. However, they are not the only attempts to protect humans from excesses of clinical interventions. International codes have been ratified to regulate certain forms of research and treatments with human subjects. For example, in response to the Nazi atrocities of World War II, a code of ethics was developed at Nuremberg trials to govern medical research. It specified that human subjects should not experience unnecessary suffering and injury, that they should not undergo procedures that risk injury or death, that voluntary consent from the subject should be provided, that the subject could withdraw at any time, and that the investigators should be qualified scientifically to conduct the research. Similar recommendations were drafted in the Declaration of Helsinki, which provided guidelines for protecting human subjects in medical experiments (World Medical Association, 1964). As with the Nuremberg codes, the Declaration stressed the need for informed consent, the opportunity for the subject to withdraw from the study, the minimization of risks, and the supervision of scientifically qualified researchers.

In the United States, federal regulations for medical and psychological experimentation have been enacted. For example, in 1966, the Surgeon General of the Public Health Service required that institutions that received federal monies for research establish review committees to consider subjects' rights and to ensure that informed consent was procured for the proposed research. This policy was extended to cover not only clinical studies but all research in the behavioral and social sciences (cf. Stolz, 1978). The Public Health Service guidelines for research have been revised and elaborated periodically (Curran, 1969). The most recent version outlines procedures that rest on institutional review of the investigator's proposed research along with review of the staff of the support agency (United States Department of Health, Education, and Welfare, 1972). Particular safeguards for client rights have been written into the guidelines. Recommendations have been made to ensure informed consent, protection of confidentiality, protection against physical, psychological, social, and legal risks, and specification of risks, benefits, and likely ratio of risks to benefits.

In 1974, Congress mandated a special commission to draft ethical guidelines for research with human subjects. The National Commission for the Protection of Human Subjects in Biomedical and Behavioral Research was established to examine research and applications in areas in which human rights have been or might be infringed upon. The Commission has studied and made recommendations for practices in research with fetuses, prisoners, individuals considered for psychosurgery, and children, with prospects for other groups as well.

Professional organizations also have set forth guidelines to protect human subjects in research and experimentation. For example, the American Psychological Association (APA) has specified basic principles designed to protect subjects who participate in behavorial research (Ad Hoc Committee on Ethical Standards in Psychological Research, 1973). Individuals must be informed of features of the research that might influence willingness to participate and their ability to terminate participation. Experimenters must avoid exposing subjects to physical and mental discomfort, harm, or danger, and must secure consent if the possibility of experiencing such risks exists.

In 1973, the American Psychiatric Association approved recommendations to cover the practice of psychiatry (American Psychiatric Association Committee on Ethics, 1973). The code pertains to the conduct of treatment and the resulting interactions with patients and colleagues rather than research and experimentation. The protection of confidentiality, given the sensitive nature of the material provided by the patient, and the adherence to a professional relationship with the patient are emphasized. The recommendations also address such topics as the policy for referral of patients to colleagues, competence of psychiatrists, the relationship of psychiatrists to other mental health professionals, and the assessment of fees.

In 1974, the APA formed a Commission on Behavior Modification to look into controversial ethical and legal issues involved with implementing treatment and conducting research in behavior modification (Stolz, 1977).[3] The Commission considered a wide range of issues—for example, accountability of treatment to clients, definition of the client's problem, selection of the goals and specific intervention for treatment, protection of client rights and confidentiality, and evaluation of the quality of treatment. The Commission decided that issuing guidelines for behavior modification was undesirable. It maintained that behavior modification was in no more need of ethical regulation and no more subject to abuse than were other intervention procedures. The primary recommendation of the Commission was that persons engaged in any psychological interventions adhere to the ethical codes and standards of their respective professions. In addition, several points were raised for consideration by individuals who implement treatment in order to sensitize therapists to the necessity of presenting treatment and its goals explicitly, protecting client rights, and evaluating treatment outcome.

Within the field of behavior modification, additional efforts have been made to regulate practice. In 1977, the Association for Advancement of Behavior Therapy (AABT), the major organization of behavior therapists in the United States, issued a statement on ethical practice for the organization (*Association for Advancement of Behavior Therapy Newsletter,* 1977). Like the American Psychological Association Commission, the committee[4] in charge of the

---

[3] Members of the Commission were Sidney W. Bijou (Chairperson), Jerome Frank, Paul R. Friedman, James G. Holland, Leonard Krasner, Hugh Lacey, Stephanie B. Stolz, David Wexler, and G. Terence Wilson.

[4] Members were Nathan H. Azrin, Todd R. Risley, Stephanie B. Stolz, and Richard B. Stuart.

recommendations for AABT decided that there was no need to establish guidelines peculiar to behavior therapy, because they would imply that behavior therapy was in greater need of being monitored than other techniques. Instead, the AABT committee formulated a set of questions of central importance for providing human services in general, independent of the conceptual basis of treatment, the type of clients, and the nature of the treatment setting. The questions resemble those developed by the APA's Commission on Behavior Modification and encompass considerations of the goals of treatment, possibilities for therapeutic procedures that might be used, the interests and voluntary participation of the client, evaluation of treatment efficacy, confidentiality, qualifications of the therapists, and referral to another treatment if necessary.

Additional attempts within behavior modification have been made to regulate professionals and their activities to ensure that client rights are not violated. One issue in the profession that has been the subject of considerable debate and attention is the certification and accreditation of behavior therapists (e.g., Agras, 1973; Davison, 1972; Franks, 1972; Lazarus, 1973; Nawas, 1973). The objective of certification and accreditation is to recognize formally those individuals whose practice of behavior therapy reflects sufficient training and skill as to make mistreatment of their clients unlikely. Whether or not this objective is achieved by certification has been a source of controversy.

The AABT entertained the possibility of certifying qualified practitioners but decided that the task extended beyond the charter of the original bylaws as an interest group. In addition, certification was not endorsed overwhelmingly by the membership. Another organization, the Behavior Therapy and Research Society, has compiled a roster of individuals who are regarded by the subcommittee of the society as qualified and competent behavior therapists. Peer recommendations, based upon experience and training in behavior therapy, are required for inclusion on the list. The society does not formally regard acceptance as certification *per se*, but the screening procedures and professional recognition implicit in being accepted function similarly to certification.

Outside of attempts to reflect on the competence of specific individuals as a means of protecting client rights, one recommendation has been made to certify specific *procedures* rather than the individuals who conduct them. Risley (1975) has reviewed behavior modification programs conducted by individuals who received adequate training in behavior modification and who would be likely to receive certification were it available. However, these individuals occasionally have engaged in questionable practices and, under the guise of treatment, have implemented procedures for which no empirical basis exists. To lessen the possibility that well-trained individuals may still mistreat their clients, Risley has advocated that specific procedures and techniques be accredited. He recommends that a procedure could be certified if it were classified as an established therapeutic or educational practice rather than as an experimental technique. Extensive empirical evidence in support of the technique would be required before it could be considered for accreditation. In addition, the procedure would need to be set forth in detail, with directions for implementation by practitioners, as judged by professional or lay monitors. Finally, the procedures would have to fall within the normally accepted practices of the society. The necessity for all these conditions to be met would depend upon the state of knowledge in the area as well as careful review by professionals and lay individuals.

Kittrie (1971) has proposed a therapeutic Bill of Rights as a safeguard to protect individuals who receive treatment that could be codified as law or merely serve as a guideline for institutions. The rights, listed below, encompass and extend many of the existing court rulings:

1. *No person shall be compelled to undergo treatment except for the defense of society.*
2. *Man's innate right to remain free of excessive forms of human modification shall be inviolable.*
3. *No social sanctions may be invoked unless the person subjected to treatment has demonstrated a clear and present danger through truly harmful behavior which is immediately forthcoming or has already occurred.*
4. *No person shall be subjected to involuntary incarceration or treatment on the basis of a finding of a general condition or status alone. Nor shall the mere conviction of a crime or a finding of not guilty by reason of insanity suffice to have a person automatically committed or treated.*
5. *No social sanctions, whether designated criminal, civil, or therapeutic, may be invoked in the absence of the previous right to a judicial or other independent hearing, appointed counsel, and an opportunity to confront those testifying about one's past conduct or therapeutic needs.*
6. *Dual interference by both the criminal and therapeutic process is prohibited.*

7. *An involuntary patient shall have the right to receive treatment.*
8. *Any compulsory treatment must be the least required reasonably to protect society.*
9. *All committed persons should have direct access to appointed counsel and the right, without any interference, to petition the courts for relief.*
10. *Those submitting to voluntary treatment should be guaranteed that they will not be subsequently transferred to a compulsory program through administrative action.* (Adapted from *The Right to be Different: Deviance and Enforced Therapy* by N. N. Kittrie, pp. 402–404. Copyright 1971 by The Johns Hopkins University Press.)

Designed to protect the fundamental rights and liberties of the individual while allowing therapeutic interventions to proceed, the Bill is formulated in general terms for application across different patients, goals, and methods of treatment. Of course, the generality of the proposed rights will require elaborate interpretation for each case, and some of the ambiguity will challenge the rationale of entire therapeutic programs. For example, Kittrie's proposal includes the right of an involuntarily confined patient to receive treatment. However, the definition of "treatment" is not without problems. Is "treatment" some intervention that a professional so labels or one which actually has been shown to effect therapeutic change? It is generally accepted that numerous treatment procedures with little scientific evidence of success are defined as curative for heterogeneous disorders and recommended and used by professionals.

As a second question, will treatment defined by a mental-health professional invariably meet legal requirements for treatment set by the judiciary? For example, normalized interactions between staff and patients may be justified by professionals under the rubric of "milieu therapy." However, this form of treatment may not be sufficiently specific or individualized to be entirely satisfactory to the courts (cf. Martin, 1975). Overall, general recommendations in the form of a bill of rights should contribute markedly in their own right, but more pointed guarantees and guidelines will be required to handle specific cases.

Some specific solutions for protecting client rights already have been proposed, notably a change in the relationship of the patient and the therapist or institution vis-à-vis treatment (Schwitzgebel, 1975). It is recommended that treatment be conceived as a contractual activity in which patients negotiate the conditions of treatment with a therapist. The contract could make explicit the goals, methods, risks, and benefits of treatment. A written agreement drafted by all involved parties extends beyond informed consent not only because the goals are explicit but also because the patient has a role in negotiating the final goals of treatment.

Along with making the goals explicit, the contract might specify the contingencies for therapeutic success and failure so that the therapist or institution is accountable. By placing treatment in terms of a written agreement, the patient has some legal power to sue for a breach of contract, to be compensated for injury, and to demand effective treatments. The contract may or may not guarantee a successful outcome. Given a particular behavior problem, the qualified efficacy of various techniques, and the vicissitudes of clinical practice, such a contract may be unreasonable. However, the therapist would specify the procedures to be used, their probable result, and other choices in the absence of effective outcome. Perhaps one of the greatest advantages of a contract from the standpoint of a patient's rights is that it could specify the conditions for cure or sufficient improvement to obtain release from confinement.

There are few examples of explicit contracts in treatment programs in which the goals of treatment are formulated clearly and in some way guaranteed in a manner to hold the therapist accountable. However, a contract was drawn up for a treatment program designed to alter the behavior of an eight-year-old boy who engaged in tantrums and negativistic behavior (Ayllon and Skuban, 1973). Therapy involved training the boy to comply with instructions and not to have tantrums in order to function in everyday life. The explicitness with which the nature and goals of treatment were presented is illustrated in the contract depicted in Figure 10.1. An extraordinary feature of the contract is that the therapist's fee was based upon the extent to which the original objectives were achieved. Usually fees are paid for providing services independent of their effects on behavior; making fees at least partially contingent upon outcome obviously would increase the accountability of the professional.

The contract model is desirable because it provides the opportunity for the patient to negotiate the goals of treatment. It is unclear if the contractual agreement by itself will provide sufficient protection for a patient. The difference in status, power, and information about treatment, as well as the patient's or inmate's confined and involuntary status, may limit the legitimacy of the arrangement. For the contract to be upheld in court, the usual conditions of informed

I. *Overview of problem and therapeutic program*

The overall objective of this therapeutic program is to develop and stabilize Mike's behavior patterns so that he may be considered for admission to school this fall. In general, this will involve strengthening some requisite behaviors such as following commands from an adult, and eliminating others, such as the screaming and tantrumming that accompany most of his refusals to follow instructions.

Mike has a discouraging behavior history for most teachers to consider working with. Because his characteristic reaction to requests is to throw tantrums, he is considered "untestable" by standard psychological means. This does not necessarily mean that he cannot do the items on a test, but rather that he has little or no control over his own behavior. His uncooperativeness quickly discourages most people from making much of an effort to work with him. What is clearly needed is an intensive rehabilitation program designed to enable Mike to build patterns of self-control which would lead to the elimination or drastic reduction of his disruptive behavior. This, in turn, would open other possibilities for developing Mike's potential, that is, the avenues which are blocked by his unmanageable behavior.

The overall goal of this 8-week program will be the development of self-control with its reciprocal outcome of decreasing or eliminating tantrums and disruptive behaviors. Implementation of this program will require that the child and his trainer engage in such activities as trips to the zoo, museums, parks, movies, swimming pools, shopping centers, supermarkets, and so on as well as having lunch and snacks together. These settings are included to expose Mike to a maximal number of normal situations where expectations of a standard of conduct are imposed by the setting itself.

As much as possible, the techniques used in the day program will be designed with the ultimate objective of utilization in the home. An attempt will be made to see that procedures used in the program are transferred to home management at the termination of treatment. The therapist will give instructions weekly to the parents by phone to insure that efforts both at home and in rehabilitation do not conflict.

II. *Behavioral objectives of therapy*

1. The objective of the therapeutic program is to teach Mike to comply with between 80–100 per cent of the verbal commands given to him by an adult(s). Compliance will be defined as Mike's beginning to perform the behavior specified by the command within 15 sec after it has been stated and then completing the specified task.

2. In addition, we intend to eliminate or drastically reduce Mike's excessive screaming and tantrumming. The goal is not to tantrum more frequently than once out of 30 commands and for no longer than 1 min at a time.

3. Evaluation of treatment outcome: The decision as to the attainment of these specific objectives will rest upon Mike's performance during a 30 min test session to be conducted in a classroom situation. At this session the therapist, the parents, and an additional person will make 10 verbal requests each of Mike, for a total of 30 verbal requests. Mike must comply with 80–100 per cent of these requests for the program to be considered a success. In addition, he must have tantrummed not more than once, and for not more than 1 min, during this final evaluation.

III. *Time and place of therapeutic intervention*

1. The therapeutic program will start on ——————————————————————————— and terminate on——————————————————————. Evaluation of the effectiveness of treatment will be held on or about the termination date of the therapeutic program.

2. Location: The meeting place will be at the ———————————————————————. Session activities, however, will involve time spent elsewhere, for example, having lunch, trips to shopping centers, amusements, and other special events. If the facility is not available, some other place agreeable can be designated as meeting and base center.

3. Days of training: Therapy sessions will be scheduled 5 days per week. The specific days may vary from week to week to comply with the objectives of the program. The family will be advised of the therapy schedule 1 week in advance.

4. Hours per day: Therapeutic sessions will be scheduled for 7 hr a day. Session time may be extended when therapeutically necessary as decided by the therapist.

5. Absences: There will be 4 notified absences allowed. The mother is expected to notify the therapist at least 1 hr before the scheduled therapy session. Any additional absences will require an additional fee of $10 per absence.

IV. *Fees*

Achievement of the behavioral objectives is expected to take 7 weeks of training from——————————— This training will cost a total of —————————. The monies will be disbursed in the following manner.

1. A check for 2/3 of the total amount will be given to the therapist at the beginning of therapy.

2. The balance of 1/3 will be paid to the therapist upon the achievement of the program objectives as specified above on about the date of termination of the program. In the event that the above objectives are not reached by this date, therapy will be discontinued and the balance will be forfeited by the therapist.

3. All expense incurred during training will be defrayed by the therapist. This will include admission to baseball games, the city zoo, swimming pools, and so on, as well as the cost of field trips, lunch, and snacks.

* * * *

By my signature I do hereby attest that I have read the above proposal and agree to the conditions stated therein.

	Parent
	Supervising Therapist
	Co-Therapist
Date	

Figure 10.1. A contingency contract for therapy. (From Ayllon and Skuban, 1973; reprinted by permission.)

consent may have to be met (Friedman, 1975). That is, the patient must be knowledgeable, competent, and submit voluntarily to the conditions of the contract.

Guidelines for the use of behavior modification procedures and the protection of client rights are being issued by various states and professional organizations (cf. Stolz, 1978; Wexler, 1975a). One of the more well known proposals was developed in Florida in response to a discovery of the abuses in a residential training facility that ostensibly ran a token economy program for mentally retarded, delinquent, and disturbed boys. The procedures, many of which were mistakenly believed to be behavior modification, included severe physical punishment, forced sexual acts, and deprivation, all administered as consequences for undesirable behavior.

These abuses led to the formation of a task force under the auspices of the Florida Division of Retardation to draft guidelines based upon psychological and legal principles against which subsequent programs could be evaluated (May, Risley, Twardosz, Friedman, Bijou, and Wexler, 1976). The guidelines included recommendations pertaining to competence, informed consent, and the least restrictive alternative doctrine (Friedman, 1975; Wexler, 1975a) and outlined procedures for selecting methods of treatment. Review committees were suggested to oversee any proposed treatment program. A peer review committee, consisting of experts in behavior modification, and a legal and ethical protection review committee, typically comprised of at least a lawyer, a behavioral scientist, and a nonprofessional person such as a parent of a handicapped client, would all represent the interests and civil liberties of the client. These individuals could judge the adequacy of treatment from different perspectives and ensure that the program combined treatment interests with the client's rights.

A three-level scheme was proposed as part of the Florida guidelines for classifying the behaviors to be modified and treatment techniques (May et al., 1976; Wexler, 1975a). The levels represent increasingly intrusive treatments to the client and, therefore, require increasingly greater scrutiny by advocacy and review panels. The first category of behaviors to be changed and techniques to be applied are those generally regarded as standard, reasonable, and conventional. Examples would be self-help responses, linguistic skills, and self-destructive acts. Positive reinforcement (using praise or other events that do not infringe upon the absolute rights of the client), extinction, and mild expressions of social disapproval would be the typical methods employed to change this class of activities.

At the second level, somewhat more intrusive procedures might be required to modify behavior. They would only be used if necessary and would represent relatively standard, reasonable, and conventional techniques. Mildly aversive events such as time-out or response cost would be considered as somewhat intrusive. Behaviors and procedures not specified previously would compromise the third tier of the guidelines. Controversial subjects for therapy—such as patterns of sexual activity, in which the direction or necessity of change could be questioned—would fit in this category. The procedures classified at this level might consist of last-resort interventions such as electric shock or drugs, or perhaps less well established therapies of ambiguous or unknown risks and benefits. However, no procedure that is highly intrusive and speculative, and that has a poor chance of success or a substantial likelihood of producing deleterious side effects would be approved.

Dividing behaviors and techniques into three levels would dictate the amount of scrutiny required before a program is approved (Wexler, 1975a). First-level behaviors and techniques might not need approval from a committee, whereas greater infringements might require specific review procedures. The committee review process and the right of the client to legal counsel might be taken on a case-by-case basis. Additionally, informed consent as well as the least restrictive alternative doctrine could be enforced by the review process. An advantage of a hierarchical arrangement of behaviors for modification and techniques is that rank-ordering dovetails with the least restrictive alternative doctrine. The less intrusive procedures are likely to be the least restrictive as well. Similarly, justification of a more aversive or confining intervention would require a demonstration that less controversial procedures were ineffective.

In general, the precise method by which patient rights can best be guaranteed remains to be determined. None of the suggested methods is flawless by any means. Indeed, variations of some of these proposals already have been employed outside of behavior modification in instances in which the courts nonetheless decided that the client's best interests were not protected. For example, in the *Kaimowitz* case, psychosurgery aimed at suppressing the destructive behavior of a sexual psychopath had been approved by two review bodies, one for scientific and one for a human rights review. And although the patient gave consent for surgery, the court ruled that voluntary and informed consent was not possible given the involuntarily confined status of the patient and the nature of the intervention.

Characteristics of different treatment populations, the conditions which bring them into treatment, the behaviors targeted for alteration, and, perhaps of most importance, the intrusiveness of the intervention will dictate solutions for protecting client rights. In addition, increased public attention to preserving individual rights may serve as a general protection. Recent litigation has heightened the sensitivity of those responsible for designing and implementing treatment to the rights of their clients, which may reduce the likelihood that threatening clinical interventions will be proposed. The litigation, accountability, and institutional and personal responsibility extend beyond the application of behavior modification to the whole mental-health treatment profession. Thus, the consequences of judicial review of how behavioral disorders are ameliorated could alter the scope of treatment, rehabilitation, and criteria for evaluating heterogeneous therapies and their techniques.

SUMMARY AND CONCLUSIONS

The application of behavior modification in institutional settings and its potential influence on society at large have heightened sensitivity to ethical and legal implications of the behavioral approach. The threat of a technology of behavioral manipulation to abridge individual freedom has been actively discussed. Writers sympathetic to behavior modification have pointed out that its techniques and the principles from which they are derived should not be criticized because of their implications. The fear that contemporary behavior modification will spawn coercive techniques to control society is based on hypothetical extrapolations extending far beyond the orientation and accomplishments of existing procedures. Moreover, coercive techniques for controlling individuals in society at large have always been available. If contemporary behavioral techniques have anything to do with social control, they probably contribute to thwarting despotic oppression in that dissenting individuals can apply behavioral principles more effectively to accomplish specific changes in their own behaviors and the behaviors of others.

Although critics of behavior modification on ethical grounds have pointed out important sources of concern, discussions have remained on the abstract plane because of their basis in hypothetical circumstances in which specific practices would be odious. Legal battles have in many ways made the ethical concerns more concrete. Restricting the scope of the decisions to cases of treatment should assuage some critics' worries about the hyperextension of behavioral techniques. The increased judicial oversight of treatment and rehabilitation, particularly with involuntarily confined patients and prison inmates, has had direct implications for behavior modification programs. Many of the decisions have curtailed the use of highly controversial aversive procedures used in the field as well as techniques outside its domain (such as psychosurgery).

Although court decisions directly pertaining to the use of reinforcement programs are relatively rare, certain related decisions have reduced or redefined the types of programs that can be conducted. For example, in token economies, back-up events that commonly have been delivered contingently may no longer be routinely withheld. Events that behavior modifiers have viewed as *privileges* to be allocated as rewards have been ruled as *absolute rights* of patients and inmates. Basic amenities of living, including living quarters, clothes, meals, access to group privileges, interaction with others, and religious services must be awarded regardless of performance except under unusual circumstances.

The behaviors typically treated in behavior modification programs have been less of a source of concern, but one outlet that has now been limited by the courts is the use of patient labor to maintain the institution. Expecting patients to perform jobs, even if considered therapeutic, has been restricted. Patients still can do some tasks, particularly those related to self-care. However, the routine reinforcement of work behavior is no longer legal.

Increased attention is being paid to a patient's right to receive and to refuse treatment. Many ambiguities remain, particularly occasions in which enforced treatment can abridge individual rights and when refusal of treatment is or is not alternative. What constitutes the most suitable treatment might be influenced by the court decision. Treatments that are the least restrictive must be employed, although there is great uncertainty about what a *bona fide* treatment might be and the dimensions along which restrictiveness might be evaluated.

The issue of informed consent is a particularly difficult problem because many individuals under treatment are incompetent and cannot give consent. Moreover, the status of involuntarily confined individuals and the duress that they may experience to provide consent further compound the dilemma. For many treatments that are proposed, consent cannot be informed simply because of the paucity of empirical evidence about their direct and inadvertent effects.

The necessity to deal with legal matters has spawned professional groups, legislative bodies, and special committees for devising guidelines for treatment. They usually are directed at balancing the requirements for treatment with the rights of the treated. General guidelines for all treatments have been recommended and the notion of a contract, whereby clients or individuals that represent the clients can directly negotiate treatment means and ends, is a promising contribution. Hierarchically classifying behavioral techniques and therapeutic goals in order of intrusiveness has been suggested to help clarify those areas that must be monitored closely. Oversight committees with both professional and nonprofessional members have been suggested for treatment programs so that individuals of diverse interests can pass judgment on the adequacy of treatment and the means to protect client rights.

11
Epilogue: New Directions

Behavior modification has matured within a relatively brief time. At its formal inception, the field represented an alternative to traditional ways of viewing abnormal behavior and its treatment. The conceptual position and specific techniques proposed were based largely upon the psychology of learning. Thus, behavior modification represented a fresh yet relatively narrow approach that could be viewed simply as an alternative to the intrapsychic-disease approach that dominated the field.

Behavior modification has expanded considerably, no longer a singular approach or narrowly defined set of techniques. It encompasses a variety of conceptualizations, research methods, and treatment techniques to explain, investigate, and alter behavior. Rather than being identified with a particular theoretical stance or narrowly circumscribed set of techniques, the field can be viewed as an empirical approach toward clinical phenomena. In the process of its own growth, behavior modification has altered several features of providing and evaluating treatment in the mental health profession at large. The traditional substantive areas of application, nature of delivering treatment services, and criteria for evaluating treatment in clinical psychology and psychiatry have been affected radically. The scope of behavior modification and how it has influenced traditional applications and their evaluation are highlighted in this final chapter.

DEFINITION AND SCOPE OF BEHAVIOR MODIFICATION

Behavior modification has grown and diversified considerably since its formal beginnings in the late 1950s and early 1960s. Given the great strides in research and applications that have marked the area, one might expect that fundamental issues about the domain and scope of the field would have been resolved long ago. Perhaps the most basic issue would be the definition and boundaries of behavior modification and behavior therapy. Over the years, the definition of behavior modification has expanded and changed considerably. Thus, the characteristics that unify individuals who refer to themselves as behavior modifiers are less clear now than 20 years ago. For example, because the field was a reaction to the prevailing view in psychiatry and clinical psychology, adherents were united in wanting to show that a behavioral approach, globally defined, was as valid or more efficacious than the intrapsychic model of conceptualizing and treating abnormal behaviors. For the time being, differences were minimized or ignored for the greater good of vitiating the claims of theories not based on the psychology of learning.

As behavior modification gained a following and established its strength through cumulative research, through texts and journals defining its domain, and through professional organizations, opposition to the intrapsychic-disease model and psychoanalysis no longer needed to be the field's dominant critical enterprise, and it was no longer necessary for researchers and clinicians to speak with one voice. The distinguishing features of dissimilar positions within behavior modification could be set forth, and assorted and innovative techniques that illuminated the differences among behavioral approaches could be presented.

By now, behavior modification is so variegated in its conceptualizations of behavior, research methods, and techniques that no unifying schema or set of assumptions about behavior can incorporate all the extant techniques. Many of the theoretical positions expressed within behavior modification represent opposing views about the nature of human motivation, the mechanisms that influence behavior and the relative influence of such factors, and the most suitable focus of treatment for a given problem. The diversity of approaches is suggested by the plethora of types of behavior modification or behavior therapy that have been discussed in the literature, for example, the qualifiers associated with the term "behavior therapy"—cognitive behavior therapy, language behavior therapy, rational behavior therapy, multimodal behavior therapy (Wilson, in press). Similarly, the multitude of concerns is illustrated by the specialized journals that deal with only specific circumscribed parts of the field (i.e., the *Journal of Applied Behavior Analysis* for interventions based on operant principles in the tradition of the experimental analysis of behavior and *Cognitive Therapy and Research* for treatment designed to modify cognitive processes).

Given the diversity of approaches, it is extremely difficult to enumerate a set of agreed-upon assumptions and features that can encompass the field. The characteristics that apply most widely, if not universally, to approaches subsumed under the rubric of behavior modification are

1. Focus upon current rather than historical determinants of behavior;
2. Emphasis on overt behavior change as the main criterion by which treatment should be evaluated;
3. Specification of treatment in objective terms so as to make replication possible;
4. Reliance upon basic research in psychology as a source of hypotheses about treatment and specific therapy techniques; and
5. Specificity in defining, treating, and measuring the target problems in therapy.[1]

These five assumptions represent unities within the heterogeneity of behavior modification. Commonality also is reflected in the rejection of different aspects of the intrapsychic-disease view of abnormal behavior and certain propositions of orthodox psychoanalysis. Behavior modifiers still generally do not believe that viewing abnormal behavior as "illness," aside from cases of diagnosed organic or physiological impairment, is profitable, that personality reorganization is essential for behavior change, and that understanding the original causes or psychodynamic concomitants of behavior is important for an individual's improvement. Instead, behavior modification is committed to the use of scientific methodology in constructing and evaluating therapy techniques. A premium is placed upon empirical validation, data, and replication to establish claims made about treatment. With the emphasis upon experimental evaluation and diversity of approaches, contemporary behavior modification is more an advocation of a scientific approach toward treatment and clinical practice rather than a particular conceptual stance.

---

[1] The material on the characteristics of behavior modification resulted from extensive discussions of the field that included W. Stewart Agras, Nathan H. Azrin, Alexander George, Walter Mischel, Stanley Rachman, G. Terence Wilson, and myself while we were Fellows at the Center for Advanced Study in the Behavioral Sciences, Stanford, California.

EXPANSION OF APPLICATIONS

Originally, behavior modification research and therapy were restricted to traditional foci within the mental health professions, for example, treatment for individuals in need of outpatient or inpatient services. Because psychological treatment constitutes the major professional service commitment of clinical psychology and psychiatry, it continues to dominate behavioral applications. However, behavior modification has been employed outside the usual confines of clinical psychology and psychiatry. For example, it has played a major role in educating normal children and helping patients with physiological and psychophysical disorders. Within the last decade, behavioral techniques have been enlisted successfully in the service of psychiatry, special education (including help for the retarded), law enforcement and correction, and other areas, as evidenced by a survey of the periodical literature of these fields (Kazdin, 1975c).

The extension of behavior modification research beyond the usual confines of treatment is evident in the applications to contemporary environmental and social problems (Kazdin, 1977b; Tuso and Geller, 1976). For example, behavior modification has been employed specifically to address pollution control, energy conservation, unemployment and job performance, racial integration, and community self-help for individuals in lower socioeconomic brackets. The following descriptions of these programs show the potential for new and different uses. To control pollution, reinforcement techniques have been employed. As a result, littering has been reduced in low-income housing projects, national campgrounds, schools, zoos, movie theaters, athletic facilities, and similar settings in which the methods were tried (e.g., Baltes, 1973; Baltes and Hayward, 1974; Burgess, Clark, and Hendee, 1971; Chapman and Risley, 1974; Kohlenberg and Phillips, 1973; Powers, Osborne, and Anderson, 1973). In these settings, behavior modification programs were designed explicitly to reduce littering. Typically, small monetary incentives were used to reinforce proper disposal or pickup of trash. Operant techniques also have been applied to augment recycling of waste products that otherwise would accumulate. For example, reinforcement programs in the form of raffles, lotteries, and small monetary incentives have increased the frequency that individuals purchase returnable rather than throwaway soft-drink bottles or collect paper that can be recycled rather than discarded as trash. The applications have elevated recycling in such settings as grocery stores, university campuses, apartments, and mobile homes (e.g., Geller, Chaffee, and Ingram, 1975; Geller, Farris, and Post, 1973; Reid, Luyben, Rawers, and Bailey, 1976).

Reinforcement techniques have increased conservation of electricity, gas, and fuel oil in the home (Kohlenberg, Phillips, and Proctor, 1976; Palmer, Lloyd, and Lloyd, in press; Seaver and Patterson, 1976). Families have received incentives for such behaviors as using appliances less than usual or merely showing an overall reduction in energy consumption as indicated by lower meter readings. In addition, programs have reduced gasoline consumption by rewarding individuals for driving less than usual (Foxx and Hake, 1977). Other attempts to decrease the use of cars were the aim of reinforcement programs designed to increase the public's use of mass transit (e.g., Everett, Hayward, and Meyers, 1974). Rewards, such as money or tickets exchangeable for items in community stores, were provided for riding buses.

Behavior modification principles have been applied to unemployment and on-the-job performance. For example, one study increased the job-procuring ability of a state unemployment agency by rewarding those who disclosed jobs that ultimately led to placement of unemployed individuals (Jones and Azrin, 1973). A more comprehensive behavioral program has helped individuals find jobs by training them in methods to seek employment, to communicate with others about job prospects, and to engage in several specific behaviors that would increase their desirability as an employee (e.g., better dress and grooming, preparing a résumé, and appropriate deportment at a job interview) (Azrin, Flores, and Kaplan, 1975).

On-the-job performance is an area in which operant procedures have been used traditionally, at least implicitly, in the form of reinforcers for excellence (e.g., raises, commissions, promotions) and aversive consequences for inadequate performance (e.g., job loss). However, recent systematic applications of feedback, praise, and incentives have been found to alter specific aspects of job performance. Incentives, including small monetary bonuses or lotteries, have reduced absenteeism, tardiness, and cash register losses from error or theft; rewards also have increased conservation of materials to save the corporation money and quicker completion of tasks during work (e.g., "New tool: 'Reinforcement' for good work," 1971; Marholin and Gray, 1976; Pedalino and Gamboa, 1974; Pierce and Risley, 1974).

Preliminary investigations have been conducted in topics dealing with sociological problems, attitudes, and biases. Behavioral techniques have been instrumental in fostering self-help skills among individuals with lower socioeconomic standing. Interest in attending community self-help meetings, as well as problem-solving and decision-making skills designed to resolve specific community issues, have resulted from such instruction (e.g., Briscoe, Hoffman, and Bailey, 1975; Miller and Miller, 1970). Operant techniques have been applied to alter the tendency of white and black children to evaluate black children negatively, a racial bias that develops early (e.g., Best, Smith, Graves, and Williams, 1975; McMurtry and Williams, 1972). Similarly, interracial cooperation has been increased in classroom programs by reinforcing instances of positive interaction across racial lines (Hauserman, Walen, and Behling, 1973).

The behavioral approach also has been adopted as part of military training. For example, reinforcement systems have been used to replace traditional methods of discipline in some basic training programs (Datel and Legters, 1970). More in line with traditional applications of treatment techniques, the military also has adopted behavioral techniques in many psychiatric treatment facilities for veterans (Chase, 1970).

USE OF PARAPROFESSIONALS

Traditionally, psychological treatment has been administered by professionals, usually in an office where patients come for visits or an institution where treatment can be provided on an inpatient basis. In both cases, the professional usually is in direct contact with the client or patient. Several changes in the mental health profession have permitted treatment to be administered by trained nonprofessionals (e.g., housewives, parents, students) and in settings that are more enmeshed with community life (e.g., half-way houses) than are traditional institutional facilities. The movement toward deprofessionalization and deinstitutionalization of treatment was stimulated by such factors as a shortage of professional therapists and the inadequacy of traditional treatment facilities (cf. Albee, 1967; Hobbs, 1964; Joint Commission on Mental Illness and Health, 1961).

Within the mental-health field there has been a tendency to use paraprofessionals as agents for psychological treatment. Thus, parents, teachers, relatives, spouses, and peers often are intermediaries between a professional mental-health worker and the client. Behavior modifiers have been particularly outspoken in advocating that individuals in the natural environment rather than professionally trained therapists manage client behavior.

Behavior modification has certain characteristics that make it particularly amenable to employing individuals in a client's everyday surroundings as treatment intermediaries. First, many problems for which individuals seek treatment are best resolved by altering behaviors in the situations in which they normally occur. Many of the contingencies of reinforcement contribute to problem behavior and need to be controlled directly and immediately. Hence, for many problems, the behavior modifier is literally not in the best position to directly effect the needed change. The role of the therapist becomes primarily that of a consultant who helps the client and his/her friends and relatives to rearrange environmental contingencies so as to support adaptive behavior.

A second feature of behavior modification that lends itself well to deprofessionalization of care is its goal of constructing therapies in such a way that they are replicable and readily implemented by others. Whenever possible, treatments are explained so that they can be followed in a relatively straightforward fashion. Explicit descriptions of methods make it more possible for individuals who have not had highly specialized professional training to try them. Finally, behavior modification increasingly has emphasized self-control as a means of changing behavior and thus would encourage individuals to alter their patterns of conduct by themselves or by enlisting others.

The acceptance of a client's peers as agents of treatment has led to much research on training paraprofessionals and information dissemination to the public. Investigations have been made of useful methods for teaching institutional staff, teachers, parents, peers, and students to apply a behavioral approach (cf. Patterson, 1976; Yen and McIntire, 1976). In addition, select behavior modification techniques have been prepared in a form that is available for public dissemination or for client use. For example, specific procedures for toilet training that parents or teachers can use without professional consultation have been detailed in a book entitled *Toilet Training in Less than a Day* (Azrin and Foxx, 1974). As another instance, systematic desensitatization has been developed and refined to the point that it can be totally self-administered treatment in overcoming fears (cf. Phillips, Johnson, and Geyer, 1972; Rosen, 1974; Rosen, Glasgow, and Barrera, 1976). Other techniques have been prepared in "package" form for the self-treatment of obesity (e.g., Hagen, 1974; Stuart and Davis, 1972) and of sexual dysfunction (e.g., Kass and Stauss, 1976). Overall, behavior modification has taken considerable steps to recognize the importance of individuals in the client's every-day environment, including the clients themselves, in administering treatment (cf. Guerney, 1969; Krumboltz and Thoresen, 1976; Mahoney and Thoresen, 1974; Tharp and Wetzel, 1969).

EXPANDED CRITERIA FOR
EVALUATING THERAPEUTIC INTERVENTIONS

Therapeutic interventions traditionally have been evaluated by the client's standing on various measures designed to reflect the problem observed in treatment. Although different therapeutic approaches stress different ways to measure a problem, the client's own reports, the therapist's ratings of improvement, or measures of overt behavior usually make up part of the evaluation. The client's performance on outcome measures serves as the main criterion for drawing conclusions about treatment, which is evaluated on the basis of whether change is produced, whether that change is statistically significant, and whether it has produced greater change than another method.

However, standards for evaluating treatment in behavior modification are no longer solely dependent on the usual outcome criteria. Although outcome questions on the measures of a client's problem remain central to evaluation of treatment, they have been augmented by other considerations about treatment and its effects. The involvement of the courts in deciding fair and reasonable treatment and increased concern about informed consent in judicial and other circles have helped to bring about this change. In addition, behavior modification has an abiding interest in extending the evaluation of therapeutic outcome to include measures of the clinical importance of behavior change.

Evaluation of treatment has broadened to include questions about its *foci*, its *procedures* for effecting behavior change, and the *clinical importance* of the changes produced. Consider first the concern with evaluating treatment procedures. Recent court decisions concerning involuntarily confined populations have firmly established the importance of obtaining the willing and informed consent from individuals participating in treatment. A person's willingness to participate will most probably depend on the specific techniques that are used.

Independent of the effects of different treatments on behavior, therapies differ in the degree to which they are acceptable to the client. Even an extremely efficacious intervention (e.g., electric shock for a particular behavior) may not be acceptable. Essentially, acceptability of treatment is a measure of consumer satisfaction and introduces a new dimension for evaluating treatment. For example, consumer satisfaction has been surveyed in select applications of behavior modification with students in educational settings and delinquents in home-style facilities. Participants have been asked the extent to which they are satisfied with a given intervention as compared to another (e.g., Drabman, Spitalnik, and Spitalnik, 1974; Phillips, Phillips, Wolf, and Fixsen, 1973). Studies also have asked paraprofessionals who administer treatment to indicate their preferences for particular procedures (e.g., Porterfield, Herbert-Jackson, and Risley, 1976; Rosenbaum, O'Leary, and Jacob, 1975). Evaluating consumer satisfaction with a treatment addressess the desirability or aversiveness of the procedures independently of their therapeutic effects. However, that index is of interest only with those techniques that have demonstrated change on outcome measures.

Assessing the therapeutic focus of treatment represents another dimension that has begun to receive attention. In many behavior modification programs, the behaviors selected for intervention ultimately are decided upon by the investigator. Or, the complaints of the clients or individuals responsible for the clients may dictate the general emphasis selected. However, it is the investigator who must decide which specific behaviors will best accomplish the overall goal. The actual behaviors that are changed only operationally define the larger category that was specified as a problem by the client. However, the behaviors may not always address what individuals in contact with the client see as the crucial problem. That is, are the target behaviors of treatment therapeutically important and do they encompass areas that a client's peers and family perceive as important? For example, whether behaviors studied in programs with delinquents are important to police officers or to others with whom delinquents may be likely to interact has been determined by ascertaining what the interested parties perceive as important (e.g., Minkin, Braukmann, Minkin, Timbers, Timbers, Fixsen, Phillips, and Wolf, 1976; Werner, Minkin, Minkin, Fixsen, Phillips, and Wolf, 1975). Once the specific behaviors desirable to individuals with whom the clients interact are identified, they can be induced in the clients. Overall, evaluation of the treatment focus attempts to ensure that the behaviors studied are significant to individuals in the participant's day-to-day environment.

Evaluating treatment outcome has been broadened in many behavior modification studies. Along with providing measures of overt behavior to reflect improvements resulting from treatment, an attempt has been made to discern the clinical magnitude of the change. Investigators have tried to determine if therapy makes a difference to the client or individuals in contact with the client. One way to assess the importance of behavior change is to compare the client's functioning with how his/her peers not considered as deviant act in similar situations. If the client's behavior deviates from that of his/her peers before treatment and conforms with his/her peers after it, the changes produced are likely to be clinically important. For example, children with behavior problems referred for treatment are more disruptive in the home and at school than are their peers in age, sex, and demographic variables but without such problems. After treatment, deviant conduct at home and school has been shown to fall within the acceptable range of the normal deportment for children (e.g., Kent and O'Leary, 1976; Patterson, 1974). Assessing the effectiveness of treatment according to how well its results bring clients within a normative range of behavior is a new dimension in behavior modification that is being introduced with diverse populations (Kazdin, 1977a).

A second way in which the clinical importance of behavior change can be assessed is to have persons in the client's everyday surroundings (e.g., teachers, relatives and others who are likely to observe him/her frequently) rate whether the changes effected with treatment have made a qualitative difference in overall performance. Subjective evaluations are solicited to supplement post-treatment data to determine if the changes in discrete behaviors are perceived by others as being important in the overall impression the client makes. For example, using behavior modification techniques to increase some vocabulary skills in children not only alters those behaviors but also increases the global ratings of creativity of the compositions as rated by individuals not involved in training (e.g., Brigham, Graubard, and Stans, 1972; Maloney and Hopkins, 1973). Thus, the discrete behavior changes appear to influence the qualitative evaluation of client performance.

Treatment effects have tended to be evaluated by looking at their social consequences. Wolf (1976) has called this emphasis *social validation*, which means examining the procedures, behaviors, and extent of change in light of the social context in which the client or consumers of treatment function. Social validation of treatment in behavior modification goes beyond demonstrating behavior change to encompass supplementary measures of the acceptability, foci, and efficacy of treatment.

These extensions of the criteria by which treatment is analyzed represent very recent developments in behavior modification. Another evaluative dimension that may eventually become prominent is cost-effectiveness—the relative costs of a treatment in money and professional time weighed against the rapidity of behavior change. Cost-effectiveness and cost-benefit analyses have yet to be included systematically in critical examinations of behavior modification programs, but they might represent a likely direction for future selections of criteria for evaluating treatment.

SUMMARY AND CONCLUSIONS

Through the course of its own growth, behavior modification has extended the domain of clinical psychology and psychiatry in general. Its expansion and breadth have obscured many of the unique substantive and conceptual characteristics with which the field was once identified. Perhaps behavior modification offers the most promise in its diversity of conceptual approaches and treatment techniques: the primary commitment of the field is to methodological rigor rather than to any particular conceptual approach. The unifying theme across techniques is that empirical validation is the chief criterion for appraising treatment. Therapeutic approaches need to be entrenched firmly in empirical evaluation. The emphasis on scientific methodology in assessing clinical phenomena rather than narrowly defined techniques or conceptual positions has greatly decreased the precision and meaning of the term "behavior modification." However, this broader conceptualization of the field has worked advantageously to improve and open up new areas of the scientific study of behavior and its alteration.

References

Ad Hoc Committee on Ethical Standards in Psychological Research. Ethical principles in the conduct of research with human participants. Washington, D.C.: American Psychological Association, 1973.

Agras, W. S. Toward the certification of behavior therapists? Journal of Applied Behavior Analysis, 1973, 6:167–173.

Aitchison, R. A., and Green, D. R. A token reinforcement system for large wards of institutionalized adolescents. Behaviour Research and Therapy, 1974, 12:181–190.

Albee, G. W. The relation of conceptual models to manpower needs. In E. L. Cowen, E. A. Gardner, and M. Zax (Eds.), Emergent Approaches to Mental Health Problems. New York: Appleton-Century-Crofts, 1967.

Aldrich, C. A. A new test for hearing in the new-born: The conditioned reflex. American Journal of Diseases of Children, 1928, 35:36–37.

Alexander, F. G., and Selesnick, S. T. The History of Psychiatry: An Evaluation of Psychiatric Thought and Practice from Prehistoric Times to the Present. New York: New American Library, 1968.

Alexander, J. Thought-Control in Everyday Life. New York: Funk & Wagnalls, 1928.

Alexander, L. Objective evaluation of antidepressant therapy by conditional reflex technique. Diseases of the Nervous System, 1961, 22(5, Section 2, Suppl.):14–23.

Alexander, L. Differential diagnosis between psychogenic and physical pain: The conditioned psychogalvanic reflex as an aid. Journal of the American Medical Association, 1962, 181:855–861.

Allen, K. E., Hart, B., Buell, J. S., Harris, F. R., and Wolf, M. M. Effects of social reinforcement on isolate behavior of a nursery school child. Child Development, 1964, 35:511–518.

American Psychiatric Association, Committee on Ethics. The principles of medical ethics with annotations especially applicable to psychiatry. American Journal of Psychiatry, 1973, 130:1058–1064.

American Psychiatric Association, Committee on Nomenclature and Statistics. Mental disorders: Diagnostic and statistical manual. Washington, D.C.: Author, 1952.

American Psychiatric Association, Committee on Nomenclature and Statistics. Diagnostic and statistical manual of mental disorders (2nd ed.). Washington, D.C.: Author, 1968.

Anderson, O. D., and Liddell, H. S. Observations on experimental neurosis in sheep. Archives of Neurology and Psychiatry, 1935, 34:330–354.

Anderson, O. D., and Parmenter, R. A long-term study of the experimental neurosis in the sheep and dog. Psychosomatic Medicine Monographs, 1941, 3(Whole Nos. 3 and 4).

Arann, L., and Horner, V. M. Contingency management in an open psychiatric ward. Journal of Behavior Therapy and Experimental Psychiatry, 1972, 3:31–37.

Argyle, M., Bryant, B., and Trower, P. Social skills training and psychotherapy: A comparative study. Psychological Medicine, 1974, 4:435–443.

Ascher, L. M., and Cautela, J. R. Covert negative reinforcement: An experimental test. Journal of Behavior Therapy and Experimental Psychiatry, 1972 3:1–5.

Ash, P. The reliability of psychiatric diagnoses. Journal of Abnormal and Social Psychology, 1949, 44:272–276.

Ayllon, T. Intensive treatment of psychotic behaviour by stimulus satiation and food reinforcement. Behaviour Research and Therapy, 1963, 1:53–61.

Ayllon, T. Some behavioral problems associated with eating in chronic schizophrenic patients. In L. P. Ullmann and L. Krasner (Eds.), Case Studies in Behavior Modification. New York: Holt, Rinehart & Winston, 1965.

Ayllon, T., and Azrin, N. H. Reinforcement and instructions with mental patients. Journal of the Experimental Analysis of Behavior, 1964,-7: 327–331.

Ayllon, T., and Azrin, N. H. The measurement and reinforcement of behavior of psychotics. Journal of the Experimental Analysis of Behavior, 1965, 8:357–383.

Ayllon, T., and Azrin, N. H. Reinforcer sampling: A technique for increasing the behavior of mental patients. Journal of Applied Behavior Analysis, 1968a, 1:13–20.

Ayllon, T., and Azrin, N. H. The token economy: A motivational system for therapy and rehabilitation. New York: Appleton-Century-Crofts, 1968b.

Ayllon, T., Garber, S., and Pisor, K. The elimination of discipline problems through a combined school-home motivational system. Behavior Therapy, 1975, 6:616–626.

Ayllon, T., and Haughton, E. Control of the behavior of schizophrenic patients by food. Journal of the Experimental Analysis of Behavior, 1962, 5:343–352.

Ayllon, T., and Haughton, E. Modification of symptomatic verbal behaviour of mental patients. Behaviour Research and Therapy, 1964, 2:87–97.

Ayllon, T., Haughton, E., and Osmond, H. O. Chronic anorexia: A behaviour problem. Canadian Psychiatric Association Journal, 1964, 9:147–154.

Ayllon, T., and Michael, J. The psychiatric nurse as a behavioral engineer. Journal of the Experimental Analysis of Behavior, 1959, 2:323–334.

Ayllon, T., Milan, M., Roberts, M., and McKee, J. Behavior modification and prison rehabilitation: Toward an effective humanism (working title), in preparation.

Ayllon, T., and Skuban, W. Accountability in psychotherapy: A test case. Journal of Behavior Therapy and Experimental Psychiatry, 1973, 4:19–30.

Azrin, N. H., Flores, T., and Kaplan, S. J. Job-finding club: A group-assisted program for obtaining employment. Behaviour Research and Therapy, 1975, 13:17–27.

Azrin, N. H., and Foxx, R. M. Toilet Training in Less Than a Day. New York: Simon & Schuster, 1974.

Azrin, N. H., and Holz, W. C. Punishment. In W. K. Honig (Ed.), Operant Behavior: Areas of Research and Application. New York: Appleton-Century-Crofts, 1966.

Azrin, N. H., and Lindsley, O. R. The reinforcement of cooperation between children. Journal of Abnormal and Social Psychology, 1956, 52:100-102.

Babkin, B. P. Pavlov, A Biography. Chicago: University of Chicago Press, 1949.

Baer, D. M. Escape and avoidance response of pre-school children to two schedules of reinforcement withdrawal. Journal of the Experimental Analysis of Behavior, 1960, 3:155-159.

Baer, D. M. Effect of withdrawal of positive reinforcement on an extinguishing response in young children. Child Development, 1961, 32:67-74.

Baer, D. M. Laboratory control of thumbsucking by withdrawal and re-presentation of reinforcement. Journal of the Experimental Analysis of Behavior, 1962, 5:525-528.

Baer, D. M. A case for the selective reinforcement of punishment. In C. Neuringer and J. L. Michael (Eds.), Behavior Modification in Clinical Psychology. New York: Appleton-Century-Crofts, 1970.

Baer, D. M., and Wolf, M. M. The entry into natural communities of reinforcement. In R. Ulrich, T. Stachnik, and J. Mabry (Eds.), Control of Human Behavior, Vol. 2: From Cure to Prevention. Glenview, Illinois: Scott, Foresman, 1970.

Baer, D. M., Wolf, M. M., and Risley, T. R. Some current dimensions of applied behavior analysis. Journal of Applied Behavioral Analysis, 1968, 1:91-97.

Bagby, E. The Psychology of Personality: An Analysis of Common Emotional Disorders. New York: Holt, 1928.

Bailey, P. The great psychiatric revolution. American Journal of Psychiatry, 1956, 113:387-406.

Ball, R. S. Reinforcement conditioning of verbal behavior by verbal and non-verbal stimuli in a situation resembling a clinical interview. Unpublished doctoral dissertation, Indiana University, 1952.

Ball, T. S. Issues and implications of operant conditioning: The reestablishment of social behavior. Hospital & Community Psychiatry, 1968, 19:-230-232.

Baltes, M. M. Operant principles applied to acquisition and generalization of nonlittering behavior in children. Proceedings of the 81st Annual Convention, American Psychological Association, 1973, 8:889-890.

Baltes, M. M., and Hayward, S. C. Control of littering in a naturalistic setting: the football stadium. Paper presented at the 82nd annual convention of the American Psycological Association, New Orleans, September 1974.

Bandura, A. A social learning interpretation of psychological dysfunctions. In P. London and D. Rosenhan (Eds.), Foundations of Abnormal Psychology. New York: Holt, Rinehart & Winston, 1968.

Bandura, A. Principles of Behavior Modification. New York: Holt, Rinehart & Winston, 1969.

Bandura, A. Modeling theory. In W. S. Sahakian (Ed.), Psychology of Learning: Systems, Models, and Theories. Chicago: Markham, 1970.

Bandura, A. Psychotherapy based upon modeling principles. In A. E. Bergin and S. L. Garfield (Eds.), Handbook of Psychotherapy and Behavior Change: An Empirical Analysis. New York: Wiley, 1971a.

Bandura, A. Vicarious and self-reinforcement processes. In R. Glaser (Ed.), The Nature of Reinforcement: A Symposium of the Learning Research and Development Center, University of Pittsburgh. New York: Academic Press, 1971b.

Bandura, A. Behavior theory and the models of man. American Psychologist, 1974, 29:859–869.

Bandura, A. Self-reinforcement: Theoretical and methodological considerations. Behaviorism, 1976, 4:135–155.

Bandura, A. Social Learning Theory. Englewood Cliffs, New Jersey: Prentice-Hall, 1977.

Bandura, A., Grusec, J. E., and Menlove, F. L. Observational learning as a function of symbolization and incentive set. Child Development, 1966, 37:499–506.

Bandura, A., and Kupers, C. J. Transmission of patterns of self-reinforcement through modeling. Journal of Abnormal and Social Psychology, 1964, 69:1–9.

Bandura, A., and Walters, R. H. Social Learning and Personality Development. New York: Holt, Rinehart & Winston, 1963.

Bandura, A., and Whalen, C. K. The influence of antecedent reinforcement and divergent modeling cues on patterns of self-reward. Journal of Personality and Social Psychology, 1966, 3:373–382.

Barber, T. X., DiCara, L. V., Kamiya, J., Miller, N. E., Shapiro, D., and Stoyva, J. (Eds.). Biofeedback and Self-Control 1974: An Aldine Annual on the Regulation of Bodily Processes and Consciousness. Chicago: Aldine, 1975.

Barlow, D. H. Aversive procedures. In W. S. Agras (Ed.), Behavior Modification: Principles and Clinical Applications. Boston: Little, Brown, 1972.

Baron, A., Kaufman, A., and Stauber, K. A. Effects of instructions and reinforcement-feedback on human operant behavior maintained by fixed-interval reinforcement. Journal of the Experimental Analysis of Behavior, 1969, 12:701–712.

Barrett, B. H. Reductions in rate of multiple tics by free operant conditioning methods. Journal of Nervous and Mental Disease, 1962, 135:187–195.

Barrett, B. H., and Lindsley, O. R. Deficits in acquisition of operant discrimination and differentiation shown by institutionalized retarded children. American Journal of Mental Deficiency, 1962, 67:424–436.

Barry, J. V. Alexander Maconochie of Norfolk Island: A Study of a Pioneer in Penal Reform. Melbourne: Oxford University Press, 1958.

Bartlett, F. L. Institutional peonage: Our exploitation of mental patients. Atlantic Monthly, July 1964, pp. 116–119.

Baum, M. Extinction of avoidance responding through response prevention (flooding). Psychological Bulletin, 1970, 74:276–284.

Bechterev, V. M. (See Bekhterev, V. M., and Bekhterew, V. M.)

Beck, A. T. Cognitive therapy: Nature and relation to behavior therapy. Behavior Therapy, 1970, 1:184–200.

Beck, A. T. Cognitive Therapy and the Emotional Disorders. New York: International Universities Press, 1976.

Beer, T., Bethe, A., and Uexküll, J. V. Vorschläge zu einer objektivierenden Nomenklatur in der Physiologie des Nervensystems. Biologisches Centralblatt, 1899, 19:517–521.

Begelman, D. A. Ethical and legal issues of behavior modification. Progress in Behavior Modification, 1975, 1:159–189.

Bekhterew, V. M. Die Anwendung der Methode der motorischen Assoziations reflexe zur Aufdeckung der Simulation. Zeitschrift für Die Gesamte Neurologie und Psychiatrie, 1912, 13:183–191.

Bekhterew, V. M. La Psychologie Objective. Paris: Alcan, 1913.

Bekhterew, W. Die Perversitäten und Inversitaten vom Standpunkt der Reflexologie. Archiv für Psychiatrie und Nervenkrankheiten, 1923, 68: 100–213.

Bekhterev, V. M. [General Principles of Human Reflexology: An Introduction to the Objective Study of Personality.] (E. Murphy and W. Murphy, trans.) London: Jarrolds, 1933.

Benedict, R. Patterns of Culture. New York: Penguin, 1946.

Bergin, A. E. Some Implications of psychotherapy research for therapeutic practice. Journal of Abnormal Psychology, 1966, 71:235–246.

Bergin, A. E. An empirical analysis of therapeutic issues. In D. S. Arbuckle (Ed.), Counseling and Psychotherapy: An Overview. New York: McGraw-Hill, 1967.

Bergin, A. E. The evaluation of therapeutic outcomes. In A. E. Bergin and S. L. Garfield (Eds.), Handbook of Psychotherapy and Behavior Change: An Empirical Analysis. New York: Wiley, 1971.

Bergin, A. E., and Garfield, S. L. (Eds.), Handbook of Psychotherapy and Behavior Change: An Empirical Analysis. New York: Wiley, 1971.

Berkowitz, B. P., and Graziano, A. M. Training parents as behavior therapists: A review. Behaviour Research and Therapy, 1972, 10:297–317.

Best, D. L., Smith, S. C., Graves, D. J., and Williams, J. E. The modification of racial bias in preschool children. Journal of Experimental Child Psychology, 1975, 20:193–205.

Bidder, F., and Schmidt, C. Die Verdauungssäfte und der Stoffwechsel: Eine physiologisch-chemische untersuchung. Leipzig: Mitau, Beyer, 1852.

Bijou, S. W. A systematic approach to an experimental analysis of young children. Child Development, 1955, 26:161–168.

Bijou, S. W. Methodology for an experimental analysis of child behavior. Psychological Reports, 1957a, 3:243–250.

Bijou, S. W. Patterns of reinforcement and resistance to extinction in young children. Child Development, 1957b, 28:47–54.

Bijou, S. W. A child study laboratory on wheels. Child Development, 1958a, 29:425–427.

Bijou, S. W. Operant extinction after fixed-interval schedules with young children. Journal of the Experimental Analysis of Behavior, 1958b, 1:25–29.

Bijou, S. W. Learning in children. Monographs of the Society for Reseach in Child Development, 1959, 24(5, Serial No. 74).

Bijou, S. W. Discrimination performance as a baseline for individual analysis of young children. Child Development, 1961, 32:163–170.

Bijou, S. W. Theory and research in mental (developmental) retardation. Psychological Record, 1963, 13:95–110.

Bijou, S. W. A functional analysis of retarded development. In N. R. Ellis (Ed.), International Review of Research in Mental Retardation (Vol. 1). New York: Academic Press, 1966.

Bijou, S. W., and Baer, D. M. Child Development, Vol. 1: A Systematic and Empirical Theory. New York: Appleton-Century-Crofts, 1961.

Bijou, S. W., and Baer, D. M. Child Development, Vol. 2: Universal Stage of Infancy. New York: Appleton-Century-Crofts, 1965.

Bijou, S. W., and Baer, D. M. Child Development: Readings in Experimental Analysis. New York: Appleton-Century-Crofts, 1967.

Bijou, S. W., Birnbrauer, J. S., Kidder, J. D., and Tague, C. Programmed instruction as an approach to the teaching of reading, writing, and arithmetic to retarded children. Psychological Record, 1966, 16:505-522.

Bijou, S. W., and Oblinger, B. Responses of normal and retarded children as a function of the experimental situation. Psychological Reports, 1960, 6: 447-454.

Bijou, S. W., and Orlando, R. Rapid development of multiple-schedule performances with retarded children. Journal of the Experimental Analysis of Behavior, 1961, 4:7-16.

Bijou, S. W., and Peterson, R. F. Functional analysis in the assessment of children. In P. McReynolds (Ed.), Advances in Psychological Assessment (Vol. 2). Palo Alto, California: Science & Behavior Books, 1971.

Bijou, S. W., Peterson, R. F., and Ault, M. H. A method to integrate descriptive and experimental field studies at the level of data and empirical concepts. Journal of Applied Behavior Analysis, 1968, 1:175-191.

Bijou, S. W., Peterson, R. F., Harris, F. R., Allen, K. E., and Johnston, M. S. Methodology for experimental studies of young children in natural settings. Psychological Record, 1969, 19:177-210.

Bijou, S. W., and Redd, W. H. Behavior therapy for children. In S. Arieti (Ed.), American Handbook of Psychiatry, Vol. 5 (2nd ed.). New York: Basic Books, 1975.

Birk, L. Behavior therapy—integration with dynamic psychiatry. Behavior Therapy, 1970, 1:522-526.

Birk, L. (Ed.). Biofeedback: Behavioral Medicine. New York: Grune & Stratton, 1973.

Birnbaum, M. The right to treatment. American Bar Association Journal, 1960, 46:499-505.

Birnbaum, M. A rationale for the right. In D. S. Burris (Ed.), The Right to Treatment. A Symposium. New York: Springer, 1969.

Birnbaum, M. The right to treatment—some comments on implementation. Duquesne Law Review, 1972, 10:579-608.

Birnbaum, P. (Ed.). A treasury of Judaism. New York: Hebrew Publishing, 1962.

Birnbrauer, J. S. Mental retardation. In H. Leitenberg (Ed.), Handbook of Behavior Modification and Behavior Therapy. Englewood Cliffs, New Jersey: Prentice-Hall, 1976.

Birnbrauer, J. S., Bijou, S. W., Wolf, M. M., and Kidder, J. D. Programed instruction in the classroom. In L. P. Ullmann and L. Krasner (Eds.), Case Studies in Behavior Modification. New York: Holt, Rinehart & Winston, 1965a.

Birnbrauer, J. S., and Lawler, J. Token reinforcement for learning. Mental Retardation, 1964, 2:275–279.

Birnbrauer, J. S., Wolf, M. M., Kidder, J. D., and Tague, C. E. Classroom behavior of retarded pupils with token reinforcement. Journal of Experimental Child Psychology, 1965b, 2:219–235.

Blache. Chorées graves: Guérison rapide par les massages et la gymnastique methodiquement appliques. Gazette Hebdomadaire de Médecine et de Chirurgie, 1864, 1:787–790.

Blanchard, E. B. Behavioral medicine: A perspective. In R. B. Williams, Jr., and W. D. Gentry (Eds.), Behavioral Approaches to Medical Treatment. Cambridge, Massachusetts: Ballinger, 1977.

Blanchard, E. B., and Epstein, L. H. The clinical usefulness of biofeedback. In M. Hersen, R. M. Eisler, and P. M. Miller (Eds.), Progress in Behavior Modification (Vol. 4). New York: Academic Press, 1977.

Blanchard, E. B., and Young, L. D. Self-control of cardiac functioning: A promise as yet unfulfilled. Psychological Bulletin, 1973, 79:145–163.

Blanchard, E. B., and Young, L. D. Clinical applications of biofeedback training: A review of evidence. Archives of General Psychiatry, 1974, 30:573–589.

Blough, D. S. New test for tranquilizers. Science, 1958, 127:586–587.

Bockoven, J. S. Some relationships between cultural attitudes toward individuality and care of the mentally ill: An historical study. In M. Greenblatt, D. J. Levinson, and R. H. Williams (Eds.), The Patient and the Mental Hospital: Contributions of Research in the Science of Social Behavior. Glencoe, Illinois: Free Press, 1957.

Bockoven, J. S. Moral Treatment in American Psychiatry. New York: Springer, 1963.

Boring, E. G. A History of Experimental Psychology (2nd ed.). New York: Appleton-Century-Crofts, 1950.

Borkovec, T. D. Effects of expectancy on the outcome of systematic desensitization and implosive treatments for analogue anxiety. Behavior Therapy, 1972, 3:29–40.

Bornstein, P. H., and Spitzform, M. Institutional sources of research in major behavioral journals: 1970–1973. Behavior Therapy, 1974, 5:661–664.

Brady, J. P. Systematic desensitization. In W. S. Agras (Ed.), Behavior Modification: Principles and Clinical Applications. Boston: Little, Brown, 1972.

Brady, J. P. Behavior therapy: Fad or psychotherapy of the future? In R. D. Rubin, J. P. Brady, and J. D. Henderson (Eds.), Advances in Behavior Therapy (Vol. 5). New York: Academic Press, 1973.

Brady, J. P., and Lind, D. L. Experimental analysis of hysterical blindness. Archives of General Psychiatry, 1961, 4:331–339.

Brady, J. P., Nurnberger, J. I., and Tausig, T. N. Experimental analysis of therapeutic variables by operant conditioning techniques. In J. Wortis (Ed.), Recent Advances in Biological Psychiatry (Vol. 3). New York: Grune & Stratton, 1961.

Branca, A. A. Semantic generalization at the level of the conditioning experiment. American Journal of Psychology, 1957, 70:541–549.

Braukmann, C. J., And Fixsen, D. L. Behavior modification with delinquents. In M. Hersen, R. M. Eisler, and P. M. Miller (Eds.), Progress in Behavior Modification (Vol. 1). New York: Academic Press, 1975.

Braukmann, C. J., Fixsen, D. L., Phillips, E. L., and Wolf, M. M. Behavioral approaches to treatment in the crime and delinquency field. Criminology, 1975, 13:299–331.

Breger, L., and McGaugh, J. L. Critique and reformulation of "learning-theory" approaches to psychotherapy and neurosis. Psychological Bulletin, 1965, 63:338–358.

Breger, L., and McGaugh, J. L. Learning theory and behavior therapy: A reply to Rachman and Eysenck. Psychological Bulletin, 1966, 65:170–173.

Bregman, E. O. An attempt to modify the emotional attitudes of infants by the conditioned response technique. The Pedagogical Seminary and Journal of Genetic Psychology, 1934, 45:169–198.

Breland, K., and Breland, M. The misbehavior of organisms. American Psychologist, 1961, 16:681–684.

Breland, K., and Breland, M. Animal Behavior. New York: Macmillan, 1966.

Brener, J., Eissenberg, E., and Middaugh, S. Respiratory and somatomotor factors associated with operant conditioning of cardiovascular responses in curarized rats. In P. A. Obrist, A. H. Black, J. Brener, and L. V. DiCara (Eds.), Cardiovascular Psychophysiology. Current Issues in Response Mechanisms, Biofeedback, and Methodology. Chicago: Aldine, 1974.

Bridger, W. H., and Mandel, I. J. A comparison of GSR fear responses produced by threat and electric shock. Journal of Psychiatric Research, 1964, 2:31–40.

Brigham, T. A. Self-control. In T. A. Brigham and A. C. Catania (Eds.), Handbook of Applied Behavior Research: Social and Instructional Processes. New York: Irvington/Halstead, 1978, in press.

Brigham, T. A., Graubard, P. S., and Stans, A. Analysis of the effects of sequential reinforcement contingencies on aspects of composition. Journal of Applied Behavior Analysis, 1972, 5:421–429.

Briscoe, R. V., Hoffman, D. B., and Bailey, J. S. Behavioral community psychology: Training a community board to problem solve. Journal of Applied Behavior Analysis, 1975, 8:157–168.

Brissaud, E. Tics et spasmes cloniques de la face. Journal de Médecine et de Chirurgie Pratiques, 1894, 65:49–64.

Brooks, C. H. The Practice of Autosuggestion by the Method of Emile Coué. New York: Dodd, Mead, 1922.

Brown, B. B. Recognition of aspects of consciousness through association with EEG alpha activity represented by a light signal. Psychophysiology, 1970, 6:442–452.

Brown, C. C. Changes in avoidance conditioning following psychotherapeutic treatment. Journal of Nervous and Mental Disease, 1957, 125:487–489.

Brown, P. L., and Jenkins, H. M. Auto-shaping of the pigeon's key peck. Journal of the Experimental Analysis of Behavior, 1968, 11:1–8.

Brown, W. Science and Personality. New Haven: Yale University Press, 1929.

Bryan, G. L., and Nagay, J. A. Use of programed instructional materials in Federal Government agencies. In A. A. Lumsdaine and R. Glaser (Eds.), Teaching Machines and Programed Learning, Vol. II: Data and Directions. Washington, D.C.: National Education Association, 1965.

Budd, K. S., and Baer, D. M. Behavior modification and the law: Implications of recent judicial decisions. Journal of Psychiatry and Law, 1976, 4:171–244.

Bugelski, B. R. The Psychology of Learning. New York: Holt, Rinehart & Winston, 1956.

Burchard, J. D., and Harig, P. T. Behavior modification and juvenile delinquency. In H. Leitenberg (Ed.), Handbook of Behavior Modification and Behavior Therapy. Englewood Cliffs, New Jersey: Prentice-Hall, 1976.

Burgess, A. A Clockwork Orange. New York: Norton, 1963.

Burgess, R. L., Burgess, J. M., and Esveldt, K. C. An analysis of generalized imitation. Journal of Applied Behavior Analysis, 1970, 3:39–46.

Burgess, R. L., Clark, R. N., and Hendee, J. C. An experimental analysis of anti-litter procedures. Journal of Applied Behavior Analysis, 1971, 4:71–75.

Burnham, J. C. On the origins of behaviorism. Journal of the History of the Behavioral Sciences, 1968, 4:143–151.

Burham, W. H. Mental hygiene and the conditional reflex. The Pedagogical Seminary, 1917, 24:449–488.

Burnham, W. H. The Normal Mind: An Introduction to Mental Hygiene and the Hygiene of School Instruction. New York: Appleton, 1924.

Burnham, W. H. The Wholesome Personality: A Contribution to Mental Hygiene. New York: Appleton, 1932.

Buros, O. K. (Ed.). The Seventh Mental Measurements Yearbook (2 vols.). Highland Park, New Jersey: Gryphon, 1972.

Burris, D. S. (Ed.), The Right to Treatment. A Symposium. New York: Springer, 1969.

Buss, A. H. Psychopathology. New York: Wiley, 1966.

Byassee, J. E. Essential hypertension. In R. B. Williams, Jr., and W. D. Gentry (Eds.), Behavioral Approaches to Medical Treatment. Cambridge, Massachusetts: Ballinger, 1977.

Bykov, K. M. New data on the physiology and pathology of the cerebral cortex. Communication at the 19th International Physiological Congress, Montreal, 1953.

Bykov, K. M. [The Cerebral Cortex and the Internal Organs] (W. A. H. Gantt, Ed. and trans.). New York: Chemical Publishing Company, 1957.

Cahoon, D. C. Issues and implications of operant conditioning. Balancing procedures against outcomes. Hospital & Community Psychiatry, 1968a, 19:228–229.

Cahoon, D. C. Symptom substitution and the behavior therapies: A reappraisal. Psychological Bulletin, 1968b, 69:149–156.

Caldwell, B. M. The effects of infant care. In M. L. Hoffman and L. W. Hoffman (Eds.), Review of Child Development Research (Vol. 1). New York: Russell Sage Foundations, 1964.

Cameron, N. A., and Magaret, A. Behavior Pathology. Boston: Houghton Mifflin, 1951.

Carcopino, J. [Daily Life in Ancient Rome: The People and the City at the Height of the Empire] (E. O. Latimer, trans. and H. T. Rowell, Ed.). New Haven: Yale University Press, 1940.

Carlson, C. G., Hersen, M., and Eisler, R. M. Token economy programs in the treatment of hospitalized adult psychiatric patients. Journal of Nervous and Mental Disease, 1972, 155:192–204.

Case, H. W. Therapeutic methods in stuttering and speech blocking. In H. J. Eysenck (Ed.), Behaviour Therapy and the Neuroses: Readings in Modern

Methods of Treatment Derived from Learning Theory. New York: Pergamon, 1960.

Catania, A. C. (Ed.). Contemporary Research in Operant Behavior. Glenview, Illinois: Scott, Foresman, 1968.

Catania, A. C. The myth of self-reinforcement. Behaviorism, 1975, 3:192–199.

Cattell, J. M. The conceptions and methods of psychology. Popular Science Monthly, 1904, 66:176–186.

Cautela, J. R. Treatment of compulsive behavior by covert sensitization. Psychological Record, 1966, 16:33–41.

Cautela, J. R. Covert sensitization. Psychological Reports, 1967, 20:459–468.

Cautela, J. R. Covert negative reinforcement. Journal of Behavior Therapy and Experimental Psychiatry, 1970a, 1:273–278.

Cautela, J. R. Covert reinforcement. Behavior Therapy, 1970b, 1:33–50.

Cautela, J. R. Covert conditioning. In A. Jacobs and L. B. Sachs (Eds.), The Psychology of Private Events: Perspectives on Covert Response Systems. New York: Academic Press, 1971a.

Cautela, J. R. Covert extinction. Behavior Therapy, 1971b, 2:192–200.

Cautela, J. R. Rationale and procedures for covert conditioning. In R. D. Rubin, H. Fensterheim, J. D. Henderson, and L. P. Ullmann (Eds.), Advances in Behavior Therapy (Vol. 4). New York: Academic Press, 1972.

Cautela, J. R. Covert response cost. Psychotherapy: Theory, Research and Practice, 1976a, 13:397–404.

Cautela, J. R. The present status of covert modeling. Journal of Behavior Therapy and Experimental Psychiatry, 1976b, 7:323–326.

Cautela, J. R., and Upper, D. A behavioral coding system. Paper presented at meeting of the Association for Advancement of Behavior Therapy, Miami, December 1973.

Cautela, J. R., and Upper, D. The behavioral inventory battery: The use of self-report measures in behavioral analysis and therapy. In M. Hersen and A. S. Bellack (Eds.), Behavioral Assessment: A Practical Handbook. Oxford: Pergamon, 1976.

Chapman, C., and Risley, T. R. Anti-litter procedures in an urban high-density area. Journal of Applied Behavior Analysis, 1974, 7:377–383.

Chappell, M. N., and Stevenson, T. I. Group psychological training in some organic conditions. Mental Hygiene, 1936, 20:588–597.

Charcot, J.-M. La foi qui guérit. Archives de Neurologie, 1893, 25:72–87.

Chase, J. D. Report of survey of token economy programs in the Veterans Administration. Washington, D.C.: Veterans Administration Department of Medicine and Surgery, 1970.

Chatterjee, B. B., and Eriksen, C. W. Cognitive factors in heart rate conditioning. Journal of Experimental Psychology, 1962, 64:272–279.

Chomsky, N. Reviews: Verbal Behavior by B. F. Skinner. Language, 1959, 35:26–58.

Ciminero, A. R., Calhoun, K. S., and Adams, H. E. (Eds.). Handbook of Behavioral Assessment. New York: Wiley, 1977.

Clark, L. P. The phantasy method of analyzing narcissistic neuroses. Psychoanalytic Review, 1926, 13:225–232.

Clonce v. Richardson, 379 F. Supp. 338 (W. D. Mo. 1974).

Cochrane, R., and Sobol, M. P. Myth and methodology in behaviour therapy research. In M. P. Feldman and A. Broadhurst (Eds.), Theoretical and Empirical Bases of the Behaviour Therapies. London: Wiley, 1976.

Cohen, H. L. Programming alternatives to punishment: The design of competence through consequences. In S. W. Bijou and E. Ribes-Inesta (Eds.), Behavior Modification: Issues and Extensions. New York: Academic Press, 1972.

Cohen, H. L., and Filipczak, J. A New Learning Environment. San Francisco: Jossey-Bass, 1971.

Cohen, L. H., Hilgard, E. R., and Wendt, G. R. Sensitivity to light in a case of hysterical blindness studied by reinforcement-inhibition and conditioning methods. Yale Journal of Biology and Medicine, 1933, 6:61–67.

Colman, A. D., and Baker, S. L. Utilization of an operant conditioning model for the treatment of character and behavior disorders in a military setting. American Journal of Psychiatry, 1969, 125:1395–1403.

Cook, S. W., and Harris, R. E. The verbal conditioning of the galvanic skin reflex. Journal of Experimental Psychology, 1937, 21:202–210.

Cooper, A. B., and Early, D. F. Evolution in the mental hospital: Review of a hospital population. British Medical Journal, 1961, 1:1600–1603.

Cooper, C. Aggression: Changing behavior. Civil Liberties, November 1973, No. 299, 3–4.

Cooper, J. E., Gelder, M. G., and Marks, I. M. Results of behaviour therapy in 77 psychiatric patients. British Medical Journal, 1965, 1:1222–1225.

Couch, R. H., and Allen, C. M. Behavior modification in rehabilitation facilities: A review. Journal of Applied Rehabilitation Counseling, 1973, 4:88–95.

Coué, E. (Ed.). Self-Mastery through Conscious Autosuggestion. New York: American Library Service, 1922.

Coué, E. How To Practice Suggestion and Autosuggestion. New York: American Library Service, 1923.

Covington v. Harris, 419 F. 2d. 617 (D.C. 1969).

Creek v. Stone, 379 F. 2d. 106 (D.C. 1967).

Criswell, J. H. Considerations on the permanence of rehabilitation. Paper presented at the 75th annual convention of the American Psychological Association, Washington, D.C., September 1967.

Cross, H. J. The outcome of psychotherapy: A selected analysis of research findings. Journal of Consulting Psychology, 1964, 28:413–417.

Crossman, E. Communication. Journal of Applied Behavior Analysis, 1975, 8:348.

Crow, W. J. The effect of training upon accuracy and variability in interpersonal perception. Journal of Abnormal and Social Psychology, 1957, 55:355–359.

Crozier, W. J., and Hoagland, H. The study of living organisms. In C. Murchison (Ed.), A Handbook of General Experimental Psychology. Worcester, Massachusetts: Clark University Press, 1934.

Cuny, H. [Ivan Pavlov: The Man and His Theories] (P. Evans, trans.). New York: Paul S. Eriksson, 1965.

Curran, W. J. Governmental regulation of the use of human subjects in medical research: The approach of two federal agencies. In P. A. Freund (Ed.), Experimentation with Human Subjects. New York: Braziller, 1969.

Dale, E. Historical setting of programed instruction. In P. C. Lange (Ed.), Programed Instruction: The Sixty-Sixth Yearbook of the National Society for the Study of Education (Part II). Chicago: University of Chicago Press, 1967.

Darwin, C. On the Origin of Species by Means of Natural Selection, or, The Preservation of Favoured Races in the Struggle for Life. London: Murray, 1859.

Darwin, C. The Descent of Man and Selection in Relation to Sex. New York: Appleton, 1871.

Darwin, C. The Expression of the Emotions in Man and Animals. London: Murray, 1872.

Datel, W. E., and Gengerelli, J. A. Reliability of Rorschach interpretations. Journal of Projective Techniques, 1955, 19:372–381.

Datel, W. E., and Legters, L. J. The psychology of the army recruit. Paper presented at meeting of the American Medical Association, Chicago, June 1970.

Davenport, B. F. The semantic validity of TAT interpretations. Journal of Consulting Psychology, 1952, 16:171–175.

Davidson, W. S., II, and Seidman, E. Studies of behavior modification and juvenile delinquency: A review, methodological critique, and social perspective. Psychological Bulletin, 1974, 81:998–1011.

Davis, G. A. Psychology of Problem Solving: Theory and Practice. New York: Basic Books, 1973.

Davison, G. C. Appraisal of behavior modification techniques with adults in institutional settings. In C. M. Franks (Ed.), Behavior Therapy: Appraisal and Status. New York: McGraw-Hill, 1969.

Davison, G. C. (Letter to the editor): The AABT, the Behavior Therapy and Research Society and accreditation. Behavior Therapy, 1972, 3:522.

Davison, G. C. Counter-control in behavior modification. In L. A. Hamerlynck, L. C. Handy, and E. J. Mash (Eds.), Behavior Change: Methodology, Concepts, and Practice. Champaign, Illinois: Research Press, 1973.

Davison, G. C., and Stuart, R. B. Behavior therapy and civil liberties. American Psychologist, 1975, 30:755–763.

Davison, G. C., Tsujimoto, R. N., and Glaros, A. G. Attribution and the maintenance of behavior change in falling asleep. Journal of Abnormal Psychology, 1973, 82:124–133.

Deese, J., and Hulse, S. H. The Psychology of Learning (3rd ed.). New York: McGraw-Hill, 1967.

Dejerine, J., and Gauckler, E. Les Manifestations Fonctionneles des Psychonéuroses, Leur Traitement par la Psychothérapie. Paris: Masson, 1911.

Dekker, E., and Groen, J. Reproducible psychogenic attacks of asthma: A laboratory study. Journal of Psychosomatic Research, 1956, 1:58–67.

Dekker, E., Pelser, H. E., and Groen, J. Conditioning as a cause of asthmatic attacks: A laboratory study. Journal of Psychosomatic Research, 1957, 2:97–108.

DeMyer, M. K., and Ferster, C. B. Teaching new social behavior to schizophrenic children. Journal of the American Academy of Child Psychiatry, 1962, 1:443–461.

Denker, P. G. Results of treatment of psychoneuroses by the general practitioner. A follow-up study of 500 cases. New York State Journal of Medicine, 1946, 46:2164-2166.

Denny-Brown, D. Theoretical deductions from the physiology of the cerebral cortex. Journal of Neurology and Psychopathology, 1932, 13:52-67.

Desoille, R. Exploration de l'Affectivité Subconsciente par la Méthode du Réve Eveillé. Paris: D'Artrey, 1938.

Desoille, R. Le Reve Éveillé en Psychothérapie: Essai sur la Fonction de Régulation de L'Inconscient Collectif. Paris: Presses Universitaires de France, 1945.

Deutsch, A. The Mentally Ill in America: A History of their Care and Treatment from Colonial Times. New York: Columbia University Press, 1946.

Dewey, J. How We Think, a Restatement of the Relation of Reflective Thinking to the Educative Process. Boston: Heath, 1933.

Diloreto, A. O. Comparative Psychotherapy: An Experimental Analysis. Chicago: Aldine, Atherton, 1971.

Dinitz, S., Lefton, M., Angrist, S., and Pasamanick, B. Psychiatric and social attributes as predictors of case outcome in mental hospitalization. Social Problems, 1961, 8:322-328.

Dix, M. R., and Hallpike, C. S. Peep-show audiometry. Proceedings of the Third World Congress of the Deaf, 1959. Frankfurt Am Main: Deutschen Gehörlosen-Bund e.V., 1961.

Dollard, J., and Miller, N. E. Personality and Psychotherapy: An Analysis in Terms of Learning, Thinking, and Culture. New York: McGraw-Hill, 1950.

Donaldson v. O'Connor, 493 F. 2d. 507 (5th Cir. 1974).

Doolittle, J. Social Life of the Chinese: With Some Account of Their Religious, Governmental, Educational, and Business Customs and Opinions. With Special but not Exclusive Reference to Fuhchau (Vol. 1). New York: Harper & Brothers, 1865.

Drabman, R. S. Behavior modification in the classroom. In W. E. Craighead, A. E. Kazdin, and M. J. Mahoney (Eds.), Behavior Modification: Principles, Issues, and Applications. Boston: Houghton Mifflin, 1976.

Drabman, R. S., Spitalnik, R., and O'Leary, K. D. Teaching self-control to disruptive children. Journal of Abnormal Psychology, 1973, 82:10-16.

Drabman, R., Spitalnik, R., and Spitalnik, K. Sociometric and disruptive behavior as a function of four types of token reinforcement programs. Journal of Applied Behavior Analysis, 1974, 7:93-101.

Duhrssen, A., and Jorswieck, E. Zur korrektur von Eysencks Berichterstattung über psychoanalytische Behandlungsergebnisse. Acta Psychotherapeutica et Psychosomatic, 1962, 19:329-342.

Dulany, D. E., Jr. The place of hypotheses and intentions: An analysis of verbal control in verbal conditioning. In C. W. Eriksen (Ed.), Behavior and Awareness: A Symposium of Research and Interpretation. Durham, North Carolina: Duke University Press, 1962.

Dulany, D. E. Awareness, rules, and propositional control: A confrontation with S-R behavior theory. In T. R. Dixon and D. L. Horton (Eds.), Verbal Behavior and General Behavior Theory. Englewood Cliffs, New Jersey: Prentice-Hall, 1968.

Dunham, P. The nature of reinforcing stimuli. In W. K. Honig and J. E. R.

Staddon (Eds.), Handbook of Operant Behavior. Englewood Cliffs, New Jersey: Prentice-Hall, 1977.

Dunlap, K. The case against introspection. Psychological Review, 1912, 19:404–413.

Dunlap, K. A revision of the fundamental law of habit formation. Science, 1928, 67:360–362.

Dunlap, K. Repetition in the breaking of habits. Scientific Monthly, 1930, 30:66–70.

Dunlap, K. Habits, Their Making and Unmaking. New York: Liveright, 1932.

Duran, D. [The Aztecs: The History of the Indies of New Spain] (D. Heyden and F. Horcasitas, trans.). New York: Orion, 1964.

Dyrud, J. E. Behavior analysis, mental events, and psychoanalysis. In J. H. Masserman (Ed.), Science and Psychoanalysis, Vol. 18: Techniques of Therapy. New York: Grune & Stratton, 1971.

D'Zurilla, T. J. Reducing heterosexual anxiety. In J. D. Krumboltz and C. E. Thoresen (Eds.), Behavioral Counseling: Cases and Techniques. New York: Holt, Rinehart & Winston, 1969.

D'Zurilla, T. J., and Goldfried, M. R. Problem solving and behavior modification. Journal of Abnormal Psychology, 1971, 78:107–126.

Edlin, J. V., Johnson, R. H., Hletko, P., and Heilbrunn, G. The conditioned aversion treatment of chronic alcoholism. Preliminary report. Archives of Neurology and Psychiatry, 1945, 53:85–87.

Edwards, A. L., and Cronbach, L. J. Experimental design for research in psychotherapy. Journal of Clinical Psychology, 1952, 8:51–59.

Eggan, F. (Ed.). Social Anthropology of North American Tribes. Chicago: University of Chicago Press, 1937.

Ellis, A. Towards the improvement of psychoanalytic reseach. Psychoanalytic Review, 1949, 36:123–143.

Ellis, A. Outcome of employing three techniques of psychotherapy. Journal of Clinical Psychology, 1957, 13:344–350.

Ellis, A. Reason and Emotion in Psychotherapy. New York: Lyle Stuart, 1962.

Ellis, A. Should some people be labeled mentally ill? Journal of Consulting Psychology, 1967, 31:435–446.

Ellis, A. The Essence of Rational Psychotherapy: A Comprehensive Approach to Treatment. New York: Institute for Rational Living, 1970.

Ellis, A. Growth through Reason: Verbatim Cases in Rational-Emotive Therapy. Palo Alto: Science & Behavior Books, 1971.

Engel, B. T. Operant conditioning of cardiac function: A status report. Psychophysiology, 1972, 9:161–177.

English, H. B. Three cases of the "conditioned fear response." Journal of Abnormal and Social Psychology, 1929, 24:221–225.

Ennis, B. J., and Friedman, P. R. (Eds.). Legal Rights of the Mentally Handicapped (Vols. 1 and 2). Practising Law Institute, The Mental Health Law Project, 1973.

Erikson, E. H. Childhood and Society (2nd ed.). New York: Norton, 1963.

Eschenbach, A. E., and Borgatta, E. F. Testing behavior hypotheses with the Rorschach: An exploration in validation. Journal of Consulting Psychology, 1955, 19:267–273.

Ethical issues for human services. Association for Advancement of Behavior Therapy Newsletter, July 1977, 4, p. 11.

Everett, P. B., Hayward, S. C., and Meyers, A. W. The effects of a token reinforcement procedure on bus ridership. Journal of Applied Behavior Analysis, 1974, 7:1–9.

Eysenck, H. J. Training in clinical psychology: An English point of view. American Psychologist, 1949, 4:173–176.

Eysenck, H. J. Function and training of the clinical psychologist. Journal of Mental Science, 1950, 96:710–725.

Eysenck, H. J. Discussion on the role of the psychologist in psychiatric practice. Proceedings of the Royal Society of Medicine, 1952a, 45:447–449.

Eysenck, H. J. The effects of psychotherapy: An evaluation. Journal of Consulting Psychology, 1952b, 16:319–324.

Eysenck, H. J. The Dynamics of Anxiety and Hysteria: An Experimental Application of Modern Learning Theory to Psychiatry. London: Routledge & Kegan Paul, 1957.

Eysenck, H. J. Learning theory and behaviour therapy. Journal of Mental Science, 1959, 105:61–75.

Eysenck, H. J. (Ed.). Behaviour Therapy and the Neuroses: Readings in Modern Methods of Treatment Derived from Learning Theory. New York: Pergamon, 1960a.

Eysenck, H. J. The effects of psychotherapy. In H. J. Eysenck (Ed.), Handbook of Abnormal Psychology: An Experiential Approach. London: Pitman Medical Publishing, 1960b.

Eysenck, H. J. Learning theory and behaviour therapy. In H. J. Eysenck (Ed.), Behaviour Therapy and the Neuroses: Readings in Modern Methods of Treatment Derived from Learning Theory. London: Pergamon, 1960c.

Eysenck, H. J. Editorial. Behaviour Research and Therapy, 1963, 1:1–2.

Eysenck, H. J. (Ed.). Experiments in Behaviour Therapy: Readings in Modern Methods of Treatment of Mental Disorders Derived from Learning Theory. Oxford: Pergamon, 1964.

Eysenck, H. J. The effects of psychotherapy. International Journal of Psychiatry, 1965, 1:99–144.

Eysenck, H. J. The Effects of Psychotherapy. New York: International Science Press, 1966.

Eysenck, H. J. Behavior therapy and its critics. Journal of Behavior Therapy and Experimental Psychiatry, 1970, 1:5–15.

Eysenck, H. J. Behaviour therapy—dogma or applied science? In M. P. Feldman and A. Broadhurst (Eds.), Theoretical and Experimental Bases of the Behaviour Therapies. London: Wiley, 1976.

Eysenck, H. J., and Beech, H. R. Counter conditioning and related methods. In A. E. Bergin and S. L. Garfield (Eds.), Handbook of Psychotherapy and Behavior Change: An Empirical Analysis. New York: Wiley, 1971.

Eysenck, H. J., and Rachman, S. The Causes and Cures of Neurosis: An Introduction to Modern Behaviour Therapy Based on Learning Theory and the Principles of Conditioning. London: Routledge & Kegan Paul, 1965.

Fahmy, S. A. Conditioning and extinction of a referential verbal response class in a situation resembling a clinical diagnostic interview. Unpublished doctoral dissertation, Indiana University, 1953.

Fairweather, G. W., Sanders, D. H., Maynard, H., and Cressler, D. L. Community Life for the Mentally Ill: An Alternative to Institutional Care. Chicago: Aldine, 1969.

Falk, J. L. Production of polydipsia in normal rats by an intermittent food schedule. Science, 1961, 133:195–196.

Falk, J. L. The nature and determinants of adjunctive behaviour. In R. M. Gilbert and J. D. Keehn (Eds.), Schedule Effects. Drugs, Drinking, and Aggression. Toronto: University of Toronto Press, 1972.

Farber, I. E. The things people say to themselves. American Psychologist, 1963, 18:185–197.

Farina, A., Gliha, D., Boudreau, L. A., Allen, J. G., and Sherman, M. Mental illness and the impact of believing others know about it. Journal of Abnormal Psychology, 1971, 77:1–5.

Farina, A., and Ring, K. The influence of perceived mental illness on interpersonal relations. Journal of Abnormal Psychology, 1965, 70:47–51.

Fattu, N., Auble, D., and Mech, E. V. Partial reinforcement in a bar-pressing situation with preschool children. Journal of Genetic Psychology, 1955, 87:251–255.

Fattu, N. A., Mech, E. V., and Auble, D. Partial reinforcement related to "free" responding in extinction with pre-school children. Journal of Experimental Education, 1955, 23:365–368.

Feather, B. W., and Rhoads, J. M. Psychodynamic behavior therapy: I. Theory and rationale. Archives of General Psychiatry, 1972a, 26:496–501.

Feather, B. W., and Rhoads, J. M. Psychodynamic behavior therapy: II. Clinical aspects. Archives of General Psychiatry, 1972b, 26:503–511.

Federal Bureau of Prisons. START. Revised program. Washington, D.C.: 1972.

Feldman, M. P., and MacCulloch, M. J. The application of anticipatory avoidance learning to the treatment of homosexuality: 1. Theory, technique and preliminary results. Behaviour Research and Therapy, 1965, 2:165–183.

Feldman, R. B., and Werry, J. S. An unsuccessful attempt to treat a tiqueur by massed practice. Behaviour Research and Therapy, 1966, 4:111–117.

Felixbrod, J. J., and O'Leary, K. D. Effects of reinforcement on children's academic behavior as a function of self-determined and externally imposed contingencies. Journal of Applied Behavior Analysis, 1973, 6:241–250.

Ferleger, D. Loosing the chains: In-hospital civil liberties of mental patients. Santa Clara Lawyer, 1973, 13:447–500.

Ferster, C. B. The use of the free operant in the analysis of behavior. Psychological Bulletin, 1953, 50:263–274.

Ferster, C. B. Withdrawal of positive reinforcement as punishment. Science, 1957, 126:509.

Ferster, C. B. Positive reinforcement and behavioral deficits of autistic children. Child Development, 1961, 32:437–456.

Ferster, C. B. Classification of behavioral pathology. In L. Krasner and L. P. Ullmann (Eds.), Research in Behavior Modification: New Developments and Implications. New York: Holt, Rinehart & Winston, 1965.

Ferster, C. B., Culbertson, S., and Boren, M. C. P. Behavior Principles (2nd ed.). Englewood Cliffs, New Jersey: Prentice-Hall, 1975.

Ferster, C. B., and DeMyer, M. K. The development of performances in autistic children in an automatically controlled environment. Journal of Chronic Diseases, 1961, 13:312–345.

Ferster, C. B., and DeMyer, M. K. A method for the experimental analysis of the behavior of autistic children. American Journal of Orthopsychiatry, 1962, 32:89-98.

Ferster, C. B., Nurnberger, J. I., and Levitt, E. B. The control of eating. Journal of Mathetics, 1962, 1(1):87-109.

Ferster, C. B., and Skinner, B. F. Schedules of Reinforcement. New York: Appleton-Century-Crofts, 1957.

Filipczak, J., and Cohen, H. L. The Case II contingency system and where it is going. Paper presented at the 80th annual convention of the American Psychological Association, Honolulu, Hawaii, September 1972.

Fishman, H. C. A study of the efficacy of negative practice as a corrective for stammering. Journal of Speech Disorders, 1937, 2:67-72.

Flanagan, B., Goldiamond, I., and Azrin, N. Operant stuttering: The control of stuttering behavior through response-contingent consequences. Journal of the Experimental Analysis of Behavior, 1958, 1:173-177.

Flanagan, B., Goldiamond, I., and Azrin, N. Instatement of stuttering in normally fluent individuals through operant procedures. Science, 1959, 130:979-981.

Flanders, J. P. A review of research on imitative behavior. Psychological Bulletin, 1968, 69:316-337.

Flugel, J. C., and West, D. J. A Hundred Years of Psychology, 1833-1933 (Rev. ed.). New York: Basic Books, 1964.

Fo, W. S. O., and O'Donnell, C. R. The buddy system: Relationship and contingency conditions in a community intervention program for youth with nonprofessionals as behavior change agents. Journal of Consulting and Clinical Psychology, 1974, 42:163-169.

Fordyce, W. E. An operant conditioning method for managing chronic pain. Postgraduate Medicine, 1973, 53(6):123-128.

Fordyce, W. E., Fowler, R. S., Jr., Lehmann, J. F., DeLateur, B. J., Sand, P. L., and Trieschmann, R. B. Operant conditioning in the treatment of chronic pain. Archives of Physical Medicine and Rehabilitation, 1973, 54:399-408.

Forehand, R., and Baumeister, A. A. Deceleration of aberrant behavior among retarded individuals. In M. Hersen, R. M. Eisler, and P. M. Miller (Eds.), Progress in Behavior Modification (Vol. 2). New York: Academic Press, 1976.

Fox, L. Effecting the use of efficient study habits. Journal of Mathetics, 1962, 1(1):75-86.

Foxx, R. M., and Azrin, N. H. Restitution: A method of eliminating aggressive-disruptive behavior of retarded and brain damaged patients. Behaviour Research and Therapy, 1972, 10:15-27.

Foxx, R. M., and Azrin, N. H. The elimination of autistic self-stimulatory behavior by overcorrection. Journal of Applied Behavior Analysis, 1973a, 6:1-14.

Foxx, R. M., and Azrin, N. H. Toilet Training the Retarded: A Rapid Program for Day and Nighttime Independent Toileting. Champaign, Illinois: Research Press, 1973b.

Foxx, R. M., and Hake, D. F. Gasoline conservation: A procedure for measuring and reducing the driving of college students. Journal of Applied Behavior Analysis, 1977, 10:61-74.

Frank, J. D. Problems of controls in psychotherapy as exemplified by the psychotherapy research project of the Phipps Psychiatric Clinic. In E. A. Rubinstein and M. B. Parloff (Eds.), Research in Psychotherapy, Vol. I. Washington, D. C.: American Psychological Association, 1962.

Frank, J. D. Persuasion and Healing: A Comparative Study of Psychotherapy. Baltimore: The Johns Hopkins University Press, 1961.

Franks, C. M. Conditioning and abnormal behaviour. In H. J. Eysenck (Ed.), Handbook of Abnormal Psychology: An Experiential Approach. London: Pitman Medical Publishing, 1960.

Franks, C. M. (Ed.). Conditioning Techniques in Clinical Practice and Research. New York: Springer, 1964.

Franks, C. M. (Ed.), Behavior Therapy: Appraisal and Status. New York: McGraw-Hill, 1969a.

Franks, C. M. Behavior therapy and its Pavlovian origins: Review and perspectives. In C. M. Franks (Ed.), Behavior Therapy: Appraisal and Status. New York: McGraw-Hill, 1969b.

Franks, C. M. Pavlovian conditioning approaches. In D. J. Levis (Ed.), Learning Approaches to Therapeutic Behavior Change. Chicago: Aldine, 1970.

Franks, C. M., and Brady, J. P. What is behavior therapy and why a new journal? Behavior Therapy, 1970, 1:1-3.

Franks, V. (Letter to the editor): The AABT, the Behavior Therapy and Research Society and accreditation. Behavior Therapy, 1972, 3:521-522.

Franks, V., and Franks, C. M. Classical conditioning procedures as an index of vocational adjustment among mental defectives. Perceptual and Motor Skills, 1962, 14:241-242.

Franzini, L. R., and Tilker, H. A. On the terminological confusion between behavior therapy and behavior modification. Behavior Therapy, 1972, 3:279-282.

Freeman, H. E., and Simmons, O. G. The Mental Patient Comes Home. New York: Wiley, 1963.

French, T. M. Interrelations between psychoanalysis and the experimental work of Pavlov. American Journal of Psychiatry, 1933, 89:1165-1203.

Fretigny, R., and Virel, A. L'imagerie Mentale: Introduction à l'Onirothérapie. Genèva: Mont-Black, 1969.

Freud, S. [New Introductory Lectures in Psychoanalysis] (W. J. H. Sprott, trans.). New York: Norton, 1933.

Freud, S. [The Problem of Anxiety] (H. A. Bunker, trans.). New York: Norton, 1936.

Freud, S. [An Outline of Psychoanalysis] (J. Strachey, trans.). New York: Norton, 1949.

Freud, S. [The Question of Lay Analysis: An Introduction to Psychoanalysis] (N. Procter-Gregg, trans.). New York: Norton, 1950.

Freudenberg, R. K., and Robertson, J. P. S. Symptoms in relation to psychiatric diagnosis and treatment. Archives of Neurology and Psychiatry, 1956, 76:14-22.

Friedman, P. H. The effects of modeling, role playing, and participation on behavior change. In B. A. Maher (Ed.), Progress in Experimental Personality Research (Vol. 6). New York: Academic Press, 1972.

Friedman, P. R. Legal regulation of applied behavior analysis in mental institutions and prisons. Arizona Law Review, 1975, 17:39–104.

Fuller, P. R. Operant conditioning of a vegetative human organism. American Journal of Psychology, 1949, 62:587–590.

Gagne, R. M. The Conditions of Learning (2nd ed.). New York: Holt, Rinehart & Winston, 1970.

Gantt, W. H. A method of testing cortical function and sensitivity of the skin: An aid in differentiating organic and psychogenic disturbances. Archives of Neurology and Psychiatry, 1938, 40:79–85.

Gantt, W. H. The origin and development of nervous disturbances experimentally produced. American Journal of Psychiatry, 1942, 98:475–481.

Gantt, W. A. H. Experimental Basis for Neurotic Behavior: Origin and Development of Artificially Produced Disturbances of Behavior in Dogs. New York: Paul B. Hoeber, 1944.

Gantt, W. H. Conditional or conditioned, reflex or response? Conditional Reflex, 1966, 1:69–73.

Gantt, W. H., and Muncie, W. Analysis of the mental defect in chronic Korsakov's psychosis by means of the conditioned reflex method. Bulletin of the Johns Hopkins Hospital, 1942, 70:467–487.

Gardner, W. I. Behavior Modification in Mental Retardation: The Education and Rehabilitation of the Mentally Retarded Adolescent and Adult. Chicago: Aldine, Atherton, 1971.

Garfield, S. L. Clinical Psychology: The Study of Personality and Behavior. Chicago: Aldine, 1974.

Garrett, H. E. Great Experiments in Psychology (3rd ed.). New York: Appleton-Century-Crofts, 1951.

Gelder, M. G., and Marks, I. M. Severe agoraphobia: A controlled prospective trial of behaviour therapy. British Journal of Psychiatry, 1966, 112:309–319.

Gelfand, D. M. (Ed.). Social Learning in Childhood: Readings in Theory and Application. Belmont, California: Brooks/Cole, 1969.

Geller, E. S., Chaffee, J. L., and Ingram, R. E. Promoting paper recycling on a university campus. Journal of Environmental Systems, 1975, 5:39–57.

Geller, E. S., Farris, J. C., and Post, D. S. Prompting a consumer behavior for pollution control. Journal of Applied Behavior Analysis, 1973, 6: 367–376.

Geller, E. S., Wylie, R. G., and Farris, J. C. An attempt at applying prompting and reinforcement toward pollution control. Proceedings of the 79th Annual Convention of the American Psychological Association, 1971, 6:701–702.

Genouville, L. Incontinence dite essentielle d'urine. L'association Française d'urologie. Procès-Verbaux, 1908, 12:97–107.

Gentry, W. D. Noncompliance to medical regimen. In R. B. Williams Jr., and W. D. Gentry (Eds.), Behavioral Approaches to Medical Treatment. Cambridge, Massachusetts: Ballinger, 1977.

Gerver, A. Vladimir Michailovitch Bechterev. In V. M. Bekhterev, [General Principles of Human Reflexology: An Introduction to the Objective Study of Personality] (E. Murphy and W. Murphy, trans.). London: Jarrolds, 1933.

Gewirtz, J. L. The roles of overt responding and extrinsic reinforcement in "self-" and "vicarious-reinforcement" phenomena and in "observational learning" and imitation. In R. Glaser (Ed.), The Nature of Reinforcement: A Symposium ofthe Learning Research and Development Center, University of Pittsburgh. New York: Academic Press, 1971.

Gewirtz, J. L., and Baer, D. M. The effect of brief social deprivation on behaviors for a social reinforcer. Journal of Abnormal and Social Psychology, 1958a, 56:49–56.

Gewirtz, J. L., and Baer, D. M. Deprivation and satiation of social reinforcers as drive conditions. Journal of Abnormal and Social Psychology, 1958b, 57: 165–172.

Gewirtz, J. L., Baer, D. M., and Roth, C. H. A note on the similar effects of low social availability of an adult and brief social deprivation on young children's behavior. Child Development, 1958, 29:149–152.

Gibb, J. R. The effects of human relations training. In A. E. Bergin and S. L. Garfield (Eds.), Handbook of Psychotherpy and Behavior Change: An Empirical Analysis. New York: Wiley, 1971.

Gilbert, T. F. Editorial. Journal of Mathetics, 1962a, 1(1):4–6.

Gilbert, T. F. Editorial. Journal of Mathetics, 1962b, 1(2):4–5.

Gilbert, T. F. Mathetics: The technology of education. Journal of Mathetics, 1962c, 1(1):7–73.

Gilbert, T. F. Mathetics: II. The design of teaching exercises. Journal of Mathetics, 1962d, 1(2):7–56.

Glicklich, L. B. An historical account of enuresis. Pediatrics, 1951, 8: 859–876.

Glickman, H., Plutchik, R., and Landau, H. Social and biological reinforcement in an open psychiatric ward. Journal of Behavior Therapy and Experimental Psychiatry, 1973, 4:121–124.

Goffman, E. Asylums: Essays on the Social Situation of Mental Patients and Other Inmates. New York: Doubleday, 1961.

Gold, S., and Neufeld, I. L. A learning approach to the treatment of homosexuality. Behaviour Research and Therapy, 1965, 2:201–204.

Goldberg, L. R. The effectiveness of clinicians' judgments: The diagnosis of organic brain damage from the Bender-Gestalt Test. Journal of Consulting Psychology, 1959, 23:25–33.

Goldberg, L. R., and Werts, C. E. The reliability of clinicians' judgments: A multitrait-multimethod approach. Journal of Consulting Psychology, 1966, 30:199–206.

Goldberg, S. R. Comparable behavior maintained under fixed-ratio and second order schedules of food presentation, cocaine injection, or d-amphetamine injection in the squirrel monkey. Journal of Phamacology and Experimental Therapeutics, 1973, 186:18–30.

Goldfried, M. R. Systematic desensitization as training in self-control. Journal of Consulting and Clinical Psychology, 1971, 37:228–234.

Goldfried, M. R., and Davison, G. C. Clinical Behavior Therapy. New York: Holt, Rinehart & Winston, 1976.

Goldfried, M. R., and Goldfried, A. P. Cognitive change methods. In F. H. Kanfer and A. P. Goldstein (Eds.), Helping People Change: A Textbook of Methods. New York: Pergamon, 1975.

Goldfried, M. R., and Kent, R. N. Traditional versus behavioral personality assessment: A comparison of methodological and theoretical assumptions. Psychological Bulletin, 1972, 77:409-420.

Goldfried, M. R., and Merbaum, M. (Eds.). Behavior Change Through Self-Control. New York: Holt, Rinehart & Winston, 1973.

Goldfried, M. R., and Pomeranz, D. M. Role of assessment in behavior modification. Psychological Reports, 1968, 23:75-87.

Goldfried, M. R., and Sprafkin, J. N. Behavioral Personality Assessment. Morristown, New Jersey: General Learning Press, 1974.

Goldiamond, I. The maintenance of ongoing fluent verbal behavior and stuttering. Journal of Mathetics, 1962, 1(2):57-95.

Goldiamond, I. Justified and unjustified alarm over behavioral control. In O. Milton (Ed.), Behavior Disorders: Perspectives and Trends. Philadelphia: Lippincott, 1965a.

Goldiamond, I. Self-control procedures in personal behavior problems. Psychological Reports, 1965, 17:851-868b.

Goldiamond, I. Stuttering and fluency as manipulatable operant response classes. In L. Krasner and L. P. Ullmann (Eds.), Research in Behavior Modification: New Developments and Implications. New York: Holt, Rinehart & Winston, 1965c.

Goldiamond, I. Toward a constructional approach to social problems: Ethical and constitutional issues raised by applied behavior analysis. Behaviorism, 1974, 2:1-84.

Goldiamond, I. Self-reinforcement. Journal of Applied Behavior Analysis, 1976, 9:509-514.

Goldiamond, I., and Dyrud, J. E. Some applications and implications of behavior analysis for psychotherapy. In J. M. Shlien (Ed.), Research in Psychotherapy, Vol. III. Washington, D.C.: American Psychological Association, 1968.

Goldstein, H., Krantz, D. L., and Rains, J. D. (Eds.). Controversial Issues in Learning. New York: Appleton-Century-Crofts, 1965.

Goldstein, L. S., and Gotkin, L. G. A review of research: Training machines vs. programed textbooks as presentation modes. Journal of Programed Instruction, 1962, 1:29-36.

Goodall, K. Shapers at work. Psychology Today, November 1972, 6:53-63, 132-134, 136-138.

Goodman, S. M. Right to treatment. The responsibility of the courts. In D. S. Burris (Ed.), The Right to Treatment. A Symposium. New York: Springer, 1969.

Gormezano, I. Classical conditioning. In J. B. Sidowski (Ed.), Experimental Methods and Instrumentation in Psychology. New York: McGraw-Hill, 1966.

Gough, H. G. Clinical versus statistical prediction in psychology. In L. Postman (Ed.), Psychology in the Making: Histories of Selected Research Problems. New York: Knopf, 1962.

Gouldner, A. W. Anti-minotaur: The myth of a value-free sociology. Social Problems, 1962, 9:199-213.

Grant, M. Gladiators. London: Weidenfeld & Nicolson, 1967.

Green, E. E., Green, A. M., and Walters, E. D. Voluntary control of internal states: Psychological and physiological. Journal of Transpersonal Psychology, 1970, 2:1–26.

Greenblatt, M., and Levinson, D. J. Mental hospitals. In B. B. Wolman (Ed.), Handbook of Clinical Psychology. New York: McGraw-Hill, 1965.

Greenspoon, J. The effect of verbal and non-verbal stimuli on the frequency of members of two verbal response classes. Unpublished doctoral dissertation, Indiana University, 1951.

Greenspoon, J. Verbal conditioning and clinical psychology. In A. J. Bachrach (Ed.), Experimental Foundations of Clinical Psychology. New York: Basic Books, 1962.

Grindley, G. C. The formation of a simple habit in guinea-pigs. British Journal of Psychology, 1932, 23:127–147.

Grings, W. W. Verbal-perceptual factors in the conditioning of autonomic responses. In W. F. Prokasy (Ed.), Classical Conditioning: A Symposium. New York: Appleton-Century-Crofts, 1965.

Grings, W. W., and Lockhart, R. A. Effects of "anxiety-lessening" instructions and differential set development on the extinction of GSR. Journal of Experimental Psychology, 1963, 66:292–299.

Gripp, R. F., and Magaro, P. A. The token economy program in the psychiatric hospital: A review and analysis. Behaviour Research and Therapy, 1974, 12:205–228.

Grossberg, J. M. Behavior therapy: A review. Psychological Bulletin, 1964, 62:73–88.

Grossberg, J. M. Brain wave feedback experiments and the concept of mental mechanisms. Journal of Behavior Therapy and Experimental Psychiatry, 1972, 3:245–251.

Grosslight, J. H., and Child, I. L. Persistence as a function of previous experience of failure followed by success. American Journal of Psychology, 1947, 60:378–387.

Grosz, H. J., and Zimmerman, J. Experimental analysis of hysterical blindness: A follow-up report and new experimental data. Archives of General Psychiatry, 1965, 13:255–260.

Gruenberg, E. M. The social breakdown syndrome—some origins. American Journal of Psychiatry, 1967, 123:1481–1489.

Guerney, B. G., Jr. (Ed.). Psychotherapeutic agents: New roles for non-professionals, parents, and teachers. New York: Holt, Rinehart & Winston, 1969.

Gurin, G., Veroff, J., and Feld, S. Americans View their Mental Health. A Nationwide Interview Survey. New York: Basic Books, 1960.

Guthrie, E. R. The Psychology of Learning. New York: Harper, 1935.

Guthrie, E. R. Association by contiguity. In S. Koch (Ed.), Psychology: A Study of a Science, Study I: Conceptual and Systematic, Vol. 2: General Systematic Formulations, Learning, and Special Processes. New York: McGraw-Hill, 1959.

Hagen, R. L. Group therapy versus bibliotherapy in weight reduction. Behavior Therapy, 1974, 5:222–234.

Hall, C. S., and Lindzey, G. Theories of Personality. New York: Wiley, 1957.

Hall, K. R. L. Observational learning in monkeys and apes. British Journal of Psychology, 1963, 54:201–226.

Hall, S. M., Hall, R. G., DeBoer, G., and O'Kulitch, P. Self and external management compared with psychotherapy in the control of obesity. Behaviour Research and Therapy, 1977, 15:89–95.

Hancock v. *Avery*, 301 F. Supp. 786 (M. D. Tenn. 1969).

Hanson, L. F., and Komoski, P. K. School use of programed instruction. In A. A. Lumsdaine and R. Glaser (Eds.), Teaching Machines and Programed Learning, Vol. II: Data and Directions. Washington, D.C.: National Education Association, 1965.

Harris, F. R., Johnston, M. K., Kelley, C. S., and Wolf, M. M. Effects of positive social reinforcement on regressed crawling of a nursery school child. Journal of Educational Psychology, 1964, 55:35–41.

Harris, F. R., Wolf, M. M., and Baer, D. M. Effects of adult social reinforcement on child behavior. Young Children, 1964, 20:8–17.

Hart, B. M., Allen, K. E., Buell, J. S., Harris, F. R., and Wolf, M. M. Effects of social reinforcement on operant crying. Journal of Experimental Child Psychology, 1964, 1:145–153.

Hartlage, L. C. Subprofessional therapists' use of reinforcement versus traditional psychotherapeutic techniques with schizophrenics. Journal of Consulting and Clinical Psychology, 1970, 34:181–183.

Hartmann, H. Essays on Ego Psychology: Selected Problems in Psychoanalytic Theory. New York: International Universities Press, 1964.

Hastings, D. W. Follow-up results in psychiatric illness. American Journal of Psychiatry, 1958, 114:1057–1066.

Haughton, E., and Ayllon, T. Production and elimination of symptomatic behavior. In L. P. Ullmann and L. Krasner (Eds.), Case Studies in Behavior Modification. New York: Holt, Rinehart & Winston, 1965.

Hauserman, N., Walen, S. R., and Behling, M. Reinforced racial integration in the first grade: A study in generalization. Journal of Applied Behavior Analysis, 1973, 6:193–200.

Hawkins, R. P., Peterson, R. F., Schweid, E., and Bijou, S. W. Behavior therapy in the home: Amelioration of problem parent-child relations with the parent in a therapeutic role. Journal of Experimental Child Psychology, 1966, 4:99–107.

Haynes v. *Harris*, 344 F. 2d. 463 (8th Cir. 1965).

Heckel, R. V., Wiggins, S. L., and Salzberg, H. C. Conditioning against silences in group therapy. Journal of Clinical Psychology, 1962, 18: 216–217.

Hefferline, R. F. Learning theory and clinical psychology—an eventual symbiosis? In A. J. Bachrach (Ed.), Experimental Foundations of Clinical Psychology. New York: Basic Books, 1962.

Hefferline, R. F., and Bruno, L. J. J. The psychophysiology of private events. In A. Jacobs and L. B. Sachs (Eds.), The Psychology of Private Events: Perspectives on Covert Response Systems. New York: Academic Press, 1971.

Hefferline, R. F., Keenan, B., and Harford, R. A. Escape and avoidance conditioning in human subjects without their observation of the response. Science, 1959, 130:1338–1339.

Heller, K., and Marlatt, G. A. Verbal conditioning, behavior therapy, and behavior change: Some problems in extrapolation. In C. M. Franks (Ed.), Behavior Therapy: Appraisal and Status. New York: McGraw-Hill, 1969.

Hendershot, C. H. Programmed learning: A bibliography of programs and presentation devices. Bay City, Michigan: National Society for Programmed Instruction, 1964.

Herrnstein, R. J. Behaviorism. In D. L. Krantz (Ed.), Schools of Psychology: A Symposium of Papers by David L. Krantz, E. G. Boring, Edna Heidbreder, R. J. Herrnstein, Wolfgang Köhler, David Shakow, Gardner Murphy, on the Occasion of the Seventy-Fifth Anniversary of the Founding of the American Psychological Association. New York: Appleton-Century-Crofts, 1969.

Herrnstein, R. J. Nature as nurture: Behaviorism and the instinct doctrine. Behaviorism, 1972, 1:23–52.

Hersen, M., and Barlow, D. H. Single Case Experimental Designs: Strategies for Studying Behavior Change. New York: Pergamon, 1976.

Hersen, M., and Bellack, A. S. (Eds.). Behavioral Assessment: A Practical Handbook. New York: Pergamon, 1976.

Hersen, M., Eisler, R. M., and Miller, P. M. Development of assertive responses: Clinical, measurement and research considerations. Behaviour Research and Therapy, 1973, 11:505–521.

Herzberg, A. Active Psychotherapy. New York: Grune & Stratton, 1945.

Hilgard, E. R., and Bower, G. H. Theories of Learning. New York: Appleton-Century-Crofts, 1966.

Hilgard, E. R., and Marquis, D. G. Conditioning and Learning. New York: Appleton-Century, 1940.

Hill, W. F. Learning: A Survey of Psychological Interpretations. San Francisco: Chandler, 1963.

Hinde, R. A. Constraints on learning: An introduction to the problems. In R. A. Hinde and J. Stevenson-Hinde (Eds.), Constraints on Learning: Limitations and Predispositions. London: Academic Press, 1973.

Hinde, R. A., and Stevenson-Hinde, J. (Eds.). Constraints on Learning: Limitations and Predispositions. London: Academic Press, 1973.

Hingtgen, J. N., Sanders, B. J., and DeMyer, M. K. Shaping cooperative responses in early childhood schizophrenics. In L. P. Ullmann and L. Krasner (Eds.), Case Studies in Behavior Modification. New York: Holt, Rinehart & Winston, 1965.

Hingtgen, J. N., and Trost, F. C. Shaping cooperative responses in early childhood schizophrenics: II. Reinforcement of mutual physical contact and vocal responses. In R. Ulrich, T. Stachnik, and J. Mabry (Eds.), Control of Human Behavior (Vol. 1). Glenview, Illinois: Scott, Foresman, 1966.

Hobbs, N. Mental health's third revolution. American Journal of Orthopsychiatry, 1964, 34:822–833.

Hogan, R. A. The implosive technique. Behaviour Research and Therapy, 1968, 6:423–431.

Holland, J. G., and Skinner, B. F. The Analysis of Behavior; A Program for Self-Instruction. New York: McGraw-Hill, 1961.

Holland, J. L., and Nichols, R. C. Prediction of academic and extracurricular achievement in college. Journal of Educational Psychology, 1964, 55:55–65.

Holmes v. Silver Cross Hospital of Joliet, Illinois, 340 F. Supp. 125 (E. D. Ill. 1972).

Holt, R. R. Clinical and statistical prediction: A reformulation and some new data. Journal of Abnormal and Social Psychology, 1958, 56:1–12.

Holz, W. C., Azrin, N. H., and Ayllon, T. Elimination of behavior of mental patients by response-produced extinction. Journal of the Experimental Analysis of Behavior, 1963, 6:407–412.

Homme, L. E. Perspectives in psychology: XXIV. Control of coverants, the operants of the mind. Psychological Record, 1965, 15:501–511.

Honig, W. K. (Ed.). Operant Behavior: Areas of Research and Application. New York: Appleton-Century-Crofts, 1966.

Honig, W. K., and Staddon, J. E. R. (Eds.). Handbook of Operant Behavior. Englewood Cliffs, New Jersey: Prentice-Hall, 1977.

Honigfeld, G., and Gillis, R. The role of institutionalization in the natural history of schizophrenia. Diseases of the Nervous System, 1967, 28:660–663.

Hoon, P. W., and Lindsley, O. R. A comparison of behavior and traditional therapy publication activity. American Psychologist, 1974, 29:694–697.

Horowitz, M. J. A study of clinicians' judgments from projective test protocols. Journal of Consulting Psychology, 1962, 26:251–256.

Hospers, J. Human Conduct: An Introduction to the Problems of Ethics, New York: Harcourt, Brace & World, 1961.

Hovey, H. B. The questionable validity of some assumed antecedents of mental illness. Journal of Clinical Psychology, 1959, 15:270–272.

Howard, K. I. The convergent and discriminant validation of ipsative ratings from three projective instruments. Journal of Clinical Psychology, 1962, 18:183–188.

Hudgins, C. V. Conditioning and the voluntary control of the pupillary light reflex. Journal of General Psychology, 1933, 8:3–51.

Hull, C. L. Hypnosis and Suggestibility: An Experimental Approach. New York: Appleton-Century, 1933.

Hull, C. L. Mind, mechanism, and adaptive behavior. Psychological Review, 1937, 44:1–32.

Hull, C. L. Principles of Behavior: An Introduction to Behavior Theory. New York: Appleton-Century, 1943.

Hull, C. L. Essentials of Behavior. New Haven: Yale University Press, 1951.

Hull, C. L. A Behavior System. New Haven: Yale University Press, 1952.

Humphrey, G. The Nature of Learning in Its Relation to the Living System. New York: Harcourt, Brace, 1933.

Hunt, H. F. Problems in the interpretation of "experimental neurosis." Psychological Reports, 1964, 15:27–35.

Hunt, H. F. Behavior therapy for adults. In S. Arieti (Ed.), American Handbook of Psychiatry, Vol. 5 (2nd ed.). New York: Basic Books, 1975.

Hunt, H. F. Recurrent dilemmas in behavioral therapy. In G. Serban (Ed.), Psychopathology of Human Adaptation. New York: Plenum, 1976.

Hunt, H. F., and Dyrud, J. E. Commentary: Perspective in behavior therapy. In J. M. Shlien (Ed.), Research in Psychotherapy, Vol. III. Washington, D.C.: American Psychological Association, Inc., 1968.

Hunt, J. McV. Toward an integrated program of research on psychotherapy. Journal of Consulting Psychology, 1952, 16:237–246.

Hunt, W. A., Wittson, C. L., and Hunt, E. B. A theoretical and practical analysis of the diagnostic process. In P. H. Hoch and J. Zubin (Eds.), Current Problems in Psychiatric Diagnosis. New York: Grune & Stratton, 1953.

Hutchinson, R. R., and Azrin, N. H. Conditioning of mental-hospital patients to fixed-ratio schedules of reinforcement. Journal of the Experimental Analysis of Behavior, 1961, 4:87–95.

Inmates of Boys' Training School v. *Affleck*, 346 F. Supp. 1354 (D.R.I. 1972).

In re Spadafora, 54 Misc., 2d. 123, 281, N.Y.S. 2d. 923 (Sup. Ct. 1967)

Isaacs, W., Thomas, J., and Goldiamond, I. Application of operant conditioning to reinstate verbal behavior in psychotics. Journal of Speech and Hearing Disorders, 1960, 25:8–12.

Ivanov-Smolensky, A. G. Neurotic behavior and the teaching of conditioned reflexes. American Journal of Psychiatry, 1927, 84:483–488.

Jackson, J. Toward the comparative study of mental hospitals: Characteristics of the treatment environment. In A. F. Wessen (Ed.), The Psychiatric Hospital as a Social System. Springfield, Illinois: Charles C Thomas, 1964.

Jacob, R. G., Kraemer, H. C., and Agras, W. S. Relaxation therapy in the treatment of hypertension: A review. Archives of General Psychiatry, 1977, 34:1417–1427.

Jacobs, A., and Wolpin, M. A second look at systematic desensitization. In A. Jacobs and L. B. Sachs (Eds.), The Psychology of Private Events: Perspectives on Covert Response Systems. New York: Academic Press, 1971.

Jacobson, E. Progressive Relaxation. Chicago: University of Chicago Press, 1938.

Jacobson, L. I. The effects of awareness, problem solving ability, and task difficulty on the acquisition and extinction of verbal behavior. Journal of Experimental Research in Personality, 1969, 3:206–213.

Jacobson, N. S., and Martin, B. Behavioral marriage therapy: Current Status. Psychological Bulletin, 1976, 83:540–556.

Jastrow, J. Freud, His Dream and Sex Theories. Cleveland: World, 1932.

Jenkins, W. O., Witherspoon, A. D., DeVine, M. D., deValera, E. K., Muller, J. B., Barton, M. C., and McKee, J. M. The Post-Prison Analysis of Criminal Behavior and Longitudinal Follow-Up Evaluation of Institutional Treatment. Montgomery, Alabama: Rehabilitation Research Foundation, 1974.

Jennings, H. S. Behavior of the Lower Organisms. New York: Columbia, 1906.

Jobson v. *Henne*, 355 F. 2d. 129 (2d. Cir. 1966), cited in 61 Calif. L. Rev. at 91.

Johnson, S. M., and Bolstad, O. D. Methodological issues in naturalistic observation: Some problems and solutions for field research. In L. A. Hamerlynck, L. C. Handy, and E. J. Mash (Eds.), Behavior Change: Methodology, Concepts, and Practice. Champaign, Illinois: Research Press, 1973.

Johnson, W. People in Quandaries: The Semantics of Personal Adjustment. New York: Harper, 1946.

Johnston, M. K., Kelley, C. S., Harris, F. R., and Wolf, M. M. An application of reinforcement principles to development of motor skills of a young child. Child Development, 1966, 37:379–387.

Joint Commission on Mental Illness and Health. Action for Mental Health: Final Report. New York: Basic Books, 1961.

Jolly, F. Ueber die sogenannte maladie des tics convulsifs. Charité-Annalen, 1892, 17:740–753.

Jonas, G. Visceral Learning: Toward a Science of Self-Control. New York: Viking, 1973.

Jones v. Robinson, 440 F. 2d. 249 (D. C. Cir. 1971).

Jones, H. E. The conditioning of overt emotional responses. Journal of Educational Psychology, 1931, 22:127–130.

Jones, H. G. The application of conditioning and learning techniques to the treatment of a psychiatric patient. Journal of Abnormal and Social Psychology, 1956, 52:414–419.

Jones, H. G. Applied abnormal psychology: The experimental approach. In H. J. Eysenck (Ed.), Handbook of Abnormal Psychology: An Experimental Approach. London: Pitman Medical Publishing, 1960.

Jones, M., Baker, A., Freeman, I., Merry, J., Pomryn, B. A., Sandler, J., and Tuxford, J. The Therapeutic Community: A New Treatment Method in Psychiatry. New York: Basic Books, 1953.

Jones, M. C. A laboratory study of fear: The case of Peter. Pedagogical Seminary and Journal of Genetic Psychology, 1924a, 31:308–315.

Jones, M. C. The elimination of children's fears. Journal of Experimental Psychology, 1924b, 7:382–390.

Jones, M. C. A 1924 pioneer looks at behavior therapy. Journal of Behavior Therapy and Experimental Psychiatry, 1975, 6:181–187.

Jones, R. J., and Azrin, N. H. An experimental application of a social reinforcement approach to the problem of job-finding. Journal of Applied Behavior Analysis, 1973, 6:345–353.

Jones, R. T., Nelson, R. E., and Kazdin, A. E. The role of external variables in self-reinforcement: A review. Behavior Modification, 1977, 1:147–178.

Kaestle, C. F. (Ed.). Joseph Lancaster and the Monitorial School Movement: A Documentary History. New York: Teachers College Press, 1973.

Kaimowitz v. Michigan Department of Mental Health, 42 U. S. L. Week 2063 (Mich. Cir. Ct., Wayne City, 1973).

Kallman, W. M., and Feuerstein, M. Psychophysiological procedures. In A. R. Ciminero, K. A. Calhoun, and H. E. Adams (Eds.), Handbook of Behavioral Assessment. New York: Wiley, 1977.

Kamiya, J. Conditioned discrimination of the EEG alpha rhythm in humans. Paper presented at the Western Psychological Association, San Francisco, April 1962.

Kamiya, J. Operant control of the EEG alpha rhythm and some of its reported effects on consciousness. In C. T. Tart (Ed.), Altered States of Consciousness: A Book of Readings. New York: Wiley, 1969.

Kamiya, J., Barber, T. X., DiCara, L. V., Miller, N. E., Shapiro, D., and Stoyva, J. (Eds.), Biofeedback and Self-Control. Chicago: Aldine, 1971.

Kanfer, F. H. Verbal conditioning: A review of its current status. In T. R. Dixon and D. L. Horton (Eds.), Verbal Behavior and General Behavior Theory. Englewood Cliffs, New Jersey: Prentice-Hall, 1968.

Kanfer, F. H. Self-regulation: Research, issues, and speculations. In C. Neuringer and J. L. Michael (Eds.), Behavior Modification in Clinical Psychology. New York: Appleton-Century-Crofts, 1970.

Kanfer, F. H., and Phillips, J. S. Behavior therapy: A panacea for all ills or a passing fancy? Archives of General Psychiatry, 1966, 15:114–128.

Kanfer, F. H., and Phillips, J. S. Learning Foundations of Behavior Therapy. New York: Wiley, 1970.

Kanfer, F. H., and Saslow, G. Behavioral analysis: An alternative to diagnostic classification. Archives of General Psychiatry, 1965, 12:529–538.

Kanfer, F. H., and Saslow, G. Behavior diagnosis. In C. M. Franks (Ed.), Behavior Therapy: Appraisal and Status. New York: McGraw-Hill, 1969.

Kant, F. Further modifications in the technique of conditioned-reflex treatment of alcohol addiction. Quarterly Journal of Studies on Alcohol, 1944, 5:229–232.

Kantorovich, N. V. [An attempt of curing alcoholism by associated reflexes.] Novoyev Refleksologii i Fiziologii Nervnoy Sistemy, 1929, 3:436–445.

Kass, D. J., and Stauss, F. F. Sex Therapy at Home. New York: Simon & Schuster, 1976.

Kassirer, L. B. Behavior modification for patients and prisoners: Constitutional ramifications of enforced therapy. Journal of Psychiatry and Law, 1974, 2:245–302.

Katahn, M., and Koplin, J. H. Paradigm clash: Comment on "Some Recent criticisms of behaviorism and learning theory with special reference to Breger and McGaugh and to Chomsky." Psychological Bulletin, 1968, 69:147–148.

Katz, M. M., Cole, J. O., and Lowery, H. A. Nonspecificity of diagnosis of paranoid schizophrenia. Archives of General Psychiatry, 1964, 11:197–202.

Katz, R. C., Johnson, C. A., and Gelfand, S. Modifying the dispensing of reinforcers: Some implications for behavior modification with hospitalized patients. Behavior Therapy, 1972, 3:579–588.

Katz, R. C., and Zlutnick, S. (Eds.). Behavioral Therapy and Health Care: Principles and Applications. New York: Pergamon, 1975.

Katzev, R. Extinguishing avoidance responses as a function of delayed warning signal termination. Journal of Experimental Psychology, 1967, 75:339–344.

Kazdin, A. E. The failure of some patients to respond to token programs. Journal of Behavior Therapy and Experimental Psychiatry, 1973a, 4:7–14.

Kazdin, A. E. Methodological and assessment considerations in evaluating reinforcement programs in applied settings. Journal of Applied Behavior Analysis, 1973b, 6:517–531.

Kazdin, A. E. Covert modeling, model similarity, and reduction of avoidance behavior. Behavior Therapy, 1974a, 5:325–340.

Kazdin, A. E. Self-monitoring and behavior change. In M. J. Mahoney and C. E. Thoresen (Eds.), Self-Control: Power to the Person. Monterey, California: Brooks/Cole, 1974b.

Kazdin, A. E. Behavior Modification in Applied Settings. Homewood, Illinois: Dorsey, 1975a.

Kazdin, A. E. Characteristics and trends in applied behavior analysis. Journal of Applied Behavior Analysis, 1975b, 8:332.

Kazdin, A. E. The impact of applied behavior analysis on diverse areas of research. Journal of Applied Behavior Analysis, 1975c, 8:213–229.

Kazdin, A. E. Developing assertive behavior through covert modeling. In J. D. Krumboltz and C. E. Thoresen (Eds.), Counseling Methods. New York: Holt, Rinehart, & Winston, 1976a.

Kazdin, A. E. Implementing token programs: The use of staff and patients for maximizing change. In R. L. Patterson (Ed.), Maintaining Effective Token Economies. Springfield, Illinois: Charles C Thomas, 1976b.

Kazdin, A. E. Assessing the clinical or applied significance of behavior change through social validation. Behavior Modification, 1977a, 1:427–452.

Kazdin, A. E. Extensions of reinforcement techniques to socially and environmentally relevant behaviors. In M. Hersen, R. M. Eisler, and P. M. Miller (Eds.), Progress in Behavior Modification (Vol. 4). New York: Academic Press, 1977b.

Kazdin, A. E. Research issues in covert conditioning. Cognitive Therapy and Research, 1977c, 1:45–58.

Kazdin, A. E. The Token Economy: A Review and Evaluation. New York: Plenum Press, 1977d.

Kazdin, A. E. Methodology of applied behavior analysis. In T. Brigham and A. C. Catania (Eds.), Handbook of Applied Behavior Research: Social and Instructional Processes. New York: Irvington/Halstead, 1978.

Kazdin, A. E., and Craighead, W. E. Behavior modification in special education. In L. Mann and D. A. Sabatino (Eds.), The First Review of Special Education (Vol. 2). Philadelphia: Buttonwood Farms, 1973.

Kazdin, A. E., and Pulaski, J. L. Joseph Lancaster and behavior modification in education. Journal of the History of the Behavioral Sciences, 1977, 13:261–266.

Kazdin, A. E. and Wilcoxon, L. A. Systematic desensitization and nonspecific treatment effects: A methodological evaluation. Psychological Bulletin, 1976, 83:729–758.

Kazdin, A. E., and Wilson, G. T. Evaluation of Behavior Therapy: Issues, Evidence, and Research Strategies. Cambridge, Massachusetts: Ballinger, 1978.

Keehn, J. D. Schedule-dependence, schedule-induction, and the law of effect. In R. M. Gilbert and J. D. Keehn (Eds.), Schedule Effects: Drugs, Drinking, and Aggression. Toronto: University of Toronto Press, 1972.

Keehn, J. D., and Webster, C. D. Behavior therapy and behavior modification. Canadian Psychologist, 1969, 10:68–73.

Keeley, S. M., Shemberg, K. M., and Carbonell, J. Operant clinical intervention: Behavior management or beyond? Where are the data? Behavior Therapy, 1976, 7:292–305.

Keller, F. S. Animals and children. Child Development, 1950, 21:7–12.

Keller, F. S. Learning: Reinforcement Theory. New York: Random House, 1954.

Keller, F. S. A personal course in psychology. In R. Ulrich, T. Stachnik, and J. Mabry (Eds.), Control of Human Behavior (Vol. 1). Glenview, Illinois: Scott, Foresman, 1966.

Keller, F. S. "Good-bye, teacher. . . ." Journal of Applied Behavior Analysis, 1968, 1:79–89.

Keller, F. S. Psychology at Harvard (1926–1931), a reminiscence. In P. B. Dews (Ed.), Festschrift for B. F. Skinner. New York: Appleton-Century-Crofts, 1970.

Keller, F. S., and Schoenfeld, W. N. The psychology curriculum at Columbia College. American Psychologist, 1949, 4:165–172.

Keller, F. S., and Schoenfeld, W. N. Principles of Psychology: A Systematic

Text in the Science of Behavior. New York; Appleton-Century-Crofts, 1950.

Kelly, G. A. The Psychology of Personal Constructs. New York: Norton, 1955.

Kendler, H. H. "What is learned?"—A theoretical blind alley. Psychological Review, 1952, 59:269–277.

Kennedy, R. E. Behavior modification in prisons. In W. E. Craighead, A. E. Kazdin, and M. J. Mahoney (Eds.), Behavior Modification: Principles, Issues, and Applications. Boston: Houghton Mifflin, 1976.

Kent, R. N., and O'Leary, K. D. A controlled evaluation of behavior modification with conduct problem children. Journal of Consulting and Clinical Psychology, 1976, 44:586–596.

Kerr, N., Meyerson, L., and Michael, J. A procedure for shaping vocalizations in a mute child. In L. P. Ullmann and L. Krasner (Eds.), Case Studies in Behavior Modification. New York: Holt, Rinehart & Winston, 1965.

Kiesler, D. J. Some myths of psychotherapy research and the search for a paradigm. Psychological Bulletin, 1966, 65:110–136.

Kiesler, D. J. Experimental designs in psychotherapy research. In A. E. Bergin and S. L. Garfield (Eds.), Handbook of Psychotherapy and Behavior Change: An Empirical Analysis. New York: Wiley, 1971.

Kifer, R. E., Lewis, M. A., Green, D. R., and Phillips, E. L. Training predelinquent youths and their parents to negotiate conflict situations. Journal of Applied Behavior Analysis, 1974, 7:357–364.

Kimble, G. A. Hilgard and Marquis' Conditioning and Learning. New York: Appleton-Century-Crofts, 1961.

Kimmel, H. D. Instrumental conditioning of autonomically mediated behavior. Psychological Bulletin, 1967, 67:337–345.

Kimmel, H. D. Instrumental conditioning of autonomically mediated responses in human beings. American Psychologist, 1974, 29:325–335.

King, G. F., Armitage, S. G., and Tilton, J. R. A therapeutic approach to schizophrenics of extreme pathology: An operant-interpersonal method. Journal of Abnormal and Social Psychology, 1960, 61:276–286.

Kish, G. B. Studies of sensory reinforcement. In W. K. Honig (Ed.), Operant Behavior: Areas of Research and Application. New York: Appleton-Century-Crofts, 1966.

Kittrie, N. N. The Right To Be Different: Deviance and Enforced Therapy. Baltimore: The Johns Hopkins University Press, 1971.

Klein, D. A Comprehensive Etymological Dictionary of the English Language (Vol. II). Amsterdam: Elsevier, 1967.

Klein, M. H., Dittman, A. T., Parloff, M. B., and Gill, M. M. Behavior therapy: Observations and reflections. Journal of Consulting and Clinical Psychology, 1969, 33:259–266.

Klopfer, W. G., and Taulbee, E. S. Projective tests. In M. R. Rosenzweig and L. W. Porter (Eds.), Annual Review of Psychology (Vol. 27). Palo Alto, California: Annual Reviews, 1976.

Knapp, T. J., Downs, D. L., and Alperson, J. R. Behavior therapy for insomnia: A review. Behavior Therapy, 1976, 7:614–625.

Knapp, T. J., and Peterson, L. W. Behavior management in medical and nursing practice. In W. E. Craighead, A. E. Kazdin, and M. J. Mahoney (Eds.),

Behavior Modification: Principles, Issues, and Applications. Boston: Houghton Mifflin, 1976.

Knecht v. *Gillman*, 488 F. 2d. 1136, 1139 (8th Cir. 1973).

Koch, S. Clark L. Hull. In W. K. Estes (Ed.), Modern Learning Theory. A Critical Analysis of Five Examples. New York: Appleton-Century-Crofts, 1954.

Koch, S. Psychology and emerging concepts of knowledge as unitary. In T. W. Wann (Ed.), Behaviorism and Phenomenology: Contrasting Bases for Modern Psychology. Chicago: University of Chicago Press, 1964.

Koffka, K. The Principles of Gestalt Psychology. New York: Harcourt, Brace, 1935.

Kohlenberg, R., and Phillips, T. Reinforcement and rate of litter depositing. Journal of Applied Behavior Analysis, 1973, 6:391–396.

Kohlenberg, R., Phillips, T., and Proctor, W. A behavioral analysis of peaking in residential electrical-energy consumers. Journal of Applied Behavior Analysis, 1976, 9:13–18.

Kondaš, O., and Ščetnická, B. Systematic desensitization as a method of preparation for childbirth. Journal of Behavior Therapy and Experimental Psychiatry, 1972, 3:51–54.

Konorski, J. Conditioned Reflexes and Neuron Organization. New York: Cambridge University Press, 1948.

Konorski, J., and Miller, S. On two types of conditioned reflex. Journal of General Psychology, 1937, 16:264–272.

Korzybski, A. Science and Sanity. Lancaster, Pennsylvania: Science Press, 1933.

Koshtoyants, K. [I. M. Sechenov (1829–1905)] In I. M. Sechenov, Reflexes of the Brain: An Attempt to Establish the Physiological Basis of Psychological Processes. (S. Belsky, trans. and G. Gibbons, Ed). Cambridge, Massachusetts: M.I.T. Press, 1965.

Kostyleff, N. L'inversion sexuelle expliquée par réflexologie. Psychologie et Vie, 1927, 1:8–12.

Kraepelin, E. [One Hundred Years of Psychiatry] (W. Baskin, trans.). New York: Citadel, 1962.

Kraft, T. Psychoanalysis and behaviorism: A false antithesis. American Journal of Psychotherapy, 1969, 23:482–487.

Krantz, D. L. The separate worlds of operant and non-operant psychology. Journal of Applied Behavior Analysis, 1971, 4:61–70.

Krasner, L. The use of generalized reinforcers in psychotherapy research. Psychological Reports, 1955, 1:19–25.

Krasner, L. Studies of the conditioning of verbal behavior. Psychological Bulletin, 1958, 55:148–170.

Krasner, L. The therapist as a social reinforcement machine. In H. H. Strupp and L. Luborsky (Eds.), Research in Psychotherapy, Vol. II. Washington, D.C.: American Psychological Association, 1962.

Krasner, L. Reinforcement, verbal behavior, and psychotherapy. American Journal of Orthopsychiatry, 1963, 33:601–613.

Krasner, L. The behavioral scientist and social responsibility: No place to hide. Journal of Social Issues, 1965a, 21:9–30.

Krasner, L. Verbal conditioning and psychotherapy. In L. Krasner and L. P.

Ullmann (Eds.), Research in Behavior Modification: New Developments and Implications. New York: Holt, Rinehart & Winston, 1965b.

Krasner, L. Behavior modification—values and training: The perspective of a psychologist. In C. M. Franks (Ed.), Behavior Therapy: Appraisal and Status. New York: McGraw-Hill, 1969.

Krasner, L. Behavior therapy. In P. H. Mussen (Ed.), Annual Review of Psychology (Vol. 22). Palo Alto, California: Annual Reviews, 1971a.

Krasner, L. The operant approach in behavior therapy. In A. E. Bergin and S. L. Garfield (Eds.), Handbook of Psychotherapy and Behavior Change: An Empirical Analysis. New York: Wiley, 1971b.

Krasner, L., and Ullmann, L. P. (Eds.). Research in behavior modification: New Developments and Implications. New York: Holt, Rinehart & Winston, 1965.

Krasner, L., and Ullmann, L. P. Behavior Influence and Personality: The Social Matrix of Human Action. New York: Holt, Rinehart & Winston, 1973.

Krasnogorski, N. I. The conditioned reflexes and children's neuroses. American Journal of Diseases in Children, 1925, 30:735-768.

Kris, E. Psychoanalytic Explorations in Art. New York: International Universities Press, 1952.

Krumboltz, J. D., and Thoresen, C. E. (Eds.). Counseling Methods. New York: Holt, Rinehart & Winston, 1976.

Kubie, L. S. Relation of the conditioned reflex to psychoanalytic technic. Archives of Neurology and Psychiatry, 1934, 32:1137-1142.

Kubie, L. S. The use of induced hypnagogic reveries in the recovery of repressed amnesic data. Bulletin of the Menninger Clinic, 1943, 7:172-183.

Kuhn, T. S. The Structure of Scientific Revolutions. Chicago: University of Chicago Press, 1962.

Laing, R. D. The Politics of Experience. New York: Pantheon, 1967.

Lake v. Cameron, 364 F. 2d. 657 (D. C. 1966).

Lancaster, J. Improvements in Education, as it Respects the Industrious Classes of the Community, Containing, Among Other Important Particulars, an Account of the Institution for the Education of One Thousand Poor Children, Borough Road, Southwark; and of the New System of Education on Which it is Conducted (3rd ed.). London: Darton & Harvey, 1805.

Landis, C. A statistical evaluation of psychotherapeutic methods. In L. E. Hinsie, Concepts and Problems of Psychotherapy. New York: Columbia University Press, 1937.

Lang, P. J., and Lazovik, A. D. Experimental desensitization of a phobia. Journal of Abnormal and Social Psychology, 1963, 66:519-525.

Lange, P. C. (Ed.). Programed Instruction: The Sixty-Sixth Yearbook of the National Society for the Study of Education (Part II). Chicago: University of Chicago Press, 1967.

Langsley, D. G., Machotka, P., and Flomenhaft, K. Avoiding mental hospital admission: A follow-up study. American Journal of Psychiatry, 1971, 127:1391-1394.

La Piere, R. T. Review of Freud: On War, Sex and Neurosis by S. Katz (Ed.), Sigmund Freud: An Introduction by W. Hollitscher, and Psychoanalysis and the Social Sciences by G. Róheim (Ed.), American Sociological Review, 1948, 13:346-348.

Lashley, K. S. The human salivary reflex and its use in psychology. Psychological Review, 1916, 23:446–464.

Lashley, K. S. Integrative functions of the cerebral cortex. Physiological Reviews, 1933, 13:1–42.

Lazarus, A. A. New methods in psychotherapy: A case study. South African Medical Journal, 1958, 32:660–664.

Lazarus, A. A. The elimination of children's phobias by deconditioning. Medical Proceedings, 1959, 5:261–265.

Lazarus, A. A. Group therapy of phobic disorders by systematic desensitization. Journal of Abnormal and Social Psychology, 1961, 63:504–510.

Lazarus, A. A. The results of behaviour therapy in 126 cases of severe neurosis. Behaviour Research and Therapy, 1963, 1:69–79.

Lazarus, A. A. Broad-spectrum behaviour therapy and the treatment of agoraphobia. Behaviour Research and Therapy, 1966, 4:95–97.

Lazarus, A. A. In support of technical eclecticism. Psychological Reports, 1967, 21:415–416.

Lazarus, A. A. Behavior Therapy and Beyond. New York: McGraw-Hill, 1971a.

Lazarus, A. A. Reflections on behavior therapy and its development: A point of view. Behavior Therapy, 1971a, 2:369–374.

Lazarus, A. A. (Letter to the editor): The AABT, the Behavior Therapy and Research Society, and accreditation. Behavior Therapy, 1973, 4:172–174.

Lazarus, A. A., and Abramovitz, A. The use of "emotive imagery" in the treatment of children's phobias. Journal of Mental Science, 1962, 108: 191–195.

Lazarus, A. A., and Rachman, S. The use of systematic densensitization in psychotherapy. South African Medical Journal, 1957, 31:934–937.

Lefcourt, H. M. Internal versus external control of reinforcement: A review. Psychological Bulletin, 1966, 65:206–220.

Lehner, G. F. J. Negative practice as a psychotherapeutic technique. Journal of General Psychology, 1954, 51:69–82.

Leitenberg, H. (Ed.). Handbook of Behavior Modification and Behavior Therapy. Englewood Cliffs, New Jersey: Prentice-Hall, 1976.

Lemere, F., and Voegtlin, W. L. Conditioned reflex therapy of alcoholic addiction: Specificity of conditioning against chronic alcoholism. California and Western Medicine, 1940, 53:268–269.

Lemere, F., and Voegtlin, W. L. An evaluation of the aversion treatment of alcoholism. Quarterly Journal of Studies on Alcohol, 1950, 11:199–204.

Lemere, F., Voegtlin, W. L., Broz, W. R., O'Hollaren, P., and Tupper, W. E. The conditioned reflex treatment of chronic alcoholism: VII. Technic. Diseases of the Nervous System, 1942a, 3:243–247.

Lemere, F., Voegtlin, W. L., Broz, W. R., O'Hollaren, P., and Tupper, W. E. Conditioned reflex treatment of chronic alcoholism: VIII. A review of six years' experience with this treatment of 1,526 patients. Journal of the American Medical Association, 1942b, 120:269–270.

Lessard v. Schmidt, 349 F. Supp. 1078 (E. D. Wisc. 1972).

Leuner, H. Guided affective imagery (GAI): A method of intensive psychotherapy. American Journal of Psychotherapy, 1969, 23:4–22.

Levin, M. Narcolepsy and the machine age: The recent increase in the incidence of narcolepsy. Journal of Neurology and Psychopathology, 1934, 15:60–64.

Levis, D. J. Integration of behavior therapy and dynamic psychiatric techniques: A marriage with a high probability of ending in divorce. Behavior Therapy, 1970, 1:531–537.

Levis, D. J. Implosive therapy: A critical analysis of Morganstern's review. Psychological Bulletin, 1974, 81:155–158.

Levitt, E. E. The results of psychotherapy with children: An evaluation. Journal of Consulting Psychology, 1957, 21:189–196.

Levitt, E. E. Psychotherapy with children: A further evaluation. Behaviour Research and Therapy, 1963, 1:45–51.

Levitt, E. E. Research on psychotherapy with children. In A. E. Bergin and S. L. Garfield (Eds.), Handbook of Psychotherapy and Behavior Change: An Empirical Analysis. New York: Wiley, 1971.

Lewin, K. Field theory of learning. In N. B. Henry (Ed.), Forty-First Yearbook of the National Society for the Study of Education. Part 2. The Psychology of Learning. Bloomington, Illinois: Public-School, 1942.

Lewis, D. Chastity; Or, Our Secret Sins. Philadelphia: George Maclean, 1874.

Lewis, N. D. C. A Short History of Psychiatric Achievement, with a Forecast for the Future. New York: Norton, 1941.

Liberman, R. P., and Ferris, C. Antisocial behavior and school performance: Comparison between Welcome Home and Rancho San Antonio. Unpublished report to the California Council on Criminal Justice, 1974.

Liberman, R. P., King, L. W., and DeRisi, W. J. Behavior analysis and therapy in community mental health. In H. Leitenberg (Ed.), Handbook of Behavior Modification and Behavior Therapy. Englewood Cliffs, New Jersey: Prentice-Hall, 1976.

Liddell, H. S. The experimental neurosis and the problem of mental disorder. American Journal of Psychiatry, 1938, 94:1035–1042.

Liddell, H. S. Emotional Hazards in Animals and Man. Springfield, Illinois: Charles C Thomas, 1956.

Liddell, H. S., and Bayne, T. L. Auditory conditioned reflexes in the thyroidectomized sheep and goat. Society for Experimental Biology and Medicine Proceedings, 1926, 24:289–291.

Lindsley, O. R. Operant conditioning methods applied to research in chronic schizophrenia. Psychiatric Research Reports, 1956, 5:118–139.

Lindsley, O. R. Characteristics of the behavior of chronic psychotics as revealed by free-operant conditioning methods. Diseases of the Nervous System, Monograph Supplement, 1960, 21:66–78.

Lindsley, O. R. Free-operant conditioning and psychotherapy. Current Psychiatric Therapies, 1963, 3:47–56.

Lindvall, C. M., and Bolvin, J. O. Programed instruction in the schools: An application of programing principles in "individually prescribed instruction." In P. C. Lange (Ed.), Programed instruction: The Sixty-Sixth Yearbook of the National Society for the Study of Education (Part II). Chicago: University of Chicago Press, 1967.

Ling, B.-C. Form discrimination as a learning cue in infants. Comparative Psychology Monographs, 1941, 17(2):166.

Lisina, M. I. The role of orientation in the transformation of involuntary into voluntary reactions. In A. V. Zaporozhets (Ed.), The Development of Voluntary Movements. Moscow: 1960.

Little, K. B., and Shneidman, E. S. Congruencies among interpretations of psychological test and anamnestic data. Psychological Monographs, 1959, 73:(6, Whole No. 476).

Livson, N., and Peskin, H. Prediction of adult psychological health in a longitudinal study. Journal of Abnormal Psychology, 1967, 73:509–518.

Loeb, J. Einleitung in die Vergleichende Gehirnphysiologie und Vergleichende Psychologie, mit Besonderer Berücksichtigung der Wirbellosen Thiere. Leipzig: Barth, 1899.

Loeb, J. The Organism as a Whole, from a Physicochemical Viewpoint. New York: Putnam, 1916.

London, P. The Modes and Morals of Psychotherapy. New York: Holt, Rinehart & Winston, 1964.

London, P. Behavior Control. New York: Harper & Row, 1969.

London, P. The end of ideology in behavior modification. American Psychologist, 1972, 27:913–920.

Lovaas, O. I., and Bucher, B. D. (Eds.). Perspectives in Behavior Modification with Deviant Children. Englewood Cliffs, New Jersey: Prentice-Hall, 1974.

Lovaas, O. I., Koegel, R., Simmons, J. Q., and Long, J. S. Some generalization and follow-up measures on autistic children in behavior therapy. Journal of Applied Behavior Analysis, 1973, 6:131–166.

Lovaas, O. I., and Simmons, J. Q. Manipulation of self-destruction in three retarded children. Journal of Applied Behavior Analysis, 1969, 2:143–157.

Lovibond, S. H. Intermittent reinforcement in behaviour therapy. Behaviour Research and Therapy, 1963a, 1:127–132.

Lovibond, S. H. The mechanism of conditioning treatment of enuresis. Behaviour Research and Therapy, 1963b, 1:17–21.

Lovibond, S. H. Conditioning and Enuresis. New York: Pergamon, 1964.

Luborsky, L. A note on Eysenck's article, "The effects of psychotherapy: An evaluation." British Journal of Psychology, 1954, 45:129–131.

Luborsky, L., Singer, B., and Luborsky, L. Comparative studies of psychotherapies: Is it true that "everyone has won and all must have prizes"? Archives of General Psychiatry, 1975, 32:995–1008.

Luborsky, L., and Spence, D. P. Quantitative research on psychoanalytic therapy. In A. E. Bergin and S. L. Garfield (Eds.), Handbook of Psychotherapy and Behavior Change: An Empirical Analysis. New York: Wiley, 1971.

Lucero, R. J., Vail, D. J., and Scherber, J. Regulating operant-conditioning programs. Hospital & Community Psychiatry, 1968, 19:53–54.

Lumsdaine, A. A., and Glaser, R. (Eds.). Teaching Machines and Programed Learning, Vol. II: A Source Book. Washington, D.C.: National Education Association, 1960.

Lumsdaine, A. A., and Glaser, R. (Eds.). Teaching machines and programed Learning, Vol. II: Data and Directions. Washington, D.C.: National Education Association, 1965.

Luria, A. R. [The Role of Speech in the Regulation of Normal and Abnormal behavior] (J. Tizard, Ed.). New York: Liveright, 1961.

Luyben, P. D., and Bailey, J. S. Newspaper recycling behavior: The effects of reinforcement versus proximity of containers. Unpublished doctoral dissertation, Florida State University, 1975.

MacCulloch, M. J., Feldman, M. P., Orford, J. F., and MacCulloch, M. L. Anticipatory avoidance learning in the treatment of alcoholism: A record of therapeutic failure. Behaviour Research and Therapy, 1966, 4:187-196.

Mackey v. Procunier, 477 F. 2d. 877 (9th Cir. 1973).

Maconochie, A. Norfolk Island. Hobart, Australia: Sullivan's Cove, Publisher, 1973. (Originally published, 1847.)

Maconochie, A. The Mark System. London: John Ollivier, 1848.

Magaret, A. Generalization in successful psychotherapy. Journal of Consulting Psychology, 1950, 14:64-70.

Mahoney, M. J. Cognition and Behavior Modification. Cambridge, Massachusetts: Ballinger, 1974.

Mahoney, M. J., Kazdin, A. E., and Lesswing, N. J. Behavior modification: Delusion or deliverance? In C. M. Franks and G. T. Wilson (Eds.), Annual Review of Behavior Therapy, Theory, and Practice (Vol. 2). New York: Bruner/Mazel, 1974.

Mahoney, M. J., and Thoresen, C. E. (Eds.). Self-control: Power to the Person. Monterey, California: Brooks/Cole, 1974.

Mahrer, A. R., and Mason, D. J. Changes in number of self-reported symptoms during psychiatric hospitalization. Journal of Consulting Psychology, 1965, 29:285.

Malinowski, B. Sex and Repression in Savage Society. London: K. Paul, Trench, Trubner, 1937.

Malleson, N. Panic and phobia: A possible method of treatment. Lancet, 1959, 1:225-227.

Maloney, K. B., and Hopkins, B. L. The modification of sentence structure and its relationship to subjective judgments of creativity in writing. Journal of Applied Behavior Analysis, 1973, 6:425-433.

Mandler, G., and Kahn, M. Discrimination of changes in heart rate: Two unsuccessful attempts. Journal of the Experimental Analysis of Behavior, 1960, 3:21-25.

Mandler, G., Preven, D. W., and Kuhlman, C. K. Effects of operant reinforcement on the GSR. Journal of the Experimental Analysis of Behavior, 1962, 5:317-321.

Marholin, D., II, and Gray, D. Effects of group response cost procedures on cash shortages in a small business. Journal of Applied Behavior Analysis, 1976, 9:25-30.

Marholin, D., II, Siegel, L. J., and Phillips, D. Treatment and transfer: A search for empirical procedures. In M. Hersen, R. M. Eisler, and P. M. Miller (Eds.), Progress in Behavior Modification (Vol. 3). New York: Academic Press, 1976.

Marinesco, G., and Kreindler, A. Des Réflexes Conditionnels; Études de Physiologie Normale et Pathologique. Paris: Alcan, 1935.

Marinesco, G., Sager, O., and Kreindler, A. Nouvelles contributions à l'étude des reflexes conditionnels dans l'hysterie. Revue Neurologique, 1931, 38(2):624-629.

Markovnikov, A. [Treatment of alcoholism by combination of persuasion with development of conditioned reflex of vomiting after swallowing alcoholic drink.] Sovetskaya Vrachebnaya Gazeta, May 1934, 807–808.

Marks, I. M. Flooding (implosion) and allied treatments. In W. S. Agras (Ed.), Behavior Modification: Principles and Clinical Applications. Boston: Little, Brown, 1972.

Marks, I. Behavioral treatments of phobic and obsessive-compulsive disorders: A critical appraisal. In M. Hersen, R. M. Eisler, and P. M. Miller (Eds.), Progress in Behavior Modification (Vol. 1). New York: Academic Press, 1975.

Marks, I. M., and Gelder, M. G. A controlled retrospective study of behaviour therapy in phobic patients. British Journal of Pychiatry, 1965, 111:561–573.

Marks, I. M., and Gelder, M. G. Transvestism and fetishism: Clinical and psychological changes during faradic aversion. British Journal of Psychiatry, 1967, 113:711–729.

Marlatt, G. A., and Perry, M. A. Modeling methods. In F. H. Kanfer and A. P. Goldstein (Eds.), Helping People Change: A Textbook of Methods. New York: Pergamon, 1975.

Martin, R. Legal Challenges to Behavior Modification: Trends in Schools, Corrections and Mental Health. Champaign, Illinois: Research Press, 1975.

Masserman, J. H. Behavior and Neurosis: An Experimental Psycho-analytic Approach to Psychobiologic Principles. Chicago: University of Chicago Press, 1943.

Masserman, J. H., and Carmichael, H. T. Diagnosis and prognosis in psychiatry: With a follow-up study of the results of short-term general hospital therapy in psychiatric cases. Journal of Mental Science, 1938, 84:893–946.

Matarazzo, J. D., Saslow, G., and Pareis, E. N. Verbal conditioning of two responses classes: Some methodological considerations. Journal of Abnormal and Social Psychology, 1960, 61:190–206.

Mateer, F. Child Behavior: A Critical and Experimental Study of Young Children by the Method of Conditioned Reflexes. Boston: Badger, 1918.

Mattocks, A. L., and Jew, C. Assessment of an aversive treatment program with extreme acting-out patients in a psychiatric facility for criminal offenders. Unpublished manuscript, California Department of Corrections, undated. (On file with the University of Southern California Law Library, Los Angeles, California.)

Max, L. W. Breaking up a homosexual fixation by the conditioned reaction technique: A case study. Psychological Bulletin, 1935, 32:734.

May, J. G., Risley, T. R., Twardosz, S., Friedman, P., Bijou, S. W., and Wexler, D. Guidelines for the Use of Behavioral Procedures in State Programs for Retarded Persons. Arlington, Texas: National Association for Retarded Citizens, 1976.

McConnell, J. V. Stimulus/response: Criminals can be brainwashed—now. Psychology Today, April, 1970, 3:14, 16, 18, 74.

McDougall, W. Physiological Psychology. London: J. M. Dent & Sons, 1905.

McDougall, W. An Introduction to Social Psychology. Boston: J. W. Luce, 1909.

McLaughlin, T. F. The applicability of token reinforcement systems in public school systems. Psychology in the Schools, 1975, 12:84–89.

McMurtry, C. A., and Williams, J. E. Evaluation dimension of the affective meaning system of the preschool child. Developmental Psychology, 1972, 6:238–246.

McReynolds, W. T., and Church, A. Self-control, study skills development and counseling approaches to the improvement of study behavior. Behaviour Research and Therapy, 1973, 11:233–235.

McReynolds, W. T., and Tori, C. A further assessment of attention-placebo effects and demand characteristics in studies of systematic desensitization. Journal of Consulting and Clinical Psychology, 1972, 38:261–264.

Mead, M. Coming of Age in Samoa: A Psychological Study in Primitive Youth for Western Civilization. New York: Morrow, 1928.

Mead, M. Sex and Temperament in Three Primitive Societies. New York: Morrow, 1935.

Mednick, M. T., and Lindsley, O. R. Some clinical correlates of operant behavior. Journal of Abnormal and Social Psychology, 1958, 57:13–16.

Meehl, P. E. Clinical versus Statistical Prediction: A Theoretical Analysis and a Review of the Evidence. Minneapolis: University of Minnesota Press, 1954.

Meehl, P. E. Psychotherapy. In C. P. Stone (Ed.), Annual Review of Psychology (Vol. 6). Stanford, California: Annual Reviews, 1955.

Meehl, P. E. Wanted—a good cookbook. American Psychologist, 1956, 11:263–272.

Meehl, P. E. When shall we use our heads instead of the formula? Journal of Counseling Psychology, 1957, 4:268–273.

Meehl, P. E. The cognitive activity of the clinician. American Psychologist, 1960, 15:19–27.

Meehl, P. E., and Rosen, A. Antecedent probability and the efficiency of psychometric signs, patterns, or cutting scores. Psychological Bulletin, 1955, 52:194–216.

Meichenbaum, D. H. The effects of instructions and reinforcement on thinking and language behaviour of schizophrenics. Behaviour Research and Therapy, 1969, 7:101–114.

Meichenbaum, D. H. Cognitive factors in behavior modification: Modifying what clients say to themselves. In R. D. Rubin, J. P. Brady, and J. D. Henderson (Eds.), Advances in Behavior Therapy (Vol. 5). New York: Academic Press, 1973.

Meichenbaum, D. H. Cognitive Behavior Modification. Morristown, New Jersey: General Learning Press, 1974.

Meichenbaum, D. H. Self-instructional methods. In F. H. Kanfer and A. P. Goldstein (Eds.), Helping People Change: A Textbook of Methods. New York: Pergamon, 1975.

Meichenbaum, D. H. Cognitive Behavior Modification. New York: Plenum, 1977.

Meichenbaum, D. H., and Goodman, J. Training impulsive children to talk to themselves: A means of developing self-control. Journal of Abnormal Psychology, 1971, 77:115–126.

Meige, H., and Feindel, E. [Tics and Their Treatment] (S. A. K. Wilson, trans.). London: Sidney Appleton, 1907.

Meignant, P. Réflexes conditionnels et psycho-pathologie: Quelques remarques concernant les perversions et les anomalies sexuelles. Gazette Medicale de France, 1935, 8:327–332.

Melin, G. L., and Götestam, K. G. A contingency management program on a drug-free unit for intravenous amphetamine addicts. Journal of Behavior Therapy and Experimental Psychiatry, 1973, 4:331–337.

Mendel, W. M. Effect of length of hospitalization on rate and quality of remission from acute psychotic episodes. Journal of Nervous and Mental Disease, 1966, 143:226–233.

Mendel, W. M. On the abolition of the psychiatric hospital. In L. M. Roberts, N. S. Greenfield, and M. H. Miller (Eds.), Comprehensive Mental Health: The Challenge of Evaluation. Madison: University of Wisconsin Press, 1968.

Mental Health Law Project. Basic Rights of the Mentally Handicapped; Right to Treatment, Right to Compensation for Institution-maintaining Labor, Right to Education. Washington, D.C.: Mental Health Law Project, 1973.

Mertens, G. C., and Fuller, G. B. Conditioning of molar behavior in "regressed" psychotics: I. An objective measure of personal habit training with "regressed" psychotics. Journal of Clinical Psychology, 1963, 19: 333–337.

Meyer, M. F. The Fundamental Laws of Human Behavior: Lectures on the Foundations of Any Mental or Social Science. Boston: Badger, 1911.

Meyer, V. The treatment of two phobic patients on the basis of learning principles. Journal of Abnormal and Social Psychology, 1957, 55:261–266.

Milan, M. A., and McKee, J. M. Behavior modification: Principles and applications in corrections. In D. Glaser (Ed.), Handbook of Criminology. Chicago: Rand McNally, 1974.

Milan, M. A., Wood, L. F., Williams, R. L., Rogers, J. G., Hampton, L. R., and McKee, J. M. Applied Behavior Analysis and the Imprisoned Adult Felon: Project I: The Cellblock Token Economy. Montgomery, Alabama: Rehabilitation Research Foundation, 1974.

Millard v. Cameron, 125 U.S. App. D. C. 383, 373 F. 2d. 468 (1966).

Miller, D. Worlds that fail: Part I, Retrospective analysis of mental patients' careers. California Mental Health Research Monograph, 1965 (Whole No. 6).

Miller, D. Retrospective analysis of posthospital mental patients' worlds. Journal of Health and Social Behavior, 1967, 8:136–140.

Miller, G. A., Galanter, E., and Pribram, K. H. Plans and the Structure of Behavior. New York: Holt, Rinehart & Winston, 1960.

Miller, L. K., and Miller, O. L. Reinforcing self-help group activities of welfare recipients. Journal of Applied Behavior Analysis, 1970, 3:57–64.

Miller, N. E. Studies of fear as an acquirable drive: I. Fear as motivation and fear-reduction as reinforcement in the learning of new responses. Journal of Experimental Psychology, 1948, 38:89–101.

Miller, N. E. Learnable drives and rewards. In S. S. Stevens (Ed.), Handbook of Experimental Psychology New York: Wiley, 1951.

Miller, N. E. Learning of visceral and glandular responses. Science, 1969, 163:434–445.

Miller, N. E. Interactions between learned and physical factors in mental illness. Seminars in Psychiatry, 1972, 4:239–254.

Miller, N. E., and Dollard, J. Social Learning and Imitation. New Haven: Yale University Press, 1941.

Miller, N. E., and Dworkin, B. R. Visceral learning: Recent difficulties with curarized rats and significant problems for human research. In P. A. Obrist, A. H. Black, J. Brener, and L. V. DiCara (Eds.), Cardiovascular Psychophysiology. Current Issues in Response Mechanisms, Biofeedback, and Methodology. Chicago: Aldine, 1974.

Miller, P. M., and Eisler, R. M. Alcohol and drug abuse. In W. E. Craighead, A. E. Kazdin, and M. J. Mahoney (Eds.), Behavior Modification: Principles, Issues, and Applications. Boston: Houghton Mifflin, 1976.

Miller, S., and Konorski, J. [On a particular form of conditioned reflex]. Journal of the Experimental Analysis of Behavior, 1969, 12:187–189. (Originally published, 1928).

Minkin, N., Braukmann, C. J., Minkin, B. L., Timbers, G. D., Timbers, B. J., Fixsen, D. L., Phillips, E. L., and Wolf, M. M. The social validation and training of conversational skills. Journal of Applied Behavior Analysis, 1976, 9:127–139.

Mischel, W. Predicting the success of Peace Corps volunteers in Nigeria. Journal of Personality and Social Psychology, 1965, 1:510–517.

Mischel, W. Personality and Assessment. New York: Wiley, 1968.

Mischel, W. Introduction to personality. New York: Holt, Rinehart & Winston, 1971.

Mischel, W., and Gilligan, C. Delay of gratification, motivation for the prohibited gratification, and responses to temptation. Journal of Abnormal and Social Psychology, 1964, 69:411–417.

Mischel, W., and Metzner, R. Preference for delayed reward as a function of age, intelligence, and length of delay interval. Journal of Abnormal and Social Psychology, 1962, 64:425–431.

Mischel, W., and Staub, E. The effects of expectancy on working and waiting for larger rewards. Journal of Personality and Social Psychology, 1965, 2:625–633.

Mitchell, W. S., and Stoffelmayr, B. E. Application of the Premack Principle to the behavioral control of extremely inactive schizophrenics. Journal of Applied Behavior Analysis, 1973, 6:419–423.

Mitford, J. The torture cure. Harper's Magazine, August 1973, p. 16.

Montgomery, A. G. Comparison of the effectiveness of systematic desensitization, rational-emotive therapy, implosive therapy, and no therapy, in reducing test anxiety in college students. Unpublished doctoral dissertation, Washington University, 1971.

Moore, B. R. The role of directed Pavlovian reactions in simple instrumental learning in the pigeon. In R. A. Hinde and J. Stevenson-Hinde (Eds.), Constraints on Learning: Limitations and Predispositions, Based on a Conference Sponsored by St. John's College, Cambridge, England. London: Academic Press, 1973.

Morales v. Turman, 383 F. Supp. 53 (E. D. Tex. 1974).

Morgan, J. J. B., and Witmer, F. J. The treatment of enuresis by the conditioned reaction technique. Journal of Genetic Psychology, 1939, 55:59–65.

Morganstern, K. P. Implosive therapy and flooding procedures: A critical review. Psychological Bulletin, 1973, 79:318–334.

Morhardt, P. E. Les reflexes conditionnel dans les névroses et dans les états allergiques. Vie Medicale, 1930, 11:825–828.

Morse, W. H. Intermittent reinforcement. In W. K. Honig (Ed.), Operant Behavior: Areas of Research and Application. New York: Appleton-Century-Crofts, 1966.

Morse, W. H., and Kelleher, R. T. Schedules as fundamental determinants of behavior. In W. N. Schoenfeld (Ed.), The Theory of Reinforcement Schedules. Englewood Cliffs, New Jersey: Prentice-Hall, 1970.

Morse, W. H., and Kelleher, R. T. Determinants of reinforcement and punishment. In W. K. Honig and J. E. R. Staddon (Eds.), Handbook of Operant Behavior. Englewood Cliffs, New Jersey: Prentice-Hall, 1977.

Moss, C. A. Directory of Behavioral Therapists in the United States and Canada. Monticello, New York: Author, 1972.

Mowrer, O. H. A stimulus-response analysis of anxiety and its role as a reinforcing agent. Psychological Review, 1939, 46:553–564.

Mowrer, O. H. On the dual nature of learning—a reinterpretation of "conditioning" and "problem solving." Harvard Educational Review, 1947, 17:102–148.

Mowrer, O. H. Learning Theory and Personality Dynamics: Selected papers. New York: Ronald, 1950.

Mowrer, O. H. Learning Theory and Behavior. New York: Wiley, 1960a.

Mowrer, O. H. Learning Theory and the Symbolic Processes. New York: Wiley, 1960b.

Mowrer, O. H. "Sin," the lesser of two evils. American Psychologist, 1960c, 15:301–304.

Mowrer, O. H., and Lamoreaux, R. R. Fear as an intervening variable in avoidance conditioning. Journal of Comparative Psychology, 1946, 39:29–50.

Mowrer, O. H., and Mowrer, W. M. Enuresis—a method for its study and treatment. American Journal of Orthopsychiatry, 1938, 8:436–459.

Mowrer, O. H., and Viek, P. An experimental analogue of fear from a sense of helplessness. Journal of Abnormal and Social Psychology, 1948, 43:193–200.

Murphy, G., and Kovach, J. K. Historical Introduction to Modern Psychology. (3rd ed.). New York: Harcourt Brace Jovanovich, 1972.

Murray, E. J., and Jacobson, L. I. The nature of learning in traditional and behavioral psychotherapy. In A. E. Bergin and S. L. Garfield (Eds.), Handbook of Psychotherapy and Behavior Change: An Empirical Analysis. New York: Wiley, 1971.

Murray, H. A. Thematic Apperception Test Manual. Cambridge: Harvard University Press, 1943.

Myasishchev, V. [Experimental evidence on the problem of objective indices in sensory disorders.] Novoyev Refleksologii i Fiziologii Nervnoy Sistemy, 1929, 3:458, 480.

Nason v. Superintendent of Bridgewater State Hospital, 233 N. E. 2d. 908 (Mass. 1968).

Nau, S. D., Caputo, J. A., and Borkovec, T. D. The relationship between credibility of therapy and simulated therapeutic effects. Journal of Behavior Therapy and Experimental Psychiatry, 1974, 5:129–133.

Nawas, M. M. (Letter to the editor): the AABT, the Behavior Therapy and Research Society and accreditation. Behavior Therapy, 1973, 4:173.

Nay, W. R. Analogue measures. In A. R. Ciminero, K. S. Calhoun, and H. E. Adams (Eds.), Handbook of Behavioral Assessment. New York: Wiley, 1977.

Nedelman, D., and Sulzbacher, S. I. Dicky at 13 years of age: A long-term success following early application of operant conditioning procedures. In G. Semb (Ed.), Behavior Analysis in Education. Lawrence, Kansas: Follow-through Project, 1972.

Neff, W. S., and Koltuv, M. Work and Mental Disorder. A Study of Factors Involved in the Rehabilitation of the Vocationally Disadvantaged Former Mental Patient. New York: Institute for the Crippled and Disabled, 1967.

Neisser, U. Cognitive Psychology. New York: Appleton-Century-Crofts, 1967.

New tool: "Reinforcement" for good work. Business Week, December 18, 1971, pp. 76–77.

New York City Health and Hospital Corporation v. *Stein*, 335 N. Y. S. 2d. 461 (Sup. Ct. 1972).

New York State Association for Retarded Children v. *Rockefeller*, 357 F. Supp. 752 (EDNY 1973).

Nietzel, M. T., Winett, R. A., MacDonald, M. L., and Davidson, W. S. Behavioral Approaches to Community Psychology. New York: Pergamon, 1977.

Notterman, J. M., Schoenfeld, W. N., and Bersh, P. J. A comparison of three extinction procedures following heart rate conditioning. Journal of Abnormal and Social Psychology, 1952, 47:674–677.

Novak, M. Is he really a grand inquisitor? In H. Wheeler (Ed.), Beyond the Punitive Society; Operant Conditioning: Social and Political Aspects. San Francisco: Freeman, 1973.

Oberndorf, C. P. A History of Psychoanalysis in America. New York: Grune & Stratton, 1953.

Obler, M. Systematic desensitization in sexual disorders. Journal of Behavior Therapy and Experimental Psychiatry, 1973, 4:93–101.

O'Leary, K. D., and Drabman, R. Token reinforcement programs in the classroom: A review. Psychological Bulletin, 1971, 75:379–398.

O'Leary, S. G., and O'Leary, K. D. Behavior modification in the school. In H. Leitenberg (Ed.), Handbook of Behavior Modification and Behavior Therapy. Englewood Cliffs, New Jersey: Prentice-Hall, 1976.

Orlando, R., and Bijou, S. W. Single and multiple schedules of reinforcement in developmentally retarded children. Journal of the Experimental Analysis of Behavior, 1960, 3:339–348.

Orlansky, H. Infant care and personality. Psychological Bulletin, 1949, 46: 1–48.

Osborn, A. F. Applied Imagination: Principles and Procedures of Creative Problem-Solving (3rd ed.). New York: Scribner's, 1963.

Osgood, C. E. Method and Theory in Experimental Psychology. New York: Oxford University Press, 1953.

The Oxford English Dictionary (Vol. VIII). London: Oxford University Press, 1961.

Palmer, A. B., and Wohl, J. Voluntary-admission forms: Does the patient know what he's signing? Hospital & Community Psychiatry, 1972, 23: 250–252.

Palmer, M. H., Lloyd, M. E., and Lloyd, K. E. An experimental analysis of electricity conservation procedures. Journal of Applied Behavior Analysis, in press.

Parloff, M. B., and Rubinstein, E. A. Research problems in psychotherapy. In E. A. Rubinstein and M. B. Parloff (Eds.), Research in Psychotherapy, Vol. I. Washington, D.C.: American Psychological Association, 1962.

Partridge, E. Origins: A Short Etymological Dictionary of Modern English (4th ed.). London: Routledge & Kegan Paul, 1966.

Patterson, G. R. An application of conditioning techniques to the control of a hyperactive child. In L. P. Ullmann and L. Krasner (Eds.), Case Studies in Behavior Modification. New York: Holt, Rinehart & Winston, 1965a.

Patterson, G. R. A learning theory approach to the treatment of the school phobic child. In L. P. Ullmann and L. Krasner (Eds.), Case Studies in Behavior Modification. New York: Holt, Rinehart & Winston, 1965b.

Patterson, G. R. Responsiveness to social stimuli. In L. Krasner and L. P. Ullmann (Eds.), Research in Behavior Modification: New Developments and Implications. New York: Holt, Rinehart & Winston, 1965c.

Patterson, G. R. Behavioral intervention procedures in the classroom and in the home. In A. E. Bergin and S. L. Garfield (Eds.), Handbook of Psychotherapy and Behavior Change: An Empirical Analysis. New York: Wiley, 1971.

Patterson, G. R. Interventions for boys with conduct problems: Multiple settings, treatments, and criteria. Journal of Consulting and Clinical Psychology, 1974, 42:471–481.

Patterson, G. R., Cobb, J. A., and Ray, R. S. A social engineering technology for retraining the families of aggressive boys. In H. E. Adams and I. P. Unikel (Eds.), Issues and Trends in Behavioral Therapy. Springfield, Illinois: Charles C Thomas, 1973.

Patterson, G. R., and Reid, J. B. Reciprocity and coercion: Two facets of social systems. In C. Neuringer and J. L. Michael (Eds.), Behavior Modification in Clinical Psychology. New York: Appleton-Century-Crofts, 1970.

Patterson, R. L. Maintaining Effective Token Economies. Springfield, Illinois: Charles C Thomas, 1976.

Paul, G. L. Insight versus Desensitization in Psychotherapy: An Experiment in Anxiety Reduction. Stanford: Stanford University Press, 1966.

Paul, G. L. Chronic mental patient: Current status—future directions. Psychological Bulletin, 1969a, 71:81–94.

Paul, G. L. Outcome of systematic desensitization, I: Background procedures, and uncontrolled reports of individual treatment. In C. M. Franks (Ed.), Behavior Therapy: Appraisal and Status. New York: McGraw-Hill, 1969b.

Paul, G. L. Outcome of systematic desensitization, II: Controlled investigations of individual treatment, technique variations, and current status. In C. M. Franks (Ed.), Behavior Therapy: Appraisal and Status. New York: McGraw-Hill, 1969c.

Paul, G. L., and Bernstein, D. A. Anxiety and Clinical Problems: Systematic

Desensitization and Related Techniques. Morristown, New Jersey: General Learning Press, 1973.

Pavlov, I. P. [The Work of the Digestive Glands] (W. H. Thompson, trans.). London: Charles Griffin, 1902.

Pavlov, I. P. The scientific investigation of the psychical faculties or processes in the higher animals. Science, 1906, 24:613–619.

Pavlov, I. P. [Conditioned Reflexes: An Investigation of the Physiological Activity of the Cerebral Cortex] (G. V. Anrep, Ed. and trans.). London: Oxford University Press, 1927.

Pavlov, I. P. [Lectures on Conditioned Reflexes] (W. H. Gantt, trans.). New York: International Publishers, 1928.

Pavlov, I. P. The reply of a physiologist to psychologists. Psychological Review, 1932, 39:91–127.

Pavlov, I. P. An attempt at a physiological interpretation of obsessional neurosis and paranoia. Journal of Mental Science, 1934, 80:187–197.

Pavlov, I. P. [Lectures on Conditioned Reflexes. Vol. 2: Conditioned Reflexes and Psychiatry] (W. H. Gantt, trans.). New York: International Publishers, 1941.

Pavlov, I. P. Experimental psychology and psychopathology in animals. Speech presented to the International Medical Congress, Madrid, April 1903. (Also reprinted in I. P. Pavlov, Selected Works. Moscow: Foreign Languages Publishing House, 1955.)

Pawlow, I. P. [Die Arbeit der Verdauungsdrüsen] (A. Walther, trans.). Wiesbaden: J. F. Bergmann, 1898.

Paynes, R.-W. The role of the clinical psychologist at the Institute of Psychiatry. Revue de Psychologie Appliquée, 1953, 3:150–160.

Pedalino, E., and Gamboa, V. U. Behavior modification and absenteeism: Intervention in one industrial setting. Journal of Applied Psychology, 1974, 59:694–698.

Peek v. Ciccone, 288 F. Supp. 329 (W. D. Mo. 1968).

People ex rel. Blunt v. Narcotic Addiction Control Commission, 295 N.Y.S. 2d. 276 (Sup. Ct.), aff'd mem., 296 N.Y.S. 2d. 533 (App. Div. 1968).

People ex rel. Stutz v. Conboy, 300 N.Y.S. 2d. 453 (Sup. Ct. 1969).

Perrow, C. Hospitals: Technology, structure, and goals. In J. G. March (Ed.), Handbook of Organizations. Chicago: Rand McNally, 1965.

Peters, H. N., and Jenkins, R. L. Improvement of chronic schizophrenic patients with guided problem-solving, motivated by hunger. Psychiatric Quarterly Supplement, 1954, 28:84–101.

Peterson, D. R. Scope and generality of verbally defined personality factors. Psychological Review, 1965, 72:48–59.

Peterson, D. R. The Clinical Study of Social Behavior. New York: Appleton-Century-Crofts, 1968.

Pfaundler, M. Demonstration eines Apparates zur selbsttätigen Signalisierung stattgehabter Bettnässung. Verhandlungen der Gessellschaft für Kinderheilkunde, 1905, 21:219–220.

Phares, E. J. Locus of Control: A Personality Determinant of Behavior. Morristown, New Jersey: General Learning Press, 1973.

Phillips, E. L., Phillips, E. A., Wolf, M. M., and Fixsen, D. L. Achievement place: Development of the elected manager system. Journal of Applied Behavior Analysis, 1973, 6:541–561.

Phillips, L., and Rabinovitch, M. S. Social role and patterns of symptomatic behaviors. Journal of Abnormal and Social Psychology, 1958, 57:181–186.

Phillips, R. E., Johnson, G. D., and Geyer, A. Self-administered systematic desensitization. Behaviour Research and Therapy, 1972, 10:93–96.

Pierce, C. H., and Risley, T. R. Improving job performance of Neighborhood Youths Corps aides in an urban recreation program. Journal of Applied Behavior Analysis, 1974, 7:207–215.

Pillsbury, W. B. The Essentials of Psychology. New York: Macmillan, 1911.

Pitres. Des spasmes rythmiques hystériques. Gazette Médicale de Paris, 1888, 5:145–148.

Platt, J. R. The Skinnerian revolution. In H. Wheeler (Ed.), Beyond the Punitive Society; Operant Conditioning: Social and Political Aspects. San Francisco: Freeman, 1973.

Pommer, D. A., and Streedbeck, D. Motivating staff performance in an operant learning program for children. Journal of Applied Behavior Analysis, 1974, 7:217–221.

Porter, R. (Ed.). The Role of Learning in Psychotherapy: A Ciba Foundation Symposium. London: Churchill, 1968.

Porterfield, J. K., Herbert-Jackson, E., and Risley, T. R. Contingent observation: An effective and acceptable procedure for reducing disruptive behavior of young children in a group setting. Journal of Applied Behavior Analysis, 1976, 9:55–64.

Powers, R. B., Osborne, J. G., and Anderson, E. G. Positive reinforcement of litter removal in the natural environment. Journal of Applied Behavior Analysis, 1973, 6:579–586.

Premack, D. Catching up with common sense, or two sides of a generalization: Reinforcement and punishment. In R. Glaser (Ed.), The Nature of Reinforcement. New York: Academic Press, 1971.

Prentice, W. C. H. Some cognitive aspects of motivation. American Psychologist, 1961, 16:503–511.

Pressey, S. L. A simple apparatus which gives tests and scores—and teaches. School and Society, 1926, 23:373–376.

Pressey, S. L. A machine for automatic teaching of drill material. School and Society, 1927, 25:549–552.

Pressey, S. L. Development and appraisal of devices providing immediate automatic scoring of objective tests and concomitant self-instruction. Journal of Psychology, 1950, 29:417–447.

Pressey, S. L. Some perspectives and major problems regarding "teaching machines." In A. A. Lumsdaine and R. Glaser (Eds.), Teaching Machines and Programmed Learning, Vol. I: A Source Book. Washington, D.C.: National Education Association, 1960.

Price, K. P. The application of behavior therapy to the treatment of psychosomatic disorders: Retrospect and prospect. Psychotherapy: Theory, Research and Practice, 1974, 11:138–155.

Quilitch, H. R. A comparison of three staff-management procedures. Journal of Applied Behavior Analysis, 1975, 8:59–66.

Quinn, J. T., and Henbest, R. Partial failure of generalization in alcoholics following aversion therapy. Quarterly Journal of Studies on Alcohol, 1967, 28:70–75.

Rachlin, H. Self-control. Behaviorism, 1974, 2:94–107.

Rachman, S. The treatment of anxiety and phobic reactions by systematic desensitization psychotherapy. Journal of Abnormal and Social Psychology, 1959, 58:259–263.

Rachman, S. (Ed.). Critical Essays on Psychoanalysis. Oxford: Pergamon, 1963.

Rachman, S. Systematic desensitization. Psychological Bulletin, 1967, 67: 93–103.

Rachman, S. Behavior therapy and psychodynamics. Behavior Therapy, 1970, 1:527–530.

Rachman, S. The Effects of Psychotherapy. New York: Pergamon, 1971.

Rachman, S. Clinical applications of observational learning, imitation and modeling. Behavior Therapy, 1972, 3:379–397.

Rachman, S. J. Observational learning and therapeutic modelling. In M. P. Feldman and A. Broadhurst (Eds.), Theoretical and Empirical Bases of the Behaviour Therapies. London: Wiley, 1976.

Rachman, S., and Eysenck, H. J. Reply to a "critique and reformulation" of behavior therapy. Psychological Bulletin, 1966, 65:165–169.

Rachman, S., and Teasdale, J. Aversion Therapy and Behavior Disorders: An Analysis. Coral Gables, Florida: University of Miami Press, 1969.

Rapaport, D. (Ed.). Organization and Pathology of Thought: Selected Sources. New York: Columbia University Press, 1951.

Ravitch, D. The Great School Wars, New York City, 1805–1973: A History of the Public Schools as Battlefield of Social Change. New York: Basic Books, 1974.

Razran, G. H. S. Conditioned responses in children: A behavioral and quantitative critical review of experimental studies. Archives of Psychology, 1933 (Whole No. 148).

Razran, G. H. S. Conditioned withdrawal responses with shock as the conditioning stimulus in adult human subjects. Psychological Bulletin, 1934, 31:111–143.

Razran, G. H. S. The law of effect or the law of qualitative conditioning. Psychological Review, 1939, 46:445–463.

Razran, G. Conditioning and perception. Psychological Review, 1955, 62: 83–95.

Razran, G. Avoidant vs. unavoidant conditioning and partial reinforcement in Russian laboratories. American Journal of Psychology, 1956, 69:127–129.

Razran, G. The observable unconscious and the inferable conscious in current Soviet psychophysiology: Interoceptive conditioning, semantic conditioning, and the orienting reflex. Psychological Review, 1961, 68:81–147.

Razran, G. Russian physiologists' psychology and American experimental psychology: A historical and systematic collation and a look into the future. Psychological Bulletin, 1965, 63:42–64.

Reese, W. G., Doss, R., and Gantt, W. H. Autonomic responses in differential diagnosis of organic and psychogenic psychoses. A.M.A. Archives of Neurology and Psychiatry, 1953, 70:778–793.

Reid, D. H., Luyben, P. D., Rawers, R. J., and Bailey, J. S. Newspaper recycling behavior. The effects of prompting and proximity of containers. Environment and Behavior, 1976, 8:471–482.

Reik, T. [Surprise and the Psycho-analyst: On the Conjecture and Comprehension of Unconscious Processes] (M. M. Green, trans.). New York: Dutton, 1937.

Reisman, J. M. The Development of Clinical Psychology. New York: Appleton-Century-Crofts, 1966.

Renelli v. Department of Mental Hygiene, 340 N. Y. S. 2d. 498 (Sup. Ct. 1973).

Reyher, J. Free imagery: An uncovering procedure. Journal of Clinical Psychology, 1963, 19:454–459.

Reyna, L. J. Experimental extinction as a function of the distribution and number of extinction trials. Unpublished doctoral dissertation, University of Iowa, 1947.

Reynolds, G. S. A Primer of Operant Conditioning. Glenview, Illinois: Scott, Foresman, 1968.

Rickard, H. C., Dignam, P. J., and Horner, R. F. Verbal manipulation in a psychotherapeutic relationship. Journal of Clinical Psychology, 1960, 16:364–367.

Rickard, H. C., and Dinoff, M. A follow-up note on "Verbal manipulation in a psychotherapeutic relationship." Psychological Reports, 1962, 11:506.

Rickard, H. C., and Mundy, M. B. Direct manipulation of stuttering behavior: An experimental-clinical approach. In L. P. Ullmann and L. Krasner (Eds.), Case Studies in Behavior Modification. New York: Holt, Rinehart & Winston, 1965.

Rimm, D. C., and Masters, J. C. Behavior Therapy: Techniques and Empirical Findings. New York: Academic Press, 1974.

Riopelle, A. J. (Ed.). Animal Problem Solving: Selected Readings. Baltimore: Penguin, 1967.

Risley, T. R. Behavior modification. An experimental-therapeutic endeavor. In L. A. Hamerlynck, P. O. Davidson, and L. E. Acker (Eds.), Behavior Modification and Ideal Mental Health Services. Calgary, Alberta, Canada: University of Calgary Press, 1970.

Risley, T. R. Certify procedures not people. In W. S. Wood (Ed.), Issues in Evaluating Behavior Modification: Proceedings of the First Drake Conference on Professional Issues in Behavior Analysis, March, 1974. Champaign, Illinois: Research Press, 1975.

Risley, T. R., and Wolf, M. M. Strategies for analyzing behavioral change over time. In J. R. Nesselroade and H. W. Reese (Eds.), Lifespan Developmental Psychology: Methodological Issues. New York: Academic Press, 1973.

Ritter, B. The group desensitization of children's snake phobias using vicarious and contact desensitization procedures. Behaviour Research and Therapy, 1968, 6:1–6.

Roberts, L. E., Lacroix, J. M., and Wright, M. Comparative studies of operant and electrodermal and heart rate conditioning in curarized rats. In P. A. Obrist, A. H. Black, J. Brener, and L. V. DiCara (Eds.), Cardiovascular Psychophysiology: Current Issues in Response Mechanisms, Biofeedback, and Methodology. Chicago: Aldine, 1974.

Roe, A. Man's forgotten weapon. American Psychologist, 1959, 14:261–266.

Rogers, C. R. Counseling and Psychotherapy: Newer Concepts in Practice. Boston: Houghton Mifflin, 1942.

Rogers, C. R. Client-Centered Therapy: Its Current Practice, Implications, and Theory. Boston: Houghton Mifflin, 1951.

Rogers, C. R., and Dymond, R. F. (Eds.). Psychotherapy and Personality Change: Co-ordinated Research Studies in the Client-Centered Approach. Chicago: University of Chicago Press, 1954.

Rogers, C. R., and Skinner, B. F. Some issues concerning the control of human behavior: A symposium. Science, 1956, 124:1057–1066.

Romanes, G. J. Animal Intelligence. New York: Appleton, Kegan Paul, 1883.

Rorschach, H. [Psychodiagnostics: A Diagnostic Test Based on Perception] (P. Lemkau and B. Kronenberg, trans., and W. Morgenthaler, Ed.). New York: Grune & Stratton, 1942.

Rosen, G. M. A manual for self-administering systematic desensitization in your home. Unpublished doctoral dissertation, University of Oregon, Eugene, 1974.

Rosen, G. M. The development and use of nonprescription behavior therapies. American Psychologist, 1976, 31:139–141.

Rosen, G. M., Glasgow, R. E., and Barrera, M., Jr. A controlled study to assess the clinical efficacy of totally self-administered systematic desensitization. Journal of Consulting and Clinical Psychology, 1976, 44:208–217.

Rosen, G. R., and Orenstein, H. A historical note on thought stopping. Journal of Consulting and Clinical Psychology, 1976, 44:1016–1017.

Rosenbaum, A., O'Leary, K. D., and Jacob, R. G. Behavioral intervention with hyperactive children: Group consequences as a supplement to individual contingencies. Behavior Therapy, 1975, 6:315–323.

Rosenthal, D. Changes in some moral values following psychotherapy. Journal of Consulting Psychology, 1955, 19:431–436.

Rosenthal, D., and Frank, J. D. Psychotherapy and the placebo effect. Psychological Bulletin, 1956, 53:294–302.

Rosenzweig, M. R. Salivary conditioning before Pavlov. American Journal of Psychology, 1959, 72:628–633.

Rosenzweig, S. A transvaluation of psychotherapy: A reply to Hans Eysenck. Journal of Abnormal and Social Psychology, 1954, 49:298–304.

Rotenstreich, N. Skinner and "Freedom and Dignity." In H. Wheeler (Ed.), Beyond the Punitive Society; Operant Conditioning: Social and Political Aspects. San Francisco: Freeman, 1973.

Rotter, J. B. Social Learning and Clinical Psychology. Englewood Cliffs, New Jersey: Prentice-Hall, 1954.

Rotter, J. B. Some implications of a social learning theory for the prediction of goal directed behavior from testing procedures. Psychological Review, 1960, 67:301–316.

Rotter, J. B. Generalized expectancies for internal versus external control of reinforcement. Psychological Monographs, 1966, 80:(1, Whole No. 609).

Rouse v. Cameron, 373 F. 2d. 451 (D.C. Cir. 1966).

Roux, R. Nouvel appareil electrique contre l'incontinence nocturne d'urine. Bulletin et Mémoires de la Société de Medecine de Vaucluse, 1908–1911, 2:337–340.

Rubenstein, C. The treatment of morphine addiction in tuberculosis by

Pawlow's conditioning method. American Review of Tuberculosis, 1931, 24:682–685.

Rubinstein, E. A., and Parloff, M. B. Research in psychotherapy, Vol. I. Washington, D.C.: American Psychological Association, 1962.

Rush, A. J., Beck, A. T., Kovacs, M., and Hollon, S. Comparative efficacy of cognitive therapy and pharmacotherapy in the treatment of depressed outpatients. Cognitive Therapy and Research, 1977, 1:17–37.

Russell, R. W. The comparative study of "conflict" and "experimental neurosis." British Journal of Psychology, 1950, 41:95–108.

Rutherford, B. R. The use of negative practice in speech therapy with children handicapped by cerebral palsy, athetoid type. Journal of Speech Disorders, 1940, 5:259–264.

Ryan, B. A. Keller's Personalized System of Instruction: An Appraisal. Washington, D.C.: American Psychological Association, 1974.

Salmon, D. Joseph Lancaster. London: Longmans, Green, 1904.

Salter, A. Three techniques of autohypnosis. Journal of General Psychology, 1941, 24:423–438.

Salter, A. What is Hypnosis; Studies in Auto and Hetero Conditioning. New York: Richard R. Smith, 1944.

Salter, A. Conditioned Reflex Therapy; The Direct Approach to the Reconstruction of Personality. New York: Creative Age Press, 1949.

Salter, A. The Case Against Psychoanalysis. New York: Holt, 1952.

Salzinger, K. Experimental manipulation of verbal behavior: A review. Journal of General Psychology, 1959, 61:65–94.

Salzinger, K., Feldman, R. S., Cowan, J. E., and Salzinger, S. Operant conditioning of verbal behvior of two young speech-deficient boys. In L. Krasner and L. P. Ullmann (Eds.), Research in Behavior Modification: New Developments and Implications. New York: Holt, Rinehart & Winston, 1965.

Sandler, J., and Quagliano, J. Punishment in a signal avoidance situation. Paper read at the Southeastern Psychological Association Meeting, Gatlinburg, Tennessee, 1964.

Santogrossi, D. A., O'Leary, K. D., Romanczyk, R. G., and Kaufman, K. F. Self-evaluation by adolescents in a psychiatric hospital school token program. Journal of Applied Behavior Analysis, 1973, 6:277–287.

Sarbin, T. R. On the futility of the proposition that some people be labeled "mentally ill." Journal of Consulting Psychology, 1967, 31:447–453.

Sarbin, T. R., Taft, R., and Bailey, D. E. Clinical Inference and Cognitive Theory. New York: Holt, Rinehart & Winston, 1960.

Sargent, H. D. Methodological problems of follow-up studies in psychotherapy research. American Journal of Orthopsychiatry, 1960, 30:495–506.

Sawyer, J. Measurement and prediction, clinical and statistical. Psychological Bulletin, 1966, 66:178–200.

Schachter, S. The interaction of cognitive and physiological determinants of emotional state. In L. Berkowitz (Ed.), Advances in Experimental Social Psychology (Vol. 1). New York: Academic Press, 1964.

Scheff, T. J. Being Mentally Ill: A Sociological Theory. Chicago: Aldine, 1966.

Schick, K. Operants, Journal of the Experimental Analysis of Behavior, 1971, 15:413–423.

Schlosberg, H. The relationship between success and the laws of conditioning. Psychological Review, 1937, 44:379–394.

Schmidt, H. O., and Fonda, C. P. The reliability of psychiatric diagnosis: A new look. Journal of Abnormal and Social Psychology, 1956, 52:262–267.

Schultz, D. A History of Modern Psychology (2nd ed.). New York: Academic Press, 1975.

Schultz, J. H. Das Autogene Training, Konzentrative Selbslentspannong; Versuch einer Klinisch-praktischen Darstellung. Leipsic: Georg Thieme, 1932.

Schultz, J. H., and Luthe, W. Autogenic Training: A Psychophysiologic Approach in Psychotherapy. New York: Grune & Stratton, 1959.

Schwartz, B., and Gamzu, E. Pavlovian control of operant behavior: An analysis of autoshaping and its implications for operant conditioning. In W. K. Honig and J. E. R. Staddon (Eds.), Handbook of Operant Behavior. Englewood Cliffs, New Jersey: Prentice-Hall, 1977.

Schwartz, L. A. Group psychotherapy in the war neuroses. American Journal of Psychiatry, 1945, 101:498–500.

Schwitzgebel, R. K. A contractual model for the protection of the rights of institutionalized mental patients. American Psychologist, 1975, 30:815–820.

Scott, W. A. Research definitions of mental health and mental illness. Psychological Bulletin, 1958, 55:29–45.

Scriven, M. The experimental investigation of psychoanalysis. In S. Hook (Ed.), Psychoanalysis: Scientific Method and Philosophy; A Symposium. New York: New York University Press, 1959.

Sears, R. R. Survey of Objective Studies of Psychoanalytic Concepts, A Report Prepared for the Committee on Social Adjustment (Bulletin 51). New York: Social Science Research Council, 1943.

Sears, R. R. Experimental analysis of psychoanalytic phenomena. In J. Mc. V. Hunt (Ed.), Personality and the Behavior Disorders: A Handbook Based on Experimental and Clinical Research (Vol. 1). New York: Roland, 1944.

Sears, R. R., and Cohen, L. H. Hysterical anesthesia, analgesia and astereognosis. Archives of Neurology and Psychiatry, 1933, 29:260–271.

Seaver, W. B., and Patterson, A. H. Decreasing fuel-oil consumption through feedback and social commendation. Journal of Applied Behavior Analysis, 1976, 9:147–152.

Sechenov, I. M. [Reflexes of the Brain: An Attempt to Establish the Physiological Basis of Psychological Processes.] (S. Belsky, trans. and G. Gibbons, Ed.). Cambridge, Massachusetts: M.I.T. Press, 1965.

Sewell, W. H. Infant training and the personality of the child. American Journal of Sociology, 1952, 58:150–159.

Shadel, C. A. Aversion treatment of alcohol addiction. Quarterly Journal of Studies of Alcohol, 1944, 5:216–228.

Shaffer, G. W., and Lazarus, R. S. Fundamental Concepts in Clinical Psychology. New York: McGraw-Hill, 1952.

Shaffer, L. F. The Psychology of Adjustment: An Objective Approach to Mental Hygiene. Boston: Houghton Mifflin, 1936.

Shaffer, L. F. The problem of psychotherapy. American Psychologist, 1947, 2:459–467.

Shapiro, D., and Surwit, R. S. Learned control of physiological function and disease. In H. Leitenberg (Ed.), Handbook of Behavior Modification and Behavior Therapy. Englewood Cliffs, New Jersey: Prentice-Hall, 1976.

Shapiro, M. B. An experimental approach to diagnostic psychological testing. Journal of Mental Science, 1951, 97:748–764.

Shapiro, M. B. Experimental Studies of a perceptual anomaly. II. Confirmatory and explanatory experiments. Journal of Mental Science, 1952, 98:605–617.

Shapiro, M. B. Experimental method in the psychological description of the individual psychiatric patient. International Journal of Social Psychiatry, 1957, 3:89–102.

Shapiro, M. B. A method of measuring psychological changes specific to the individual psychiatric patient. British Journal of Medical Psychology, 1961a, 34:151–155.

Shapiro, M. B. The single case in fundamental clinical research. British Journal of Medical Psychology, 1961b, 34:255–262.

Shapiro, M. B. The single case of clinical-psychological research. Journal of General Psychology, 1966, 74:3–23.

Shapiro, M. B., Marks, I. M., and Fox, B. A therapeutic experiment on phobic and affective symptoms in an individual psychiatric patient. British Journal of Social and Clinical Psychology, 1963, 2:81–93.

Shapiro, M. B., and Ravenette, A. T. A preliminary experiment on paranoid delusions. Journal of Mental Science, 1959, 105:295–312.

Shaw, F. J. A stimulus-response analysis of repression and insight in psychotherapy. Psychological Review, 1946, 53:36–42.

Shaw, F. J. Some postulates concerning psychotherapy. Journal of Consulting Psychology, 1948, 12:426–431.

Sherman, J. A. Reinstatement of verbal behavior in a psychotic by reinforcement methods. Journal of Speech and Hearing Disorders, 1963, 28: 398–401.

Sherman, J. A. Use of reinforcement and imitation to reinstate verbal behavior in mute psychotics. Journal of Abnormal Psychology, 1965, 70:155–164.

Sherrington, C. S. The Integrative Action of the Nervous System. New Haven: Yale University Press, 1906.

Shipley, J. T. Dictionary of Word Origins. New York: Philosophical Library, 1945.

Shlien, J. M. (Ed.). Research in Psychotherapy, Vol. III. Washington, D.C.: American Psychological Association, 1968.

Shoben, E. J., Jr. Psychotherapy as a problem in learning theory. Psychological Bulletin, 1949, 46:366–392.

Shoemaker, H. A., and Holt, H. O. The use of programed instruction in industry. In A. A. Lumsdaine and R. Glaser (Eds.), Teaching Machines and Programmed Learning, Vol. II: Data and Directions. Washington, D.C.: National Education Association, 1965.

Sidman, M. Tactics of Scientific Research: Evaluating Experimental Data in Psychology. New York: Basic Books, 1960.

Simmel, E. C., Hoppe, R. A., and Milton, G. A. (Eds.). Social Facilitation and Imitative Behavior: Outcome of the 1967 Miami University Symposium on Social Behavior. Boston: Allyn & Bacon, 1968.

Singer, J. L. Imagery and Daydream Methods in Psychotherapy and Behavior Modification. New York: Academic Press, 1974.

Skinner, B. F. On the conditions of elicitation of certain eating reflexes. Proceedings of the National Academy of Sciences, 1930, 16:433–438.

Skinner, B. F. On the rate of formation of a conditioned reflex. Journal of General Psychology, 1932, 7:274–286.

Skinner, B. F. Two types of conditioned reflex and a pseudo type. Journal of General Psychology, 1935, 12:66–77.

Skinner, B. F. Two types of conditioned reflex: A reply to Konorski and Miller. Journal of General Psychology, 1937, 16:272–279.

Skinner, B. F. The Behavior of Organisms: An Experimental Analysis. New York: Appleton-Century, 1938.

Skinner, B. F. Walden Two. New York: Macmillan, 1948.

Skinner, B. F. Are theories of learning necessary? Psychological Review, 1950, 57:193–216.

Skinner, B. F. Science and Human Behavior. New York: Macmillan, 1953a.

Skinner, B. F. Some contributions of an experimental analysis of behavior to psychology as a whole. American Psychologist, 1953b, 8:69–78.

Skinner, B. F. A new method for the experimental analysis of the behavior of psychotic patients. Journal of Nervous and Mental Disease, 1954a, 120:403–406.

Skinner, B. F. The science of learning and the art of teaching. Harvard Educational Review, 1954b, 24:86–97.

Skinner, B. F. A case history in scientific method. American Psychologist, 1956, 11:221–233.

Skinner, B. F. Verbal Behavior. New York: Appleton-Century-Crofts, 1957.

Skinner, B. F. Teaching machines. Science, 1958, 128:969–977.

Skinner, B. F. What is the experimental analysis of behavior? Journal of the Experimental Analysis of Behavior, 1966, 9:213–218.

Skinner, B. F. Contingencies of Reinforcement: A Theoretical Analysis. New York: Appleton-Century-Crofts, 1969.

Skinner, B. F. An autobiography. In P. B. Dews (Ed.), Festschrift for B. F. Skinner. New York: Appleton-Century-Crofts, 1970.

Skinner, B. F. Beyond Freedom and Dignity. New York: Knopf, 1971.

Skinner, B. F. Cumulative Record: A Selection of Papers (3rd ed.). New York: Appleton-Century-Crofts, 1972.

Skinner, B. F. Answers for my critics. In H. Wheeler (Ed.), Beyond the Punitive Society; Operant Conditioning: Social and Political Aspects. San Francisco: Freeman, 1973.

Skinner, B. F. About Behaviorism. New York: Knopf, 1974.

Skinner, B. F., and Morse, W. H. Fixed-interval reinforcement of running in a wheel. Journal of the Experimental Analysis of Behavior, 1958, 1: 371–379.

Skinner, B. F., Solomon, H. C., and Lindsley, O. R. Studies in behavior therapy, Metropolitan State Hospital, Waltham, Massachusetts, Status Report I, November 30, 1953.

Skinner, B. F., Solomon, H. C., Lindsley, O. R., and Richards, M. E. Studies in behavior therapy, Metropolitan State Hospital, Waltham, Massachusetts, Status Report II, May 31, 1954.

Sloane, R. B., Staples, F. R., Cristol, A. H., Yorkston, N. J., and Whipple,

K. Psychotherapy versus Behavior Therapy. Cambridge, Massachusetts: Harvard University Press, 1975.

Sluchevski, I. F., and Friken, A. A. [Apomorphine treatment of chronic alcoholism.] Sovetskaya Vrachebnaya Gazeta, June 1933, 557–561.

Smith, S., and Guthrie, E. R. General Psychology in Terms of Behavior. New York: Appleton, 1921.

Solomon, R. L., and Wynne, L. C. Traumatic avoidance learning: Acquisition in normal dogs. Psychological Monographs, 1953, 67(4, Whole No. 354).

Solomon, R. L., and Wynne, L. C. Traumatic avoidance learning: The principles of anxiety conservation and partial irreversibility. Psychological Review, 1954, 61:353–385.

Sommer, R., and Osmond, H. Symptoms of institutional care. Social Problems, 1961, 8:254–263.

Soskin, W. F. Influence of four types of data on diagnostic conceptualization in psychological testing. Journal of Abnormal and Social Psychology, 1959, 58:69–78.

Spence, K. W. Cognitive versus stimulus-response theories of learning. Psychological Review, 1950, 57:159–172.

Spence, K. W. Cognitive factors in the extinction of the conditioned eyelid response in humans. Science, 1963, 140:1224–1225.

Spence, K. W. Cognitive and drive factors in the extinction of the conditioned eye blink in human subjects. Psychological Review, 1966, 73:445–458.

Spence, K. W., Rutledge, E. F., and Talbott, J. H. Effect of number of acquisition trials and the presence or absence of the UCS on extinction of the eyelid CR. Journal of Experimental Psychology, 1963, 66:286–291.

Spielberger, C. D., and DeNike, L. D. Descriptive behaviorism versus cognitive theory in verbal operant conditioning. Psychological Review, 1966, 73:306–326.

Staats, A. W. Learning theory and "opposite speech." Journal of Abnormal and Social Psychology, 1957, 55:268–269.

Staats, A. W. (Ed.). Human Learning: Studies Extending Conditioning Principles to Complex Behavior. New York: Holt, Rinehart & Winston, 1964.

Staats, A. W. A general apparatus for the investigation of complex learning in children. Behaviour Research and Therapy, 1968a, 6:45–50.

Staats, A. W. Learning, Language and Cognition: Theory, Research, and Method for the Study of Human Behavior and its Development. New York: Holt, Rinehart & Winston, 1968b.

Staats, A. W., and Butterfield, W. H. Treatment of nonreading in a culturally deprived juvenile delinquent: An application of reinforcement principles. Child Development, 1965, 36:925–942.

Staats, A. W., Finley, J. R., Minke, K. A., and Wolf, M. Reinforcement variables in the control of unit reading responses. Journal of the Experimental Analysis of Behavior, 1964, 7:139–149.

Staats, A. W., Minke, K. A., and Butts, P. A token-reinforcement remedial reading program administered by black therapy-technicians to problem black children. Behavior Therapy, 1970, 1:331–353.

Staats, A. W., Minke, K. A., Finley, J. R., Wolf, M., and Brooks, L. O. A reinforcer system and experimental procedure for the laboratory study of reading acquisition. Child Development, 1964b, 35:209–231.

Staats, A. W., Minke, K. A., Goodwin, W., and Landeen, J. Cognitive behavior modification: "Motivated learning" reading treatment with subprofessional therapy-technicians. Behavior Research and Therapy, 1967, 5:283–299.

Staats, A. W., Staats, C. K., Schutz, R. E., and Wolf, M. The conditioning of textual responses using "extrinsic" reinforcers. Journal of the Experimental Analysis of Behavior, 1962, 5:33–40.

Stahl, J. R., and Leitenberg, H. Behavioral treatment of the chronic mental hospital patient. In H. Leitenberg (Ed.), Handbook of Behavior Modification and Behavior Therapy. Englewood Cliffs, New Jersey: Prentice-Hall, 1976.

Stampfl, T. G. Implosive therapy: The theory, the subhuman analogue, the strategy, and the technique. Part I: The theory. In S. G. Armitage (Ed.), Behavior Modification Techniques in the Treatment of Emotional Disorders. Battle Creek, Michigan: Veterans Administration Hospital, 1966.

Stampfl, T. G. Implosive therapy: An emphasis on covert stimulation. In D. J. Levis (Ed.), Learning Approaches in Therapeutic Behavior Change. Chicago: Aldine, 1970.

Stampfl, T. G., and Levis, D. J. Essentials of implosive therapy: A learning-theory-based psychodynamic behavioral therapy. Journal of Abnormal Psychology, 1967, 72:496–503.

Staudt, V. M., and Zubin, J. A biometric evaluation of the somatotherapies in schizophrenia. Psychological Bulletin, 1957, 54:171–196.

Stayer, S. J., and Jones, F. Ward 108: Behavior modification and the delinquent soldier. Paper presented at Behavioral Engineering Conference, Walter Reed General Hospital, 1969.

Steinman, W. M. Generalized imitation and the setting event concept. In B. C. Etzel, J. M. LeBlanc, and D. M. Baer (Eds.), New Developments in Behavioral Research: Theory, Method, and Application. Hillsdale, New Jersey: Lawrence Erlbaum, 1977.

Stevenson, I. The comparative and clinical status of conditioning therapies and psychoanalysis: Discussion. In J. Wolpe, A. Salter, and L. J. Reyna (Eds.), The Conditioning Therapies: The Challenge in Psychotherapy. New York: Holt, Rinehart & Winston, 1964.

Stokes, T. F., and Baer, D. M. An implicit technology of generalization. Journal of Applied Behavior Analysis, 1977, 10:349–367.

Stolz, S. B. (Ed.). Report of the American Psychological Association Commission on Behavior Modification. Washington, D.C.: American Psychological Association, 1977.

Stolz, S. B. Ethics of social and educational interventions: Historical context and a behavioral analysis. In T. A. Brigham and A. C. Catania (Eds.), Handbook of Applied Behavior Research: Social and Instructional Processes. New York: Irvington/Halstead, 1978.

Stolz, S. B. Ethical issues in behavior modification. In G. Bermant, H. Kelman, and D. Warwick (Eds.), The Ethics of Social Intervention. Washington, D.C.: Hemisphere, in press.

Stolz, S. B., Wienckowski, L. A., and Brown, B. S. Behavior modification: A perspective on critical issues. American Psychologist, 1975, 30:1027–1048.

Stoyva, J., and Kamiya, J. Electrophysiological studies of dreaming as the prototype of a new strategy in the study of consciousness. Psychological Review, 1968, 75:192–205.

Strupp, H. H. The outcome problem in psychotherapy revisited. Psychotherapy; Theory, Research and Practice, 1963, 1:1–13.

Strupp, H. H., and Luborsky, L. (Eds.). Research in Psychotherapy, Vol. II. Washington, D.C.: American Psychological Association, 1962.

Stuart, R. B. Trick or Treatment: How and When Psychotherapy Fails. Champaign, Illinois: Research Press, 1970.

Stuart, R. B. Situational versus self-control. In R. D. Rubin, H. Fensterheim, J. D. Henderson, and L. P. Ullmann (Eds.), Advances in Behavior Therapy (Vol. 4). New York: Academic Press, 1972.

Stuart, R. B., and Davis, B. Slim Chance in a Fat World: Behavioral Control of Obesity. Champaign, Illinois: Research Press, 1972.

Stumphauzer, J. S. (Ed.). Behavior Therapy with Delinquents. Springfield, Illinois: Charles C Thomas, 1973.

Subcommittee on Constitutional Rights, Committee on the Judiciary, United States Senate, Ninety-Third Congress. Individual Rights and the Federal Role in Behavior Modification. Washington, D.C.: U.S. Government Printing Office, 1974.

Subotnik, L. Spontaneous remission: Fact or artifact? Psychological Bulletin, 1972, 77:32–48.

Sulzer-Azaroff, B., and Mayer, G. R. Applying Behavior-Analysis Procedures with Children and Youth. New York: Holt, Rinehart & Winston, 1977.

Szasz, T. S. The myth of mental illness. American Psychologist, 1960, 15:113–118.

Szasz, T. S. The Myth of Mental Illness: Foundations of a Theory of Personal Conduct. New York: Hoeber-Harper, 1961.

Taffel, C. Anxiety and the conditioning of verbal behavior. Journal of Abnormal and Social Psychology, 1955, 51:496–501.

Taft, R. The ability to judge people. Psychological Bulletin, 1955, 52: 1–23.

Tasto, D. L. Self-report schedules and inventories. In A. R. Ciminero, K. S. Calhoun, and H. E. Adams (Eds.), Handbook of Behavioral Assessment. New York: Wiley, 1977.

Taylor, J. G. The Behavioral Basis of Perception. New Haven: Yale University Press, 1962.

Taylor, J. G. A behavioral interpretation of obsessive-compulsive neurosis. Behaviour Research and Therapy, 1963, 1:237–244.

Terhune, W. B. The phobic syndrome. A study of 86 patients with phobic reactions. Archives of Neurology and Psychiatry, 1949, 62:162–172.

Tharp, R. G., and Wetzel, R. J. Behavior Modification in the Natural Environment. New York: Academic Press, 1969.

Thimann, J. Conditioned-reflex treatment of alcoholism: I. Its rationale and technic. New England Journal of Medicine, 1949a, 241:368–370.

Thimann, J. Conditioned-reflex treatment of alcoholism. II. The risks of its application, its indications, contraindications and psychotherapeutic aspects. New England Journal of Medicine, 1949b, 241:406–410.

Thompson, T., and Grabowski, J. (Eds.). Behavior Modification of the Mentally Retarded. New York: Oxford University Press, 1972.

Thoresen, C. E., and Mahoney, M. J. Behavioral Self-Control. New York: Holt, Rinehart & Winston, 1974.

Thorndike, E. L. Animal Intelligence: Experimental Studies. New York: Macmillan, 1911.

Thorndike, E. L. Human Learning. New York: Century, 1931.

Thorndike, E. L. The Fundamentals of Learning. New York: Columbia University Teachers College, 1932.

Thorndike, E. L. An Experimental Study of Rewards. New York: Columbia University Teachers College, 1933.

Thorndike, E. L. The Psychology of Wants, Interests, and Attitudes. New York: Appleton-Century, 1935.

Thorne, F. C. Rules of evidence in the evaluation of the effects of psychotherapy. Journal of Clinical Psychology, 1952, 8:38-41.

Tissié, P. Tic oculaire et facial droit accompagné de toux spasmodique, traité et guéri par la gymnastique médicale respiratoire. Journal de Medecine de Bordeaux, 1899, 29:326-330.

Tolman, E. C. Purposive Behavior in Animals and Men. New York: Century, 1932.

Tolman, E. C. Theories of learning. In F. A. Moss (Ed.), Comparative Psychology. New York: Prentice-Hall, 1934.

Tolman, E. C. Cognitive maps in rats and men. Psychological Review, 1948, 55:189-208.

Tolman, E. C. A cognitive motivation model. Psychological Review, 1952, 59:389-400.

Tourney, G. A history of therapeutic fashions in psychiatry, 1800-1966. American Journal of Psychiatry, 1967, 124:784-796.

Trexler, L. D., and Karst, T. O. Rational-emotive therapy, placebo, and no-treatment effects on public-speaking anxiety. Journal of Abnormal Psychology, 1972, 79:60-67.

Tribby v. Cameron, Id. at 328, 379 F. 2d. at 105. See also Dobson v. Cameron, 127 U.S. App. D.C. 324, 328-329 n.2, 383 F. 2d. 519, 523-524 n.2 (1967) (en banc) (Burger, J., concurring).

Troland, L. T. The Fundamentals of Human Motivation. New York: Van Nostrand, 1928.

Truax, C. B. Reinforcement and nonreinforcement in Rogerian psychotherapy. Journal of Abnormal Psychology, 1966, 71:1-9.

Tuso, M. A., and Geller, E. S. Behavior analysis applied to environmental/ecological problems: A review. Journal of Applied Behavior Analysis, 1976, 9:526.

Twitmyer, E. B. A Study of the Knee Jerk. Philadelphia: Winston, 1902.

Ullmann, L. P. Institution and Outcome: A Comparative Study of Psychiatric Hospitals. Oxford: Pergamon, 1967.

Ullmann, L. P., and Krasner, L. (Eds.). Case Studies in Behavior Modification. New York: Holt, Rinehart & Winston, 1965.

Ullmann, L. P., and Krasner, L. A Psychological Approach to Abnormal Behavior. Englewood Cliffs, New Jersey: Prentice-Hall, 1969.

Ullmann, L. P., and Krasner, L. A Psychological Approach to Abnormal Behavior (2nd ed.). Englewood Cliffs, New Jersey: Prentice-Hall, 1975.

Ulman, J. D., and Klem, J. L. Communication. Journal of Applied Behavior Analysis, 1975, 8:210.

Ulrich, R. Behavior control and public concern. Psychological Record, 1967, 17:229–234.

Ulrich, R., Stachnik, T., and Mabry, J. (Eds.). Control of Human Behavior, Vol. 1. Genview, Illinois: Scott, Foresman, 1966.

Ulrich, R., Stachnik, T., and Mabry, J. (Eds.). Control of Human Behavior, Vol. 2: From Cure to Prevention. Glenview, Illinois: Scott, Foresman, 1970.

Ulrich, R., Stachnik, T., and Mabry, J. (Eds.). Control of Human Behavior, Vol. 3: Behavior Modification in Education. Glenview, Illinois: Scott, Foresman, 1974.

United States Department of Health, Education, and Welfare, Public Health Service, National Institutes of Health. The Institutional Guide to DHEW Policy on Protection of Human Subjects. DHEW Publication No. (NIH) 72-102, Bethesda, Maryland: U.S. Government Printing Office, 1972.

Verplanck, W. S. The control of the content of conversation: Reinforcement of statements of opinion. Journal of Abnormal and Social Psychology, 1955, 51:668–676.

Voegtlin, W. L. The treatment of alcoholism by establishing a conditioned reflex. American Journal of the Medical Sciences, 1940, 199:802–810.

Voegtlin, W. L., and Lemere, F. The treatment of alcohol addiction: A review of the literature. Quarterly Journal of Studies on Alcohol, 1942, 2:717–803.

Voegtlin, W. L., Lemere, F., and Broz, W. R. Conditioned reflex therapy of alcoholic addiction. III. An evaluation of present results in the light of previous experiences with this method. Quarterly Journal of Studies on Alcohol, 1940, 1:501–516.

Voegtlin, W. L., Lemere, F., Broz, W. R., and O'Hollaren, P. Conditioned reflex therapy of chronic alcoholism. IV. A preliminary report on the value of reinforcement. Quarterly Journal of Studies on Alcohol, 1942, 2: 505–511.

Vogel, M. D. The relationship of GSR conditioning to drinking patterns of alcoholics. Quarterly Journal of Studies on Alcohol. 1961, 22:401–410.

Vygotsky, L. S. [Thought and Language]. (E. Hanfmann and G. Vakar, Eds. and trans.). Cambridge, Massachusetts: M.I.T. Press, 1962.

Wahler, R. G. Setting generality: Some specific and general effects of child behavior therapy. Journal of Applied Behavior Analysis, 1969, 2:239–246.

Wahler, R. G. Deviant child behavior within the family: Developmental speculations and behavior change strategies. In H. Leitenberg (Ed.), Handbook of Behavior Modification and Behavior Therapy. Englewood Cliffs, New Jersey: Prentice-Hall, 1976.

Walton, D. Experimental psychology and the treatment of a ticqueur. Journal of Child Psychology and Psychiatry, 1961, 2:148–155.

Wanklin, J. M., Fleming, D. F., Buck, C., and Hobbs, G. E. Discharge and readmission among mental hospital patients. Archives of Neurology and Psychiatry, 1956, 76:660–669.

Watson, J. B. Psychology as the behaviorist views it. Psychological Review, 1913, 20:158–177.

Watson, J. B. Behavior: An Introduction to Comparative Psychology. New York: Holt, 1914.

Watson, J. B. The place of the conditioned-reflex in psychology. Psychological Review, 1916, 23:89–116.

Watson, J. B. Psychology, from the Standpoint of a Behaviorist. Philadelphia: Lippincott, 1919.

Watson, J. B. Behaviorism. Chicago: The People's Institute, 1924.

Watson, J. B., and Rayner, R. Conditioned emotional reactions. Journal of Experimental Psychology, 1920, 3:1–14.

Watson, R. I. Measuring the effectiveness of psychotherapy: Problems for investigation. Journal of Clinical Psychology, 1952a, 8:60–64.

Watson, R. I. Research design and methodology in evaluating the results of psychotherapy. Journal of Clinical Psychology, 1952b, 8:29–33.

Watson, R. I., Mensch, I. N., and Gildea, E. F. The evaluation of the effects of psychotherapy: III. Research design. Journal of Psychology, 1951, 32:293–308.

Webster's Third New International Dictionary of the English Language (unabridged). Springfield, Massachusetts: G. & C. Merriam, 1967.

Weimer, W. B., and Palermo, D. S. (Eds.). Cognition and the Symbolic Processes. Hillsdale, New Jersey: Lawrence Erlbaum, 1974.

Weitzman, B. Behavior therapy and psychotherapy. Psychological Review, 1967. 74:300–317.

Wells, C. E., and Wolff, H. G. Formation of temporary cerebral connections in normal and brain-damaged subjects. Neurology, 1960, 10:335–340.

Wendt, G. R. The development of a psychological cult. American Psychologist, 1949, 4:426.

Werner, J. S., Minkin, N., Minkin, B. L., Fixsen, D. L., Phillips, E. L., and Wolf, M. M. "Intervention package." An analysis to prepare juvenile delinquents for encounters with police officers. Criminal Justice and Behavior, 1975, 2:55–83.

West, J. The History of Tasmania. Launceston, Tasmania: H. Dowling, 1852.

Wexler, D. B. Token and taboo: Behavior modification, token economies, and the law. California Law Review, 1973, 61:81–109.

Wexler, D. B. Behavior modification and other behavior change procedures: The emerging law and the proposed Florida guidelines. Criminal Law Bulletin, 1975a, 11:600–616.

Wexler, D. B. Reflections on the legal regulation of behavior modification in institutional settings. Arizona Law Review, 1975b, 17:132–143.

Wheeler, H. (Ed.). Beyond the Punitive Society; Operant Conditioning: Social and Political Aspects. San Francisco: Freeman, 1973.

Whitree v. State, 56 Misc. 2d. 693, 290 N. Y. S. 2d. 486 (Ct. Cl. 1968).

Whytt, R. An Essay on the Vital and Other Involuntary Motions of Animals (2nd ed.). Edinburgh: J. Balfour, 1763.

Wiest, W. M. Some recent criticisms of behaviorism and learning theory: With special reference to Breger and McGaugh and to Chomsky. Psychological Bulletin, 1967, 67:214–225.

Wilder, J. Facts and figures on psychotherapy. Journal of Clinical Psychopathology, 1945, 7:311–347.

Wildman, R. W., II, and Wildman, R. W. The generalization of behavior modification procedures: A review—with special emphasis on classroom applications. Psychology in the Schools, 1975, 12:432–448.

Wilkins, W. Desensitization: Social and cognitive factors underlying the effectiveness of Wolpe's procedure. Psychological Bulletin, 1971, 76:311–317.

Williams, C. D. The elimination of tantrum behavior by extinction procedures. Journal of Abnormal and Social Psychology, 1959, 59:269.

Williams, J. L. Operant Learning: Procedures for Changing Behavior. Monterey, California: Brooks/Cole, 1973.

Williams, R. B., Jr., and Gentry, W. D. (Eds.). Behavioral Approaches to Medical Treatment. Cambridge, Massachusetts: Ballinger, 1977.

Wilson, G. T. On the much discussed nature of the term "behavior therapy." Behavior Therapy, in press.

Wilson, G. T., and Evans, W. I. M. Behavior therapy and not the behavior "therapies." Association for Advancement of Behavior Therapy Newsletter, November 1967, 2:5–7.

Winett, R. A., and Nietzel, M. T. Behavioral ecology: Contingency management of consumer energy use. American Journal of Community Psychology, 1975, 3:123–133.

Winett, R. A., and Winkler, R. C. Current behavior modification in the classroom: Be still, be quiet, be docile. Journal of Applied Behavior Analysis, 1972, 5:499–504.

Winkler, R. C. Reinforcement schedules for individual patients in a token economy. Behavior Therapy, 1971, 2:534–537.

Winters v. Miller, 446 F. 2d. 65 (2d. Cir. 1970), reversing 306 F. Supp. 1158 (E.D. N.Y. 1969), cert. denied 404 U.S. 985, 92 S. Ct. 450. 30L. Ed. 2d. 369.

Wolf, M. M. Social validity: The case for subjective measurement or how applied behavior analysis is finding its heart. Paper presented at the 86th annual convention of the American Psychological Association, Washington, D.C., September, 1976.

Wolf, M. M., and Risley, T. R. Reinforcement: Applied research. In R. Glaser (Ed.), The Nature of Reinforcement: A Symposium of the Learning Research and Development Center, University of Pittsburgh. New York: Academic Press, 1971.

Wolf, M., Risley, T. R., and Mees, H. Application of operant conditioning procedures to the behaviour problems of an autistic child. Behaviour Research and Therapy, 1964, 1:305–312.

Wolpe, J. The genesis of neurosis. An objective account. South African Medical Journal, 1950a, 24:613–616.

Wolpe, J. Need-reduction, drive-reduction, and reinforcement: A neurophysiological view. Psychological Review, 1950b, 57:19–26.

Wolpe, J. Experimental neuroses as learned behaviour. British Journal of Psychology, 1952a, 43:243–268.

Wolpe, J. The formation of negative habits: A neurophysiological view. Psychological Review, 1952b, 59:290–299.

Wolpe, J. Objective psychotherapy of the neuroses. South African Medical Journal, 1952c, 26:825–829.

Wolpe, J. Primary stimulus generalization: A neurophysiological view. Psychological Review, 1952d, 59:8–10.

Wolpe, J. Reciprocal inhibition as the main basis of psychotherapeutic effects. Archives of Neurology and Psychiatry, 1954, 72:205–226.

Wolpe, J. Psychotherapy by Reciprocal Inhibition. Stanford, California: Stanford University Press, 1958.

Wolpe, J. The prognosis in unpsychoanalysed recovery from neurosis. American Journal of Psychiatry, 1961, 118:35–39.

Wolpe, J., and Lazarus, A. A. Behavior Therapy Techniques: A Guide to the Treatment of Neuroses. New York: Pergamon, 1966.

Wolpe, J., and Rachman, S. Psychoanalytic "evidence": A critique based on Freud's case of Little Hans. Journal of Nervous and Mental Disease, 1960, 131:135–148.

Wolpe, J., and Reyna, L. J. Editorial. Journal of Behavior Therapy and Experimental Psychiatry, 1970, 1:1–2.

Wolpe, J., Salter, A., and Reyna, L. J. (Eds.). The Conditioning Therapies: The Challenge in Psychotherapy. New York: Holt, Rinehart & Winston, 1964.

Wolpe, J., and Theriault, N. Francois Leuret: A progenitor of behavior therapy. Journal of Behavior Therapy and Experimental Psychiatry, 1971, 2:19–21.

Woolfolk, A. E., Woolfolk, R. L., and Wilson, G. T. A rose by another name . . .: Labeling bias and attitudes toward behavior modification. Journal of Consulting and Clinical Psychology, 1977, 45:184–191.

Woodworth, R. S. Dynamic Psychology. New York: Columbia University Press, 1918.

Woodworth, R. S. Experimental Psychology. New York: Holt, 1938.

The World Book Encyclopedia (Vol. 15). Chicago: Field Enterprises Educational Corporation, 1975.

World Medical Association. Human experimentation: Code of ethics of the World Medical Association. British Medical Journal, 1964, 2:177.

Wyatt v. Stickney, 344 F. Supp. 373, 344 F. Supp. 387 (M. D. Ala. 1972) affirmed sub nom. Wyatt v. Aberholt, 503 F. 2d. 1305 (5th Cir. 1974).

Yates, A. J. The application of learning theory to the treatment of tics. Journal of Abnormal and Social Psychology, 1958a, 56:175–182.

Yates, A. J. Symptoms and symptom substitution. Psychological Review, 1958b, 65:371–374.

Yates, A. J. Behavior Therapy. New York: Wiley, 1970a.

Yates, A. J. Misconceptions about behavior therapy: A point of view. Behavior Therapy, 1970b, 1:92–107.

Yen, S., and McIntire, R. W. (Eds.). Teaching Behavior Modification. Kalamazoo, Michigan: Behaviordelia, 1976.

Yerkes, R. M., and Morgulis, S. The method of Pawlow in animal psychology. Psychological Bulletin, 1909, 6:257–273.

Zeiler, M. Schedules of reinforcement: The controlling variables. In W. K. Honig and J. E. R. Staddon (Eds.), Handbook of Operant Behavior. Englewood Cliffs, New Jersey: Prentice-Hall, 1977.

Zeisset, R. M. Desensitization and relaxation in the modification of psychiatric patients' interview behavior. Journal of Abnormal Psychology, 1968, 73:18-24.

Zilboorg, G., and Henry, G. W. A History of Medical Psychology. New York: Norton, 1941.

Zimmerman, E. H., and Zimmerman, J. The alteration of behavior in a special classroom situation. Journal of the Experimental Analysis of Behavior, 1962, 5:59-60.

Zimmerman, J., and Grosz, H. J. "Visual" performance of a functionally blind person. Behaviour Research and Therapy, 1966, 4:119-134.

Zubin, J. Evaluation of therapeutic outcome in mental disorders. Journal of Nervous and Mental Disease, 1953, 117:95-111.

Zubin, J. Failures of the Rorschach technique. Journal of Projective Techniques, 1954, 18:303-315.

Zubin, J. Classification of the behavior disorders. In P. R. Farnsworth, O. McNemar, and Q. McNemar (Eds.), Annual Review of Psychology (Vol. 18). Palo Alto, California: Annual Reviews, 1967.

Zubin, J., Sutton, S., Salzinger, K., Salzinger, S., Burdock, E. I., and Peretz, D. A biometric approach to prognosis in schizophrenia. In P. H. Hoch and J. Zubin (Eds.), Comparative Epidemiology of the Mental Disorders. New York: Grune & Stratton, 1961.

Author Index

Subject Index